Strategic Challenges

**RELATED TITLES FROM POTOMAC BOOKS
AND NATIONAL DEFENSE UNIVERSITY PRESS**

The Armed Forces Officer
by the U.S. Department of Defense

*African Counterterrorism Cooperation:
Assessing Regional and Subregional Initiatives*
edited by Andre Le Sage

Seeing the Elephant: The U.S. Role in Global Security
by Hans Binnendijk and Richard L. Kugler

Capacity Building for Peacekeeping: The Case of Haiti
edited by John T. Fishel and Andres Saenz

Congress at War: The Politics of Conflict Since 1789
by Charles A. Stevenson

Strategic Challenges

America's Global Security Agenda

Edited by Stephen J. Flanagan
and James A. Schear

Institute for National Strategic Studies

National Defense University Press

Potomac Books, Inc.

Washington, DC

Library of Congress Cataloging-in-Publication Data
Strategic challenges : America's global security agenda / edited by Stephen J. Flanagan and James A. Schear.— 1st ed.
       p. cm.
    Includes index.
    ISBN-13: 978-1-59797-120-1 (hardcopy : alk. paper)
    ISBN-13: 978-1-59797-121-8 (pbk. : alk. paper)
    1. United States—Foreign relations—2001– 2. War on Terrorism, 2001– 3. Weapons of mass destruction—International cooperation. 4. Security, International. I. Flanagan, Stephen J. II. Schear, James A., 1953–
    JZ1469.S77 2008
    355'.033573—dc22

                                                                          2007051455

Printed in the United States of America on acid-free paper that meets the American National Standards Institute Z39-48 Standard.

Potomac Books, Inc.
22841 Quicksilver Drive
Dulles, Virginia 20166

First Edition

10 9 8 7 6 5 4 3 2 1

To Ambassador Robert B. Oakley

Mentor, friend, and colleague. An exceptional leader in efforts to promote peace and security amidst the post–Cold War disorder

Contents

Illustrations

FIGURES

TABLES

Foreword

The past 6 years have seen dramatic shifts in America's global security priorities. While the 9/11 attacks and their aftermath still dominate the strategic landscape, Islamist militancy and terrorist violence are far from the only challenges confronting senior leaders. The United States also faces the prospect of widening proliferation of weapons of mass destruction, rising or rebounding powers whose impact upon global stability remains unclear, the spillover effects of ethnosectarian conflict in volatile regions, and vulnerability of the homeland to natural or manmade disasters. Dealing with these challenges has placed and will continue to place enormous demands on the U.S. Armed Forces and highlights the need for enhanced cooperation with international and interagency partners to achieve better unity of effort. This agenda will test the skill, tenacity, and imagination of U.S. policymakers well beyond the next administration.

Two years ago, the National Defense University's Institute for National Strategic Studies (INSS) undertook a study of the emerging global security environment at the request of the Chairman of the Joint Chiefs of Staff and in context of the then-ongoing Quadrennial Defense Review 2006. This effort assessed the interplay of key geostrategic, military-technical, and regional security trends, how catalytic intervening events might alter the future strategic landscape, and what such changes would imply for U.S. defense strategy and posture through the end of the decade. The first chapter of this volume is a revised and updated version of that assessment, which sets the framework for analysis in subsequent chapters.

This volume presents a trenchant analysis by INSS experts of seven major national security challenges that the United States will confront in the coming decade, including countering global terrorism; combating the threats posed by the proliferation of mass destruction weapons; protecting the American homeland; defusing conflicts in unstable regions; engaging other major powers; adapting alliances and partnerships; and transforming the U.S. defense strategy and military posture. The authors provide a cogent and balanced evaluation of the progress made, and pitfalls encountered, in addressing these challenges since 2001. They then advance a set of practical strategy and policy options for consideration by future administrations. The final chapter presents a synthesis of the entire book and integrated strategy for managing American security in this volatile period. This book offers some unique perspectives on these vexing issues, reflecting the broad policy, operational, and analytic experience of the Institute's civilian and military fellows.

Since it was established in 1984, INSS has earned a well-deserved reputation as a source of objective, incisive analysis on a wide range of strategic policy issues facing our country. Building upon its innovative work on the implications of globalization for national security prior to 2001, INSS was ready to respond to a rising tempo of post-9/11 calls from the Joint Chiefs of Staff, the Office of the Secretary of Defense, the unified commands, and other U.S. Government agencies to assess strategy and policy options.

Outreach is an important element of the National Defense University's mission. Our many publications and conferences seek to inform the wider public debate on contemporary national and international security issues. I am delighted to make the insights of INSS experts available to all those who share an abiding concern about America's security and the future of international peace and stability.

LtGen Frances C. Wilson, USMC
President, National Defense University

Acknowledgments

Truth be told, good analytic work is rarely the solitary activity it is often presumed to be. Most every step along the path—from developing initial arguments and clarifying key assumptions to digging up the best sources, testing hypotheses, and debating conclusions—requires the help of supportive, inquisitive colleagues. In that spirit, we wish to acknowledge a number of individuals whose contributions were absolutely vital to the success of this endeavor.

First and foremost are this volume's lead chapter authors and contributors whose talents, expertise, and creativity have helped the Institute for National Strategic Studies to keep up with ever-increasing demand for its analysis on complex international security and defense policy issues over the past several years. We are delighted that this volume can give their insights a wider circulation than is often possible in the context of specific project work for audiences within the U.S. Government interagency community.

We also are deeply indebted to a number of colleagues and friends of the Institute—Michael Bell, Chester Crocker, Jack Gill, Jamie Laughrey, Robert Oakley, Stewart Patrick, Jeffrey Simon, and Judith Yaphe—who offered helpful critiques, comments, and feedback on particular parts of the manuscript. In addition, we are most grateful to Michael Casey, Zachery Devlin-Foltz, Arnold Dupuy, William Lahneman, Kaley Levitt, Bindi Patel, Nisha Singh, Ambar Ramos, Samuel Rosmarin, and Tamara Shie, who met our herculean demands for research assistance with great skill and dedication. On the production side, this volume benefited greatly from the meticulous editing of Lisa Yambrick and George Maerz, as well as the eternal patience of David Gurney, Director of National Defense University Press. We extend our sincere thanks to all these outstanding colleagues for their efforts.

Finally, we have benefitted from the love and support of two very understanding spouses, Lynn Wansley Flanagan and Jane Stromseth, as we devoted too many evenings and weekends to completing this manuscript. We hope the final product makes a constructive contribution to the wider public debate on strategies and policies for securing America's future and promoting international peace and stability.

Stephen J. Flanagan
James A. Schear

Chapter One

The Emerging Global Security Environment

CHARLES D. LUTES, M. ELAINE BUNN, AND STEPHEN J. FLANAGAN

What trends will define the global security environment through the second decade of the 21st century? A fair question, to be sure, but not one that the United States grapples with very easily. As a democratic society, America's time horizons tend to be short. Washington's natural proclivity is to connect judgments about trends and policy choices to the electoral calendar—in this case, to the results of the 2008 election. Yet there is no reason to suppose that the country's most pressing strategic challenges could be made to fit neatly into electoral cycles. Each of the challenges analyzed in this volume took time to emerge; none is fully amenable to solution in the near term. As a point of departure, therefore, it is essential to take a longer view of the key trends that shape the way these challenges are perceived and ultimately addressed.

Forecasting is an inherently risky business. Most "futures studies" attempt to predict the strategic environment 15 to 20 years hence. Invariably, predictions that are fairly linear extrapolations of current trends are prone to error because certain discontinuous or catalytic events may intervene to throw these trends drastically off course. However, inability to predict the future does not mean that it is completely unknown.[1]

Looking at trends for policy insight in the near- to mid-term, while considering potential intervening events, is a worthwhile exercise for prioritization and risk management. This chapter explores America's probable strategic position in the period 2007 to 2020.

If the current futures literature is correct, the global security environment for the next two decades will feature accelerating, and possibly momentous, changes in the international system. The large-scale trends most often cited are increasing globalization (with both beneficial and disruptive side effects); the continued rise of China and India; the quickening pace of technological innovation; the accelerating proliferation of mass disruption/destruction technologies; the growing power/capacity of nonstate actors relative to nation-states; the persistence of corrosive regional, ethnic, and religious conflicts; and increasing resource scarcity and environment degradation.

The strategic environment of the next decade will be marked by continued, possibly heightened, instability and the potential for catalytic events that would suppress or accelerate one or more of these trends. Since no forecast or estimate posits a peer military competitor within the next 20 years, the United States will likely remain preeminent, but not unchallenged, on the world stage, seeking to shape the forces of change in ways favorable to its national interests. Yet the character and quality of U.S. global leadership will be largely determined by its ability to accurately assess these changes and their key drivers. More critical will be the ability of the United States and its partners to adapt to potential intervening events, some predictable and some not, that can dramatically alter the security landscape. U.S. global influence will also hinge on its ability to sustain alliances and partnerships and convince diverse audiences around the world that its vast power is being employed in a principled fashion to widen the circle of freedom and prosperity.

GEOSTRATEGIC TRENDS

The emerging global geostrategic environment will be heavily shaped by two interrelated trends: the continued pace of change due to globalization, and the preeminence of the United States as the lone, comprehensive superpower. *Globalization*, defined as a dynamic process of rapidly growing, if uneven, cross-border flows of goods, services, money, people, technology, ideas, cultures, values, crime, and weapons throughout the world,[2] will continue to be a dominant influence on the evolving security order by deepening interdependence and empowering certain actors while alienating and marginalizing others. Globalization is not bringing geopolitics or ideological struggles to an end. Rather, globalization's influences interact with traditional regional and ethnic rivalries and are exacerbating many transnational threats. While most futurists describe the inevitability of a globalized society, some point out that catastrophic events or a major global recession could intervene to slow or reverse its course.[3] As the United States seeks to advance its global economic and security interests and promote democracy, civil society, and the rule of law in this environment, it will be challenged by instability arising from strains on governance, economic dislocation, and political convulsions. It will also be challenged by radical ideologies—particularly the jihadist vision of ridding the Muslim world of Western influence, corrupt regimes, and restoring the caliphate—and dissenting views of global order—such as the notion of "sovereign democracy" embraced by Russia, China, and other members of the Shanghai Cooperation Organization who see vigorous U.S. promotion of democracy and human rights as representing unwarranted interference in the internal affairs of sovereign states. With these conditions, volatility will likely be the dominant feature for the foreseeable future.

1. *Globalization is an overarching "mega-trend"[4] altering the world economic, cultural, and security landscape, but between now and the end of the next decade, volatility will increase as shifts in traditional power structures occur.*

An expanding and increasingly integrated global economy combined with a continued technological revolution, particularly in the areas of information and biotechnology, will kick the forces of globalization into high gear over the next decade. This trend both enables, and is enabled by, the flows of energy, money, people, security, technology, and information without regard to international borders.[5] An increasing portion of the world's population will be connected to the globalization grid. This "flattening" of the world due to globalization is not simply about how governments, business, organizations, and people communicate and interact; it is about the emergence of completely new social, political, and business models. These profound changes will, over the long term, alter the way in which governments approach conflict on the international stage. The speed and breadth of change will determine the potential for disruption, as opposed to an orderly transfer of power from the old to the new.[6]

The "dark side" of globalization, including terrorism and organized crime, will continue to exacerbate regional tensions and transnational threats, to challenge the security of the United States and other advanced democracies integrated into the global economy, and to fuel competition and instability in the international system.

Globalization will also enhance the influence and reach of many regional actors in world politics. According to a U.S. Joint Forces Command assessment of the future operational environment:

> Expanding webs of social, economic, political, military, and information architectures will afford opportunity for some regional powers to compete on a broader scale and emerge on the global landscape with considerable influence. In addition, regional power structures are likely to change continuously, as regional conflicts, civil wars, and transnational actors reshape existing norms. It can be expected that nations, transnational actors, and non-state entities will challenge and redefine the global distribution of power, the concept of sovereignty, and the nature of warfare. Local conflicts and wars will be commonplace and will always carry the risk of escalation into broader conflicts.[7]

As societies either transform or resist change, additional challenges will arise in the form of ethnic and religious extremism, nationalism, authoritarianism, and problems of governance. These challenges will be particularly acute in the geographic "arc of instability" or the "gap" countries that are not well integrated into the world economy and have weak or inflexible governance and are, therefore, being buffeted by the winds of globalization.[8] While the global economy expanded by about 30 percent during the 1990s and is continuing to grow at an average of about 3 percent a year, the gap between the richest and poorest countries is widening. The modern industrial powers possess 70 percent of the world's wealth but have only 28 percent of the world's population. Their per capita wealth is four to seven times greater, on average, than the vast number of far poorer countries that house nearly three-quarters of the world's people. While some developing countries are growing fast, the overall disparity between the rich and poor has actually widened because both clusters are growing at similar rates, and rapid population growth in the poorer countries can lower per capita income.[9] It will take decades for some developing countries to achieve moderate wealth.

Most of the gap countries in sub-Saharan Africa, the Middle East, and South Asia are also burdened with the two demographic factors most closely associated with the likelihood of an outbreak of civil conflict: a high proportion of young adults (aged 15 to 29 years) and a rapid rate of urban population growth.[10] By 2035, about 60 percent of the world's population will live in urban areas. Ungoverned rural areas with populations disconnected from the global economy and extremely urbanized areas with high unemployment can serve as havens for those who defy or feel marginalized by the existing social order. These forces can result in pockets of dislocation even in countries well integrated into the global system. Fueled by resonant ideologies, disenfranchised actors tend to drive instability on a local scale with strategic effects by pursuing terrorism, organized crime, and arms or drug trafficking. Additionally, the potential for escalation to catastrophic violence will continue to rise, as the international community remains unable to deal effectively with the increasing proliferation of weapons of mass destruction and potential new capabilities with capacity for catastrophic effect.

2. *The United States will continue to dominate the world stage, but its geopolitical power may begin to erode over the next decade. At the same time, Asia's preeminent population giants with dynamic economies—China and India—will continue their slow, uneven rise.*

The policies and actions of the United States will be major factors shaping the security environment and will continue to dominate the geopolitical landscape for the foreseeable future. As the leading promoter of democratic political change around the world and as the most important engine of economic, cultural, and informational globalization, U.S. actions and the way others react to them will be the leading influence on the levels and types of instability. As the most capable global actor, the U.S. military will be the default option for coping with rising instability as other tools are likely to be inadequate or insufficiently developed. No peer military power or power bloc will emerge to either challenge U.S. supremacy or relieve it of its global security burden before 2020. However, in some respects American supremacy may get in the way of effective influence. What will challenge the United States is the weight of its own commitments, further hampered by international unease about U.S. dominance and rising opposition to American security and foreign policies, even among long-time friends and allies.

Against this backdrop, the rising powers of China and India will gain momentum. Chinese and Indian economic growth will provide them with increased leverage, tempered by the demands of their growing populations for natural resources, a healthy environment, better governance, and a more robust social safety net. Over the next few years, the trajectory of China's military modernization program should become clearer as a means to either maintain its sovereignty and respond to a crisis over Taiwan or intimidate its neighbors and mount a larger challenge to U.S. global power. However, the United States may be limited in its ability to influence China's military trajectory, particularly if it is primarily intended to increase regional influence rather than compete directly with U.S. global power.

3. *International partnerships will be increasingly complex and difficult to manage. As a result, coalition building will need to be tailored for each distinct strategic challenge or contingency.*

With the international system itself in profound flux, some of the institutions that are charged with managing global problems may instead be overwhelmed by them. Regionally based institutions will be particularly challenged to meet the complex transnational threats posed by terrorism, organized crime, and weapons of mass destruction (WMD) proliferation.[11]

Increasingly, the United States will be expected to fill this void, but to do so multilaterally. As *The National Defense Strategy of the United States* of 2005 notes, the Nation "will continue to play leading roles on issues of common international concern and will retain influence worldwide. . . . [However,] our capacity to address global security challenges alone will be insufficient. . . . Our leading position in world affairs will continue to breed unease, a degree of resentment, and resistance."[12] However, differences in interests and policies with longtime allies and partners will continue to hamper building permanent coalitions for international action.

While the United States must retain a resilient global network of alliances and partnerships, as discussed in chapter seven of this volume, some allies and partners will decide not to act with the United States or will lack the capacity to do so.[13] As threats become more globally distributed and closer to home, some countries may be reluctant to become involved in out-of-area coalition activities. Additionally, many allies will be unable to keep pace with U.S. military transformation efforts, hampering the interoperability of future coalitions. This will be difficult to manage in part because it will be very case-dependent—that is, an ally or group of allies that cooperates very closely with the United States in one region might take a neutral (or even opposing) position in another.

MILITARY-TECHNICAL TRENDS

Against the backdrop of these geopolitical trends, rapid technological change is unlikely to transform the character of warfare profoundly. That said, the United States and its allies and partners will need to hedge against disruptive developments in dynamic areas of research and development such as information and communication technology, cognitive science, biological sciences, robotics, and nanotechnology.[14] Conflict between two evenly matched great powers is also unlikely during this period, and thus there is little prospect of heavy force-on-force campaigns. Instead, the reliance of the United States on advanced technology, precision warfare, and information dominance will be asymmetrically challenged by various regional powers and in substate conflict with the potential for escalation to catastrophic violence that threatens not only military forces, but the homeland as well. In planning its transformation agenda, the U.S. Government and Armed Forces must consider how best to adapt to these trends.

1. As the capacity of nonstate actors to employ power improves, substate warfare will be the most dominant form of conflict through 2020.

As the case of the A.Q. Khan proliferation network showed, the flow of weapons technology and knowledge is increasingly out of the control of the international community and individual states.[15] The ability of individual actors and groups of actors to gain and employ power will continue over the next decade,[16] as national governments struggle to meet the challenge of stateless, decentralized networks that move freely across borders.

Countering terrorism will remain a focus of U.S. security policy for the foreseeable future, as the global jihadist insurgency, examined in chapter two, continues its struggle over the legitimacy of the existing world order. This transnational insurgency marks the transition of warfare to a "fourth generation" in which the political, social, economic, and technical changes since World War II—and as a result of globalization—offer asymmetric advantages to an unconventional enemy.[17] Such an insurgency is likely to last decades and will require consistent and dedicated focus by the United States, its partners, and other states with an interest in the preservation of the established international system. Continued instability in the Middle East and Africa will exacerbate the conditions that cause insurgencies, civil war, and ethnic strife. These conflicts will also occupy U.S. policymakers over the next decade or more.

In the meantime, other lower level forms of warfare will distract governments globally. The "five wars of globalization" include fights against the illegal international trade in drugs, arms, intellectual property, people, and money.[18] As globalization enables the expansion of illegal markets and boosts the size and resources of criminal networks, it makes the task of fighting global criminals more difficult. The fundamental changes that have given the five wars new intensity over the last decade are likely to persist in the next.

Although substate warfare is likely to dominate the next decade, it would be imprudent to rule out the possibility of state-on-state warfare. In an increasingly interconnected world, a major regional crisis could reverberate well beyond the affected region or the immediate causes of conflict.[19] Miscalculation and escalation in one or more regional crises or desperation on the part of rogue state regimes may spark conflict that plunges several military powers, including the United States, into war. Lingering tensions between China and Taiwan, India and Pakistan, and on the Korean Peninsula will continue, and flare-ups into actual fighting, with opportunities for serious escalation, will be a possibility. Additionally, aggressive or destabilizing actions by states such as Iran, North Korea, or Syria could result in unwanted escalation and even, in extreme cases, the use of WMD. Any of these scenarios, unpredictable in their occurrence in the next 5 to 10 years, will have strategic effects that significantly alter the security environment during that timeframe and beyond.

2. *Threats to the U.S. homeland, infrastructure, and deployed forces will continue to grow and diversify, and countering weapons of mass destruction or mass effect will prove increasingly difficult.*

As chapter three outlines, global proliferation of a wide range of technology and weaponry will affect the character of future conflict, resulting in a greater diversity of threats against the United States and its global interests.[20] Those who seek to confront the United States will develop adaptive strategies, tactics, and force designs to exploit perceived U.S. vulnerabilities and to counter or mitigate U.S. strengths.[21]

Today, the U.S. homeland is a key target, a reality that will grow over time.[22] Various adversaries consider U.S. soil part of the battlespace, challenging traditional U.S. notions of the homeland as a "sanctuary" and the U.S. military's operational role within that space. Additional terrorist attacks against the homeland are very likely over the next decade. Terrorists probably will be most original not in the technologies or weapons they use but rather in their operational concepts—the scope, design, or support arrangements for attacks.[23]

Strong terrorist interest in acquiring chemical, biological, radiological, and nuclear weapons, combined with the ongoing dissemination of know-how for their production and inadequate security over some countries' existing weapons, increases the risk of a major terrorist attack involving WMD. Of greatest concern is that terrorists might acquire biological agents or a nuclear device, either of which could cause mass casualties. As chapter four notes, bioterrorism appears particularly suited to the smaller, better informed groups. Adversaries may use nontraditional chemical agents to counter U.S. forces and interests globally.

The probability of WMD falling into the hands of terrorists will increase significantly over the next decade as the global nonproliferation regime begins to break down. In response to the nuclear programs of Iran and North Korea, additional states may embark on a nuclear course. Preventive action will become riskier as the possession of chemical, biological, and/or nuclear weapons by Iran, North Korea, and Syria, and the possible acquisition of such weapons by others (to include nonstate actors), increases the potential costs of any military action by the United States against them or their allies.[24] Overt use of WMD by state actors can likely be deterred, but the risk of transfer of WMD materials to terrorists, either wittingly or unwittingly, increases dramatically as more states gain access to the requisite technologies.

3. *Information is a vital domain in current and future warfare. Adversaries will seek opportunities for information advantage by negating U.S. information strengths and exploiting weaknesses.*

According to the late Vice Admiral Arthur Cebrowski, "The new strategic common is the domain of information and cognition that includes the channels of mass media and finance."[25] Technology trends point to potential disruptive advances in cyber operations, and space or directed-energy weapons could seriously endanger U.S. security.[26] A range of potential adversaries—from "super-empowered individuals" (hackers), to terrorists, to state actors—can be expected to attempt cyber attacks to disrupt critical information networks and, even more likely, to cause physical damage to information systems.[27] Innovative and adaptive operational schemes will be employed by adversaries to negate U.S. information advantages. Adversaries will also take advantage of the easy flow of information and global media to promote their ideology, recruit new adherents, and spread anti-American messages. While very few countries or groups have the financial resources to launch space programs, access to space will not be denied them. Adversaries will seek ways to degrade or negate U.S. advantages in commercial communications and bandwidth, battle command and control, intelligence, surveillance, and reconnaissance, and weapons through asymmetric attacks, including direct attacks on U.S. spacecraft and ground control systems.[28]

REGIONAL TRENDS

As globalization continues, traditional geographic groupings will continue to lose salience in international relations.[29] Over the next decade, the rising powers of China and India, and perhaps others such as Brazil and Indonesia, may begin to alter traditional power balances in their respective regions. Competition for allegiances will be more open and less fixed than in the recent past. Some of these governments may band together to balance U.S. dominance or even form hostile coalitions to constrain U.S. options. Chapter six examines U.S. relations with the other major powers, and chapter seven explores the state of U.S. alliances and partnerships on a global basis.

The ranks of fragile, failing, or failed states may grow as a result of economic collapse, resource competition, repressive rule, and failed social infrastructure. Pakistan, Indonesia, Iran, Saudi Arabia, Syria, and many other states in sub-Saharan Africa and Central Asia will be stressed by growing internal pressures. As discussed in chapter five, the United States will almost certainly face new pressures to help reconstitute governance and support security transitions and reconstruction activities in the world's most unstable areas.

1. *Europe will enjoy relative stability, although some lingering tensions—for example, in the Balkans—could erupt into conflict. Worries over future European Union (EU) expansion (beyond the current 27 members), differences over the EU's institutional arrangements, as well as social problems and economic stagnation exacerbated by aging, declining populations in most EU countries, will occupy much of Europe's attention and dilute its policy consensus on defense and foreign policy. Europe will be a less capable and sometimes reticent partner for the United States in managing global challenges.*

Europe seems poised to turn further inward over the next decade. European policies will continue to reflect debate between the dominant opinion favoring close transatlantic ties and those seeking a stronger "European identity" as a potential counterweight to American power. That said, significant changes in European political leadership are unfolding, and a slow movement away from the counterweight school is by no means excluded. Absent a significant intervening event, the potential expansion of the European Union, especially to include Turkey, will cause fissures among key EU states and, potentially, between certain EU governments and their publics.

Both U.S. and European relations with Turkey remain strained and are at a strategic crossroads. As the Turks have watched the EU raise the bar on integration, the North Atlantic Treaty Organization (NATO) equivocate on security commitments during the Iraq war, and both the Kurdistan Workers Party regroup and a Kurdish proto-state be formed in U.S.-occupied northern Iraq, they have begun to hedge their bets and ponder a "Eurasian option." Turkey's growing energy dependence on Russia is also creating a corrosive new dynamic. Growing Turkish nationalism and anti-Americanism could move Turkish politics away from its pro-Western leanings. Turkey could remain a critical partner in advancing a number of common Euroatlantic interests in Southwest Asia and the greater Middle East, but this will require restoring mutual trust and creating a new framework for relations.

A consistent, unified European position on most challenging security matters will remain elusive, and there will be considerable ambivalence toward partnering with the United States on specific military operations, especially operations outside Europe carrying the risk of major combat. Europeans will probably maintain a presence in Afghanistan through NATO but are unlikely to sustain a military commitment to Iraq much beyond 2008. Despite ambitious rhetoric within EU structures, European governments will be reluctant to invest heavily in redundant structures or to adopt standards in training and interoperability that diverge from NATO's. Should humanitarian crises arise in Africa or elsewhere, there may be support for "autonomous" EU operations to exert European influence, but for ongoing or sustained operations, there would likely be calls for cooperation with NATO, in part to secure U.S. participation. Investment in transformation for European militaries is likely to be low and will not keep pace with U.S. transformation. Few European governments have given much thought to the prospect of participation—for example, in a NATO context but under UN Security Council mandate—in an eventual peacekeeping mission as part of an Israeli-Palestinian settlement. This mission would involve major political and military investment by the Europeans, although it is one they would be hard pressed to refuse, as demonstrated by their sizable, if somewhat hesitant, contributions in 2006 to reinforce the UN mission in Lebanon.

The most significant security threat is the specter of catastrophic terrorism in a major urban area in Europe. Although the Europeans are more accustomed to lower level terrorism, the psychological impact of a WMD event would be hard to predict. The ripple effects could include economic destabilization, ethnic tensions directed against growing Muslim communities in Europe, inward orientation to focus on domestic security matters, and concern about possible U.S. reactions.

Enduring security issues in Europe include the persistence of such transnational problems as increased trafficking in arms, drugs, and humans along its southeast corridors. Unresolved tensions with respect to Kosovo's final status, Bosnia-Herzegovina, Moldova/Transnistria, and Armenia-Azerbaijan could spark conflict. There are also persistent concerns about Russia's reliability as an energy supplier and tendency to use energy as an instrument of political intimidation. New and longstanding tensions between Russia and its neighbors—Georgia, Ukraine, Moldova, and even Belarus, as well as the Baltic states—could have wider implications for European security.

2. In the Middle East, expanding Islamist extremism, challenges to governance, and long-held grievances will continue to fuel instability.

The road into the next decade will weave through unpredictable terrain in the Middle East as unresolved issues fester. Three significant and interrelated drivers will continue to play out in the region: ongoing Islamist extremist violence; Israeli-Palestinian tensions; and U.S. policies. Also, Syria could be teetering on the brink of instability that could result in civil war, takeover by Islamic extremists, or outright collapse, all with enormous consequences for stability in the region. Additional instability may also result as populations chafe under unrepresentative regimes. Saudi Arabia and Bahrain (with its 25 percent Sunni population governing 75 percent of the population that is Shi'a) are candidates for turmoil.

The passing of Yasser Arafat and Israel's 2006 withdrawal from Gaza held some promise of a new politics of realism in settling the Arab-Israeli dispute. However, the Palestinian Authority's inability to control extremist violence and the polarization of the leadership struggle between Hamas and Fatah have precluded diplomatic progress on a settlement. Israel has created de facto borders by building a barrier separating the Jewish state from the West Bank, but it could lead to further unrest and violence.[30] Even an interim two-state solution based on the Oslo Accords seems unlikely in the next few years, and a final settlement will clearly be a generational effort.

The sustained insurgencies in Iraq and Afghanistan have implications far beyond their borders. The growing restlessness by the American public may precipitate major reductions of U.S. forces before the fragile governments of these countries are firmly established. The United States will most likely still be involved in counterinsurgency efforts with forces stationed in or near both countries for a decade or more. Complete withdrawal from Iraq would be fraught with risks until greater stability and the legitimacy of the Iraqi government can be enhanced, but Sunni and Shi'a communities increasingly anxious to manage their own security may demand it. With few coalition partners likely to offer replacement forces, the United States may have to shoulder this commitment alone. Failure by the United States, coalition partners, and neighboring states to achieve stability in both Iraq and Afghanistan would likely increase various forms of extremism and terrorism throughout the region. Pakistan would be particularly threatened, as would the energy-rich countries of the Persian Gulf and Central Asia. If there is still a stalemate in the Israeli-Palestinian dispute, the psychological spillover would seriously exacerbate these problems.

Iran's nuclear ambitions may be delayed through sanctions and incentives but are unlikely to be abandoned. Prospects for significant political change within the Persian state are low in the near term, and even a more moderate government would not change the course of what is a unifying nationalistic desire to obtain nuclear status. While Tehran may have put its nuclear weapons program on hold in 2003, Iran is likely to have the capability to produce such weapons during the next decade, either overtly or behind a veil of ambiguity.[31] In dealing with the prospect of a nuclear-armed Iran, the United States has two basic options: freeze the Iranian nuclear program with hopes of rolling it back (and constraining it to peaceful applications), or live with the program while containing its negative impacts by reinforcing U.S. security commitments to allies and friends in the region.[32]

3. *In Asia, a rising China and India will continue to reshape the power dynamics in the region, and an unpredictable North Korea will require significant U.S. attention.*

China will remain the most significant driver of change in Asia for the foreseeable future. The challenges China poses in the near- to mid-term are more political, economic, and cultural than military.[33] Governments in the region do not view China as a near-term military threat; barring a misstep, the rise of China will likely pull more countries toward its influence than push countries away. Most U.S. allies in the region will want the benefits of good relations with both China and the United States; they will not want to choose between them. Resolution of the Taiwan issue is unlikely to occur before the 2008 Taiwan presidential elections, but if the Chinese Nationalist Party returns to power, it is possible that China and Taiwan could reach an interim agreement or be on a long-term path toward peaceful reunification even in the next few years. Conflict over the issue is always a wildcard and could happen if miscalculation occurs by either side. War over the Taiwan Strait that would involve U.S. intervention would dramatically change the regional dynamics for years to come. The next 5 years will be critical to shaping U.S. relations with China and will require continued U.S. engagement in the region. The United States will be best served by a multidimensional relationship with China that emphasizes cooperation with all nations in the region over military competition.

The North Korean situation is the most unpredictable in the region. Pyongyang remains an erratic partner in the Six-Party Talks, which have been marked by several lengthy boycotts by North Korea, including after the conclusion of the September 19, 2005, statement of principles. The October 9, 2006, North Korean nuclear test appears to have inspired more forceful Chinese diplomacy with Pyongyang and led to the February 2007 agreement in which North Korea agreed to freeze, and ultimately dismantle, its main nuclear complex at Yongbyon. Much work remains to achieve a verifiable agreement concerning the elimination of existing weapons stockpiles and other nuclear programs. Without successful implementation of the Six-Party framework, North Korea will retain its status as a nuclear power with uncertain reactions in the region. After Pyongyang's test, Japan and South Korea sought and received U.S. assurances that extended deterrence still applies. However, in the long term, Japan could be tempted to embark on its own program. The prospects for additional global proliferation will increase significantly. Overt use of force on the peninsula, in the form of preemptive or preventive force, or even a blockade, could spark a dangerous conflict and require significant U.S. military involvement for years to come to deal with its aftermath. The possibility of total North Korean collapse is not especially high, since China and South Korea would intervene to prevent a total failure. Overall, the prospects for resolution on the peninsula in the next 5 years are not good but will require significant U.S. attention to ensure the situation does not become catastrophic. Additionally, the North Korean issue will pose a test case for U.S. alliance management with South Korea and Japan.

In other areas of the region, a bipolar dynamic may gradually emerge, with a U.S./Japan–centered axis on one hand, and a China-centered one on the other. In Southeast Asia, Chinese presence and influence will grow, but opportunities for U.S. involvement will remain as nations such as the Philippines, Indonesia, and Thailand look for help with problems such as terrorism, insurgency, piracy, pandemic flu, and other natural or manmade disasters.

The rise of India will be the governing dynamic in South Asia over the next 20 years, and India may emerge as an even stronger counterweight to China in Asia. Rising India will put additional pressures on an already precarious Pakistan, as even a minor crisis between the two continues to run the risk of escalation and nuclear miscalculation. Pakistan continues to strike a delicate balance between supporting U.S. antiterrorism efforts and controlling the appeal of radicalism within its own populace. Pakistan has shown a remarkable penchant for "muddling through" with an alternating series of military and civilian governments. While unlikely to implode, particularly if it can allow some political liberalization and secure affordable energy supplies essential to continued growth, Pakistan will not become notably more stable and successful over the next 5 years, and any crisis or instability in Pakistan will have significant consequences beyond its borders.

4. Russia and Central Asia will struggle with the challenge of political modernization and will have to cope with weakening of state institutions, limited sovereignty, poor governance, and even the risk of state failure.

The Russian economy is booming, thanks to the high prices of oil, gas, and other export commodities, as well as prudent fiscal policies instituted by the Russian government. However, a declining Russia and the geopolitical vacuum left in its wake in Eurasia will remain the defining feature of regional dynamics. With population losses of as much as 1 million per year, Russia will struggle to adequately police its borders; deal with domestic and international terrorism; address problems related to smuggling and WMD proliferation; build a sustainable, diversified economy; and project power and influence around its periphery.[34] Moreover, the Russian foreign policy establishment will be increasingly preoccupied by the problem of managing its relationship with the rising China, which, many in Moscow fear, will be a difficult partner to handle given Russia's weakness in the Far East. China, and to a lesser degree India, will expand their influence in Central Asia, but no nation is likely to fully fill the vacuum of power left by Russia's loss of power and influence in the region. Russia's own leadership transition in 2008, when President Vladimir Putin's term in office expires, looks increasingly like a serious challenge for Russia's young political system. Russia's handling of this domestic challenge is likely to have considerable impact on its international position and relations with the United States and Europe.

In Central Asia too, leadership transition will be a serious test facing the key regional powers of Kazakhstan and especially Uzbekistan. In Kyrgyzstan and Turkmenistan, leadership transition is already under way, and its outcome looks uncertain. None of the region's young states is well equipped to deal with it, having invested heavily in personality-based regimes. Leadership transition could trigger regime failure and instability, opening doors to clan, tribal, and regional rivalries that may transcend state borders and lead to turmoil and violence in large portions of Central Asia. Significant and protracted instability could become the defining characteristic of

Central Asia, including failed and failing states, or states with limited sovereignty; radical Islamic movements; organized crime; and trafficking in weapons, WMD materials, and narcotics.

The United States will confront the difficult task of dealing with unstable and undemocratic partners in Central Asia, where U.S. economic and security assistance will be welcome, but U.S. pursuit of democratization and wide-ranging reforms will be viewed as a major threat to national and regional stability. This view will be shared not only by the former Soviet states of Central Asia, but also by their biggest partners and neighbors—China, Russia, Iran, and even U.S. allies and partners Turkey, Pakistan, and India. Instability in Central Asia will continue to complicate U.S. military access in the region. Central Asian rulers will want to trade base access for political support and security assistance, thus confronting the United States with difficult choices. In military operations, the United States will need to adapt to the limited capacity of these nations rather than expecting them to adapt to U.S. approaches.

The United States will have to find a way to cooperate with and assist Russia, while in effect competing with it for influence in Central Asia, Eastern and Central Europe, and the South Caucasus. Outside its immediate periphery, such as in the Middle East, where Russian influence has declined and is likely to stay low, Russia too will be a difficult partner, trying to hold on to the remnants of its great power status. Russia is likely to be a challenging partner even in areas where U.S. and Russian interests may coincide and cooperating could be mutually beneficial, such as in matters related to WMD proliferation, terrorism, and other transnational issues.

5. Africa will remain outside the mainstream of economic globalization and will continue to struggle with serious problems such as HIV/AIDS, terrorism, and internal conflict.

Africa will continue to struggle with significant problems that have prevented its development in the past. HIV/AIDS is the most serious challenge facing Africa today and will grow in its devastation during this time. This crisis is hampering economic growth, as well as decimating the ranks of African armed forces and severely limiting their manpower and capacity to deal with security issues.[35]

Continued terrorist activity in parts of Africa is a virtual certainty as many states lack the security capacity necessary to break up terror cells, thwart arms trafficking, or prevent well-coordinated attacks. These problems, coupled with the existence of several failed or weakened states with significant Muslim populations and the growth of Islamist extremism in Nigeria and parts of western, central, and northeastern Africa, could aid and abet the continent's emergence as a new regional battleground in the war on terrorism.[36]

As demonstrated by the crisis in Sudan's Darfur region, civil strife with potential for mass violence will continue to plague a number of African countries. While the sources of these conflicts are most often local, the United States and other members of the international community may be drawn in to provide emergency assistance, peacekeepers, or conflict mediation. In addition to ongoing and known conflicts in Somalia, Sudan, and the Democratic Republic of Congo, flashpoints triggering pressures for new or expanded international interventions could well arise elsewhere in Africa's diverse western, central, and southern subregions.

6. *Latin America will remain at peace, but countries with weak governance will struggle to dampen transnational security problems. A growing sense of community, persistent anti-American sentiment, and an expanded set of trading partners outside the hemisphere will increase independence from U.S. influence.*

Latin America's differing approaches to democracy will continue. Good governance will be hampered in some countries by disgruntled masses, inadequate infrastructure, and growing pains of globalization, and in others by unwillingness to push through crucial structural reforms. Populist alternatives, particularly Hugo Chavez's Bolivarian movement in Venezuela, will continue to trample democratic norms and threaten regional stability. In the shadow of U.S. primacy, Latin governments will pursue their own course and frequently disagree with the United States, particularly if Washington remains vague about regional interests and fails to maintain steady engagement with these governments as respected partners. This strained relationship expands opportunities for greater influence by China, Japan, India, and several European countries, which are already actively courting many Latin American states economically. With a reversal of these trends, effective cooperation on common regional and global concerns is possible with a number of current and potential partners in the hemisphere. The governments in the Andean ridge and the Caribbean basin will struggle to correct longstanding socioeconomic problems and counter those transnational forces that exploit weak governance and foster populism and extremist violence.

The most explosive potential crisis in the region is the implosion of Cuba in the wake of Fidel Castro's death. Such a scenario could trigger intervention by the United States and other governments in the region, as well as many private citizens, with disparate and conflicting goals. The result could be civil war and a massive humanitarian crisis that would taint hemispheric relations for decades.

As a whole, the countries of the Western Hemisphere will continue to struggle with the ability to deal collectively and cooperatively with the multidimensional challenges presented by the five wars of globalization (illegal trade in drugs, arms, intellectual property, humans, and money).[37] Over the next decade, the United States, which has an intense interest in countering illicit trade—especially since most trafficking routes lead to the homeland and could readily be used by terrorists—will have to develop new ways to partner with Mexico and other countries in Central America and the Caribbean boundary area. A perception of subordination to the United States will have to give way to greater mutual trust and assistance in improving and integrating the region's police, border security, and military surveillance and response systems to address powerful transnational threats.

DISRUPTIVE EVENTS

The geostrategic, military-technical, and regional trends considered thus far provide context for the security environment of the coming decade. They represent the plausible, if not probable, trajectory. However, these trends can be drastically altered by discontinuous events with significant strategic consequences: witness, for example, the 9/11 terrorist attacks and the subsequent reactions of the United States and international community. Some of these events can be considered strategic shocks or wildcards: events that are very unlikely and cannot be fully anticipated, such as cascading natural disasters, worldwide economic collapse, or the sudden rise of a charismatic leader.[38] For other types of events, trend lines point to the possibility of their occurrence; however, whether and how they will unfold are unknowns. Examples of these types of events are familiar scenarios such as war on the Korean Peninsula or a WMD event on the U.S. homeland. Whether "known unknowns" or "unknown unknowns," these uncertainties harbor strategic consequences that can shape the security environment beyond recognition of the current trends. In mitigating risks, it is less important to predict the specific event than it is to characterize the strategic effects that might arise from similar events.[39] The following considers the strategic effects resulting from possible disruptive events over the next decade.

1. A catastrophic WMD event or a sustained terrorism campaign inflicting substantial losses at home or abroad could fundamentally alter international and domestic security "rules."

The 9/11 attacks on the World Trade Center and the Pentagon changed the prism through which America viewed its security environment and ultimately its policies for dealing with that environment. Similarly, a catastrophic WMD event or a sustained terrorism campaign against the United States and its allies would significantly change the international security environment over the next decade. Some types of WMD attacks—for example, a large-scale contagious biological attack—could disrupt the flow of trade and people, causing systemic effects so important as to alter the forces of globalization.

Sustained or catastrophic attacks occurring overseas would have unpredictable effects on the international community. Some countries that previously viewed 9/11 primarily as an American problem may change their perception and align with the United States in a more aggressive policy to combat terrorism and WMD worldwide. Others may interpret events differently and choose to distance themselves from U.S. international policies and focus on individual interests. If fear became a dominant driver, it could interrupt the process of globalization by significantly increasing the security costs associated with international commerce, encouraging restrictive border control policies, and adversely affecting trade patterns and financial markets.[40] As the most capable provider of security, the U.S. military would see an increasingly active role globally.

Sustained or catastrophic attacks on the homeland would renew fears among the American public and could create conditions and expectations for new roles for the military. In responding to catastrophic or parallel attacks, the U.S. military would likely be tasked for substantial support to overwhelmed civil authorities, diluting efforts to combat threats in-depth. In a sustained campaign, the military may be required to assist in providing some measure of internal security while simultaneously combating threats overseas. If the homeland becomes a significant new front in the war on terrorism, dramatic changes in the roles and expectations of the military, particularly the roles of the National Guard and Reserves, are likely.

2. Regional crises that lead to wider instability, conflict, or failed states may severely tax U.S. ability to respond to broader challenges.

As the regional trends indicate, lingering tensions have the potential to ignite into crisis or conflict. Although many of these scenarios are well known, the strategic implications are not well understood in the context of the global security environment. Preparations for such contingencies often do not project beyond the immediate crises themselves, even though the strategic effects of such events would change the landscape dramatically.

Well-known scenarios include escalation of tensions on the Korean Peninsula, over the Taiwan Strait, and between India and Pakistan. Although these types of state-on-state conflict are avoidable (and unlikely) in the next several years, miscalculation and escalation could occur. Direct involvement of U.S. forces is considered a given in the first two cases, and some type of intervention role may be required in the third. The potential for a WMD exchange looms large in these conflicts, and the ability of local forces to manage the consequences of such an exchange while continuing to engage in warfare is limited. Any one of these scenarios, if it came to pass, would irrevocably alter the face of the region and would likely involve U.S. force commitments for years, possibly decades, to come. Even though the potential for such conflict remains relatively low, their extreme consequences—military, diplomatic, humanitarian, and economic—warrant continued attention.

On the positive side, peaceful resolution of these regional tensions would also have lasting strategic consequences that may shift the trend lines significantly, although not as dramatically as crisis or conflict. For example, a unified Korean Peninsula with nuclear weapons would likely spark new tensions with Japan and possibly China and trigger a regional arms race. Alternatively, a unified Korea without nuclear weapons would enable (and probably require) reconfiguration of U.S. forces in the region. A peaceful solution to the Taiwan issue would strengthen China's power in Asia and alter regional security dynamics. Further easing of India-Pakistan tensions is a distinct possibility, although it would likely have the least strategic impact for the United States. One other scenario worth considering in this context is a significant breakthrough in Israel's disputes with its Arab neighbors and the Palestinians, perhaps along the lines of the historic "land for peace" concept revived by Saudi King Abdullah that would trade full recognition of Israel by the Arab world in exchange for Israel's withdrawal from West Bank lands it occupied after the 1967 war and pave the way for a Israeli-Palestinian settlement. Such an agreement might require an international peacekeeping presence in the near term but over the long term would reduce the anti-American resentment in the region and remove a crucial rhetorical point for Islamic radicals.

In cases of failed or failing states, the international community will likely turn to the United States for assistance in quelling instability in both these countries and their neighbors. A different type of intervention may be required in the event of failure or implosion of WMD states, particularly Pakistan, North Korea, or Syria. These scenarios present unique operational challenges. Although the primary U.S. objective may be to locate, secure, and eliminate the existing stockpiles of WMD, it may not be able to do so without simultaneously addressing the stability of the state. This implies a longer-term commitment to stability and reconstruction operations for which the larger international community may or may not provide assistance.

3. *Wider proliferation of WMD introduces another plausible set of scenarios with strategic consequences: U.S. intervention in WMD states such as Iran, North Korea, or Syria.*

If left unchecked, the nuclear aspirations of Iran and North Korea will be fully realized and Syria might use the threat of its chemical and biological capabilities to support aggressive activities in the region. As significant as these events would be, the reaction and policies of the United States will have more of a global effect. Should the United States choose military intervention, it would carry enormous long-term implications for U.S. forces. Standoff preemptive strikes would likely have only short-term effectiveness and would harden the resolve of these adversaries to gain WMD capabilities. That said, a credible threat of such strikes must remain on the table to deter them from possible use or transfer to third parties. More significant intervention, involving the use of special operations or other ground forces, would be difficult, given the U.S. involvement in Iraq. Such commitment would also critically impact the ability of the United States to respond to other crises at home or abroad.

4. *Energy insecurity, resource scarcity, and natural disasters could create instability and uncertainty and have consequences for U.S. policy.*

Ensuring the reliable flow of energy resources from producers to consumers has long been a cornerstone of U.S. national security strategy, particularly in the Middle East, but changes in energy production and distribution patterns have already called into question many of the traditional ways in which the United States has understood the energy security problem. Future changes, both foreseen and unforeseeable, promise to transform the challenge of ensuring energy security even more dramatically. Global primary energy demand is projected to increase by just over one-half between 2006 and 2030. Over 70 percent of the increase in demand comes from developing countries, with China accounting for 30 percent of that growth. [41] Rising oil and gas demand, if unchecked, will accentuate the vulnerability of consuming countries to a severe supply disruption and resulting price shock. The continued concentration of energy resources in unstable areas and significant changes in resource distribution patterns will provide security challenges for the United States and all consuming countries.

Resource scarcity will be an increasing source of humanitarian crises and instability. This will be particularly acute if the predictions of the effects of global warming are realized. For instance, the International Panel on Climate Change reported that by 2020, between 75 million and 250 million people in Africa are expected to face starvation and malnutrition due to lack of fresh water supplies, a 50 percent reduction in crop yields from rain-fed agriculture, and severe drought.[42]

Lastly, the United States may also become involved in humanitarian assistance response to natural or manmade disasters, including a global pandemic. In these cases, the United States would likely be part of larger international efforts but may be compelled to respond to provide leadership, expertise, and substantial personnel. The length of such commitments could vary from a few months to several years and could well tax certain limited U.S. Government capabilities. In the case of naturally occurring pandemic disease, the United States could be caught between an impulse to assist vulnerable countries and a requirement (on force protection and public health grounds) to quarantine "hot zones." The manner in which the country responds to such challenges will impact its ability to engender support in the international community for its other security policies. A devastating global pandemic could also change the rules of international behavior and bring globalization to a halt.

5. *Asymmetric challenges to key American vulnerabilities, such as information or space, could significantly hamper the military's—and the country's—ability to carry out key missions.*

Even the greatest U.S. military advantages may also be an Achilles' heel. Adversaries continue to look for asymmetric means to negate U.S. advantages. The U.S. ability to effectively use the information domain provides a unique opportunity for its adversaries. Daily battles against the nuisance of hackers and cyber terrorists could be taken to a higher level in the next decade by some individuals, groups, or even state adversaries. Most vulnerable is the civilian information infrastructure, against which a mass effect attack would likely require significant military assistance for attribution and response. Cascading effects in such attacks are extremely unpredictable. Less likely would be direct attacks on the military information infrastructure, but since the military is so reliant on commercial systems for day-to-day operations, its ability to carry out its missions would be severely impacted.

Space systems are increasingly vulnerable to attack as well, as graphically demonstrated by China's January 2007 antisatellite weapon test. Although it is unlikely that nonstate actors would have the technological capability to attack U.S. space assets, rudimentary capability by state adversaries could be employed to great effect. Bursts of solar energy, electromagnetic pulse, satellite jammers, and space debris could effectively negate U.S. advantages for long durations and significantly impact commercial uses of space.

CONCLUSION

Over the coming decade, the international community will struggle to manage the accelerating pace of change and turmoil stemming from globalization. While the United States will remain preeminent on the world stage, its influence and ability to manage this turmoil will hinge on better integrating various elements of national power, sustaining alliances and partnerships, and maintaining cooperative relations with the other major powers. Widening economic inequality and the global jihadist insurgency with its anti-Western ideology will remain particularly vexing challenges to a stable world order for the foreseeable future. Threats to the U.S. homeland, critical infrastructure, and deployed forces will continue to evolve and diversify. Countering weapons of mass destruction or mass effect will prove increasingly difficult, and the probability of such weapons coming into the hands of terrorists will increase significantly. Climate change and resource scarcity will be growing causes of humanitarian crises and instability.

Europe and Latin America will remain fairly stable with limited risk of conflict. However, extremist violence and long-held grievances will continue to fuel instability in the Middle East and South Asia. A rising China and India will reshape the power dynamics in Asia, which, while stable, retains worrisome flashpoints on the Korean Peninsula and in the Taiwan Strait. Russia and Central Asia will face the challenges of political modernization and weak state institutions. Africa will remain outside the mainstream of economic globalization and will continue to struggle with serious problems such as HIV/AIDS, terrorism, and internal conflict.

Several plausible intervening events could disrupt these trends and significantly alter the emerging security landscape. A catastrophic WMD event, a sustained terrorism campaign inflicting substantial losses in the United States and other developed countries, or a global pandemic could fundamentally alter international and domestic security "rules" and bring globalization to a halt. Crises on the Korean Peninsula, over the Taiwan Strait, or in South Asia that triggered wider regional conflicts or involved the use of WMD could also have dramatic ripple effects on the international order. Even more extensive proliferation of WMD could trigger preemptive military action against the proliferant governments or grant them capacity for regional hegemony. Asymmetric challenges to key U.S. information systems or space assets, along with significant energy disruptions, could significantly alter the country's security and economic vitality. The United States and its partners need to develop adaptive plans and capabilities to mitigate the risks of these scenarios.

Chapter Two

Countering Global Terrorism

JOSEPH MCMILLAN AND CHRISTOPHER CAVOLI

The cliché that the events of September 11, 2001, changed everything may be something of an exaggeration, but the attacks of that day undoubtedly changed the American people's understanding of the world in which they live. As a result of 9/11, Americans see themselves confronted by a shadowy enemy, one bent on waging war against them and capable of inflicting catastrophic damage. The global primacy that once made the United States safe now makes it a target for those who harbor grievances against not only particular U.S. policies but also the global status quo in general. The realization that American citizens at home are now the vulnerable targets of unseen and largely unknown forces has had an undeniable effect on the national psyche. As a result, any attempt to analyze the strategic challenges facing America in the coming decades must start with the challenge of terrorism.

THE STATE OF PLAY

In contemplating the magnitude of the task at hand, it is best to keep sight of the substantial progress made since 9/11. The most tangible achievement has been the disruption of and damage to the al Qaeda leadership made possible by the ouster of the Taliban regime in Afghanistan, although, as a July 2007 National Intelligence Estimate made clear, the surviving capability of al Qaeda to carry out strikes against the U.S. homeland remains substantial.[1] Equally important has been the creation of a de facto international counterterrorist coalition that is operating around the globe in a number of less visible functional areas. The disruption of terrorist financial networks, the exchange of intelligence and law enforcement information so local authorities can track and arrest terrorist leaders and operatives, and the improvements in border and customs control are just three examples. The coalition extends to the military sphere as well, with U.S. and coalition forces cooperating against terrorists in places ranging from the Philippines to the African pan-Sahel to the Mediterranean Sea.

Important steps have also been taken at home, with the creation of the Department of Homeland Security and the Homeland Security Council, the establishment of U.S. Northern Command within the Department of Defense, and the enactment of a range of preparedness and security measures that better position U.S. authorities than they were before 9/11 to prevent or respond to another attack. The congressional 9/11 Commission has made extensive recommendations for further reform; some have already been implemented, such as the appointment of a Director of National Intelligence. A national strategy for combating terrorism has been developed, as well as a military strategic plan to implement the military aspects of it. Last but not least, the U.S. Government's general approach to terrorism has been put on a more realistic footing, with the realization that terrorism is truly a national security problem, not simply a matter for the judicial system to deal with as a species of criminal misconduct.

Nevertheless, U.S. strategy toward terrorism continues to face a number of major challenges, both practical and conceptual. The groundswell of global sympathy the United States enjoyed in the immediate aftermath of the 9/11 attacks has largely dissipated, not just in the Islamic world but also among the populations of many of America's closest allies, particularly since the 2003 invasion of Iraq and the ensuing insurgency. At best, this drop in international public support for the war on terrorism stems from honest disagreements over the nature and severity of the threat and the relevance of Saddam Hussein's regime to that threat; the underlying causes of terrorism; and the strategy for dealing with it. At worst, it reflects a misperception that U.S. policy and strategy toward terrorism are guided by uncontrolled use of force and disregard for international norms. Although little better than caricature, such perceptions nonetheless shape popular attitudes and limit foreign governments' willingness to associate openly with the United States in combating terrorism.

Meanwhile, as then-Director of Central Intelligence George Tenet reported to Congress in early 2004, U.S.-led successes against terrorist command and control structures in Afghanistan have caused a metamorphosis in the nature of the threat. The U.S. enemy is no longer simply al Qaeda as an organization but rather a more dispersed, less coherent movement of Sunni jihadists inspired but not controlled by al Qaeda.[2] As U.S. strategy recognizes, combating this worldwide movement will require close cooperation with foreign governments[3]—the same ones whose people have become so disaffected with the U.S. approach to the struggle. Moreover, it will require an understanding of the nature of the appeal that the violent, radical Islamist movement seems to hold for many in the world's Muslim community.

In short, the questions that then-Secretary of Defense Donald Rumsfeld asked his senior staff over 4 years ago are even more pertinent now than they were then. Noting the considerable progress made on the tactical battlefields, Rumsfeld suggested that far less had been accomplished on the strategic battlefield of politics and ideas: "Are we capturing, killing, or deterring and dissuading more terrorists every day than the *madrassas* and the radical clerics are recruiting, training, and deploying against us? Does the U.S. need to fashion a broad, integrated plan to stop the next generation of terrorists?"[4] Answering these questions is crucial to success in the struggle against terrorism. To answer them, it is necessary to go back to basics.

THE NATURE OF THE THREAT

The principal terrorist threat to the United States stems from a number of more or less affiliated groups—all extremely small compared to the size of the world's Muslim population[5]—that are conducting a global insurgency inspired by a radical, violent interpretation of the teachings of Sunni Islam. If one takes the rhetoric of these groups at face value, the objective of the insurgency is eschatological in character: to bring about the divinely ordained endstate of a universal Islamic caliphate on earth. Whether this rhetoric *should* be taken at face value remains a matter of considerable debate. Undoubtedly, there are differences of view among terrorist leaders themselves as to the relative priority of establishing Islamist governments within the majority-Muslim world, getting the United States and Israel out of the Middle East, and stemming the tide of Western cultural influences as objectives on the path to "restoring" the universal caliphate.

Despite these inconsistencies and ambiguities, or perhaps because of them, the politico-religious doctrine espoused by jihadist ideologues is flexible enough to serve as the principal factor uniting and coordinating a far-flung assortment of disparate groups. This use of ideology as a surrogate for formal structures of command and control is one of the defining strategic characteristics of the jihadist insurgency.

IS JIHADIST EXTREMISM JUST A SUNNI ISSUE?

Our characterization of the principal terrorist threat facing the United States as stemming from radical strains of Sunni Islam may be surprising in view of the military capabilities exhibited by the Iranian-sponsored Shi'ite group Hezbollah against the Israel Defense Forces in July and August 2006. While Hezbollah's operational skills as a terrorist group probably surpass those of al Qaeda and related Sunni terrorist groups, the fact is that Hezbollah has thus far shown no interest in attacking American targets except when U.S. military forces become engaged in a conflict to which Hezbollah was a party, as in the case of the bombing of the U.S. Marine barracks in Beirut in 1983. The same could be said of the attacks by Moqtada al-Sadr's Jaysh al-Mahdi Army against U.S. military and Coalition Provisional Authority assets in Iraq in 2004. Other Shi'ite groups have also generally avoided attacks on American targets, with the principal exception of the bombing of Khobar Towers in Saudi Arabia in 1996.

None of this is to say that Hezbollah and other Shi'ite extremist organizations should be taken lightly, but whatever risk to U.S. interests is presented by these groups should not be conflated with the much more virulent and widespread threat posed by violent Sunni *salafis*. Indeed, there is some risk that conflating these diverse threats could ultimately drive them together to make common cause against us. Notwithstanding evidence of sporadic cooperation between Iranian authorities and radical Sunni groups, especially allegations that Afghan Taliban leaders had found sanctuary in Iran following the U.S. invasion in 2001, the viciousness of the violence carried out by Abu Mus'ab al-Zarqawi's followers against Iraqi Shi'a and by similar groups elsewhere, such as Sipah-e-Sahaba in Pakistan, demonstrates clearly the intense fundamental antagonism between the two camps.

Moroccan terrorists attacking Madrid or Kashmiri terrorists attacking New Delhi do not need to be controlled by the al Qaeda leadership in order to do what al Qaeda wants done. Such groups understand the strategy and tactics of the jihadist movement and share enough of its agenda to act in concert with al Qaeda and each other, even without direct contact. The only coordination needed may be a resonant ideological message and the capability to communicate it—a capability that is almost universally available in the electronic age. Consequently, it is impossible to define a single center of gravity or even a single network node against which force can be decisively used.

The second defining strategic characteristic of the jihadist insurgency, and particularly of the elements most directly influenced by al Qaeda, is its reliance on mass-effect terrorism not just as one among many instruments but also as the weapon of first choice. Al Qaeda and its associated groups place especially high value on suicide attacks rather than standoff attacks or the covert placement of timed or remotely controlled weapons. This characteristic suggests that jihadist leaders may consider terrorism less a device for weakening the will of the Western societies they target than a means of galvanizing support among Muslims through the production of high-profile martyrs, an example par excellence of what 19th-century anarchists called "propaganda by deed."[6] The writings of such jihadist theorists as Ayman al-Zawahiri and his ideological mentor, the late Sayyid Qutb, are almost as attentive to the synergy between words and action as those of such anarchist luminaries as Prince Pyotr Kropotkin and Mikhail Bakunin (see figure 2–1).

The practice of making and disseminating videotapes in which operatives place the terrorist act in a religious context lends credence to the idea that the audience for jihadist terrorism is not the targeted group but rather the community from which the terrorists spring. If this assessment is correct, then terrorism is, for the jihadists, not merely a tactical choice but a strategic one. In any case, it is clear that jihadist leaders fully understand that the ultimate objective of the insurgency is winning the support of the world's Muslim population. As Ayman al-Zawahiri wrote to the Jordanian terrorist Abu Mus'ab al-Zarqawi in Iraq in 2005, "I say to you: that we are in a battle, and that more than half of this battle is taking place in the battlefield of the media. And that we are in a media battle in a race for the hearts and minds of our Umma."[7]

Jihadist leaders and ideologues also understand that their war against the West is sustained and fed by a multitude of discontents in the Islamic world—that unhappy Muslims are an essential underpinning of the jihadist movement. An aggrieved Islamic population provides materiel, money, assistance, and, above all, new recruits to terrorist organizations. The terrorists do not create the market for their ideas; they exploit an already existing market by providing an attractive explanation for all the ills that afflict the Muslim world and a seductively simple solution to them. By framing this explanation and solution in religious terms, they benefit from the emotional resonance that Islamic imagery and terminology carry among believers, provide moral cover for the use of violence, and escalate the stakes for would-be bystanders by introducing issues of personal salvation or damnation into the motivational calculus.

The discontent that attracts people to the jihadist cause need not track closely with the specific program that the terrorists espouse. The trick that Osama bin Laden, Ayman

FIGURE 2–1. PROPAGANDA BY WORD AND DEED IN ANARCHISM AND JIHADISM

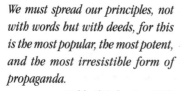

We must spread our principles, not with words but with deeds, for this is the most popular, the most potent, and the most irresistible form of propaganda.

Mikhail Bakunin, 1870

Anyone who understands the particular character of this religion will also understand the place of struggle with the sword, which is to clear the way for struggle through preaching.

Sayyid Qutb, ca. 1964

al-Zawahiri, and their colleagues have mastered is to portray all grievances felt by Muslims as aspects of one global struggle between the "House of Islam" and the "House of War."[8] Moreover, they have shown a knack for inspiring to jihad many who are not directly touched by the perceived inequities suffered by Muslims but who, thanks to education, modern communications, and individual psychological susceptibility, feel a sense of vicarious aggrievement with those who are objectively downtrodden. As a result of these skills, al Qaeda and similar groups have been able to exploit local conflicts of economic, political, or ethnic origin, imbue the aggrieved parties with religious fervor, and co-opt them into the global insurgency, creating an ever-expanding support base that strengthens the hard-core movement both materially and politically.[9] In other words, they are achieving the first objective of al Qaeda as set forth in a set of draft bylaws found in the Kandahar house of al Qaeda's deceased military commander, Abu Hafs al-Masri: "spreading the sentiment of jihad among the Muslim nation."[10]

DYNAMICS OF THE CONFLICT

Understanding the war being waged against us as an insurgency, albeit one of unprecedented scope, yields a number of important insights about the nature of the conflict.

FIGURE 2–2. CIRCLES OF INSURGENT SUPPORT

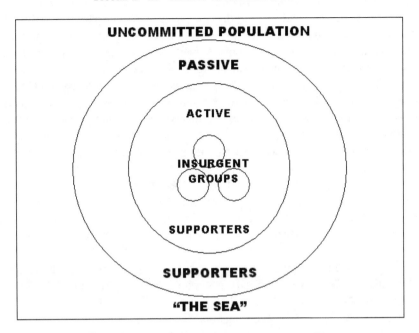

The first of these is that, like most insurgencies, the global jihadist insurgency is conducted on multiple levels by a range of distinct actors (see figure 2–2). If one visualizes these actors as inhabiting a series of concentric circles, the center circle is occupied by the core group of insurgents—top leaders, mid-level commanders, and frontline fighters—who actively prosecute the violent struggle. This core group makes common cause with similar groups pursuing the same objectives under separate leadership. Occupying the next circle out are the insurgency's active supporters: those who raise money, provide logistic support and ideological justification, or serve as communications links between groups and between leaders and fighters. A third, considerably larger, circle is composed of passive supporters—those who identify with the insurgency's objectives and may express support for it rhetorically, but who, if they provide any material aid, do so only incidentally or indirectly and perhaps without full knowledge of the ultimate use to which that aid will be put.

Finally, beyond this third ring is the enormous pool of uncommitted members of the community upon whose sympathy the insurgency's success depends. This sympathy need not be strong; public indifference between the terrorists and the forces fighting them may suffice from the terrorists' point of view because the global jihadist insurgency is a fight over the legitimacy of the existing order. The long-term success or failure of any insurgency depends on the beliefs and attitudes of the populace. Do they believe that the governments under which they live have a valid right to rule? Can these governments command their own peoples' respect and obedience as a matter of justice? Is the international order basically fair or unfair? If the majority of people accept the government or the international order as fundamentally legitimate, notwithstanding whatever disagreements they may have with some particular policy, they will feel a moral obligation to the maintenance of that order. In that case, insurgents will find it difficult to recruit new fighters, generate financial and material support, and move with impunity among the population. When governments call for assistance in combating terrorists, they will get it, or at least enough of it to make a difference.

Conversely, if most people do not accept the existing order as legitimate, discontent can lead quickly to mass alienation. A radical, violent ideology then mobilizes the most susceptible among this alienated population to take up arms. Not everyone will resort to violence; the decision to become a terrorist depends on a multitude of highly individual factors. But if the existing order is not legitimate, even people who do not subscribe to the agenda of violence will tend to reject cooperation with governments prosecuting the struggle against the insurgents. They may well sympathize with the insurgents' ends, but even if they do not, they are not prepared to take personal risks on behalf of a system to which they are not emotionally and morally committed.

The Sum of All Grievances

The jihadist insurgency has been successful at adapting its radical ideology to convert particular grievances harbored by people in different countries—lack of job opportunity in one place, foreign occupation in another, corrupt rulers in a third—into a broad disgruntlement with the entire status quo. As a result, the already tenuous legitimacy of many states in the Islamic world has been seriously weakened. More to the point, however, is that, as a transnational insurgency, the jihadist critique has as much to do with the legitimacy of the international order, of which the United States is the dominant member, as it does with the domestic legitimacy of any state within which discontented Muslims find themselves living.[11]

Inasmuch as the conflict is about legitimacy, the established order can prevail only if it can convince uncommitted community members that it is prosecuting the struggle with legitimate means. This dynamic creates a serious conundrum for the forces combating an insurgency, particularly a terrorist one. Providing for the safety of its people is one of the fundamental responsibilities of any government; waiting passively for insurgents to strike detracts from its legitimacy in proportion to the terrorists' capacity to inflict harm. Thus, given the immense destructive power in the hands of modern terrorists, those combating terrorists are compelled to seize the offensive by discovering, disrupting, and destroying terrorist cells before they can strike. Yet a perception by the public, whose support the insurgents are seeking, that official authorities are unfairly using excessive force, violating the generally accepted rules of the game (for example, by disregarding guarantees of civil liberties in a democratic society), or inflicting collateral damage on innocent bystanders also damages the legitimacy of the established order. This is especially true when the fight against the insurgents is seen as being conducted by or on behalf of outsiders, as was once the case with colonial powers fighting liberation movements and is now the case with U.S. antiterrorist operations on foreign soil. Insurgent groups often try to goad governments and out-side forces into attacking them in ways that further alienate potential terrorist sympa-thizers from the established order.

While the use of violence by the state (or by a foreign power) tends to erode the user's legitimacy, the opposite is usually true for the insurgents themselves (see figure 2–3). Resorting to violence is seen as demonstrating seriousness of purpose, and the greater the level of violence inflicted by an insurgent group, the more credible it ap-pears as an alternative to a state incapable of fulfilling its most fundamental responsi-bility: providing security. Since the insurgents begin by rejecting the rules of the game, they tend to be held less accountable by a disaffected public for the consequences of their actions. In fact, in the case of international terrorists, the targets are often outsid-ers to the society on whose support the success of the insurgency depends. From their own point of view, the only side that appears to be causing damage to the population is the side seeking to combat the terrorists.

There are two important exceptions to this general pattern. It is sometimes pos-sible for the government to apply force overwhelmingly, skillfully, accurately, and efficiently, thereby inflicting a decisive blow against the insurgents with minimum effect on the surrounding population. It is also occasionally the case that insurgents overplay their hands. They may misjudge the degree and types of violence the society is prepared to countenance, as did the Armed Islamic Group in Algeria, or they may undertake a particular campaign that has a disproportionately negative impact on the people in whose name they pretend to act, as did the terrorist group Islamic Jihad when it destroyed the tourist industry by attacking Westerners in Upper Egypt.

FIGURE 2–3. VIOLENCE-LEGITIMACY PARADOX IN INSURGENCIES

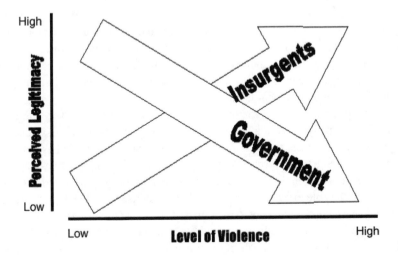

Similarly, the April 25, 2006, bombings in the Egyptian resort town of Dahab, apparently the work of al Qaeda, drew sharp condemnation from across the Muslim political spectrum, including the leadership of the Egyptian Muslim Brotherhood and the Hamas government of the Palestinian Authority. Important strategic implications derive from both the general pattern and the exceptions.

Cold War Analogies?

Of course, the matter of legitimacy does not depend entirely on questions of use of force. Inasmuch as an insurgency is about winning popular support, it is a campaign of persuasion, and in this campaign, ideas matter. In this sense, as President Bush has noted,[12] our struggle bears a certain resemblance to the great ideological struggle of the 20th century, the struggle against communism. As in the Cold War, the battle of ideas will have to be conducted over many decades. Just as the jihadists of today offer a unified theory that purports to account for the ills facing their target audience and use that theory to co-opt fundamentally nonreligious conflicts into the global jihad, so the communist ideologists of the last century offered a unified theory—Lenin's doctrine that imperialism arose from the inevitable economic competition between capitalist states—to co-opt national liberation movements into the communist orbit. But the resemblance is deceptive, given six fundamental differences between the Cold War experience and the present conflict.

First, the ideological conflict between East and West during the Cold War manifested itself in large part—although not exclusively—as a struggle to gain or hold geographic territory by force. While ideological subversion played an important role in the conflict, it was nevertheless significant that one could trace the front lines between the two sides on a map. This is not the case with the jihadist insurgency, in which, despite theoretical claims lodged by Islamists to the whole of the territory ever governed by Muslims, the forward edge of the battle area cannot be found on a map but rather along the nongeographic cleavage lines existing in a multitude of states.

Second, liberal democracy and Marxist communism were closely related intellectually, both flowing from the same secular, rationalist 18th-century spring called the European Enlightenment. That the West could provide freedom, prosperity, and equality more effectively than the communist East was ultimately decisive because both sides measured their performance against the same yardstick. That is not the case in the struggle against violent, radical Islam.

Third, despite much of the rhetoric, the threat posed to the West by the jihadist insurgency is not truly existential in the sense that the jihadists could put an end to the Western world as it exists today. Part of the reason that this struggle has not taken a predominantly geographic form is that the jihadists lack military forces capable of territorial conquest. Even if they were to obtain weapons of mass destruction (WMD), they would not be able to wipe out the United States or its way of life the way the Soviet Union could have done. This is not to minimize the danger posed by the jihadist movement; its capacity for damage to the United States and its people may be less than was the Soviet Union's, but the probability that it will use that capacity is much greater.

Nevertheless, it would be an exaggeration to say that the physical survival of American society is at stake the way it was during the Cold War.

Fourth, because the ideas espoused by radical Islamists are so antithetical to those held almost universally within Western societies, there is also no significant danger that the jihadists and their allies will be able to subvert Western societies from within. While radical Islamist ideology does have significant appeal in unassimilated Muslim communities in some European countries, in no European country does the Muslim population exceed about 8 percent of the total, and far from all Muslims are drawn to radical solutions.[13] On this side of the Atlantic, there seems to be even less support for the ideology espoused by al Qaeda, or even for political Islam in its more moderate forms. All this is in sharp contrast to the presence in Western countries, throughout most of the Cold War, of large, well-organized communist parties, some of them consistently enjoying the support of 30 to 40 percent of the electorate.

Fifth, in the geographic areas where Muslim populations dominate and sympathy for the jihadist cause is substantial, the insurgents and their ideological allies still do not bear the burden, as the Soviet communists did, of having to put their ideas into practice by running an actual country. As long as radical Islamists are not required to act on their teachings, there will be no practical contradictions to undermine the credibility of the theory. The radical Islamist ideology can remain an elegant, self-contained construct, like Marxism before the Bolshevik Revolution. Seen in this light, al Qaeda's and the Taliban's loss of control over Afghanistan may not have been an unmitigated failure for the Islamists; they can once again project an image that is untainted by practical failures of governance. Of course, the fact that the jihadists are not in power also makes them more difficult to deter; compared to the government of a conventional territorial state, they have little to lose that a power seeking to deter them can hold at risk.

Finally, the standards by which to judge strategic victory or defeat in the struggle against Islamist terrorism are much less clear than was the case during the Cold War. It is, of course, possible to identify near-term victories and defeats; another successful major terrorist attack on the United States would be a defeat, while the destruction of a terrorist network, as in Afghanistan, would be a victory. Over the longer term, however, such categories become less useful, if only because the meanings of *victory* and *defeat* are themselves unclear. The United States and the West are unlikely to "lose" the long-term fight with jihadism in the sense that they might have lost the Cold War; the inexorable progress of the global information revolution almost guarantees that the propagation of Western ideas and values will continue, for better and for worse. Interaction between the West and the Islamic world is simply not going to cease, as the jihadists and other radical Islamists demand. Nor would the ills afflicting Muslims suddenly be cured if it did. In short, it is extremely difficult to conceive of what any plausible scenario of defeat would look like.

It is no easier to identify what plausible outcome would constitute a genuine victory. Absent an enemy that occupies a given territory or commands regular military units, it is difficult to imagine how an enemy capitulation would appear. It may therefore be preferable to think not in terms of victory or defeat but rather of the success or failure of a counter-jihadist strategy. Long-term hostility, a pervading sense of "us versus them" between the Islamic world and the rest of the world, with all the dangers and disorder that such hostility implies, would clearly be failure. U.S. antiterrorist policy would obviously be judged to have failed if U.S. citizens are constantly at risk of being struck by mass-effects terrorism far into the future. The country would pay a high cost in money, manpower, and morale if it were forced to remain in a state of elevated terrorist alert for decades on end. Even if the U.S. homeland could be kept safe, American citizens would not be immune from the consequences of chronic disorder afflicting more than a billion people—people who own half or more of the world's proven natural gas supplies and over two-thirds of its oil, and who, thanks to demographic and immigration trends, comprise a growing share of the population of U.S. European allies and trading partners. Such an outcome would also represent a policy failure.

A STRATEGIC CONCEPT FOR THE WAR ON JIHADIST TERROR

One of the most difficult dilemmas confronting the United States in dealing with jihadist terrorism is that it may be possible to win an unbroken series of tactical victories and never suffer a tactical defeat, yet still find ourselves in the end confronting a strategic failure. This conundrum, hinted at by Secretary Rumsfeld's questions to his staff, is also implicit in the vast literature on combating insurgencies dating back to the 1960s: the use of force to eradicate insurgents, including terrorists who enjoy popular sympathy, can fuel long-term hostility unless it is adroitly managed in the context of a strategy for addressing the broader political and social aspects of the struggle.

Once the jihadist terrorist movement is understood as a global insurgency, the need to approach the struggle against it with a counterinsurgency mindset becomes obvious. U.S. strategy must work toward two objectives at once. It must prevent terrorists from acting effectively now and in the future. *At the same time*, it must break the connective tissues between the terrorist-insurgent movement and the population from which it draws its strength.

The use of military force remains an essential, but not the only, element for pursuing the first objective. Obviously, as illuminated by the force-legitimacy paradox discussed above, the use of excessive force can damage the legitimacy of the United States, strengthen that of the jihadists, and lead to strategic failure. Yet underutilization of force can yield the same result. Obviously, to allow the American people to remain at high risk of a mass-casualty terrorist attack into the distant future would be a strategic failure in its own right. But not suppressing existing terrorists would have other strategic consequences as well. Each terrorist success has the effect of burnishing the insurgency's credibility among Muslims who are alienated from the status quo. The jihadists become heroes for standing up to an enemy that appears muscle-bound in its powerlessness against them. Meanwhile, the continuing sense of threat felt by target societies and the defensive measures they adopt in response are an effective way of persuading Muslims who are not already sympathetic to the jihadist cause that the Islamist vision of the world as divided into two irreconcilably hostile camps is an accurate depiction of reality.

Excessive or inadequate use of force in a counterinsurgency conflict can lead to strategic failure, but even the proper balance of force cannot promise strategic success. Insurgents can thrive politically, even in the face of utter military rout. Ultimate success against insurgents depends on dividing them from their base of popular support. What Robert Taber wrote of guerrilla insurgencies in 1965 applies equally to the jihadist insurgency 40 years later:

> Without the consent and active aid of the people, the guerrilla would be merely a bandit, and could not long survive. If, on the other hand, the counterinsurgent could claim this same support, the guerrilla would not exist, because there would be no war, no revolution. The cause would have evaporated, the popular impulse toward radical change—cause or no cause—would be dead.[14]

A strategy to combat jihadist terrorism must therefore provide for simultaneously carrying out two fundamentally different sets of tasks that are not merely different but often in tension with one another. The war on terrorism will see American leaders—and the leaders of other states resisting the jihadist insurgency—repeatedly called upon to balance the operational benefits of active attacks on terrorist leaders and networks against the strategic risk that such attacks will reinforce the appeal of the jihadist cause. Meanwhile, the process of severing the tissue connecting jihadists with their popular base is bound to be a prolonged one. The crisis of legitimacy from which sympathy for jihadists arises did not develop overnight and will not be resolved overnight. As with any effort to alter social attitudes and behavior, progress will be difficult to gauge, and many initiatives that at first seem to have great potential for breaking those key linkages between the people and the insurgents will turn out to be over-ambitious, inappropriate to the culture in which they are attempted, or simply derived from flawed premises.

Suppression of Terrorists: Minimum Effective Force

How can terrorists be prevented from acting, and how can their capabilities to strike in the future be eliminated without generating an even greater flood of new terrorists? The answer derives from recalling what the jihadists are trying to achieve with their terrorist strategy: to galvanize their own support base, weaken the legitimacy of the existing order, and draw ever more Muslims into their ideological orbit. Accordingly, the most strategically potent approach to the suppression of jihadist insurgents is exactly the reverse of the conventional approach, in which overwhelming, decisive force is used after all other remedies have been exhausted. Instead, as illustrated by one of the exceptions to the force-legitimacy paradox described above, the minimum effective force should be used at a point early enough that it can still be effective, before the insurgents have a chance to move up the violence ladder themselves.

This means a strong emphasis on the use of diplomatic, intelligence, financial, and law enforcement tools for destroying terrorist capabilities in preference to even the most carefully calibrated uses of military means. Furthermore, these tools should be wielded wherever possible by local authorities, for several reasons. First, reliance on local authorities to maintain order in the territory under their nominal control reinforces local government legitimacy; outside intervention undermines it. Second, host country authorities, however flawed, usually have a better chance than outsiders of penetrating the social networks that enable and protect insurgent operatives, making the need to resort to overt violence less likely. This is especially important in operations against the jihadists' active support base of fundraisers and apologists, who will be seen by many of their countrymen as law-abiding citizens against whom the use of military force would be beyond the pale.

Of course, however useful and important such nonviolent instruments of statecraft may be, there will still be times when violent means must be employed. In these cases, given the impact the use of force will have on perceptions of legitimacy, this use of force, whether overt or covert, must be sharply focused at times and places where it can be rapidly effective, intensive rather than extensive, avoiding prolonged engagements and reducing the probability of unintended casualties that will further alienate the populace on which the jihadists depend.

This means that major conventional operations should not be the norm in future military action against jihadist terrorism. Any efforts to achieve regime change by military force should be pursued with particular care. If the jihadists play on the existing order's lack of legitimacy for their popular appeal, then the perception that new governments are being installed at the point of foreign, let alone infidel, guns will only fan the flames of the transnational insurgency. Furthermore, as the cases of Afghanistan and Iraq demonstrate, a regime change strategy can easily require subsequent employment of substantial numbers of combat troops—in the tens of thousands—for years at a time. This is a situation tailor-made for radical Islamist propagandists, as the U.S. experience in Iraq has painfully proven.

Instead, the employment of force should focus on eradicating specific terrorist assets or capabilities that pose a clear and present danger and cannot be dealt with by other means. For the same reasons that nonviolent means should be favored over violent ones, host country forces should be in the lead if possible when violence must be used. Failing that, the United States should look for ways to act in concert with host country forces or at least with the host country's knowledge and consent. However deficient host country forces' legitimacy may be in the eyes of their people, it is almost always greater than that of U.S. forces.

Criteria for Use of Force

Ultimately, there will be situations in which immediate action is imperative but the host government either cannot or will not act. In such cases, the United States should consider whether a third party with a modicum of local legitimacy might be able to conduct the operation with less blowback than direct U.S. involvement might trigger. Finally, when no other option exists, the United States must have the capability to apply force itself. When that is necessary, three considerations should be kept paramount in the design of the operation.

First, force must be employed quickly, effectively, and precisely. Second, conducting such operations effectively, while minimizing the damage done to the political half of U.S. strategy, necessarily requires exquisite intelligence about the location and identity of targets. Each use of force comes at a political cost; U.S. officials cannot afford to miss, let alone to hit, a target that turns out to be wrong. Finally, the visibility of the operation should be minimized, even more so when the host government is complicit in the U.S. action and could have its legitimacy undermined by public knowledge of its cooperation with foreign forces.

Since each use of force in this war comes at a cost, it is important that shots hit their mark. The nature of the enemy means that the calculus involved in these decisions will be quite different from that used in targeting a conventional adversary. Where it might be more cost-effective when fighting a conventional state to focus on the enemy's will rather than his capabilities, this is not the case when fighting a terrorist insurgency. Operating against the enemy's will to fight requires a high confidence in one's ability to affect the enemy's *strategic* calculus, not simply his military calculus, through the application of what is by nature a very blunt instrument. This level of confidence in the fight with the present enemy is lacking. Indeed, there is every possibility that terrorist organizations foresee that anything the United States might do in the military sphere will ultimately redound to their advantage.

This is not to say that the jihadists are correct in this assessment; in fact, there may well be things the United States can do militarily that can inflict serious political damage on them. Nevertheless, it cannot be assumed that jihadist leaders believe this to be so. Certainly, if their political strategy centers around the creation of high-profile martyrs to galvanize the Islamic *umma* to action, they will respond to U.S. attempts at coercion quite differently than would the rulers of a conventional state with power and resources to preserve. A U.S. strategy that involves the use of force should focus on destroying capabilities, not affecting enemy calculations.

Finally, structuring the use of force in this war requires deep skepticism about the possibility that a single operation or even a single campaign could bring down the jihadist enemy in the way that Clausewitz taught that the destruction of the enemy's center of gravity could bring down a conventional foe. The potency of the jihadist threat arises from the ability of those who inspire the movement to link widely separated groups on the basis of a common agenda without a centralized command and control structure. Much of the recent military operational theory that focuses on attacking an enemy's decisionmaking capabilities is therefore of limited applicability. Moreover, the ties among different members of the terrorist networks are informal, constantly shifting and adapting, making it both difficult and pointless to attack those linkages militarily in the way one might attack nodes connecting the members of a traditional alliance or a national command structure. Finally, even if these links could be severed, the jihadists' global reach stems not only from the connections among terrorist bodies, but also from the ability of each separate organization, and increasingly of each individual, to apply the fruits of globalization to the common cause. In the 21st century, a local terrorist with a global agenda is a global terrorist, and the elusive network of which he is a part does not present opportunities for single-point-failure attacks. Rather, a counterinsurgency strategy must focus on the enemy's strategy.

Insurgents and People: Cutting the Ties that Bind

At its root, an insurgency strategy is about establishing connections between the insurgents and the populations from which they draw sustenance and whose political support they seek to win. Successful counterinsurgents must sever these connections. The task of designing an effective strategy to separate the insurgents from their popular base of support is even more complex than designing an effective strategy for the use of force. No single approach can achieve the rupture between insurgents and population everywhere in the Islamic world. What makes any given Muslim sympathize with the insurgents varies from place to place, group to group, and person to person. The fact that people support violent insurgencies because they reject the legitimacy of the existing order does not mean that all who are receptive to Osama bin Laden's appeal share the same discontents or that they see the complex questions of legitimacy the same way. A Berber villager may be perfectly satisfied that King Mohamed VI is the legitimate ruler of Morocco by virtue of biological descent from the Prophet yet might still reject the legitimacy of an international system that permits militarily stronger countries to "impose" their social values through the process of globalization. A Saudi student may reject the status quo in his country not because of disagreement with how the present rulers came to power but because these rulers have not been able to act effectively to end the Israeli occupation of the Palestinian territories or prevent the American invasion of Iraq.

Some of the discontents that make people susceptible to the jihadist appeal are obviously common to much of the Islamic world—unhappiness at the relative weakness of Islam vis-à-vis the West, resentment against the intrusion of alien ideas into traditional societies, a sense of powerlessness in the face of relentless globalization. Other discontents, however, are peculiar to individual countries, and even the grievances that are more widely felt manifest themselves in different ways from place to place.

Neutralizing the jihadist appeal to Islamic populations, therefore, depends on following the injunction on the popular bumper sticker: "think globally, act locally." In effect, the global insurgency must be unraveled through a series of local counterinsurgency campaigns, using classical counterinsurgency approaches, addressing each specific combination of global and local grievances and concerns that drive popular support for the insurgency. Rather than assuming the existence of a single universal solution, whether it be democracy, peace, development, or education, U.S. planners must analyze the factors that lead specific groups to support, sympathize with, or tolerate terrorist activity. The strategy should seek to affect those factors, case by case, along six mutually reinforcing lines: building capacity for governance, strengthening systemic legitimacy, defusing regional flashpoints, controlling cultural confrontation, addressing material discontents, and countering the jihadist ideological appeal.

Building capacity for governance. The jihad at the center of this globalized insurgency challenges the validity of the entire international state system. The very ideology of jihad focuses on overcoming that system, whether explicitly or implicitly, in its quest to restore a rightly guided caliphate. A fundamental requirement of combating jihadism, then, is to bolster the international order, a task most readily fulfilled by reinforcing the institutions—the states—comprising that order. Strengthening states, and then working cooperatively with them to fulfill the responsibilities of sovereignty, can greatly complicate the jihadists' mission.

There are two aspects to this effort: increasing the capacity of states to govern, and increasing their will to fulfill the responsibilities of statehood. States must control their own territory, including the control of physical ungoverned spaces, in ways that prevent it from being used to incubate threats to other states. At worst, persistent inability to exercise control over the national space is a manifestation of actual or impending state failure. In other instances, governments have made conscious decisions to stay out of tribal quarrels and similar conflicts, assuming that as long as such disputes could be geographically contained, they would pose no danger to the rest of the population. But this is no longer the case. Outside organizations with broader agendas take advantage of the disorder in places such as Pakistan's Federally Administered Tribal Areas, Bangladesh's Chittagong Hills Tract, and Yemen's Hadhramaut to find sanctuaries where they can organize, train, and plan—and where they can work to co-opt these local conflicts into the wider transnational struggle.

The United States must therefore help other governments generate the political will, physical capability, and conceptual creativity to take responsibility for what transpires in such areas. It is a primary task of a counterinsurgency strategy to identify those areas and to assist the state in question in coming to terms with its responsibilities. It goes without saying that this effort is neither a fast nor an inexpensive one, and it will require significant insight to embark upon such extensive foreign work in places where U.S. interests are not immediately obvious.

States face the even more complicated task of finding ways to gain control of less obvious sanctuaries. Some of these sanctuaries resemble the ungoverned spaces of failing states in that they are definable geographic zones in which state authority is limited, such as the immigrant-populated suburban ghettos surrounding many major European cities. Others derive from the basic social contract characteristic of the modern West, especially in urban areas, under which people generally respect one another's privacy and tolerate even the most diversely unorthodox attitudes and behaviors. Still other sanctuaries exist within the web of legal protections and constitutional rights upon which democratic polities are founded. Dealing effectively with these virtual lacunae in governance is easier said than done, even more so in a well-governed country than in a badly governed one. Navigating the tangle of tradeoffs between civil liberties and security is enormously tricky, and it is a rare country that would endeavor to tackle these issues without imminent concern. The United States must be very careful how it pushes its partners in this regard; while steps must be taken, the potential for them to backfire is enormous.

Increasing capacity for governance also means improving the ability of key states to deliver the services expected of them by their populations. To some extent, the problems of uncontrolled spaces and unserviced spaces overlap; it is hard to induce construction workers, power line repairmen, teachers, and doctors to work in areas into which even the army and police are unprepared to venture. But the problem is not merely geographic. Many regimes in the Middle East and South Asia have failed, for various political and bureaucratic reasons, to provide such basic institutions of government as functioning courts of law. Citizens seeking the most modest action by local administrations often meet with prolonged delays. The same applies, only more so, to the social services—housing, health care, education—that 21st-century governments, even in the Third World, are expected to furnish.

Across the Islamic world, radical organizations increasingly are moving into the political vacuum created by these governmental shortcomings. In some areas of Pakistan, the state's failure to provide an adequate system of public education has been offset by the provision of *madrassa*s by Islamic political parties and affiliated organizations.[15] In many Egyptian villages, the only functioning clinic is run not by the health ministry but by an Islamist nongovernmental organization. In the legal area, recognizing that justice delayed is justice denied, people turn away from the slow, inefficient, and often corrupt official judicial system and turn instead to informal arbitration, often provided, once again, by radical Islamist groups.[16] This process weakens even further the ability of state authorities to control the national space; they become outsiders in their own land, and jihadists and other radicals occupy the void.

The United States must refocus a major portion of its foreign assistance programs on correcting such governance deficits, an initiative that would overlap significantly with the task of addressing material discontents. At the same time, it is also clear that reinforcing other states' will to use capacity once it is built is as critical as building the capacity itself. To do this, the United States must foster an atmosphere that recognizes terrorism as *mala in se*—evil in itself—establishing the fundamental illegitimacy of the tactic.

Second, a broader consensus must emerge on the nature of the danger that terrorism presents to the general global welfare. This will take careful consultation throughout the world, and likely some level of abstraction: how does the U.S. Government convince Slovaks of the threat it thinks they face? On the other hand, the international community has already officially recognized many of the damaging consequences of terrorism. United Nations (UN) Security Council Resolution 1377, adopted in the months following 9/11, pointed out that terrorism not only endangers innocent lives and challenges the international state system but also "threaten[s] social and economic development . . . and undermine[s] global stability and prosperity." The more it can be shown that the tactics of the jihadists harm the people on whose behalf they claim to act, whether economically (as in Upper Egypt) or physically (as at the World Trade Center and in terrorist attacks in Saudi Arabia), the more leverage there will be to turn the Muslim populace against the jihadists. There is evidence that this process has already begun to some extent; even the leaders of Egypt's al-Gama'at al-Islamiyah, the hard-line militant group formerly headed by Shaykh Umar Abd ur-Rahman, have condemned al Qaeda for the damage it has inflicted on the Islamic *umma* by provoking the United States to war.[17]

Finally, there must be a global effort to stress the responsibilities of statehood, rather than the rights that have been more heavily emphasized in the postcolonial period. If the United States and its partners can develop a global grassroots consensus that terrorist methods are evil in themselves and demonstrate at the mass level the tangible damage done in the terrorist cause, perhaps popular pressure can be brought to bear on governments reluctant to fulfill those responsibilities.

Strengthening legitimacy. Given that insurgencies are intrinsically about the legitimacy of the established order, it follows that one way of combating an insurgency is to reinforce the legitimacy of the system that is under challenge. But what exactly does *legitimacy* mean, and how might one go about strengthening it?

The concept of legitimacy was introduced into modern social science by the German sociologist Max Weber. He described legitimacy as the attitude, shared by people subject to a particular set of social relationships, that the order within which those relationships exist has binding moral authority behind it. Legitimacy may derive from a variety of sources—tradition, religious belief, logical deduction from abstract principles, conventional acceptance of a tacit social contract, and others. The key to whether a particular social order is legitimate is not the source upon which its legitimacy is based. In fact, most social orders derive their legitimacy from a combination of prescription, revelation, convention, and legality.[18] The key is whether the order derives its powers, in Thomas Jefferson's formula, "from the consent of the governed," keeping clearly in view that the formal mechanisms of democracy are far from the only means by which consent is expressed.[19]

Ordinarily, one thinks of governments as the entities that are legitimate or illegitimate. A legitimate government is able to induce compliance with its rules without the constant use of overt coercion. Conversely, an illegitimate government is frequently threatened with disorder, instability, and domestic turmoil. As Weber used it, however, the concept of legitimacy is relevant to all sorts of social relationships, not just political ones. In a globalized world, in which economic, intellectual, and other social relationships increasingly transcend cultural and political boundaries, it is only reasonable to expect that how people perceive the legitimacy of the wider international order will become increasingly important. If large numbers of people in a variety of countries view the global order as illegitimate, it should not be surprising if the result is the growth of a transnational insurgency.

Arguably, that is precisely what is now manifest. Most Muslims clearly do not view the U.S.-led international order as legitimate. By large majorities, they believe that it is wrong for the United States to possess unrivalled and unchecked power and that the United States uses that power, as in the war on terrorism, in an attempt to dominate the world.[20] Even more widespread is the view that traditional cultures ought to be protected against the impact of globalization.[21] In some measure, Muslims and others who feel their lives affected by forces they do not accept as having moral authority over them are perceived as lending support to groups that promise to combat what they see as an illegitimate international order. One cannot target the international order in the abstract, however. Instead, one targets the dominant force in that international order—the United States.

Efforts to alleviate a perception that the international order is illegitimate undoubtedly will be complicated by differences in how the international order itself is understood. Many in the Islamic world, like most Europeans, have come to reify the "international community" as something that has an existence and significance above and beyond that of the sovereign states that comprise it. Americans, by contrast, tend to view international organizations as instruments through which sovereign entities pursue and harmonize their respective interests, not as entities in their own right. The issue is complicated by the fact that America's preponderant power, and its own claims to a special historical mission, often lead to expectations that it will behave other than simply as another state among states pursuing its own interests. When it does not live up to these constructs, the United States is judged more harshly than other states are.

Nevertheless, there are steps aside from purely rhetorical ones that the United States can take to alleviate perceptions that its international role is illegitimate. Most obviously, it can pay greater heed to the UN function as a validating mechanism in the eyes of foreign public opinion. While the political benefits of giving greater attention to the United Nations would certainly not be as dramatic as some might contend, they would not be negligible, either, particularly in regions such as Europe, where supranational organizations are widely seen as vested with legitimacy in their own right. The payoff would be less clear in the Islamic world, where regard for the UN is quite low,[22] although the disrepute in which the body is held among Muslims may be driven by their perception that it functions mainly as an instrument of U.S. policy. In addition, therefore, the United States should seek to promote the development of more—and more effective—multilateral institutions in which Arab and Muslim interests can be articulated and represented within both regional and functional contexts. This effort should include shaping a regional security landscape that includes multilateral institutions of varying degrees of formality, structures by which Arab and other Islamic states could interact collectively with the Group of 7 (similar to the Group of 8 arrangement by which Russian interests and concerns are represented), and other initiatives through which predominantly Muslim states can be integrated into institutions that transcend the Islamic/non-Islamic divide.

Weak legitimacy contributes to the jihadist phenomenon at the national level as well. The tendency of Arab regimes to lack legitimacy has been commonplace among regional specialists ever since Michael Hudson in 1977 described this lack as "the central problem of government in the Arab world today."[23] It was to this legitimacy deficit that Hudson attributed the pervasive instability, unpredictability, and repression that characterize Arab domestic and international politics. The same problem exists in many non-Arab Muslim countries as well.

This legitimacy deficit stems in part from the lack of a strong sense of shared identity within many Arab states; loyalty to the wider Arab "nation" on the one hand and to subnational tribal, ethnic, sectarian, and local affinity groups on the other often overwhelms loyalty to the territorial nation-state that theoretically exercises sovereignty. It is partly a result of internal inconsistencies within the popular political value systems of many Arab countries; decades of progressive rhetoric extolling democracy, equality, liberation, and unity have been overlaid on centuries of religious rhetoric extolling justice, tradition, and the importance of rightly (that is, religiously) guided government. The combination produces a mix of inflated expectations that any government would be hard pressed to fulfill. Also responsible is the transplant into the Arab (and wider Muslim) context of postcolonial and anticolonial political structures that not only do not match well with underlying social structures but also were in many instances expressly designed to destroy traditional modes of social organization. The influence of classical theories about the nature of the Islamic state, which generally deprecate the concept of multiple, independent sovereigns within the community of believers, also is a contributing factor. Finally, it stems in part from the failure of the region's governments to keep up with evolving expectations, driven by the information revolution, about the role ordinary people should play in determining their own destiny.

These sources suggest several areas in which U.S. efforts to enhance systemic legitimacy should be focused. Most obviously, it is important for regional states to develop political systems that are congruent with existing values and expectations and that have processes built in that can shape these expectations over time while building a sense of national loyalty and solidarity to supplement—and perhaps supplant—the higher and lower order loyalties that now characterize many Muslim societies. Such systems must also find ways to accommodate public demands for participation that are not only effective but also consistent with each society's dominant beliefs and attitudes.

Obviously, this means that one size will not fit all. The notion of what constitutes legitimate governance varies with culture. This variance can be seen in how different populations value competing ideals. Asked to choose whether it was more important for the government to guarantee that no one was in need or to leave people alone to pursue their own goals, Lebanese participants in the Pew Global Attitudes Project opted for noninterference by a margin of 52 to 47 percent. Yet in neighboring Jordan, social protection was valued over individual freedom by nearly two to one. In South Asia, Muslim Pakistan and predominantly Hindu India both opted for noninterference, while Muslim Bangladeshis lined up overwhelmingly in favor of social protection.[24]

Furthermore, public perceptions in different countries are sharply at odds with many Americans' assumptions. For example, a 2002 Pew report found that citizens of Pakistan and Uzbekistan, two countries considered by Americans to be dictatorships with little legitimacy, had overwhelmingly positive views of their governments (72 percent and 88 percent, respectively). Meanwhile, the government of Jordan—which

Americans tend to view favorably—got positive marks from less than half of its people.[25] Moreover, from an American perspective, Muslim attitudes on right governance may seem internally inconsistent. As has been widely remarked, majorities in almost all Muslim countries say they want democracy. In Jordan, according to the Pew research, 68 percent believed democracy can work in their country, yet only 28 percent thought it was very important to have honest, contested elections.[26]

Not only must U.S. strategy accept that "all politics is local," it must also recognize that any system that is construed by the public as externally imposed will likely be perceived as illegitimate ipso facto. Given the strongly negative attitudes now existing toward the United States, this is especially true of concepts that are perceived as "made in the USA." Pew surveys have found a strongly positive reaction throughout most of the Islamic world to the proposition that democracy is a good system, but the support falls off sharply if the question is rephrased to specify "American-style democracy." Even if the source is not the United States, however, foreign models will be viewed with intense suspicion. As the British discovered in the wake of their disappointing efforts to mobilize the Arab masses against the Ottoman Empire in World War I, disliking the government one has is a far cry from welcoming an alternative imposed from without.[27] Any efforts the United States and other outsiders make to promote political reform must therefore be as low-visibility as possible and painstakingly deferential to local popular (although not necessarily regime) sensitivities.

Western efforts should therefore focus on fostering the *process* of political development rather than on establishing fixed benchmarks of democracy and freedom against which every country will be graded. Moreover, U.S. planners must recognize, as Thomas Carothers has pointed out, that "there are very real, deeply rooted, historical, sociopolitical, and economic reasons why the democratization of Arab societies will prove unusually slow, difficult, and conflictive."[28] An early order of business must be nurturing the grassroots skills necessary for sustainable democracy: aggregating diverse individual interests into politically effective coalitions; ascertaining constituent desires and needs and converting that knowledge into effective action; managing contention without having it devolve into enmity; developing budgets that reconcile competing needs; and so on. The West should assist in the formation of both political and nonpolitical organizations and networks that cut across existing social groups as a means of building a broader sense of identity and loyalty as well as to reinforce the skills of self-rule just discussed. Finally, U.S. policy should promote the development of indigenous cadres of political and constitutional scholars who can take a leading role in shaping political arrangements that satisfy the many competing needs peculiar to each country.

Initiatives to strengthen the legitimacy of regimes that are under insurgent assault must go hand in glove with efforts to build their capacity and will to control their national space. Since the very question in dispute in an insurgency is the legitimacy of a regime, it might be counterproductive to enhance the capability of a questionably legitimate regime to use force against its own population, unless one can be sure that force will be used judiciously and wisely. If U.S. policy can encourage steps that enhance domestic legitimacy, however, there would be less concern that the capabilities that are provided at the same time will be used counterproductively.

At the same time, there are tradeoffs to be made between *good governance*, understood as effective administration in a technocratic sense, and *good politics*, understood as the effective representation of public needs, values, and desires and their reconciliation into public policy. For example, while embezzlement and extortion to line the pockets of politicians are undeniably corrosive, other forms of behavior that are conventionally defined as corrupt, such as those practiced by old-fashioned urban political machines in the United States, may in fact play an important role in integrating otherwise marginalized groups into the political process.

Defusing regional flashpoints. For the same reason, assertive U.S. diplomacy to seek resolution of the conflicts that characterize what some have called the *arc of instability* has a vital role in the political component of a strategy against jihadist terrorism. Conflict resolution is particularly important with respect to the chronic hotspots on the periphery of the Islamic world—Israel-Palestine, India-Pakistan-Kashmir, and Russia-Chechnya, to name three—but also with respect to smaller wars and potential wars (see figure 2–4).

Such conflicts are related to the war on terrorism in three ways. First, as the earlier discussion of the relationship between violence and legitimacy noted, high ambient levels of violence favor the political agenda of insurgent groups. Given that the international community confronts a transnational insurgency, the dynamics of which are heavily influenced by the phenomenon of globalization, it will be apparent that violence between Muslims and non-Muslims *anywhere* will have a political effect on Muslims *everywhere*. There was a time when Muslims in Indonesia or Mali would have been relatively indifferent to what was happening to Muslims in the Balkans or the Caucasus; that time has passed. The growth of 24-hour satellite television news and the availability of the Internet guarantee that wars will be heavily reported. Meanwhile, a growing sense of Islamic solidarity, fueled in part by this reporting, creates a heated political environment that is ripe for exploitation by jihadist ideologues.

Second, wars, especially small wars that do not involve disciplined regular forces, are perfect breeding grounds for co-optable discontents. Atrocities are relatively frequent, and the cataclysm of armed conflict is personalized to a great extent, a phenomenon amplified by the fact that these wars often center on deep identity markers such as race, ethnicity, or religion. Furthermore, the societies involved frequently lack the social development and infrastructure to mitigate the effects of war. People come into contact with their deepest emotions and are then left with little explanation or recourse for the tragedy that has befallen them and continues to burden them. This is fertile ground for the seductively simple ideology of the jihadists. Moreover, the targeted population is already armed and has crossed the line into the application of violence.

Third, dissatisfaction with the way these conflicts are playing out is persistently and overwhelmingly cited in public opinion polls as a principal reason for anti-American

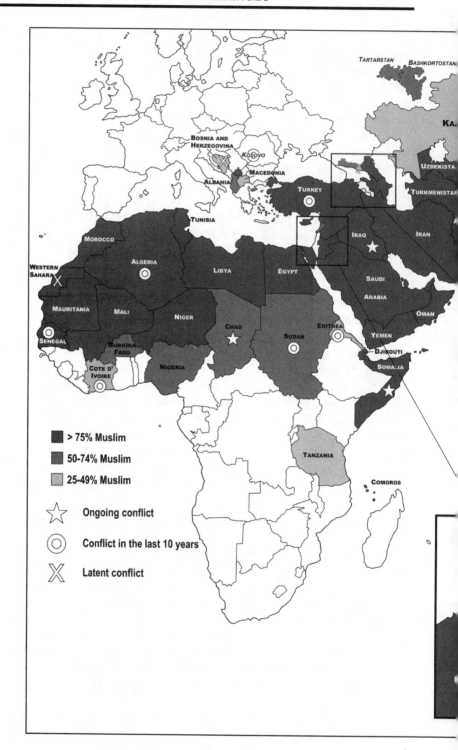

Figure 2–4. Major Conflicts and Tensions in the Muslim World

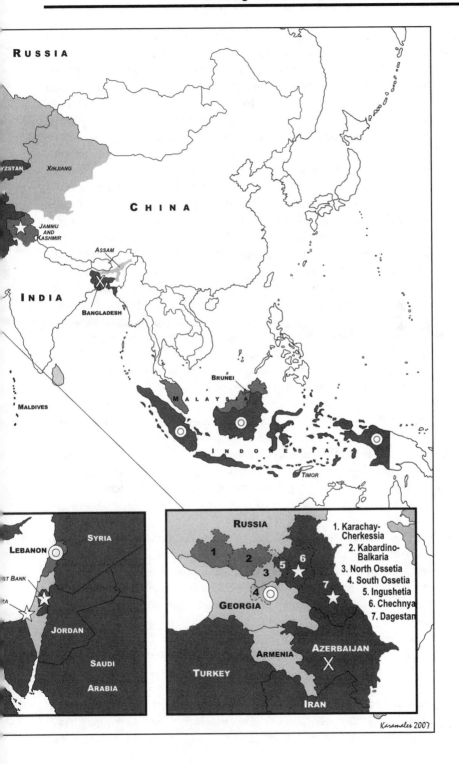

Karamales 2007

sentiment in the Islamic world. Which conflict specifically generates the most intense anti-American attitudes varies from place to place. Pakistanis look to Kashmir, Turks to the Balkans and Chechnya, while Arabs cite the plight of the Palestinians.[29] It matters little that blaming the United States is in many instances totally at odds with the facts of the war concerned. What matters is that the conflicts exist, Muslims identify with their coreligionists whom they see as being killed or oppressed, and jihadist ideologues convert that volatile mix of emotions into opposition to America.

This is not to argue that even successful conflict resolution will quickly or automatically solve the terrorism problem. Experience has shown that those who are irreconcilably opposed to peaceful compromise tend to step up violence whenever a negotiated settlement seems promising, precisely for the purpose of derailing further progress. They will not automatically stand down once a resolution is reached if it does not satisfy their maximalist demands. Nevertheless, fair solutions that are accepted by the bulk of the community concerned will cause the insurgents to lose political traction over time. A key part of a global counterinsurgency must therefore be to deprive the insurgents of the raw material that war zones provide. Prompt mediation of extant conflicts, as well as preventive measures in zones of potential conflict, is imperative.

Although this effort is largely diplomatic, it may likely come to require the occasional provision of peacekeeping or monitoring forces as a confidence-building measure. Obviously, coalition-based burden-sharing is indicated, as well as a careful analysis of which conflicts in fact contain the raw ingredients to feed Islamist extremism; there is a balance to be struck in the extent to which U.S. forces get involved in such operations. Nevertheless, it is clear that U.S. forces require greater capability in this area, and force structure and training should be substantially adjusted with the probability of such operations in mind. Even so, the scale of this effort could swell quickly beyond the U.S. ability to sustain it, and careful diplomacy would be needed to keep expectations in line with what the United States sees to be the key problems on which its influence can be decisive.

Controlling cultural confrontation. Fueling a broad intercivilizational confrontation between Islam and the West is a key goal of the jihadists. Creating a state of enduring hostility would validate the radical interpretation of the world as permanently divided into two irreconcilable camps between which there can be nothing but hatred and violence. If the radicals can plausibly characterize this confrontation as "Islam in danger," they can play on the widely accepted doctrine that every believer is under a personal obligation to participate in what is known as "defensive jihad," a struggle not to spread the faith to new areas but to protect the *umma* against assault from without.[30]

Americans may understand the world as a non–zero-sum system in which the safety, prosperity, and liberty of some need not come at the expense of the safety, prosperity, and liberty of others. But this understanding is not as widely shared as one may wish. Many in the Islamic world and elsewhere, including those most susceptible to the jihadist appeal, take for granted that if some are powerful, others must be helpless; that if some are rich, others must be poor. Radical Islamist propagandists are expert at ensuring that the *some* in this formulation is the United States and the West, while the *others* are the Muslims.

It is therefore directly contrary to U.S. interests to stoke the fires of cultural conflict. American policy should avoid any validation of the jihadists' portrayal of Islam as a culture under siege. There are at least five areas where the heat should be lowered.

In first instance, the United States must seek to prevent the emergence of conditions that could precipitate its own overreaction. A WMD attack on the United States, for instance, could prompt massive and perhaps unfocused retaliation. A variety of attacks, or even simply the persistent fear of attacks, could trigger a significant alteration of the legal status of Muslims in America or Europe and provide putative evidence of the civilizational nature of the conflict. Despite the intense and continuing negative reaction they provoked in the Islamic world, the immigration restrictions on visitors from selected Muslim countries imposed in the wake of 9/11 are a relatively mild prototype of what might come in the aftermath of another, more deadly attack. In a sense, therefore, the United States must protect itself and its allies against attack as much to prevent the ignition of wider conflict as to fulfill the more immediate requirement to defend the lives of its people.

Second, officials must be exceptionally careful of their rhetoric about the conflict. Statements that heighten the level of confrontation play into the hands of the jihadists and undermine the U.S. position. Even the terminology used to describe the conflict becomes part of the way it is fought out in the public discourse of the region. In this chapter, for example, we have used the term *jihadists* to identify the terrorist enemy because jihad is what they themselves claim to be pursuing. But it is important to be aware that both *jihad* and its derivative, *mujahideen* (those who fight in a jihad), are words that have positive, not negative, connotations in Arabic. Thoughtless use of them can easily reinforce the radicals' message that fighting the United States is indeed a sacred duty. Moreover, words can not only fan the flames within the Islamic world, but also, to the extent that they harden American perceptions that the country faces the archetypal clash of civilizations, make it more difficult domestically to follow the subtle political strategy necessary to quash the insurgency in the long run. The Bush administration has generally shown an excellent understanding of this dynamic in its carefully phrased characterizations of the nature of the conflict, although the same cannot be said for the inflammatory statements of other prominent Americans, which jihadists seize upon as evidence that Islam truly is under assault.

The U.S. Government has been less sensitive, however, to the way that pronouncements on the universality of American values, the superiority of American ways (such as the U.S. style of democracy), and the importance of American power sound through the zero-sum, us-versus-them filters described above. The problem here is not what Americans say to Muslims but what Americans say to each other that is overheard in a world of instant global communications. The eschatological vision of history implicit in much American political rhetoric can inadvertently create the impression that the United States is delivering the world to a cataclysmic moment in history. Perhaps this kind of sweeping, visionary rhetoric seems useful for arousing Americans' political will to conduct preventive diplomacy and capacity building, but its effect when heard through Muslim ears is to create precisely the overheated sense of history in the making that reverberates with the jihadist narrative.

Third, although there are no easy ways to control it, what is widely perceived as American cultural imperialism often becomes part of the general picture of confrontation between Islam and the West. Obviously, all U.S. cultural contact with the Islamic world cannot and should not be curtailed. American popular culture is at the same time one of the most popular U.S. exports—and a multi-billion-dollar business—as well one of its most unpopular. At the other extreme, it would be out of tune with fundamental U.S. values to prohibit American Christian organizations from undertaking missionary activities in the Muslim world as they do elsewhere. Nevertheless, both the decadence of American rock videos and the perceived heresy articulated by American missionaries fuel the flames of jihad, and it is important not to lose sight of that fact.

Fourth, at home, the sense of confrontation should be alleviated by encouraging a level of intercultural education and understanding that allows policymakers and citizens alike to see past stereotypes and preconceptions that could ensnare Americans in the trap of jihadist intentions for intercivilizational conflict. This, of course, involves significant upgrading of the quality and quantity of university-level programs in Islamic studies and related fields. It also involves continued efforts to foster intercultural dialogue and contact. This simple goal is complicated greatly by the natural impulse to assure security by limiting contact. Nevertheless, the requirements of security and intercultural dialogue can and must be squared.

Finally, a U.S. military presence in any predominantly Muslim country has become an easy target for jihadist ideologues to generate sympathy for their insurgency. Given the transnational nature of this insurgency, it does not even matter if people in the host country welcome the American presence; that U.S. troops are on Muslim soil is enough to stoke the propaganda furnaces elsewhere. The potential this presence has to exacerbate intercultural tensions is magnified by the U.S. insistence—well-founded as it may be—that American troops enjoy extraterritorial immunity from host country legal jurisdiction, a policy that to most people in the Islamic world recalls the hated capitulations imposed on the Ottoman Empire by the British, French, and Russians during the age of imperialism. Misconduct by U.S. forces under these circumstances— even misconduct far short of what occurred at Abu Ghraib prison or Haditha in Iraq— has a dramatically negative effect on American interests in the war on terrorism.

This is not an argument for eliminating the U.S. forward presence in the Middle East or South Asia, certainly not until the situations in Iraq and Afghanistan are substantially more stable. It is an argument for lowering the visibility of U.S. forces to the greatest possible extent commensurate with mission accomplishment. As the transformation of the U.S. Armed Forces described in chapters seven and eight moves forward, high priority should be given to steps that would permit the delivery of effective power from longer range, enabling U.S. military planners to return to thinking of the Middle East primarily as a place *to which* American forces occasionally deploy, not as one *from which* they routinely operate.

Addressing material discontents. One of the most acrimonious debates in U.S. policy circles since 9/11 has been over whether poverty is related to terrorism. One side sees social injustice as the root of all terrorism—the imagery is usually of the slums of Cairo and Karachi as breeding grounds for terrorists—and contends that only through a massive investment in economic development can there be real progress in solving the underlying causes of the problem. The other side points, accurately enough, to the fact that neither the 9/11 hijackers nor most other jihadist terrorists come from desperately poor families. On the contrary, they say, Osama bin Laden is an enormously wealthy man, scion of perhaps the richest family in Saudi Arabia after the House of Saud itself, while the leading ideologists of the jihadist movement are physicians, professors, and lawyers from reasonably affluent backgrounds.

Both sides are missing three key points. First, as scholars of rebellion and insurgency have known for at least three decades, it is not absolute deprivation but, in Ted Robert Gurr's classic formulation, "discontent arising from the perception of *relative* [emphasis added] deprivation [that] is the basic, instigating condition for participants in collective violence." Gurr defines relative deprivation as a discrepancy between what people actually have and what they think they are rightly entitled to have. A sense of relative deprivation may arise if objective conditions fall and expectations stay the same, if objective conditions stay the same and expectations increase, or even if objective conditions improve but expectations increase faster.[31]

Second, a person may be inspired to political violence not because he personally is relatively deprived, but because he feels a sense of vicarious aggrievement on behalf of those who are objectively downtrodden.[32] This concept seems to be a powerful one in explaining why relatively well-educated men planned and conducted the 9/11 attacks, just as it was university students and recent graduates who were responsible for the left-wing terror campaigns in Europe and North America in the 1960s and 1970s. Individuals learn to sympathize with others unlike themselves through formal education. Educated people are more likely than uneducated ones to read newspapers, to watch and listen to news of the outside world on television and radio, and to be able to access modern communications technologies like the Internet. With this awareness comes a sense of identification with the poor and deprived that is only strengthened if the principal markers of one's identity—religion, race, or ethnicity—are held in common with the downtrodden.[33] In other words, just because poor people do not rebel does not mean poverty does not cause rebellion.

Third, to ensure that the measures taken to build capacity for governance and to enhance systemic legitimacy become self-sustaining, it will be necessary to develop the economic base to support them. Without educational systems that prepare citizens to think critically for themselves, participatory political systems will be easy prey for radical demagogues. Without economies in the success of which people feel themselves to have a stake, it will be difficult to obtain the kind of collective sacrifice for the sake of the common good that successful self-government demands.

Addressing material discontents is a corollary to political reform, not a substitute for it, but it is a particularly important corollary considering that people in much of the Islamic world have been conditioned for 40 or more years to measure the performance of their governments in terms of material benefits delivered. This was the basis of the social contract that Gamal Abdel Nasser struck with the people of Egypt to justify his authoritarian Arab socialist state, and it was the justification by which King Faisal of Saudi Arabia secured public support to overrule the conservative religious establishment in the cause of modernization.[34] Ultimately, this is a fragile basis on which to construct a system of government, and indeed a major objective of U.S. efforts to enhance systemic legitimacy must be to help regional states construct more enduring affective foundations for their polities. But if the evolving political systems cannot do a better job of delivering what people expect in the short term, there may be never be an opportunity to lay this lasting foundation.

The Bush administration has recognized the connection between terrorism and lack of development and has made a start on applying resources to the problem, but much more remains to be done. To be sure, the foreign operations budget has increased by more than 50 percent since fiscal year 2001, with $23.7 billion in fiscal year 2007 compared with $14.9 billion in the last Clinton administration budget (see figure 2–5). But most of that increase is attributable to two programs, the HIV/AIDS Initiative and the Millennium Challenge Corporation. The latter, although heralded in part as a response to the terrorist threat, in fact does little to address the core issues, since it provides economic assistance only to countries that already achieve high marks on quality of governance. As noted earlier, the most pressing developmental needs in connection with countering terrorism lie precisely in countries where good governance is wanting. Beyond these two initiatives, substantial resources have been devoted to Afghanistan, Pakistan, and Iraq, but largely at the expense of existing programs. Even the Middle East Partnership Initiative, the flagship program for dealing with legitimacy and governance deficits, is funded at only $120 million in the 2007 budget, roughly one-twentieth what Israel receives in foreign military financing alone.

Of course, throwing money at the problems in the Islamic world will not solve them. What is needed is to look closely, country by country, province by province, at initiatives that can contribute to the development of a political and economic environment hostile to jihadist terrorism. U.S. planners should explore mechanisms for moving these funds to where they can contribute the most decisively to this objective, including direct transfers to civil society groups and even nonradical faith-based organizations that can use the resources effectively. While simply increasing spending is not a sufficient response, it is a necessary one. If budgetary realities make it impossible to increase the foreign operations top line, then radical changes within the existing allocation will be essential, including breaking the iron grip that Israel and Egypt have on more than 25 percent of the budget.

FIGURE 2–5. U.S. FOREIGN OPERATIONS BUDGET, 2001–2007

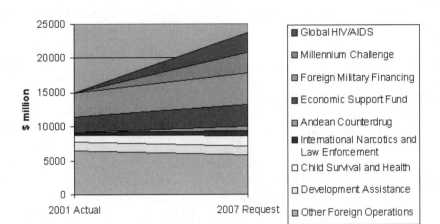

Countering the jihadist ideological appeal. In a sense, every U.S. action to counteract the population's toleration, sympathy, and support for the jihadists can be construed as "countering the jihadist ideological appeal." More narrowly defined, however, this term refers to efforts to undercut support for terrorists by discrediting the ideological justification for their actions.

The ideological appeal of jihadist rhetoric operates on various levels: as diagnosis, as motivation, and as prescription. The diagnosis it offers of the world's ills is broadly congruent with fundamental beliefs and attitudes held by many Muslims, while the symbolism and historical allusions it uses as motivation resonate deeply in the Islamic psyche. This means there is a very real danger that direct critiques of the jihadist ideology—especially by outsiders—will be interpreted even by people who are inclined against terrorism as attacks on Islam itself. It also calls into question the idea that problems in communicating the anti-jihadist message can be overcome by better marketing or by sharper logical arguments.

Better strategic communication is not the elegant solution to the ideological threat that it is often assumed to be for two reasons. First, the underlying assumption of a communications-centered strategy is that the target population is fundamentally receptive to the U.S. message—that if they truly understood the United States and its ideals, they would approve of them. To assume this is tantamount to assuming that cultural differences either do not exist or do not matter. The United States prides itself on being a tolerant society in which everyone is free to express beliefs without interference from the government. But the American commitment to tolerance stems in part from the premise, memorably expressed by Justice Oliver Wendell Holmes, that "the best test of truth is the power of the thought to get itself accepted in the competition of the market."[35] It is delusional to think that the best communications strategy in the world is going to persuade believing Muslims that the "marketplace of ideas" is a better test of moral truth than the revelation contained in the Koran.

Moreover, effective strategic communications across cultural boundaries are extraordinarily difficult. The best possible translation of a message originally crafted in a spare, logical, Anglo-Saxon rhetorical style will not resonate among people whose rhetoric is exuberant and emotive and whose educational experiences emphasized rote memorization over logical deduction and critical analysis.[36] When American commentators lament the lack of media outlets in the Arab world that take a "dispassionate, analytical approach to news,"[37] they are revealing an important cultural blind spot; Arab television and radio stations do not take this approach because no one would watch or listen.

Even if U.S. Government agencies could deliver effectively crafted messages in the appropriate rhetorical style, they could never isolate the Muslim world from the welter of other communications emanating from American society. The very nature of Holmes' marketplace of ideas guarantees that viewpoints contrary to the carefully crafted administration message will continue to be expressed, publicized, and seized upon by foreign audiences. Finally, planners must recognize that insofar as strategic communication is intended to burnish the image of the United States, it must overcome an enormous degree of cognitive dissonance among the target audience. Muslim perceptions of the United States are now so overwhelmingly negative that even the most favorable information is immediately discounted, while unfavorable information is automatically accepted and incorporated into the anti-American canon.

Defeating the jihadists ideologically is an essential component of ensuring their demise, but Muslims themselves must accomplish it. Radical Islamist ideology must be attacked, but if it is the United States that does the attacking, the radicals will only gain greater credibility within their target audience. The only way Muslims will be able to get on with the vital task of sorting out how Islam will deal with modern realities is for external players to stay out of the open debate. If non-Muslims take sides, the argument becomes one between the indigenous defenders of the faith and the lackeys of infidel powers. The more visibly the United States is involved in the question of what Islam means and what Muslims ought to believe, the more the debate is about America and not about Islam.

Ideally, as in the case of political reform discussed above, what Muslims need are authentic voices from within the Islamic community offering alternative visions by which they can understand the world and interact with it. Muslims need to find their own ways to come to terms with the challenges of modernity, and they need to discover for themselves, through their own logical processes, that jihadist solutions are untenable. The visions articulated by these voices need not be congruent with U.S. desiderata to serve the broader purpose of undermining the vision expounded by the jihadists. A traditional mainstream religious perspective or even a *salafi* (fundamentalist) perspective that eschews violence would probably be more effective than a highly Westernized secular perspective in drawing the susceptible away from the apocalyptic world view of the jihadists. In fact, growing numbers of *salafi* intellectuals are articulating the view that Osama bin Laden and his followers constitute a deviant sect, a development whose significance should not be underestimated.[38]

As survey data have consistently shown, most Arabs, and possibly most Muslims, seem to accept the jihadists' diagnosis of the ills besetting their world. The jihadists' emotional, religion-based rhetoric resonates strongly, motivating people to believe that action is needed to right these wrongs. But there is as yet no consensus beyond a small portion of the world's Muslim community that the jihadists' prescription—the call for jihad to reestablish the caliphate—is the right action to take. If the jihadist ideology is to be successfully undercut, alternative diagnoses of the problem need to be developed and reinforced by equally compelling motivations to action, and the jihadist prescription needs to be replaced by one more congruent with the inclinations of the mass of the Islamic *umma*.

The United States may be able to facilitate this process to ensure that these alternative indigenous voices can be heard and that the jihadist diagnosis is questioned and debated, but it must do so in a way that is neither visible nor attributable. For example, adapting the original concept of Radio Free Europe (RFE) in the early stages of the Cold War, the United States could make available broadcast facilities, Web servers, and other distribution media for the free use of commentators and scholars offering alternative ideas to those propagated by the jihadists and their sympathizers. Unlike Voice of America and other overt U.S. strategic communications media, the content of these RFE-like operations would be developed by people from the region with minimal U.S. policy restrictions placed upon them. Foundations could be established, appropriately distanced from the U.S. Government, to fund research and writing and to assist non-jihadist scholars in forming their own intellectual and political networks across the region. A corporation could be formed to subsidize indigenous film and television production reflecting non-jihadist values.

By itself, an effective critique of the radical movement (assuming one could be developed) articulated by Muslims who oppose its goals and methods would not be decisive in countering the jihadist ideological message. The insurgency is about the legitimacy of the status quo, not of the insurgents. Discrediting the radical vision ideologically is a good thing, and all the better when the radicals discredit themselves by rejecting concepts, such as democracy, that demonstrably have wide appeal within the Islamic world. However, no amount of tarnish on the reputation of the insurgents can rectify the legitimacy deficit from which support for the insurgency arises. That must be addressed separately.

Furthermore, while the internal debate about what it means to be a Muslim in the 21st century moves ahead over a period of years, the international community is still faced with the immediate problem of keeping the people of the region from becoming terrorists, supporting terrorists, and tolerating terrorists. This is not a matter of changing their values and beliefs. Altering values is extraordinarily difficult, even over the extended timeframe in which the war on terrorism must be fought. Moreover, a deliberate attempt to alter Muslims' understanding of right and wrong will inevitably provoke a defensive reaction that can only aggravate their sense of being a culture under siege, playing directly into the hands of the insurgents. Instead of calling into question fundamental elements of religion and culture—trying to *prescribe* what Muslims ought to *be*—U.S. policy should look for opportunities to *proscribe* certain things they must not *do*. As *The National Military Strategic Plan for the War on Terrorism* correctly observes, the United States has no problem with mainstream Muslims "who may differ from each other and from the average American in any number of ways," provided that they oppose the use of violence against noncombatants.[39] The key, therefore, must be quietly empowering and facilitating the messages, articulated by people inside the Islamic *umma*, that Islam considers terrorism evil in itself and that the insurgents are incorrectly construing what the Prophet and his successors said on the subject of jihad. The aim should not be a quantum shift in the ideological center of gravity of the entire Islamic community but rather a series of relatively small shifts in Muslims' attitudes toward what the faith means for specific practical behaviors.

As part of this effort, U.S. strategists should identify and seek to reinforce the elements within each of the diverse cultures comprising the Islamic world that tend to favor peaceful coexistence and tolerance against those elements that are amenable to violence. Obviously, most Muslims most of the time do not participate in the global campaign of violence called for by al Qaeda and its allies. What leads them to stay in their neighborhoods and villages, quietly going about their lives?

Some of the factors that affect any person's receptivity to the call to religiously justified violence are themselves religious in nature. For example, most mainstream Muslims, and even many within the radical *salafist* movement, fear and abhor *fitnah,* or disorder. Traditional Islamic political philosophy holds that governments exist partly to implement the holy law and partly to suppress *fitnah* within the Islamic community. It may be possible for opponents of violence to relabel the self-proclaimed supporters of jihad as supporters of *fitnah* instead. It is also important to recognize that in most of the Islamic world, with the principal exception of Saudi Arabia, traditional, conservative Islam is bound up with a number of cultural practices, especially the Sufi-influenced veneration of saints and their tombs, that radical Islamists are determined to eradicate. Reinforcing people's emotional commitment to traditional ways, and highlighting the *salafist* radicals' own promises to destroy those traditions, may be an effective way to undercut the radical appeal.

In addition, while a person living within a particular society may perceive his religion to be part of an integrated whole with the rest of his social life, an outside observer can see that in fact many forces besides religion shape how the members of any society conduct themselves. Moreover, the dictates of religious belief itself are understood and interpreted quite differently from one Muslim country to another. To separate publics morally from the insurgents, U.S. strategy needs to identify these positive factors and find ways to reinforce behavior that conforms to them. For example, it is a widely shared belief among Muslims that men have a religious obligation to ensure the safety and well being of the women and children in their families. Can this belief be played upon to discourage suicide terrorism? Tribal peoples in South Asia and

Arabia have strong cultural imperatives of hospitality. Can the obligation of hospitality be used, in conjunction with the traditional Islamic teaching that permits and protects non-Muslim "guests" within the "House of Islam," to counter insurgent calls for attacks against foreigners in these countries?

At the same time, U.S. planners also need to be aware of the prejudices and jealousies that divide communities within the Islamic world and how they might discourage participation in the transnational insurgency. For example, many Afghans believe that the Arabs who dominate al Qaeda were "dismissive and abusive of Afghans, considering them unsophisticated 'hicks.' Afghans, for their part, resented the imperiousness evinced by al Qaeda in Afghanistan and felt increasingly exploited by them."[40] Despite decades of rhetoric about Arab solidarity, negative stereotypes about other groups remain rampant throughout the Arab world, with northern Arabs from Syria and Iraq tending to see Gulf Arabs as lazy and uncultured, and Gulf Arabs seeing those to their north as abrasive and obnoxious. These antagonisms could well serve to help unravel the transregional ties that unite the insurgent movement.

Finally, curbing the jihadists' ideological appeal includes not only countering it directly but also countering its effects, particularly in the area of recruiting new terrorists. U.S. planners need to understand better, country by country and district by district, what leads people to join terrorist organizations. How do they first come under jihadist influence, and what can be done to thwart the jihadist recruiters?

For example, research in rural Pakistan has shown that parents often send their children to Islamic *madrassa*s because there is no functioning state school, or because they realize that graduates of state schools cannot find jobs unless they enjoy the patronage of someone wealthy or powerful, or because they cannot afford even the modest fees charged at government schools, let alone the cost of uniforms and supplies. In contrast, many radical *madrassa*s operate free of charge. Not only do they cover room and board, they even pay a subsidy to the child's parents to cover the value of his lost labor. The *madrassa*s' sponsoring groups often take on the responsibility for finding employment—perhaps as a teacher in another *madrassa*—for the otherwise unemployable graduate.[41] If these *madrassa*s contribute to public sympathy for jihadist organizations, then it would make sense to take steps through targeted assistance to make state schools (as well as *madrassa*s sponsored by less extreme religious communities) more competitive.

Effectively blocking extremist fundraising efforts can also make an important contribution to undercutting the jihadist ideology. Americans generally think of a financial contribution to a cause as a manifestation of an existing commitment, but as commentator and former political operative Christopher Matthews points out, "The most effective way to gain a person's loyalty is not to do him or her a favor, but to let that person do one for you."[42] Making a tangible contribution to a movement gives the contributor a psychological stake in its success and therefore conditions him to make ever greater sacrifices on its behalf. Inducing the states where fundraising takes place to prohibit such activities is one way of undercutting this dynamic; another is to foster the creation of alternative organizations to which people can contribute and in which they can make the concomitant psychological investment, but to a more benign purpose, such as bona fide philanthropic and political action groups.

A third example: it has been suggested that the sense of drift and ennui that afflicts young men in places like southwestern Saudi Arabia (from which 12 of the 9/11 hijackers originated) leads them to seek companionship in organizations such as al Qaeda, which give them a sense of purpose. If this is the case, are there things that could be done to offer alternative outlets and opportunities? Could something as seemingly trivial as organized sports leagues or youth organizations divert at least some portion of potential terrorist recruits to other outlets? The answer obviously depends on what young men in each culture have been taught to value. But the U.S. Department of Defense is one of the world's most proficient institutions at figuring out what motivates males between the ages of 17 and 23 and using that knowledge to influence their behavior. The same methodologies used to encourage U.S. recruiting efforts—although not the same specific incentives—should be equally applicable to thwarting jihadist recruiting efforts.

IMPLEMENTING THE STRATEGY: PRACTICAL CHALLENGES

For even the best of strategies, the devil is in the details of practical implementation, and this is no less true in the war on terrorism. While it would be possible to develop a long list of challenges that must be overcome to carry out our proposed approach, the most serious of them fall into three major categories: balancing military and political actions, integrating and harmonizing the instruments of national power, and managing shifting coalitions.

Balancing Military and Political Actions

The success of the strategic concept outlined here depends on achieving synergy between actions designed to eradicate jihadist terrorists and their structures and those designed to isolate jihadists from the wider Muslim population. The two sets of actions are inextricably linked with one another. The kinetic actions the United States takes in the name of eradicating terrorists will inevitably affect public attitudes toward the United States, its partners, and the jihadists. The poorly planned or ineptly executed use of force can put U.S. planners squarely on the horns of the Rumsfeld dilemma, generating new terrorists faster than the old ones can be killed. Conversely, progress in severing the bonds that connect jihadists to the local community will not only complicate the terrorists' own operations but also make it easier for the United States and its partners to employ force against them accurately, effectively, and early. Keeping actions along these two lines in balance and ensuring that they are mutually reinforcing will therefore be the most important and demanding practical challenge in the years ahead.

U.S. and allied leaders must continuously weigh the near-term benefits to be gained from using force in pursuit of the first objective of the strategy against the long-term benefits to be gained from the political and economic initiatives employed under the second. This is emphatically not an argument for eschewing the use of force in the name of "addressing root causes." It is rather an argument for seeking what theorists of nuclear war call *escalation dominance*. As suggested by the historic experiences with national insurgencies mentioned earlier, using intense, proactive, precisely targeted force over a relatively brief time span can yield a net decrease in the overall level of violence—thereby advancing the political element of the strategy—if it has the effect of preventing jihadists from taking actions that rally their supporters and provoke the United States to more visible, less discriminate retaliatory measures of longer duration. This is particularly true if force can be used decisively before the insurgents have a chance to develop an initial level of credibility.

At the same time, all actions—both kinetic and nonkinetic—do have rhetorical consequences in any struggle for hearts and minds. Policymakers must remain mindful that ultimate success in the war on terrorism hinges on being able to change the way people in the Islamic world perceive the legitimacy of the U.S.-led international order, the legitimacy of their own governments, the credibility of the jihadist diagnosis and prescription for the problems facing the Islamic world, and the viability of alternative solutions to those problems. Despite the reservations expressed above about the potential of strategic communications for fundamentally altering attitudes and beliefs in a foreign culture, they must nevertheless play an important role in the struggle.

To borrow from the old anarchist vocabulary, strategic communications are "propaganda by word"; the messages that are sent through U.S. actions are "propaganda by deed." For either type of propaganda to be effective, however, the deeds and the words must reinforce each other. Jihadist leaders understand this; an intercepted letter from Abu Mus'ab al-Zarqawi apparently intended for Osama bin Laden envisioned Iraq as "an arena of jihad in which the pen and the sword complement each other."[43] The interplay between word and deed must also be clearly understood. If deed and word cannot always reinforce each other, they should at least be mutually consistent, and when that is not possible, the deeds must be conducted in such a fashion as to minimize the exploitable differences. All too often, U.S. strategic communications have been focused on explaining away apparent inconsistencies between American words and American actions. U.S. decisionmakers will therefore need to develop a process to ensure that the long-term political effects of kinetic actions, and the strategic communications challenges involved in persuasively linking actions and objectives, are taken into account throughout the planning and decision process. The need for such integration between the elements of the strategy necessarily leads to the second challenge.

Integrating and Harmonizing the Instruments of Power

The two critical components of the strategy outlined here—attacking the enemy's leadership, operatives, and support systems while winning or maintaining the support of the population—require the application of diplomatic, informational, political, military, intelligence, law enforcement, and foreign assistance instruments, all of which must be utilized simultaneously and with unity of effort on both the national and international levels.

Unfortunately, the U.S. Government is not organized to pursue these two goals effectively and to balance the tensions that will emerge between them. In an organization so large and complex, an infinite number of organizational permutations can be generated to correct these shortcomings, and this is not the place to explore them all. However, some enduring principles could help inform choices among various options.

Unity of effort. A primary goal of any reorganization must be to establish and maintain unity of effort in the application of the relevant elements of national power in this global counterinsurgency. A single entity or process must be established to set goals and procedures; orchestrate, harmonize, and deconflict actions; and receive feedback and modify plans accordingly. This entity or process must include means to compel participation and compliance among agencies. It is quite clear that the leadership of all the departments and agencies involved in fighting the war against terrorism abroad appreciate the importance of unity of effort and cross-agency cooperation and coordination. Yet actually achieving this unity of effort remains elusive. The entire history of the Department of Defense from 1947 to the passage of the Goldwater-Nichols Act in 1986 demonstrates that traditional processes of coordination are not good enough, so the U.S. Government must develop legal vehicles for officers and officials to exercise operational control of assets across departmental and agency boundaries. This will include, under some circumstances, giving officials of other agencies operational control of military personnel, and vice versa.

Echelonment. At the same time, any organizational solution must recognize that local insurgencies—the co-optation of which must be prevented—begin and grow for reasons as varied as their number. A global counterterrorism strategy must therefore develop and execute specific solutions tailored to local conditions. Moreover, since each of these local solutions will involve a combination of military, diplomatic, informational, intelligence, and other measures, they must be subject to the same local and regional unity of effort as exists at the national strategic level. Entities or processes that correspond to the strategic organization described above must be established at operational and tactical levels.

As a matter of reality, such interagency cooperation is typically better at the tactical level than at higher levels, provided that it can be practiced "off the scope" of higher headquarters. Institutionalizing such flexibility would require overcoming the pressures parent agencies put on individuals' conduct as well as a willingness on Washington's part to devolve authority and responsibility to lower levels. In other words, the U.S. Government needs to make its own organizations function more like a network of networks and less like a series of rigid hierarchies.

Authorities for overseas operations. An effective counterinsurgency will also require accepting that even local insurgencies operate freely across international borders. There will be times when high-priority regional efforts in support of national strategy must trump the country-specific concerns of reluctant chiefs of U.S. diplomatic missions. Maintaining unity of effort across these lines will likely require reexamination of the legal mandate that chiefs of mission be in charge of all U.S. Government activities in their countries other than military operations under combatant commanders. Not all such interagency operations will be led by military forces, and therefore in many cases it may be necessary for cross-border unity of effort to be under the control of an official who is neither the American Ambassador nor the regional combatant commander. Chief of mission oversight of U.S. activities in a particular country serves the national interest well in most circumstances, but it is easy to see that in the war on terror, there will also be situations where it does not. The nature of the terrorist challenge demands that agencies be open to new modes of organization to meet and defeat new threats.

Agility. As the threat in the global insurgency changes, the U.S. Government must be able to build, modify, and dismantle quickly the organizations established to contend with it. No single solution to organizational challenges can last; the threat will mutate too rapidly. It is not necessarily clear in advance which organizations will be valuable and which will not. This implies that any new organizations should begin as temporary structures; as they prove their worth, they can be made permanent. The speed with which the threat can change also suggests that interagency policymaking structures need to be more flexible. At the national level, having a deputies committee that replicates the duties of the principals committee, with subordinate groups mostly confined to making recommendations for deputies' or principals' approval, may be an excellent structure for making deliberate policy; however, as a crisis management mechanism, let alone a warfighting one, it is cumbersome and risks being unresponsive.

Interagency culture. Ultimately, organizational structures will not help much unless there is a culture of true interagency cooperation in planning and execution, not only for the global counterinsurgency but also for other complex contingencies. Programs must be developed to create and perpetuate such a culture. This could include interagency training and education; more cross-agency career paths, such as the National Security Officer Corps envisioned in the 2006 *Quadrennial Defense Review Report*;[44] and evaluation and promotion systems that reward interagency work.

Specialization. The two main elements of the proposed global counterinsurgency strategy require competencies that are not likely to be found in any single organization. As the discussion of unity of effort suggests, these skill sets must be applied under the direction of a single process or entity. That does not mean, however, that the different organizations in which they are found should be cobbled together merely on the grounds that the people involved are all engaged in achieving a common national objective. Organizational cultures and biases exist because they promote the competencies that the organization requires to do its job effectively. What is needed is an interagency philosophy comparable to the military concept of jointness properly understood—that is, the effective application of specialized skills, wherever they may be found, toward a common strategic objective.

Managing Shifting Coalitions

Success in the struggle against jihadist terrorism will depend in large part on the ability of the United States to marshal and manage the support of an array of other governments. Thus, while it is important to ostracize states that intentionally support or harbor terrorists, it is also vital to encourage and empower potential partners and focus their efforts on the common cause. This is not a simple task under the best of circumstances. Doing it in the context of the war on terrorism is particularly difficult because threat perceptions differ so radically from one state to another, and for good reason. While the rulers of many Muslim states share the U.S. perspective on jihadist terror—indeed, they see it as even more of an existential threat—they may well see some of the proposed political cures as worse than the disease. Meanwhile, the United States and many of its European allies have surprisingly different perspectives about the origins of the threat. For the United States, the danger of jihadist terror is an external threat; the terrorists come from somewhere else, so it makes sense to try and fight them as far away from U.S. shores as possible. For many European countries, the danger is an internal one, leading them to treat it less as a matter of national defense and more as a domestic policy issue. Other countries see little danger to themselves except insofar as they are perceived as collaborators with one side or the other.

These differing perspectives mean that the antiterrorist coalition will not be a neat, united alliance but a series of overlapping groupings that shift from time to time and mission to mission. Such groupings will only be viable, however, if participants believe a general commonality of purpose connects the various missions served by them; attempts to de-link completely one coalition from the context of other missions will be perceived as cavalier treatment of the national interests of members. Keeping coalition partners on board will therefore require a variety of political actions, including a major effort to rebuild the international public consensus, outside as well as inside the Islamic world, that a *war* on terrorism is justified. It will also require genuine two-way dialogue with potential partners on the nature, implications, and causes of the terrorist threat, conducted well in advance of specific requests for assistance. This dialogue must take place on both the military and civilian sides of U.S. bilateral and multilateral relationships.

The United States also needs to reexamine the benefits that it looks to gain from having coalition partners in the war on terrorism. In the past, exercises in coalition building have often emphasized the public image benefits in the U.S. political context (maximizing "flags in the sand") over the military contribution coalition partners can make. The political drive for more countries to be involved often clashes with military effectiveness and leads to the underutilization of capabilities that are offered. Furthermore, U.S. policymakers tend to tap the same countries over and over, often beyond the point that they can realistically contribute. This approach may undermine the most important contribution some partners can make: to ensure that terrorists cannot operate within their own national space. Moreover, it may sometimes be more important for a key country not to condemn or oppose something the United States needs to do than to make a troop contribution of marginal value. Adroit coalition management, especially the inclusion of the concerns, capabilities, and goals of partner countries in U.S. strategic calculus, is a sine qua non of success against a global threat.

CONCLUSION

It has become commonplace to say that the war against global terrorism will be prolonged and that progress will be hard to gauge and victory difficult to ascertain. That is all true, perhaps more so than many who repeat the words fully realize. A struggle conducted along the lines we have laid out, which we believe to be the only way it can be successfully conducted, will be fought largely out of public view. The American public as well as people in other countries will gradually lose sight of the progress of the war.

As a result, American leaders may find it difficult to muster support for the measures necessary to prevail in the political side of the conflict. This will be all the more difficult considering that what we are recommending is, in effect, a number of local counterinsurgencies being conducted in parallel as elements of a grand transnational counterinsurgency. As in any counterinsurgency, success is most probable if the insurgency is nipped in the bud before violence gets out of hand. As a result, it will be important for the United States to take action in a number of seemingly obscure places long before the problems attract the attention of humanitarian pressure groups and the international media.

In the case of nonkinetic actions, leaders will face the challenge of getting Americans to care about solving problems whose connection to the terrorist threat may not be immediately obvious. In the case of kinetic actions, Americans and foreigners alike will occasionally be shocked when news of a U.S. operation against terrorists in some faraway place suddenly appears on the front pages. When that happens, many will reflexively criticize America's supposed preference for force over peaceful conflict resolution or the relentlessness of its supposed war against Islam. To mitigate the criticism, U.S. leaders should ensure that, when action is necessary, it takes place in the environment of the grassroots global revulsion against terrorist methods for which the President has called. The United States must continue working assiduously toward the creation of such an environment, even as it combats jihadist terrorists militarily and jihadist terrorism politically. As long as it may take, the task is not hopeless. With prudent defensive measures and regenerated international support and cooperation, it is possible to prevent terrorists from doing catastrophic harm to U.S. citizens and interests and from raising the temperature of intercultural confrontation to the boiling point.

Samora Machel, the head of the Front for the Liberation of Mozambique in the 1970s and 1980s, was once asked how he could conduct a guerrilla war in a country almost devoid of natural geographic sanctuaries, such as mountains. He replied, "Our people are our mountains." By strengthening control over inadequately governed spaces, helping other countries correct the legitimacy deficits under which their governments labor, lowering the ambient level of violence by working to resolve regional conflicts, and seizing the initiative to provide better solutions to tangible grievances than those offered by the jihadists, U.S. strategy can sever the bonds between the terrorists and their mountains—the very people they seek to mobilize to their cause. When that happens, the eradication of the terrorists that remain will not be long in coming. And if, by that time, U.S. efforts have altered the environment in which jihadism flourishes, choking off the support that keeps it alive and eliminating the conditions that breed future jihadists, they will have ensured that jihadist terror organizations, once eradicated, do not revive.

Chapter Three

Combating WMD Threats

CHARLES D. LUTES

The proliferation of weapons of mass destruction (WMD)—and the specter of these weapons falling into the hands of terrorists—defines what may well be America's gravest strategic challenge in the years ahead. At a time when partisan debate over national security has become more commonplace, no one seriously disputes the stakes in this case.[1] While Cold War–era WMD threats were enormous, they also were kept at bay, mainly through a posture of deterrence, buttressed by alliance commitments and arms limitation. However, in today's security environment with a diversity of threats, this combination of policies no longer suffices. In the post-9/11 era, we cannot escape the fact that for certain types of actors, the acquisition of WMD may inevitably equate to the use of such capabilities, most likely targeted against the United States and its interests, either at home or abroad. Faced with this central problem and a pernicious mixture of aggravating factors—most notably, the lack of secure control over the former Soviet Union's far-flung WMD complex; continued pursuit of WMD capability by North Korea, Iran, and other pariah regimes; and the growth of shadowy networks of terrorists and nonstate suppliers—the United States finds itself at a crossroads. The path to greater security requires a more holistic, comprehensive policy to deal with these strategic threats.

President George W. Bush's first National Security Strategy,[2] released in the fall of 2002, provided a clear shift in the way the U.S. Government views the WMD threat. Further articulated in the subsequent publication of *The National Strategy to Combat Weapons of Mass Destruction*,[3] the U.S. approach to WMD represented a fundamental change from past reliance on deterrence and passive defensive measures. These documents were the result of an evolution in thinking more than a decade in the making: from deterrence to defense to an active offense in combating the threat of WMD by any adversary.

This chapter assesses the looming challenges in the WMD policy area from the perspective of the paradigm change over the last decade. As emphasis has shifted from a traditional Soviet-style threat to one of rogue states and terrorists, U.S. policy responses have adapted. While undergoing this transition, the United States has dealt with some nettlesome WMD-related problems with a mixed degree of success. The containment policies of the 1990s may have kept some adversaries in check but were also marked by significant intelligence gaps, which eventually led to the 2003 Iraq invasion. Libya's renunciation of WMD marked a triumph for the international community but also

61

illuminated the extensive nature of the network of suppliers led by Pakistani scientist A.Q. Khan. Rising to the forefront of concerns are Iran and North Korea, whose nuclear aspirations challenge not only the United States, but also the future of international nonproliferation regimes. Additional challenges are raised by the problems of "loose nukes" and "failed states"—that is, how to secure worldwide stockpiles of fissile material and how to protect such material in the event of a failure or adversarial shift of governance in current WMD states. Underlying all these concerns are the ultimate danger and unpredictability of WMD-armed terrorists and the need for a tailored deterrence strategy to counter the variety of actors on the proliferation scene. This chapter argues that the policy options for all of these issues must not be constrained to a single paradigm; instead, U.S. policy must include a comprehensive toolkit of options that leverages all capabilities and instruments of national power. At the same time, new and flexible responses must be developed in conjunction with the international community to prevent catastrophic consequences.

THE PARADIGMS OF PROLIFERATION

The strategic challenge of adversaries with weapons of mass destruction has been with us since the end of World War II, and until 1990 the perception and management of this threat varied little, given that it emanated from one principal peer state adversary—the Soviet Union—that shared with the United States similar principles of mutual deterrence. With the fall of the Berlin Wall, followed closely by the 1991 Persian Gulf War and the collapse of the Soviet Union, U.S. strategic planners shifted attention away from the Soviet threat to one posed by the acquisition of WMD by so-called rogue states that rejected international norms of behavior. The post–Cold War period proved to be a transitional one, as U.S. policy drifted in its understanding of and concern for the problem of rogue states. However, the mass destruction that occurred on September 11, 2001, by terrorist-hijacked commercial airliners galvanized attention on how globalization had facilitated the emergence of a new set of strategic, nonstate actors and the potential catastrophic consequences that could arise should they gain access to WMD.

During each of these periods, U.S. policy has been marked by unique assumptions and emphases to address the perceived threats of greatest concern, often with mixed success. In today's security environment, WMD threats represent a diverse set of challenges that require a full range of response options. Figure 3–1 depicts the shifting paradigms of U.S. WMD policy by considering both the challenges and responses in the Cold War, post–Cold War, and post-9/11 periods. Taken individually, each paradigm tends to suffer from a certain policy myopia by overemphasizing particular threats and responses, and discounting or ignoring others.

The Cold War Paradigm

The Cold War paradigm was formed by the U.S. peer competition with the Soviet Union and its vast nuclear arsenal. In the great power context of that era, it is not surprising that the traditional nation-state was the primary unit of analysis for considering

FIGURE 3–1. CHALLENGES AND RESPONSES:
THE STRATEGIC PARADIGMS OF WEAPONS OF MASS DESTRUCTION

	Cold War	Post–Cold War	Post-9/11
Challenges			
Adversaries and Actors	Traditional states	Rogue states	Terrorist networks, rogue states
Capabilities	Nuclear	Nuclear, chemical, missiles	Nuclear, biological, missiles
Dominant Responses			
Preventing Proliferation	Nonproliferation treaties and regimes	Cooperative Threat Reduction	Interdiction, preemption, Cooperative Threat Reduction
Preventing Use	Deterrence	Containment	Preemption
Defense/Mitigation	Civil defense	Passive defense (U.S. forces), theater missile defense	Missile defense, passive defense, (homeland) consequence management

adversaries and other actors. Those with nuclear capabilities were generally treated as either friend or foe: the nuclear capabilities of Britain and France were considered additive to that of the United States in countering those of the Soviet Union and China. Deterrence, with its attendant mutually assured destruction strategic calculus, was big-stakes poker that only great powers could play. To ensure it remained that way, the U.S. deterrence shield was extended to reassure major allies (for example, Japan and West Germany), and extensive diplomatic efforts via nonproliferation negotiations were mounted in order to restrict through consent the continued spread of the fearsome power of the atom, as well as chemical and biological capabilities with mass destruction potential.

Overall, the Cold War paradigm was a system based on a fragile notion of stability. As long as all the actors remained more or less frozen in place, the system worked. The Non-Proliferation Treaty (NPT), signed in 1968, was an attempt to freeze the then-current system of five nuclear powers. Its apparent success was felt so strongly, in fact, that the need for defense was considered not only unnecessary, but actually dangerous. With the signature of the 1972 Anti-Ballistic Missile (ABM) Treaty, the only defenses that remained in the United States were the increasingly neglected popular civil defense shelters and the exhortation to "duck and cover" in case of nuclear attack. Despite periods of intense competition between the major powers, the Cold War period was marked by relatively few fundamental challenges to this system: the world held its breath as South Africa developed, then rejected, nuclear weapons; and it did little to thwart India, Pakistan, and Israel from quietly developing such capability without signing the NPT.

The Post–Cold War Paradigm

The collapse of the Soviet Union subverted the Cold War system's stability. In the post–Cold War euphoria, some thought the threat of large-scale destruction had been averted forever. Calls for a "peace dividend" assumed Western nuclear arsenals to be irrelevant. Yet despite the initial optimism, new WMD challenges emerged. The spread of WMD to other nations again became a heightened issue. Where once there had been one (Soviet) nuclear power, now there were four, as the newly independent states of Ukraine, Belarus, and Kazakhstan were "born" nuclear. Furthermore, the security and stability of the stockpile in the former Soviet states created a new concern that loose nukes could find their way to aspiring nuclear powers or perhaps even terrorists. New creative approaches were needed to address the changing nature of the nuclear threat. Successful diplomatic strategies led to the return of nuclear weapons to Russia by Ukraine, Belarus, and Kazakhstan. Another success was the Nunn-Lugar Act of 1991, which established cooperative threat reduction as a method for securing nuclear material in the states of the former Soviet Union.

Yet with the demise of the traditional peer nuclear competitor, new adversaries appeared on the horizon. Rogue regimes, notably in North Korea and Iraq, dared to defy U.S. supremacy and viewed weapons of mass destruction as the means to do so. Exploiting weaknesses in the nonproliferation regimes, these rogues developed secret nuclear programs and intentionally worked to thwart the efforts of inspectors from the International Atomic Energy Agency (IAEA), as well as of U.S. diplomats. By the early 1990s, a new sizeable forward deployment of U.S. conventional forces in Southwest Asia (in the wake of the 1991 Gulf War), along with the longstanding defense arrangements in Northeast Asia, sought to contain both the regional and nuclear appetites of these rogue states.

While nuclear ambitions proved difficult to satisfy, the rogues, specifically Iraq, Iran, North Korea, Syria, and Libya, acquired chemical capabilities as a means to gain leverage against their regional enemies and potentially against the deployed military forces of the United States. Despite overwhelming coalition success in Operation *Desert Storm*, the United States realized its battlefield vulnerability against the potential of Scud-delivered chemicals. The ability to execute regional war plans, designed to contain the rogue states and prevent their aggression, was considered at risk by the asymmetric threat of chemical weapons and, to a lesser extent, biological weapons. To protect against this, the U.S. military began to emphasize passive defense measures in the mid-1990s by investing in more capable chemical suits and medical countermeasures. The objective of this investment was to increase confidence in the U.S. ability to fight through a chemical or biological attack so that the military would not have to rely on a noncredible nuclear retaliation to counter such use.

In 1993, Secretary of Defense Les Aspin announced a major policy shift in creating the Defense Counterproliferation Initiative (CPI) to increase military response to the WMD problem.[4] Aspin suggested that the United States would maintain its emphasis on proliferation prevention through the standard nonproliferation and arms control policies, but that it would add "protection" against weapons of mass destruction as a major policy goal. Aspin viewed *protection* in the broadest sense and believed the CPI would be a means to, in his words, "deal with Saddam Hussein with nukes," either in a *reactive* or a *preemptive* mode—primarily the former, but also the latter when no other option provided a better means of defense.[5] After Aspin's short tenure, the emphasis of the CPI soon devolved to a focus on passive defense capabilities, reinforced in 1994 when Congress mandated the consolidation of all Department of Defense (DOD) chemical and biological defense programs in order to "allow military forces of the United States to survive and successfully complete their operational missions—in battlespace environments contaminated with chemical or biological warfare agents."[6] Yet with all this emphasis on protection of military forces, little investment, outside of a research and development effort in missile defense aimed at future rogue state capabilities, was made to protect the U.S. populace, as WMD attacks on the homeland seemed improbable in the foreseeable future.

The Post-9/11 Paradigm

The post–Cold War paradigm was violently shattered on September 11, 2001, by terrorists who found a new way to inflict mass casualties by hijacking commercial airliners and crashing them into the World Trade Center and the Pentagon. Following the 9/11 attacks, the United States suffered a series of random anthrax attacks, the perpetrator of which has yet to be determined. With these acts against the homeland, the rules that defined the new world order changed. A new type of adversary had jumped to the front of the pack, and with it, a new nightmare scenario invaded the public conscience: a determined terrorist network armed with weapons of mass destruction attacking U.S. cities.

Meanwhile, the threat from rogue states became conflated with the terrorist threat. The "axis of evil" (Iraq, Iran, and North Korea) presented not only a direct threat, but also an indirect one through support to terrorist networks. The fear that these states might develop WMD capabilities and provide them to terrorists who are deemed de facto "undeterrable" represented a significant shift in thinking. No longer would rogue states be content with a few nuclear weapons as bargaining chips to gain international prestige; the concern was that they would be irrational enough to use them through their terrorist surrogates. Alternatively, such irrationality coupled with a burgeoning ballistic missile program could hold hostage the United States or regional competitors with just a handful of weapons.

The initial assumption was that an apparent disregard for self-survival by rogue states and terrorists invalidated the concept of deterrence and the entire Cold War paradigm. With the realization that the threat may be as great or greater against the populace than that against operating military forces, the emphasis on defensive measures from the post–Cold War paradigm seemed inadequate. The decision by the Bush administration was to go on the offensive: "We must be prepared to stop rogue states and their terrorist clients before they are able to threaten or use weapons of mass destruction against the United States and our allies and friends."[7] The policy choice was to deal proactively with adversaries before they *acquired* WMD rather than have to deal with them reactively after acquisition when the threat of *use* may become imminent. This new emphasis on preventive action translated to a spectrum of measures from interdiction of WMD shipments on the high seas to the invasion of Iraq in April 2003. It colored the way in which America approached the world after September 11.

The post-9/11 paradigm is important for understanding the Bush administration policies against the WMD threat since 2002. Evaluating the successes and setbacks during that time also requires an understanding of the Cold War and post–Cold War paradigms and assumptions upon which the majority of preexisting military and inter-agency capabilities were built. In today's security environment, remnants of each paradigm may exist in programs and concepts of operations tailored for legacy threats. In evaluating WMD strategies for the future, it is important to consider the multidimensional nature of the threat as it has evolved over the years, and the various responses that have been designed for dealing with WMD challenges. The task for decisionmakers is to employ the right mix of policies for each unique challenge, all within a comprehensive strategy.

SUCCESSES AND SETBACKS

In the post-9/11 context, the Bush administration, wary of "a perfect storm" of rogue regimes, terrorism, and WMD, has employed a muscular approach to eliminate the conditions before the storm fully matures. The record has been decidedly mixed. Iraq, the centerpiece of the new strategy, has yet to establish a viable democracy, and regime change there has neither enhanced stability nor inspired political transformation of the broader Middle East. One thing seems certain: the estimation by the United States of the Iraqi WMD threat was vastly off the mark. On the other hand, the Libyan renunciation of its WMD program appears to vindicate aggressive policies. The intelligence windfall from the Libyan program has exposed the depth and breadth of the proliferation problem, and particularly the role of Pakistani scientist A.Q. Khan, further bolstering the concern that the threat may be greater than originally anticipated. The following sections look in greater detail at the recent record with Iraq, Libya, and the Khan network with an eye toward lessons that might inform looming policy choices vis-à-vis Iran, North Korea, and others.

Iraq

The 2002 National Security Strategy explicitly articulated a long-held yet rarely discussed policy option—the preventive use of force against gathering threats and preemptive use of force against imminent threats:

> The United States has long maintained the option of preemptive actions to counter a sufficient threat to our national security. The greater the threat, the greater is the risk of inaction—and the more compelling the case for taking anticipatory action to defend ourselves, even if uncertainty remains as to the time and place of the enemy's attack. To forestall or prevent such hostile acts by our adversaries, the United States will, if necessary, act preemptively.[8]

For the Bush administration, the threat that had been gathering for over a decade was the WMD programs of Saddam Hussein. Weary of the containment policies of the previous decade that enabled Iraq to play shell games with United Nations inspectors, the United States employed its new strategy of preventive war by invading Iraq in the spring of 2003. In the swift completion of major combat operations followed by a protracted insurgency and stability operations, the original rationale for war seems all but forgotten. The long and fruitless search for evidence of an ongoing WMD program leaves the United States with more questions than answers. With the benefit of retrospective intelligence, it seems clear that the Iraqi WMD program did not pose an immediate threat to U.S. interests. What is less clear are the different options the United States might have pursued with the benefit of perfect knowledge of Iraqi capability and intent. The choice of preventive war, predicated on the interpretation of prewar intelligence establishing Iraq as a grave danger, has both positive and negative consequences that have yet to fully play out. The full lessons from the Iraq experience are still to be written, but this section discusses two WMD-related issues: the important role of intelligence in informing policy options to counter WMD programs, and the preparedness of U.S. military forces to deal with WMD once encountered.

In the run-up to Operation *Iraqi Freedom*, the U.S. Intelligence Community judged that Iraq had "chemical and biological weapons as well as missiles with ranges in excess of UN [United Nations] restrictions; if left unchecked, it probably will have a nuclear weapon during the decade."[9] Some key judgments from that 2002 National Intelligence Estimate (NIE) were as follows: [10]

Since inspections ended in 1998, Iraq has maintained its chemical weapons effort, energized its missile program, and invested more heavily in biological weapons; most analysts assess Iraq is reconstituting its nuclear weapons program.

How quickly Iraq will obtain its first nuclear weapon depends on when it acquires sufficient weapons-grade fissile material. If Baghdad acquires sufficient weapons-grade material from abroad, it could make a nuclear weapon within a year. Without such material from abroad, Iraq probably would not be able to make a weapon until the last half of the decade.

Baghdad has begun renewed production of chemical warfare agents, probably including mustard, sarin, cyclosarin, and VX.

All key aspects—[research and development], production, and weaponization—of Iraq's offensive BW [biological warfare] program are active and most elements are larger and more advanced than they were before the Gulf War. Iraq maintains a small missile force and several development programs, including for a UAV [unmanned aerial vehicle] that most analysts believe probably is intended to deliver biological warfare agents.

Although the Intelligence Community predicted with high confidence the ongoing nature of Iraq's nuclear, chemical, biological, and missile programs, it acknowledged that it had low confidence in its ability to assess when Saddam might actually employ WMD, whether he would engage in a clandestine attack against the U.S. homeland, or whether, in desperation, he would share chemical or biological weapons with al Qaeda. From this intelligence, the imminent threat was that Iraq would soon *acquire* a significant WMD (especially nuclear) capability. In line with the post-9/11 paradigm, the Bush administration chose to eliminate this threat before it became an imminent threat of *use*.

As was subsequently revealed, the October NIE, and most all intelligence estimates—to include those of our allies—were wrong. The postwar Iraqi Survey Group (ISG), despite nearly a year and a half of investigation, found almost nothing to support the prewar estimates. Several specific key findings were as follows:[11]

> ISG discovered further evidence of the maturity and significance of the pre-1991 Iraqi Nuclear Program but found that Iraq's ability to reconstitute a nuclear weapons program progressively decayed after that date.

> While a small number of old, abandoned chemical munitions have been discovered, ISG judges that Iraq unilaterally destroyed its undeclared chemical weapons stockpile in 1991.

> In practical terms, with the destruction of the Al Hakam facility, Iraq abandoned its ambition to obtain advanced weapons quickly. ISG found no direct evidence that Iraq, after 1996, has plans for a new BW program or was conducting BW-specific work for military purposes.

The ISG report did assess that Saddam Hussein had the desire and intent to reconstitute a WMD program after sanctions were lifted, but that he had neither a strategy nor perhaps even the means to do so. In hindsight, the state of Saddam's weapons program was not an imminent threat to *acquire* WMD capability (much less *use* WMD). The program was in fact moribund.

The issue of why the Intelligence Community was so far off the mark has been the subject of at least six separate inquiries or investigations; the most notable is the White House–appointed Commission on the Intelligence Capabilities of the United States Regarding Weapons of Mass Destruction, chaired by former Senator Charles Robb (D–VA) and Judge Laurence Silberman. The commission's assessment was stark: "We conclude that the Intelligence Community was dead wrong in almost all of its prewar judgments about Iraq's weapons of mass destruction. This was a major intelligence failure."[12] As these inquiries point out, a key lesson of the Iraq experience is the fragility of intelligence in determining capability and intent in the post-9/11 world.

Such fragility was demonstrated before in the midst of another major international transition: the end of the Cold War. The Intelligence Community was originally organized to monitor, assess, and combat a relatively static Cold War adversary. The deterrence concept required extensive knowledge of Soviet capabilities and an appreciation of their role in its communist society. And yet, even with all that analytical focus, the Intelligence Community was unable to predict the Soviet collapse.

As the intelligence agencies turned to post–Cold War threats, most notably Iraq and North Korea, they were ill equipped to infiltrate a closed society with human intelligence capabilities. Ambiguities about actual WMD capabilities were dealt with by extrapolating assumptions concerning Saddam's intent. With relatively few hard facts, intelligence assessments about WMD can be a lens that either magnifies (as in the case of Iraq) or diminishes (as in the case of al Qaeda) the actual threat according to the assumptions and beliefs of the policymakers. The desire for "exquisite intelligence" will never be fully satisfied, and the range of policy options for dealing with WMD programs must be able to account for that fact.

Just as the Intelligence Community was a product of the Cold War and post–Cold War environments, so too was the military that went to war in Iraq. To paraphrase former Secretary of Defense Donald Rumsfeld, it was the military we had, not the one we wish we had. Since the end of *Desert Storm*, the U.S. military had maintained a moderate presence in the Persian Gulf region designed to contain and marginalize the aspirations of Saddam. As Iraq continually tried to outwit the United Nations Special Commission on Iraq, charged with verifying its compliance with postwar UN Security Council Resolutions to disarm, this force became the stick to keep Saddam in line. U.S. Central Command (USCENTCOM) had been refining war plans for dealing with the regime since *Desert Storm*. The original design of Operation Plan (OPLAN) 1003, the plan for the invasion of Iraq, was primarily a plan for regime removal. As refined for Operation *Iraqi Freedom*, the revised version, OPLAN 1003V, had dual purposes: regime change *and* WMD removal.[13] In the new paradigm, WMD had become the objective, not just a condition, yet the military was ill equipped to deal with it.

Initially, USCENTCOM planners assumed they could neutralize the most threatening of Iraq's WMD through direct attack and defer elimination of the remainder until after major combat operations.[14] Yet with a force developed primarily to fight through a WMD attack on its way to Baghdad, General Tommy Franks was faced with a dilemma: "We could defend our troops, but we would never preempt regime use of WMD, because intelligence on the threat was not actionable: We knew the Iraqis had WMD, but we didn't know where it was being hidden."[15] In the fall of 2002, military planners began to realize that many of their assumptions regarding the removal of Saddam's WMD were wrong: that it was "somebody else's mission"; that it could be deferred to post-hostilities; or that it was a secondary objective. The Department of Defense scrambled to put together a WMD elimination capability that could operate both during and after major combat operations.

Despite the technical nature of exploiting, disabling, and eliminating nuclear, biological, and chemical weapons, a field artillery brigade was chosen as the core command and control element to conduct this mission. An ad hoc team of experts to support this element did not come together until March 2003, just before hostilities commenced. A separate special operations task force was also involved in finding WMD, but the coordination between these units was minimal.[16] As operations commenced, the WMD problem proved to be more complex than anticipated. Insufficient forces were available to guard sensitive sites as major combat elements drove rapidly to Baghdad. Many suspected sites were found to have no clear connection to WMD programs. Integrated command and control over the disparate elements in the WMD hunt became a problem. By April, it was apparent that a new approach was needed to focus more on forensic analysis in finding clues to the vanishing WMD program. The Iraqi Survey Group was formed as an intelligence mission and devoted the next year and a half to finding traces of the program.

The military forces and Intelligence Community that planned and executed Operation *Iraqi Freedom*, with culture and capabilities formed in the Cold War and post–Cold War era, were ill equipped to deal with WMD removal as a major objective of the war plan. The lack of a significant Iraqi program avoided any serious consequences. However, it also means that to date, progress has been slow in correcting these deficiencies. The Defense Department has taken initial steps to better define the counter-WMD mission and has charged U.S. Strategic Command with the responsibility to implement it. The 2006 Quadrennial Defense Review (QDR) has set the Department of Defense on course to remedy the deficiencies in the WMD elimination area. In addition to emphasizing the capabilities required to conduct such a mission, DOD will create a standing joint task force charged with preparing for and conducting such missions in the future.[17] The Intelligence Community is in the early stages of implementing reforms advocated by the 9/11 Commission. Today, however, the U.S. capacity for detecting and removing a nation-state's WMD capability is little better than it was before 9/11. In dealing with terrorists, it is virtually nonexistent.

An epilogue to the Iraq experience: the policy choice of forcible regime removal has ramifications in our efforts to deal with other WMD challenges. Clearly, the threat in Iraq has been removed where it once was contained. The true efficacy of this approach lies not only in what happens in post-Saddam Iraq, but also what happens in other countries. Policymakers must pay close attention to the individual lessons learned by Libya, Iran, and North Korea.

Libya

One person who took careful note of the fate of Saddam Hussein was Libya's Muammar Qadhafi. Feeling the effect of years of economic sanctions following the downing of Pan Am Flight 103 over Lockerbie, Scotland, Qadhafi was anxious to seek rapprochement with the West. In 2002, he initiated diplomatic relations with Great Britain. In March 2003, with U.S. troops about to roll toward Baghdad, Qadhafi decided he did not want to be next. He sent his son Saif to engage British intelligence officers on Libya's weapons programs.[18] The Central Intelligence Agency (CIA) soon joined in covert negotiations. The final impetus to striking a bargain was the October 2003 interception of a German-registered ship, the *BBC China*, bound for Libya with thousands of centrifuge parts. This operation was the first major success under the rubric of the new Proliferation Security Initiative (PSI), developed by the Bush administration as a muscular multilateral approach to preventing proliferation by interdicting critical WMD components in shipment. Faced with indisputable evidence of an active nuclear program, Libya invited British and U.S. intelligence into the country to discuss terms of a possible disarmament. While accounts vary as to how much negotiation took place, there was at least an implicit agreement that in exchange for a complete and verifiable disarmament, the United States would not seek to remove Qadhafi as it had Saddam, and the potential existed for the lifting of sanctions.

In late December 2003, the Libyan government announced its intention to eliminate its nuclear, chemical, and long-range missile programs in order to rejoin the community of nations. Since that time, the CIA has reported the extent of Libyan cooperation in four key strategic areas:[19]

Nuclear: Libya admitted to ongoing fuel cycle projects at 10 sites intended to support a nuclear weapons program. Libya pledged voluntarily to relinquish its nuclear weapons program, abide by the NPT (to which it had been a party since 1975) and its 1980 safeguards agreement with the International Atomic Energy Agency, and submit to intrusive inspections called for by the NPT Additional Protocol. Furthermore, Libya disclosed the involvement of the Pakistani A.Q. Khan network in providing centrifuge and component designs.

Chemical: Libya revealed a chemical weapons plant at Rabta, which produced significant quantities of sulfur mustard gas, and stored equipment for a possible second factory for manufacturing mustard and nerve agent. Libya agreed to abide by the Chemical Weapons Convention and requested assistance in destroying chemical warfare stockpiles.

Biological: Libya had at one time acquired equipment and developed capabilities related to biological weapons, but now claims the program is extinct.

Ballistic Missiles: Libya provided extensive information concerning its Scud missile inventory and revealed the assistance it received from North Korea in an effort to develop longer-range missiles.

The Libyan renunciation was clearly a windfall for advocates of a hard-line emphasis in U.S. policy. Although judging the effect of the soft power of economic sanctions and possibly years of British diplomacy on Qadhafi's decision is difficult, there is little doubt that he understood the hard power of the U.S. invasion in Iraq and the PSI interdiction of his critical centrifuge components. In the end, Libya's lesson was that the price of pursuing WMD was just too high. When George W. Bush surveyed the components of the Libyan nuclear program at Oak Ridge National Laboratory in July 2004, he rightfully credited both diplomacy and action:

Libya is dismantling its weapons of mass destruction and long-range missile programs. This progress came about through quiet diplomacy between America, Britain, and the Libyan government. This progress was set in motion, however, by policies declared in public to all the world. The United States, Great Britain, and many other nations are determined to expose the threats of terrorism and proliferation—and to oppose those threats with all our power. We have sent this message in the strongest diplomatic terms, and we have acted where action was required.[20]

Economic and political developments have been largely positive for Libya since its WMD renunciation. In June 2004, Washington reestablished diplomatic relations with the opening of an independent liaison office in Tripoli. Sanctions were lifted in September 2004. Since then, foreign investment and tourism have risen, brightening Libya's economic prospects.

The critical lessons learned by U.S. and British intelligence experts once again exposed the fragility of information concerning adversaries' WMD programs. Libya was much farther along in the uranium enrichment process than anyone had previously known. With attention and resources diverted to monitoring Iraq and North Korea, the Libyan program was hardly more than a blip on anyone's radar screen. More troubling was the extent and breadth of the A.Q. Khan supplier network as revealed through this intelligence windfall. So while the positive side lies in how much we have learned through the Libyan experience, the downside is discovering how little the Intelligence Community knew previously. In the words of the Silberman-Robb Commission: "We conclude that collection and analytic efforts with regard to Libya's weapons programs and in support of the U.S./U.K.-led efforts represent, for the most part, an Intelligence Community success story."[21] However, based on this experience, the commission also offered a warning: "It is apparent to us that the Community is not well-postured to replicate such successes."[22]

A.Q. Khan Network

The same incident that caused Libya to change its strategic calculus uncovered an extensive network of WMD proliferators. In October 2003, Italian coast guard cutters, operating within the PSI framework, pulled alongside the *BBC China*, a German-flagged cargo vessel bound for Libya.[23] Upon inspection, authorities found precision machine tools, aluminum tubes, molecular pumps, and other components for building approximately 10,000 P–2 gas centrifuges designed for enriching uranium to specifications required for a nuclear weapon. These components were traced back to a publicly traded Malaysian engineering company called Scomi Precision Engineering. Scomi had manufactured the parts at the behest of a Sri Lankan middleman name Buhary Sayed Abu Tahir. From his front company in Dubai, SMB Computers, Tahir arranged to deliver the parts to Libya for its nascent nuclear weapons program. Tipped by British and American intelligence, the Italian authorities ensured the cargo never arrived at its destination. The seizure of the *BBC China*'s cargo began the chain of events that led Muammar Qadhafi to "come in from the cold" and renounce his WMD programs in December of 2003. Just as significantly, this interdiction operation was the strand that unraveled the shadowy proliferation network of Tahir's boss and mentor, A.Q. Khan.

The godfather of Pakistan's nuclear weapons program, Khan is a legendary and celebrated figure around Islamabad for his years of secretive work in developing the first "Islamic bomb." As a scientist working in the Netherlands for the European nuclear services firm Urenco in the 1970s, Khan had access to blueprints for uranium enrichment technology, which he stole and brought back to Pakistan. Khan was appointed by Prime Minister Ali Bhutto to run Pakistan's nuclear research program, with the goal of countering India's nuclear aspirations with a weapon of its own. Running counter to the nonproliferation norms of the international community, Khan was forced to pursue this goal with the utmost secrecy. However, Pakistan's indigenous scientific and engineering infrastructure was underdeveloped for the task. So Khan did what any good entrepreneur would do: he outsourced. He developed a contact list of suppliers and manufacturers, many of whom did not realize the ultimate objective of the science project undertaken at the Khan Research Laboratories. By 1998, however, there was no doubt. To the surprise of the international community, Pakistan completed five underground nuclear tests and joined an elite club of nuclear weapons states.[24]

For A.Q. Khan, the patriotic fervor surrounding this achievement was not enough. A shrewd businessman, he realized a match between his network of suppliers and a burgeoning market for nuclear arms. North Korea, Iran, Iraq, Syria, and Libya were foremost on a list of countries at least window-shopping for such capability. Continuing investigation into the Khan network points to a significant role, beginning in the early 1990s, in the development of Iranian and North Korean enrichment technology. In exchange, North Korea appears to have shared its ballistic missile technology with Pakistan.[25] The investigation of the Libyan program continues to reap an intelligence bonanza uncovering the extent of Khan's cooperation with rogue regimes worldwide.

While there is considerable debate over the role of the Pakistani government with regard to Khan's activities, it is unlikely that officials in Islamabad had full knowledge of the scope and scale of the Khan network. As it continues to be exposed, the web of alleged Khan sponsors and suppliers is breathtaking. Starting with the stolen centrifuge designs from the Netherlands and augmented by weapons designs from China, the syndicate also included engineering assistance from Britain; vacuum pumps from Germany; specialized lathes from Spain; furnaces from Italy; centrifuge motors and frequency converters from Turkey; enrichment parts from South Africa and Switzerland; aluminum from Singapore; and centrifuge parts from Malaysia, all orchestrated from an administrative hub in Dubai. Despite mounting evidence, however, it is unlikely that the full extent of the network that IAEA Director General Mohamed ElBaradei dubbed the "Wal-Mart of private-sector proliferation"[26] will ever be fully known.

Now that A.Q. Khan is under house arrest in Pakistan but unavailable to Western authorities for interrogation, vexing questions remain. It is clear that Khan met with, and possibly sold components to, officials in a number of aspiring nuclear states. In addition to the traditional rogues in the axis of evil, published reports have linked Khan to potential customers in Egypt, Saudi Arabia, Sudan, Malaysia, Indonesia, Algeria, Kuwait, Burma, and Abu Dhabi. Not known is whether these or other customers represent more problematic clients: terrorists or other nonstate actors with nuclear desires. What is known, regrettably, is that a man who did so much to damage nonproliferation efforts remains a hero in his own country.

LOOMING ISSUES AND CHOICES

Against the backdrop of Iraq, Libya, and the exposure of the A.Q. Khan network, the United States faces some tough choices in dealing with proliferation issues over the next decade. The remaining rogues—Iran, North Korea, and, to a lesser extent, Syria—seem to have learned a different lesson than Libya and appear to be accelerating their drive toward WMD capability. The questionable safety and security of nuclear material in the former Soviet Union and the potential for instability in countries with WMD present perplexing challenges. Most daunting of all is the nexus of WMD and terrorism, where most of the traditional policy tools have little to no effect. In dealing with this wide range of problems, policymakers cannot be wedded to a particular paradigm. President Bush himself recognizes that "different threats require different strategies."[27] To address these challenges will require coordination of all elements of national power as well as those of the global community.

Rogue Realism: Iran and North Korea

Watching from the sidelines, the remaining members of the axis of evil have taken their cue from the U.S. invasion of Iraq: they could be next. North Korea accelerated its program while Iran shifted gears, putting its weaponization program on hold but continuing its pursuit of weapons-grade material. Mohamed ElBaradai observed, "The fundamental issue is that countries look at know-how as a deterrent. Once you get into areas of deterrence, you get into security and insecurity. If you have nuclear material, the weapon part is not far away."[28]

During the Cold War, the nuclear club remained exclusive. Technology barriers certainly were a factor. However, it may have been the global norms set by the nonproliferation regimes, and the ability of the United States and the Soviet Union in the bipolar geopolitical environment of the Cold War to secure compliance (with France and China being the notable exceptions), that played more strongly in avoiding President John F. Kennedy's fear of a world with 20 or more nuclear powers. When the Non-Proliferation Treaty was signed in 1968, only the "big five" had nuclear weapons: the United States, Soviet Union, Great Britain, France, and China. Later they were joined by India, Pakistan, and Israel, the only nonsignatories to the NPT. With North Korea's acknowledgment in October 2002 that it possessed highly enriched uranium, followed in January of 2003 by its withdrawal from the NPT, the world saw its first crack in the nonproliferation armor. With Iran close behind, the prospect is that the entire set of norms could unravel.

Consequences could be dire. U.S. allies and partners South Korea, Japan, Taiwan, Turkey, Egypt, and Saudi Arabia, among others, may no longer feel sufficiently comfortable under the U.S. nuclear umbrella and may be tempted to convert their fuel cycle technology to security purposes. In fact, investigations into undeclared nuclear activity in South Korea,[29] Taiwan, and Egypt[30] may be just the tip of the iceberg. At least 18 countries have had nuclear programs at one or another time, most abandoning them before signing the NPT.[31] But that means that many countries may be able to develop nuclear technology if the NPT fails.

From the U.S. perspective, the unwillingness or inability of the IAEA, the United Nations, and the world community to hold North Korea and Iran accountable for their NPT obligations means that the treaty may already be irrelevant. In February 2004, President Bush announced proposals to close loopholes in the NPT and other nonproliferation regimes, such as the Nuclear Suppliers Group, by strengthening IAEA inspections and safeguards; improving restrictions on export of sensitive technologies to include criminal penalties for transfer to nonstate actors; advancing the PSI; and expanding the G–8 Global Partnership to eliminate and secure sensitive materials, which builds on U.S.-Russian Cooperative Threat Reduction activities.[32] He also challenged the IAEA and the international community to enforce global norms, particularly in the cases of Iran and North Korea. The response has been disappointing.

Handling a proliferating rogue state does not consist, as is often portrayed, of making a choice among discrete courses of action: diplomacy or force, carrots or sticks, soft or hard power. It is instead a delicate balancing act along a spectrum of responses. Diplomacy in the absence of credible threats of force can lack effectiveness, as a proliferating nation would be more than happy to take advantage of perceived overflexibility. On the other hand, an overreliance on forceful responses risks alienating the proliferating nation, as well as allies and the larger international community, and may cause negotiations to break down altogether. The difficulty in achieving such balance continues to plague U.S. strategy in dealing with the nuclear ambitions of North Korea and Iran. As the chessboard of negotiations and strategic capabilities continuously changes, the United States and its allies must constantly reexamine their tactics and adjust their responses to unfolding realizations.

The Bush administration has opposed separate bilateral talks with North Korea and Iran on nuclear issues. The administration's position was that previous bilateral talks with North Korea had been counterproductive and allowed Pyongyang to raise extraneous issues and more easily drive wedges between Washington and its allies. Moreover, U.S. officials noted, the Iranian and North Korean nuclear programs threaten many countries, and multilateral talks bring the weight of the wider international community to bear on Pyongyang and Tehran. Some in the Bush administration view such engagement as a Cold War artifact, ill suited to the post-9/11 realities, in that it rewards countries that fail to live up to their international obligations.

Regarding Iran, Washington chose to pressure the IAEA to refer Iran to the UN Security Council for possible sanctions. However, the opposition of the United Kingdom, Germany, and France (the EU–3), who separately negotiated two agreements with Iran to suspend their uranium enrichment program, initially stymied that effort. Iran soon violated the first agreement and in February 2006 broke the second by announcing it had resumed uranium enrichment, claiming it had a right to a peaceful nuclear program without interference. Abandoning its diplomatic tact, the EU–3 joined the United States in spearheading a call by the IAEA Board of Governors to refer the matter to the UN Security Council. Reluctance by Russia and China to support punitive sanctions has diminished the effect of this endeavor. However, Beijing and Moscow did support imposition of UN Security Council sanctions on Iran in December 2006 and March 2007 that prohibited trade with Iran in nuclear materials and ballistic missiles, froze assets of individuals and institutions involved in Tehran's nuclear programs, imposed an embargo on Iranian weapons exports, and barred nations and banks from making any new loans to Iran. Some in the United States believe that the engagement efforts by the EU–3 have merely allowed Iran to buy time and perhaps get closer to developing the technology it needs to make a weapon. Indeed, neither the EU–3 negotiations nor political developments in Iran over the past few years have diverted Tehran from its systematic pursuit of nuclear technology that could contribute to a weapons program, including uranium enrichment and a heavy water reactor.[33] The Bush administration has conditioned initiation of any bilateral talks with Tehran on nuclear issues upon Iran's suspension of its nuclear enrichment and reprocessing activities.[34]

This skeptical view toward negotiation is understandable, given the U.S. experience in North Korea. In 1994, the United States and North Korea signed the Agreed Framework, which called upon Pyongyang to freeze operation and construction of nuclear reactors suspected of being part of a covert nuclear weapons program in exchange for two proliferation-resistant nuclear power reactors. The agreement also called upon the United States to supply North Korea with fuel oil pending construction of the reactors. Many charge that this agreement simply allowed the North Koreans to continue to work clandestinely on a uranium enrichment program while attempting to reap benefits offered (but not always delivered) by the United States.

Despite this, the United States has been willing to engage with North Korea through the framework of the Six-Party Talks involving the United States, North Korea, South Korea, China, Japan, and Russia. In this forum, the United States initially insisted on the unconditional demand of complete, verifiable, and irreversible disarmament (CVID), which China, South Korea, and Russia viewed as inflexible and counterproductive. During the round of talks in June 2004, Washington softened its stance on CVID as a measure of good faith, yet no agreement was reached. North Korea rejected a planned meeting in September 2004, citing the revelation of South Korea's experimentation with uranium processing. This was clearly a cover for Pyongyang's desire to wait out the U.S. elections in hopes of gaining a more favorable position with a different administration. After the election, North Korea first agreed to another round of talks, but later declared that it had nuclear weapons capability and again pulled out before talks began.

Following a 13-month boycott by North Korea, the fourth round of talks opened in July 2005 with hints of new flexibility by Pyongyang and Washington. However, longstanding differences—including over North Korea's demands that they retain nuclear plants for power generation and that the U.S. nuclear guarantee to South Korea be part of the negotiations, as well as over the timing of North Korea's disarmament and the compensation it would receive in return—clouded the prospects. Finally, in September 2005, the discussions yielded agreement on a joint statement of principles for denuclearization of the Korean Peninsula, improvement of bilateral relations, and regional cooperation. The statement was immediately subject to differing interpretations, particularly by the Democratic People's Republic of Korea (DPRK). The U.S. Government made clear its view of the main tenets, which were generally endorsed by all the other parties: all nuclear weapons and all elements of the DPRK's nuclear programs will be declared and completely, verifiably, and irreversibly dismantled; the DPRK will return, at an early date, to the Nuclear Non-Proliferation Treaty and come into full compliance with International Atomic Energy Agency safeguards; and various benefits, particularly the right to pursue nuclear energy for peaceful purposes at the "appropriate time," will only accrue to the DPRK when it has met these two obligations, demonstrated a sustained commitment to cooperation and transparency, and ceased proliferating nuclear technology.[35]

Continued North Korean intransigence, including a failed July 2006 test of the long-range Taepo Dong II missile and a successful October 2006 test of a nuclear device, further dimmed the prospects for another 18 months. However, Pyongyang's nuclear test galvanized diplomacy, and in February 2007 the six parties reached agreement on initial steps to implement the joint statement of principles, wherein Pyongyang agreed to disable its main nuclear facility at Yongbyon and the United States undertook bilateral talks on normalization of relations with North Korea.[36]

Kim Jong Il's motivations are difficult to judge, although he clearly is trying to enhance the survival of his regime and gain some economic rewards. How much the United States and the other participants in the Six-Party Talks are willing to offer in terms of economic incentives or security guarantees remains to be seen. The participants have differing interests that have precluded development of a unified strategy in dealing with North Korea and are sometimes at odds with one another. To date, this has strengthened the North Korean position in being able to play against these fissures.

Future prospects are, as a rule, difficult to predict. From its post-9/11 viewpoint, the Bush administration is concerned that either North Korea or Iran would be willing to use a nuclear weapons capability not to deter the United States, but instead to hold it hostage. The growing ballistic missile program in each country provides grist for those who maintain that these unstable regimes would actually use these weapons as a means for deterring the United States or others from responding to local aggression or subversion. As former Deputy Secretary of Defense Paul Wolfowitz commented concerning the President's decision to withdraw from the ABM Treaty and develop defenses against long-range ballistic missiles:

> To those who say the threat is still a remote one far in a distant and uncertain future, the fact is that the short-range threat is here with us today even as we worry about the dangers of a possible conflict in the Persian Gulf or on the Korean Peninsula. And while a longer-range threat may still be a few years away, thanks to the historic change

that the President was able to achieve, we may now be in a position to be able to respond before that threat emerges.[37]

Even more troublesome is the possibility of a terrorist link and the potential for nuclear capabilities to migrate from rogue states to terrorist organizations. Terrorists may not be deterrable, and they also may provide a means for rogue states to attack the United States or other adversaries with WMD with little or no attribution.

Thus, as the efficacy of diplomacy has been greatly challenged in recent years, the option of forceful action has been a subject of ongoing discussion. Throughout its dealings with Iran and North Korea, the United States consistently has not ruled out the use of force. In line with its post-9/11 approach, the Bush administration retains the right to use force as a tool to prevent the further development of a rogue nuclear program. Yet with more than 185,000 troops tied down in counterinsurgency and stability operations in Iraq and Afghanistan, how much and what kind of force can be used? For instance, a large-scale military operation by the United States would face considerable difficulty. Not only would formidable military capability in either Iran or North Korea make this task difficult, but also the task of reconstruction, particularly on the Korean Peninsula, would be staggering. Even if the troops were available, it is questionable that the international community would tolerate another American adventure.

What about a long-range strike against WMD facilities? The Israelis were successful in striking the Iraqi Osirak reactor in 1981, which delayed, but did not eliminate, Iraq's quest for nuclear weapons. Both Iran and North Korea took note, choosing to disperse and hide many components of their programs. The United States has difficulty finding and striking hard and deeply buried targets, especially given the dearth of human intelligence in these closed societies. Punishment strikes against better characterized regime sources of power would be easier to execute but probably would engender unintended consequences. In North Korea, it would likely trigger hostilities on the peninsula, beginning with a hail of artillery on Seoul. In Iran, such strikes may not touch off an immediate retaliatory response, but they would likely inflame moderates and students against the United States. Furthermore, Iran might use surrogates, such as Hezbollah, to launch terrorist counterstrikes against U.S. interests around the world or military operations against U.S. allies in the Middle East—a capability illustrated quite starkly by Hezbollah's attacks against Israel from Lebanon in August 2006. Iran is also quite capable of further complicating the U.S. efforts to stabilize Iraq.

A milder form of preemption, such as a stepped-up interdiction campaign under the auspices of the Proliferation Security Initiative, could have some positive effect in stemming the shipment of materials to and from these countries. However, if, as some believe, Iran and North Korea already have all the components they need to continue their programs, interdiction is unlikely to slow them down. As can be seen, acts of force are riddled with complications and therefore must be approached delicately.

Safeguards: Deterrence and Assurance

What, then, are the prospects? No single paradigm will work here. To develop a comprehensive strategy, the United States must maximize all available tools to convince North Korea and Iran to renounce their programs. In looking at the range of solutions, we must consider the ramifications to the worldwide nonproliferation regime, the efficacy of engagement, and the threat of force in eliminating nuclear challenges.

However, another consideration remains: what to do if worldwide efforts to stem Iranian and North Korean WMD programs fail. Despite the rhetoric that a nuclear-armed rogue state is not acceptable, the United States must consider the reality that it might occur.

To prepare for this eventuality, the Bush administration is developing a strategy of *tailored deterrence*.[38] Traditional Cold War deterrence breaks down in the face of extremist governments, state-sponsored terrorism, and nuclear arsenals with fragile security infrastructures. A policy of tailored deterrence would include a set of military, economic, and political measures designed to stem proliferation within and from the rogue state and to other states; deter the rogue state from using WMD; and insulate the United States and its allies from blackmail. Certain measures may have to recognize the reality of rogue state possession. For instance, though contrary to the official U.S. nonproliferation stance, assuring that the rogue state's WMD arsenal is secured and safeguarded from unintentional use and from theft would also be in the interest of the United States.

Inherent to the idea of tailored deterrence is the need to adjust U.S. measures to the unique situation posed by each proliferating state. North Korea and Iran serve as good examples. While a military strike on North Korea's facilities may evoke the grave consequence of retaliation, the price of isolating North Korea would be small. Its economic ties to neighboring states are minimal, and as long as vigilant eyes are kept on North Korea's WMD program, proliferation to other states or nonstate actors could be managed. This contrasts with Iran, however, which has strong economic ties to other countries, particularly China, through its oil reserves. Isolation is less likely an option, and the issues of terrorism and extremist agendas among the heads of state complicate the prospects of stemming proliferation and guarding against blackmail.

A policy of tailored deterrence would be needed to deal with these contingencies. Regarding North Korea, maintaining sanctions while keeping diplomatic channels open via the Six-Party framework or other means could prove to be a capable policy, at least for the short term. On the other hand, dealing with Iran would require a different deterrent strategy. Economic sanctions may have only limited value due to many nations' reliance on Iranian oil. Using military force should be kept as an option, though the level of threat the United States voices to Iran will need to depend on Tehran's perceived willingness to regulate its WMD programs and responsibly attend to diplomatic gestures. In the end, much will depend on assumptions: what credence do we give to extremist rhetoric, such as demands for Israel to be wiped off the map, and what do we believe Iran's capability and/or willingness is to keep WMD out of the hands of terrorists?

For tailored deterrence to work effectively, the United States must have a much deeper and richer base of understanding of its adversaries' motivations and the contexts for which decisions are made.[39] As mentioned before, in cases beyond the Cold War with the Soviet Union, traditional intelligence methods have proven ill equipped to provide this kind of understanding. As the Intelligence Community develops the ability to incorporate deeper cultural and social analyses in its assessments, tailoring deterrence to specific adversaries can begin to become reality.

In facing the reality of a nuclear North Korea or Iran, the United States will also have to consider a tailored assurance strategy to ensure that global proliferation does not spiral out of control. North Korea's October 2006 nuclear test has led some Japanese and South Korean political leaders to reconsider their countries' nuclear options. In the Middle East, a nuclear Iran may change the calculus of Turkey, Saudi Arabia, and Egypt. U.S. nuclear guarantees to these key allies may no longer be sufficient to prevent the nuclear dominoes from falling. Should that occur, regional balances of power will be forever altered in unpredictable ways.

As Senator John McCain (R–AZ) has contended, "There is only one thing worse than military action, and that is a nuclear-armed Iran."[40] Though his view is certainly debatable, his statement cuts right to the heart of the matter. If Washington perceives diplomatic actions to be failing, it must decide to either use force or learn to live with a WMD-armed rogue state. Once a rogue state attains WMD capability, the consequences of using force multiply exponentially. In the cases of North Korea and Iran, the countries at greatest risk for retaliation would be South Korea, Japan, and Israel, staunch U.S. allies. Developing a policy of tailored deterrence must therefore be addressed now in order to realistically assess the consequences of a WMD-armed North Korea and Iran and whether the use of force is justified and necessary.

Stemming Supply: Loose Nukes, Bugs, and Failed States

The U.S. strategy for combating weapons of mass destruction is designed to address both the demand and supply problems represented by the rogue states and terrorists. A supply problem requiring urgent attention is that of unsecured nuclear and biological materials. In Russia, which holds half of the world's plutonium and highly enriched uranium, safeguards and security are insufficient to prevent terrorist theft or diversion. The Nunn-Lugar Cooperative Threat Reduction (CTR) program, devised in 1991 as a nonproliferation "Marshall Plan" to deal with the breakup of the Soviet Union, has had some notable success. Specifically, it secured all weapons in the former Soviet republics of Ukraine, Belarus, and Kazakhstan; ensured the deactivation of some 6,382 nuclear warheads; decommissioned or destroyed more than 1,400 delivery systems; eliminated over 200 metric tons of highly enriched uranium; and shifted more than 22,000 nuclear scientists to peaceful endeavors.[41] Yet even with that progress, success remains elusive: up to two-thirds of Russia's weapons-grade material remains inadequately secured.[42] To be sure, securing nuclear material is dangerous, difficult, and expensive. Bureaucratic disputes and lingering mistrust between the United States and Russia have not helped. For instance, a disagreement with Russia over worker liability has caused some parts of the program to languish.

President Bush reaffirmed his support for CTR and proposed expansion of the program beyond the former Soviet space. To do so, in February 2004, the Department of Energy announced the creation of its Global Threat Reduction Initiative (GTRI) to bring several programs under one umbrella with a mission to remove or secure high-risk nuclear and radiological materials and equipment around the world.

In 2002, the United States enlisted its G–8 partners to form the Global Partnership against the Spread of Weapons and Materials of Mass Destruction. The G–8 pledged more than $20 billion through 2012: $10 billion from the United States, with another $10 billion being sought from other donor nations. With goals of expanding the number of donor nations and contributing to threat reduction efforts in Russia, the Global Partnership also places a priority on the destruction of chemical weapons, dismantlement of decommissioned nuclear submarines, disposition of fissile material, and employment of former scientists. At the 2005 Gleneagles summit, 13 additional donor countries joined the partnership, and Ukraine joined Russia as a recipient.[43] While international pledges have been lagging, U.S. contributions have totaled about $1 billion annually in recent years, with about 40 percent of those funds coming from DOD CTR programs and 50 percent from DOE GTRI activities.[44]

FIGURE 3–2. APPLYING COOPERATIVE THREAT REDUCTION TECHNIQUES TO THE GLOBAL NUCLEAR PROBLEM

Category	Areas of Concern	Tasks
Traditional	Russia	• Reducing number of highly enriched uranium (HEU) sites and accelerating the blend down of HEU • Extending/tightening control over nuclear weapons and materials • Interdicting nuclear smuggling • Securing and dismantling smaller warheads • Safely disposing of existing plutonium and ending future production • Reducing and monitoring nuclear weapons stockpiles
De Facto Nuclear Weapons States	India, Pakistan	• Improving physical control • Improving accountability • Preventing leakage to unauthorized recipients • Preventing export of nuclear, weapons, materials, and equipment • Hardening transportation links against attack • Purchasing HEU for resale as fuel for commercial nuclear power plants • Diverting technical and scientific expertise to civil purposes
Former Noncooperative States	Libya	• Preventing export of nuclear weapons, materials, and equipment • Assisting in the conversion of defense industries or weapons laboratories to civil operations
Noncooperative Proliferators	North Korea, Iran	• Improving physical control • Improving accountability • Diverting technical and scientific expertise to civil purposes • Preventing leakage to unauthorized recipients • Preventing export of nuclear weapons, materials, and equipment • Eliminating means of delivering nuclear weapons • Assisting in the conversion of defense industries or weapons laboratories to civil operations • Supporting alternative power sources • Removing nuclear weapons, fissile materials, and equipment for producing weapons-useable fissile material from countries of concern
Sources of Highly Enriched Uranium	Global	• Improving HEU security at research reactors • Transferring HEU materials from regions of concern to original sources • Converting HEU reactors to low enriched uranium

Cooperative threat reduction techniques can be applied globally to the nuclear proliferation problem beyond the former Soviet countries. Figure 3–2 provides examples of the type of tasks that should be accomplished.

In recent years, the CTR has emphasized the securing and destruction of biological and chemical weapons in the former Soviet Union states. The fiscal year 2006 CTR Annual Report to Congress stated the following objectives:

- dismantle FSU [Former Soviet Union] states WMD and associated infrastructure
- consolidate and secure FSU WMD and related technology and materials
- increase transparency and encourage higher standards of conduct
- support defense and military cooperation with the objective of preventing proliferation.[45]

The stress placed on *securing* and *preventing* the proliferation of all forms of WMD was a notable shift from the original CTR concern on the *destruction* of nuclear materials.

A nontrivial subset of the loose nukes problem is the nightmare scenario of major instability in a nuclear weapons state. Pakistan is the most cited case. President Pervez Musharraf has dodged several assassins' bullets to date, and the fate of Pakistan's nuclear weapons should he lose his grip on power is unknown. While Pakistan may be a center of gravity in the war against terrorism and WMD proliferation, the United States must carefully navigate its policy options to ensure Islamabad does not become the "center of catastrophe."

A possible failure of governance also could occur in North Korea. Although the self-induced elimination of Kim Jong Il's regime would certainly be seen as a positive development, it could become a nightmare if the international community did not react quickly enough to find and secure whatever stockpiles of weapons the regime may have been hiding. Doing so is imperative to ensure that WMD does not fall into the hands of terrorists or nonstate proliferators.

Shadow Networks: Terrorism and WMD Suppliers

The most distinguishing feature of the post-9/11 paradigm is the emergence of radical Islamist extremism. Substate transnational terrorism represents a perplexing new security challenge, one exacerbated by the potential acquisition of WMD. Osama bin Laden has proclaimed the acquisition of WMD a "religious duty," but no one believes al Qaeda would stop there. It is almost universally assumed that radical terrorists are pursuing WMD to inflict as many casualties as possible against the United States or its interests. With this assumption, the line between adversary acquisition and attempted use has been erased. Prevention must occur before the terrorists obtain weapons, technology, or know-how to achieve this goal. This narrows the range of options available to the United States and is a fundamental reason for the more aggressive WMD policies of the post-9/11 period.

Existing nonproliferation regimes may be inadequate to deal with the emerging threat of nonstate proliferation. International norms, the basis of these regimes, are predicated on an assumption that only states have the requisite resources to develop nuclear weapons. The Khan experience, viewed through a new set of assumptions in a post-9/11 world, indicates that this basic premise is flawed. For this reason, the Bush administration has begun prodding the international community to move from a position of *cooperative agreements* to one of *cooperative action.*

In keeping with its changed worldview, the United States has developed a more proactive approach to attack both ends of the problem. To curb demand, the war on terrorism seeks to defeat terrorist groups in the short term while undermining terrorist ideology and support over the long term. Against rogue states, international pressure backed by threat of force is aimed at isolating outlaw regimes. However, the experience in Iraq shows the complications of such policy, especially conducted with limited international consensus.

The Bush administration has pursued parallel strategies for combating terrorism and weapons of mass destruction and for ensuring homeland security.[46] At the nexus of WMD and terrorism, these strategies converge to emphasize the role of state sponsors in providing terrorist networks the material, technology, and know-how to build nuclear, radiological, chemical, and biological weapons. As a result, the policy options have focused on reducing the supply originating from rogue states, "loose WMD" in traditional states, and potential failed states.

The nexus of WMD and terrorism has clearly colored Bush administration policies on Iraq, Iran, North Korea, and Libya, with mixed results. Perhaps the lesson is that not all WMD problems can be viewed exclusively through the terrorism lens. Likewise, all WMD solutions cannot be viewed exclusively as state solutions. Yet there have been some successes in this state-centered approach that can have a real and positive effect on the terror problem. One, discussed earlier, is the idea of securing the world's nuclear material through initiatives like CTR. Another is the creative new policy option of interdiction as embodied in the Proliferation Security Initiative.

Announced in May 2003, the PSI initiative quickly gained momentum to target shipments of WMD materials and technology en route from proliferators to consumers. Billed as "an activity, not an organization," PSI has eschewed the bureaucratic and political trappings of traditional international regimes. By engaging with like-minded nations, the United States has been able to rapidly engender cooperation designed to isolate WMD proliferators. Within a few months of its first announcement, PSI held successful maritime exercises. By October 2003, PSI had its first major success with the interception of the *BBC China,* which isolated Libya as a WMD consumer and helped convinced Qadhafi to come in from the cold. By building a global network dedicated to stop WMD transshipment, the United States has developed an effective tool in defeating transfers between proliferating states. The jury is still out on how effective it may be in dealing with nonstate proliferation networks, but the concept holds promise.

This model of cooperative action should be extended to other global efforts to prevent WMD from reaching terrorists. Clandestine WMD development outside of state auspices will be the most difficult to detect, particularly in areas other than nuclear.

To further build an antiproliferation network, the United States will need to engage a range of nonstate actors to include corporate enterprises, financiers, and scientists. Extended collaboration among these network partners will enhance awareness of those seeking or developing dangerous capabilities. This type of cooperation can also serve to isolate terrorist groups and proliferators by reinforcing international norms and denying critical technological expertise required to create such weapons.

TOWARD A NEW PARADIGM

The paradigms of proliferation are useful in highlighting the changing threat perceptions from the Cold War through today. According to Secretary of State Condoleezza Rice, "after 9/11, there is no longer any doubt that today America faces an existential threat to our security—a threat as great as any we faced during the Civil War, the so-called 'Good War,' or the Cold War."[47] The post–Cold War period proved to be a transitional interlude allowing minimal breathing space to deal with new dangers. The success of the post-9/11 period will be judged by our ability to use these paradigms as a guide, to recognize that most of the capabilities to combat WMD were designed during the Cold War and post–Cold War world. Some may still be viable for today's problems; others may not. Today's policymakers will need the acumen to understand the context in which they were developed: to discard those that are irrelevant for certain contexts, but not to throw the baby out with the bath water. Looking across the paradigms provides a rich set of tools for dealing with WMD in today's context of state and nonstate actors, competitors, rogues, terrorists, proliferators, suppliers, and middlemen. Bridging the paradigms will require a robust strategy of cooperative action to enhance the commitment of the international community to deal with its WMD problems, while isolating the intransigent few.

The U.S. Government is showing signs of addressing the complexity and depth of the WMD problem in a more holistic manner. For example, the final report of the 2006 Quadrennial Defense Review recognizes the strategic shifts that have taken place since the last QDR in September 2001.[48] Combating WMD, a topic that was lightly addressed in the 2001 report, has been elevated to prominence in the department's strategic calculus. DOD has placed priority on efforts to detect, track, interdict, and eliminate WMD, capabilities that were clearly deficient judging by the experiences with Iraq, Libya, and A.Q. Khan. It envisions a future force that is "organized, trained, equipped, and resourced to deal with all aspects of the threat posed by weapons of mass destruction."[49]

The concept of tailored deterrence has also been introduced into the military's strategic lexicon as a nod to the realities that, despite our best preventive efforts, rogue or nonstate adversaries may in fact develop WMD capabilities. In its vision for tailored deterrence, the 2006 QDR suggests:

> The Department is continuing to shift from a 'one size fits all' notion of deterrence toward more tailorable approaches appropriate for more advanced military competitors, regional WMD states, as well as nonstate terrorist networks. The future force will provide a fully balanced, tailored capability to deter both state and nonstate threats—including

WMD employment, terrorist attacks in the physical and information domains, and opportunistic aggression—while assuring allies and dissuading potential competitors.[50]

Yet critics of the report believe that it does not go far enough in making the fundamental choices and prioritization that are necessary for a comprehensive WMD strategy.[51] The concern is that the QDR did not make adequate guidance on the department's full range of combating WMD responsibilities. For example, critics point out that too much of the current effort is focused on detecting and defending against weapons once they are in an adversary's possession, rather than developing a strategy for denying adversaries access to fissile materials and weapons in the first place.

Despite its critics, the QDR at least rhetorically begins to address the combating WMD mission in a more holistic manner than in previous attempts. The extent to which priority and resources are developed around this vision for combating WMD, and the extent to which it is embraced by the rest of the interagency and international partners, remains to be seen. However, there is promise in the 2006 QDR and other U.S. Government efforts that the lessons of the past have begun to merge with the realities of today in building a new, broader-based paradigm for dealing with WMD-armed adversaries.

Chapter Four

Protecting the American Homeland

Thomas X. Hammes, James A. Schear, and John A. Cope

Ａmerica's sense of vulnerability has grown enormously in recent years, propelled initially by the terrorist attacks of September 11, 2001, and again by Hurricane Katrina's devastating impact upon the city of New Orleans and the gulf coast in September 2005. Granted, these two disasters could not have been more different. One was an armed attack; the other was a natural catastrophe. One caught the country by surprise; the other was a foreseeable event, tracked by forecasters prior to impact. One brought the country together in the face of a newly perceived threat from a foreign source; the other aggravated domestic social divisions and bitter discontent. Despite these differences, both events illustrated very starkly the all-too-human fallibility of public institutions charged with protection of the U.S. homeland.

The attacks of 9/11 were more than just treacherous and tragic—they were novel. Within the span of 90 minutes during an otherwise normal morning rush hour, 19 terrorists armed with box cutters commandeered 4 commercial aircraft and struck at the symbolic pinnacles of America's economic and military power, inflicting mass casualties, emboldening Islamist extremists worldwide, and bringing the U.S. civil aviation system to a screeching halt. The events revealed the shocking extent to which public thinking about *how* to defend the country had become out of step with modern threats. Hurricane Katrina, by contrast, struck at a large urban area whose susceptibility to massive flooding had long been well established. What it revealed was the shocking extent to which disaster responders at all levels of government and in the private sector, even with the benefit of timely warning and a known vulnerability, were incapable of mounting a coherent response.

Without question, the spectacle of governmental disarray in the face of catastrophic threats, whether natural or manmade, is an unnerving one for the American public, and the traumas of the past several years have spawned a massive effort to analyze past mistakes, promote reform, and ensure better preparedness.[1] Even so, the paramount strategic challenge on homeland security for the George W. Bush administration and its successor is not to turn America into an impregnable fortress but to identify and aggressively close avoidable gaps in how the U.S. disaster management community attempts to prevent or respond to catastrophic threats.

The road ahead will not be easy. Overall, the ability of the Federal Government to adapt to changing circumstances has been sluggish, uneven, and mired in bureaucracy. In fact, the very nature of a U.S. Government response to any public problem is bound to be bureaucratic. The federal form of government, as discussed below, complicates the problem because it creates distinct cultures at and within the various levels of government as well as significant legal and organizational restrictions that often impede the provision of assistance to state and local law enforcement, emergency management, and public health organizations. The net result is a response impeded by institutional checks and balances—as was intended by the framers of the Constitution.

On the terrorist front, future efforts to attack the American homeland are a virtual certainty. Al Qaeda and its affiliates, at the very least, clearly have the motive. Can they be deprived of the means and opportunity? The greater public vigilance that has accompanied post-9/11 homeland security enhancements very likely has raised the bar to certain kinds of opportunistic attack options. Any future hijackers, for example, whether bent upon suicide missions or not, would have to reckon with the defiance of commercial airline passengers, such as those on United Flight 93 who rushed the cockpit after learning of the other attacks via cell phone conversations. The traumas of 9/11 have forever changed the rules of behavior during a hijacking. But as old attack options recede, newer ones may come to the fore; terrorists will seek new ways to cause massive damage. Therefore, it is essential that U.S. leaders focus on those kinds of attacks that would cause the most damage to U.S. citizens and economy.

Over the next few years, one of the most pressing challenges confronting the Nation will be dealing with threats posed by attacks of catastrophic scale, involving weapons of mass destruction (WMD) and weapons of mass disruption (WMd). In doing so, it may not be possible to prevent all forms of attack on the United States, or even all WMD/d attacks, but there is much that public institutions at all levels can do to improve the security of the Nation and its air, land, and maritime approaches within the constraints of a democratic, federal government. Furthermore, the focus should be directed at those efforts that have dual benefits: ones that defend/mitigate against more than one form of catastrophic attack and also improve the ability of all levels of government to prevent/respond to daily emergencies throughout the country.

Enhancing preparedness in the face of natural disasters is a somewhat different challenge. Truly catastrophic events with a regional or national impact—say, another massive gulf coast hurricane, a west coast earthquake, or a pandemic flu outbreak—are going to happen sooner or later, but they also constitute a small subset of all the emergencies that occur in any given year—emergencies for which America's long-standing approach of relying on local and state responders, with Federal responders acting in support, works reasonably well. Deterrence or prevention are not the issues here, but rather the approach of having local responders lead until they get overwhelmed by disasters that exceed what multiple jurisdictions or states can handle. The Katrina experience raises difficult questions that apply to all kinds of hazards: under what kinds of extreme circumstances should the Federal Government shift its posture from one of reactively assisting state and local levels to one of proactively supporting or leading a disaster response, and how should such a shift be achieved?

This chapter assesses the challenges of thwarting catastrophic attacks and coping with human impacts of megadisasters, whether natural or manmade. It begins by exploring the distinctive problems of WMD/d attacks, highlighting the difficulties in building stronger defenses against such threats. Following that, it turns to an examination of the organizational and operational problems of mitigating the effects of massive damage. It concludes with a balance sheet that weighs recent improvements against continuing shortfalls and identifies a number of key areas where innovation is needed.

PREVENTING CATASTROPHIC ATTACKS

There are two major components to protecting the homeland from catastrophic damage. The first is prevention, which applies in the case of possible terrorist attacks. The second is minimizing the consequences of the damage that a successful attack or a large-scale disaster can inflict. Minimizing damage must include not only the emergency response capabilities that mitigate immediate damage to life and property but also rapid recovery to curtail long-term economic damage. The Bush administration's *National Strategy for Homeland Security* highlighted each of these as an essential element in mounting stronger defenses against catastrophic threats, while also acknowledging—correctly—that capabilities for detecting such threats were "modest" and that U.S. response capabilities were "dispersed throughout the country, at every level of government."[2] The following sections take a closer look at each area to see why these missions are so challenging and where the critical gaps remain.

Preventing WMD Attacks

Weapons of mass destruction are generally defined as chemical, biological, radiological, nuclear, and high-yield explosives (CBRNE) weapons. While this label is appropriately inclusive, its implicit hierarchy does not reflect the level of hazards involved in the various types of attack. The actual hierarchy should be *biological, nuclear, chemical,* and *high-yield explosive*. Radiological devices are treated here as a weapon of mass disruption rather than mass destruction and will be analyzed in that context.

Biological threats. A well-thought-out biological attack has the potential to be, by far, the most destructive form of attack—in terms not only of casualties but also of adverse economic and financial impacts. If such an attack were conducted with a contagious agent such as smallpox or plague, it could kill tens of millions worldwide and effectively shut down global trade for a significant period of time. Such an attack could involve the near-simultaneous release of the agent or volunteers infected with the agent in major population centers worldwide. Under such a scenario, the use of a contagious agent combined with the high mobility of today's society would ensure the spread of the disease over most of the globe before the symptoms were identified. The intent would be to overwhelm the public health system in every nation simultaneously and thereby stymie international assistance. Such an attack would almost certainly bring about a sudden drop in international travel and commerce—a pattern that would be powerfully reinforced if movement control restrictions or quarantines were imposed by national authorities as a public health necessity.

It is beyond the scope of this chapter to discuss the sources of biological agents, but a quick survey of a library or the Internet will confirm the availability of a number of biological agents, even infectious ones. The use of anthrax and ricin in attacks on Capitol Hill in 2001 and 2003 indicates both are available. In addition, anthrax and plague are available in many university labs. In fact, not until after the Capitol Hill attacks did some states even pass laws requiring that such agents be registered. North Carolina, for instance, passed its law in November 2001.[3] Documents captured in 2003 revealed that al Qaeda was close to producing anthrax bacteria in labs in Afghanistan.[4]

The very nature of a biological attack makes it nearly impossible to prevent and often even to identify the perpetrators. U.S. law enforcement authorities still do not know who conducted either the 2001 anthrax or the 2003 ricin attacks on Capitol Hill. While efforts at preventing proliferation of biological weapons must continue, the exceptional advances in the biological sciences and biotechnology will change the world even more radically than did the last two decades' advances in computer sciences. Today, graduate students using a well-equipped university lab can do biological research that used to require government sponsorship.

The actual effect of the advances in the biological fields is to create the conditions where small networks can create and disseminate contagious agents. The only way to prevent such an attack is to penetrate the small group necessary to conduct it. Thus, it pits U.S. human intelligence (HUMINT) collection ability—the shortcomings of which were highlighted by the 9/11 Commission—against what may be the toughest target in the HUMINT world, a small group of close friends bound by an ideological belief. Like nearly all terrorist cells, such a cell is easy to arrest if identified. But the chances of identifying it prior to an attack are not good. Therefore, the single biggest step in preventing biological attack is to recognize its potential and focus intelligence organizations on identifying and tracking key indicators of research/production of such weapons. This will require innovative outreach programs to tap into the broad, diverse, and scattered biological research field worldwide. However, the rapidly lowering technical and financial barriers to such research, combined with its exceptional potential profit and need for secrecy, make it virtually impossible to track all the entities involved in such research. Thus, defense against this most dangerous of threats must include a heavy emphasis on mitigation of the impact of such an attack. This will be discussed later in the chapter.

Nuclear threats. The next most dangerous type of WMD attack is a nuclear attack. Such an attack in a heavily populated urban area could result in hundreds of thousands of casualties, displacement of hundreds of thousands of people, and billions of dollars in economic losses.[5]

Despite numerous media reports to the contrary, the difficulty of building such a device precludes all but a major organization with extensive facilities from doing so. If a terrorist group cannot make a nuclear device, it would have to steal or purchase one on the black market. Besides the basic difficulty of buying and transporting the device, there is the problem of detonating it. The safeguards in such a device are specifically designed to prevent it from going off except when delivered as designed and properly prepared for detonation. Still, it is well established that various terrorist groups, al Qaeda in particular, have been trying hard to obtain such a device.[6] Despite the great difficulties inherent in obtaining and using a nuclear device, the fact that al Qaeda has made it a priority combined with the devastating effect of a nuclear detonation means the United States must orchestrate all available resources to defend against such a contingency.

A nuclear weapon generally can be delivered in two ways. A conventional military attack would deliver the warhead by missiles or aircraft; an unconventional attack would deliver the weapon by hand, truck, or ship. There has been a great deal of discussion of suitcase nuclear weapons, but small size is not a requirement. Terrorists are not restricted to very small weapons. If they obtain or build a larger weapon, they can simply deliver it by truck or ship rather than by hand.

The United States has been spending approximately $10 billion annually for missile defense and by some estimates could substantially increase this amount over the next 10 years.[7] This is despite the fact that the missile system being placed in operational status has not undergone the normal Department of Defense (DOD) testing process to determine if it works. Further, this money is being spent against a rogue state threat that has not yet emerged. By contrast, the United States is spending only a fraction of that amount to defend against existing delivery systems: ships and trucks entering the United States. Intercepting this type of threat requires a layered effort that increases control of existing nuclear weapons and material, fights nuclear proliferation, and scans transportation methods to ensure weapons do not enter the country. In contrast to major increases on spending for missile defense, the combined spending on the U.S. Government's nonproliferation and Cooperative Threat Reduction programs (better known as the Nunn-Lugar legislation) continues to be only just over $1 billion per year and may be facing reductions in the future.[8]

The last layer of defense, cargo screening, must be funded out of the Department of Homeland Security (DHS) budget. That budget, only $34.8 billion for 2007,[9] must cover all aspects of operating the second largest organization in the U.S. Government. The fact that police and intelligence operations around the world have yielded several successes against those attempting to sell material has injected a vital element of uncertainty into the trade in nuclear materials. Since 2002, the United States has enlisted the support of major trading partners for the Container Security Initiative (CSI). Launched by the U.S. Customs Service (now U.S. Customs and Border Protection, or CBP), CSI seeks to identify and prescreen high-risk seaborne containers before they are shipped. As of fall 2006, roughly 90 percent of all transatlantic and transpacific cargo imported into the United States has been subjected to nonintrusive CSI prescreening. However, the system still lacks truly global reach and is necessarily dependent upon CBP officials and host nation customs administrations being able to agree upon and implement criteria for identifying high-risk cargo containers before these containers leave ports heading for the U.S. homeland.[10]

Osama bin Laden sees "CBRN weapons as 'war winners' and intends to use them to pin a strategic defeat on Islam's foes."[11] He or likeminded fanatics would clearly deliver them by unconventional means. The entire problem of unconventional delivery of nuclear weapons is receiving only a fraction of the resources it should. U.S. public officials should rethink priorities on defense against nuclear attack and focus on those enemies who have actually conducted major attacks against the United States and are actively seeking nuclear weapons.

Chemical threats. Chemical attacks pose graver threats than do high-yield explosives, not so much because of their greater potential for creating casualties but simply because of the widespread presence of hazardous chemicals in modern society. The evidence of al Qaeda's attempts to develop chemical warfare agents uncovered by seizure of documents and videotapes in Afghanistan received great publicity, but the fact is they had created only small quantities of chemical agents. Further, those chemicals were in Afghanistan and would have required both movement to the United States and some form of dissemination device before they could be used. In contrast, there has been very little coverage of the extensive network of hazardous chemicals that are a part of daily life in every major U.S. city. The potential for a terrorist attack using commercially available chemicals is much greater than that from the use of synthesized chemical warfare agents. The accident at the Bhopal chemical plant in 1984 caused more casualties than the combined 9/11 attacks. According to a BBC News report on the 20th anniversary of the accident, 3,500 died immediately; 15,000 subsequent deaths have been attributed to it; and up to 500,000 people have been adversely affected physically.[12]

In the face of such a pervasive threat, the U.S. response has been spotty at best. On the plus side, many cities have begun using a nontoxic chemical for water purification, thus removing a potential source of toxic chemicals. In other areas, such as rerouting large, hazardous material shipments around major population areas, the overall record is unacceptably poor. In fact, as recently as April 2007, public officials were still debating the feasibility of rerouting freight trains carrying toxic chemicals away from downtown Washington, where they pass within a few hundred yards of the U.S. Capitol and the National Mall.[13]

Clearly, defense against a chemical attack lies mainly with the commercial concerns that own the chemicals, the plants, and the transportation assets. The problem is that they have no incentive for raising the security levels unless it is made mandatory. The firm that spends the extra money on security must pass those costs along to consumers, who are free to purchase the same materials from firms that have not spent the money on security. The U.S. Government thus far has failed to come up with an effective, equitable way to ensure that all commercial firms and government agencies that produce, store, transport, and use these chemicals provide effective security for them.

The first step in an effective defense against chemical attack is to understand the country's vulnerability to such attacks and then establish the necessary regulations to ensure the safeguarding of the production, storage, and transportation of these chemicals. Given the natural tension between businesses that do not wish to deal with (often absurd) government regulations and the requirement for those regulations to protect the American people, this will be an exceptionally difficult step.

High-yield explosives. High-yield explosives have the potential to cause tens of thousands of deaths. If the 1993 al Qaeda attack on the World Trade Center had been better executed, it could have brought Tower One down in the middle of the business day and killed upwards of 35,000 people. All of the materials needed for that attack—1,500 pounds of urea nitrate fertilizer, a timer, and a delivery van—were purchased or rented in the United States from commercial sources.[14]

In fact, the potential for much larger explosive attacks—even on the scale of nuclear yields—exists in the United States. In 1947, the Texas City disaster occurred when a ship filled with ammonium nitrate fertilizer caught fire, exploded, and ignited another ship, which also exploded.[15] The surrounding area was devastated to a distance of about three-quarters of a mile with major damage occurring to residential neighborhoods 1½ miles from the site. This explosion was clearly an accident but caused devastation equaling that of a low-yield nuclear weapon. The Oklahoma City bombing, which used ammonium nitrate mixed with fuel, was not an accident. Yet even in the face of these experiences, only a few states restrict the sale of ammonium nitrate, require large quantity sales to be reported, or even regulate how large quantities are transported.

While many government facilities have been hardened against truck bombs, it is not practical to harden most large commercial buildings or port facilities against this type of device. Nor is it possible to harden bridges and port facilities against the power of a ship-sized high-yield explosive. The critical aspect of defense against this kind of attack is to protect the production facilities, check who buys the materials, and require security for them while in transit. Once again, the tension between business practices and government regulation will have to be balanced, but regulation will have to be tightened.

Preventing Mass Disruption Attacks

Weapons of mass disruption are those designed mainly to cause major political, economic, or social disruptions. While these attacks will cause some casualties, the focus is not on killing people but on disrupting the lives of as many as possible and inflicting as much economic damage as possible. These would include attacks on transportation systems, agriculture, and communications networks as well as the use of radiological weapons. While attacks on other systems such as water and food can result in a high degree of anxiety in the general population, the effort required to create a major disruption in either greatly exceeds that of attacking the more vulnerable networks.

As the bombings in Madrid in 2004 and London in 2005 starkly illustrated, transportation systems are the most obvious and accessible targets. By their very nature, they are open to surveillance by would-be attackers. Many such systems have entire books written about them that are readily available at public libraries. Increasing amounts of information are also available on the Internet. Further, the potential impact of the attacks can be gauged by observing what happens when an accident closes a particular chokepoint. Finally, the normal fear of heights and water ensures that an attack on one bridge or tunnel will initially reduce traffic on similar venues. Like the 9/11 attacks, such an attack will create enormously disruptive demands for increased security on similar facilities nationwide. While such attacks will not kill thousands, they will intimidate hundreds of thousands.

A second form of attack upon the transportation system would not target a node but instead use an explosion inside a standard shipping container in an attempt to shut down the system. By creating distrust concerning the contents of containers, ships, rail cars, and trucks, the terrorists can hope to immobilize the U.S. transportation network for a period of time to achieve economic rather than physical damage.

In the same way, attacks on agriculture will be about inflicting economic damage. The most effective and easiest attacks on agriculture would be those conducted against livestock herds with agents such as anthrax bacteria and foot and mouth virus.[16] Anyone who observed the extensive disruption and huge economic cost of naturally occurring mad cow disease or anthrax can easily understand the impact of an attack widely disseminated across the feed lots of the Midwest. Further, the biological agents necessary for such an attack are present in many university laboratories since they are the subjects of important scientific research.

The U.S. communications system is also very vulnerable and subject to both cyber and kinetic attacks. While the U.S. Government has extensive experience in dealing with cyber attacks, it has no experience in dealing with a kinetic attack that targets key nodes specifically to cause maximum disruption. In particular, the country's increasing reliance upon fiber optic networks combined with the vulnerability of those systems and the lack of redundancy in certain segments of the paths make these networks attractive targets. The information concerning the location of these networks is not classified. In fact, in one reported case, a graduate student mapped the entire network in the United States, loaded it on his laptop, and was able to drill down to determine the vulnerability of any part of the system.[17]

The impact of another form of communications-related attack has already been demonstrated by the anthrax attacks on Capitol Hill. Although the attacker apparently took precautions to target the attack on specific offices (even including a warning in the envelopes sent to Capitol Hill), he or she apparently was unaware the envelopes would contaminate the postal system as they passed through. As a result, the attacks shut down the U.S. postal system serving Capitol Hill and other government offices. If the attacker had instead chosen to shut down the postal service nationwide, this could have done by mailing a larger number of contaminated letters from various locations so as to ensure maximum coverage of the U.S. Post Office and commercial carriers' systems of distribution centers. Then, by notifying the media, he or she could have forced testing on all sites with probable positive results and the subsequent costly and time-consuming cleanup. The $27 million cleanup cost for the single attack on

Capitol Hill did not include the economic cost of disruption, such as renting office spaces while waiting for the cleanup.[18] The combined cost of cleanup and disruption of service could easily climb into the billions.

As previously noted, radiological attacks are designed to deny specific areas rather than to create massive casualties or direct damage. Radiological devices cause damage by creating a long-term radiological hazard. The radiological material can be disseminated by a small bomb and will contaminate the immediate vicinity. Such an attack will most likely be against a symbolic target such as the Lincoln Memorial or a key transportation node such as the Metro Center subway station in Washington, DC. The objective is to deny access to the site until an extensive, expensive, and time-consuming cleanup is completed. Very small terror cells can carry out WMd attacks with little expertise or support. Thus, this type of attack can also only be disrupted by penetrating those small cells.

Preventing an attack with either WMD or WMd requires that U.S. intelligence and security assets remain inside the terrorists' Observe-Orient-Decide-Act Loop.[19] This is an exceptional challenge. The contest matches hierarchical Federal, state, and local bureaucracies against a networked enemy. The U.S. Government was specifically designed with a separation of powers to slow down action. Networks are specifically designed to speed action. Despite substantial efforts at reform, including the establishment of the Office of the Director of National Intelligence and National Counterterrorism Center, it is by no means clear as yet whether or how much these efforts will in fact improve the performance of U.S. intelligence services against terrorist cells.[20] One key requirement is to ensure all elements focus on the needed capabilities to deal with this enemy rather than with the internal processes and bureaucratic turf battles that are an inevitable part of any major reorganization.

MITIGATING CATASTROPHIC DAMAGE

Mitigating threats to life and property ranks among the highest responsibilities for public officials at all levels of government. No matter how skillful the United States becomes at thwarting catastrophic attacks, the country could never have absolute protection against terrorist violence. Nor can the country escape its inherent vulnerabilities to other types of large-scale disasters—be they floods, wind storms, earthquakes, pandemics, toxic materials spills, or major power failures—that could expose hundreds of thousands of citizens to life-threatening perils and bring disaster-prone regions to a standstill. The really hard question is how the instrumentalities of government can best be organized and operated in a fashion to ensure they will aid and abet solutions, not simply compound problems.

When catastrophic threats are the issue, certain features of the U.S. constitutional framework, as well as differing authorities and practices of Federal, state, and local government agencies, can pose serious obstacles to the effective management of megadisasters.

One aspect of the U.S. system is both a strength and a weakness: the constitutionally mandated principle of state sovereignty. States and their local municipalities traditionally assume the role of leading the response to threats to public safety, with the Federal Government providing assistance in a supporting mode. State governors, in particular, by law and customary practice must be the ones to request Federal involvement in matters of law enforcement or public safety.[21] By law, governors also command the National Guard assets of their states when these are not federalized for national or overseas missions, and conversely the President's use of Active duty military forces for disaster mitigation in the homeland requires the affirmative request of the governor(s) of the affected states.[22] This is normally seen as a strength, since local first responders and political leaders are vastly better informed about their communities than a distant Federal response system is. Yet it can also be a problem when local assets are overwhelmed and the governor requests Federal assistance, since it sets up a tension over command responsibility when significant Federal assets come into play.

The second complicating feature of U.S. disaster response capabilities at the Federal level is its highly distributed character. At the heart of this system sits the Department of Homeland Security, which has the lead in building a nationwide approach to domestic incidents, regardless of cause, size, or complexity, and in administering the National Response Plan (NRP). The NRP provides the overall agreed roadmap Federal response, striving as it does for a comprehensive all-hazards approach to management of domestic incidents; it forms the basis of how the Federal Government coordinates with state, local, and tribal governments and the private sector during incidents; and it establishes protocols for prevention and consequence management activities.[23]

Having a roadmap is one thing; exerting real directive power is another. Core responsibilities under the NRP are parceled out to those Federal departments that provide or regulate critical services (such as health care and transportation) in day-to-day life. The Federal Emergency Management Agency (FEMA), as a component of DHS, acts as a headquarters element, relying heavily on commercial procurement and intergovernmental coordination protocols in order to mobilize and direct Federal disaster assistance to those who need it. In so doing, FEMA is empowered to act as the Federal Government's main point of contact with state and local emergency managers, and it provides training and quality assurance for certain types of missions. However, the agency does not itself possess legions of garrisoned emergency personnel, fleets of trucks or aircraft, or stockpiles of critical assistance. The involvement of so many agencies at the Federal level compounds the challenge of empowering local first responders. Assistance from Washington often arrives in fragments, with no coordination even among Federal assets and each wanting to be in charge of their particular part of the mission.

The third attribute is the multimission character of America's most muscular disaster responder: the U.S. military. With their own robust transportation, communications, planning, personnel, and logistics infrastructures, and with an expeditionary orientation, the U.S. Armed Forces possess enormous capacity to conduct rapid, decisive disaster relief operations. Yet they also, unavoidably, have a predominantly overseas orientation, focusing on missions aimed at deterring or defeating foes, reassuring friends, and dissuading would-be adversaries. Consequently, only a fraction of U.S.

forces are dedicated to homeland missions—a factor that necessarily impedes any extensive reliance on them for disaster response contingencies.

Taken together, the cumbrous quality of this system's architecture is striking. It has a horizontal layered structure (Federal, state, and local levels) that is also rife with vertical stovepipes (between Federal agencies). It would not be an optimal system design even if disaster management were the *sole* function of government or if public resources were not a practical constraint. In reality, of course, elected officials and public bureaucracies have to balance competing priorities all the time. It also needs to be emphasized that the current U.S. response system, complex as it is, works well for the majority of the disasters that occur in any given year; and it is built upon the sensible proposition that state and local responders will have the best knowledge of the needs and vulnerabilities of the communities in which they serve. The issue, again, is whether the United States can meet the challenge of truly catastrophic disasters mainly by enhancements to the current system, or whether a new paradigm is needed.

To consider this question, we first look at the distinctive operational challenges posed by large-area threats, and then at the organizational challenges, and finally at the implications of putting the military in charge of this mission.

Large-Area Threats

Biological mitigation. As stated earlier, biological threats have by far the most potential to kill or injure Americans. Either contagious or noncontagious attacks or naturally occurring pandemics could have devastating effects. In the wake of the 9/11 attacks, public concerns were heightened by a widely publicized game simulation— dubbed *Dark Winter*—that postulated a smallpox attack occurring simultaneously in three states. Before the end of the 13th game day, the outbreak had spread to 25 states and 15 countries.[24] It highlighted the fact that U.S. authorities were woefully unprepared to deal with the effects of a biological attack. The two most effective countermeasures—immunization and isolation—could not be carried out for a number of reasons. In particular, there was no decisionmaking process that allowed local, state, and Federal officials to coordinate critical actions in dealing with the outbreaks. The result was uncoordinated action. In the after-action brief, it was noted that even if the relevant officials had been able to decide quickly whom to immunize, there were neither sufficient doses of vaccine nor a process to rapidly distribute and administer the stocks on hand. Isolation was also impossible because most states no longer had quarantine laws on the books or procedures for establishing and enforcing such laws if they existed.

Since 2001, the Federal Government has been able to acquire sufficient doses of smallpox vaccine to cover the entire population of the United States—roughly 300 million. This notable achievement, however, is marred by several shortfalls: the country still lacks well-developed processes for mass immunization; the U.S. public health system has atrophied badly in many parts of the country; and there are no vaccines available for many other biological threats including plague, tularemia, and Marburg. In addition, little or no progress has been made on quarantine laws, procedures for quarantine, or training for public safety officials in establishing and enforcing quarantine measures. Finally, there is inherent uncertainty about the extent of likely public cooperation. A 2003 national survey in Canada found that "only 55.8 percent of respondents would take 'whatever vaccine was promoted by the national government and its medical advisors.'"[25] Americans trust their government even less than Canadians. Thus, while the vaccine to deal with smallpox is available, there is no guarantee the American people will take it, even if the system to distribute it effectively were fully developed. Similarly, medicines for other biological agents have been stockpiled, but if the confusion witnessed after the anthrax attacks is any indication, it remains unclear whether the U.S. public health system would be able to clearly inform the public what medicine is appropriate, effectively distribute available stocks, or ensure that citizens take their prescribed dose when they get it.

After the command, control, communication, and trust issues, the most frequently noted deficiency in the U.S. biological defense system is the weakened state of the public health systems. While some jurisdictions have made progress in integrating their medical systems into an early warning system of the onset of an attack, most have not. Further, public health systems have little capability to respond even if they do receive timely notice. They lack medicines, equipment, personnel, and procedures to deliver a surge capacity to meet the health care needs of affected populations over the period of time characteristic of a contagious disease crisis.[26]

Nuclear effects mitigation. The same lack of a preplanned or coordinated response will limit U.S. ability to minimize casualties from a nuclear attack. Organizations already exist that can analyze a blast quickly, determine the downwind hazard, and make recommendations to evacuate or shelter in place. However, those organizations are neither distributed around the country, nor do they regularly exercise with the decisionmakers who must validate and disseminate their recommendations. Further, much like the inability to isolate, there is little or no ability to organize and execute a mass evacuation or to effectively promulgate and enforce a shelter in place decision. This is a critical deficiency, since a very large percentage of the casualties caused by a nuclear event will result from post-blast radiation exposure.

Finally, disaster responders have very little capability to enter a contaminated area and extract casualties. First responders will enter, but most lack individual radiation dosimeters to ensure they do not receive so much radiation that they themselves become casualties.

Chemical effects mitigation. Mitigating the effects of the third major form of attack—toxic chemical agents—also requires an effective and rapid decision on whether to evacuate or shelter in place. Some areas of the country that are collocated with chemical plants have effective, rehearsed plans; they have an immediate incentive to develop and rehearse the plan. However, most communities that lie along major transportation routes used by bulk chemical haulers and some communities with major chemical plants still do not have evacuation plans.

Thus, the country lacks effective responses to most potential chemical attacks. Further, those areas that have rehearsed consistently identify shortages in equipment, personnel, and medical facilities necessary to locate, extract, decontaminate, and treat the massive casualties such an attack will create. After the decision and capability to evacuate a contaminated area, the two biggest challenges are extraction/decontamination of casualties and treatment when they arrive at medical facilities. More than a decade after the sarin gas attacks on Tokyo, the United States still does not have adequate capability to deal with the casualties created by such an event. Surprisingly, there are no established standard operating procedures for dealing with those victims who self-evacuate from the scene. Key questions remain unanswered, such as how these victims can be treated while preventing them from contaminating medical facilities. Individual hospitals have worked through some of the procedures, but a lack of investment in on-site decontamination facilities means the hospitals may be forced to simply close their doors and try to keep people out. Thus, they will not be able to treat the casualties who are decontaminated and transported to the hospital. This is only one of the as-yet unresolved challenges in dealing with a chemical attack.

High-yield explosives. High-yield explosive devices will create many of the same problems that a nuclear device would: massive casualties, extensive fires, monitoring requirements, extraction from a hazardous environment, and extensive infrastructure damage. While there would be no requirement to monitor for radiation, monitoring for air quality would still be essential. The only major difference is that large-scale evacuation will not likely be necessary except for those areas where monitoring determines the atmosphere is dangerous.

Mitigating Mass Disruption Attacks

Mitigation of attacks designed to achieve mass disruption is a different kind of problem. The very nature of these attacks makes them unusually difficult to defend against. However, if prior planning has been done, it also makes the consequences somewhat easier to deal with than weapons of mass destruction. What is needed is a coherent plan for what actions to take in the event of such an attack. For instance, the widely postulated example of an explosion in a shipping container should not be allowed to shut down every port in the United States. Preplanning is needed to determine which, if any, ports should be closed and what other actions should be taken. Whether the attack is a single container explosion or multiple explosions, if the response is immediately closing all ports, the terrorist has achieved his goal.

Each type of WMd attack needs to be talked through in a tabletop exercise, decision points determined, and decision trees developed and then rehearsed with the elected officials who will have to make those choices. Homeland Security Presidential Directive 8 of 2003 directed DHS to establish a National Exercise Program (NEP) that identifies and integrates national-level exercise activities in order to enhance collaboration among all levels of government and with the private sector. The cornerstone of the

NEP is the biennial Top Officials (TOPOFF) exercise series. TOPOFF 3 in April 2005, which simulated a coordinated terrorist attack involving biological and chemical weapons, was the most comprehensive terrorism exercise ever conducted in the United States. It involved a broad range of Federal authorities, officials from the states of Connecticut and New Jersey, as well as officials in the United Kingdom and Canada.[27] It is essential that decisionmakers understand the implications of their decision before the crisis occurs. In particular, they must carefully prepare a public information program that will minimize the disruption the terrorists achieve.

Mitigating Other Types of Catastrophes

Intuitively, the job of mitigating megadisasters caused by events other than WMD/d attacks ought to be less stressing. For instance, gaining access into affected areas, assuming the means, should be easier for emergency personnel. While the risk of hazardous materials exposure could be an impediment to movement within storm- or earthquake-damaged areas, the most likely locations of toxic substance contamination could be easier to pinpoint in advance (chemical storage facilities, industrial plants, and so forth) and would not be as pervasive as with widespread dispersion of nuclear, radiological, or chemical-biological agents in large-scale attack scenarios. The decontamination of evacuated victims ought to be much less of an issue as well.

That said, some missions may still prove to be Herculean in their scope. Hurricane Katrina was enormous in terms of its geographical range, human costs, and associated impacts, triggering in its wake the largest mass dislocation on the U.S. homeland since the 1930s (see table 4–1).[28]

TABLE 4–1. HURRICANE KATRINA: THE IMPACT

Affected area (square miles)	93,000
Fatalities	1,330
Homes damaged or destroyed	300,000
Property damage	$96 billion
Displaced people	770,000
Oil spills (gallons)	8 million
Federal assistance (as of August 2007)	$8.3 billion

Sources: The White House, *The Federal Response to Hurricane Katrina Lessons Learned* (Washington, DC: U.S. Government Printing Office, 2006); Federal Emergency Management Agency Fact Sheet, August 27, 2007, available at <http://www.fema.gov/pdf/hazard/hurricane/2005katrina/gc_fs_pa_2_year_anniversary.pdf>.

Hurricane Katrina destroyed or irreparably damaged some 300,000 homes and triggered the exodus of over 700,000 people from affected areas—the largest mass dislocation on the U.S. homeland since the 1930s.[29] While most disaster relief planning and operational concepts proceed from a strong preference to move assistance into populations sheltering in place, precisely to avoid human dislocations, mass evacuation and relocation proved to be absolute necessities in this particular case. And yet these operations—despite the knowledge of flooding threats—were improvised and chaotic.[30] For those trapped by flood waters, search and rescue operations also proved to be extremely difficult to mount over expansive urban areas. And amidst all these other problems, the breakdown of public order overwhelmed local police, who were reeling from the displacement of personnel and their families and the loss of equipment. In fact, the inherent strengths of local emergency responders (knowing the local terrain, living in the communities) suddenly became a liability; they were victims, too.

The System's Inherent Weaknesses

On paper, the current U.S. disaster response system has clear pathways that should enable it to function coherently when stressed by higher levels of damage. Applicable laws and regulations prescribe the sequence of steps: local jurisdictions expend their own resources, then request state assistance if the disaster exceeds their capacities; the states in turn do the same until the point at which they—via the governor—request the President to issue a major disaster declaration, thereby making Federal aid available, when the disaster is of "such severity and magnitude that effective response is beyond the capabilities of the State and the affected local governments."[31] Clear though this sequence is, however, the system's adaptability is highly dependent upon a number of variables that have proved troublesome in real-world situations.

First, there is a certain presumption that local jurisdictions on the cusp of being overwhelmed can still coherently identify their needs and direct incoming state or Federal assistance to where it is needed most. However, experience shows that being overwhelmed in megadisasters consists of more than simply running out of supplies— it also encompasses individuals losing their ability to identify needs, establish priorities, and communicate them promptly. One can well imagine the futility of the dialogue that ensues when frustrated higher authorities exhort the local responders to "tell us what you need" and the locals in desperation reply: "Send us whatever you can!" When first responders no longer know what they need or where the assistance needs to go, the result can only be disabling confusion. The current Federal system is not well configured to provide immediate, small-scale help to assist local authorities in evaluating the magnitude of a particular disaster. U.S. Northern Command (USNORTHCOM) has made progress in training liaison teams for early deployment, but the sheer number of jurisdictions within the United States means these teams can only exercise with a small fraction of their local counterparts.

Second, operational exigencies under the present layered system place a huge burden on FEMA, as the main Federal point of contact, to build and sustain close working relationships with state and local responders. This, in turn, requires FEMA to maintain a robust regional presence to assist states in disaster planning, exercising, and anticipating necessary actions when a particular crisis erupts. However, after FEMA's incorporation into DHS in 2003, the size and quality of the agency's field staffs spread across its 10 regional offices reportedly atrophied, as DHS in some cases moved key programs and personnel back to Washington and reallocated staff and resources to other priorities.[32] The result on balance has been to make FEMA a more distant, less effective partner. Nor is FEMA, DHS, or any other individual or agency below the President empowered under the National Response Plan to direct actions across the various Federal departments or agencies that actually provide the assistance. This is a third significant weakness in the current system.

FEMA by design is less a provider of operational capability than a supply broker, mediating between demands for relief assistance from the state and local level and Federal sources of supply. In a given crisis situation, when key suppliers are identified under the NRP's various emergency support functions, they fall into alignment within the National Incident Management System. There is good reason to question how adept this interagency structure is at managing really catastrophic situations. One criticism of the system is that if Federal agency field staff find themselves dissenting from instructions they receive from senior officials on the spot, they will tend to refer the matter up their own supervisory chain back to Washington to get the decisions reversed, compounding the coordination problem.[33]

This vertically stovepiped system also inhibits rapid action even when local and Federal personnel could liaise directly between field elements. As a former commanding officer of the Marine Corps Chemical Biological Incident Response Force (CBIRF), this chapter's principal author can attest to the Federal bureaucracy's frustrating inability to transmit a request quickly or clearly. When responding to the anthrax attacks of October 2001, the Capitol Police requested CBIRF assistance in conducting biological sampling of office buildings on Capitol Hill. Due to a longstanding relationship between CBIRF and the Capitol Police, the request was coordinated at the local level while the official request was being routed through the bureaucracy. When it finally emerged from the formal system, the official tasking bore no resemblance to the capabilities requested and needed by the Capitol Police. Had CBIRF responded with the forces directed, they would have been of very little use in the crisis. In this case, the chain of command was able to ignore the formal tasking and simply did what was necessary to get the job done. However, close relationships between Federal and local assets are rare, and in most instances, U.S. citizens must count upon the bureaucracy to get the requirements right.

Fourth, and most significantly, the current U.S. disaster response system fails to grapple directly with the touchy issue of when or how, if at all, command of relief operations should be handed off in catastrophic disaster situations. The general principle that the Federal level gets involved as and when the state or local authorities become overwhelmed and request the assistance does not translate well into specific guidance for how and when to transfer command responsibility—a prerogative that state governors are loath to cede. Due to the wide spectrum of local and state capabilities, this decision will almost have to be made on a case-by-case basis. There is no reason to presume a priori that when Federal personnel arrive on site in significant numbers, they should be in charge. Decisionmaking will have to factor in the degree of the disaster, capabilities and capacities of local responders, and even personalities of key local authorities.

Ultimately, what compels consideration of a command transfer is the mounting human cost of a faltering response: the lengthening food lines, lack of potable water, inadequate shelter, spreading disease, and, in the worst cases, escalating violence as desperate victims turn predatory. By then, however, critical time has been lost. As the bipartisan House Select Committee on Hurricane Katrina put it: "How can we rely on the overwhelmed to acknowledge they are overwhelmed, and then expect them to direct and manage the process of coming to their rescue?"[34] To every extent possible, the focus must be on developing the kinds of organizations and standard operating procedures that can provide immediate assistance to local authorities but in a fashion that keeps them effectively in charge of the effort.

Should the Military Be the Lead Responder?

In the wake of Hurricane Katrina, President Bush asked whether the U.S. military should be assigned the lead role in responding to certain extremely dire disaster situations. Though he took some heat from various governors, the President was right to raise the question.[35] In addition to the capacities mentioned earlier, the Armed Forces certainly possess a lot of relevant experience. They have long conducted these types of missions overseas: the Asian tsunami relief effort in 2004–2005 and more recent operations in Pakistan's earthquake-devastated areas are good examples. At the same time, giving the job to the military will not necessarily make things easier.

First, given its other primary missions, the U.S. military is never going to be more than the responder of last resort (after others have tried and failed), so there is still the problem of figuring out when to call for military assistance—a trickier task than it might first appear, given that a disaster's full magnitude and impact may not always be initially apparent.

Another challenge is that, clearly defined roles notwithstanding, nonmilitary Federal agencies may well be prey to countervailing pressures to underfund key disaster preparedness programs if they know a muscular second responder is waiting in the wings. In some past migration emergencies, U.S. immigration agencies were all too quick to seek a lead role for DOD, not necessarily because a particular problem had reached a catastrophic level, but simply because they had run out of money. To help guard against this tendency, executive branch managers and their congressional overseers need to work toward more clearly defined capabilities goals up to which civilian first responders can build and against which the U.S. Armed Forces can plan, and by so doing help to foster better awareness of what each sides brings to the table.

Beyond this problem, it is worth stressing that military disaster responders are not uniformly strong in all areas. Disaster assessments are a case in point. U.S. forces have unparalleled intelligence and reconnaissance capabilities, but they also pay closest attention to current or future battlefields, not necessarily to disaster-prone regions; on occasion, key systems or people were not where they needed to be when disasters struck.

For disasters occurring on the U.S. homeland, getting personnel on the ground should be much easier than in overseas cases. The trickier part will be in translating the assistance distribution assessments into agreed decisions concerning the type, destination, and mode of delivery for assistance flowing in. In some past disasters, civilian and military logisticians have found themselves at loggerheads over what Pentagon planners clinically refer to *requirements validation*. In a disaster of this magnitude, the requirements validation should be used only to prioritize assets, not to restrict them. In a disaster, the American people need effectiveness more than efficiency.

Finally, no military disaster response mission can succeed without direct civilian involvement. Mass evacuations and quarantine-like restrictions of mass movement are two such cases. There is a world of difference between rescuing a family from a rooftop of a flooded house or restricting contagious victims to a hospital ward, and moving thousands of stranded people from a stadium complex or, conversely, cordoning off an entire community or refugee camp. Enabling movement on a mass scale may exceed what even the military can provide, prompting a Dunkirk-like mobilization of all the civil transportation assets that a region can muster. Correspondingly, in establishing large-scale restrictions on movement, which may be necessary in some refugee situations and conceivable in certain biomedical emergencies, military enforcement of perimeter controls will be hard or impossible to sustain without civil law enforcement operating inside the restricted zone.

In such situations, the National Guard, operating under Title 32 authority (under the command of a state governor), is the appropriate instrument to use for these types of missions, given that guard units will have law enforcement authority and extensive prior contact with and knowledge of local communities. What are plainly needed are improved procedures to reduce the time interval for mobilization from days to hours.

Ultimately, the military is no panacea for America's catastrophic response needs. National leaders cannot presume to solve the country's megadisaster response problems simply by calling upon a force that is not optimized for the job and that has other core missions. However, in the context of specific planning, and with the prior agreement of all parties, giving the military a clear lead in certain truly desperate situations may be the best course to ensure a rapid response and avoidable loss of life.

ASSESSING THE BALANCE SHEET

As the foregoing suggests, homeland security's two highest priorities—preventing mass destruction and disruption attacks and responding to catastrophic hazards of all kinds—are enormously demanding missions, both conceptually and in terms of available resources. A number of gaps in America's approach are painfully apparent. Even so, it would be wrong to infer that no progress has been made over the past half-decade. America is undoubtedly a tougher target to hit now than it was on September

10, 2001. The question is how to balance advances and successes against areas plagued by persistent, yet fixable, shortfalls.

On the plus side, improved efforts can be seen across a wide range of areas, both large and small:

- The single most important advance has been the deepening understanding of terrorist threats to the United States. After the initial massive disruptions from 9/11, leaders have begun to make more rigorous, detailed evaluations of the actual vulnerabilities and capabilities of their communities.
- Most potential target areas have conducted vulnerability assessments that allow their leaders to determine how best to apply their resources to defend actual rather than assumed vulnerabilities. Further, the studies have helped them understand the magnitude of a potential attack and begin preparations for mitigation and recovery. Conversely, the studies have shown that some assumed vulnerabilities are not actually problems and do not need resources expended to protect them.
- Due to a massive focus on civil passenger flight, many vulnerabilities in U.S. civil aviation systems have been reduced. Improved screening of passengers, strengthened cockpit doors, and passenger awareness all make it more difficult for terrorists to hijack another aircraft.
- Federal stocks of smallpox vaccine stocks have grown to the point where nationwide coverage is now attainable.
- Many states have established 24-hour command centers. Those that have not done so have made arrangements to quickly man such a center in a crisis. The most encouraging aspect of the command centers is the efforts to integrate the wide range of local, state, Federal, and private resources available in a crisis. Most have integrated National Guard Bureau crisis managers to speed the response of local guard forces and provide a vital communications and translation node between Federal and other response agencies.
- In the wake of Katrina, the Pentagon has given expanded authority to USNORTHCOM to stage forces and equipment prior to the onset of a catastrophic disaster. As a result of its 2006 Quadrennial Defense Review, DOD also has launched a $1.5 billion initiative to improve medical countermeasures against genetically engineered biohazards, as well as new programs for improved interagency communications.[36]
- The National Counterterrorist Center (called the Terrorism Threat Integration Center when it was established in 2003) has enabled a much greater degree of fusion of intelligence from all elements of the government.
- Terrorist information has been consolidated into a single integrated watch list via the new Terrorist Screening Center.

These steps are rightly viewed as major advances in America's effort to secure the homeland. On the downside, however, a number of glaring shortfalls still need to be remedied:

- America's public health infrastructure remains woefully unprepared to deal with a major biomedical emergency. The flu shot fiasco during the winter of 2004–2005 is an indication of some of the issues; even the doses that were available were not distributed quickly and effectively. While preparedness activities have been spurred on by the administration's *Implementation Plan for the National Strategy for Pandemic Influenza*, issued in May 2006, the pace of progress remains modest in relation to the threat.[37] The U.S. public health system is not yet capable of executing a nationwide crash immunization program, even though, at least in the case of smallpox, sufficient stocks of vaccine are now available. Effective epidemiological monitoring should be developed nationwide by investing in public health offices at the local and state levels.

- Given the increasing probability of genetically modified biological agents, the current system of developing and producing vaccine remains entirely inadequate. Though increased spending on the defense side may help, and amidst some encouraging advances in this field, research is not being funded at anywhere near the level of that targeted against other, much less deadly threats. In this respect, investments in the public health system provide a double benefit. The United States will be better prepared not only for attack but also for the inevitable naturally occurring outbreaks of new forms of flu or other viruses. Given the Centers for Disease Control and Prevention estimate that flu kills an average of 36,000 Americans per year, investment in public health systems has enormous payoff.[38]

- Even if steps are taken to rapidly create, manufacture, distribute, and administer vaccines, the United States still lacks a fully effective, nationwide surveillance system to provide the critical early understanding that an attack has occurred. Once again, the long-term failure to fund the U.S. public health system caused a previously functioning system to atrophy badly.

- Despite improvements, bureaucratic inflexibility is all too often the norm, not the exception. This is true across all Federal agencies that are designated to respond in a crisis. While government personnel have shown the ability to adapt rapidly in a crisis, all planning, coordination, and interagency work is still conducted by vertically stovepiped agencies, while state and local first responders wrestle with a lack of transparency. As a result, the critical training and coordination necessary to be ready to respond in a crisis are often stifled. Training events are not executed due to bureaucratic inertia or objections concerning areas of responsibility.

- The national security bureaucracy continues to pose obstacles to the sharing of information with state and local authorities. The incredibly slow and cumbersome system required to obtain security clearances has severely restricted the number of people with whom the Intelligence Community and the Department of Defense can share information. Further efforts are required to ensure wider dissemination of national intelligence to state and local authorities, and conversely, to ensure that those same authorities provide

Federal agencies with timely tactical information that might provide early warning of a major attack.

- On the military side, there is still strong reluctance to build a dedicated operational capability for catastrophic response. The Department's 2005 *Strategy for Homeland Defense and Civil Support* asserts that homeland defense is the department's number one priority.[39] On the counterterrorism side, it acknowledges that civil authorities will have the lead in defending against and mitigating most WMD and WMd attacks. However, it then assigns support to civil authorities as only a secondary mission; no DOD assets will have the primary mission of going to the aid of civil authorities. While the department has created an Assistant Secretary of Defense for Homeland Defense, U.S. Northern Command, a Joint Task Force Civil Support, two Response Task Forces (East and West), and the Guardian Brigade to command the defense of America, DOD has not actually created any new units specifically trained, equipped, and tasked to provide support to civil authorities in a crisis since the creation of CBIRF in 1996.[40]

The single biggest weakness is that the U.S. homeland security approach relies upon large, slow, highly bureaucratic organizations that are designed to ensure everyone works—and stays—in their own lane. Perhaps a dense bureaucratic landscape is inevitable, given the Federal form of government and the value Americans attach to state and local sovereignty, but it also puts us at a serious disadvantage. America's enemies face no similar problems; they are arrayed in agile, flat networks.

LOOKING AHEAD

Over the next several years, the United States must face up to a large number of challenges if it is to sustain momentum on homeland security. As discussed earlier, the most difficult long-term problems are structural. The consolidation of 22 agencies into the Department of Homeland Security was a step toward integrating U.S. security. However, each agency was a bureaucracy in its own right, and bureaucracies are very good at resisting change. For example, the creation of the Department of Defense in 1947 required the consolidation of only two departments—the War Department (land and air forces) and the Navy Department—and both had the same mission: protect the United States from outside enemies. Yet it took 40 years and several changes of the law before the various Services actually learned to fight jointly.

The challenge is much more difficult at DHS. The missions of some of the agencies are actually in conflict with each other. Further, there is no incentive in the original legislation to develop genuine interagency operations. Everyone knows they are necessary, but there is no formal process or reward system to encourage actions that improve interagency cooperation and training. In response to the nationbuilding problems encountered in Iraq and Afghanistan, there is increasing discussion of "Beyond Goldwater-Nichols" legislation to unify Federal agencies for counterinsurgency and nationbuilding operations. In working through these issues, consideration should be given to how the United States can improve its domestic response and coordination as well, starting with those agencies now located inside the formal DHS structure.

A second critical area is the lack of integration between Federal agencies not inside DHS. Federal interagency response currently is at a similar level to where joint operations were in the early 1980s. Thus, any new legislation must include incentives for increased jointness not just within DHS, but also between all Federal agencies involved in preventing and responding to catastrophic events. Rethinking this legislation would provide dual benefits in that it prepares us better for both homeland security and overseas operations. The 2006 *Quadrennial Defense Review Report* highlights this shortfall, but the problem is not fundamentally the Pentagon's to solve.

A third critical area, highlighted by Hurricane Katrina, is improving crisis communication and coordination, not only among all levels of government but also with the American public. All too often, first responders and affected communities do not know what the Federal Government (and in some cases even their state governments) will provide in a catastrophic event. This problem has been consistently identified in major exercises. The very nature of the federal form of government means this will be a continuing problem and will only be overcome by well-funded, regular training and exercises involving all levels of government. Local responders will only be able to count on those assets with which they have planned and trained. In the absence of that planning and training, they will have to assume they are on their own and duplicate Federal and state resources to ensure they have them when they are needed.

An issue separate from the problems of coordinating among different levels of government is the failure to clarify the division of responsibility between private and government sectors for security, response, and recovery. This is an issue across the board for biological, chemical, nuclear, and high-yield explosives responses.

There is a final key feature of the U.S. homeland security architecture sorely in need of strengthening—the international dimension. Consistent with the defense-in-depth concept embedded in the *National Strategy for Homeland Security*, a fresh look should be given to various ways and means of bolstering defensive barriers along the most likely geographic approaches to the American homeland.

To the north, defense in depth builds upon a mature security relationship with Canada and benefits from its depth of at least 2,000 miles. The North American Aerospace Defense Command (NORAD), collocated with USNORTHCOM, coordinates airspace warning and response. In May 2006, the United States and Canada agreed, in connection with indefinite renewal of their bilateral air defense cooperation under the NORAD agreement, to initiate integrated surveillance of the continent's maritime approaches and internal waterways to improve warning of terrorist and other threats.[41] U.S. and Canadian authorities will retain responsibility for acting on warnings of threats in the maritime domain or along inland waters. The Canadian government has a single operational military headquarters, Canada Command, to manage air, ground, and naval responses to domestic emergencies and crises and expedite defense collaboration with the United States. While the lengthy U.S.-Canadian frontier would be impossible to seal off against penetrations by criminal or terrorist networks, two-way communication and coordination are good.

Looking south, the picture is more complex and difficult. The United States has not one but many neighbors—Mexico, Cuba, Colombia, Venezuela, and the Central American and Caribbean states—spread across a vast area that is prone to weak or capricious governance, rising crime, permeable borders, and the corrupting effects of chronic smuggling, trafficking, and associated transnational problems. Moreover, the quality of bilateral cooperation between these countries and the United States varies greatly, ranging from firm partnerships to outright hostility. The region as a whole lacks a strong geostrategic identity and a commonly held perception of threats and ways to mitigate them.

There are no easy paths toward improved security cooperation in the greater Caribbean basin, and simply to assert that protection of the U.S. homeland should be the organizing principle underlying such cooperation is a surefire way not to elicit it. Concerns about terrorism on their own are not enough to galvanize cooperation; what is needed is a two-way effort that links U.S. antiterrorism priorities with their overriding anxieties about public order and criminal activities. On its face, this ought to be possible. Proceeds from transnational crime are known to support terrorist organizations, and their members exploit the lines of flow used by traffickers. If countries in the greater Caribbean zone are able to improve public safety and the capacity to control and diminish trafficking and smuggling, that will also shrink whatever opportunities terrorist networks may have to exploit these permeable zones for ingress into the U.S. homeland.

Given its size and proximity to U.S. borders, Mexico's role will be pivotal. However, instead of trying to integrate Mexico into a U.S.-centric scheme—which will simply fuel Mexican neuralgia over subordination to U.S. command—Washington should find ways to encourage Mexico's leadership in the development of a Caribbean basin initiative on security and disaster response. The goal would be an agreement that provides a legal basis for separate, "locally owned" air, maritime, and land surveillance and response systems covering both geographic corridors and the Caribbean Sea. The heart of the partnership could be a "Mexico-Caribbean Basin Surveillance System," as described in more detail in chapter seven, based in and led by Mexico and staffed by military, police, and intelligence officers from participating countries. Once established and strengthened, this system could collaborate with NORAD as an equal command, providing a southern hub for international information-sharing and coordinated national enforcement actions.[42]

SUMMING UP

Given the evolving threat environment, homeland security enhancements should rank at the very top of the priority lists of all levels of government in the United States through and beyond the end of this decade. Yet it is also true that U.S. public attitudes toward homeland safety and security are by no means constant. As a continent-sized country separated from most others by vast oceans, Americans have long been prone to the complacency derived from an exaggerated sense of the protection that geographical distance affords. Occasional doses of reality—whether on December 7, 1941, or on September 11, 2001—have not fully immunized us from that tendency. The national mood thus tends to vacillate between periods of casual distraction and bouts of heightened, sometimes panicky, vigilance.

The good news is that United States clearly has become a much tougher target for terrorist attacks since 9/11. The sobering news is that the existing U.S. disaster response system is not yet robust enough to deal effectively with catastrophic attacks or megadisasters. Nor, it should be stressed, are there overwhelming pressures at this point to fundamentally redesign the country's current preparedness architecture. If there were, one would be hearing public voices arguing that the prerogatives of city mayors or governors should be usurped by the Federal Government, or that FEMA should be transformed into an operational field agency with embedded logistics, or that the U.S. military should become something other than, in USNORTHCOM parlance, the "heavy lifters of last resort."[43]

Absent any new political pressures for a major expansion of Federal authority, the only real public policy option strategy available is to remedy shortfalls, as noted previously, with a view to making the current cumbersome system more robust. Such a strategy could well prove effective, provided the result is more genuine two-way communication between Washington and the states, based on a clearer mutual understanding of the kinds of circumstances that could trigger a massive Federal response. Such developments, however, take time, patience, and sustained effort—and the interval until the next disaster strikes is anyone's guess.

Chapter Five

Defusing Conflicts in Unstable Regions

JAMES A. SCHEAR

The United States faces no tougher strategic challenge in the coming years than to develop more effective ways of fostering stability in regions plagued by chronic violence and disorder. The strategic imperative for doing so can be summed up in one word: vulnerability. More Americans than ever before recognize the growing connection between their own welfare and the fate of war-torn lands that lie beyond the frontiers of the developed world.[1] Ironically, just as the community of globalized nations is expanding, the pathologies that its frontiers used to fence out no longer seem so distant. A British diplomat summed up this sense of anxiety quite well: "We may not be interested in chaos but chaos is interested in us."[2]

Indeed, few people today profess a laissez-faire attitude about corrosive regional violence in the developing world. For much of the latter 20th century, upheavals in Asia, Africa, and Latin America were overshadowed by the East-West nuclear confrontation. As Cold War rivals, the United States and the Soviet Union each mounted interventions to check the other's influence in the geopolitical space left by retreating European colonial powers. A whole generation of aspiring Third World leaders and insurgent fighters sustained itself in part by trading anticommunist credentials or nonaligned loyalties for assistance from Washington or Moscow. Since the Cold War's demise, it has become possible to analyze these regions much more on their own merits, without the distorting effects of great power rivalry. Unfortunately, historical, political, and cultural differences still cloud the prism through which Americans try to comprehend the forces shaping stability and conflict in these volatile areas.

Al Qaeda's attacks of September 11, 2001, have become the paradigmatic examples of the kind of hazards that the United States seeks to thwart in its efforts to help build stability in turbulent areas. In that case, it was Taliban-ruled Afghanistan that provided an auspicious environment for the growth of a lethal force that could reach halfway around the globe with devastating effect. "Afghanistan," as then-CIA director George Tenet put it, "was less a state sponsor of terrorism than a state sponsored by terrorism."[3]

As argued in chapter two of this volume, al Qaeda strength since 9/11 has been mainly inspirational, and the group represents only one strand of militancy now preying upon various parts of the Muslim world.[4] But therein lies a core strategic problem: the growth of violent nonstate actors emboldened by a coherent worldview that can parasitically latch on to and fuel geographically disparate "fault-line conflicts," [5] besieging or subverting weak governmental structures and impeding their access to outside support. The fact that such groups can thrive in the high ambient temperature created by violent conditions has forced a wholesale reexamination of the dangers of letting certain regional conflicts fester without active efforts at remediation. The 2002 U.S. National Security Strategy's stark observation that "America is now threatened less by conquering states than we are by failing ones" has echoed throughout official speeches and policy pronouncements of the past few years.[6]

To be sure, Islamist militancy is not the only driving force behind heightened American concerns. The world's most chronically insecure regions also tend to generate the bulk of global population displacement. They are the prime source of massive illegal flows of narcotics, arms, human trafficking, and, potentially, disease pandemics. They also are—in extreme cases—venues for genocidal violence, as witnessed in Rwanda more than a decade ago and, more recently, in the Darfur region of western Sudan. Finally, these regions are home to the majority of global energy reserves; they exert great influence on both the supply and demand sides of the market for weapons and technologies of mass destruction. In some cases, they lay astride vital lines of global commerce.

Confronted with diverse and converging threats, the first impulse of any responsible policymaker is to take remedial action—a fair enough reaction, since denial is never a good option. But what kinds of action make the most sense? It is fanciful to imagine that under one policy rubric, one could devise a universally applicable formula for defusing ethnosectarian conflict in Iraq, or pacifying the remote provinces of southeastern Afghanistan, or dislodging Hezbollah from southern Lebanon, or thwarting genocidal violence wherever it may flare up. Rejecting the discredited strategies of bygone eras—be they isolationism, appeasement, or imperial-style dominion—is much easier than developing strategies worthy of sustained support. Achieving stable, democratic governance is a worthy objective, but it too lacks a clear roadmap for successful exportation or incubation.

As this chapter argues, the problems plaguing unstable regions are too diverse and interwoven to lend themselves to a single, generalized approach. The principal tools for dealing with them are not all that mysterious. Good intelligence is essential for gaining a clear understanding of combustible situations and the spillover hazards they pose. Diplomacy has an indispensable role to play in clarifying the extent of common ground, if any, among key parties and inducing their cooperation while mobilizing international support for the remediation effort. Military capabilities may also be crucial as a buttressing element for diplomacy or, in strictly operational terms, as an instrument for suppressing or disrupting the most immediate threats or helping to stabilize a fragile, postconflict environment. A range of reconstructive and developmental instruments—humanitarian relief, infrastructure repair, essential public services, development aid, and macroeconomic stimulation—may be equally essential, along with security assistance, to help quell insurgencies and enable local leaders to provide responsive governance and public safety for their citizens over the long term. The challenges lie in tailoring strategies that incorporate these various instruments to the distinctive features of individual regions and in orchestrating their cooperative and coercive elements in a compatible fashion.

Nowhere are the obstacles to conflict stabilization more forbidding than in present-day Iraq and Afghanistan. While the latter clearly is better off in 2007 than it was in late 2001, when the U.S.-led intervention toppled the Taliban regime, the country's transition out of civil war has failed to achieve the momentum toward normalcy for which many had hoped. In contrast, Iraq's future looks very uncertain. Although the belated "surge" of U.S. forces into Baghdad, coupled with a greater emphasis upon population protection, has helped tamp down communal violence, Iraq's fledging national government appears incapable of bridging the ethnic and sectarian divisions that have embroiled the country and imperiled its reconstruction. Both sets of experiences teach sobering lessons about the difficulties of building stability in the wake of intervention. Whether these lessons will translate into improved U.S. performance over time remains an open question. While the Iraqi and Afghan experiences have shown deficiencies in the U.S. approach, they also risk draining away high-level attention and political support from institutional reforms that could better prepare the United States for deciding when and how to undertake such missions in the future.

To gain better perspective on the challenges of defusing regional conflicts, this chapter starts by considering the magnitude of the problem. Specifically, from a U.S. perspective, how should we assess the hazards of regional violence? Second, this chapter looks closely at the question of response. What strategies present themselves in coping with the problem of regional conflict? Third, it explicates the lessons of recent experiences. What do Afghanistan, Iraq, and other interventions teach about the perils and opportunities of conflict stabilization? Finally, this chapter turns to the all-important question of capacity building. Based upon past and current experiences, what are the key ingredients in getting America's house in order?

CURRENT TRENDS: HOW OMINOUS?

Stretching from the Andean ridge of Latin America to sub-Saharan Africa and across a vast arc from the Maghreb to Southeast Asia, a large portion of humanity—upwards of 2 billion people—lives in the shadow of instability and episodic violence. Dubbed variously as the "transitional world," a "premodern world," "a zone of turmoil and development," a "nonintegrating gap," a "southern belt of strategic instability," or a "neo-Hobbesian world of turmoil," this region defies easy labeling.[7] Within it one finds many stark contrasts: widespread poverty interspersed with pockets of wealth and commercial vibrancy; globally connected urban areas amidst remote rural expanses; quiescent tribal areas alongside zones of chronic communal strife; centers of culture tolerance close by oppressively patriarchal societies; and radicalized groups bent upon violence within moderately inclined communities. However, two broad generalizations about this area hold true.

Twin Challenges: Irregular Warfare and State Weakness

The first concerns the character of warfare. Whenever conflicts erupt in this region, they are typically irregular in character (an ironic twist on Western military lexicon, as if the commonplace is somehow less regular than our expected norm). These wars are called irregular because they are not waged between large mechanized armies, navies, or fleets of strike aircraft. Their most common variant is substate conflict, waged by insurgent or militia groups against a central authority or each other. Whether in Monrovia, Mogadishu, Baghdad, or Kabul, the graphic imagery of conflict is all too familiar: looted storefronts, bullet-scarred buildings, bombed-out cars, mass graves, booby traps, widely scattered landmines, or unexploded ordnance. Suicide attacks may also become commonplace, especially (though not only) where Islamist fighters are engaged in the fighting; and where one of the warring parties presents large moving targets, such as convoys, remote-controlled improvised explosive devices (IEDs) planted along roadsides also become a weapon of choice.

The landscape of irregular warfare is densely populated. Among its most visible victims are fleeing civilians, dead livestock, destitute farmers, child soldiers, and communities bereft of young men and essential services. Less visible are groups threatened by targeted violence—be they Darfurian villagers, Afghan teachers, or urban professionals in Baghdad. As for the fighters and their enablers, it is a diverse mix. Transnational terrorists who flock to a local conflict to inflate their global agenda will be the focus of greatest concern to the United States, but they are only one constituency. One also finds rapacious warlords and rebel groups that conduct terror and/or guerrilla campaigns to advance local agendas; predatory militias—land pirates, essentially—that kill or extort for a living rather than for a cause; despotic state leaders who repress their citizens or threaten neighbors; and criminal syndicates that engage in the smuggling/trafficking of a wide range of commodities—narcotics, people, small arms, timber, diamonds, weapons of mass destruction (WMD) components—usually in tandem with one or more of the above mentioned groups.

A second commonplace feature of this region is the prevalence of weak state structures with limited reach and, as a consequence, large tracts of rural or urban space that are essentially ungoverned. Although state collapse—most often in the midst of grinding civil war—is the most severe form of the phenomenon, that remains comparatively rare. The more typical situation is not the absence of a government, but rather a dysfunctional or corrupted state authority. In some cases, governmental institutions never existed or were merely the artifact of empires; in other cases, they have been hollowed out by years of chronic civil war. Whatever the circumstances, when a government's practical reach extends no farther than the suburbs of its capital city, if that, it might be considered sovereign as a matter of international law but not in control of very much at home. Other, more subtle forms of dysfunction are paralyzed decisionmaking or public service deficits.[8] However the weakness is manifest, the question is always the same: who fills this vacuum?

The answer varies considerably. In some locales, tribes and clans fill the governance gap, enforcing traditional codes and employing local methods of dispute resolution. Heightened tribal authority may result from escalating internal threats; Kamajor hunters in Sierra Leone, for example, were mobilized by village chiefs to fend off predatory militia during that country's civil war. In other cases, the mobilizing threat has been external: the Pashtun tribes in Pakistan's tribal areas have stoutly resisted encroachments by Islamabad, as they had done with the British Empire that preceded it. Yet tribal authority has fared less well in other situations. Warlords siphoned away power from tribal elders in the Afghan war in the years prior to the Taliban's ascent. Elsewhere, communally based mass organizations have emerged as primary nonstate authorities, often supported by armed paramilitary loyalists—for example, the Jaysh al-Mahdi in Iraq or Hezbollah in south Lebanon—that mobilize against a local enemy (Ba'athists, Israel, and so forth) while also providing social services, albeit closely tied to a militant agenda. A rekindled neo-Taliban movement appears to be seeking to do just that in southeastern Afghanistan's contested zones. In still other cases, urban gangs or drug traffickers will act as de facto authorities, providing social services, protection, and favors in return for loyalty.[9] Consequently, whatever civic or national identity a local population may possess resides uneasily or even pales in comparison with other, possibly more authentic, popular loyalties based on kinship, culture, or religion.[10]

Severity of the Impact

How significant is this overall pattern of irregular warfare and state weakness for global stability? There is clearly grist for an argument that cautions against an overly alarmist assessment.

To start with, recent survey data indicate that the numbers of conflicts and battle deaths and the frequency and intensity of genocidal violence worldwide have declined markedly, albeit unevenly, since the height of the Cold War, along with attendant population displacement.[11] While indirect casualties (for example, war-induced privation as a distinctive causation) should not be ignored, they are difficult to measure; and the low-intensity conflicts characteristic of irregular warfare simply will not produce the scale of casualties seen in major conventional wars of the past century. Second, while mass casualty terrorism poses an unambiguous threat, the weak states that could serve as attractive incubators for long-range terrorist attacks may not be all that numerous. A state abutting vast areas of remote space (such as Chad) is going to be less of a hazard than one (such as Afghanistan) that has a stronger neighbor (in this case, Pakistan) that is plugged in to global transportation and information networks.

A third reason not to feel undue alarm is found in great power relations. When compared with previous eras, these relationships are relatively unpolarized by ideology or fettered by the kind of rigidly opposed, interlocking alliance structures that plagued previous eras, in one instance catapulting an assassin's tragically lucky break into a world war.[12] In particular, no emerging or great power aspires to overturn the existing global economic system, which has generated unparalleled growth.[13] These powers, along with the larger community of modern, well-governed states—which includes many U.S. allies and partners—recognize that they are stakeholders in a globalizing economy. True, geopolitics is not free from rivalry, resentment at American preeminence, or the presence of legacy conflicts that could explode in places like the Taiwan Strait or the Korean Peninsula. But no current or aspiring great power would be immune from damage inflicted by its own capricious acts; and surely none has an ideological disposition that would blind it to these realities.

Finally, it would be unwise to hype unduly the distinctive power of nonstate actors. They are enabled by larger trends—Internet communications, global trafficking networks, and the like—and may attract strong local allegiance, but not all nonstate actors are capable or equally problematic. While some are sustained by the black market or illicit transactions, such as the drug trade, others clearly rely on state sponsors. Hezbollah's sizable missile stockpile, as evidenced by its bombardment of Israel during the summer of 2006, as well as its battlefield skills and the rapid assistance it delivered to Lebanese communities after the war, exceeded what it could muster on its own. Moreover, to the extent that a nonstate entity takes on roles as a public service provider to local populations, the more state-like it will tend to become, which opens opportunities to maneuver it into the larger political structure. Those pressures have been evident with Fatah, the longest governing party in the Palestinian territories. Whether the same tendencies would ultimately affect the behavior of the more extremist groups, Hamas or Hezbollah, remains an open question.

The arguments against undue alarm need to be weighed carefully, but they are not ultimately dispositive. With regard to nonstate actors, the United States remains primarily concerned with the subset of militant Islamist groups that are unequivocally irreconcilables, having a global target set and a propensity for suicidal violence and mass casualty terrorism. While the number of attractive state hosts for such groups may not be numerous, it is the lethality of their attack options, not the location of their cadre, that remains the core issue for policymakers. The threat is real enough.[14] Jihadism has not lost its magnetic qualities for certain sizable disaffected constituencies since 9/11. While it is not the only manifestation of violent militancy within the Muslim world, it continues to provide a coherent worldview for committed operatives as well as a powerful magnet vis-à-vis pools of would-be recruits, especially in diaspora communities scattered throughout Europe.

As noted earlier, such groups thrive in the climate of widespread ethnosectarian conflicts. For them, the struggle is a war of civilizations, pitting defenders of Islamic faith, culture, and identity against either "apostates" within the Muslim world or non-Muslims elsewhere. Their propensity to latch on to and leverage local conflicts—whether in Somalia, Kashmir, Indonesia, Chechnya, or Iraq—for their own larger purposes is well established. Less clear is the extent of additional means and opportunity they gain through active involvement in these conflicts—namely, some combination of a safe haven and financial backing that enables them to hide, train, and equip themselves, possibly with WMD, and to put into effect operations that place high-value targets at risk.

Beyond the continued threat of mass casualty terrorism, there is no a priori reason why the number of conflicts, battle deaths, or acts of mass violence against civilians will continue to decline as patterns of warfare evolve. The planet has not yet witnessed major conflict between two nuclear-armed regional adversaries in the developing world, but the continued spread of the enabling technologies increases the odds that it will happen someday. As for instances of large-scale genocide, they are comparatively rare. Several key ingredients—ethnic hatred, interspersed populations, and a predator-prey relationship where one side is disproportionately vulnerable to targeted mass violence inflicted by the other—must all be present simultaneously. Still, if those conditions coalesce, mass killing can certainly erupt and spread rapidly. No observer of the Rwandan genocide, in which hundreds of thousands of people were massacred, largely with machetes and small arms in little more than 100 days, could reasonably conclude it was a low-intensity conflict.

Systemic vulnerabilities? To obtain a clearer overall perspective on the international system's vulnerability to regional violence, it is worth assessing the risks along the vertical and horizontal axes.

Vertical escalation consists of regional crises or conflicts that pit a regional power against a global intervener. The potential combinations here are comparatively few but well known, and WMD proliferation is the most likely catalyst: the familiar scenarios posit either a radical state (for example, Iran) "going nuclear" or a nuclear weapons state (such as Pakistan) "going radical."[15] From the regional stability viewpoint, the most troublesome aspect of nuclear (or WMD) proliferation is when a state's motivation for acquisition is to gain a deterrence cover for its own aggressive designs against neighbors. This is not to say proliferation for other reasons—national prestige, financial profit, global influence, or regime survival—is any less problematic, only that the most immediately threatening variant is one in which WMD directly enables the conduct of other forms of warfare. Imagine how the world might be different if an aggressive, oil-rich and *nuclear-armed* Iraq had invaded Kuwait in 1990 under the cover of its own deterrent umbrella. Precisely that kind of specter would amplify pressures for preventive action by outsiders.

Vertical escalation hazards also arise in the desperate acts of possible victims, not just would-be aggressors. In today's international system, one can discern a cohort of states and state-like entities that senses existential threats and whose countervailing actions would risk drawing the United States or other great powers into confrontations, or worse, with the threatened state's nearby foes or with each other. The list here is diverse: Israel (vis-à-vis Iran, Syria, and Palestinian Islamists), Georgia or Ukraine (vis-à-vis Russia), the Kurdish areas of northern Iraq (vis-à-vis Turkey or Iran), Taiwan (vis-à-vis China), or, in some scenarios, Pakistan (vis-à-vis India). Here, too, the threat of reverberating instabilities or fears of an unbroken cycle of onward proliferation could factor into the calculations of a great power intervener.

Though vertical escalation would be the most dramatic pathway to regional violence—witness the invasion of Iraq, or possibly a future confrontation with Iran—the greater vulnerability in today's system is *horizontal escalation*. Captured well by Chester Crocker's concept of regional "conflict systems," horizontal escalation occurs when instabilities and tension between states are enflamed by substate violence spreading across permeable borders; when flows of refugees, rebel groups, criminals, arms traffickers, or illicit goods—the symptoms of conflict in one arena—become causal or aggravating factors for turmoil in another; and where a "regional patchwork of ethnic or communal minorities adds critical tinder to the mix."[16] The result can be a "hybrid" conflict, which has regional as well as internal dimensions and, in the most extreme cases, in which anarchy has approached a level in which no entity (not even contending militia groups) can fully secure its own turf.[17]

Such conflict systems already are deeply embedded in parts of Africa and Eurasia. Among the most notable ones are the Horn of Africa (around the Somali hub), West Africa (spreading eastward from Liberia and Sierra Leone), Central Africa (spanning the Democratic Republic of Congo and most of its neighbors), and Central/South Asia (covering parts of Afghanistan, Pakistan, and Central Asia). Close behind these zones are two other regions sitting on the cusp of major lateral escalation: Southwest Asia/ Middle East, where Iraq's sectarian violence could be the trigger for a widening intra-Islamic conflict, and the pan-Sahel area, where genocidal violence in western Sudan threatens to spill over into neighboring Chad and Central African Republic. On the other hand, one can also find examples of regions that have survived and begun their long climb out of the abyss. Indochina, Central America, and Southern Africa were all disfigured by violence in the late 1980s, and the wars of Yugoslav succession dominated the Balkan landscape during much of the 1990s. That these formerly war-ravaged regions have achieved considerable (if not necessarily complete) success in conflict mitigation may hold valuable lessons for similar efforts today.

Competing yardsticks. In the end, the vulnerabilities afflicting international order are not hard to identify. More controversial is the task of weighing the costs and impacts of these conflicts when they threaten to break out or actually explode. The initial yardstick for impact assessment is bound to be humanitarian—the numbers of lives lost, people displaced, livelihoods disrupted, and so forth—but decisive policy actions rarely hinge upon such measures alone. Were it otherwise, history might have recorded different outcomes to the mass slaughter of Cambodians, Rwandans, Bosnians, or Kurds, or to the starvation of North Koreans.[18] What usually drives, and frequently embroils, policy decisions on response is the question of spillover impacts. Will a failure to act somehow imperil U.S. national security or regional interests? Will it disrupt global prosperity? The challenge here is to move beyond a generalized recognition of a spillover hazard toward a more nuanced approach that can tackle individual types of concerns, be they terrorism, energy, crime, or disease pandemics.[19]

It is not impossible to imagine the spread of regional violence on a scale sufficient to disrupt the liberalizing global order. The current system relies upon unimpeded routes of supply and distribution across the entire globalizing world, not just for energy and other resources but also increasingly for distributed production and consumer markets. Several kinds of events could disrupt that. An outbreak of pandemic disease certainly could do so, though a contagion's source would be just as likely to spring from a region experiencing rapid growth, like Southeast Asia, than one torn apart by ongoing conflict. Another kind of disruption would be spreading civil unrest in a major regional state—Mexico, Brazil, Egypt, South Africa, Turkey, Nigeria, Saudi

Arabia, Venezuela, Indonesia, or Pakistan, among others—whose destabilization would trigger reverberations well beyond its borders. These are, for the most part, modernizing but still internally fractious countries that, by virtue of their location, resource base, demographic size, or socioethnic composition, already play a substantial role in global stability. China and India no longer fit within this cohort, though in some extreme scenarios they could fall back into it. A crash of a major state could no doubt inflict economic harm—skyrocketing energy prices, trade disruptions, and the like—as well as broader geostrategic damage, if its implosion made it a conveyer belt for displaced populations or bad actors. The international system has not faced such a collapse since the demise of the Soviet empire and the rise of the post–Cold War global economy.

Ultimately, no one could predict the exact sequence of events that might trigger disruption on a scale that could fragment the globalizing community and stymie its progressive tendencies. But the fear of fragmentation—of being taken off "the grid"— is bound to be palpable for any fragile country struggling to stay afloat. "Disconnectedness defines danger," as Thomas Barnett aptly summed it up.[20] What a senior U.S. military commander once observed about Afghanistan holds true in a more global sense: "Show me where the road ends, and I'll show you where the Taliban begins."[21]

CHALLENGES OF DEVISING STRATEGY

U.S. policymakers have struggled mightily since the Cold War to devise sensible options for meeting the myriad challenges posed by chronic regional volatility and episodic violence. The journey has been a rocky one. Major remedial actions have more often reflected a kneejerk response to immediate crises brought to prominence by continuous media coverage than some larger strategic design. Working in tandem with coalition partners or via international organizations is inevitably complicated and time-consuming. And good roadmaps have been hard to find, given that each case always has some unique attributes.

Rhetorically, the term *exporting stability* has great cachet in current policy and international circles. But what does it really mean? The label conveys a sense of general intent, but little more. For some audiences, especially among U.S. allies, providing stability is primarily about the orchestration of diplomatic mediation, consensual peacekeeping, humanitarian aid, or development assistance. For others, the term is shorthand for more ambitious and at times coercive measures—for example, no-fly zones, aerial bombardments, ground assaults, occupation, or democracy promotion in the wake of ousting dictatorial regimes. To one degree or another, all of these (and other) tasks represent gradations of foreign intervention, an undertaking that for the United States poses great irony. No great power has been more interventionist in modern times than the United States, and yet none arguably has been more ambivalent about the mission.

America's Approach

Three factors stand out in explaining this ambivalence.[22] First, the United States has always seen the geographical terrain in question as peripheral to its core interests.

America's formative preoccupations were with the great powers of Europe, not with weak or undeveloped regions. Indeed, from the late 19th through the mid-20th century, the United States saw itself as a counterweight to European imperial aggrandizement and, later, as a defender of international order against aggressive great powers like Nazi Germany or imperial Japan. One can forgive some understandable dissent on this point by Haitians, Nicaraguans, Panamanians, Filipinos, Mexicans, and the U.S. Marine Corps, but the U.S. national psyche has never been greatly influenced by its experiences in those places where Americans dug canals, chased bandits, secured trading routes, sent missionaries, or otherwise exerted a degree of colonial influence.[23] Consequently, U.S. diplomatic and military institutions never really absorbed the civil administrative and "foreign legion" traditions of that bygone era—traditions that were deeply engrained in Europe's counterpart institutions during the 20th century, though less so today.

Second, America's latter-day experiences in unstable regions are dominated by two overwhelmingly negative cases: Vietnam and Somalia. For many Americans, especially on the political left, Vietnam stands for the proposition that counterinsurgency can never be won and should never be waged. While the cases of Malaya (the 1950s), Cambodia (1991–1993), Sierra Leone (2000–2002), or the Andean region (mid 1990s–present) could be cited as evidence that counterinsurgency strategies can work, if done properly, these are not—except for the Philippines, in an earlier era (1899–1902)—primarily *American* experiences. Somalia, on the other hand, convinced many that nationbuilding could never be a realistic objective for outside interveners. Again, one can cite contrapuntal cases—southern Africa and Central America (1990s), Southeast Asia (1960s), not to mention postwar Japan, Germany, and South Korea—but these examples tend to be overlooked or questioned for relevance.

A third factor contributing to U.S. neuralgia about foreign interventions is the presence of so many diaspora communities in modern America, be they Cuban, Jewish, Arab, Somali, Chinese, Armenian, West African, Haitian, Vietnamese, or others. In a nation built largely by immigrants, interest-group politicking based on ethnic heritage and loyalty to homeland is hardly a new phenomenon. Such constituencies can be instrumental in achieving longer-term solutions, especially if they have the wherewithal to contribute economic revitalization through remittances and direct investment. But they also, inevitably, bring their own set of historical grievances into debates surrounding U.S. policies affecting their countries of origin, at times giving those debates a sharp partisan edge.

While by no means the only ones in play, these factors nonetheless go some distance toward explaining why the United States has found it so difficult to keep a steady hand in its dealings with unstable regions. They have fed into, and amplified, larger divisions among contending schools of thought about America foreign policy and made national consensus elusive.[24] The results show up in certain recurring patterns of U.S. behavior: a strong preference for decisive applications of force against clearly defined enemies; concern about the costs of prolonged involvement; risk aversion in some (though not all) cases; limited patience with indigenous actors and foreign partners; eagerness to retain freedom of action; and sensitivity to fleeting political support at home. All of these traits are bound to influence subjective judgments about when and how to respond to dire regional circumstances whenever objective conditions (for example, terrorist attacks, looming WMD proliferation, or genocidal violence) coalesce in a way that confronts the country with hard choices.

Which Priorities?

Which priorities, then, should the United States try to advance when responding to regional violence? The 2002 U.S. National Security Strategy stressed the need for multinational collaboration: "[R]egional crises can strain our alliances, rekindle rivalries among the major powers, and create horrifying affronts to human dignity. When violence erupts and states falter, the United States *will work with friends and partners* [emphasis added] to alleviate suffering and restore stability."[25] In its 2006 update of the strategy, the Bush administration stressed the central role of indigenous actors: "Outsiders generally cannot impose solutions on parties that are not ready to embrace them, but outsiders can sometimes help create the conditions under which the parties themselves can take effective action."[26] While these particular themes are sensible, the authoritative policy statements from which they are drawn shy away from articulating a larger strategic logic for conflict stabilization or enumerating specific priorities. Instead, everything is portrayed as important: Liberia is highlighted as well as the West Bank and Gaza; Venezuela is cited as well as Uganda; Nepal as well as Darfur.[27]

And therein lies a basic predicament for the United States. More than anything else, strategy is about making hard choices—specifically, about how one should apportion finite resources (the means) against an array of desired goals (the ends). In the case of conflict management, two challenges arise. First, any overall strategic design will have to rank-order hazards and thus must give some regions higher priority than others. In a unipolar world, Washington's disinclination to play regional favorites is understandable, especially when the transcendent priority of U.S. national security, defeating global terrorism, already inclines the United States toward an intense preoccupation with the Islamic world—a fact not lost on friends or adversaries in East Asia, sub-Saharan Africa, and Latin America.[28] Secondly, conflict stabilization strategies are usually viewed as instrumental to other priorities (countering terror, building democracy, expanding prosperity), and their distinctive value (beyond getting the guns to fall silent) is often hard to read.

It was not always this way. Cold War–era regional stabilization efforts had a clear, distinctive theme: *preventing escalation* that would embroil hostile, nuclear-armed superpowers. Deterrence remained the principal anchor for stability, to be sure, but in places like Cyprus, the Golan Heights, and Kashmir, international peacekeeping missions composed largely of neutral or nonaligned countries deployed under a United Nations (UN) banner to shore up precarious ceasefires between hostile parties. Although small by today's standards, these so-called interposition missions achieved important calming effects along contested front lines in a bifurcated interstate system.

Yet absent any diplomatic follow-through, these missions also had a calcifying effect, for the most part freezing rather than resolving conflicts.

By the late 1980s, escalation prevention had given way to another strategic objective: the *strategic disengagement* of the superpowers and their proxies. With the Cold War's subsidence, a window opened for internationally brokered disengagements or peace settlements: as peacekeepers flowed in, foreign combatants (for example, the Cubans in Angola, the Vietnamese in Cambodia, and the Soviets in Afghanistan) flowed home; and local adversaries turned toward the negotiating table as their outside patronage slowly dried up. This phase of regional stabilization produced mixed results: it aided and abetted positive transitions in Central America, sub-Saharan Africa, and Southeast Asia, but it failed to halt new or continued turmoil in places like Afghanistan, the Balkans, the Caucasus, Central Asia, or the Horn of Africa, where the ebbing of Cold War tides and, ultimately, the collapse of the Soviet empire exposed shaky regimes or pent-up animosities.

Since the late 1990s, and more particularly since 9/11, the focus has shifted yet again, toward the goal of stabilizing countries in the midst of violent transitions. The circumstances are by now familiar ones: an oppressive regime is evicted from a contested region (Kosovo, East Timor) or toppled altogether (the Taliban in Afghanistan, Saddam and the Ba'athists in Iraq) by an intervening coalition of foreign and local actors, or conversely, a fledging internationally recognized government attempts to consolidate its authority in the face of violent spoilers (Sierra Leone in 2000, Democratic Republic of Congo since 2003, Afghanistan since 2004–2005, Iraq since 2005). Either way, the overriding task facing outside interveners and their local beneficiaries is to shape a new political dispensation in which public security, economic development, accountable government, and the rule of law can all be built over time.

As it has unfolded, this new phase—*transconflict stabilization*—has been a response to situations where underlying conflicts of interest generally were not ripe for settlement as a consequence of a stalemated civil war or superpower disengagement. Not surprisingly, for international actors, the biggest obstacle to success in these situations has been political: war or state collapse tends to be everyone's second choice at the local level, certainly not as attractive as winning outright but preferable to a national unity government where factions would have to get along and distasteful accommodations would be necessary.[29] And for the United States, as discussed below, the depth of investment and patience required for successful reconstruction, nation building, and counterinsurgency activities has been hard to muster.[30]

Recalibrating the Paradigm

What is the next step in this progression? Is history a prologue for the future, or should the United States consider a radical change in its approach to regional stabilization? Candidly, neither path will be easy.

The problem with a "stay the course" approach is the number of criticisms that have accumulated over time. Nation building is a quagmire, the argument goes; these missions are just too ambitious a goal when the recipient is a large, fragile state; moreover, the

U.S. track record is mixed at best and in Iraq is verging on a major failure; in any case, the mission of American soldiers is to fight and win wars, not act as "social workers"; and finally, our allies and partners are stretched thin and losing their enthusiasm for the mission. On the other hand, a radical shift away from active involvement in regional stabilization could be dangerous and self-defeating. Here, too, the litany of arguments is familiar: the key to winning wars (as opposed to battles) is securing the peace that follows victory; chronic regional violence empowers extremists and criminals, undermines partners, and propels incentives for further WMD proliferation; and, finally, as a democratic country with the capacity to act, the United States has a moral duty to confront genocide when it flares and a national interest in deterring its outbreak elsewhere.

Building a new strategic design for U.S. regional stabilization activities amidst these conflicting impulses will not be easy, but it is essential. No matter how events in Iraq and Afghanistan ultimately unfold, the prevailing threat conditions set forth above will continue to generate pressures for large-scale stabilization activity. Conceivably, a few such actions might occur on the heels of wars of necessity, akin to the invasion of Afghanistan following al Qaeda's 9/11 attacks. Most will likely be more volitional in nature—that is, actions taken in response to third-party crises where U.S. leaders sense that significant national security or humanitarian interests would be imperiled unless someone acts. Those interests can best be advanced by shaping U.S. regional stabilization efforts around three overarching objectives:

- Mitigating "fault-line" conflicts. A central task of the strategy must be to defuse the kinds of ethnosectarian conflict that impart energy and fervor to transnational terrorist groups or that threaten to spur the spread of WMD capacity. To the extent that ethnosectarian conflict involving Muslim communities can be defused through locally focused efforts aimed at resolving specific grievances, these conflicts can gradually be decoupled from each other and from the global struggle that jihadist groups seek to advance, thereby shrinking the latter's recruiting pool and their geographical room for maneuver.[31] In this sense, conflict stabilization contributes very directly to the larger counterterror campaign.
- Strengthening "anchors," plugging "gaps." The aim here is to assist modernizing states whose collapse would trigger massive human displacement, major disruptions to global commerce or transportation, or the spread of militants with irreconcilable agendas. These states often, though not always, sit along volatile ethnosectarian boundaries that bisect Afro-Eurasia.[32] This approach has a clear preventive posture, directed mainly toward countries with whom the United States is at peace (or even allied) but where threatening nonstate groups seek sanctuary. The locus of such activity would be the provision of capacity-building assistance that can help the national governments and near-neighbors secure their own territories and win the trust and confidence of local populations.[33]

- Building humanitarian protection. Finally, the strategy must give a strong impulse to international capacity-building measures aimed at thwarting mass violence or acts of genocide that invariably implicate U.S. humanitarian concerns but at times fall short of engaging U.S. national security interests. In these cases, there is no real internal capacity to build, at least initially; the states in question are usually fractured, if not failing, or are part of the problem. The focus should be mobilizing international capacity for protective action as a first step toward rolling back the violence.[34]

Taken together, these priorities do not point to a radically new paradigm; threats that could metastasize into direct assaults upon the United States or its allies and key partners will still receive paramount attention. What these priorities require is a recalibrated approach that seeks a better balance between direct intervention and indirect action, between U.S.-led operations and regionally led actions where the United States plays an enabling role, between a heavy military footprint and a lighter, more diverse, and sustained presence, and between the direct provision of essential stabilization assistance to affected populations and indigenous capacity building.

None of these adjustments will be effective without a stronger foundation for coalition building. The old adage "we can't go it alone" is sensible enough but suggests the only problem is burdensharing. In fact, a large American presence, military or civilian, is just plain counterproductive in certain locales, especially where our embrace of local allies can stigmatize them as puppets and our adversaries can be drawn together by the common bond of anti-American sentiment. Like it or not, the United States has become a highly polarizing power: attracting some, repelling others. Consequently, intelligent choices about when and how to intervene require a thoroughgoing knowledge of not only the conflict dynamics that roil a given region but also how American involvement would alter those dynamics.

MODES OF STABILIZATION

While the priorities set forth above might represent a reasonable point of departure for a recalibrated regional stabilization strategy, there remains the critical question of methods. How should such complex activity be orchestrated? Weighing the benefits and limitations of various approaches begins, as it must, with a brewing crisis situation—specifically, its causes and threatening consequences and how to mitigate both. Then there is the challenge of helping to build an indigenous base for stability sufficient to prevent the reoccurrence of conflict after international interveners have departed. And finally, policymakers must ask themselves: how do we strengthen U.S. capabilities needed for each of these tasks? The first two issues are considered below, before turning to the latter in a subsequent section.

Three Options

Any number of instruments may be useful in dealing with threats to stability, but specific policy actions usually boil down to three basic choices. One can try to *contain* the problem, in part by denying attack options and/or material support to the various parties. Alternatively, one can try to *engage* the problem, initially with diplomacy, alleviating both symptoms and causes in a generally (but not always) consensual way. Finally, one can attempt to *compel* a desired outcome, most often through direct or indirect use of force. These are not exclusive choices, to be sure; for instance, engagement may also involve a degree of pressure, and compellence may involve the use of inducements. Let us consider how each would support the broader objective set forth above.

Containment: erecting barriers. A posture of containment has enormous appeal in crisis situations, especially in the early phases. From the policymaker's perspective, the logic runs something like this: "This crisis is still unfolding; direct intrusions into the conflict now would be costly, and it's not clear who would benefit or what the end result would be; in any case, the belligerents have far greater stakes in this fight than we do. What we want, above all, is to stop this thing from escalating or spreading." Employed in the right way, containment/denial should not preclude more ambitious measures. There is also, always, the hope that restricting the conflict in some fashion might lead to a stalemated situation, wearing the parties out over time and inducing a negotiation.

Recent history is replete with examples of containment. Multilaterally imposed sanctions—aimed at cutting off outside support—have been commonplace during phases of active conflict. Since the 1980s, the UN Security Council has imposed comprehensive sanctions against Serbia and Montenegro and Iraq, as well as more targeted arms embargos against all of the other former Yugoslav republics, Afghanistan, Sudan, Somalia, Liberia, Sierra Leone, Eritrea, Ethiopia, Rwandese rebels, and the Democratic Republic of Congo.[35] Sanctions come into play most often in situations of threatened or actual cross-border aggression, civil war, genocide, regime collapse, or as punishment for acts of terrorism (for example, the air embargo against Libya after the bombing of Pan Am 103). In cases where an internationally recognized government finds itself fighting one or more rebel groups, such as in Colombia or Sri Lanka, they tend to be seldom used.

A more stringent form of containment involves efforts to deny certain attack options. No-fly zones have been employed in places such as the former Yugoslavia and Iraq, usually with the intention of trumping the capability of the stronger belligerent(s) or protecting vulnerable populations or associated international operations. Maritime interception operations, employed in parts of the Mediterranean, the Gulf of Aden, the Persian Gulf, and the Indian Ocean since 9/11, can be useful in denying aggressive states or terrorist groups easy transit or staging opportunities. In a different way, the reflagging of Kuwaiti oil tankers during the Iran-Iraq war of 1980–1988—in effect, sailing these vessels under American protection—was an attempt, albeit not a completely successful one, to achieve the same general objective: namely, to put oil transit activity off-limits to the belligerents through a localized form of deterrence.

Containment concepts also have been attempted directly on the battlefield, drawing upon the well-established humanitarian concepts of neutral areas or undefended locations to which noncombatants and war wounded could be evacuated.[36] Thus, safe areas were designated during the war in Bosnia-Herzegovina in the early 1990s, and in Colombia, a mutually agreed demilitarized area was set up as a place where civilians in rebel areas could find safety. Such measures may provide some immediate relief, but they are enormously difficult to sustain. And if they actually provide important attack options to one side or are abused as a sanctuary for the other's forces, they will unravel sooner or later.

Equally difficult to sustain is the protected relief of civilian populations, in effect containing the hardships that civilians would otherwise suffer. Used most visibly under UN auspices in Croatia and Bosnia in the early 1990s, this technique of containment became embroiled in the belligerents' conflicting war aims and finally collapsed as the Bosnian war reached a culminating point in late 1995. In other venues, however, humanitarian assistance has played a more useful containment role. Food deliveries, including by air, to civilians during the Kosovo conflict in 1998–1999 enabled many to shelter in place rather than flee, greatly containing refugee-related impacts in neighboring countries until the very end, when Belgrade finally upped the ante and began mass cleansing throughout the province. The United States also on occasion has mounted major foreign disaster relief operations out of concern in part that natural disasters could generate political instabilities in fragile areas.[37]

What is required to make containment work? Without question, diplomacy is an indispensable tool, not only for the establishment of a sanctions regime, but also for the onerous job of prodding countries to comply once the sanctions are agreed. Operationally, the range of instruments suitable for containment missions tends to be fairly heavy on the intelligence and military sides. Surveillance assets are needed to monitor compliance with internationally agreed sanctions. Combat aircraft are needed to police no-fly zones, and naval assets would be used to police maritime approaches. Civilian and military observers on the ground are extremely valuable, if they can be protected, as well as logistics units, light infantry, and mechanized units to provide escort to relief supplies or undertake preventive, protective, or interpositional operations.

From the stabilization standpoint, the value of containment is mainly indirect: to interpose barriers or filters that control how a conflict interacts with its external environment. Containment's greatest benefits, clearly, are that it can be a responsive first step, a natural complement to more ambitious steps, a vital means for collaborating with friendly actors and stigmatizing bad actors in the immediate region, and the foundation for multinational actions that enjoy broad legitimacy. Especially significant in some cases could be the provision of capacity-building assistance with a containment orientation at the operational level—for example, the training, equipping, and mentoring of border control elements—that can help regional "anchor" states to exert greater control over their territory.

On the other hand, containment can also be very onerous to implement. In fault-line conflicts, as seen in Iraq and Afghanistan, physically interdicting the ingress of foreign fighters has proved practically impossible when they blend in with or are drawn from an ethnosectarian group that spans both sides of a given border. More generally, there is a risk that containment will result in open-ended commitments (such as on the Korean Peninsula, 1953–2007) and political stalemates, and the job of sustaining widespread adherence to sanctions is frustratingly hard. It also can, if done maladroitly, hamper other options.[38]

Finally, containment presumes a degree of detachment from the conflict that may be difficult to sustain in practice. Often, the population, rather than the leadership, suffers the most under large-scale sanctions. Indeed, from the humanitarian protection standpoint, there is a "let the fires burn" quality to this posture that can prove controversial unless it provides an agreed measure for more ambitious action as and when the violence begins to overwhelm whatever containment barriers have been set up.

Engagement: building bridges. The essence of the engagement option is the deal. Faced with an outbreak or escalation of mass violence, the United States and other outside parties may decide that the spillover consequences are sufficiently high to warrant active involvement. This, in turn, raises two questions: what should the character of the "intervention" be—partisan, impartial, diplomatic, military, or other— and would some investment in mediation help pave the way?

In any given conflict situation, the character of the intervention will depend critically upon judgments concerning the claims and objectives of the combatants. If, for example, there is a national government that can plausibly claim to represent the legitimate aspirations of the people, an intervention will most often take the form of military or economic assistance to that entity. From the U.S. standpoint, Colombia, the Philippines, and Georgia, among other countries, all fit this model. Post-Taliban Afghanistan and post-Saddam Iraq would shift toward this model, too, if the transitions now under way in each country eventually yield more stable, representative governments. The job of diplomacy in this "partisan" mode is narrowly tailored to the task of ensuring that external assistance achieves its intended impact of helping to defeat or marginalize rebel forces, shoring up local public support for the government, and building state structures in contested areas that will deliver a modicum of public security and essential services to the people.[39]

The more complicated form of third-party intervention is a more evenhanded one, where no single party has both the means and legitimacy to lay uncontested claim to outside support. In these cases, the job of diplomacy is settlement brokerage. In theory, the belligerents can deliver something that the outsiders want: peace and the restoration of civil order. The outsiders in turn have the wherewithal to deliver on things that the belligerents may want: legitimacy, resources, access, and security guarantees. The terms of the trade will be a cessation of hostilities, at least, in exchange for external commitments. The belligerents then each have to decide whether they are better off with the deal at hand or the prospect of continued fighting, while outsiders will look hard at what their commitments can buy. As an international mediator once put it, "A little peace, a little commitment; a lot of peace, a lot of commitment."[40]

Engagement definitely implies a more activist stance than containment. For the policymaker, the logic goes something like this: "Suppressing this conflict through force would be too risky and complicated, but we can't sit passively by and let this thing boil over; let's work the entry conditions diplomatically, which will reduce both the scale of the force we need to send and the risks it will face in helping to reestablish a durable peace." Translating this general impulse into action requires a clear sense of both how the diplomatic process should be orchestrated and which operational concepts and resources would be required to implement the deal.

There is no standard model for negotiating settlements. The most streamlined arrangement involves one mediator and two parties, on the model of Henry Kissinger's "shuttle diplomacy" following the 1973 Yom Kippur War between Egypt and Israel. A more recent example is the U.S. mediation of the 1998–2000 Eritrea-Ethiopia conflict, where lead negotiator Anthony Lake, in close coordination with the United Nations, brought both sides to a package deal involving border demarcation, phased disengagement, the interposition of a peacekeeping force, and the restoration of local control in disputed areas. A more complex mechanism is the Six-Party Talks on North Korea's nuclear programs, in which Beijing is playing the pivotal, bridging role between Pyongyang, Washington, Tokyo, Seoul, and Moscow. Even more elaborate models include the 1995 Dayton negotiations orchestrated by U.S. mediator Richard Holbrooke that produced the settlement of the conflict in Bosnia-Herzegovina, as well as the French-Indonesian co-chaired multinational negotiation (involving 19 states) that produced the Cambodia peace agreement of 1991.

The toughest initial question when structuring a settlement process is whom to include beyond the immediate belligerents. The answer is not all that hard (though the politics often is): anyone with the ability to implement, support, or spoil the deal needs to be involved. In civil wars, especially, interactions between the factions and their external patrons can be a decisive factor in determining outcomes. It is hard to imagine success at the Dayton negotiations without direct involvement of Bosnia's immediate neighbors, and occasional tormenters, presidents Slobodan Milosevic and Franjo Tudjman, as well as the backing of Russia and European Union members of the so-called Contact Group. Similarly, Cambodia's peace process probably would have ground to a halt without active intercessions by the Thai and Chinese governments to keep the reluctant Khmer Rouge engaged. In the Middle East context, the Baker-Hamilton Iraq Study Group pushed hard for a new international support group to include all parties that have a stake in preventing the country from "falling into chaos."[41] Of course, not all outsiders may be willing or able to secure their clients' forbearance—something that the offer of inclusion may help to expose and stigmatize.

As for the settlement itself, the contours of the deal usually clarify themselves fairly quickly. In civil wars, the central trade often involves power sharing for demobilization: those with the greatest hold on power—for example, Hun Sen in Cambodia, José Eduardo dos Santos in Angola, Alhaji Ahmad Kabbah in Sierra Leone—will agree to share power under a transitional formula, often leading to national elections, while rebel groups disarm, demobilize, or merge into a new unified army. In separatist conflicts, the overriding question is how much political autonomy there will be: either a loose confederation (Bosnia, possibly a future Iraq), or a reversion of territory to its original owner (Eastern Slavonia to Croatia) or outright independence (East Timor, possibly Kosovo). Where the final destination is agreed, these arrangements can work fairly well; where the outcome is not clear, the process can quickly bog down.

A distinctive challenge for engaging "fault-line conflicts" is devising ways to pull apart, rather than drive together, potentially reconcilable militants, their irreconcilable allies, and external patrons. Whether in Iraq's Anbar province, south-central Somalia, Pakistan's tribal areas, or Indonesia's Aceh province, success lies in a combination of pressures and inducements attractive enough to incline indigenous actors toward a cooperative posture, leaning away from elements that seek to leverage the conflict for their own larger purposes.[42] This is best done through a bottom-up approach, keyed to addressing local issues, though buttressed wherever possible by the alluring prospect of a pathway to trade, development, and greater coupling to centers of economic growth within the region.[43]

As for local issues, while no two negotiations are alike, there are inevitably some problems that stand in the way of agreement. Wherever forced displacement has occurred, the repatriation of refugees or internally displaced persons to areas from which they were cleansed—in the Balkans or Afghanistan or possibly a future confederated Iraq—will have to be resolved. In some cases, the verified withdrawal of foreign fighters (as in Cambodia, Angola, Afghanistan, and elsewhere) can prove troublesome, as have demands for amnesty for past crimes. Another chronic problem is the reform of dysfunctional or repressive police forces, whether in Central America or Iraq. And in many chronic conflicts, securing central control over, and fair distribution of, natural resources (diamonds, oil, timber, and so forth) in a fashion that binds the country together and denies would-be spoilers independent access to revenue sources looms large.[44]

Whichever way the process is structured, a central question is the proper role of international institutions, both global and regional. Three roles are most visible. At the global level, *international legitimization* of the process via endorsement of a UN body, normally by means of a Security Council resolution, is always highly desirable. The second possible role is *mediation/facilitation*, usually provided by the Secretary-General or his representatives, either as the mediator (for example, Cyprus) or as an independent troubleshooter assisting a national mediator by reaching out to difficult-to-engage constituencies (for example, Lakhdar Brahimi's intercessions with Shi'a clerics in Iraq in 2004). The third function is the *provision of field services*, ranging from things as straightforward as border demarcation by the UN cartographer, to more extensive types of support in the form of peacekeepers, electoral assistance, food, and refugee assistance provided by the World Food Program, the UN High Commissioner for Refugees, or World Bank funding for national reconstruction programs.

For the United States, there is no preset formula for involving international organizations in conflict remediation. Burden sharing is always desirable, but the United Nations, the North Atlantic Treaty Organization (NATO), the Organization for Security and Co-operation in Europe, the African Union, and the Association of Southeast

Asian Nations are all actors in international conflict resolution, and their value-added should be weighed in relation to the kinds of advantages (such as operational capacity or local legitimacy) they might bring in responding to a particular crisis. Inevitably, choices will be influenced by the strength of the international consensus favoring the use of one institution over another, how a specific organization is viewed within the country or region under threat, and the availability/desirability of alternate modes of supply, such as states acting in coalitions of the willing. What is clear, however, is that major mediation would probably rule out anything but a background role for the United States except in a few improbable cases (for example, Israel and the Palestinians).

In finalizing the package, a genuinely hard issue for mediators is the problem of establishing local ownership of the process. Whenever the parties fail to agree on how to do something, or who should do it (policing, elections management, and so forth), a default tendency is the international provision of a domestic service.[45] The basic principle that outsiders should assist rather than govern whenever possible is straightforward enough, but drawing the line is difficult. Too little support can cause the remediation effort to falter; too much support breeds an unhealthy dependency.

As the foregoing implies, the tools of engagement are necessarily diverse. Diplomacy is an absolutely vital instrument, one that should include all parties with a stake in the outcome but also be structured with a clear division of labor in mind.[46] On the operational side, the military capabilities for stabilization or peace support operations draw heavily from what in U.S. parlance are called *combat support elements*—logistics, transportation, communications, and engineering units, as well as contingency planners, military police, civil affairs, forensic specialists, medical units, and their protective cover.

Compared with a containment posture, the civilian-led field activities for engagement are much more extensive: humanitarian relief, reconstruction, public security, and governance assistance, to include the justice sector/rule of law reform, civil administration, human rights monitors/trainers, and elections specialists. Such contributions come through governments, international organizations, and large nongovernmental organizations. Task-built organizations with a civil-military character also play valuable roles in areas such as humanitarian demining and unexploded ordnance removal, and disarmament, demobilization, and reintegration programs.

The synchronization of these instruments can be complex and prone to friction. To greater or lesser degrees, the stabilizing elements of the posture will exist in tension with their more remedial elements, which can be quite *destabilizing*. Electoral processes create winners and losers, as do reconstruction projects. War crime tribunals and even truth and reconciliation commissions involve assigning culpability. A freed-up media can stir public anger. All this amplifies pressure upon the military and police elements to have the necessary capacity in place to react quickly to problems. For their part, the military components will also seek to forge a close link in the eyes of local communities between their presence and the provision of humanitarian and developmental assistance. As a former U.S. commander observed: "You need to address development to offset some of the negatives when you bring a modern force into a third world country that is just getting by day-to-day."[47] This linkage (discussed below) becomes even more vital in situations of active insurgency.

Ultimately, engagement efforts succeed or fail on their ability to establish through diplomacy a reasonable set of entry conditions for an international presence in a war-torn region. That is not to say that conditions must be benign, only manageable. The key is whether the consent that the (former) belligerents give at the strategic level proves durable enough to withstand resistance within their ranks at lower levels. If it does, then the interveners—or better yet, the locals themselves—can enforce discipline by applying measured force against spoilers. If it does not, then the interveners are no longer operating in an engagement mode.

For the policymaker, the upsides of engagement are considerable. Done selectively, under auspicious circumstances, engagement has a better chance of alleviating the causes of violence than a containment posture, and it correctly puts the onus upon the parties to cooperate as a condition for international involvement. Even so, several downsides are clear. It takes time to work the conditions diplomatically. If the conflict does not lend itself to the calming effects of diplomacy—say, it is genocidal, with a predator-prey dimension—or if the spillover effects cannot be contained, engagement will just be a wheel-spinning exercise. Also, the conditions for a consensual transition and international assistance may not prove durable. Parties can hedge their bets or change their minds. Local consent can erode. The choices then are rather inauspicious: an ignominious withdrawal or a quagmire.

Compellence: wielding the hammer. Compellence as a method of stabilization is best viewed as a high-risk, high-payoff approach, one that usually comes to the fore when other options have been tried and found insufficient.[48] For a besieged policymaker contemplating the step, the reasoning runs something like this: "We've tried other options, to no avail. The threats are serious and growing; we cannot afford to let this situation fester. Time is not on our side. Let's alter the political and military landscape through coercive pressure or force to gain a positive outcome."

Several questions flow from this line of reasoning. Given that force does not lend itself to impartial application, against whom or what does one act? And who or what is the beneficiary? Do the benefits justify the costs and risks? And what must be done to safeguard our investment?

In the current climate, the use of coercive means to achieve regional stabilization is regarded as synonymous with the toppling of aggressive or dictatorial regimes. In fact, the applications have been more diverse:

- On the lower end of the ladder, externally enabled indigenous force has been targeted against spoilers in order to bring them into compliance with an internationally agreed transition process. Thus, the British-trained Sierra Leone army, supported by U.S.-trained West African troops (the latter operating under UN command), pushed back and eventually marginalized the rogue elements of the Revolutionary United Front (RUF) in 2001–2002, pulling Sierra Leone out of a downward spiral.

- Higher on the ladder are instances in which external force has been applied against spoilers with the consent of their patron. Thus, for example, with Jakarta's (reluctant) consent in the face of strong outside pressures, an Australian-led intervention into East Timor secured that region (now country) from rampaging pro-Indonesian militias after a referendum there in August 1999 yielded a pro-independence outcome. Similarly, in the wake of the Dayton Accords, UN-assigned troops in Croatia's Eastern Slavonia region drove hostile Serb militia out of the Djeletovci oil fields with the tacit consent of Belgrade, once it was clear that the region would revert to Zagreb's control.[49]
- Still higher are coercive campaigns, involving initially (or mainly) airpower, that have been aimed at reversing aggression or breaking an untenable stalemate. The classic examples are the U.S.-led Operation *Desert Storm* (1991), which helped to evict the Iraqis from Kuwait; NATO's Operation *Deliberate Force* (1995), which eventually brought the Bosnian Serbs to the Dayton Accords; and NATO's Operation *Allied Force* (1999), which compelled the withdrawal of the Serb army and militias from Kosovo province.
- Finally, at the highest level are forced-entry campaigns, utilizing airpower along with ground expeditionary forces, which have been conducted with the explicit aim of deposing a threatening regime. The U.S.-led Operation *Enduring Freedom* (OEF) in the wake of the 9/11 attacks toppled Afghanistan's Taliban regime and scattered its al Qaeda sponsors, and Operation *Iraqi Freedom* (OIF), begun in March 2003, ousted Saddam Hussein.

If these cases are noteworthy for the diversity of force applications they illustrate, they also show that the utility of a given action hinges very much upon the context in which it is used. Defeating a rebel group that has no popular following (say, the RUF in Sierra Leone) will be much easier than attempting to suppress insurgent groups that enjoy support among some segments of the population (for example, Ba'athists in Iraq). Coercing a spoiler into a compliant posture may be easier if he has lost a patron's support than if he has not. Forcing a party to evacuate territory (for example, Kosovo) or halt egregious behavior may be easier if compellence is focused more on those objectives than on posing an existential threat to the perpetrator. Broadly speaking, when compellence removes obstacles to a settlement whose outlines are already visible, stabilization is going to be much easier to achieve than in cases where the use of decisive force simply upsets a status quo and triggers a scramble for power and influence. The fundamental consideration for policymakers must always be whether force solves more problems than it creates. Even when problems are solved, there are consequences that have to be anticipated or offset.

One such consequence is an upsurge in crime and civil disorder in the wake of decisive force. In communal settings, especially, looting and retributive attacks will tend to flare up as soon as organized combat subsides. This progression has unfolded repeatedly—in Sarajevo, Port au Prince, Baghdad, and other places. Partisans of the side being suppressed or deposed will begin to disperse; local police will have already disappeared; hostile crowds begin to form; stores and public buildings come under attack. All this poses hard choices for outside interveners: what can be done to halt the looters? Should lethal force be used? Whose cooperation will be needed to calm things down? Unless outsiders can muster forces of truly intimidating size, they will always be reluctant to intervene in mass looting. The violence, after all, is not directed at them, and trying to stop it will only draw fire and alienate the public.[50] It is more tempting to try to ride out the violence in hopes that the public's steam will get vented than to get caught in the middle.

Beyond this problem lies the larger issue of malign adaptation by either foes or friends. For the foes—against whom force is used—there is always the option of fighting asymmetrically. While Iraqi Ba'athists and the Taliban provide the best current examples of this, one can find less celebrated (and less successful) attempts by ousted regime elements to reconfigure themselves as guerrilla fighters: pro-Indonesian security forces in East Timor, the Haitian armed forces under ousted dictator Raoul Cedras, or the so-called Armed Forces Revolutionary Council in Sierra Leone are three apt cases. To make the transition requires several ingredients—access to resources, an influx of fighters, recruiting networks, communal loyalty, safehavens, and, at times, outside backing—that may not always be available.

As for the friends (more aptly, the beneficiaries of compellent action), the principal hazard is falling prey to a winner-take-all mentality—a natural impulse, especially in communal conflict. Having endured (in many cases) years of repression and the deprivations of conflict, the decision whether to accommodate former tormenters, or elements thereof, is never going to be an easy choice, even if dispassionate calculations might show it to be the best option. Indeed, in the absence a Nelson Mandela–like unifying figure, and in the midst of continued deep-seated grievances, any act of reconciliation may well prove impossible. This leaves outside interveners with few options than to try to rein in the winners—for example, the Kosovo Liberation Army, or the Northern Alliance in Afghanistan, or the Shi'a militia in south-central Iraq—while attempting to maneuver them and their erstwhile enemies into a posture of forbearance, a predicate for building durable postconflict institutions.

Generally, effective compellence requires all of the tools required for effective engagement. It also requires combat-capable expeditionary forces for the entry phase of operations, as well as forces sufficient to maintain a safe and secure environment until security functions can be handed back to local actors. Depending on the situation, this latter mission may entail a major investment in human intelligence gathering and the training of indigenous forces, to harden postconflict recovery against attacks by spoilers. Finally, a creative blending of international military and civilian assets may be required for the purpose of assisting indigenous actors in revitalizing rural economies and extending new forms of security and civil administration into war-torn areas—a classic element in counterinsurgency.

Without question, compellence ranks as the most ambitious and costly choice on the menu of remediation. Its upside is the possibility of decisively halting dangerous situations that generate threats to national or global security interests and that careful diplomacy cannot attenuate. It also can have a salutary dissuasive value vis-à-vis a range of dangerous actors in unstable regions. Its main downsides are the complications that arise from the ownership that intervening parties assume for a messy situation when they take this dramatic step. Having entered the fray as "partisans" unavoidably complicates the interveners' subsequent ability to reengage politically with communities (such as the Pashtuns in Afghanistan, Sunnis in Iraq, or Serbs in Kosovo) that found themselves on the other side of the fight. In addition, international organizations that trade on their presumptive neutrality as a means of obtaining safe access into unstable areas—which is to say, most nongovernmental aid providers, particularly the International Committee of the Red Cross—find they have less independent room for maneuver in situations where they are viewed as tools of the interveners. Accepting the protective cover of the interveners limits their access to affected populations; eschewing the protection exposes them to risk, at times with potentially devastating consequences.[51]

AFGHANISTAN AND IRAQ: DISTILLING THE LESSONS

Each in its own way, Afghanistan and Iraq have come to symbolize cautionary tales about the challenges of mounting effective compellent action as a remedy for looming regional threats. While definitive judgments regarding these two U.S.-led interventions will rest ultimately with future historians, the extensive chronicling of both endeavors provides more than enough grist for reaching preliminary conclusions about the choices that policymakers and field commanders made at various stages and the consequences of their actions. The challenge, not surprisingly, lies in distilling applicable lessons—amidst inevitable debate over what the "right" lessons are—and figuring out how these ought to be reflected in the U.S. approach to regional stabilization.

The Afghan Intervention: Treading Lightly

For much of the 1990s, the Afghan civil war seemed too distant and complicated for the international community to do much about. The departure of Soviet forces in 1989 under the terms of a UN-brokered disengagement agreement had led to the fighting among the mujahideen factions, the rise to power of the Taliban movement, and a growing al Qaeda presence in the country. Following al Qaeda's attacks on U.S. Embassies in eastern Africa in 1998, Washington struck al Qaeda sites with cruise missiles and imposed financial sanctions on the Taliban, but a major intervention to root out the problem was never viewed as a realistic option. The 9/11 attacks changed that perception fundamentally, and barely a month later, on October 7, 2001, the United States launched Operation *Enduring Freedom* to overthrow the Taliban.

The early phases of OEF and Afghan postwar stabilization have been well chronicled and need not be recounted here in detail.[52] Using mainly airpower and small groups of Special Operations Forces and U.S. Marines, the intervention succeeded in tipping the balance decisively in favor of the Taliban's principal opponent, the Northern Alliance, which seized Kabul in early November. Al Qaeda was dislodged, although Osama bin Laden and his immediate cohort escaped. The intervention benefited greatly from timely diplomatic and political initiatives. With strong support from the United States and other Security Council members, the United Nations brokered the so-called Bonn Agreement among major Afghan factions that established an interim administration and a UN assistance mission, and called for the deployment of an international peace-keeping force (the International Security Assistance Force, or ISAF). A moderate Pashtun leader, Hamid Karzai, emerged as a consensus choice to lead the new transitional administration, itself a precarious balance between the Northern Alliance (mainly Tajiks, Uzbeks, and Hazaras) and the more numerous Pashtun tribes, whence the Taliban had first emerged.

These developments imparted much-needed early momentum to the Afghan transition process. Between 2002 and 2005, the Bonn Agreement's roadmap—to include the adoption of a new constitution as well as presidential and parliamentary elections—was followed, and a new, internationally recognized Afghan government came into being. The initial deployments of ISAF troops into Kabul, criticized by some as too timid, helped to counterbalance the Northern Alliance's armed presence there, inducing stability in a tense capital city—something many desperate Baghdadis could only yearn for in the subsequent conflict in Iraq.[53] Meanwhile, President Karzai, backed by occasional U.S. muscle-flexing, succeeded in sidelining a number of warlords, thus reducing the prospect of factional infighting that had loomed so large immediately after the Taliban's fall. The U.S.-led effort to build a new Afghan national army achieved some significant milestones toward creating an indigenous force with national loyalty. Finally, ISAF's subsequent outward expansion in 2004–2005 under the NATO banner helped to extend a presence to less volatile areas of the countryside.

Underlying these positive developments were two basic factors that have clearly worked in favor of the transition. The first was (and remains) a favorable comparison with the situation that preceded it. Difficult though current circumstances might be, very few Afghans yearn for the days of seemingly endless civil war or harshly repressive rule by Talibs. The second positive factor is a distinctively Afghan sense of nationhood. Despite the country's interethnic and tribal tensions, its remote impoverished regions, neighbors with a penchant for meddling, and provincial suspicion of strong central government, there are no longstanding separatist or irredentist claims weighing against the concept of national unity among Afghans. Thus, while each of the contending groups might in principle wish to dominate its competitors, leaving the Afghan union seems to be no group's second choice—a fact that works in favor of indigenous nation building.

Unfortunately, neither these factors nor the auspicious start of the transition process more generally has been able to prevent a progressive loss of momentum since 2006. The principal obstacles are easy to spot: the inherent weakness of state institutions, the death of human capital, inadequate international resources, and a lack of visible progress at the local level to give Afghans hope. As a senior U.S. official put it: "There's no transmission belt that goes between Kabul and the local government. You lost a whole generation of . . . people that can take a government plan and make it real on a local level."[54] Hence, while warlords and other negative actors have been dislodged in some cases, the fact remains that they and their backers in the illicit economy still exert disproportionate influence on the fledging government and aggravate divisions at the provincial level and in the security forces, which are already struggling with corruption.[55]

By far the most daunting problems, however, are found in southeastern Afghanistan and parts of neighboring Pakistan, where turbulent local conditions have abetted the resurgence of a neo-Taliban opposition that is upping the size and frequency of attacks and utilizing tactics honed in the Iraq war.[56] Amidst the violence, the halting pace of reconstruction and economic development and the nonexistent or corrupt government services have frustrated public expectations and provide no real alternative to a booming illicit economy, anchored by the opium trade as well as cross-border smuggling of all kinds and mercenary employment. Ironically, NATO's 2006 expansion into these areas has been greeted less as a sign of international resolve than of weakness, given the widespread perception that the alliance was filling a void in lieu of more capable American units. Overall, one detects an uncomfortable sense that the Afghan transition is losing momentum and public support. Its trajectory is very unclear, and its fate is inextricably linked to Pakistan's ability to curtail the exploitation of its frontier regions as sanctuaries and staging areas for Taliban attacks.

Toppling Saddam: Treading (Too) Lightly

On March 19, 2003, barely 17 months after the invasion of Afghanistan, the United States embarked upon Operation *Iraqi Freedom,* a campaign that, in the President's words, was intended to "disarm Iraq, to free its people and to defend the world from grave danger."[57] In one sense, OIF marked the end of an era: a messy 12-year stalemate following a ceasefire in the 1991 Gulf War characterized by acrimony over sanctions, Iraqi obstruction of UN disarmament resolutions, and periodic confrontations between Iraq, the United States, and its allies over enforcement of two no-fly zones designed to protect Iraq's Kurdish and Shi'a populations from air assaults by Baghdad. In ending one era, however, OIF also ushered in a new chapter in the turbulent history of Iraq, whose destiny in the near term—either a weak, barely unified state that manages to hold together, or an imploding failed state—is not yet clear.

As a target for compellent action, Iraq could not have been more different from Afghanistan (see table 5–1). Though weakened by years of tyranny, sanctions, agricultural and industrial mismanagement, and the regime's exploitation of tribal politics in Saddam's later years, the Iraq of 2003 had not suffered extensive damage from uncontrolled civil strife. The Kurdish areas were largely left alone, thanks in large part to the northern no-fly zone; and the Shi'a rebellion of 1991 had been put down mercilessly by Saddam's Republican Guards. The country possessed large, accessible oil reserves, a highly urbanized society, a public education system, and an extensive, albeit decaying, infrastructure. It also, notably, occupied a prime cultural and geostrategic position: the cradle of Mesopotamian civilization, the sacred heartland of Shi'ite Islam, and the crossroads between the Arab and Persian worlds. Unlike Afghanistan, no one could fairly claim that Iraq was some remote hinterland.

TABLE 5–1. IRAQ AND AFGHANISTAN: A COMPARISON

	Iraq	Afghanistan
Population	27,500,000	31,890,000
Life expectancy (years)	69.31	43.77
Literacy rate (percent)	74.1	28.1
Urban population (percent)	66.9	22.9
Shi'a Muslim (percent)	60–65	19
Sunni Muslim (percent)	32–37	80
Size (km²)	437,072	647,500
Roads (km)	45,500	34,500
Paved roads (km)	38,500	8,000

Sources: *CIA World Factbook*, "Afghanistan," available at <https://www.cia.gov/library/publications/the-world-factbook/geos/af.html>, "Iraq," available at <https://www.cia.gov/library/publications/the-world-factbook/geos/iz.html>; United Nations Department of Economic and Social Affairs Population Division, "World Population Prospects, 2005," available at <http://esa.un.org/unpp/>.

Yet ironically, Afghanistan turned out to be a guidepost for Iraq postwar planning. In a highly publicized speech a month before OIF was launched, then–Secretary of Defense Donald Rumsfeld lauded the merits of a "tread lightly" approach: "The objective is not to engage in what some call nation-building. Rather it's to try to help [the Afghans] so that they can build their own nation. This is an important distinction. . . . [I]t can really be a disservice in some instances because when foreigners come in with international solutions to local problems . . . they can create a dependency." He went on to observe: "Some ask what lessons our experience in Afghanistan might offer for the possibility of a post-Saddam Iraq. . . . The President has not made any decision with respect to the use of force in Iraq, but if he were to do so that principle would hold true."[58] Iraq, Rumsfeld added, offered several advantages not available in the Afghan case that would help keep America's postwar role limited. One was resources—specifically, a solid economic infrastructure and oil wealth. The other advantage he cited, somewhat surprisingly, was time to prepare for the contingency.[59]

In retrospect, this view clearly dominated U.S. planning for postwar Iraq, as extensive chronicling makes clear. First, the overall size of the coalition ground invasion force—roughly 150,000 troops—was much lighter than U.S. military planners had foreseen for such a contingency during the 1990s, when substantial stabilization tasks were assumed. Reinforcing units that could have been used for such missions were withheld once it became clear that Saddam's forces would quickly capitulate.[60]

Second, the postwar planning office, the Office for Reconstruction and Humanitarian Assistance (ORHA), operated essentially as a coordination hub with contracting and advisory capacity; it had no specific plan to restore law and order and certainly no ability to tap operational capacity to do so. Nor did ORHA or its more prominent successor, the Coalition Provisional Authority (CPA), have any capacity to deliver administrative services in lieu of functioning ministries. The core assumption was that while Iraq's leadership would be toppled, the government's ministries could be kept intact.[61] Consequently, on both the military and civilian sides, the United States and its partners lacked sufficient size and strength to take on stabilizing missions more demanding than those presumed in a relatively straightforward restoration of Iraqi authority.[62] Throughout this period, the Pentagon's civilian leadership had strongly contested any suggestion that more troops might be needed to stabilize postwar Iraq than to topple Saddam.[63]

As is now known, realities on the ground soon belied any hope of an easy or straightforward transition. The institutions of government simply did not hold. Once the Iraqi army was defeated, its soldiers fled. The weaker and less professional police simply dissolved. Looting broke out in Baghdad and quickly spread. Militia organizations began to fill the public security vacuum. On the Sunni side, the Fedayeen Saddam, a paramilitary force loyal to the regime and constituted to blunt any Shi'a uprising in southern Iraq, had surprised coalition forces with their harassing attacks in the drive to Baghdad. This had not been the Fedayeen's primary mission, but their tactics within a few months became hallmarks of a growing Sunni insurgency in the central and western parts of the country. Meanwhile, the armed elements of the victorious Shi'ite groups—the Badr Brigades and the Jaysh al-Mahdi—were expanding their presence in Baghdad and southern Iraq, while Kurdish peshmerga fighters consolidated their positions in the three predominantly Kurdish northern provinces.

Despite these disorders, the first few months of the postwar phase were fairly permissive for the U.S. presence. During this timeframe, the CPA launched some of its most ambitious initiatives. On the institutional front, it issued decrees in May 2003 to evict Ba'ath party members from the management layers of public employment and to formally dissolve the Iraqi army and national police. On the political front, it appointed an Interim Governing Council to draft a transitional administrative law—essentially an interim constitution—that laid out steps leading to adoption of a new, permanent constitution. Operationally, U.S. forces began a drawdown and consolidation phase, leaving large tracts of Sunni-dominated Anbar province and the borders of western Iraq essentially uncovered, while U.S. commanders wrestled with the issue of how OIF forces should organize for the conduct of postwar missions. In specific hot spots in central and northern areas, large security sweeps or reported instances of cultural insensitivity or excessive force by U.S. military units triggered a public outcry that played into the hands of the resistance, as would the detainee abuse scandal at Abu Ghraib prison a year later.[64]

Some of these actions were controversial even at the time; others had reverberations that only became clearer in hindsight. The CPA's orders on de-Ba'athification and formal dissolution of the Iraq army fell into the former category. Emblematic of an ambitious "tear-down, rebuild" strategy, they were driven largely by concerns that merely rehabbing Saddam-era institutions would not go nearly far enough to satisfy Iraq's long-repressed Shi'ite community.[65] This concern was not unfounded, to be sure, and the strategy they came to symbolize might have worked had the United States and its coalition members been prepared to play the role of a direct, if interim, provider of public security and services. Absent that willingness, however, these tear-down steps greatly aggravated an already tense situation. Government ministries and the public service sector, already only barely functional, simply hemorrhaged skilled personnel.[66] Tens of thousands of bureaucrats and former soldiers joined the ranks of the unemployed and disaffected precisely as underground dissident groups were expanding their influence in the Sunni heartland.

The steady growth of Sunni insurgent elements, and the marriage of convenience of some of them with jihadist terrorist groups, reinforced already strong American instincts to ramp up a major security capacity-building effort during 2004–2005. Iraqi forces, it was assumed, would be more adept at operating in the local environment than U.S. forces could ever be; they would be in a much better position to earn public trust and confidence, progressively depriving insurgents of an attractive target. But the requisites of this strategy—a truly national security force and a fully representative government that would rise above ethnosectarian loyalties—have been enormously difficult to achieve in practice. The so-called Iraqi Civil Defense Corps (essentially, local militia) proved unreliable in cross-sectarian situations, and even the more professional Iraqi national army that has since come into being has been plagued by questions about its sectarian sympathies and ability to operate effectively in all areas.[67] More broadly, the Herculean task of forging an inclusive national government introduced its own turbulence. The two legislative elections during 2005, required as they were to move the country from a CPA-appointed interim government to a transitional administration (under Ibrahim al-Jaafari) and ultimately a permanent government under Prime Minister Nouri al-Maliki by May 2006, opened the door to a politicizing, sectarian presence in the (de-Ba'athified) public sector as newly appointed ministers filled the void with their own loyalists. The result has been a fractious government that is hard pressed to dispel suspicions that it lacks an even-handed approach to questions of security and civil protections.

For Sunni insurgent groups, the prospect of a new, genuinely national Iraqi government must have been an unsavory prospect, since it would close the door to any return of a Sunni-dominated regime. This may well explain the clear shift—a malign adaptation—in their targeting of Shi'a communities during 2006. Provoking the Shi'a into a sectarian war would drive a huge wedge through a fragile national government, isolate Sunni collaborators from their base of support, make any national reconciliation effort much more problematic, and force an already Shi'ite-dominated government into a more partisan posture. Such conflict had been a consistent goal of the Iraq war's most visible jihadist, Jordanian terrorist Abu Mus'ab al-Zarqawi. With the February 2006 bombing of al-Askari Mosque in Samarra, one of Shi'a Islam's most revered shrines, the door to cross-sectarian violence swung open and, ironically, outlived its principal architect, who died violently in June 2006.

Even so, to label Iraq's conflict as merely an ethnosectarian conflict or a civil war is to greatly oversimplify the reality.[68] Quite apart from Sunni-on-Shi'a violence, the country's major ethnic and sectarian communities are all highly factionalized. Thus, Sunni tribal groups and former Ba'athists have taken up arms against jihadist elements in Anbar province; and the militia of contending Shi'ite factions appeared locked in a spiral of escalating strife in southern cites such as Basra. Meanwhile, Kurdish, Arab, and Turkmen groups are vying for control in and around Kirkuk. Criminal gangs extort, kidnap, and plant bombs for a living. Within Iraq's major contested areas, the violence has been too chaotic to be labeled as war.

Critical Lessons for Stabilization?

For better or worse, American experiences in post-Taliban Afghanistan and post-Saddam Iraq will have a decisive influence upon how the United States chooses to use its power and influence in the years ahead, and with what practical effect. Developments in each country are going to be shaped by a variety of factors: internal power balances within each of the governments in question, as well as the behavior of their opponents, neighboring states, and the larger international community. How these factors will interact is anyone's guess.

Both Afghanistan and Iraq now have democratically elected and internationally recognized governments—a notable achievement but one that comes at a price, for those who would undermine or overthrow these governments are numerous and difficult to dislodge. By late 2007, President Karzai was attempting to forge greater tribal collaboration along Afghanistan's rugged frontier with Pakistan—a difficult task in light of Pakistan's own internal instability—while NATO's ISAF contributors were confronting flagging domestic support for a sustained counterinsurgency campaign in Afghanistan's contested zones.[69] In Iraq, meanwhile, the path of events, at least in the near term, was pointing toward somewhat greater stability. The U.S. military surge appeared to be having some beneficial effects in and around Baghdad, while a spreading Sunni tribal "uprising" against al Qaeda–inspired violence, most notably in Anbar province, was expanding with the assistance of U.S. forces.[70] Yet the great unknown associated with a strategy of empowering armed Sunni elements at the provincial level was how to accomplish this goal without also sowing the seeds of future confrontation between those tribes and a Shi'a-dominated national government.[71] Overall, the political track of Iraq's stabilization—dominated by bitter division among its ethnosectarian communities—provided scant reason for optimism about the country's ability to survive as a unified entity. [72]

Of the two cases, Iraq's situation has been much more burdensome for the United States, and the extent of America's involvement there has deprived Afghanistan of critical U.S. attention and resources at a moment when its own transition appears to be flagging. The cruel irony is that the Iraqi campaign took flight on the wings of good intentions and the buoyant effect of initial success in Afghanistan; it was seen more as a strategic opportunity to transform the Middle East region than the huge liability it would become. Had President Bush, his leadership team, and the U.S. Congress known then what they know now, it is hard to imagine the United States would have made the same, fateful decision to launch the war in 2003, let alone to prosecute it in the manner that it was.

What lessons do these contingencies teach? Surely the most obvious one is that the United States risks losing wars if its postintervention stabilization activities are not accorded a priority commensurate with the task at hand, in much the same fashion that the United States considers the options and capacities of its foe when preparing to fight and win battles. There is good reason to believe that this essential insight, even if not yet fully acted upon, is at least more widely appreciated.[73]

Another critical lesson is the need to keep the quality of "ripeness" in mind when considering compellent action of any type. Not all conflicts are equally ripe from the standpoint of postconflict stabilization. It is commonplace for the United States to judge how easy or hard an armed intervention might be when humanitarian concerns are paramount. By contrast, when interventions are launched mainly on national security grounds, there is a tendency to accept a difficult postconflict stabilization mission as a cost of doing business. That may well be inevitable, even justifiable, so long as policymakers and commanders are clear-eyed about the kinds of problems the country is likely to encounter once the action is launched. In the case of Iraq, key planning assumptions were overly optimistic; the tenor of public statements prior to OIF accentuated the factors conducive to rapid stabilization; and potential problems, such as widespread looting and sabotage, were late in being highlighted or even acknowledged.[74]

In comparing these two cases, the great irony is that the intervention of necessity in Afghanistan turned out to be far more amenable as a target for postconflict stabilization than Iraq, often dubbed the intervention of choice. True, the Afghan war had not reached a "mutually-hurting stalemate," to use William Zartman's famous term, where victory appears so impossible to achieve that all sides opt for a cessation of hostilities as their preferred outcome.[75] Even so, most Afghans had grown weary from years of endless fighting, and the Taliban's hold on power was very tenuous. Not much force was needed to dislodge them. The key factors abetting the stabilization effort in 2001–2002 were Pakistan's quick about-face, abandoning the Taliban in support of the U.S. action; the emergence of Hamid Karzai as a unifying leader from within the very Pashtun community that had produced the Taliban; and the fortuitous fact that the capital city, Kabul, did not become a contested zone.[76]

By contrast, Iraq was anything but ripe for stabilization. The act of toppling Saddam was akin to prying the lid off an overheated pressure cooker, one in which a number of unresolved ethnosectarian pressures bubbled just below the surface. Inevitably, these pent-up tensions were going to be released—tensions that in the Afghan case had been consumed by years of civil war. What is more, any real effort to build democratic order in Iraq would mean shifting the reins of power to a long-repressed majority, in effect convincing the winners to be generous in their victory and the losers to be gracious in accepting their minority status in a new dispensation. In Afghanistan, this kind of far-reaching adjustment was not required. It was required in Iraq, but the psychological hurdles on both sides have been enormous. General Anthony Zinni was prescient when he observed in 1999, "Saddam is going to go. . . . it will be sooner than anyone thinks. The trouble is that the problem begins when Saddam goes."[77]

The "unripeness" of Iraq or any other case is not an argument against intervention per se; decisive force may need to be used when the stakes really are high. But it is an argument for planning that includes rigorous alternative scenarios, realistic assumptions, and, above all, a preparedness to commit necessary resources to the mission. This is a third important lesson that clearly was not observed in Iraq. There was substantial planning for a contingency that did not occur—a humanitarian crisis on the scale of the 1991 Gulf War aftermath—but much less for the contingency that actually did occur—the collapse of Iraqi state institutions. Moreover, an ambitious tear-down and rebuild strategy was very much at odds with U.S. preferences for a modest and diminishing postwar military presence, aimed mainly at capacity building, a preference driven (not unreasonably) by concerns about a large Western force quickly taking on the trappings of an occupier in a Muslim nation.[78]

A fourth lesson—apt in both cases—concerns the regional environment. Stabilization efforts have little hope of success unless neighboring states see it as being in their interests to buy into the process. If they have reason to be hostile, or if their own abutting territory is remote and difficult to govern, spoilers will seek sanctuary, and the presence of refugee populations will serve as a ready recruitment pool. What is needed from the stabilizers' perspective is a strategy of counterleverage and inducement aimed at driving wedges between spoilers and their external patrons. This kind of wedge-driving strategy has been accomplished in the past, but it takes time, ingenuity, and a major investment in painstaking diplomatic engagement.[79]

The fifth lesson concerns coalition management in the context of regional stabilization. U.S. policymakers have long approached the coalition-building challenge with a degree of ambivalence; while multinational coalitions can help to distribute burdens, symbolize international resolve, and provide sustained presence, they can also reduce flexibility when national caveats are invoked that produce internal frictions over rules of engagement and concepts of operation. Whether the benefits outweigh costs in any given case is not always a straightforward calculation. To compound matters, neither Iraq nor Afghanistan fits the more typical post–Cold War model of a regionally led stabilization mission in which the United States provides vital enabling assistance but not the bulk of the troops. In these cases, in fact, the Americans provided the mass and the partners assisted by filling key niches.

The implications of this role reversal have not been so apparent in Iraq, where OIF's contested international legitimacy and the absence of major Islamic troop contributors have relegated coalition partners, with a few exceptions, to purely supporting roles. In Afghanistan, however, ISAF has assumed growing significance, starting in Kabul and then expanding into relatively secure areas to the north and west. It also has piloted novel ways of bringing developmental and diplomatic expertise to its headquarters. Unfortunately, its progressive expansion to more turbulent areas of southeastern

Afghanistan has been widely seen as a cover for U.S. disengagement and hence as a sign of weakness—a perception that resurgent Taliban elements have been eager to exploit. The lesson here is straightforward: in nonpermissive environments, multinational coalitions—even relatively robust ones—function best when their mission is to secure rear areas. Casting them as substitutes for U.S. military power in contested areas is bound to be a gamble.

This brings us to the final lesson: the need to prepare for the future. The Iraqi and Afghan experiences have illustrated clearly that relative to high-intensity combat, the United States remains underinvested in capabilities that are critical to the task of stabilizing war-torn countries or regions. If circumstances arise in which the United States must bear the main burden, even within a multinational context, what steps must Washington take to better utilize its resources and people to conduct these difficult operations, now and in the future?

GETTING AMERICA'S HOUSE IN ORDER

In conflict stabilization missions, success hinges upon harmonizing and, ultimately, integrating the activities of many different departments and agencies. Changing the way governments operate is never easy, but it is absolutely essential for two reasons. The first is America's uneven post-9/11 track record. The United States finds itself bogged down in two highly significant and expensive missions that have not gone as well as expected. There is plenty of scope for legitimate debate about the factors that drove the country to intervene, particularly in the case of Iraq, but less room for dissent on the proposition that failure in either case, or both, would carry hugely negative consequences for the United States and for regional and global security more broadly.

Second, the road is not likely to end with Iraq and Afghanistan. As this chapter's earlier discussion of trends indicated, the United States will almost certainly face future situations where it deems that large-scale stabilization operations are warranted, either for reasons of national security or because significant diplomatic and humanitarian interests are at stake. If so, that will usher in tough decisions on whether and how to lead or support such missions, and in concert with which international partners. The past, in short, is a prologue.

Given these imperatives, why then should reform be such a daunting task? The answer is simple: it is not just about resources. America's military, diplomatic, intelligence, and development assistance communities have viewed their primary missions, to greater or lesser degrees, in ways that give short shrift to this complex endeavor. Consequently, any effort at real reform must seek to alter deep-set institutional identities, cultures, and mindsets, and to do so in a larger political climate that harbors ambivalence toward anything resembling Vietnam-like counterinsurgency or Somalia-like nation-building excursions. For every advocate who would see greater U.S. investment in these missions as a safeguard against ill-considered or wasteful intervention, one could find a critic who would see such activity as simply opening the door to new quagmires.

Charting a New Course

In the wake of OIF's initial setbacks, the Bush administration took some notable steps to launch a process of reform within the Executive Branch. It created a new State Department office to focus specifically upon regional stabilization. This entity—the Office of the Coordinator for Reconstruction and Stabilization (S/CRS)—received explicit tasking by the President to serve as a coordinating hub for interagency work on country-specific risk assessments as well as on conflict prevention, mitigation, and mission planning, including the integration of civilian and military contingency plans.[80] Secretary of State Condoleezza Rice also launched a larger initiative on "transformational diplomacy" as a vehicle for repositioning and retooling America's diplomatic capacity to lend greater assistance to developmental, stabilization, reconstruction, and democratic reform activities in the world's most populous and turbulent regions.[81] Meanwhile, the Pentagon's leadership was already pressing ahead with a new departmental directive that identified stability operations as a "core" U.S. military mission that "should be given priority comparable to combat operations."[82]

Taken collectively, these initiatives represent a positive and commendable impulse for reform. The hard question is how effectively the vision animating the policy can be implemented.[83] Clearly, those leading the effort on these initiatives find themselves buffeted by strong cross currents. While the Iraq and Afghanistan contingencies have created pressures for change and provide a venue for testing new operational concepts, the sheer size and complexity of these missions distract high-level attention, energy, and resources from systemic reform efforts. The Office of the Coordinator for Reconstruction and Stabilization has had difficulty gaining visibility or funding, despite some useful piloting efforts. What is more, the designation of the State Department as interagency lead for this mission has not settled the larger problem of building a productive civil-military division of labor. Defense leaders have expressed their unhappiness over the State Department's inability to recruit adequate numbers of field personnel for civilian missions in Iraq and Afghanistan.[84] State officials, for their part, have been uncomfortable with the presumption in Defense guidance that the U.S. military should be prepared to carry out reconstruction and governance activities when civil capacity is not available.

Without question, the barriers to reform are enormous. One of the most unyielding remains the civilian community's dearth of qualified personnel—as a U.S. military officer observed, its lack of "bench strength." The State Department and its U.S. Agency for International Development (USAID) are still feeling the effects of major post–Cold War personnel cuts. USAID's numbers alone dropped from a peak of 15,000 during the height of Vietnam War to less than 2,000 by 2002.[85] While it has recovered slightly, the agency continues to grapple with skyrocketing retirement eligibility within its ranks and has had to rely heavily on private contractors for its field work as well as, more problematically, for the management and oversight of its programs.[86] Beyond the human resources problem, the prevailing development philosophy of the past two decades—enshrined in the so-called Washington Consensus[87]—has focused largely on reducing state barriers to trade and investment, while official aid flows for poverty alleviation, public health, and other priorities have steered increasingly toward service delivery via nongovernmental implementing partners. While these steps were logical responses to excessive regulation and corruption risks, comparatively little attention was paid to areas where the public administration of recipient states needed to be strengthened.[88] Hence, beyond the ambit of democracy reform—which itself is viewed as more promotional than developmental priority—governance building has been a neglected area.

The Pentagon is not without its own problems. The U.S. Armed Forces certainly took their share of post–Cold War cutbacks. During the 1990s, the prevailing mantra—derived largely from the Army's doctrinal perspective—was "train for war, adapt for peace." The skills needed for peacekeeping or stabilization missions, it was argued, could be honed with "just-in-time" training because they constituted a lesser included case of military operational art. Left unclear, however, was exactly within which larger category these skills were included. Multipurpose light infantry units traditionally have covered "operations other than war" contingencies (for example, peacekeeping and humanitarian assistance), but the equipment necessary for stabilization operations in today's environment may need to be heavier (more armored) and more mobile than the light infantry possesses, while the specialty skills are more akin to those embedded in U.S. Special Operations Forces (SOF): civil affairs, psychological operations, cultural and regional expertise, or unconventional warfare. Not only are these SOF capabilities more specialized and require longer lead times to build, but they also typically are scarce resources that are pulled in competing directions and, oftentimes, zealously guarded for other missions, such as strategic reconnaissance and direct action in the counterterror campaign.

For the Pentagon's stability operations reformers, then, the question is where to embed the expertise. To say everyone plays a part is analytically correct. Bureaucratically, however, firm ownership of the mission needs to be established, or else it will founder. That has not yet occurred.

A Down Payment on Reform

The job of achieving major institutional change will require a long-term commitment that bridges administrations and elicits sustained congressional support. This surely will not happen overnight. Within the next few years, the optimal reform strategy is to find the right combination of near-term steps that can provide pressure points for larger changes. Seven priorities deserve close attention:

Improving situational awareness. Despite the controversies swirling around the U.S. Intelligence Community in recent years, it need not be a Sisyphean task to improve American understanding of regional instability or conflict dynamics. Substantial pressures are already being felt by the community to improve its utilization of open sources, its human collection, and its analytic work on sociocultural phenomena and transnational threats. Improved performance in all these areas will work to the benefit of stabilization priorities. The State Department's effort, led by S/CRS, to pilot more rigorous conflict assessments is a positive initial step and, if institutionalized, could serve as an important baseline for progress. The key ingredient is consistent consumer (that is, policymaker) demand that focuses analytic attention on the right kinds of information requirements.[89] Improved situational awareness would help greatly in shaping choices regarding the terms of entry (for example, forceful or negotiated) in particular contingencies, and in anticipating how U.S. presence would reshape conflict dynamics within a given country or region. It would also help in recapturing the concept of ripeness as part of the calculus policymakers must go through for mobilizing expeditionary operations that will have stabilization or reconstruction mission elements.

Building balanced planning expertise. Arguably, no chasm between the defense and civilian parts of the Executive Branch is wider than in the sphere of planning. The U.S. military is steeped in a culture that demands extensive planning activity and has dedicated staffs devoted to this task, especially in the joint community. Civilian agencies do not abjure planning (in contrast to the stereotype that most military counterparts have of them), but their planning focus is largely programmatic, not expeditionary, and it is typically performed by the same (often understaffed) Embassy teams that carry the burden of implementation. The tempo of stabilization activities across government is closing this gap. However, there have long been mutual inhibitions regarding the involvement of interagency partners in the Defense Department's so-called deliberate and adaptive planning processes, and the current Presidential directive on this topic conveys the clear intent that civil and military planning ought to be integrated but assigns no ultimate responsibility.[90] There is no a priori reason why mere coordination cannot suffice, provided the principals are in sync and two-way communication is good. The key element for stabilization planning, at either the strategic or operational level, is to ensure the process includes regional experts who know a given region's sociopolitical environment, program managers and specialists who know the instrumentalities to be utilized by the mission, and strategists who can bridge both worlds and offset the parochialism of the other two communities.

Meeting doctrinal, equipment, and force sizing needs. Stability operations have never fit comfortably under the rubric of high-intensity conventional warfare, except possibly when employed to separate large hostile (but consenting) armies in places like the Golan Heights. In today's less permissive environments, stabilization is best viewed as a subset of irregular warfare, and it shares with counterinsurgency, another species of irregular warfare, many similar doctrinal precepts: to wit, a focus on winning over civil populations rather than simply suppressing enemies; establishing a safe and secure environment; the requirement for good intelligence and cultural awareness; keeping use of force to a minimum effective level; and assisting in building local self-reliance. From this standpoint, the U.S. Army–Marine Corps collaboration on developing new counterinsurgency doctrine provides a valuable assist to education and training on stabilization methods throughout the land forces more broadly.[91] In addition, many of the systems that are critical for irregular warfare—armored vehicles, nonlethal weapons, rapidly deployable demining/explosive ordnance disposal capacity, and air defense countermeasures—are also quite relevant for stability operations, especially in urban settings, and chronic equipment shortfalls in these areas need to be remedied. The big challenges associated with counterinsurgency are less about the principles by which it is conducted than about recognizing the circumstances when it may be warranted, and how in particular to prevent one's operation from becoming hostage to faulty or deliberately misleading intelligence in situations where local actors attempt to manipulate the outside intervener for their own purposes. As for force sizing and shaping, the key issue is determining how much interagency capacity can reliably be counted on in future contingencies. The State Department recognizes that it cannot maintain the full spectrum of skilled personnel that might be needed for various aspects of stabilization or counterinsurgency missions, and it has been looking at ways to develop a civilian reserve corps that could tap into expertise in and outside of government. How best to prepare, field, and protect these civilians in nonpermissive environments and to care for injured or wounded personnel remain difficult unresolved questions.

Assisting governance-building activity. The United States has poured enormous energy into the training and equipping of indigenous military and police organizations as a vital part of the stabilization repertoire, not only in Iraq and Afghanistan but also in the Balkans, West Africa, and East Asia. While this capacity-building mission has encountered its share of serious strains—including a tempo of activity well in excess of what U.S. Special Operations Forces, as the traditional training resource, could provide—it is outpacing the more difficult process of assisting the growth of indigenous governance and rule of law institutions. This governance effort needs to be strengthened at two levels: top-down assistance at the level of national ministries, in the form of embedded advisors, and bottom-up assistance where government is a local service provider, in the form of district or provincial-level reconstruction teams (PRTs). Afghanistan has been a useful venue for experimentation with the PRT concept, but U.S. and coalition partners have had less success in assisting ministerial consolidation. Both approaches are key to ensuring that an enabled indigenous security sector does not overwhelm the government it is meant to support.

Civil-military training. Once it became clear that the forces committed to OEF and OIF would have to stay in the field much longer than expected, it would have been logical for civilian and military agencies to consider ways to develop joint predeployment education and training opportunities for new echelons of personnel rotating into theater. In fact, such efforts have lagged considerably, impeding early familiarity with the mission's civil-military division of labor at the field level and missing an opportunity to shorten the timeframe in which newly arriving personnel begin to contribute more than they are absorbing. The highest priority for joint training would be for personnel to be embedded in ministries and deployed in civil-military settings such as PRTs.

Forging closer links to international and regional organizations. While the United States remains preoccupied with the conduct of its own operations, it has significant interests across a growing range of multinational stability operations. The NATO stabilization effort in southeastern Afghanistan is a vital endeavor, and the alliance has staked its credibility on a successful outcome. Less well understood is an ongoing surge in UN field operations, driven in part by new or expanding peacekeeping missions in southern Lebanon, Nepal, Haiti, and Sudan, and the likelihood of new starts in Chad, Somalia, and the Central African Republic. These missions rely upon a coalition of troop-contributing countries from the developing world—most notably in South Asia—as well as the financial and enabling assistance of major funders in Europe and North America. Washington has a clear security interest in working with both communities to strengthen the capacity of the United Nations and key regional organizations to meet expanding commitments, and it has a number of ongoing initiatives, such as the Global Peace Operations Initiative, that might be optimized for this purpose.

Strengthening lessons learned. For its educational value, nothing compares to operational experience. Greater priority should be accorded to innovating new methods for distilling experiences of previous as well as ongoing operations. In fact, although the lessons learned enterprise has been a perennial favorite for reformers, strengthening the process has been hard to accomplish in practice. Parts of the U.S. military perform this mission exceptionally well, but efforts across the defense community—let alone the interagency community—are uneven. Moreover, on the military side, the analytic work has focused mainly at the tactical level, which—although clearly a necessary element in unit training—is not sufficient for judging the impacts of practices in key areas like governance, development, or reconstruction.[92] Finally, it has been difficult to capture insights from non-U.S. stabilization efforts, and building stronger channels of communication for such purposes with the United Nations and regional organizations remains a work in progress. U.S. Joint Forces Command is playing a useful role as a locus for integrated efforts, and it benefits from collaborative relations with civilian agencies; but the learning process overall is only as strong as its constituent parts, beginning with collection and ending with acceptance, absorption, and dissemination by commanders and policymaking levels of government.

A FINAL WORD

Can these reforms succeed? It is too early to say. The foregoing list of priority areas is only a starting point—a reasonable line of attack against the institutional, political, and other barriers that currently stand in the way of major enhancements in U.S. stabilization capabilities. And those barriers are truly formidable. With so much turbulence in present-day Iraq and Afghanistan, and yet with so much at stake in those transitions, America's traditional ambivalences about this issue will be on display for a long time to come: driven, on the one hand, by a palpable sense of weariness with costly, open-ended entanglements but anchored, on the other hand, by an abiding concern with the threatening or disruptive potential of uncontrolled regional violence.

Taken together, the three key tasks outlined above—mitigating "fault-line" conflicts that could bolster transnational terrorist groups or spur the spread of WMD, strengthening modernizing states whose collapse would have ripple effects, and building stronger humanitarian protection capability—provide a hierarchy for sorting through priorities but not a detailed guide to action. A posture of selective engagement built around these priorities may have the best chance of generating a broad consensus within an increasingly restive American body politic in the foreseeable future. That means, unavoidably, a greater stress upon building the capacity of would-be partners to act, coupled with a heightened concern for how U.S. involvement might alter the conflict dynamics in a given situation. It does not mean passivity or risk aversion, but it does mean greater caution. While Iraq may have insulated the Nation from future contingencies whose necessity is less than immediately clear, the experience has not changed the larger realities that require the United States to be prepared to lead or support major regional stabilization efforts in the face of spreading instability or escalating violence.

Chapter Six

Engaging Other Major Powers

JOSEPH MCMILLAN, EUGENE B. RUMER, AND PHILLIP C. SAUNDERS

C hina, Russia, and India each play major roles in the international system, and each one presents unique foreign policy challenges for the United States and other countries. All three exert substantial influence beyond their borders, due in varying degrees to geographic or demographic size, economic clout, or military capabilities. While China and India are increasingly confident, rising powers, an uncertain, declining Russia is looking for ways to preserve its international influence.

Each of these three powers faces greater challenges at home than abroad. Any external threats they will have to confront are likely to be exceeded by the challenges of social, economic, and political modernization brought on by domestic pressures and globalization. Their ability to tackle these challenges successfully should not be taken for granted. The failure of any one of these countries is likely to be fraught with far-reaching consequences for all of them and their neighbors, as well as the United States. All three countries are, in some sense, evolving states—aspiring to be, but not yet in the camp of, modern, well-governed states that are deeply integrated into the global economy and clear about which international norms they will embrace. This leads to some uncertainty about their role in the international system over the next decade and how to best encourage their evolution in positive directions.

A NEW MAJOR POWER DYNAMIC

During the latter half of the 20th century, ideological differences kept U.S.-Soviet relations implacably hostile, U.S.-China relations hostile to circumspect, and U.S.-Indian relations distant and sometimes strained. Today, there is no fundamental polarizing issue among the great powers. How well the United States manages its relations with each will be a major test for American leadership in the years ahead. As the 2006 U.S. National Security Strategy (NSS) observed, "We must seize the opportunity—unusual in historical terms—of the absence of fundamental conflict between the great powers. Another priority, therefore, is preventing the reemergence of great power rivalries that divided the world in previous eras."[1]

U.S. stakes in China, Russia, or India should not be mistaken for identical interests and priorities—far from it. Despite substantial mutual dependencies—trade, energy, and certain global and regional security concerns—that the United States has to take into account in its dealings with these countries, each of these relationships represents a mix of cooperative and competitive elements that require continuous and careful balancing. While important strides have been made over the past decade in major power cooperation to combat terrorism, thwart proliferation of weapons of mass destruction (WMD), and stabilize certain regional conflicts, differences over the proper handling of some of these issues as well as divergent national interests on these and other matters (particularly the role of democratic governance) could limit effective joint action.

For the United States, working effectively with these powers will not be easy. All three bilateral relationships are in flux. There is no tradition of stable relations and regular consultations to fall back upon. All three countries are wary of U.S. dominance in the international system, have criticized the U.S. exercise of its military power, and have concerns that the U.S. military presence in neighboring regions (for example, Japan, Georgia, and Pakistan) is aiding or abetting local problems. All three remain unconvinced that adapted U.S. alliances and security partnerships in their regions (as discussed in chapter seven) can be used to advance mutual security interests.

As a matter of sheer economic power, dynamism, and geopolitical ambition, China represents the biggest challenges and opportunities for U.S. policy. Successful beyond belief in its historic task of modernization, with two decades of rapid economic growth, it is quickly emerging as the only potential peer competitor to the United States in Eurasia and the world. Neither Russia nor India is likely to match China in the years to come in terms of their geopolitical ambition or impact on U.S. interests. Its appetite for energy alone, projected to continue to grow at very high rates for the foreseeable future, is bound to make China an ever more ambitious player in global energy markets.

As China continues to reassert its great power status, the challenge for U.S. diplomacy is likely to be far more complicated than Cold War–style containment or straightforward great power competition for resources, access, and influence. The complicating factor here is that China's future growth and social cohesion are not to be taken for granted. A China that stumbles in its pursuit of economic and political modernization would be fraught with numerous negative consequences, both economic and strategic, for the United States.

Russia, buoyed by high energy and commodity prices after a period of economic decline, domestic turmoil, and international contraction in the 1990s, is resurgent and seeking to capitalize on its newfound prosperity as an energy superpower. This concept, articulated by President Vladimir Putin, implicitly acknowledges the loss of Russia's superpower status. But the country's wealth, legacy, and size make it more than just a mere regional power, and Moscow thus seeks to carve itself a special place in the international system. Whether Russia succeeds at this remains to be seen, but the competitive spirit has returned to U.S.-Russian relations throughout the regions around Russia's periphery, as well as in several global hotspots—the Persian Gulf, the Levant, and the Korean Peninsula.

For the United States, growing tensions with Russia pose a difficult foreign policy challenge. Russia retains considerable ability to act as a spoiler, able to undercut any number of important initiatives—from solving Kosovo's final status to stopping Iran's pursuit of nuclear weapons. But U.S. efforts to contain or punish Russia not only would be of questionable effectiveness, but also would risk undermining Russia's still-fragile recovery. The consequences of a stumbling Russia would adversely affect a variety of U.S. interests—from renewed concerns about WMD proliferation to global oil shocks to impact on Russia's neighbors—Ukraine, Georgia, or Kazakhstan. Moreover, U.S. pressures on Russia in retaliation for its policy vis-à-vis Ukraine, Kosovo, Iran, or Central Asia could unintentionally undermine Russia's already precarious position relative to China. The United States would punish Russia but at the same time would deny itself the potential opportunity for delicate geopolitical balancing between the two Eurasian powers.

India's status as a relative newcomer to the club of major powers and the absence of geopolitical rivalries with the United States make it the most likely of the three Eurasian great powers to become a U.S. partner. But these very same factors that make the relationship between the United States and India so promising also represent significant constraints on this nascent partnership. India's status as a great Eurasian power cannot conceal the nation's poverty, uneven development, and growing pains that indicate that it is far from realizing its full potential. Moreover, just as with China, India's impressive recent progress is encouraging, but sustainment of that progress is hardly guaranteed.

India's domestic modernization requirements in turn impose a series of constraints on its policies, both domestic and international, as well as on its ability to act as a full-fledged partner to the United States. While U.S.-Indian relations do not suffer from any inherent contradictions, India's needs, from defense and security to energy and trade, could on occasion trump considerations of strategic partnership with the United States. The question, then, is how those elements of competition and cooperation will balance each other. In situations requiring tradeoffs in relation to the United States and third parties—Iran, China, Pakistan, or Russia, to name just a few countries that figure quite differently on respective U.S. and Indian agendas—the United States is unlikely to be in a position to take India's partnership for granted.

Thus, for the foreseeable future, U.S. relations with these three major powers will not be as adversarial and zero sum as in the past. Given U.S. global reach and other power asymmetries, each of these countries has more at stake in promoting relations with the United States than in joining with each other to counterbalance U.S. power. Achieving balance is the main challenge for the United States as it strives to promote its interests with regard to these major powers while protecting and advancing its principles.

This chapter assesses the key strategic challenges that the United States confronts in managing relations with the three main centers of global power—China, Russia, and India. The outlook for the individual powers in the next 10 to 15 years is explored, with a focus on domestic factors as drivers of international behavior; the uncertainty surrounding the outcome of domestic change in these countries and its impact on their international behavior; the relationship of mutual dependency each has with the United States; and the resulting constraints on U.S. ability to influence their behavior at home and abroad through pressure or incentives.

CHINA: THE RISING POWER

Of all the major powers, China poses the most difficult challenges for the United States. Yet concerns about potential future conflicts have not stopped economic, political, and military interactions from deepening over the last two decades. China has become important to a wide range of U.S. interests, from the management of North Korea to the availability of cheap consumer goods. For its part, the United States is a key market and is uniquely positioned to facilitate or obstruct Chinese goals such as Taiwan unification and China's emergence as a great power.

China's increasing global economic role has created concerns that economic growth is underwriting an ambitious military modernization program that threatens Taiwan and that may alter the balance of power in the Asia-Pacific region. These concerns are reinforced by China's growing influence in Asia and increasing economic and diplomatic involvement in regions such as Latin America and Africa. Some Americans worry about the ability of U.S. firms and workers to compete with goods produced by inexpensive Chinese labor and with state-owned firms that have access to capital at below-market rates.

To complicate matters further, China's progress has been uneven. Political reforms have lagged and economic development has benefited some regions more than others, thus adding to internal pressures and raising concerns about the country's long-term stability.

The view from Beijing is equally ambivalent. Leaders and scholars recognize the importance of the United States for China, and Beijing seeks stable, cooperative relations with Washington. Yet many Chinese elites believe that the United States seeks to subvert the Chinese political system and to contain the country's economic and military potential. Evidence cited includes U.S. economic sanctions, efforts to limit Chinese acquisitions of military and dual-use technology, alleged tacit support for Taiwan independence, and even the accidental bombing of the Chinese embassy in Belgrade in 1999.

RECENT TRENDS IN U.S.–CHINA RELATIONS

Given these concerns, most observers have been surprised by the stability in Sino-U.S. relations during the George W. Bush administration and give it relatively high marks for its handling of China. During the 2000 presidential campaign, then-Governor Bush and prominent campaign advisors called for treating China as a "strategic competitor" rather than a "strategic partner."[2] The new administration's regional approach deliberately deemphasized China's importance relative to U.S. allies in Asia and sought to improve ties with democratic India as a potential counterweight. The collision between a U.S. EP–3 reconnaissance plane and a Chinese fighter in April 2001 might easily have sent relations into a tailspin, but the incident was resolved diplomatically and did not leave a broad negative impact on relations. By the time

Secretary of State Colin Powell visited China in July 2001, the Bush administration's references to "strategic competitor" were replaced by statements about "constructive, forward-looking relations" with China.[3]

The shift toward a more cooperative relationship with China was under way prior to the September 11 terrorist attacks on the United States. The reordering of U.S. security priorities following 9/11 reinforced this trend, as the war on terror displaced China as the top concern on the U.S. security agenda. Chinese leaders exploited the opportunity to improve relations by declaring support for the war on terror. Bush administration officials praised Chinese leaders for choosing the right side and pursued a series of summit meetings with them, including one in October 2002 with Jiang Zemin at President Bush's ranch. The shift in the U.S. agenda made it easier for China to cooperate with the United States and has shielded China from U.S. demands that are harder to satisfy. China has not emerged as a target of the Bush administration's campaign of democracy promotion. In 2003, the administration declined to support a United Nations Human Rights Commission resolution calling for investigation of human rights conditions in China.

The Bush administration's overall approach to China reflects considerable continuity with the policies in place by the second term of the Clinton administration.[4] Rather than defining China as an ally or an adversary, the United States has tried to reap the economic and security benefits of cooperation while hedging against the potential emergence of China as a threat.[5] This approach reflects uncertainty about China's political and military evolution.

The U.S. strategy has two elements. The first emphasizes cooperation and integration into global institutions (including the global economy) as a means of influencing Chinese behavior and political evolution in positive directions. The second emphasizes maintenance of U.S. military capabilities and alliances as a hedge against the possibility of China becoming aggressive or threatening. The challenge is to keep the two elements in balance, so that overemphasis on cooperation does not leave the United States in an unfavorable position and overemphasis on the military dimension does not stimulate nationalism and push China toward confrontation. One additional concern is that treating China as an inevitable threat could become a self-fulfilling prophecy.

Whereas the Clinton administration's approach to China downplayed the military dimension of U.S. strategy and employed ambiguity and quiet diplomacy rather than sanctions to address concerns such as Chinese proliferation activities, the Bush administration's approach reflects the view that differences should be expressed frankly and that clear statements of U.S. commitments and capabilities reinforce deterrence and reduce the likelihood of challenges to U.S. interests.

The Bush administration has frequently used sanctions against Chinese firms for violations of U.S. nonproliferation laws and has been vocal about disagreements on issues such as missile defense and space weapons. It has also been more open than the Clinton administration about efforts to improve U.S. military capabilities in Asia and to increase security cooperation with Japan, India, and Taiwan. In addition to authorizing the sale to Taiwan of advanced weapons (including diesel submarines that had been denied by previous administrations), President Bush clarified the U.S. security commitment by declaring that the country would do "whatever it takes" to help Taiwan defend itself.

Within the context of a hedge strategy, the Bush administration has sought to increase cooperation with China on a range of important economic and security issues, including energy security, nonproliferation, and counterterrorism. It has also sought to shape Chinese thinking about its own long-term interests by proposing the vision of China as a responsible stakeholder that helps maintain the current international system. This concept, elaborated in a 2005 speech by then-Deputy Secretary of State Robert Zoellick, recognizes China's increasing impact on the international system and seeks to obtain Chinese support in sustaining the global institutions and norms that have contributed to its remarkable economic success.[6] It represents an effort to expand the scope of U.S. and Chinese common interests and to place potential conflicts of interests within a larger framework of cooperation.

China's options in dealing with the United States are limited. The traditional strategy for middle powers to constrain a dominant power is to seek formal or informal allies to create a balance of power. However, the current U.S. position is so powerful that other countries are reluctant to align themselves overtly against the United States.

The failure of China's 1999–2001 campaign to mobilize international opposition to U.S. ballistic missile defense (BMD) plans shows the limits of such a strategy. For China, its "strategic partnership" with Russia was a crucial means of dissuading the United States from pursuing BMD. Yet Russia ultimately made its own arrangements with the United States by signing the Strategic Offensive Reductions Treaty in May 2002, without taking China's strategic interests into account. Other countries may also be concerned about U.S. dominance, but their unwillingness to oppose the United States limits China's options. Chinese leaders also recognize that provocative behavior is likely to backfire and result in a more confrontational U.S. policy toward China.

Hence, China apparently has decided to accommodate the United States and acquiesce to U.S. policies that run counter to Beijing's preferences. China has accepted a number of U.S. actions with minimal or pro forma complaint, including sales of advanced weapons to Taiwan, deployment of U.S. military forces to Central Asian bases not far from China's borders, diplomatic pressure on North Korea and Iran, and the U.S. invasions of Afghanistan and Iraq.

The decision to accommodate Washington has had a positive impact on the tone of bilateral relations. Chinese official media have moderated criticism of the United States; Chinese officials have participated in dialogues with their U.S. counterparts on a range of economic and security issues; and China has increased security cooperation where U.S. and Chinese strategic interests coincide (such as counterterrorism and in joint efforts to respond to the North Korean nuclear weapons crisis). Zoellick's speech sparked widespread debate in China about how to translate the concept of responsible stakeholder and whether it was in China's interests to accept the current rules and norms of the international system. Chinese president Hu Jintao eventually endorsed the concept during his April 2006 summit with President Bush, agreeing that "China and the United States are not only stakeholders, but they should also be constructive partners."[7] Hu's phrasing highlighted China's view that both countries have global responsibilities and placed acceptance of the stakeholder concept within the context of an ongoing, positive U.S.-China relationship.

While avoiding direct confrontation with Washington, China has sometimes pursued policies such as economic assistance to North Korea and efforts to limit U.S. influence in Central Asia that complicate U.S. diplomatic strategies and make it harder for the United States to achieve its objectives. China has also accelerated efforts to improve its military capabilities; its military budget rose by approximately 17 percent in 2001 and 2002, with double-digit real increases continuing in 2003, 2004, and 2005 (see table 6–1). The official 2006 military budget was approximately $35 billion, but the Defense Intelligence Agency estimates China's total defense spending was between $70 billion and $135 billion in 2006.[8] China's 2007 defense budget was announced as $44.9 billion, which was cited as a 17.8 percent increase over the 2006 figure.[9]

MANAGING A MULTIFACETED RELATIONSHIP

The relative stability of U.S.-China relations during the Bush administration's tenure conceals underlying tensions and potential conflicts. The wide range of U.S. interests affected by China requires an approach that can deal with both the cooperative and competitive dimensions of Sino-U.S. relations.

In some areas, shared interests make cooperation the dominant element of the relationship. Examples include stability in the Asia-Pacific region, a global system that supports trade and economic development, a denuclearized Korean Peninsula, and counterterrorism. Common and overlapping interests provide a foundation for cooperation on bilateral and multilateral bases. The task is defining and aligning U.S. and Chinese interests and finding ways to cooperate effectively. The existence of common interests does not guarantee that cooperation will actually take place.

In other areas, engagement is an important way to encourage China to redefine its interests and change its behavior. Examples of areas where engagement is appropriate

TABLE 6–1. CHINESE DEFENSE SPENDING, 2001–2006

	2000	2001	2002	2003	2004	2005	2006
Renminbi	121.29	144.20	169.44	190.79	211.70	247.76	283.80
Dollars (in billions)*	15.21	18.08	21.24	23.92	26.54	31.06	35.58

*Converted from renminbi at a rate of 7.98 RMB=$1 US.

Sources: State Council Information Office, *White Papers on China's National Defense* (2000, 2002, 2004) and *White Paper on China's Endeavors for Arms Control, Disarmament, and Non-Proliferation* (2005); "China's Defense Budget to Increase 14.7% in 2006," *People's Daily*, March 5, 2006, available at <english.people.com.cn/200603/05/eng20060305_247883.html>.

include nonproliferation, human rights, constructive Chinese participation in multi-lateral institutions, economic policy, protection of intellectual property rights, and environmental protection. In these cases, common interests may exist but go unrecognized, or the two countries may have differing priorities. Sanctions and incentives may sometimes play a useful role in sensitizing China to U.S. concerns and stimulating policy change. However, the core mechanisms are education and inclusion in international institutions and organizations in order to influence Chinese thinking and definitions of interests. This process seeks to build and strengthen groups within China—in and outside of the government—who believe that the changes the United States seeks are also in China's interest.

Engagement has had a significant impact on Chinese economic policy and nonproliferation behavior. In both areas, Chinese leaders and officials have been exposed to Western views and learned how international mechanisms work, built a core of technical expertise within China, and eventually redefined China's national interests and policies. In economic policy, fellowships in Western universities, technical advice from the World Bank and Western experts, and participation in international organizations have dramatically increased the sophistication of Chinese economic policymakers and supported reforms that have moved China toward a more market-oriented economy.

A similar process has occurred in nonproliferation, where China has gradually shifted from a stance of regarding it as inherently discriminatory against developing countries to a position where China now accepts nonproliferation norms and participates in key organizations (including export control regimes that had previously been anathema), and it has passed domestic export control laws that meet international standards. Although the United States still has concerns about Chinese proliferation behavior, China has made remarkable progress, considering where it started.[10]

Nonetheless, tensions between Chinese policies and U.S. interests sometimes call for more assertive policies. The United States seeks to deter China from undertaking certain actions such as invading or attacking Taiwan or using force to pursue Chinese claims in territorial and resource disputes. Deterrence in the Taiwan Strait is complicated by the fact that the United States is trying to deter or discourage both China and Taiwan from challenging the status quo. A degree of ambiguity about the circumstances under which the United States would intervene in a conflict is therefore unavoidable.

China's ongoing military modernization program could complicate or delay U.S. military intervention in the event of a Taiwan crisis and represents a potential challenge to U.S. ability to deter China. But deterrence does not rest solely on the military balance. A conflict with the United States would set back China's economic modernization substantially. This enhances U.S. deterrence by making the use of force against Taiwan costly and unattractive to Chinese decisionmakers.

Along with deterrence, dissuasion is an element of U.S. policy toward China that aims to avert future conflicts by shaping Beijing's strategic choices. It involves discouraging China from going after capabilities or objectives that would threaten U.S. interests. Dissuasion alters the Chinese calculus by imposing costs or denying gains, maintaining U.S. advantages, exploiting Chinese weaknesses, and/or providing more acceptable alternatives.[11] Dissuasion can be thought of in a narrow technical sense (efforts to discourage China from developing antisatellite weapons) or a broader strategic sense (efforts to discourage China from challenging the U.S. global position). Some conceptions of dissuasion are compatible with the U.S. hedging strategy, especially those that work indirectly by influencing China's cost-benefit analysis.

Deterrence and dissuasion are most effective when employed for specific, limited objectives. The United States must also be prepared for competition with China. Competition can entail efforts to win political support for specific regional and global initiatives or more general efforts to encourage countries to embrace broad political and cultural values. Competition is a normal part of how states pursue their interests and does not necessarily imply a hostile relationship.

KEY STRATEGIC CHALLENGES FOR THE UNITED STATES

The United States and China have a complex, multifaceted relationship that cannot be reduced to a simple slogan or phrase. Depending on the issue and the time period under consideration, the United States may need to rely on cooperation, engagement, deterrence, dissuasion, or competition to pursue its interests regarding China. This complexity does not mean that the two countries are fated to be enemies, but it does mean that a degree of ambivalence and tension is unavoidable.

China's Domestic Developments

Chinese leaders are focused on the domestic tasks of maintaining social stability and preventing challenges to Communist Party rule. Economic growth is viewed as a critical means of building legitimacy and maintaining stability. But the economic reforms that have promoted growth and raised living standards have also created serious social problems such as unemployment, an inadequate social safety net, and a collapsing rural healthcare system. One measure of these problems is the increasing number of protests in China. A senior public security official admitted that there were more than 74,000 large-scale public protests involving 3.7 million people in 2004.[12]

Protests generally have local causes, but they also reflect underlying systemic problems. One major issue is the declining legitimacy of the Chinese Communist Party, due to problems such as economic inequality resulting from reforms that benefit some individuals and regions more than others; the gap between southeastern coastal areas that have been the winners of reform and northeastern rustbelt and interior provinces that have been hard hit by economic restructuring; and corruption among government and party officials.

Protests to date have remained isolated and have not presented a major threat to the regime. However, Chinese leaders are worried about the revolutions that toppled governments in Georgia, Ukraine, and Kyrgyzstan. The immediate response has been a crackdown on press freedom and intensified controls on nongovernmental organizations (NGOs) and the Internet.[13]

The longer-term response appears to be efforts to address underlying causes by reducing the tax burden on rural residents and seeking economic policies that will produce more balanced growth with fewer negative environmental and social side effects. Reports from the Communist Party's fifth plenum in October 2005 suggest that the next 5-year program will stress common prosperity and sustainable development.[14] However, Chinese leaders will still emphasize economic growth for fear that a prolonged economic downturn or slowing of the growth rate would aggravate social problems and stimulate increased protests.

The more important question is whether China can continue rapid growth without significant political reforms. Party goals of building a "harmonious society" cannot compensate for the lack of effective political institutions to represent diverse and competing social interests. But Chinese leaders appear determined to prevent the emergence of any organized political groups and to resist any independent monitoring of government officials by the press or the public. Instead, the party seeks to rely on intraparty supervision and anticorruption campaigns that are unlikely to be effective. Technocratic approaches and scientific management are unlikely to solve the serious social problems China faces. The party maintains considerable coercive tools, but an economic slowdown would greatly increase the challenge of maintaining social stability.

Instability in China would pose a variety of challenges for the United States. Chinese leaders would likely respond to widespread instability with a political crackdown, possibly involving the use of force, to maintain order. This would raise the profile of human rights issues in U.S. China policy and heighten concerns that China was moving toward greater authoritarianism rather than democracy. Chinese leaders would likely also seek to accelerate economic growth via increased exports to ameliorate underlying social problems. This might lead to increased government subsidies or incentives for exporters, further aggravating U.S. concerns about China's trade practices and undervalued currency.

The Chinese leadership might be tempted to blame domestic problems on outside influences to justify a political crackdown and harness nationalist sentiment behind government policy. Although authoritarian regimes sometimes seek foreign conflicts to unify the population and divert attention from domestic problems, Chinese leaders are unlikely to engage in foreign adventures that would further aggravate their troubles.

Taiwan

Another strategic challenge is Taiwan. The "one China" framework whereby the United States recognizes the People's Republic of China as the sole official government of China while maintaining unofficial economic and cultural relations with Taiwan has been remarkably successful for pursuing U.S. interests while facilitating economic, social, and political development on both sides of the Taiwan Strait. The U.S. long-term objective is a peaceful resolution of the dispute over Taiwan's status that is acceptable to the Taiwan people. U.S. short-term policy seeks to maintain stability and prevent unilateral challenges to the status quo (as defined by the United States) by either side.[15] The United States also encourages dialogue and cooperation between China and Taiwan.

However, a number of trends are gradually eroding the stability of the status quo and challenging the viability of the "one China" framework.[16] Taiwan's growing sense of separate identity and efforts by leaders to highlight its separate status have raised concerns in Beijing about "creeping independence." Beijing has had difficulty formulating an effective response to gradual moves toward independence, with leaders seeking to reinforce the credibility of threats to use force (most recently through an antisecession law) while simultaneously pressing the United States to rein in Taiwan.

China has also accelerated its military modernization efforts, with a focus on weapons that can be used to delay or deter U.S. military intervention in the event of a conflict. These trends are occurring against a backdrop of growing economic integration and interdependence across the Taiwan Strait and an increasing role of domestic politics of both sides in cross-strait relations.

The United States has been forced to become more deeply involved simply to maintain the status quo. Both China and Taiwan regularly push the United States to back their position in the dispute. For Taiwan, this involves attempts to obtain symbolic gestures of U.S. support, such as congressional resolutions, diplomatic support for Taiwan's participation in the World Health Organization, or permission for Taiwan leaders to make transit visits through the United States. Democratization has given Taiwan's appeals for support more legitimacy, allowing a push for greater U.S. recognition of its elected leaders. Taiwan's successes include President Clinton's February 2000 statement that any resolution of the island's status must be "peaceful and acceptable to the Taiwan people" and President Bush's April 2001 statement that the United States would do "whatever it takes to help Taiwan defend itself."[17] However, Taiwan leaders have been unable to win U.S. endorsement of their claim that Taiwan is already an independent sovereign state.

At the same time, China regularly pushes the United States to reaffirm its "one China" policy and to make statements opposing Taiwan independence. China also tries to use previous U.S. commitments and cooperation in other areas to limit U.S. political and security ties with Taiwan (with arms sales being a particular sore point). An important success was President Bush's statement in a meeting with Chinese Premier Wen Jiabao in December 2003 that the United States opposes "comments and actions made by the leader of Taiwan" that "indicate that he may be willing to unilaterally change the status quo."[18]

Changes in the military balance are also increasing U.S. involvement. Taiwan's technological edge is eroding, as China's military modernization efforts begin to pay dividends. Over the past decade, China has acquired advanced Russian weapons systems[19] and has begun producing higher quality weapons that incorporate advanced technologies. China's expanding deployments of short-range ballistic missiles (now estimated at 700 to 800 missiles) are increasing the People's Liberation Army's (PLA's) military reach.[20]

As the military balance has shifted, U.S. officials and military planners have focused on the practical issues involved in the event of a military conflict. One response has been increased U.S.-Taiwan security cooperation that includes strategic defense dialogues, visits by military officers and senior civilian officials, educational exchanges, observation of exercises, and assessment team visits.[21] The United States has long used ambiguity about the circumstances under which it would intervene to discourage destabilizing actions by both China and Taiwan. However, a clearer U.S. commitment to deter a possible Chinese attack could erode this ambiguity and encourage Taiwan to shirk responsibility for its own defense or engage in risky behavior, believing that China would not risk a conflict with the United States.

Can the "one China" framework be sustained indefinitely? It requires that China, Taiwan, and the United States compromise and tolerate ambiguity about Taiwan's status. Beijing is focused on stopping Taiwan independence, but unification remains its long-term objective. The signals emanating from Taiwan are contradictory. On the one hand, strong support for the status quo exists on the island, while support for independence may be declining, as evidenced by public approval for Nationalist Party chairman Lien Chan's visit to mainland China. On the other hand, democratization and the development of a separate identity have encouraged political leaders to assert Taiwan's independence. A key question is whether its leaders will see economic integration and the changing military balance as grounds for accommodation with Beijing or as a narrow window to achieve independence. The United States has to reckon with the possibility that developments in either China or Taiwan could cause a major crisis.

The United States could respond to these challenges through diplomatic efforts to promote cross-strait dialogue and political and military confidence-building measures. One interesting suggestion is to explore an interim agreement for 20 to 50 years whereby China would agree not to use force and Taiwan would agree not to declare independence.[22]

Absent major domestic political changes, both China and Taiwan are likely to use negotiations to pursue their long-term political objectives. The possibility of a conflict (and the growing U.S. role in cross-strait relations) may make it increasingly difficult to manage the Taiwan issue within the broader U.S.-China relationship.

Nuclear Modernization and Ballistic Missile Defense

The potential for a military confrontation over Taiwan complicates a third strategic challenge: the interaction between Chinese strategic force modernization and U.S. ballistic missile defenses. China will soon begin deploying a new generation of mobile land-based intercontinental ballistic missiles (ICBMs) and sea-launched ballistic missiles (SLBMs) on nuclear submarines (see table 6–2).[23] These new missiles will improve the survivability of China's nuclear deterrent and double or triple the number of Chinese nuclear warheads that can reach the continental United States.[24] Interactions between China's strategic modernization and U.S. BMD deployments could generate an action-reaction spiral that would lead to a strategic arms race. Even if this outcome is avoided, increased strategic mistrust and suspicion could spill over into bilateral relations in potentially destabilizing ways.

Deployment of even a thin U.S. BMD system would threaten China's goal of a credible strategic nuclear deterrent. Chinese leaders are determined not to accept permanent vulnerability to U.S. nuclear leverage. The size, perceived effectiveness, and potential expandability of U.S. missile defenses are likely to have a direct impact on the pace and scope of China's strategic modernization. China will most likely respond

TABLE 6–2. CHINA'S MISSILE FORCES

Inventory Total	Launchers	Missiles	Estimated Range
DF–5A (CSS–4) ICBM	20	20	8,460+ km
DF–4 (CSS–3) ICBM	10–14	20–24	5,470+ km
DF–3/3A (CSS–2) ICBM	6–10	14–18	2,790+ km
DF–21A (CSS–5 Mod 1/2) MRBM	34–38	19–50	1,770+ km
JL–1 SLBM	10–14	10–14	1,770+ km
DF–15 (CSS–6 SRBM)	70–80	275–315	600 km
DF–11 (CSS–7 SRBM)	100–120	435–475	300 km
JL–2 SLBM	Developmental	Developmental	8,000+ km
DF–31 ICBM	Developmental	Developmental	7,250+ km
DF–31A ICBM	Developmental	Developmental	11,270+ km

Source: Department of Defense, *Military Power of the People's Republic of China 2006.*

by increasing force levels and deploying new technologies as necessary to maintain a credible nuclear deterrent.[25] This could involve a significant increase in the number of Chinese ICBMs aimed at U.S. targets, retention of older strategic missile systems, deployment of countermeasures to penetrate or defeat U.S. missile defenses, and the possible deployment of multiple warheads on China's DF–5A ICBMs.

Although the U.S. BMD system has very limited operational capabilities against Chinese ICBMs, the United States is exploring a wide range of systems and technologies, including boost-phase, mid-course, and terminal defense systems. The Missile Defense Agency is also considering future concepts that might include space-based weapons.[26] Chinese planners therefore confront considerable uncertainty about the ultimate size and effectiveness of future U.S. missile defenses. More advanced U.S. BMD architectures would likely result in correspondingly larger increases in China's ICBM force.[27]

This situation is further complicated by changes in U.S. nuclear doctrine. The new strategic triad concept introduced in the 2002 Nuclear Posture Review highlighted the role of conventional strike capabilities in targeting an adversary's weapons of mass destruction.[28] Moreover, once the Chinese Type 094 submarine is operational, U.S. Navy efforts to shadow it on patrol increase the possibility of an incident.

From a political standpoint, the key question is whether China's strategic modernization and U.S. missile defense deployments are viewed as rational responses to real strategic vulnerabilities or as indicators of hostile political intentions. This issue will receive increasing attention as Chinese deployments of new strategic missiles are reported, especially given ongoing debates about the possible need for new nuclear weapons designs to improve the capability and reliability of the U.S. arsenal. The fact that China will be expanding its nuclear forces at a time when the United States is reducing its arsenal will highlight the question of Chinese strategic intentions.

Uncertainty about the ultimate size and effectiveness of U.S. missile defenses and China's reluctance to discuss its force structure plans create a high potential for misperception on both sides. Most Chinese officials and analysts dismiss U.S. fears of rogue state missile threats and view China as the real target of U.S. missile defenses. U.S. interest in space-based weapons and the range of BMD technologies being explored raises the possibility of a surprise technological breakthrough. These factors are likely to cause China to overestimate the effectiveness of U.S. missile defenses and plan for a nuclear force structure that U.S. officials will view as excessive.

There is considerable U.S. ambivalence about a strategic deterrence relationship with China.[29] Some former officials have argued that the United States must maintain overwhelming strategic superiority so that China's limited nuclear retaliatory capability is neutralized.[30] However, it is unclear that U.S. missile defenses will ever have the technical capability to negate China's current nuclear forces reliably, much less defend against the larger forces China would likely deploy in response. An explicit U.S. effort to nullify China's nuclear deterrent would have an extremely damaging effect on bilateral relations and likely limit future security cooperation. These issues are further complicated by Chinese concerns about potential U.S. development of space weapons and by the U.S. belief that China plans to deploy antisatellite weapons to target U.S. space assets.[31]

The potential negative political effects of such strategic interactions might be limited through mutual strategic reassurance.[32] The United States could clarify the technical parameters of its planned BMD architecture and discuss China's potential responses. At some point, the United States might be able to offer assurances about the ultimate scope of its BMD system, while China might offer greater transparency about its modernization plans, possibly including force structure levels keyed to specific missile defense architectures.

The Bush administration has expanded consultations with Chinese officials on a range of political, economic, and security matters, including some discussion of strategic nuclear issues. Addressing Chinese concerns without allowing Beijing to dictate U.S. policy could help avert misperceptions and potentially moderate the size of China's nuclear buildup. However, this approach would require accepting the inevitability of a nuclear deterrent relationship with China, a controversial position in the United States. Moreover, any serious strategic dialogue requires reciprocity in the form of greater transparency about China's nuclear doctrine and planned force structure.

While a franker dialogue on strategic issues would be useful, the potential for a U.S.-China conflict over Taiwan to escalate to the nuclear level raises the stakes and will make it hard for either side to react passively to improvements in the other's strategic capabilities. The negative U.S. reaction to recent remarks by a Chinese general that China was prepared to use nuclear weapons if attacked by Washington during a confrontation over Taiwan highlights the potential for strategic issues to affect broader relations, as does the U.S. outcry over China's successful test of a ground-based antisatellite weapon in January 2007.[33]

Chinese Influence in Asia

China's expanding influence in Asia poses a fourth strategic challenge. Many expected that China's military actions to defend its territorial claims in the South China Sea and use of "missile diplomacy" against Taiwan in 1995–1996 signaled a more aggressive regional stance that would eventually cause Asian countries to balance against China. But as Beijing became aware of regional concerns, it moderated its behavior and sought to reassure its neighbors that its rising power would not threaten them. One initial means was the articulation of a "New Security Concept" that emphasized the importance of dialogue and negotiations as means of resolving disputes. China's settlement of numerous land border disputes, signature of the Declaration on Conduct of Parties in the South China Sea, and accession to the Association of Southeast Asian Nations' (ASEAN's) Treaty of Amity and Cooperation have all helped reassure China's neighbors.

Chinese diplomacy has become more sophisticated, embracing multilateralism and launching new initiatives aimed at spurring regional cooperation.[34] China has taken the initiative in establishing new organizations such as the Shanghai Cooperation Organization (SCO) and the ASEAN + China grouping. China has supported the ASEAN initiative for an East Asian Summit, including the major Northeast and Southeast Asian countries as well as Australia, India, and New Zealand. China has also proposed cooperation on nontraditional security issues within the ASEAN + 3 (China, Japan, South Korea) framework. These initiatives have created new venues for regional cooperation without the United States.

China's efforts to reassure its neighbors have calmed regional fears about its rising power. Asian countries increasingly view China as a partner and market opportunity rather than a potential threat. Beijing's embrace of multilateralism and cooperation on issues of concern to Asian governments contrasts positively with a perceived U.S. unilateralism and narrow focus on fighting terrorism. The result has been a substantial increase in Chinese influence, including with traditional U.S. allies such as Australia and South Korea.

The desire to benefit from China's future economic growth further increases Beijing's leverage. China has signed a China-ASEAN free trade agreement that includes provisions benefiting ASEAN's poorer members. Arguments that neighboring countries will benefit economically from China's rise figure prominently in speeches by Chinese leaders.[35] China is now the leading trading partner for Japan, South Korea, and Taiwan (see table 6–3 and figures 6–1 and 6–2). Asia has been the primary focus of China's diplomacy, but the need for energy, natural resources, and markets has prompted an expansion of Chinese activities in Latin America, Africa, and the Middle East.[36]

Beijing's reliance on economic and political tools is preferable to the use of military instruments, but China's increasing influence complicates U.S. efforts to advance its own regional interests. China's growing ties with U.S. friends and allies in Asia could limit the U.S. ability to respond to Chinese actions that threaten U.S. interests.

TABLE 6–3. DEPENDENCE ON IMPORTS FROM AND EXPORTS TO CHINA

	Percent of Total Imports				Percent of Total Exports			
	1993	1998	2002	2004	1993	1998	2002	2004
East Asia	6.24	9.62	13.17	15.89	6.64	6.99	12.35	16.32
Japan	6.53	10.56	14.37	16.16	6.42	7.29	12.83	16.68
South Korea	3.30	6.70	10.21	11.89	6.25	11.31	17.69	25.19
Taiwan	1.91	3.70	5.85	8.07	15.20	15.04	29.15	37.22
ASEAN	2.29	4.02	6.64	8.43	2.94	3.83	7.71	11.03
South Asia	3.54	3.83	5.79	7.59	1.57	2.59	4.03	7.53

Source: United Nations COMTRADE database.

FIGURE 6–1. CHINESE EXPORTS TO WORLD, 2004

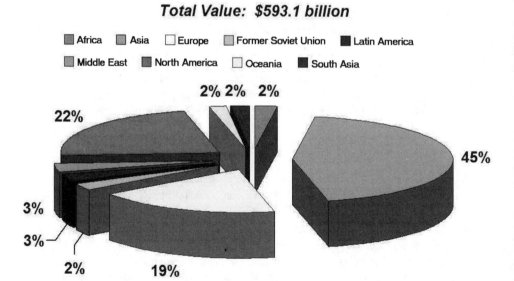

Total Value: $593.1 billion

FIGURE 6–2. CHINESE IMPORTS FROM WORLD, 2004

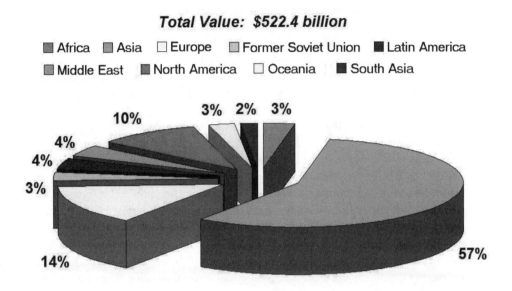

Total Value: $522.4 billion

■ Africa   ■ Asia   □ Europe   ▨ Former Soviet Union   ■ Latin America
■ Middle East   ■ North America   □ Oceania   ■ South Asia

3% 4% 4% 10% 3% 2% 3% 14% 57%

This is already evident in the U.S. alliance with South Korea, where Seoul has pointedly rebuffed suggestions that the U.S.–Republic of Korea alliance might be used in a Taiwan contingency. China's preference for regional institutions that exclude the United States and U.S. ambivalence about supporting multilateral organizations in Asia raise the possibility that the United States could be shut out of key decisions about Asia's future. China's increasing influence could eventually affect the viability of the U.S. alliances in Asia.

A U.S. response must recognize that Asian countries do not want to be forced to choose between China and the United States, especially in the event of a military crisis over Taiwan. However, most Asian governments welcome a continuing U.S. presence, to balance China and reduce their vulnerability to Chinese demands. The United States should broaden its regional agenda to place greater emphasis on economic development and on nontraditional security issues of interest to Asian governments.

Greater U.S. responsiveness to Asian concerns might also increase the willingness of countries to cooperate on counterterrorism. One important role for the United States is to provide alternative modes of security cooperation within Asia, including options that fall short of formal alliances or security partnerships. As the U.S. response to the South Asian tsunami indicated, the United States has resources and unique capabilities that make it the preferred partner for cooperation in many areas, but these resources must be applied more actively and within the context of a broader regional strategy.

China as a Potential Strategic Rival

A final strategic challenge involves China's long-term potential as a great power. China has enjoyed the most rapid economic growth in the world over the last 25 years and is the only potential peer competitor for the United States. As China moves up the technology curve, many Americans will view it as a looming economic and strategic challenge. Senior U.S. policymakers have expressed concerns about the purposes behind China's increasing military spending and modernization efforts.[37] These factors lead many U.S. analysts to worry about China's eventual challenge to the U.S. global position.

This anxiety is reinforced by the realpolitik worldview of Chinese leaders, who are committed to realizing the goal of a "rich country, strong army," as well as China's role as a successful "communist development state" where the Communist Party plays a leading role in fostering economic development. Some observers argue that the Chinese approach of reforming the economy while limiting political reforms represents a new model with considerable appeal to developing countries.[38] Chinese leaders remain committed to Communist Party rule and have explicitly rejected multiparty democracy. The human rights Americans care about most—political rights, freedom of speech, and freedom of religion—are the areas in which China has made the least progress, while recent crackdowns on press freedom and NGOs have eroded the limited advances that had been made.

The prospect of an authoritarian, increasingly nationalist, and stronger China highlights questions about its future behavior. Besides Taiwan, China has a host of unresolved maritime and territorial disputes.[39] These issues are complicated by the existence of considerable natural gas and possible oil resources in the disputed territories. China's increasing demand for energy has prompted concerns that Beijing might defend its maritime claims more aggressively and seek to develop a blue-water navy to protect its sea lines of communications to the Middle East.

These concerns have been part of the China debate since the mid-1990s, but several recent developments are increasing their salience. The first is a sense that China is improving its military capabilities more rapidly than expected. This reflects the cumulative impact of double-digit real increases in Chinese military spending since 1999; "software" reforms in training, education, doctrine, and logistics that are improving PLA operational capabilities; and increased Chinese deployments of both Russian and domestically produced weapons systems. Analysts disagree about the significance of some of these developments, but most agree that Chinese military modernization is moving faster than anticipated in the late 1990s.

A second factor is the realization that integration in the world economy and membership in international and regional organizations have given China new opportunities to influence these institutions. While membership in these organizations influences China's foreign policy choices (through socialization and by raising the costs of aggressive policies), it also presents opportunities for China to employ political and economic levers to exercise influence. This is a logical consequence of China's integration into international organizations, but it has caught many observers by surprise.

China's increasing ability to influence the rules and operations of international institutions may limit the degree to which those institutions can shape China's international behavior and political evolution.

A third factor is impatience that economic growth and integration in the world community have not produced dramatic changes in the Chinese political system. There has been significant progress in building the legal institutions that are a precondition for establishing the rule of law, but key political decisions remain firmly in control of the Communist Party. Although Chinese citizens enjoy greater freedom in their daily lives, they do not enjoy freedom of speech or full political rights. It is logical to expect the military and the core institutions of Communist Party control to be the last to liberalize, but the slow pace of political change in China has led some to question the assumptions underpinning engagement.

Despite these concerns, the hedge strategy the United States has pursued since the mid-1990s remains the most appropriate way of responding to the long-term challenges posed by China. Alternative strategies such as containment have high costs and limited benefits. A containment strategy would require the United States to significantly increase military spending and to develop expensive new capabilities such as space weapons to negate Chinese asymmetrical warfare options. Containment would not only require the United States to forego the benefits of cooperation with China, but also have a destabilizing impact in Asia as the United States tried to force unwilling countries to act against their perceived interests by lining up against China. In addition, containment would impose high economic costs on American businesses and consumers, including significant damage to the global competitive position of U.S. companies.

A better approach is to continue engaging China while simultaneously working to improve the U.S. strategic position. This requires enhanced efforts to engage Chinese leaders and to strengthen bilateral cooperation. The Bush administration has launched a number of initiatives, such as the "senior dialogue" and the "strategic economic dialogue," that could play a beneficial role in this respect. The "responsible stakeholder" concept outlines a useful framework for long-term U.S.-China cooperation. Nevertheless, there are significant operational challenges to using this framework as a basis for bilateral relations.[40] With Deputy Secretary Zoellick's departure, it will also be important to identify a senior member of the administration who can help coordinate relations with China across the economic, security, and diplomatic domains.

The United States should have patience and modest expectations about how quickly political change will come in China. But the United States should also respond to the competitive aspect of China's increasing power and influence by developing a foreign policy agenda with greater appeal to other countries. The United States has more hard and soft power assets than China, but these tools must be applied systematically. The United States also needs to sustain the economic foundations of its power over the long term by bringing its budget and trade deficits under control and devising policies to increase the U.S. savings rate.

WHAT NEXT?

Despite recent relative stability in Sino-U.S. relations, bilateral tensions are likely to increase significantly over the next few years. Congress has been reluctant to challenge the Bush administration on China policy, but this may be changing. Increased congressional activism is currently focused on economic issues such as surges in Chinese textile imports, the ballooning U.S. trade deficit with China, and concerns about the impact of an undervalued Chinese currency on U.S. manufacturers. But this does not mean that issues such as Taiwan, China's relations with North Korea, human rights, and the ongoing Chinese government crackdown on the press, Internet, and NGOs have been put to rest. Heightened congressional activism may challenge the administration's efforts to set clear priorities and to implement its China policy. Renewed Chinese efforts to link cooperation with U.S. concessions on issues such as Taiwan would make U.S. policymaking with regard to China much more difficult.

The U.S.-China relationship will continue to be characterized by ambiguity and ambivalence. The complex mix of cooperative and competitive elements in the relationship will require patience and persistence. The multifaceted nature of U.S.-China relations requires the United States to simultaneously cooperate with China to pursue common interests, engage China to alter its behavior, and deter China from unwanted military actions. All these activities take place within a broader context where the United States is attempting to influence China's political evolution and long-term strategic choices in positive directions. Maintaining the balance between aggressively pursuing short-term U.S. economic and security interests and longer-term efforts to shape Chinese thinking about its global interests will be difficult. Leadership, vision, and patience will be necessary for the United States to take full advantage of the benefits that cooperation with China offers while successfully meeting the strategic challenges China poses to U.S. interests.

RUSSIA ON THE REBOUND

Russia does not provide the key organizing principle for U.S. foreign policy that the Soviet Union did through most of the second half of the 20th century. Still, the complex relationship with Russia remains one of the principal challenges for U.S. foreign policy. Russia's fortunes and actions remain an integral and critical part of the Eurasian security environment. Devoid of the major confrontational features that characterized it during the Cold War, the relationship falls short of the promise of partnership it held out in the early 1990s and combines elements of cooperation with competition.

As expectations of partnership between the United States and Russia fade and competitive aspects of the relationship reassert themselves, America's biggest challenge vis-à-vis Russia is to navigate carefully between two distinct postures—selective cooperation in areas deemed too important to be neglected, such as nuclear proliferation or terrorism, and an approach best described as *neocontainment* that places much greater emphasis on competitive tools and aspects of the relationship, including competition of ideas, geopolitical balancing, and even diplomatic isolation in instances where U.S. and Russian interests and policies contradict each other. U.S.-Russian disagreements over political developments in Ukraine, Georgia, and Uzbekistan fall into the latter category.

Some might argue that this is a strategic partnership in the truest meaning of the term—a partnership that is limited to issues that both sides believe are truly strategically important. If so, this partnership falls far short of the early post–Cold War expectations and, if sustained along its current trajectory, could become quite competitive. However, the competitiveness of this relationship is likely to be limited by Russia's internal conditions and the huge stake the United States has in a stable and secure Russia.

SHORT-TERM RESURGENCE AMIDST LONG-TERM DECLINE

The presidency of Vladimir Putin has been a period of economic prosperity and political stability unprecedented in recent Russian history. However, a host of long-term, structural indicators point to problems that are not being addressed and in the long run will hamper Russia's reemergence as a major actor.

After a Bust—A Boom, and Then?

Judging by its macro indicators, the Russian economy in 2007 is booming. With 2006 growth rates in excess of 7 percent, the federal budget running a surplus, Russian Central Bank reserves topping the $400 billion mark,[41] repayment of its international debts, and relatively low inflation, the country's macroeconomic picture is the envy of many less fortunate nations and exceeds the wildest expectations of Russian and foreign economists of less than a decade ago. The 1998 financial crisis when the country slipped dangerously close to the brink of economic and political chaos is but a distant memory.

But experts inside and outside of Russia also agree that these impressive macroeconomic statistics do not yet reveal the entire picture, which remains quite bleak. Indeed, the reason that explains the spectacular growth of the Russian economy for over half a decade also explains why the country's finances collapsed in 1998: the price of oil. As figure 6–3 illustrates, Russian economic health remains heavily dependent on the economy's ability to export hydrocarbons. Despite numerous warnings by foreign and Russian economists, it has proven unable to diversify its exports and wean itself from this habit. When the price of oil hovered near $10 a barrel in 1998, Russian finances collapsed. With the price of oil in excess of $90 a barrel, the Russian economy is booming. This addiction to oil steers Russia toward the boom-bust cycle of development, in which the nation's economic well-being is determined disproportionately by external factors, such as the price of oil and other commodities in the world.[42]

Russian dependence on hydrocarbon exports underscores the need to sustain and expand production of oil and gas as a guarantee of continuing economic success. This in turn highlights another challenge for Russia: its questionable climate for domestic and foreign investment necessary to develop new oil and gas fields and carry their output to markets in Europe, Asia, and even the United States.[43] The Russian investment

FIGURE 6–3. RUSSIAN GROSS DOMESTIC PRODUCT GROWTH AND CRUDE OIL PRICES

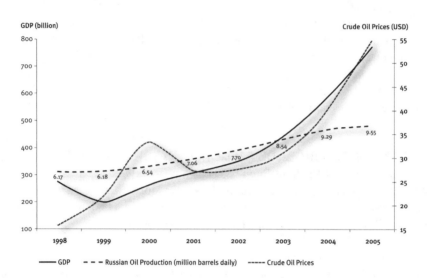

Source: BP Statistical Review 2006; International Monetary Fund

climate, hampered by a litany of familiar problems—fragile rule of law, pervasive corruption, inadequate infrastructure, and an arbitrary tax regime—remains weak.

This list of longstanding problems was recently joined by yet another—growing government intervention in the running of the economy, especially its strategic sectors such as oil and gas. Growing government involvement in these strategic sectors, including renationalization of some assets, legislation limiting the foreign role in Russian hydrocarbon development, and stepped-up political oversight of key Russian energy companies, does not bode well for the investment climate in this critical segment of the country's economy.[44]

Another aspect of Russia's long-term decline, which is both systemic and reflective of its socioeconomic conditions, is its continuing demographic crisis.[45] Despite the rapid growth of the country's economy and substantial increases in its per capita income—$10,700 in 2005[46]—key social indicators continue to decline. The Russian population continues to shrink, reaching the level of just under 141 million in 2007[47]—less than Pakistan. Life expectancy for Russian males is now 59. Overall life expectancy is 65—lower than India (68) and China (72).[48]

The conditions underlying these statistics point to a long-term systemic crisis in Russia's socioeconomic sphere, one that is recognized routinely by Russian and foreign demographers. The long-term nature of this crisis and the sheer scale of the remedies required to restore the country's population conditions to general demographic health and well-being suggest that it will not be overcome in the next 10 to 15 years and that Russia will have to suffer its consequences with regard to its domestic development as well as its international position.

The long-term outlook for the Russian economy remains bleak. Buoyed by high oil and commodities prices in the near term, it has sidestepped the measures needed to secure long-term sustainable growth.

However, Russia's current economic recovery is a factor that has significant regional impact. Relative to the economies of most of its neighbors, Russia's is a veritable powerhouse, whose recovery has been the critical factor in renewed economic growth among the states of the former Soviet Union. Russia remains the biggest trading partner these countries have. As its economy surged with the inflow of petrodollars, Russia became a key outlet for excess labor from the less endowed economies of the Caucasus, Central Asia, and Ukraine, generating a steady flow of guest worker remittances to their native lands. Thus, Russian economic growth has been an important element of the still-fragile socioeconomic balance in the territories of the former Soviet Union.

Russia's recovery lacks durable foundations for sustainable economic development—through further exploitation of its hydrocarbon reserves or otherwise. But its petrowealth and position as a critical supplier in the global energy marketplace give it confidence and clout that it will not shy away from using in its own neighborhood and beyond.

Political Consolidation Amidst Uncertainty

The long-term outlook for Russian domestic politics is mixed at best. President Putin's term in office has been marked by much greater stability than that of Boris Yeltsin in the 1990s. But beyond that, Russian domestic politics resembles the situation with the country's economy: near-term consolidation has been achieved at the expense of long-term development of institutions and mechanisms needed to secure a stable, sustainable political system for Russia.

Stability in Russian domestic politics during Putin's administration has been accompanied by steady accumulation of authority in the hands of the federal government at the expense of other institutions and power centers. The roles of regional governors, the Duma, the Federation Council, independent business, media, political parties, and NGOs in the country's political and economic life have been reduced.

However, the Kremlin's enhanced power and authority have done little to strengthen what it calls the *vertical of power*—meaning top-down, centralized administration and the erosion of regional government—and make the country more secure from terrorist attacks, or produce a more dynamic and effective policy process, or result in a sustainable model for political succession.[49] In fact, the record of the past few years suggests the opposite. The terrorist attack in Beslan in 2004, the embarrassment suffered by the government with the social welfare reform in 2005, and the longstanding failure to address the numerous problems facing the Russian military are just a few examples of this disconnect between the Kremlin's nominal power and real capacity to deliver.[50]

By "strengthening the vertical of power," the Kremlin has marginalized virtually all potential challengers to its authority—from big business to the Communist Party. At the same time, in doing so, the Putin administration has also succeeded in weakening its own independent bases of support, as well as the institutions and power centers that in the long run have the potential to ensure balance, separation of power, and political stability in the country: political parties, independent legislature and elected governors, independent media, and business. Once consolidated, the vertical of power became like a narrow pole—tall, but precariously balanced on a narrow base.

Having marginalized virtually all independent power centers, the Kremlin has empowered the vast federal bureaucracy and undercut its own ability to control it. Without independent political parties, a business community capable of standing up to the bureaucracy, independent major media outlets to mobilize public opinion, and NGOs, the Putin administration has made itself hostage to the bureaucracy.

The vertical of power does not appear to be particularly effective in relation to the regional governors, either. The latter have accepted their newly diminished status with docility. But the ability to achieve its desired outcomes and control developments in the country's far-flung regions continues to elude the Kremlin. Having abolished gubernatorial elections and achieved full control of gubernatorial appointments, the Kremlin appears to have opted for a peculiar bargain with its regional prefects: political loyalty to the president in exchange for the license to run their fiefdoms with impunity. The result has been a system approaching feudalism, which gives regional barons almost unlimited power over their subjects with no recourse to federal, let alone local, law enforcement.[51]

One important feature of the Kremlin's political strategy has been the absence of a vision or a set of ideas to guide its policies. The legacy of the 1990s, with their social, political and economic upheavals in the name of democracy and market, made it politically difficult for the new, post-2000 leadership to insist on the same set of principles as the rationale for their policies. The idea of strengthening the state appeals to many Russians, given the nation's long-standing tradition of a powerful central state. But while it has championed the idea of a strong state, until quite recently, the Kremlin did not define its vision of that state—democratic or authoritarian, federal or centralized.

When it did so, it appears to have acted out of necessity. The Kremlin's chief political strategist, Vladislav Surkov, articulated the vision in early 2006 under the title of "sovereign democracy."[52] The *sovereign* part of the label is clearly intended to signal the strength of Russian state institutions and their dominance over institutions of civil society and is fully consistent with the historical Russian legacy of a strong sovereign. The *democracy* part signals that the Kremlin does not intend to dismantle the country's democratic institutions and will develop and nurture them as befits a modern, enlightened leading nation and a member of the Group of 8 (G–8).

However, the word *sovereign* in this context is also intended to signal that the Kremlin has no intention to compromise Russian sovereignty by submitting to the terms and conditions demanded from it by the international community, which of late has become increasingly critical of the Putin administration for dismantling Russian institutions of civil society. According to the Kremlin's sovereign democracy blueprint, Russia will develop its own brand of democracy, free of foreign influence and interference.

This idea suffers from several obvious shortcomings. It is clearly reactive, intended to counter external pressures on the Putin administration to reverse its relentless pursuit of the vertical of power. It has xenophobic, isolationist overtones that will hamper Russia's consolidation of its position in the club of industrialized democracies. And by marginalizing institutions of civil society as foreign imports, it does little to broaden the base for the vertical of power and thus leaves it as precariously balanced as ever.

The political calm of the Putin era—relative to the turmoil that had marked the Yeltsin presidency—is not to be confused with the development in Russia of key foundations necessary for long-term political stabilization. To the contrary, it appears that with political authority concentrated at the top of the vertical of power, Russian domestic politics has become more precarious and more dependent on the well-being and ability of a single leader. The leader himself appears to be less erratic and more focused than his predecessor, but the system remains fundamentally no different and arguably no more stable than it was during the 1990s.

The prospect of presidential transition scheduled for 2008, when Putin's second term expires, has already generated considerable political uncertainty. Despite the appearance of political consolidation, Russian observers have noted that the Kremlin is in the throes of an internal struggle, which they have described as a "fight under the carpet."[53] The Kremlin's move to dismiss many long-serving governors in the run-up to the parliamentary and presidential elections, in 2007 and 2008 respectively, is a further sign of the ongoing political struggle, the uncertainty that is unnerving to the country's political elite, and the leadership's concern about its stability and sustainability of the present system.

Most arguments that Russia is retreating from democracy ignore the fact that Russia in the 1990s was not a democracy either. The government's control of the media is harmful to press freedom in Russia. But so was ownership of major media outlets by powerful businessmen who subordinated editorial policies to their business interests throughout the 1990s. Russian oligarchs of the Yeltsin era bear much responsibility for the population's widespread cynicism toward the media.

The notion that Russian democracy is dead or dying does not fully account for widespread grassroots unrest triggered in recent years by the Russian government's unpopular social welfare reforms, abuses of conscripts in the military, and prosecutorial misconduct—all matters that are nonpolitical in nature but indicative of the population's potential for mobilization on topics it cares about. Most of this unrest has been focused on local issues that bear directly on citizens' everyday lives, but it is nonetheless significant as an indicator that elements of civil society are alive in Russia and hold out the promise of change in the long run.

Concerns about Russian democracy's demise ignore the impact of such factors as the ever-expanding access to the Internet in many Russian cities in towns; cell phone use; and ability for Russians to go abroad and for foreigners to travel deep into the Russian heartland. Russia is no longer cut off from the outside world by the iron curtain. All this is having an impact in many, often immeasurable ways—from the emergence of hundreds of civic organizations at the grassroots level to academic debates about globalization and its impact on Russia. None of these phenomena promise quick change, but they are signs that changes are taking place in Russian society.

Democracy remains a distant prospect in Russia. The Kremlin's attempts to accumulate power in the office of the presidency at the expense of other public and private institutions have occurred against a background of disasters and setbacks that have highlighted the government's shortcomings and failures and its inability to act in a crisis, respond to new challenges, and cope with their aftermath. The Kursk submarine disaster, the simmering conflict in the North Caucasus, the growing threat of domestic terrorism, the hostage dramas in Moscow and Beslan, and the political and social crisis triggered by welfare reform have brought to light the fact that far from being authoritarian, the Russian state is dangerously weak.

An authoritarian system may be the true goal of President Putin and his political advisors. Having concentrated a great deal of decisionmaking authority and resources under its control, the Kremlin should be omnipotent. Yet real power, the ability to formulate and execute policies, to produce results, to deal with crises and their aftermath, to effect change—all that so far has proven elusive to the degree that various branches of the Russian government and the country's far-flung provinces appear out of control, driven not by a centrally imposed vision of national interest and will, but by narrow, parochial concerns or corporate interests of local elites. Rather than democracy or authoritarianism, the result may be a precariously unstable vertical of power in a country that is ungovernable and teeters on the brink of internal confusion and chaos.

The Military

Defining Russian military capabilities is difficult. The military undoubtedly has benefited from sustained recent growth in defense spending, which is currently estimated at approximately $30 billion.[54] The chronic payment arrears that plagued the Russian military in the 1990s and pushed hundreds of thousands of military officers and their families into poverty have been addressed. Bigger defense budgets have enabled improvements in training and experimentation with military reform. By all accounts, despite significant problems and continuing budget woes, the Russian military is an improved institution from its nadir of the 1990s.

Nonetheless, progress has been limited at best. Any mention of progress relative to the Russian army's condition during the 1990s cannot escape the fact that this is growth from a low starting point. Increased defense spending has had some positive effect, but measured in percentage points, this growth translates into rather modest numbers in dollar or ruble equivalents.

At approximately 1 million, the Russian military is currently a shadow of its strength during the Soviet era. Financially, transition to an all-volunteer force, modernization of weapons and equipment, training, proper maintenance, procurement, and other expenses necessary to ensure the military's combat readiness remain elusive goals being deferred until better times.[55] Nonetheless, some progress in this area appears to have been made, with top priority being given to elite branches of the military, such as the airborne troops, and absolutely essential strategic capabilities, such as the Strategic Rocket Forces.

Conceptually, the Russian military continues to face significant challenges as well. It has the experience of the war in Afghanistan and two wars in Chechnya in its doctrinal baggage. However, large theater-wide conflict still appears to be one of the top contingencies on the minds of Russian military planners and forecasters, if only as the rationale for the large standing military organization. Russian military sources tend to justify the requirement for a large standing army in terms of Russian geography, history as a continental power, and tradition of large-scale warfare.[56]

Russian thinking about future warfare and requirements for it seems to reflect relatively little accounting for or appreciation of the strategic circumstances surrounding Russia in the Eurasian landmass at the outset of the 21st century. Improved relations with the North Atlantic Treaty Organization (NATO), China, and the United States and the ensuing diminished likelihood of a large-scale war in the European or Far Eastern theater seem to weigh less on the minds of Russian military planners than the imbalance between Russia's own military capabilities and those of its key neighbors and other major powers.[57]

Yet despite its diminished circumstances in comparison with the Soviet-era military, the Russian military remains the biggest and most capable military force among the states of the former Soviet Union. Its stocks of military equipment; its defense-industrial complex (which remains capable of producing many types of weapons that are obsolete, but on which other ex-Soviet militaries depend); its contingent of airborne troops; its modest long-range power projection capabilities (which are a far cry from the days of the Cold War, but are nonetheless significant in crisis circumstances and vis-à-vis inferior opponents among the Commonwealth of Independent States); its intelligence capabilities; and, perhaps, most importantly, its tradition and culture of reliance on force in pursuit of national objectives make the Russian military force one to be reckoned with in the space of the former Soviet Union.

The long-term outlook for the Russian military, however, remains uncertain at best. The near-term gains realized in recent years have helped address some of the most glaring shortcomings of the previous decade. However, given the contingencies that Russia is more likely to face in Eurasia (instability in one or more of its neighboring states, or crises in the North Caucasus) than a large-scale war in the European theater, the Russian military's recent progress almost certainly will not be enough to meet future challenges.

KEY STRATEGIC CHALLENGES FOR THE UNITED STATES

Russia's Relations with Former Soviet States

Against the background of continued tensions over Russia's domestic political developments, the United States must face squarely the problem of Moscow's assertive behavior with respect to the former Soviet states, where it maintains important ties. Russian rhetoric and involvement in a series of hotspots around its periphery—in

Ukraine, Georgia, and Moldova—as well as its continuing military presence in Georgia[58] and Moldova despite those countries' objections have given rise to widespread concerns that Russian neoimperialism is on the march.

Those concerns, however, are sometimes driven more by Russia's rhetoric than by its actions. Russian media and academic discussions point to the emergence and strengthening of a consensus across the entire political spectrum in favor of restoring control over the neighborhood that is the former Soviet Union. But there appears to be little will to act on that consensus among the general public, or even foreign policy and political elites.

Moreover, Russia's preoccupation with its periphery and the contentious nature of discussions about its role there ignores one important fact: this is the only region in which Russia still is a major player. Beyond its immediate neighborhood, it is a second-rate power, and within its own neighborhood, it is having to compete for influence with powerful newcomers—the United States, the European Union, and China. As the United States and its European allies seek to expand the Euroatlantic zone of stability and security by promoting market economics and democratic principles throughout Russia's neighborhood, they encounter growing Russian resistance, moti-

TABLE 6–4. COMPARISON OF RUSSIA AND THE COMMONWEALTH OF INDEPENDENT STATES

	Population 2004	GDP per Capita (2005 US$)	Active Military	Reserve Military	Current Account Balance (2004 US$ Billion)
Russia	143,420,309	5,325	1,037,000	20,000,000	+58.563
Armenia	2,991,360	1,667	48,160	210,000*	-0.148
Azerbaijan	7,868,385	1,500	66,490	300,000	-2.604
Belarus	10,310,520	3,020	72,940	289,500	-1.220
Georgia	4,693,892	1,422	11,320	—	-0.432
Kazakhstan	15,185,844	3,691	65,800	—	+0.533
Kyrgyzstan	5,146,281	462	12,500	—	-0.075
Moldova	4,446,455	853	6,750	66,000	-0.071
Tajikistan	7,163,506	338	7,600	—	-0.083
Turkmenistan	4,952,081	985	26,600	—	+0.082
Ukraine	47,732,079	1,775	187,600	1,000,000	+6.804
Uzbekistan	26,851,195	415	55,000	—	+0.989

Sources: International Institute for Strategic Studies, *The Military Balance 2005–2006*; International Monetary Fund; Economist Intelligence Unit.

* Possible number reported with military service within 15 years

vated largely by suspicions that U.S.-European pursuits are designed to encircle Russia and diminish its influence.

The record of the last few years suggests that Russia lacks an effective long-term strategy for wielding its limited—but significant, in the context of a collection of rather small and impoverished states (see table 6–4)—resources to achieve its stated goal of increased control and influence in the former Soviet lands. The record of Russian involvement in the affairs of neighboring states that were once provinces of the Soviet Union suggests that Russian influence there is a good deal less than the rhetoric would lead one to believe. Parties backed by Russia lost in Ukraine's Orange Revolution[59] and Georgia's Rose Revolution. Russia's client regime collapsed in the Georgian province of Adjaria, and the candidate favored by Russia lost the presidential race in Georgia's breakaway province of Abkhazia, long considered to be a Russian protectorate. This is hardly a record to justify claims of growing Russian influence in the former Soviet lands. More recently, even Russia's relations with such staunch allies as Belarus suffered major setbacks.

Russia continues to wield considerable residual influence among its neighbors—influence resulting from a combination of geography, history, and culture rather than diplomatic skill. The Russian language is the lingua franca among Russia's neighbors; Russia remains a major market for their agricultural products not needed elsewhere; and Russian railroads and pipelines carry their oil, gas, and other exports to foreign markets (see figure 6–4).

Moreover, of late Russian standing in the region was enhanced by the U.S. policy of democracy promotion, which stands in stark contrast to Moscow's pragmatic approach of accepting existing leaders and regimes as they are. In this light, for example, the best-known example of Russia's ostensibly restored influence—in Uzbekistan—appears to be more a matter of political convenience for Uzbek leaders looking for new partners after being rejected by the United States than a victory of Russian diplomacy.

In short, Russian influence in the former Soviet lands is a product of factors largely outside of Russia's control—post-Soviet inertia, geography, and political convenience—that Moscow adjusts to or takes advantage of, rather than an integrated strategy to restore the old empire.

However, opportunistic, tactical moves by Russia could still cause considerable damage to its neighbors as well as to U.S. interests in the region. Unable to act as a manager of strategic trends in its neighborhood, Russia can act as a spoiler. The fact that Russian policy is opportunistic and lacks a long-term vision is no reason to ignore it. The challenge for the United States is to steer a course between pursuing its own interests and avoiding counterproductive rivalry with Russia in the region. Neocontainment could be self-defeating, since weakening Russia is not in U.S. interest. The most productive strategy would be one that would get Russia to accept the need for long-term, systemic change in the former Soviet lands. That, however, is an ambitious goal that will depend on Russia's own internal condition and openness to overall reform. As a long-term objective, it has no peers. For the near and medium

FIGURE 6–4. SELECTED OIL AND GAS PIPELINE INFRASTRUCTURE IN THE FORMER SOVIET UNION

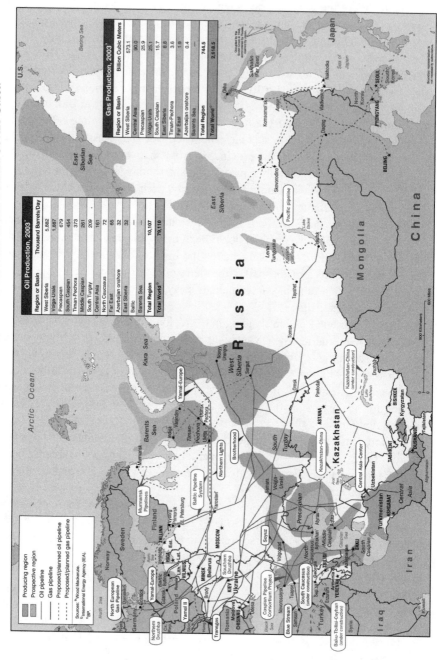

Oil Production, 2003[a]	
Region or Basin	Thousand Barrels/Day
West Siberia	5,862
Volga-Urals	1,887
Precaspian	679
South Caspian	454
Timan-Pechora	373
Middle Caspian	261
South Turgay	209
Central Asia	161
North Caucasus	72
Far East	65
Azerbaijan onshore	32
East Siberia	32
Baltic	—
Barents Sea	—
Total Region	**10,107**
Total World[b]	**79,110**

Gas Production, 2003[b]	
Region or Basin	Billion Cubic Meters
West Siberia	573.1
Central Asia	90.0
Precaspian	25.9
Volga-Urals	25.1
South Caspian	15.7
East Siberia	8.8
Timan-Pechora	3.6
Far East	1.9
Azerbaijan onshore	0.4
Barents Sea	—
Total Region	**744.5**
Total World[b]	**2,518.5**

Producing region
Prospective region
Oil pipeline
Gas pipeline
Proposed/planned oil pipeline
Proposed/planned gas pipeline

Sources: [a] Wood Mackenzie.
[b] International Energy Agency (IEA).
[c] BP.

term, it appears unrealistic. The United States therefore has few options but to walk a fine line between containment and cooperation.

Beyond the Immediate Neighborhood

Outside the former Soviet lands, Russian behavior is less likely to adversely affect U.S. interests. On numerous occasions, Russia has tabled ambitious proposals for solving international crises, thus laying claim to the status of a real great power. Its ability to implement those proposals has proven glaringly inadequate. Dealings with North Korea and Iran, both nations that Russian diplomats view as much weaker than and beholden to Russia, have been a disappointment for Moscow. Russian settlement proposals have been either brushed aside by its supposed client states, as in the case with North Korea, or exploited as a delaying tactic, as has been the case with Iran.

Russian diplomacy of the Putin era has few accomplishments to its credit. U.S.-Russian relations not only have failed to reach their full potential, but also are reeling from disagreements over the role of democracy in foreign policy, NATO's open door policy, and Russia's tendency to throw its weight around its neighborhood. Unlike China, Russia has not been able to stake out a sufficiently prominent place on the U.S. foreign policy agenda for these disagreements to be overlooked for the sake of realpolitik considerations.

Moreover, in the recent past, Russian diplomacy has even succeeded in undermining previously strong ties to Europe. Frictions in Russian-European relations appeared during the past few years over issues ranging from access to Kaliningrad to Russian interference in Ukrainian politics in the run-up to the Orange Revolution. The tipping point was the decision by the Russian government to cut off gas supplies to Ukraine in the winter of 2006 in a transparent attempt to influence Ukrainian parliamentary elections, while at the same time jeopardizing gas deliveries to customers downstream in Central and Western Europe. The move dealt a serious blow to Russian claims to be a reliable energy supplier to Europe and the world, just as Russia assumed the presidency of the G–8 in a session in which members agreed to work on improving energy security worldwide.

As relationships with Europe and the United States sputtered, Russian diplomacy could boast of very few achievements in Asia. The relationship with China, normalized on the surface and replete with high-level declarations and visits, is being regarded with growing anxiety among Russia's political class. No number of treaties or visits can make up for the fact that China is emerging as the biggest foreign policy challenge for Russia, one that has deep domestic roots.[60]

Russia's biggest worry over the long term may be the growing imbalance between the depopulating and underdeveloped (but resource-rich) Far East and Siberia on the one hand and the overpopulated and resource-poor neighboring provinces of Northeast China on the other hand, which could lead to cross-border tensions and conflict. Illegal Chinese migration is already the subject of sensationalist coverage in Russian newspapers. A leading foreign policy association, the Council for Foreign and Defense Policy, conducted a discussion in 2001 on the subject of whether Russia will be able to hold on to Siberia and the Far East in the face of China's relentless expansion.[61]

Many among the Russian elite voice concerns about China's rise and fears that China will be a very difficult partner to deal with as it matures as a great power. Still, few in Russia's foreign policy establishment can articulate a strategy for balancing China. The prospect of a partnership with Japan has reached a dead end as Russia seems unable even to contemplate some sort of a compromise with Japan over the disputed Kuril Islands. The prospect of a partnership with the United States seems equally remote at the moment, since it would require domestic political adjustments in Russia that the Kremlin is not ready to undertake.

The Putin administration has attempted to rebuild Moscow's traditional partnership with India, but for many in Russia's foreign policy establishment, this too must have been a rude awakening. Because memories of India as a poor, underdeveloped, postcolonial nation still predominate among Russia's political class, the idea of India as a Eurasian power with global aspirations and a rapidly growing high-tech sector is a novel one that will take a while to get used to. The prospect of a junior partnership with India, even if it would serve to balance China or avoid submission to U.S. political demands, is not an attractive one to Russian elites. Besides, even that strategy is not guaranteed to succeed, since India is likely to have much more at stake in a good relationship with China than with Russia—another reversal of fortune that Russian elites will take time to digest.

Thus, Russia finds itself in a rather unfavorable diplomatic position. It has no natural allies or friends on the continent. All other major Eurasian powers, as well as Europe and the United States, have much more at stake in each other than in Russia. Its reputation as a great power and as a partner to Europe and the United States has been tarnished. Its domestic conditions are such that beyond the short and mid-term, it is likely to need allies and partners, but its political class currently is not prepared to accept the terms on which these partnerships and alliances can be struck.

For the United States, this presents a significant policy challenge. An isolated and weak Russia is not in the U.S. interest. Yet it appears likely to grow increasingly unstable at home and difficult to deal with abroad, as prospects for long-term systemic change become ever more remote. Furthermore, in the near and mid-term, Russia's considerable resources enable it to act as a spoiler and cause considerable harm in its own neighborhood. The task of managing relations with this kind of Russia—countering its negative influence while keeping it engaged and protecting U.S. interests— will remain a major challenge of U.S. foreign policy for the foreseeable future.

A Difficult Tradeoff: Iran versus Democracy and Neighborhood Role

In the coming years, the U.S./European-Russia agenda is likely to be dominated by three issues: Iran's nuclear ambitions; Russia's retreat from democracy; and Russia's role and aspirations in its own neighborhood. The United States and its European allies could face a difficult tradeoff. In order to secure Russian cooperation on Iran, they may have to put aside their objections to Moscow's heavy-handed policies toward its neighbors and the Kremlin's pursuit of authoritarian forms of government at home.

Although Russian-Iranian relations have shown signs of tension triggered by Iran's reported lateness in its payments to Russia and Russia's frustration with its erratic partner, the relationship is of considerable mutual convenience and is unlikely to be altered abruptly by either side. Western pressures on Russia for a tougher line toward Iran are unlikely to produce the desired result in the context of overall deteriorating relations between Russia and the West. However, over time, Russian frustrations with Tehran's behavior, combined with Western enticements, could lead to a more constructive Russian position. This is likely to be an evolutionary rather than a revolutionary change.

Russia's attempts to influence Iran to accept its compromise proposal for joint uranium reprocessing on Russian territory have not been successful, even though Russian officials have insisted on the viability of that option long after Iran appeared to have lost interest in it. However, Russia still has an important role to play in the diplomatic efforts to contain Iran's WMD ambitions. As a permanent member of the Security Council, Russia has a key role to play in Security Council decisions regarding Iran.

However, getting Russian accession to the position embraced by the United States and its European allies will not be easy, even if this is the only card Russia has to play to restore its relationship with the United States and Europe on the course of real partnership. To understand why, it is necessary to understand the Russian calculus vis-à-vis Iran, Europe, and the United States.

Russia's political class does not view Iran and its nuclear ambitions as a major threat to Russian security. Alexei Arbatov, a leading Russian national security expert, wrote in 1999:

> Now, for Russia, the emergence of 2–3 [new] nuclear powers would bad news, but in principle not revolutionary. Their [weapons] will not necessarily be aimed at Russia even if they are geographically closer to it than to the United States. In this sense, some in Russia may even welcome quietly China's nuclear program and nuclear proliferation, which somehow can compensate the growing disparity between the Russian federation and the United States in the area of strategic nuclear weapons and tame the political arrogance and high-handedness of Washington.[62]

A form of pragmatism has characterized Russian-Iranian relations. The Iranian government has been careful not to criticize Russia with regard to its brutal suppression of Chechnya or interference in neighboring countries. Iran has trod carefully in Central Asia and the Caucasus, including in Tajikistan, to which it has ethnic and linguistic ties. As a result, Moscow does not see Iranian support to radical extremists in the Middle East as a direct threat to its own interests. Iran has been a steady buyer of Russian armaments and has valued its relationship with Russia as a major power and a member of the Security Council. Iran is also an important entry point to the Persian Gulf, into which Russia otherwise has very few openings.

Russian officials and analysts understand that Iran's nuclear ambitions are high on the agenda of the international community in general and Russia's principal interlocutors—the United States, United Kingdom, Germany, and France—in particular.

Russian policymakers most likely view their involvement in the Iranian nuclear crisis as a great power prerogative, as well as a function of their interests in that country.

However, Russian officials appear to be more concerned about a U.S. intervention than about Iran's ambitions as such. U.S. intervention, they fear, would jeopardize Russian commercial interests; complicate relations with the United States, Israel, and others; cause further regional destabilization; and set off other ripple effects that Russia may be ill equipped to handle.

A number of important enticements from the United States and its European allies would be required to convince Russia to take a more vigorous stance regarding Iran on the issue of WMD and join the U.S.-European position at the expense of its relationship with Iran. For Russia, a key issue on its foreign policy agenda is its position in the immediate neighborhood and the U.S. policy of promoting democracy there. As long as Russia continues to feel squeezed out of its own strategic backyard, its support for the U.S.-European position on Iran's WMD will be lukewarm at best.

Moscow's tradeoff on this issue of strategic importance for the United States is likely to be a compromise on the issue of strategic importance to Russia—its role in the former Soviet lands. Russian officials and foreign policy experts probably realize that an exclusive Russian sphere of influence in its neighborhood is long gone. But they do not want this region to become a zone of Russia's exclusion where, as they see it, U.S. promotion of democracy leads to Russian loss of influence and instability. Thus, a compromise solution may be possible if the United States will accept that Russian acquiescence to its position on Iran carries a price that, at the very least, entails reordered U.S. priorities and perhaps longer timelines in pursuit of democratic peace in the former Soviet lands. At the most, the price could be U.S. acquiescence to a major Russian role in its neighborhood—an objective of Russian foreign policy since the early 1990s and a controversial issue that will remain high on the U.S. policy agenda.[63]

Another set of issues where any tradeoff will be difficult to achieve concerns the situation inside Russia and the democracy deficit there. The U.S. position in this context may be helped by the fact that relatively few Russians appear to be actively interested in U.S. support for Russian democracy, thus limiting opportunities for the United States to promote democracy inside Russia. But it will be difficult for U.S. policymakers and legislators to ignore domestic trends in Russia and engage in high-level diplomacy with its leaders pursuing a strictly pragmatic agenda.

All of this points to few areas for compromise where the United States and Russia could reach common ground from which to renew cooperation and work toward improved relations. The lack of common ground and opportunities for meaningful tradeoffs points to a relationship that is bound for a difficult phase in which all three issues—Iran, Russian domestic politics and relations with neighbors—will remain contentious and in which little progress is to be made in the years to come.

WHAT IS TO BE DONE?

Having failed to win Russia as an absolute friend in the years since the Soviet collapse, the United States is finding itself in the midst of a debate about its relationship with Russia in which the latter is sometimes treated as an absolute enemy. As the foregoing discussion makes clear, however, despite major disagreements between Russia and the United States, neither the state of Russia's democracy nor Russia's policy toward its neighbors warrants the latter option. Moreover, its internal conditions are reason enough to worry that a policy of neocontainment could backfire and either lead to a new destabilization of Russia or harden its already emerging anti-Western consensus and push its domestic politics into an even more irredentist direction.

Despite Russia's diminished status and capabilities, it remains an important factor in the international arena, especially in its immediate neighborhood, where the United States has taken an increasingly active role with the expansion of the Euroatlantic security framework—NATO and Partnership for Peace—into Eastern Europe, the Baltic region, the Caucasus, and even Central Asia. Russia no longer has the means to serve as the security manager in the vast regions around its periphery, but it still wields considerable influence by virtue of its geographic position and economic and cultural ties. For the United States, displacing it from its neighborhood entirely is neither feasible nor desirable.

Russia's domestic circumstances appear to be sufficiently precarious despite the image of stability and consolidation peculiar to the Putin era. While domestic political consolidation has occurred at the expense of NGOs, independent political parties, and press freedoms, it is still too early to write off the future of democracy in Russia. A number of grassroots developments point to the emergence of civil society that in the long run could prove far more meaningful for a representative political system taking hold in Russia than current debates about the fate of Russian democracy would lead one to believe.

The United States has no choice but to balance its interest in Russia's domestic arrangements against other interests. These include the security of Russia's nuclear arsenal and its proliferation policies; its position on Iran; and its ability to sustain exports of hydrocarbons. Washington should also pursue a dialogue with Russia on U.S. missile defense development plans as part of a revived strategic dialogue and should cautiously explore President Putin's 2007 proposal to develop missile defense capabilities jointly. While Russian performance is not to be taken for granted in any of these areas, it appears that U.S. leverage to promote its desired outcome is quite limited.

In reality, U.S.-Russian relations are neither as bad as critics charge nor as good as optimists hope they can be. Although the relationship has fallen far short of its potential, it also has avoided many very real downturns and has steered clear of the worst. For the United States, the association remains one that could facilitate pursuit of its geopolitical and strategic objectives—stability and peace in Europe, balanced relations with China, combating global terrorism, counterproliferation, and energy security. It is a relationship that could seriously complicate U.S. pursuit of these objectives and the prosecution of the war on terror in Eurasia, as well as elsewhere in the world, if it were to turn sour. Since being founded at the end of the Cold War on the realization that the road ahead would be difficult and would involve change that would be nothing short of generational, the relationship has relied on a mixture of competition and partnership, confrontation and cooperation, and has paid off in a number of key areas—NATO and European Union enlargement, Cooperative Threat Reduction, cooperation in the war on terror, and so forth. It has paid off for the United States through perseverance and adherence to the long view. There is little in the balance of Russia's domestic trends or international behavior to warrant a fundamental reassessment of U.S. commitment to that relationship, let alone a radical departure from it.

INDIA: THE TRANSFORMING POWER

While China and Russia often capture the public spotlight as global actors, the idea that India will be a driving force in the transformation of global strategic reality is less familiar. Those who foresee India playing such a prominent role in the international power structure argue that a combination of demographic forces, developing military capabilities, and economic expansion makes India's rise to world power almost inevitable. Such a rise is "a virtual certainty," says the National Intelligence Council's 2004 report, *Mapping the Global Future*, "barring an abrupt reversal of the process of globalization or any major upheavals." The only important questions, the report contends, are whether the rise of India takes place smoothly and how it exercises its newfound global power vis-à-vis the rest of the international community.[64]

During the last two U.S. administrations, the logic of this assessment has increasingly shaped American policy toward India. It was expressed most directly in a background briefing by three unnamed officials in March 2005, in which the principal briefer stated that the goal of U.S. policy "is to help India become a major world power in the 21st century. We understand fully the implications, including military implications, of that statement."[65]

Those implications became much clearer on July 18, 2005, when on the occasion of a visit by Prime Minister Manmohan Singh, the Bush administration announced an agreement to share civilian nuclear technology with India, notwithstanding India's secret development and testing of nuclear weapons and its nonadherence to the Non-Proliferation Treaty.

Nothing could have signaled more dramatically than this break with previous policy that the United States was serious about a new relationship with India. Under Secretary of State Nicholas Burns' explanation of the President's action was a concise statement of the "rising India" thesis:

Within the first quarter of this century, [India] is likely to be numbered among the world's five largest economies. It will soon be the world's most populous nation, and it has a demographic structure that bequeaths it a huge, skilled, and youthful workforce. It will continue to possess large and ever more sophisticated military forces that, just like our own, remain strongly committed to the principle of civilian control. And, above all else, India will thrive as a vibrant, multi-ethnic, multi-religious, and multi-lingual democracy characterized by individual freedom, rule of law, and a constitutional government that owes its power to fair and free elections. As the President phrased it succinctly,

'This century will see democratic India's arrival as a force in the world.' And, as such, it is in our national interest to develop a strong, forward-looking relationship with the world's largest democracy as the political and economic focus of the global system shifts inevitably eastward to Asia.[66]

Considerable attention has been paid to the Bush-Singh nuclear agreement from a nonproliferation point of view,[67] but the fundamental strategic premise from which the agreement derives—that India will be a potent global force in the relatively near future and therefore can be a valuable strategic partner for the United States—has not been subjected to the same degree of scrutiny.

ASSESSING INDIA'S GLOBAL ROLE

How certain is it that India will actually play the kind of role in the world that futurists project for it, and what will it mean for the United States? These questions will be considered in light of the four factors identified by Burns as impelling India toward a prominent place in the global power structure—the country's demography, military capability, economy, and political system.

Demography as Destiny?

Demography offers the strongest argument for projecting India to be a major global power. India's population already exceeds 1 billion and is growing at a rate of 1.4 percent a year, putting it on a path to reach 2 billion by 2060. Moreover, with nearly a third of the population under the age of 15, there is little likelihood that the growth rate will slow any time soon. By contrast, China's population of 1.3 billion is growing less than half as fast as India's, and with only a fifth of its population under age 15, China is not facing the same jump in birth rates in the next decade, when the cohort of those born since 1995 enters their child-bearing years.

Moreover, India's population growth rate presently is constrained by high infant mortality (54.6 infant deaths per 1,000 live births, compared with China's 23.1 and Russia's 15.1) and relatively low life expectancy (64.71 years compared with 72.58 years in China). As health conditions improve, declining infant mortality and rising life expectancy will further fuel population growth. India's democratic political system will make it difficult for any Indian government to institute compulsory limits on family size as Beijing has done. In short, India is destined to be the world's most populous country by mid-century, with any leveling off not occurring until well in the future.

Being the most populous country on earth undoubtedly carries with it a substantial weight in world affairs, yet it is striking that the very factors that demographers cite as liabilities when they appear in other developing countries, particularly high birth rates and an enormous youth bulge, are said to be assets in the case of India. *Mapping the Global Future* treats the burgeoning Indian population almost exclusively in terms of millions of well-educated new members of a workforce fueling the global economy.[68]

TABLE 6–5. KEY INDIAN MILITARY CAPABILITIES

	Active Personnel	Major Force Structure	Key Equipment (estimated)
Army	1,100,000	3 armored divisions 8 separate armored brigades 32 infantry divisions 10 separate infantry brigades 1 commando/airborne brigade 2 artillery divisions	3,978 main battle tanks 2,800 other armored vehicles 12,675 artillery pieces 12 attack helicopters 150 utility helicopters 3,500 surface-to-air missiles 2,339 antiaircraft guns
Navy	55,000		1 aircraft carrier 63 major surface combatants 16 submarines 15 amphibious ships 14 mine warfare ships 34 combat capable aircraft 91+ helicopters
Air Force	170,000	39 fighter/attack squadrons 10 transport squadrons 3 attack helicopter squadrons 22 transport helicopter squadrons	852 combat capable aircraft 288 transport aircraft 6 tankers 60 attack helicopters 236 support/utility helicopters
Strategic Forces		1 IRBM group 3 SRBM regiments	24 Agni IRBM 45 Prithvi SRBM
Paramilitary Forces	1,720,000		

Source: International Institute for Strategic Studies, *The Military Balance 2006.*

The other side of the coin is that the Indian economy will have to grow even faster if it is to keep up with the life expectations of these millions of new workers. If it does not, India risks facing either an acceleration of the already serious brain drain or a revolution of rising expectations on the part of those who are left behind, or both. Furthermore, the tendency for most social violence to be committed by young men between the ages of 15 and 25 raises the prospect that India may be facing a wave of crime or political unrest as the proportion of its population in that age group rises. Managing these risks will necessarily absorb an enormous share of the country's political and administrative capacity for at least the next several decades.

Military Capabilities

The numbers behind India's standing as a significant military power are almost as impressive as its general demographics. With 1.3 million men under arms, it possesses the world's third largest active armed forces, ranking just behind China and the United States and ahead of North Korea and the Russian Federation. In 1998, India became the world's sixth self-declared nuclear weapons state and is now estimated by independent analysts to have as many as 150 nuclear weapons. The Indian armed forces are widely respected as professional, well trained, and committed to the principle of democratic civilian control. They are capable of carrying out the tasks assigned to them by their government, particularly the defense of Indian territory against external aggression, as well as providing valuable capabilities to international peacekeeping missions under United Nations (UN) Security Council mandates.[69]

When it comes to applying Indian military capabilities (see table 6–5) to the objectives that India and the United States may have in common on a wider global stage, however, a number of key limitations must be taken into account. While each of these limitations can be overcome over time, none are amenable to quick fixes.

India's ability to play a major military role as a U.S. strategic partner is severely constrained by a crisis of block obsolescence. For example, the Indian Air Force (IAF) is, by regional standards, a modern, technology-intensive air force and, by any standards, a well-trained and well-led one, evinced by recent exercises with the U.S. Air Force. But these positives notwithstanding, the harsh reality, fully understood by the service's leaders, is that most of India's fighter fleet is already two generations out of date. The issue is not merely qualitative but quantitative as well; because of a combination of aging equipment and inadequate maintenance, the IAF routinely loses more than 20 fighters and the lives of some 8 pilots every year.

Making matters worse is the notoriously inefficient Indian defense industrial establishment. Hindustan Aeronautics Limited's Light Combat Aircraft, which was supposed to be the backbone of the modern IAF, has now been in development for more than 22 years, with at least another 5 to go before it reaches full operational capability. Similar problems afflict other major weapons development programs, from tanks to missiles to submarines. Until the weaknesses of the armaments industry are corrected, India will remain dependent on foreign suppliers to equip its forces, and its ability to conduct the full range of defense diplomacy will be limited by the lack of credible potential as a major armaments supplier.

The armed forces' materiel problems are further aggravated by consistently inadequate budgets. In percentage terms, defense spending growth has been striking. From 2002 through 2006, the total defense budget grew by more than 50 percent, with further increases of 12.6 and 8.5 percent projected for 2007 and 2008 respectively.[70] But in absolute terms, the numbers are less impressive. Estimated defense spending for 2006 was on the order of $22 billion in terms of purchasing power parity, compared with China's estimated actual defense spending of $70 billion or more.[71] Moreover, the inefficiencies of the financial and procurement processes, aggravated by an understaffed and inexpert administrative hierarchy in the Ministry of Defence, ensure that Indian defense budgets are chronically underexecuted—a large portion of the money appropriated is never spent.[72]

The Indian military is also facing serious difficulties manning the force, a problem that will only get worse as the economy continues to grow. According to a parliamentary report in April 2007, the army is understaffed by more than 13,000 officers. The navy and air force are beginning to experience similar shortages, with applications for commissions declining and increasing numbers of officers leaving the service short of a full career.[73] These shortfalls are the direct result of competition from the rapidly growing private sector and a marked change in the way young Indians are attracted to private sector rather than public sector careers.[74]

Even if all these problems could be corrected, there are also structural realities that limit India's ability to play a strategic partnership role in military terms. The Indian armed forces are predominantly a conventional light infantry force. Of the 1.3 million men on active duty in the armed forces, 1.1 million are in the army, with the air force accounting for about 150,000 and the navy for 55,000. Within the army, armor and mechanized infantry account for only about 15 percent of the maneuver brigades, and even these heavy units have only a limited capability for power projection or sustainment.[75] This is not a shortcoming of the force in the context of its current mission, which is focused on the defense of Indian territory against external (and, to a lesser degree, internal) threats. As Christine Fair points out, "The Indian Army does not see itself as a force projection army," and both military officers and civilians in the Indian national security establishment prefer to keep it that way.[76] It would, however, be an important constraint on using Indian forces in the types of missions the United States typically expects its major strategic partners to support.

This primarily internal emphasis is less true of the air force and navy, both of which have come to see value in being able to operate out of area. Thus, the IAF has led the way in establishing India's first foreign base, in Tajikistan. That the base is fairly modest and its purpose uncertain is less important than the fact that the Indian armed forces have taken this first step toward a role beyond homeland defense. Similarly, and characteristically, the Indian navy also sees a need to operate farther from home, particularly in securing the sea lines of communication between India and the Persian Gulf and between India and the western Pacific. It has welcomed the opportunity to cooperate with the U.S. Navy in this regard since 9/11. Yet realization of the navy's ambitions is seriously hampered by the service's lack of political clout in the Indian defense establishment. Not for nothing has the navy been called the "fourth of India's three services." Without more money, more people, and more support ships—which could come only at the expense of an army that is already alarmed at its shrinking (47 percent) share of the defense budget[77]—it is hard to see how the navy could sustain an out-of-area presence on a continuing basis. Given the lack of any joint mentality and of a more effective defense decisionmaking structure, it is equally hard to see how these resources can be extracted.

The concept of jointness is only slowly gaining serious support in the Indian defense establishment. Despite the problems in interservice coordination that surfaced during the Kargil conflict with Pakistan in 1999, the key recommendations of a ministerial review group aimed at achieving greater jointness remain unfulfilled, including the appointment of an overall Chief of Defence Staff.[78] The failure to act on these recommendations is a result not only of inertia and service parochialism but also of resistance from the most important power center in the Indian national security establishment, the civilian cadres of the Indian Administrative Service (IAS) who staff the central offices of the Ministry of Defence. For the Indian armed forces to develop the joint culture that would be necessary to work effectively with their U.S. counterparts in a high-threat environment, it will be necessary to persuade the IAS establishment that interservice integration and a greater voice for senior uniformed leaders in national security decisionmaking will not jeopardize civilian control of the military. Considering that the IAS sees itself as the "steel frame" of India, and that its officers enjoy constitutional protection against political interference with the way they execute their duties, this will not be an easy task.[79]·

Economy

The concept of a "rising India" rests primarily on the basis of the country's economic potential. In absolute terms, of course, a country of a billion people is almost bound to possess substantial economic resources, so it may be surprising that India's gross domestic product, at $887 billion, ranked only as the world's thirteenth largest as of 2006.[80] However, after decades of mostly disappointing growth, the Indian economy has taken off in recent years, achieving annual growth rates that have consistently been in the 6 to 8 percent range, occasionally as high as 10 percent. The boom has been driven by the information technology sector, concentrated in several of the country's southern states, and to a lesser degree by steps taken to dismantle portions of the Nehruvian socialist economic legacy.

Based on these trends, India is expected to vault from thirteenth to fourth among the world's largest economic powers by 2025 and to surpass the combined output of the European Union by 2035. *Mapping the Global Future* predicts that, given the growth of the Indian, Chinese, and other Asian economies, international economic trends over the next two decades will be increasingly affected by the monetary policies of Asian central banks, including the Reserve Bank of India, and by the market demands of Indian and other Asian consumers. Furthermore, as is already becoming apparent, India's continued industrialization and concomitant urbanization will make it a global economic player in one area that has become increasingly salient: competition for scarce energy resources. The U.S. Department of Energy predicts that India's oil requirements will double between now and 2020, reaching 4.4 million barrels per day. Natural gas consumption will rise even faster.

Assessing India's ability to leverage its potential economic power is as complex as assessing its ability to leverage its military capabilities. While impressive, the economic development of the last decade has been strikingly uneven, both geographically and sectorally. The world-class information technology sector, for example, has sometimes been referred to as "an island of excellence in a sea of mediocrity." Even in the information technology sphere, where India is now a global player, the information revolution has left the overwhelming majority of the Indian people behind—less than 2 percent of the population has access to the Internet. At a less advanced technological level, India's billion people share fewer than 50 million main telephone lines and 26 million cellular telephones. Only one percent of Indians living in rural areas have telephones of their own.

India's 2006 per capita gross domestic product of $797 was only slightly higher than Senegal's.[81] Even though the poverty rate has dropped by 10 percentage points in the past decade, 53 percent of Indian children are malnourished by international standards, 25 to 30 percent of the population still lives below the official poverty line, and most of the rest are constantly challenged to stay above it.[82]

Most forecasters predict that these shortcomings will be redressed in the coming decades as the economic growth rate continues to exceed the increase in population. Indeed, according to Organization for Economic Co-operation and Development statistics, India's per capita gross domestic product increased by nearly as large a percentage in the 16 years from 1980 to 1996 as it did in the 160 years from 1820 to 1980.[83] Yet these predictions still put India's per capita income at barely a fifth of that of the United States as far into the future as 2050. This would put India in roughly the same position vis-à-vis the United States then as Brazil and Thailand are now. While this would reflect a major improvement from India's current position—with a per capita income of about 8 percent that of the United States—it nevertheless suggests that even by 2050, the country will still be grappling with a number of serious shortfalls in internal development.

Success in dealing with those shortfalls depends in part on the ability of Indian leaders to generate a political consensus to address underlying structural problems, such as irrational energy pricing that penalizes industrial growth, generous agricultural subsidies that encourage inefficiency, an antiquated and overburdened judicial system, and labor and investment laws that reduce India's attractiveness as a target for foreign capital. Other limiting factors are less tractable in the short term, such as the inadequacy of the country's physical infrastructure and—despite the dazzling successes in some parts of the country—a nationwide human capital deficit that is reflected by a literacy rate of 60 percent and a ranking of 128 on the UN human development index.[84]

Most economists still project India to be a major international economic force given its gross economic weight (a function primarily of the sheer size of its population) even if per capita income and other indicators of internal economic development remain low.[85] Of course, gross economic product does make a difference to a country's international stature, as the example of China already bears out. But in a democracy such as India, popular preferences concerning resource allocation will be a critical factor in determining the role the country ultimately plays in the international economy.

Much of the analysis that projects India as a dynamic force on the international economic scene partakes of a certain amount of economic determinism, as if rising prosperity will necessarily make a billion people stop acting like Indians and start acting like Americans. Yet heretofore Indians have not, as a group, evinced a hunger for foreign consumer goods, perhaps because of a lack of wherewithal, but maybe also because Hindu culture places a low value on material possessions, or because of the strong tradition of *swadeshi*—national self-reliance—that was a key element of the independence struggle and has continued to shape Indian economic behavior ever since.

Whatever the reason for this proclivity for buying domestic, India's weight in international commerce is minuscule for a country its size. The country's total two-way trade in 2006 was only about $300 billion, about the same as Sweden's. The same preference for self-reliance is reflected in international capital flows. Although international investment both into and out of India is growing exponentially, the country still has a very long way to go before it can be considered a significant factor in the global capital market. In 2004, the UN Conference on Trade and Development valued Indian holdings outside India at some $7 billion, one-fortieth the amount of foreign investment by the smallest of the G–7 economies. Meanwhile, although new foreign investment flowing into India in 2005 was nearly twice what had come in as recently as 2000, it was still dwarfed by the flow into the Chinese economy by a ratio of more than 16 to 1.

Many Indian planners and economists have come to realize that meeting the country's ambitious economic growth targets depends on external trade and foreign investment, two things that have historically held a low priority in Indian thinking given the *swadeshi* legacy. As a result, India has reached out to potential economic partners, such as the United States, Europe, China, and the ASEAN states, much more energetically than has been the case in the past. These initiatives are not universally popular, however. They face strong lingering skepticism about the virtues of international commerce in a country that sees itself as having lost its independence some 250 years ago precisely because it allowed foreign commercial interests access to its markets.

Domestic Politics and Foreign Policy

For many Americans, the most compelling argument in support of a U.S. embrace of a rising India—and one the Indian government spares no effort to emphasize—is India's record as a thriving multiparty, multiethnic, and multireligious democracy. Notwithstanding a series of recurring regional insurgencies, serious human rights problems in Kashmir, and the occasional suspension of self-government in various states under so-called president's rule, India has been in most respects the model democracy in the developing world. Political debate is robust, the press is unfettered, and elections are free and open. Many would argue that this record equips or even destines India to play a special political role in countering the appeal of radical, antidemocratic ideologies based on an ideal of religious intolerance. In fact, President Bush cited these shared democratic values rather than a commonality of interests as the basis for the strengthening of ties between the countries during Prime Minister Singh's July 2005 visit:

> India and the United States share a commitment to freedom and a belief that democracy provides the best path to a more hopeful future for all people. We also believe that the

spread of liberty is the best alternative to hatred and violence. Because of our shared values, the relationship between our two countries has never been stronger. [86]

Yet it is precisely from the nature of India's democratic political system that the greatest uncertainties about the country's international role arise. Because India is a democracy, decisions about what part India is to play on the global stage cannot be made and imposed from the top down, nor can there be any certainty that strategic decisions, once made, will not be altered or even reversed. On the contrary, these decisions will reflect the consensus of the Indian body politic at the time they are made, a consensus that will shift from time to time based on short-range calculations made by hundreds of millions of Indian voters.

On some aspects of India's world role, there is a broad and rather stable consensus, while on others there is considerable diversity and instability. For example, the over-whelming majority of Indians believe their country, as the home of a billion people and the seat of an ancient civilization, should rightfully be given the respect and rec-ognition of a major power. Accordingly, Indian governments ever since independence have envisaged India as playing such a global role, although this vision has usually manifested itself more in postcolonial rhetoric and a quest for status than in serious efforts to apply Indian political, military, or economic power beyond the confines of South Asia. India remains profoundly intent on attaining formal public acknowledg-ment of what it considers its proper place in the world; witness its determination to attain a permanent seat on the UN Security Council. Indeed, New Delhi's acquisition of nuclear weapons can be interpreted to some extent as part of this quest for recogni-tion of India's great power status.

If aspiring to international respect is something on which all Indian factions agree, so is the determination that, as India gains power and prestige internationally, it must not sacrifice its peculiarly Indian identity. In the broadest terms, this translates into an aversion to becoming "Westernized." But beyond that surface unanimity are sharp divisions among liberals, Nehruists, and traditionalists about what India's identity really is or should be. These divisions, moreover, do not necessarily coincide with party lines; they exist between different parties in the governing and opposition coali-tions and even, in the larger parties, between factions of the same party.

Nor is there by any means a national consensus on the nature of Indian relations with the United States. While two successive governments led by different parties have pursued a strong relationship with Washington, support for this course is far from unanimous, especially with respect to military ties. The leftist parties on which the Singh government depends for its survival are adamantly opposed to the defense framework agreement and mounted public protests against the relationship when U.S. Air Force F–16s arrived in India for exercises in 2005. A number of leftist parties have threatened to bring down the government if it persists in its current course of military cooperation with the United States.[87] Even those who basically support good ties with the United States are not in full accord on the extent and types of cooperation to be pursued. The Bharatiya Janata Party (BJP) under which U.S.-Indian relations started blossoming in the 1990s has strongly opposed Prime Minister Manmohan Singh's proposed "123" agreement on nuclear cooperation with the United States as being detrimental to Indian sovereignty.

The ability of Indian governments to take decisive actions that would realize the country's untapped potential internationally is further limited by the salience of local interests and concerns in Indian politics. In any large democracy based on single member districts, there are bound to be tensions between protecting the interests of local constituencies and building a national consensus around a national agenda. This is especially true in a country where the challenges of domestic development—health, education, electrification, transportation, and administration of justice—are so pressing.

This same focus on local issues has meant that few parliamentary politicians are interested in international issues and even fewer have any real expertise in them,[88] leaving the void to be filled inadequately by a growing think tank community in New Delhi and the career diplomats of the Indian Foreign Service.[89]

The argument that India's rise to global power is all but inevitable based on its demographics, military capability, and economic strength does not take into account that this rise depends at least equally on choices that are made by Indians, both consciously and unconsciously. The examples of previous rising powers that are often cited as exhibiting parallels with India illustrate the importance of such choices. In the mid-1860s, the United States and the collection of kingdoms and principalities that would soon become Germany had almost the same population (about 32 million each). Both were coming out of major wars—one that restored national unity, one that achieved it—at the end of which each country's army exceeded a million men. The U.S. gross domestic product in 1870 was nearly 40 percent greater than Germany's, its international two-way trade about 10 percent greater.[90] On the face of it, the two countries would have seemed in similar positions as potential world powers. If anything, the stronger U.S. economy would have given it a slight edge. Yet the actual trajectories followed by the two countries brought Germany to acknowledged great power status at least 40 years before the United States.

The question, then, is what kind of choices Indians are likely to make about their international role given these demographic, military, economic, and domestic political considerations. It is quite clear from Indian elections and Indian political discourse that the main concern of the country's billion people is economic development, not the attainment of global power as it has traditionally been understood.

Even in the area of national security policy, India's main strategic focus has historically been inward, not outward. For centuries, the principal issues facing Indian rulers have been the struggle against disunity within the subcontinent and the need to protect the heartland against invaders from beyond the mountains. While Indian traders ranged far afield, maintaining a substantial commercial presence in Southeast Asia and the East Indies, the Persian Gulf, and East Africa, their activities were traditionally viewed by the Indian political class as peripheral, certainly nothing that would require diverting the strategists' attention from the classic problems of subcontinental unity and landward defense.[91]

It is thus a comparatively recent development for Indian leaders to recognize that events outside South Asia affect their country's welfare and security in tangible and not merely symbolic ways. India's increasing interdependence with the greater world is being driven in part by changes within India itself. As industrialization and urbanization progress, for example, it has become apparent that India has a vital interest in the stable supply of energy at reasonable prices. Moreover, as already mentioned, Indian planners and economists recognize that continued rapid growth requires external trade and foreign investment despite the domestic political costs to be incurred from pursuing such foreign links.

External events have had an even greater role in reorienting the way Indian leaders across the political spectrum understand India's international role and interests. Perhaps the most important was the collapse of the Soviet Union in 1991 and Russia's continued decline as a global power ever since. Although India had already begun seeking closer relations with the United States by the early 1980s, especially in the area of technological cooperation, the end of the Cold War nevertheless had a decisive impact on India's international position. On the one hand, it necessitated a rethinking of the value of India's historic relationship with the Soviet Union. While India remains close to post-Soviet Russia, particularly as a source of military technology and equipment, it no longer sees the same value it once did in diplomatic alignment with Moscow, particularly since it is clear that Russia can no longer deliver on any tacit commitments to India's security or other interests. On the other hand, the demise of the Soviet Union left behind a transformed global system in which the United States is the single dominant actor. This impelled Indian decisionmakers from both major parties to seek better relations with Washington as the remaining global superpower.

What has not changed in Indian strategic thinking is just as important as what has. Part of the Indian identity that leaders of all stripes are determined to preserve is the country's independence from any international power bloc. The salience that Indian strategic thinkers and decisionmakers place on preventing any kind of outside limitations or even significant outside influence on India's freedom of action is an important intellectual legacy of the period of British domination. It was such outside pressures that India's founding prime minister, Jawaharlal Nehru, saw as one of the key threats to the attainment of Indian greatness.[92] His vision of what India is and ought to be—a major power, but one radically unlike the former imperialist masters—continues to shape the way Indians think of the country's world role.

Thus, even as decisionmakers have sought improved relations with Washington in the wake of the Soviet collapse, they have simultaneously placed a premium on reaching out to other centers of power, including the European Union and especially China, in an attempt to hedge against American global hegemony. Just as the Indian armed forces have stepped up the intensity of their bilateral interaction with the United States, they have done the same with the Chinese military, including the exchange of observers at national military exercises and the conduct of a series of bilateral naval exercises.

New Delhi's strong preference for a multipolar world in which it can balance rival powers against one another to India's advantage could turn out to be one of the most formidable barriers to achieving the close partnership the United States and India claim to seek, especially if it is occasionally manifested by India's aligning with China in opposition to American initiatives instead of the other way around.

The Indian commitment to the United Nations as the primary if not the only source of international legitimacy also remains unchanged and is another potential cause of friction in the would-be strategic partnership. It is important to keep in mind that in the past 3 years, governments led by both the Congress Party and the BJP have refused American requests to get involved in the stabilization of Iraq, explicitly because of the lack of a UN Security Council mandate for the Iraq operation. In the last two decades, the United States has come to structure its approach to maintaining international peace and stability around coalitions of the willing, with formal regional security organizations relegated to a secondary role. Absent a fundamental shift in India's approach to this core issue—a shift that is unlikely given the broad popular consensus about this subject within the Indian body politic—it is difficult to foresee active Indian participation in such coalitions, at least not with military forces and probably not with active diplomatic or financial support.

AMERICA'S STRATEGIC CHALLENGE: HARMONIZING INTERESTS AND MANAGING EXPECTATIONS

The U.S.-Indian relationship is a work in progress. While a shared commitment to democracy is a positive attribute in bilateral relations, it is by no means a sufficient foundation for the kind of robust strategic partnership that U.S. and Indian leaders claim to contemplate.[93] A truly successful partnership must be based partly on identifying where the two countries' interests converge and diverge and partly on the ability and willingness of each partner to meet the other's expectations.

There are substantial areas in which Indian and American interests converge—defeating terrorism inspired by a violent interpretation of radical Islam, encouraging the spread of democracy and respect for human rights, and promoting the prosperity of what will one day be the world's most populous economic unit. There are also areas of serious divergence. Even where the two countries share common concerns, such as the growing presence and influence of China in Southeast Asia and the Indian Ocean, the relative weight they put on these concerns and the lengths to which they are prepared to go to deal with them differ widely.

There are also areas of direct competition, most notably as rival importers of hydrocarbon fuels, a competition that will intensify as Indian economic development succeeds.[94] At a more fundamental level, the current leaders of the two countries have basically different visions of the proper functioning of the international system that will have to be harmonized for a strategic partnership to be truly effective.

This directly affects the question of whether the United States can or will fulfill the expectations that India will have of this relationship. American leaders must consider whether they are prepared to recalibrate the way they conduct international policy to conform to the Indian vision of the global system. Is the United States prepared to deliver on India's number one agenda item: formal recognition of India's world power status with a permanent seat on the UN Security Council?

While the United States was willing to give symbolic recognition of India's great power status by accepting the reality of its possession of nuclear weapons, it has thus far declined to go so far as to support India's ambition of attaining a permanent council seat. An immediate confrontation has been averted by pointing to the need to address broader reform of the United Nations, but at some point New Delhi's determination to attain a permanent seat (with veto) and Washington's resolve to prevent the addition of more veto-wielding members are bound to come into open conflict.

On the military front, Indian leaders say frankly that the main benefit they want from the bilateral relationship is access to military-related technology without restrictions or linkages of any kind. The Indian view was expressed by Foreign Secretary Shyam Saran, the senior career official in the Ministry of External Affairs, in December 2005, when he asked rhetorically how it could be desirable for the United States to operate a technology denial regime against a country it claims to consider a strategic partner. The reality is that the entire world is under a U.S. technology denial regime of some kind; there are some defense technologies that are not available for export to anyone, even America's closest allies. To U.S. officials, this is a natural state of affairs; to Indian officials, it is an indication of skepticism about Indian promises to keep the technology secure.

Conversely, as the United States looks to India as a strategic partner, it must ask itself what role India will be prepared to play in those areas where interests converge. India's potential power is tremendous, certainly within Asia and probably beyond. What remains to be seen is whether this potential power will or even can be exerted in practical terms.

Politically, a strategic partner is typically expected to work with the United States and other states within the partner's region to enhance security and stability. India obviously does share many of the principal U.S. security interests in South Asia—particularly in the end of the terrorist wars in Nepal and Sri Lanka, the stabilization of Bangladesh, the cessation of Islamist militant movements across the Kashmiri line of control, and the return of democracy and stability to Nepal. But the United States must understand that its newly benign view of Indian capabilities and intentions vis-à-vis these neighbors is not yet shared by those neighbors themselves. This calls into question how effective India can be in helping the United States achieve this shared objective.

Meanwhile, strategic partners have usually been expected to defer to Washington's judgment on matters the United States considers critical to its own interests outside the partner's immediate region, with serious tension often ensuing if this deference is not forthcoming. If U.S. experience with European allies is any gauge, there will be many occasions for such tensions with an Indian political class that expects to be deferred to, not to defer. [95]

The most pressing national security problem confronting the United States in South Asia today—defeating the Pakistani and Afghan manifestations of the globalized jihadist insurgency—is one in which India can play only a marginal role, primarily as a result of the nearly 60 years of animosity between India and Pakistan. For example, the administration points favorably to India's role as an important donor in the reconstruction of Afghanistan, and in fact India has committed some $600 million to projects ranging from road construction to power lines to schools. At the end of August 2005, the two countries signed a series of formal cooperation agreements covering education, agricultural research, and health care. Finally, President Hamid Karzai and Prime Minister Singh jointly called for tougher action against militancy, referring specifically to the importance of Pakistan's role in the struggle.[96] All of these developments sound praiseworthy when viewed from Washington, but in Pakistan—a country whose cooperation is vital to U.S. success in the war on terrorism—they look like the creation of an Afghan alignment with India against Pakistan.

The facile solution to Pakistan's concerns is for the United States to simply dehyphenate its relations with the two major South Asian powers. *Dehyphenation* is a shorthand phrase for the principle that "U.S. relations with each state should be governed by an objective assessment of the intrinsic value of each country to U.S. interests rather than by fears about how U.S. relations with one would affect relations with the other."[97] While it may sound plausible in theory, ignoring the effect that U.S. relations with one of these two countries would have on relations with the other—and on the bilateral dynamic between the two—would be impossible in practice.

Clearly, it behooves the United States to conceive of India in a more global context than it has typically done in the past, but doing so cannot negate the fact that the regional context also remains critically important. To evaluate American strategy options toward India without taking Pakistani equities into consideration would be like building a strategy toward Pakistan based solely on its role in fighting al Qaeda while disregarding the activities of A.Q. Khan or the status of the line of control in Kashmir.

All this cautions against placing a greater burden on the evolving U.S.-Indian strategic relationship than it is able to bear, a counsel to temper expectations on both sides and not allow the glowing statements of shared democratic values to blind us to very real obstacles that lie in the way of productive cooperation. Yet this does not negate in the least the extremely high importance that Washington is and ought to be placing on putting ties with India on a firm, stable, and durable footing, or the investment that the American public and private sectors will increasingly be making in the development of the Indian economy. There is considerable merit to the concept, articulated by Ashley Tellis, that the United States has an inherent interest in the development of independent power centers in Asia that by their very existence prevent the achievement of hegemony over the continent by any single state.[98]

India may turn out to be a major power unlike any that has come before. To the extent that the country remains true to what most Indians want it to be, its might will not be manifested in an ability to project military force, as that of the classical European powers and the United States has been. Nor, as long as India's external trade and investment remain negligible compared to other global centers, will it carry the kind of clout exercised by the European Union, postwar Japan, or even the "Asian tigers." Some have suggested that a rising India's influence will be felt not in these traditional areas of hard power but in the soft power of cultural clout, be it the success of Indian democracy and development "radiating" throughout Asia[99] or the subtly subversive

TABLE 6–6. COMPARING THE GREAT POWERS

	Population (million)	GDP Per Capita	Active Military Size	Est. Defense Expenditure ($billion)*	Defense Expenditure as Percent of GDP	Total Two-Way Trade ($billion)	Total External Debt ($billion)
Russia	144	$4,043	1,212,700	25.1	4.3	333.1	223.2
China	1,300	$1,462	2,255,000	62.5	3.3	1,242.6	275.5
India	1,100	$691	1,325,000	19.6	2.6	87.5	123.9
United States	294	$39,796	1,433,600	465.0	4.0	2,340.0	8,353.5

Sources: World Bank, *Key Development Data and Statistics: Country Profiles*, available at <www.worldbank.org>; U.S. Department of the Treasury, Office of International Affairs, available at <http://www.treasury.gov/tic/deb2ad04.html>; International Institute for Strategic Studies (IISS), *The Military Balance, 2004 and 2005–2006*. All figures are 2004.

*Defense expenditure data is derived from IISS estimates, which attempt to account for undisclosed expenditure and variation between countries, and have been adjusted to express all values in nominal terms.

social messages of individual choice and moderate sexual liberation conveyed by the ubiquitous movies produced by India's "Bollywood" film industry. While the role of a cultural hub is a comfortable one for most Indians, it remains to be seen how effective soft power can be without the hard edge of more conventional power to back it up.

Whatever kind of power India turns out to be, it is clear that the United States will be better off having positive relations with it than not. Tensions will arise along the way, and they will be aggravated by many differences, both stylistic and substantive, that have often caused serious friction in the past. Yet as Sumit Ganguly aptly points out, it has been precisely the lack of a broad-based relationship that has allowed such points of contention to dominate the agenda and derail promising opportunities for cooperation in the past.[100] It will be necessary for American decisionmakers to work through these irritations frankly yet patiently, slowly building the ties across a multitude of fronts, if the world's two largest democracies are to cooperate as successfully as has long been so optimistically envisioned.

MANAGING GREAT POWER RELATIONS

Nothing demonstrates better the passing of the age of absolutism from America's foreign policy than its relationships with the three major powers discussed in this chapter (see table 6–6). Unlike the Cold War, the United States has neither absolute friends nor absolute enemies among the major centers of global power. With all three of them, the relationship is bound to have elements of cooperation and competition, agreement and discord, incentives and coercion, and even the potential for conflict with China or Russia. In other words, it is likely to be a "normal" relationship where the degree of partnership or hostility is likely to be determined by the mix of U.S. interests rather than pursuit of victory guided by fierce competition of ideas.

In a stark departure from the all-out competition with the Soviet Union that resulted in the latter's demise, U.S. relationships with the major centers of global power are devoid of the same competitive spirit. The United States has enormous stakes in all three of these powers and must always, even in the most competitive aspects of these relationships, contend with the realization that victory can be costly. Even U.S. victory in the Cold War proved to be costly, for despite the peace dividend, the United States had no choice but to pay for a variety of Cold War legacy projects—from the Chernobyl nuclear disaster in Ukraine to the security of the nuclear stockpile in Russia to the environmental projects in Central Asia.

The war on terror has some fiercely competitive aspects, especially when it comes to the battle of ideas. But its prosecution, as well as dealing with many regional and global problems, requires the United States to pursue cooperative strategies toward the three major powers of Eurasia. This has a moderating effect on U.S. competition with China or Russia, whose cooperation may be required in pursuit of important U.S. interests. The U.S. stake in cooperative relations with those two nations is likely to limit the U.S. agenda for democracy promotion with regard to both of them.

Despite major changes in the world and U.S. foreign policy since the terrorist attacks of September 11, 2001, U.S. policy toward the three major powers has shown a remarkable degree of continuity. Current U.S. policies toward China, Russia, and India may reflect changes in emphasis from the 1990s but are not fundamentally different from U.S. policies of the previous decade.

U.S. policy toward China, particularly since 2005, has encouraged it to act as a responsible stakeholder in the international system, rather than as a member or observer. The goal of this policy is to encourage Chinese behavior that does not merely participate in the international system, but actively strengthens it. On the one hand, it recognizes China's enhanced status and rights as a shareholder. On the other hand, it appeals to China's sense of responsibility. This policy appeals to China's self-interest as a member of major international arrangements—the world system of free trade and attendant agreements on intellectual property rights, transparency, and fair pricing; the global nonproliferation regime; environmental treaties; and so forth. The extent of China's ability to act as a responsible stakeholder will be tested over the next several years. But the prospect of a cooperative China invested in the international system creates a powerful incentive for the United States to carefully calibrate the mix of cooperative and competitive tools in its approach to Beijing.

A stumbling China would pose at least as much of a challenge to U.S. interests in Eurasia and beyond as a successful China pursuing a deliberate, focused strategy intended to expand its power and influence. Aside from the economic fallout and impact on U.S. trade and investment in China, domestic unrest could result in a more nationalistic foreign policy as Beijing seeks to deal with internal problems or a less coherent policy that the United States would be ill equipped to counter for fear of aggravating the central government's weakness and generating even greater unpredictability in its behavior.

The novelty of this approach to Beijing lies in its unequivocal recognition of China's status as a major shareholder in the international system. However, the essence of this policy is not new and reflects the longstanding U.S. practice vis-à-vis China, Russia, and India of co-opting potential partners on the assumption that they are more likely to be cooperative inside than outside the tent, even before they are ready for full membership responsibilities. This was the logic of extending G–8 membership to Russia. Shareholder responsibility is a concept that is to a large degree being currently extended in U.S. policy toward India in the expectation that it will continue its progress as a stakeholder in the international system and will work to strengthen it.

However, to be effective, shareholder responsibility has to be a two-way street. It implies mutual responsibility, shared interests, and substantial stakes in each other held by the shareholders, including the United States. Its application to the three Eurasian powers would reaffirm the longstanding U.S. practice of balancing its diverse interests, combining elements of cooperation and competition, and mixing coercion with rewards—a practice that has proven its effectiveness in the long run and one to which there is no realistic alternative.

Moreover, the global agenda pursued by the United States is not shared by the three major Eurasian powers, whose priorities are heavily concentrated on their domestic agendas. Whenever they see the global agenda of the United States encroach upon their respective domestic agendas, they are likely to oppose it even if they agree with the United States on the endstate. There exist profound disagreements among the three Eurasian players on the means to achieve regional and global security. Chief among them are differences with respect to the role that democratic governance can and should play as an instrument of foreign policy and long-term stability. These differences pit the United States squarely against the three Eurasian great powers, which tend to view interests and their balance as the more reliable basis for achieving long-term stability and security.

In the case of India, U.S. democracy promotion does not strike the same neuralgic notes as it does with Russia and China. But India's support for this cause is likely to be tempered by skepticism about its efficacy, desire to protect India's own interests regarding third parties, and longstanding postcolonial suspicion of big power interference in the internal affairs of other nations.

Moreover, while U.S. interests appear to be well served by the flourishing relationship with India, U.S. leverage in more contentious circumstances could be quite limited. One reason is India's internal weakness as a nation suffering from widespread poverty and underdevelopment, combined with the long-term U.S. interest in seeing India overcome this weakness. Applying sanctions to India in retaliation for policies that run contrary to U.S. interests could be counterproductive and backfire. Another reason is the relative novelty of the U.S.-Indian partnership and its vulnerability to Indian public opinion, still sensitive to external pressures after the colonial experience.

Two of the three Eurasian powers—China and Russia—at least rhetorically find themselves on the receiving end of U.S. efforts to promote democracy. Both have been targets of U.S. criticism for their failure to observe democratic norms at home. Both have viewed U.S. criticism as a challenge to their sovereignty and national pride. In the case of China, U.S. support for democratic governance worldwide is superimposed on longstanding tensions over Taiwan. In the case of Russia, U.S. support for democracy has been viewed as a tool to limit Russian influence in the territories around its periphery that Moscow has viewed as its traditional sphere of influence. Thus, Washington's democracy promotion efforts will continue to constrain relations with China and Russia, barring unexpected political shifts in those countries. The 2006 National Security Strategy discussion of the limits of great power cooperation underscores that the United States cannot be indifferent to a state's treatment of its own citizens because "states that are governed well behave well."[101] The strategy concludes that close relations with the United States can only be cemented by governments that expand liberty and respect the rule of law and the dignity of the individual.

As Central Asia has emerged as a locus of great power competition, the Shanghai Cooperation Organization has become an important venue for its prosecution. Russia, China, and the four Central Asian member states are clearly interested in positioning the SCO as an international counterweight to the United States, but divergent interests among the members and the need for cooperation with Washington on certain issues make it unlikely that the SCO will develop into an anti-U.S. alliance, particularly if the United States remains engaged in the region.

The SCO evolved out of the Shanghai Five, a 1996 Chinese initiative to promote confidence-building measures and disarmament along China's borders with Russia and Central Asian states. A secondary motive was to legitimize increased Chinese influence in Central Asia without upsetting Russia. Heads of state have held annual summits since 1996 and ministers of foreign affairs, defense, economy, and trade, as well as justice and law enforcement officials, have held meetings to explore multilateral cooperation.

Statements from the 2006 and 2007 SCO summits were more restrained than those from 2005, when the summit declaration called for a timetable for the withdrawal of U.S. military forces from bases in Uzbekistan and Kyrgyzstan. But the 2006 and 2007 summits did echo previous calls decrying—not so obliquely—U.S. democracy promotion efforts as interference in the internal affairs of sovereign countries. The 2006 summit declaration stated that "differences in cultural traditions, political and social systems, values and model of development . . . should not be taken as pretexts to interfere in other countries' internal affairs" and pointedly noted that "model[s] of social development should not be exported."[102] The authoritarian SCO governments have a mutual interest in resisting U.S. pressure on human rights and democratization, which they feel will invite repetition of the revolutions that overthrew leaders in Georgia, Ukraine, and Kyrgyzstan.

Some observers view increasing SCO security cooperation—and especially combined military exercises—such as Peace Mission 2007, which took place in Russia during August 2007 under a counterterrorism rubric—as an indication that the SCO might evolve into an anti-U.S. military alliance. However, member states also have important interests that require cooperation with the United States, particularly stabilization of Afghanistan. Divergent national interests, institutional weaknesses, Sino-Russian rivalry, and the reluctance of Central Asian states to subjugate their autonomy and national interests to either Moscow or Beijing will likely limit the SCO's ability to act collectively. For example, Kazakhstan denied Chinese troops transit rights through its territory to participate in Peace Mission 2007.

This does not mean the United States should ignore the organization; rather, it should maintain its bilateral engagement with Central Asian governments, open a dialogue with China and Russia about regional stability, and try to work directly with the SCO. Concrete U.S. assistance in some forms of SCO cooperation, such as measures to improve border security to counter terrorism and drug trafficking, would likely be welcome by members. The United States could continue to push economic and political liberalization as necessary for long-term stability. While it would enhance the SCO's legitimacy, U.S. participation as a formal or informal observer would make it harder for member states to dodge responsibility for anti-U.S. statements.

Thus, in managing its relationships with the three major powers of Eurasia, the United States finds itself facing a new and very different set of challenges and opportunities than it did during the Cold War era. With two rising and one rebounding power in Eurasia, the task facing the United States, as the only truly global power, can be described as managing two takeoffs and one landing. All four players—the United States, China, India, and Russia—have enormous stakes in making these processes as smooth as possible. Turbulence in one could easily lead to significant disruptions for others. The incentives for all in avoiding disruptions are hard to overestimate, as are the consequences of failure to do so. The long-term goal—of a stable Eurasia resting on three regional and one global pillar—would serve everyone's interests well.

Chapter Seven

Adapting Alliances and Partnerships

STEPHEN J. FLANAGAN, LEO G. MICHEL, JAMES J. PRZYSTUP, AND JOHN A. COPE

To advance its interests in today's complex global security environment, the United States must continue to strengthen cooperation with allies and partners and expand and adapt these relationships to deal with new challenges. While the United States remains the foremost power in the world, none of the 21st-century threats—including international terrorism, proliferation of weapons of mass destruction (WMD), regional conflict, and failed states—is amenable to unilateral solutions. The 31 U.S. treaty allies, along with many close partners, are among the countries that are benefiting most from globalization and an open economic system.[1]

A NETWORK FOR GLOBAL SECURITY

These U.S. allies and close partners form a capable core group of states that share a stake in maintaining global peace and stability, including through the promotion of security, prosperity, good governance, and the rule of law. Despite differing approaches and capabilities to deal with specific problems, these countries can augment and complement U.S. actions in the advancement of mutual interests and help avoid military and political overextension. Moreover, allied and partner support and involvement grant greater legitimacy to U.S. actions, and effective alliance relations diminish the inclination of countries to counterbalance U.S. power. Better cross-regional integration of the activities of U.S. alliances and partnerships could create a global web of relationships for effective common action.

In its 2002 National Security Strategy (NSS), the Bush administration recognized that U.S. North Atlantic Treaty Organization (NATO) and Asian allies not only buttress regional peace and stability, but also are essential partners in combating terrorism and promoting freedom and economic development around the world. The administration called for an expanded NATO with new structures and military capabilities to deal with threats to the security of member states wherever they arise and encouraged Japan and South Korea to play an expanded role in regional and global affairs. However, senior administration officials articulated a clear preference for flexible, mission-based coalitions, given potential constraints that allies might impose on U.S. military operations, and elected to pursue the initial antiterrorism campaign in Afghanistan outside NATO.[2] In the Western Hemisphere, the NSS highlighted the value of "flexible coalitions with states that shared our priorities, particularly Mexico,

Brazil, Canada, Chile, and Colombia," while affirming a willingness to work with inclusive regional institutions.[3] The administration's emphasis on shifting, ad hoc coalitions strained relations with many longtime allies and partners who have seen it as reflecting both a diminished U.S. commitment to existing security obligations and a propensity for unilateral action.

At the outset of its second term, the Bush administration undertook essential steps to restore a broader strategic dialogue with European allies in the aftermath of disagreements over the Iraq war and to accelerate the process of adapting East Asian alliance relationships, with some noteworthy progress. The 2006 U.S. National Security Strategy and Quadrennial Defense Review (QDR) were unequivocal about the centrality of allies and international partners, as well as unified interagency efforts at home and abroad, to realize U.S. strategic goals. The QDR called for changes throughout the U.S. Government to conduct integrated, civil-military operations and for the Defense Department to enhance its ability to work with and bolster the capabilities of international partners.[4]

The global nature of America's security interests and the unpredictability of where threats to those interests will emerge led U.S. defense planners in recent years to shift from a primarily regional to a global approach in managing operations of the U.S. Armed Forces. The Global Posture Review, completed in 2004, reassessed U.S. overseas basing requirements. It concluded that the United States needs rapid, assured access to a wider array of lesser military facilities and operating locations overseas that are closer to areas of potential instability and conflict so that many large Cold War–era operating bases could be consolidated.[5] Maintenance of effective consultations and security cooperation activities with allies and partners is essential to successful implementation of both this realignment and long-term U.S. defense strategy.

The alliance adaptation process is more advanced in the transatlantic context, where NATO has undergone major adjustments of its membership, missions, and capabilities over the past 15 years. In addition to integrating 10 new Central and Eastern European members since 1999, NATO has undertaken a range of unforeseen and challenging operations—from conducting a high-intensity air campaign in Kosovo, to helping defend U.S. airspace in the wake of 9/11, to building security in Afghanistan and supporting disaster relief in Pakistan. NATO has also advanced its security cooperation with Partnership for Peace (PFP) members in the Caucasus and Central Asia and worked to build dialogue and practical cooperation with countries of the broader Middle East. In the process of taking on emerging global challenges, NATO is building new partnerships with the European Union (EU), United Nations (UN), African Union, Australia, New Zealand, Japan, and South Korea. Still, NATO's future remains far from assured, as its members continue to debate its 21st-century missions.

Terrorism, instability in the Middle East and Southwest Asia, energy security, lingering ethnic turmoil in the Balkans, and uncertainties surrounding Russia's future direction remain common European and American security concerns. In recent years, the United States and Europe have worked closely to advance counterterrorism cooperation, support democracy in Ukraine, and stop Iran's acquisition of nuclear weapons.

However, the ability and/or willingness of European governments to work with and alongside the United States—in NATO or bilaterally—to address these problems is constrained by a lack of consensus on strategy, slow or stagnant economic growth, and doubts about American leadership.[6] To sustain the transatlantic relationship, the United States faces three key challenges: to encourage a fragmented, often reluctant Europe to become a fuller partner in managing security affairs along its periphery and globally; to restore European confidence in American leadership post-Iraq and demonstrate that it really welcomes such a partnership with Europe; and to find the right institutional arrangements and division of labor, particularly with the EU, to advance many common interests.

In the Middle East, U.S. security ties to Israel remain robust, but fragile partnerships with moderate Arab states have been weakened by differences over counterterrorism activities, the Israeli-Palestinian conflict, the Iraq war, and U.S. democracy promotion activities. The lingering turmoil in Iraq and the large U.S. military presence in that country are rallying points for jihadists that also impede improved relations with Arab partners. Iran's regional assertiveness and determination to acquire nuclear capability further complicate security dynamics in the region. The future of U.S. partnerships in this region will turn on how successful Washington is in balancing its support of Israel's security with efforts to promote a durable resolution of the Israeli-Palestinian conflict, building cooperation with moderate Arab states, reshaping its military presence, and promoting gradual political and economic change.

U.S. security cooperation with the states of South and Central Asia has gained new importance, given the war in Afghanistan, the requirements of U.S. global military strategy, and Central Asia's contribution to world energy supplies. A new, multifaceted strategic partnership with India has been initiated, and Pakistan and Afghanistan have become valuable partners in the struggle against terrorism. Cooperation with the states of Central Asia, earlier concerned with post-Soviet legacy issues, has been refocused on countering terrorism and transnational threats.

In East Asia, complex and difficult negotiations with Japan and the Republic of Korea (ROK) have resulted in agreement to transform the U.S. military posture in the region to meet the security challenges of the post-9/11 world while also reinforcing defense commitments to longstanding allies. At the same time, both Japan and the ROK have become more engaged in international security affairs: Japan, with deployments to the Indian Ocean, Iraq, and other parts of the Middle East, and the ROK with deployments to Iraq and Afghanistan. Similarly, Australia has supported the United States in Afghanistan and Iraq, while assuming greater responsibilities for stability in the South Pacific region. Security cooperation with other treaty allies (Thailand and the Philippines), new partners in Southeast Asia (Singapore, Malaysia, Indonesia, and Vietnam), and Mongolia has advanced in recent years. The key strategic challenges for the United States in sustaining trans-Pacific relationships will be to transform the alliances with Japan and South Korea into fuller partnerships for addressing regional and global security concerns and open to cooperation with other countries, to build consensus on dealing with China's rising influence and military capabilities, and to show how security relationships with the United States can work to bolster and complement other forms of regional cooperation.

There has been uneven progress since 2001 in adapting security relations in the Western Hemisphere, which remain largely bilateral. The United States and Canada have increased counterterrorism and border cooperation. The two governments agreed to renew the North American Aerospace Defense (NORAD) Agreement indefinitely and to expand it to include maritime surveillance, although differences on missile defense issues remain. While U.S. and Mexican law enforcement and immigration officials have developed pragmatic cooperation on border security, military-to-military ties have remained circumspect. U.S. cooperation with Chile, Brazil, and several Central American governments on regional and global security concerns has produced concrete results and shows promise. U.S. support to Colombia's counterinsurgency efforts remains critical to strengthening that country and to containing and managing conflicts, narcoterrorism, and other transnational threats in the Andean ridge. Multilateral approaches to security are still tentative, although members of the Organization of American States (OAS) agreed in the 2003 Declaration on Security in the Americas to strengthen cooperation on an array of transnational security issues. However, state weakness, sovereignty concerns, populist movements, and wariness of U.S. power and unilateralist tendencies have tempered wider hemispheric cooperation. The key challenges to the United States in advancing hemispheric security cooperation are to overcome lingering suspicions and doubts about its policies and commitment and to help build consensus on a comprehensive vision and strategy for regional security.

Africa is an increasingly important U.S. trading partner and an enormous untapped market for U.S. investors, as well as the source of 10 percent of the oil the United States imports and significant quantities of many other natural resources. The continent's many weak and failed states contribute to instability in the international system and have attracted al Qaeda and other terrorist groups. Thus, the United States is nurturing partnerships with regional leaders in South Africa, Nigeria, Kenya, and Ethiopia and supporting efforts by the African Union and subregional organizations to build African capabilities to maintain regional peace and stability and mitigate global terrorism. The United States provides equipment and training in peacekeeping operations and other contingencies to military units in selected African countries through the Africa Regional Peacekeeping and African Contingency Operations Training and Assistance programs. The Secretary of Defense created a new U.S. Africa Command in 2007 to enhance U.S. peacetime military engagement, training activities, and contingency planning.

Against these regional developments, several overarching factors are complicating the adaptation of U.S. security partnerships around the world. Many friends and allies feel that Washington has been overly focused on combating terrorism and has an excessively militarized strategy. Widespread opposition to U.S. policies toward Iraq and the broader Middle East has led to steep drops in favorable public attitudes toward the

United States. The pace of transformation of the U.S. Armed Forces continues to widen the gap in capabilities between them and allied and partner militaries, making effective combined operations more difficult. Some allies are concerned that the re-alignment of U.S. military deployments and shifting global interests could diminish bilateral security commitments or engage them unwittingly in regional conflicts (see table 7–1). This chapter explores these and other challenges ahead in restoring confidence in U.S. leadership, adapting alliances, and building new partnerships in various regions and identifies promising policy options to advance those goals.

TABLE 7–1. U.S. FORCES AROUND THE WORLD

	Total Number of Personnel
Europe	96,119
Asia and the Pacific (excluding United States and its territories)	74,530
North Africa/Middle East/ South Asia	5,452
Western Hemisphere (excluding United States and its territories; including South and Central America and Caribbean)	2,059
Sub-Saharan Africa	1,699
Former Soviet Union	108

Source: Department of Defense (DOD), Washington Headquarters Services, Director-ate of Information Operations and Reports, *Department of Defense Active Duty Person-nel Strengths by Regional Area and by Country (309A)* (September 30, 2006), available at <http://siadapp.dior.whs.mil/personnel/MILITARY/history/hst0609.pdf>; approxi-mately 23,000 of the 100,000 authorized forces in Europe are actually deployed to Operations *Enduring Freedom/Iraqi Freedom*. Additionally, U.S. European Command's (USEUCOM's) Strategic Theater Transformation plan calls for the closure of several hundred bases and installations in Europe and the return of over 40,000 military person-nel, 65,000 DOD civilians, and 57,000 family members to the United States by 2012. For example, it is anticipated that the U.S. Army component of USEUCOM will be reduced over the next 5 years from 63,000 to about 28,000 Soldiers stationed in Europe. The majority of U.S. forces in Asia are located in South Korea and Japan; efforts to realign these forces are currently under way in both countries.

TRANSATLANTIC SECURITY RELATIONS: TENSIONS AND TRANSFORMATION

Close security bonds between the United States and its European allies, anchored in NATO since 1949, have survived many difficult tests from the 1956 Suez Crisis to the 1999 Kosovo air campaign. Ultimately, the Alliance remained strong because its members did not allow their differences to rival their overriding shared interests and values.[7]

But will the past be prologue? In recent years, signs of trouble have not been hard to find. The wave of European solidarity with the United States following 9/11 ebbed substantially within 6 months of those attacks. By early 2003, sharp differences over Iraq divided the Alliance, and widespread concerns about perceived U.S. "unilateralism" led to plummeting European public opinion of the United States and support for its policies.[8] Even those who had long held that transatlantic ties are irreversible began to worry that Europe and the United States had increasingly diverging values, interests, and capabilities.

But more hopeful signs also emerged. Since 9/11, the United States and European governments have strengthened their practical diplomatic, intelligence, financial, and law enforcement cooperation in combating terrorism.[9] The enduring value of their military cooperation, already demonstrated in the Balkans, has improved in Afghanistan and, to a limited degree, in Iraq. While a common Middle East strategy remains elusive, even those European governments most critical of the U.S.-led invasion of Iraq have acknowledged that Iraq's stabilization—as well as the promotion of reforms in the Arab world—is a shared European-American interest. U.S. endorsement of EU diplomatic efforts to block Iran's capability to develop nuclear weapons, the EU's deferral of plans to lift its embargo on arms sales to China, and important Franco-American cooperation on Lebanon and Syria have also enhanced transatlantic relations. While the Europeans, as a group, have not transformed their military capabilities as far or as fast as the United States would like, most have understood the need for change, initiated some restructuring and modernization efforts, and are looking for ways to do better within constrained budgets. More broadly, the allies overwhelmingly want to keep the United States engaged in European security affairs, while the United States looks increasingly toward its allies to share the burdens of managing global stability, including preventing or addressing threats and conflicts that emanate from outside the North Atlantic region.

KEY CHALLENGES IN TRANSATLANTIC RELATIONS

Early in his second term, President Bush pronounced a renewed commitment to close cooperation and strategic dialogue with NATO allies, and his unprecedented meeting with the European Council and Commission in February 2005 signaled a willingness to work with the EU as a fuller partner. While the tone of transatlantic relations has perceptibly improved, the longer term success of the reconciliation process will depend on how the United States and its allies address five major challenges:

- managing the "threat perception gap"
- formulating convergent strategies to address common global challenges
- narrowing the "capabilities gap"
- achieving a close and complementary—not competitive—relationship between NATO and the EU
- expanding NATO's partnerships along Europe's periphery and beyond.

Differing Threat Perceptions

For four decades, there was broad Alliance consensus on the overarching risk of Soviet-led aggression, but a gap in transatlantic perceptions of security threats began forming in the 1990s. In 1991, NATO acknowledged that the principal new security risk was instability in Central and Eastern Europe, but only passing references were made to risks emanating from WMD proliferation and terrorism.[10] However, as a result of its preponderant military role in the 1990–1991 Gulf War coalition and its continuing global commitments, the United States became more focused than its allies on preventing and, if necessary, defeating emerging threats to U.S. and Western interests arising from WMD proliferation, rogue states, and nonstate actors.[11] European officials, increasingly preoccupied with escalating violence in the former Yugoslavia, seemed slower to appreciate the changing global security environment, more anxious to reap a "peace dividend," and less motivated to help educate elite and public opinion on the new risks.

For a brief period following 9/11, the threat perception gap seemed to vanish. The celebrated phrase of a *Le Monde* editorialist—"We are all Americans"[12]—conveyed a profound sense of shared vulnerability to a common threat. Ironically, the aftermath of 9/11 might have contributed to a widening threat perception gap within the Alliance. The United States viewed the attacks as evidence that "asymmetric threats"—especially the potentially catastrophic consequences of a nexus among terrorists, WMD proliferation, and hostile states—were real, not theoretical. Hence, Washington declared, as a central tenet of its national security strategy, a "war on terrorism."

However, 9/11 has not shifted the security paradigm of most Allied governments, political elites, or general publics to the same degree as experienced in the United States. A number of allies—especially the United Kingdom, France, Germany, Italy, Spain, and Turkey—have dealt with *conventional terrorism* for decades, and improved intelligence and law enforcement tools have helped them to contain it.[13] While European officials acknowledge that 9/11 demonstrates the growing potential for *catastrophic terrorism*, many in their publics appear to view the threat as abstract and, in any event, aimed more at the U.S. homeland than European territory and populations. Despite arrests in several European countries of suspected terrorists in possession of materials indicating interest in biological or chemical weapons, as well major terrorist attacks in Madrid and Istanbul in 2004 and London in 2005, the U.S. notion of a "war on terrorism" still does not resonate well with European publics—particularly when it is used as a justification for U.S. military intervention in Iraq, which remains unpopular with a majority of European public opinion. Moreover, a substantial body of

European opinion holds that Arab-Israeli tensions and the plight of the Palestinians remain the leading cause of international terrorism and that the global targeting of American citizens and interests by Islamic terrorists is explained largely by unwavering U.S. support for Israel. European opinion generally favors a "more evenhanded" approach to Israel and the Palestinian Authority, and a few allies with large and growing Muslim minorities are especially concerned by the risk of increased domestic unrest, or even terrorist attacks against their homeland or interests, if their Middle East policies appear too closely aligned with those of Washington.

The Cold War consensus on threat assessment will not be recreated any time soon. Because of its size, power, symbolic value, and global presence, the United States will remain the principal target of international terrorists and adversary of the nexus of terrorism, WMD, and rogue states. Thus, some divergences with a number of allies and partners are probably inevitable. However, threat perceptions are not immutable. As happened in Bosnia, Kosovo, and Afghanistan, once allies and partners have committed their forces to work together in a dangerous environment, their operational experience tends to produce a greater convergence of views on threats to those forces. U.S.-European cooperation on transforming the broader Middle East and promoting Arab-Israeli reconciliation, if sustained and productive, could help to alleviate corrosive transatlantic arguments on the root causes of terrorism.

The changing capabilities of potential adversaries will influence threat perceptions as well. For example, through increased bilateral and multilateral dialogue and information-sharing—including within NATO—the United States and a number of allies have drawn closer together in assessing potential ballistic and cruise missile threats. Revelations about the A.Q. Khan network, evidence of continuing North Korean exports of ballistic missiles and related technology, and Iranian testing of medium-range ballistic missiles as Tehran proceeds with its nuclear programs eventually could strengthen the voice of allied officials interested in missile defense cooperation with the United States. However, absent more widespread and major (that is, mass casualty) terrorist attacks in Europe, at least some allies will not view asymmetric strikes as the primary direct threat to their national security. As is the case today, these divergences are likely to persist among Europeans, not just between Europeans and Americans.

Diverging Strategies

The threat perception gap is closely related to transatlantic differences over the legitimate use of military force. A common threat assessment can facilitate, but not guarantee, agreement on strategy. Allied divergences over the application or legitimacy of military force are not new. Allies differed on the role of nuclear weapons during the Cold War and on the conduct of air operations in Kosovo.[14] More recently, some analysts have advanced the concept that Americans and Europeans "no longer share a common 'strategic culture.'"[15] Broadly speaking, they argue that the United States, as the sole remaining military superpower, is more prone to "unilateral" pursuit of its security interests and less wedded to "multilateral" solutions. They also contend that American policymakers appear overconfident, in European eyes, in the U.S. ability to fundamentally change longstanding geopolitical problems that Europeans view as intractable—for example, the fostering of democracy in the Arab world. These analysts view Europeans as conditioned by their relative military weakness and success in building—incrementally but durably—a peaceful and prosperous EU. Thus, Europeans are said to opt consistently for "multilateral" institutions and international agreements to rein in threats and, if necessary, legitimize any military action to contain them, while ultimately relying on U.S. power if military action is unavoidable.[16]

The extent and depth of this perceived strategic divide is debatable and can easily be overdrawn. At least some of the European complaints of U.S. "unilateralism" have stemmed from an amalgam of highly charged transatlantic disagreements over nondefense issues—for example, the use of capital punishment in the United States and the U.S. rejection of the Kyoto Protocol on environmental protection. Among transatlantic disagreements over security-related regimes—for example, the U.S. decisions not to ratify the Comprehensive Test Ban Treaty, to withdraw from the Anti-Ballistic Missile Treaty, to reject the draft verification protocol to the Biological and Toxin Weapons Convention, and not to join the International Criminal Court or accept its jurisdiction over U.S. citizens—only the latter has evoked serious and sustained criticism among European opinion writ large.

Still, for many Europeans, the U.S. response to 9/11 seemed to validate the "unilateralist" theme. The U.S. decision not to seek NATO leadership of military operations against al Qaeda and the Taliban was widely perceived in Europe as a U.S. rejection of collective action and a vote of no confidence in the European allies.[17] Moreover, this perception was reinforced by U.S. official statements, beginning in early 2002 and elaborated in the U.S. National Security Strategy, of the need for preventive and even preemptive actions to forestall threats from terrorist groups or rogue states that could not be deterred.[18] Many Europeans consider the use of military force only a "last option" that also should be linked either to self-defense against an actual attack or cloaked in the legitimacy of a mandate established by an existing international organization, preferably the United Nations.

The European Security Strategy (ESS), adopted by the European Council in December 2003, identifies many of the same threats as the U.S. National Security Strategy, to include global terrorism, WMD proliferation, state failure, and organized crime (and the nexus of these four), as well as regional conflicts. However, it also argues that in an era of globalization, European security and prosperity depend on an "effective multilateral system" and rule-based international order. The contrast with President Bush's call for "effective multilateral *actions*" (emphasis added) is evident.

The ESS also emphasizes different prescriptions, particularly with regard to terrorism and nonproliferation. While noting the military has a role in dealing with terrorism, the ESS advocates "preventive engagement" as its preferred tool in forestalling attacks. With regard to proliferation of WMD, the ESS advocates strengthening the International Atomic Energy Agency, tightening export controls, enforcing universal adherence to international treaty regimes, and using preventive engagement when signs of proliferation are detected. This reflects much greater satisfaction with these regimes than exists in Washington, which has pushed for more proactive approaches (such as the Proliferation Security Initiative and new suppliers' controls) to address this threat.

Even if American and European threat assessments were to become more convergent, it is not clear that Europe as a whole would endorse preventive or preemptive actions advocated by the United States as essential to head off threats from terrorist groups or rogue states. Notwithstanding the caveats used by the Bush administration in describing those concepts, many European officials and opinion leaders believe the terms suggest an *offensive* and primarily *military* strategy that is fundamentally at odds with NATO's core function of collective *defense*. They also fear that other regional powers could use a U.S. "preemption doctrine" to justify aggressive military actions against their neighbors.

Moreover, the transatlantic and intra-European debate over the legitimacy of using military force absent an explicit UN authorization (or, as in *Allied Force* in Kosovo, a NATO mandate) is unlikely to fade any time soon. Even allies and partners that supported the U.S. decision to use military force against Iraq have faced strong domestic political pressure (and, in some cases, national legal requirements) to condition any contribution to the coalition stabilization force on a UN imprimatur. In particular, there is little prospect that the EU will dilute policy statements that effectively require UN authorization for virtually any EU-led military operation, although its most militarily capable members, the United Kingdom and France, will be careful to preserve their freedom of action.

Gaps in Capabilities and "Usability"

The transatlantic threat perception gap and strategic divergences are reflected in the third key source of tension in transatlantic security relations: the widening capabilities gap. The United States has contributed far more resources to NATO than any other single ally since 1949, but today's capabilities gap has its roots in the 1990s. Overall European defense spending has been nearly flat since 1995 (see Figure 7–1). While defense expenditures as a percentage of gross domestic (GDP) are an imperfect indicator of defense effort or capabilities, the gap between U.S. and European spending levels during the last decade is significant. According to NATO data, from 1995 to 2006, the U.S. average was 3.7 percent (based on current prices), compared with 1.93 percent for 16 other allies combined—all but 4 of whom spent less than 2 percent.[19] The contrast between average U.S. and European spending for investment and research and development (R&D) was even more striking. The United States outspends Europe 6 to 1 in defense R&D and devotes 35 percent of its defense expenditure to investment (from a budget more than twice as large as that of European budgets combined), compared to the European level of about 20 percent.[20] All of NATO Europe spends about $12 billion annually for defense R&D, whereas the United States spent close to $75 billion in 2006. These disparities in defense investments explain, in large part, the transatlantic capabilities gap that became obvious during the NATO-led crisis

FIGURE 7–1. ALLIED DEFENSE SPENDING TRENDS, 1995–2005

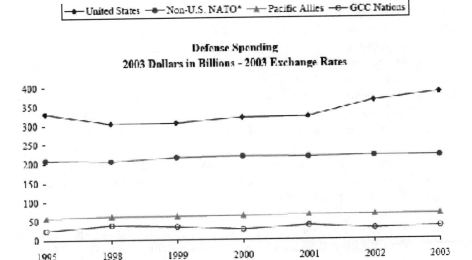

Source: U.S. Department of Defense, "2004 Statistical Compendium on Allied Contributions to the Common Defense," available at <www.defenselink.mil/pubs/allied_contrib2004/allied2004.pdf>.

response operations in Bosnia and Kosovo and that were later confirmed in Operations *Enduring Freedom* and *Iraqi Freedom* in key areas relevant to modern warfare, including strategic lift; aerial refueling; sustainability and logistics; deployable command, control, communications, computers, intelligence, surveillance, target acquisition, and reconnaissance; and precision strike weapons.

An equally problematic transatlantic gap relates to limited European countries' ability to deploy and sustain significant elements of their armed forces in expeditionary operations. While the 24 European allies have a total of 2.4 million military personnel, only 3 to 5 percent of these forces are capable of deployments outside their territory for even short periods.[21] In addition, some allies continue to place national restrictions or caveats on how those forces provided to NATO operations can be used, thus limiting the flexibility of allied commanders. This reflects both political and legal constraints and the consequences of declining defense budgets, lagging training and standards, and—in some cases—continued reliance on conscription. This situation has repeatedly reduced the usability of European forces, particularly in Afghanistan, and made it problematic for NATO to undertake certain commitments. Too many

European armed forces are still configured for the old requirements of territorial defense rather than the current demands for expeditionary operations.

Given the U.S. defense spending increases authorized or planned since 9/11 (a 36 percent overall increase in the U.S. defense budget between fiscal years 2001 and 2006, including growth of 38 percent for procurement and 45 percent for research and development), the gap is likely to widen further over the next few years.[22] In 2006, the United States spent more than twice as much on defense as all 25 EU members combined. Continuation of these trends could end the ability of all but a very few allies to operate militarily with the United States in any demanding scenario. Not only technical military problems are at stake. The capabilities gap might be spawning an intellectual, cultural, and even linguistic divide between the U.S. military and many of its allied counterparts that makes it increasingly difficult to discuss operational issues and concepts.

Under considerable U.S. pressure, allied leaders agreed at the November 2002 Prague Summit to a package of interrelated initiatives designed to meet current and emerging security threats, including:

- creation of a flexible, multiservice NATO Response Force (NRF) ready to move quickly and conduct forced entry and sustain operations for 30 days or longer wherever the North Atlantic Council (NAC) decides it is needed
- streamlining NATO's military command arrangements
- a Prague Capabilities Commitment, under which individual allies pledged to improve their capabilities in critical areas[23]
- a new NATO Missile Defense feasibility study to examine a broad range of defense options.[24]

The Prague initiatives were, in essence, an American challenge to European allies in the wake of complaints about their initial exclusion from Operation *Enduring Freedom,* but the results of those initiatives are mixed.

On the positive side, realization of full operational capability of the NRF in November 2006, if sustained over the long term, will narrow the gap in capabilities and commitment.[25] In June 2003, NATO defense ministers formalized a headquarters reduction and created two strategic commands—one for operations and one for transformation. The latter, Allied Command Transformation, was established with tight links to the U.S. Joint Forces Command as a way to advance European transformation through the transfer of lessons learned in U.S. exercises and experiments with new operational concepts. At the 2004 Istanbul Summit, NATO leaders agreed to further measures to enhance the operational effectiveness of their forces; these included a goal of having 40 percent of each nation's land forces prepared and equipped for foreign deployment, with 8 percent of those land forces capable of sustained foreign operations.[26] Meanwhile, two of the strongest contributors to alliance military potential, the United Kingdom and France, have followed through on multiyear defense budget increases announced in 2002 and, for the most part, have directed new investments toward capabilities in the priority areas identified by NATO, including strategic lift, power projection platforms, precision strike weapons, modern intelligence and surveillance systems, and improved defenses against WMD. (France, however, also plans to spend nearly one-fifth of its investment funds to modernize its nuclear systems.) Additionally, a few smaller allies have made modest budget increases coupled with important force modernization efforts.

On the other hand, some allies are implementing force structure reductions of 40 to 50 percent, and their governments are likely to reinvest the resources that supported these forces in nondefense programs. Procurement plans and investments for transformation of many allied militaries are lagging because of inadequate resources. Simply put, those allies are struggling to maintain existing defense budgets in the face of sluggish economies and/or competing domestic priorities.[27] Germany, once a powerhouse of NATO conventional capabilities, is unlikely to reverse several years of relatively low spending on defense—approximately 1.4 percent of its GDP in 2005—any time soon, despite its relatively large commitments to crisis management operations, especially in the Balkans and Afghanistan. Italy, Spain, and Poland are restructuring their forces to become more efficient and deployable over the long term, but their weak investment levels will likely hold back their pace of development.

As envisaged at Prague, allies have begun to examine possibilities for significantly increased role specialization. This means that smaller, less capable allies are focusing their national contribution to Alliance capabilities in a select number of critical areas—for example, nuclear/biological/chemical (NBC) detection and protection assets, explosive ordnance disposal, military police, special operations forces, or combat support and combat service support units. Larger, more capable allies will still be expected to contribute a broad spectrum of combat and support units and assets. NATO has accommodated a limited degree of de facto role specialization for many years, given the disparity of capabilities among allies. While attractive in principle, role specialization will have to be carefully applied to avoid several potential pitfalls. Allies want reassurance that critical capabilities would be available if needed; since no ally is formally obligated by the 1949 Washington Treaty actually to participate in a NATO military operation, NATO defense planners need to ensure some redundancy in critical capabilities. Similarly, to preserve the principle that allies should accept shared risks and burdens, the role specialization effort must not encourage allies to accept only low-cost, low-risk force goals. In addition, specialization may be constrained by domestic political realities; to maintain parliamentary and public support for their armed forces, some allies might find it necessary to preserve elements of their traditional territorial defenses that are no longer needed by NATO.

As allies implement the Prague commitments, they are pursuing greater multilateral cooperation to enhance capabilities while better managing costs, including pooling arrangements and multilateral procurement programs, which could be combined with role specialization. Multinational cooperation, however, comes with its own set of requirements and limitations. Reaching agreement on a consortium's overall requirement, national shares, and financing for and access to the military system in question can be complex and politically sensitive. Unless procurement numbers are sufficiently robust, expected economies of scale will not be realized. Synchronizing budget and procurement cycles among several allies and partners to ensure funds are available when needed has always been challenging and will remain so if, as projected, overall defense investment remains stagnant. A renewed commitment to multinational cooperation, albeit promising, will not prove to be a panacea.[28]

Multinational cooperation will be shaped, in turn, by intra-allied and transatlantic defense industrial concerns. The competition among Europeans to reap long-term economic, commercial, and technological benefits from defense-related sales within and outside Europe risks becoming even more contentious. Within several European governments and defense-related industries, suspicions persist that U.S. policies regarding enhanced NATO capabilities reflect, at least in part, an interest in promoting U.S.-based industries. Some European officials have voiced concern that the United States exacerbates the capabilities gap by restricting, essentially for commercial reasons, defense-related technology transfers to potential European industrial partners. Such concerns have prompted several allies to call for significantly increased defense industrial cooperation within the EU, to include greater pooling of defense-related research and development resources and more cooperation through its European Defence Agency.

Competition for defense sales is nothing new, and European governments arguably are at least equally as interested as the United States in seeing that their defense resources benefit their domestic economy.[29] Moreover, the cases where U.S. technology transfer controls have impeded close transatlantic cooperation are relatively few and reflect, for the most part, legitimate national security concerns over possible transfers of that technology to third parties. In addition, as U.S. officials have pointed out, the technologies needed to correct many of the most pressing alliance capability shortfalls—for example, in NBC defenses, strategic lift, aerial refueling, secure, deployable, and interoperable communications, and even precision strike weapons and unmanned aircraft systems—already exist in Europe. If they are not addressed, transatlantic frictions in these areas could divert attention and energy from the overriding national security imperative of achieving the Prague commitments. Both sides of the Atlantic have legitimate interests in a strong and efficient domestic defense industrial base, but the case for increasing transatlantic cooperation is equally compelling. Moreover, the level of defense industrial cooperation achieved in the Prague context will have important implications for intra-alliance cooperation on missile defense, an area where command and control, resource, and technology transfer issues likely will be even more daunting.

NATO–EU Relations and "Dual Enlargement"

Any U.S. strategy to shape future transatlantic security relations must take into account the transformation of not just NATO's membership, structures, and capabilities, but also those of the EU. It must take into account a critical distinction between the two organizations: the United States has a preeminent role in the former but no seat at the table in the latter.

In theory, the logic of establishing close, cooperative, and transparent NATO–EU links over a wide spectrum of defense-related matters appears overwhelming. Given their broadly overlapping memberships—21 of 27 EU member states are also members of NATO, and 4 of the others are in PFP—NATO and the EU draw upon essentially the same European force pool. As every European state has only one army, air force, or navy and one defense budget, it makes no military or budgetary sense to structure, equip, or train those forces differently for NATO-led or EU-led missions. Moreover, decisions to commit those forces to actual operations are among the most politically sensitive for any ally or EU member. Thus, as a rule, one would not expect European states to develop significantly different threat assessments within NATO and the EU or to be less protective of their national prerogatives in one organization than in the other.

In practice, after a slow start and some difficult negotiations, a solid foundation for NATO–EU links has taken shape. In late 2002, the NAC agreed to provide the EU with assured access to NATO operational planning capabilities, and the two organizations issued a declaration of principles for their "strategic partnership" that emphasizes the need for close cooperation on crisis management and capabilities development. In early 2003, the organizations agreed on further details regarding their practical cooperation—a package of arrangements known as "Berlin Plus"—that include provisions for NATO support to EU-led operations.[30] During this same period, NATO and the EU worked together closely in Bosnia, where the EU Police Mission replaced a similar UN-led police task force in January 2003, and in Macedonia, where NATO's stabilization operation was replaced by an EU mission in March 2003. In late 2004, NATO concluded its Stabilization Force Mission in Bosnia-Herzegovina, and the EU deployed a new military mission, *Althea*, under Berlin Plus arrangements.

However, NATO–EU cooperation remains uneven. The NAC and the EU's Political and Security Committee meet periodically, as do the NATO and EU military committees, but their meetings thus far have been focused on the implementation of Berlin Plus arrangements in Bosnia. They have not addressed broader strategic issues, such as cooperation involving Russia, Ukraine, Africa, or the broader Middle East. NATO–EU cooperation on capabilities development has been disappointing overall, and the organizations were slow to establish permanent military liaison arrangements to facilitate transparency and cooperation on missions beyond Bosnia. Although both organizations have provided assistance to the African Union's monitoring and peacekeeping effort in Darfur, their cooperation was nearly scuttled by a diplomatic spat over their respective roles, with a small number of EU states initially seeking to block NATO involvement.[31]

Such tensions reflect, in part, an internal EU tug-of-war over the strategic direction of its Common Foreign and Security Policy (CFSP), which provides the overarching framework for EU defense-related activities, or European Security and Defense Policy (ESDP). For some EU members—of which France has been the most vocal—CFSP/ESDP serves a grander vision of the EU as a leading "pole" in a "multipolar" world. Although French officials have been careful, at least since 2002, to avoid public suggestions that the EU should serve at times as a counterweight to the United States, implicit in their descriptions of multipolarity is the notion that a more militarily capable and autonomous EU would allow it to balance and, in some cases, restrain U.S. dominance of global affairs. Multipolarity advocates have been deliberately vague on how it would be constituted and applied, but some envision building, within the EU, a collective defense alternative to NATO. That said, a number of EU leaders, such as former British Prime Minister Tony Blair and German Chancellor Angela Merkel, have openly criticized the "counterweight" notion and emphasized the need for a complementary and cooperative NATO–EU relationship that strengthens European capabilities within the alliance as well as the EU. Their reasons for doing so are strategic and tactical: they fear that NATO–EU competition will damage transatlantic security and political bonds essential for collective defense and challenging crisis management operations, and the capabilities development necessary for both; and they believe that European influence on U.S. policies is maximized by emphasizing shared interests and developing convergent policies, not by offering alternative EU policies intended to rein in Washington.

That NATO and the EU have adopted different tones and approaches to defense and security issues should come as no surprise. The two organizations had virtually no contact before 1999, and they have somewhat different memberships, purposes, structures, and institutional cultures. It is a positive sign that their operational experience, especially in the Balkans and Darfur, has provided valuable lessons learned for possible collaboration in future crisis management contingencies. However, closer practical cooperation between the two is desirable and likely for a number of reasons:

- First, the nature of contemporary security threats—especially international terrorism and WMD proliferation, areas where NATO and EU assessments appear to be growing closer—have made such cooperation imperative, and the two organizations have complementary tools to address them.
- Second, notwithstanding the current inclination of a few EU members to demonstrate the Union's potential for "autonomous" military operations, there is not a single member (including France) that is both willing and capable of assuming within the EU a role similar to that of the United States in NATO— that is, as the catalyst, builder, integrator, and shepherd of large, complex, and high-risk military operations.[32] Most EU members will be inclined to seek NATO support for any large-scale or high-intensity EU-led mission where their forces would be exposed to significant combat risk.[33]
- Third, given the pressures on European defense spending, there is little appetite among most EU members for investing in operational planning structures that would duplicate those of NATO.[34] Nor is it likely that most EU members will invest in capabilities required for EU missions that would not be compatible with their NATO or PFP force planning goals.
- Fourth, with regard to force structures, allies who are also EU members have accepted that the NRF and the EU's more modest rapid reaction capability, known as the EU Battlegroups, can be mutually reinforcing. The capability,

training, and interoperability standards and benefits that accrue to European forces participating in the NRF will be applicable, in many cases, to the EU Battlegroups as well. While arrangements are needed to deconflict any potential dual-tasking of specific European units for concurrent NATO-led and EU-led rotations, this should be manageable through increased transparency and liaison contacts.[35]

Still, some transatlantic tensions are inevitable. All EU members likely will see important reasons (including safeguarding employment for their national firms) to increase defense industrial cooperation within the EU. The focus for such cooperation will be the European Defence Agency.[36] At the same time, several factors will temper any inclination to establish a "fortress Europe." Despite its problems, transatlantic defense industrial cooperation generally has improved over the past decade, and promising new models—for example, European participation in the large U.S. Joint Strike Fighter program—are in place. Such cooperation will remain very attractive for Europeans anxious to gain access to the larger U.S. defense market and overseas military sales and to advanced U.S. technologies. Most European governments also will see such cooperation as necessary to maintain a high level of interoperability with the U.S. military.

The dual enlargement process has given added impetus to a broad convergence between NATO and the EU. At the strategic level, there is a solid consensus among the Central and Eastern European members of both organizations that both institutions are vital to their supreme national interests, and that any pressures to "choose" between the two would be damaging to those interests. At the practical level, the new members are among the least able to afford any duplication of NATO structures by the EU or any defense capabilities investments under EU auspices that do not meet their NATO force goals as well.

U.S. policies will play a central role in determining the level of NATO–EU cooperation. Perceptions of U.S. unilateralism have the effect of increasing sympathy for the argument that greater European unity is needed to balance or constrain American power and influence. Paradoxically, they also provide fodder for those who suggest that the longstanding U.S. commitment to the defense of Europe *and* European integration are rapidly eroding and that Europe, as a consequence, must prepare for an eventual U.S. disengagement from European security affairs sooner rather than later. It should be noted, in this context, that the perceived shift in U.S. attitudes toward cooperation with the EU since President Bush's visit to EU headquarters in February 2005 has helped to promote a less contentious atmosphere for NATO–EU relations and tempered European perceptions of American unilateralism—although polling in 2006 suggests that European publics remain considerably more negative regarding American policies and President Bush than was the case in 2002.[37]

NATO's Expanding Partnerships

In the early 1990s, NATO developed the Partnership for Peace to promote stable, democratic transitions in the communist countries of Central and Eastern Europe and to build practical cooperation with them and the successor states of the Soviet Union on common security problems. PFP programs helped partners develop the interoperability required to join NATO peacekeeping missions in the Balkans and also facilitated the preparations of several states for NATO membership.[38] The 10 Central and Eastern European countries that joined NATO since 1999 have added limited additional military capabilities, but they have made valuable niche contributions to recent alliance operations and shown a strong commitment to alliance principles.

After 9/11, previous PFP cooperation activities facilitated U.S. and NATO operations in the Caucasus and Central Asia. At their first meeting after the 9/11 attacks, partner defense ministers agreed on steps to increase cooperation and capabilities against terrorism. Forces from 11 partner countries have participated in or supported the International Security Assistance Force and Operation *Enduring Freedom* in Afghanistan, and 9 partners supported stabilization efforts as part of Operation *Iraqi Freedom*.[39] Since creation of the NRF, partners have been working to identify and develop small niche units that they might contribute to future NATO operations. NATO and its partners have also launched the Partnership Action Plan Against Terrorism to strengthen efforts of partner countries in this area and provide a framework for further multinational cooperation.

Ukraine's stability and independence are important to long-term U.S. and allied interests in Central and Eastern Europe, and Ukraine has been a significant contributor to common efforts to bring peace to the Balkans and Iraq. U.S. and European support for democracy, free markets, and the rule of law support these goals as well as Ukraine's integration into Euro-Atlantic institutions.[40] Ukraine's progress along this course will also be a safeguard against any Russian efforts to intimidate its neighbors or reassert a sphere of influence. Ukraine struck a careful balance between East and West in the first decade of its independence. However, events since 9/11 demonstrated to its leaders that Ukraine's security and development require enhanced relations with Europe and the Unites States. While Victor Yushchenko and other democratic reformers who came to power in the Orange Revolution of 2004 favor eventual NATO membership, this remains a deeply divisive issue internally, with very low public support.[41] Victor Yanukovich, who returned to power in August 2006 as prime minister of a "grand coalition" government, is strongly opposed to membership, and the coalition agreement calls only for "mutually beneficial cooperation with NATO."

U.S. interests in the stability and prosperity of the Mediterranean and the broader Middle East can also be advanced through cooperation with allies and partners. The U.S. and EU security strategies both recognize that weak governance, undemocratic regimes, and economic rigidity in the broader Middle East are exacerbating economic disparities, social problems, and regional tensions that provide a fertile environment for terrorism and armed conflicts. When the Bush administration first advanced its ideas on how to strengthen governance, democratic institutions, civil society, and the rule of law in the broader Middle East, some European capitals were concerned that this approach would be perceived by various Arab regimes as threatening and as an effort to force certain models of democratic polity. As consultations ensued, U.S. and European leaders participating in the 2004 G–8 Sea Island Summit were able to reach agreement on a measured, long-term program to support democratic, social, and economic reform in the region under the rubric of the Partnership for Progress and a Common Future and the Forum for the Future dialogues among government ministers and business and civil society leaders.

Each side of the Atlantic brings certain strengths to this vast challenge. The EU has had political consultations and economic and social cooperation with Mediterranean countries for over a decade through the Barcelona Process. NATO's Mediterranean Dialogue, initiated in 1994, has been a forum for confidence-building consultations and practical cooperation with seven countries in the Mediterranean basin. In 2004, NATO moved to build dialogue and practical cooperation with states in the broader Middle East by establishing the Istanbul Cooperation Initiative (ICI). Through ICI, the alliance is offering countries in the region, focusing initially on members of the Gulf Cooperation Council, bilateral cooperation on issues of mutual interest including defense reform, counterterrorism, proliferation of WMD, and civil emergency planning. As with the Mediterranean Dialogue, ICI partners can participate in selected NATO exercises and related education and training activities that could improve the ability of their armed forces to operate with those of the alliance.[42]

Recalibrating the U.S.-European "Terms of Engagement"

Although NATO has served since 1949 as the conceptual "anchor" of the transatlantic security relationship, U.S. vital interests in Europe have always extended beyond military considerations. Europe will remain an indispensable economic partner for the United States, with two-way trade and investment serving as an engine for growth and prosperity in North America, Europe, and globally. The strong and vibrant democracies in most of Europe are natural partners and models for U.S. efforts to foster good governance, democratic principles, and market-based growth in the broader Middle East and elsewhere. America's European allies and partners are supporting many nondefense programs that help maintain global stability. The 13 other members of NATO who are also members of the Organization for Economic Co-operation and Development's Development Assistance Committee, with roughly the same gross national income (GNI), provided 2 to 3 times what the United States did in foreign assistance between 1995 and 2005.[43] In 2005, Official Development Assistance (ODA) for these countries totaled $55.7 billion, twice the $27.7 billion provided by the United States (see table 7–2). These 13 governments allocated an average of 0.5 percent of GNI to ODA, compared with 0.2 percent for the United States. In recent years, these governments have also provided about 40 percent of assessed contributions to UN peacekeeping operations and about 5 times more personnel than the United States to UN and other multinational peace operations. In fashioning an equitable transatlantic division of labor for addressing global security challenges, these broader contributions to stability that help reduce threats to the Euro-Atlantic community should be taken into fuller account. However, Washington will remain reluctant to treat Europe as a full partner until it demonstrates a willingness to enhance lagging defense capabilities.

TABLE 7–2. U.S. AND KEY ALLY EXPENDITURES ON OFFICIAL DEVELOPMENT ASSISTANCE AND DEFENSE, 2005

	2005 Official Development Assistance (ODA) (in US$ millions)	2005 ODA as percent of gross national income	Defense spending (in US$ millions)	Defense spending as percent of gross domestic product (GDP)
United States	27,622	0.22	503,353	4.0
Non-U.S. NATO	55,731	0.50	238,333	1.6
Japan	13,147	0.28	44.3	1.0
Australia	1,680	0.25	17.8	2.7
South Korea	752	0.10	21.0	2.6

For purposes of comparison, "Non-U.S. NATO" includes 13 of the 15 other longtime NATO members who are also members of the Development Assistance Committee of the Organization for Economic Co-operation and Development (excludes Iceland and Turkey). Figures for official development assistance as percent of GNI and defense spending as percentage of GDP for these countries are averages.

Sources: Organization for Economic Co-operation and Development, Development Co-operation Directorate, "Final Official Development Assistance Data for 2005" (Paris: Organization for Economic Co-operation and Development, December 6, 2006), available at <http://www.oecd.org/dataoecd/52/18/37790990.pdf>. NATO data is from NATO International Staff, "NATO-Russia Compendium of Financial and Economic Data Relating to Defence," December 18, 2006, available at <http://www.nato.int/docu/pr/2006/p06-159e.htm>. Data on Asian defense spending is from the *CIA World Fact Book 2006*, available at <https://www.cia.gov/library/publications/download/download-2006/index.html>.

Worries over future EU expansion (beyond the current 27 members), differences over the EU's institutional arrangements (especially after the setbacks to the EU Constitution suffered in the spring of 2005), and social problems and economic stagnation exacerbated by aging, declining populations in most EU countries will occupy much of Europe's attention and likely will dilute its policy consensus on defense and foreign policy. By 2025, 48 percent of Europe's working age population (ages 15–64) will be retired and over 65, and the armed forces recruitment pool (ages 16–30) will fall by over 15 percent. These demographic trends are expected to increase public expenditures for the elderly from 11–16 percent in 2006 to 17–33 percent of national GDPs over the next four decades, thereby diminishing resources available for defense at a time when military personnel costs would be rising.[44] Europe will remain an essential, but sometimes reluctant, partner for the United States in managing global challenges—especially those requiring robust and full-spectrum military capabilities—over the next few decades. Several steps seem warranted to adapt and recalibrate transatlantic security and defense cooperation.

New NATO strategic concept. NATO's 1999 strategic concept needs to be updated to reflect the multifaceted, global nature of the security threats that Allies confront in the early 21st century, particularly terrorism, WMD proliferation, and stabilization of weak states, and a consensus needs to be reached on steps to address these new challenges. Allies should initiate efforts to prepare a new concept at the 2008 Bucharest Summit, while recognizing that the next administration will need some time to conduct a policy review and formulate its approach before completing work on a new concept.

Integrated security planning. Long-term success in combating international terrorism, WMD proliferation, and other transnational threats, as well as maintaining homeland security, will demand transatlantic cooperation in military and many non-military arenas—including diplomatic pressure, intelligence exchanges, and coordinated customs and immigration efforts. In addition, the "external ministries" responsible for such efforts need to integrate their work with relevant "internal ministries," to include justice, police and law enforcement, transport, environment, health, and others. However, these external and internal entities do not come together in NATO. Although NATO's capabilities for critical infrastructure protection, civil-emergency planning, disaster response, WMD consequence management, energy security, and air defense remain relevant, the United States needs to deepen operational cooperation bilaterally with the EU, and, where appropriate, through improved NATO–EU relations and bilateral efforts with individual European governments.[45] Given the enormity of what is at stake, the United States and European governments, as well as NATO and the EU, should take further steps to enhance planning to disrupt and manage the consequences of a terrorist attack involving WMD to ensure that the mechanisms for rapid, multinational, cross-agency consultations and operational cooperation would function in the face of such threats.

Work with the EU. One way to advance more integrated approaches to transatlantic security would be to improve the strategic dialogue between NATO and the EU. This dialogue would help bring together the talent, ideas, and resources of all of the transatlantic actors and the Euro-Atlantic community's two most important institutions to identify common threats, concerns, and possible solutions. This dialogue should address major global security concerns such as Iran's nuclear program and China's emerging role in the international system and military buildup. As NATO–EU cooperation on the Balkans has proved, the two organizations can consult and work together without compromising, in any way, the autonomous decisionmaking processes of either. A positive step in this direction was taken by NATO foreign ministers at their

April 2005 meeting in Vilnius, when they agreed to hold "informal" discussions on strategic issues among foreign ministers of all 32 NATO and EU member states. Such informal meetings have taken place, but they are not a substitute for the broader range of practical, staff-to-staff contacts needed at all levels of the two organizations to ensure their complementarity and cooperation.

With the advent of active EU involvement in security and defense matters, transatlantic security relations have come to resemble, from Washington's perspective, a three-dimensional chess board of bilateral, NATO, and EU players—with the critical distinction being that the United States is "not in the room" when EU members debate and decide on security- and defense-related matters potentially affecting, directly or indirectly, U.S. interests. This change can have important consequences. At a minimum, it raises the risk that EU statements or decisions will be misread by the United States, whose diplomats have limited rights to observe EU deliberations. It also raises the risk that EU decisions on security matters will be influenced, to some degree, by backroom deals on controversial nonsecurity issues (ranging from agricultural and industrial policies to social legislation) that traditionally dominate the EU's agenda. At worst, it opens the prospect that European states, having agreed after laborious negotiations on a specific policy within the EU, refuse to budge from that position in discussions with NATO—creating, in effect, an "EU caucus" within the alliance.

The United States can mitigate such risks through various steps. For example, it can improve its internal mechanisms to spot emerging issues at the EU and engage EU members, both bilaterally and at NATO, before EU policies are set in stone. It can do a better job of holding European governments accountable where they take one position in bilateral talks and a significantly different position within EU councils. In addition, it can continue to push at NATO for expanded staff-level and informal contacts with the EU, which can help anticipate and avert contradictory efforts within the two organizations. More broadly, Washington can make clear, through both statements and actions, that it welcomes European efforts to increase their capabilities within the EU and NATO frameworks.

NATO decisionmaking. If NATO's ongoing initiatives to transform its structures and improve its capabilities stall or even collapse, the U.S. ability and incentive to cooperate militarily with its allies will diminish even more. This would have grave consequences for political solidarity within the alliance. However, as the allies work to ensure NATO has the capabilities and structures needed to respond to 21st-century threats, they also could usefully consider ways to improve NATO's decisionmaking process. Since 1949, NATO has developed a tradition of taking decisions by consensus. This requirement exemplifies for many the "one for all, all for one" ethos of NATO's collective defense commitment. Under the so-called consensus rule, no ally can be forced to approve a position or take an action against its will. The United States has relied on the consensus rule as much as any other ally to protect its interests, to shape the views of others, and to integrate the good ideas offered by others to improve its proposals. For these reasons, discussion of changing that rule has been, until recently, taboo in Brussels as well as Washington.[46]

NATO's experience in February 2003, when a few allies blocked Turkey's request to begin NATO military planning for its defense against Iraq, exposed a possible weakness in current NATO practices: NATO's military commanders have inadequate discretionary authority to conduct contingency operational planning. Specifically, the NAC retains the authority for initiating and approving all operational plans developed in response to an actual or fast-breaking crisis. This arrangement serves to "politicize"—and potentially delay—a decision to undertake robust military planning.

The NAC has granted some discretionary authority to the Supreme Allied Commander, Europe (SACEUR), to prepare generic contingency plans for a range of potential military missions. This brings NATO's approach closer to that used by the United States for its combatant commanders, whose contingency planning is considered prudent business as usual and does not prejudice the President's decisionmaking power to commit forces to a specific operation. However, generic planning has its limits. If the NRF is to be able to meet its rapid deployment goals, it would be desirable for the NAC to allow SACEUR to refine these generic contingency plans in response to emerging crises. Under this procedure, the NAC would retain its power to decide whether any of the planning options is executed, but the availability of those options would shorten the overall time needed for the NATO decisionmaking cycle. Moreover, allies who are EU members logically should favor such a procedure, as more robust planning within NATO would enhance the EU's ability to mount crisis response missions where NATO as a whole has decided not to engage.

A recalibration of NATO procedures also might be useful for decisions to authorize a military operation. The consensus rule would continue to apply to any NAC decision to launch an operation. However, in a departure from current practice, the NAC could mandate a NATO Committee of Contributors (NCC), chaired by the Secretary-General, to carry out the operation on behalf of the Alliance. The NCC would be comprised of those allies prepared to contribute forces or capabilities to the operation, and it would enjoy full access to NATO common assets. The NCC would approve the concept of operations, rules of engagement, activation order, and other steps needed to implement the operation. The Secretary-General would periodically brief allies who are not on the NCC regarding significant developments affecting the operation, but those allies would have no voice in determining the day-to-day management of the operation. The NCC would make it easier for a group of allies to draw on NATO assets and proceed with the Alliance's political blessing to implement "non–Article 5" crisis response missions. At the same time, by removing the ability of those who are not engaged in the operation to influence its day-to-day conduct, the NCC could accelerate decisionmaking and avoid the "war by committee" image attributed to Operation *Allied Force*.[47]

Further enlargement. NATO heads of state and government reaffirmed at the 2004 Prague and 2006 Riga Summits that the fifth round of enlargement would not be the last and that the Alliance's door remains open. Albania, Macedonia, and Croatia— which have NATO Membership Action Plans and cooperate on regional security under the Adriatic 3 Charter—have contributed troops to the International Security Assistance Force and supported NATO missions in the Balkans. If any or all of these countries are assessed to be stable democracies willing and able to advance NATO principles and security in Europe and beyond, the 2008 Bucharest Summit should invite them to join NATO to close a gap in the transatlantic space and advance their integration into Europe. This action would also provide Bosnia and Herzegovina, Serbia, and Montenegro, admitted to PFP at the Riga Summit, with positive incentives to follow in the footsteps of the Adriatic 3, which is the best way to enhance long-term stability in the Balkans. Beyond Southeastern Europe, Georgia's interest in joining the Alliance raises difficult questions about NATO's ultimate geographic scope. Article 10 of the Washington Treaty states that membership is open to any "European State in a position to further the principles of this Treaty and to contribute to the security of the North Atlantic area." Should the Alliance's open door policy apply to all countries on the periphery of Europe or even outside of Europe? Maintenance of an unrestricted open door policy and an active set of partnerships seems the best way for NATO to continue to promote positive reforms within and effective cooperation with nonmember governments, including Ukraine and Russia.

Reinvigorating PFP. The original strategic rationale for PFP—enhancing stability among and practical cooperation with the countries along NATO's periphery—has become even more compelling in the context of the Alliance's further enlargement, the global spread of terrorism, growing Western interests in Southwest and Central Asia, and Russia's internal political crisis and aggressive behavior toward its neighbors. How should the Alliance build cooperative partnerships with states that are unlikely to ever be members or that do not aspire to membership? To retain its relevance and effectiveness, PFP must be transformed, adequately resourced, and better integrated with bilateral and regional efforts to address new security challenges. NATO should develop new, tailored PFP programs, including ones on military education and training, security sector reforms, border security, and subregional military cooperation, in the Balkans, greater Black Sea region, and Central Asia. NATO infrastructure funds could also be used to improve bases in these regions to facilitate PFP activities and NATO operations relevant to the security of all. Successful programs of subregional cooperation in Southeastern Europe could also be adapted to or extended across the Black Sea.[48] PFP and the NATO-Russia Council could also be used to mitigate Russian suspicions and develop informal "rules of the road" with respect to the expanded role of U.S. and NATO involvement in Central Asia and the Caucasus and to managing tensions between Russia and its neighbors.

Ukraine and Russia. Given the continuing political divisions within Ukraine on NATO membership, the United States should work with the EU and European governments to bolster Kyiv's defense, security sector, and other reforms, while maintaining active engagement and cooperation with NATO through the NATO-Ukraine Council. Ukraine can remain a valuable partner in pursuing mutual security interests and enhance its sovereignty without joining the alliance. However, a more structured dialogue on membership is warranted as Kyiv is ready. Moscow continues to profess its openness to cooperation with NATO on common security concerns including counterterrorism, WMD proliferation, theater missile defense, and airspace management. It remains to be seen how serious this cooperation will become. While the United States and other allies cannot ignore Russia's retreat from democracy, the Alliance should maintain a willingness to work with Moscow on mutual security interests so long as it respects the sovereignty of its neighbors and other international commitments.

Broader Middle East. To the south, NATO's decade-long dialogue with Mediterranean neighbors has borne few practical results, and it will take time to overcome unfamiliarity and suspicions in the broader Middle East about the ICI. Nevertheless, NATO and the EU can build capacity and limited cooperation in this region through dialogue, training, and exercises as some of these countries are gradually showing openness to such cooperation. At the Riga Summit, NATO governments launched a Training Cooperation Initiative to expand participation by Middle East partners in NATO training and education programs and to explore joint establishment of a security cooperation center in the region.[49]

Global partners. Since 2001, NATO has undertaken operational military cooperation with countries beyond Europe's periphery to counter terrorism and promote stability. Australia, New Zealand, Japan, and South Korea, whom NATO has dubbed *contact countries*, have either worked with the Alliance in Afghanistan or supported stabilization efforts in Iraq. The development of these relationships reflects NATO's need for a wider circle of partners beyond PFP to respond to complex global threats. At the November 2006 Riga Summit, NATO heads of state and government recognized the value of partnerships with contact countries but deferred for future study and NAC decisions U.S. proposals to improve political and operational military consultations with these countries.[50] NATO needs to develop mechanisms to facilitate routine political consultations with capable, like-minded democracies around the world that are interested in working with the Alliance; better integrate their armed forces into the planning and conduct of those NATO-led operations where they elect to participate; and improve their interoperability with NATO forces. Whether the Alliance should use such partnerships with countries outside Eurasia that share NATO's core values and have common interests to evolve, over time, into a global alliance of democracies, is an intriguing question that merits further consideration.[51]

MIDDLE EAST PARTNERSHIPS

U.S. security relationships in the Middle East are essential to advancing America's strategic interests in the region: maintaining peace and stability, ensuring access to vital energy resources, combating extremist ideologies, and preventing hegemony.

With the exception of the U.S.-Israel security partnership, these relationships are less robust and more fragile than those in other parts of the world where U.S. interests face far less immediate risk. While ensuring Israel's security has been a central pillar of U.S. Middle East policy since the 1960s, the interests of the two countries are not identical, and the relationship has, at times, been strained. U.S. security relationships with moderate Arab countries in the Middle East are constrained by limited common interests and longstanding rivalries among partners and have become even harder to maintain in recent years, given unwavering U.S. support for Israel and the lack of progress toward resolving Israeli-Palestinian tensions. The lingering turmoil in Iraq, where the U.S. presence is likely to remain a magnet and rallying point for jihadists for years, further complicates these efforts, as does Iran's determination to acquire nuclear capabilities and expand its regional influence.

Israel: A Special Relationship

The United States supported establishment of the State of Israel in 1948 and has been strongly committed to that country's security and well-being for nearly five decades. Extensive political, economic, and personal ties, as well as shared democratic values and many common interests, have sustained the relationship. With the strongest military in the Middle East, Israel has been Washington's closest partner in the region, and the two governments are generally aligned in the United Nations and other international fora.[52] Israel has been the largest recipient of U.S. economic and military assistance since 1976 and between 1985 and 2005 has received an average of $3 billion annually in Economic Support Funds (ESF) and Foreign Military Financing (FMF) grants, along with a substantial amount of other grants and loan guarantees.[53] In light of Israel's growing prosperity, U.S. and Israeli officials agreed in 1998 to eliminate U.S. ESF—then $1.2 billion—over 10 years, while increasing FMF from $1.8 billion to $2.4 billion. In fiscal year (FY) 2006, Israel received $237 million in ESF and $2.26 billion in FMF grants; the latter figure accounted for 48 percent of the U.S. foreign military assistance budget and about 20 percent of Israel's defense budget.[54] U.S. security assistance has been premised on the notion that as Israel takes calculated risks for peace in the Middle East, the United States will help reduce those risks. Thus, the United States provided Israel an extra $1.2 billion in FY 2000 to fund implementation of the Wye Agreement and $200 million in FY 2002 in antiterror assistance. In addition, the United States has funded—and provided technological assistance for—collaborative military research and development programs in Israel through the U.S. defense budget, most significantly more than $1 billion since 1988 for the Arrow anti-tactical ballistic missile system.

Formal U.S.-Israel security consultations are conducted through annual meetings of the Joint Political-Military Group (JPMG), which reviews regional security, defense cooperation, and security assistance issues. The JPMG is supplemented by a high-level Strategic Dialogue, which meets biannually, and, since 1996, a Joint Counterterrorism Group. The United States provides Israel data from its missile early warning system, and there is a hotline between the Pentagon and the Israeli Defense

Ministry.[55] There is a broad array of bilateral military planning and combined training exercises.[56] As close as bilateral security relations have been, there is no formal U.S. security guarantee to Israel or mutual defense treaty—although there have been calls for one from time to time, including the notion that Israel should become a member of NATO.[57] Israeli governments have had mixed feelings about the benefits of a defense treaty, and U.S. administrations have been generally hesitant to make such a commitment, primarily because of the negative impact it would have on U.S. relations with the Arab world. In early 1987, the Israeli government sought and was granted status as a major non-NATO ally, which gives it lower prices on U.S. defense articles and allows Israeli industries to compete equally with NATO countries and other close allies for U.S. military production contracts.

During the Cold War, Israel's strategic location, military and intelligence capabilities, and vibrant democracy were manifestly instrumental to advancing U.S. interests in the Middle East, particularly limiting Soviet influence and countering the efforts of Syria and other radical states to destabilize the region. However, the balance between Israel's strategic value to the United States and other U.S. interests in the Middle East have shifted over the past decade, particularly after 9/11, as Washington has sought to improve relations with moderate Arab states and promote democratic development in the region as an antidote to extremist violence. So, too, the perception on the Arab street and much of the world of the United States as Israel's unconditional patron has diminished Washington's ability to mediate disputes and promote regional stability.[58] Thus, the United States did not seek direct involvement of Israeli forces in the 1991 Gulf War and the 2003 Iraq war for fear of disrupting the international coalitions. The two governments have also had differences over Israeli use of security assistance and arms transfers to third countries. The Secretary of State has certified to Congress on several occasions that Israel "may have violated" agreements that limit use of U.S. military equipment to defensive purposes, particularly in connection with operations in Lebanon in 1978–1981.[59] Concerns have also surfaced about Israeli transfer of U.S. military equipment to third countries without requisite approvals, most prominently a 1996 Israeli contract to sell an airborne early warning radar to China (later cancelled in response to U.S. pressure).

The issue of strategic value arose again during Israel's 2006 military operations in Lebanon. Seeing the conflict as a proxy war between the United States and Iran, some observers argued that Israel had an opportunity to show its value to the United States and deal a setback to the Iranian-backed Lebanese Shi'a Hezbollah organization and Iran, a development that even a number of Arab governments would have quietly welcomed.[60] However, Israeli forces found Hezbollah a more formidable adversary than expected, and the widespread killing of innocent civilians and destruction of Lebanese infrastructure stirred rage against Israel and the United States throughout the Muslim world. Nonetheless, public support for Israel remained quite strong in the United States, with nearly 60 percent of Americans surveyed in two polls during the war expressing the belief that Israeli military operations were about right or not strong enough.[61] A majority of the American political leaders and the public still see Israel as an embattled partner in maintaining vital U.S. interests in the Middle East and in combating terrorism. While this partnership rests on a solid foundation, the potential for significant divergences between Washington and Tel Aviv remain, particularly over handling of the Palestinian issue and Iran's nuclear program.

Egypt: A Wary Partner

Cooperation with Egypt has been a cornerstone of U.S. efforts to promote peace, stability, democracy, and economic development in the Middle East for over three decades. However, bilateral relations have been strained in recent years by policy differences over the Israeli-Palestinian conflict, the 2003 Iraq war, and U.S. counterterrorism strategy. Washington's vigorous democracy promotion initiatives in Egypt and the broader Middle East have also been unwelcome to the Mubarak government and angered elites and many average Egyptians, who see this as infringement on Egyptian sovereignty. [62] Nonetheless, military and counterterrorism cooperation at the operational level has continued, and the two countries still share interests in maintaining regional peace and stability and in combating extremist violence, which was the basis of the relationship charted by Egyptian President Anwar Sadat and U.S. Secretary of State Henry Kissinger in 1973.

Egypt is the second largest recipient of U.S. foreign assistance. The United States has provided Egypt an annual average of close to $2 billion in economic and military assistance since 1979. Recently, Egypt has received about $1.3 billion in U.S. Foreign Military Financing annually, which has helped it modernize and improve the operational reliability of its armed forces, among the largest in the region. Many Egyptian officers have trained in the United States under the International Military Education and Training program, building relationships that help sustain bilateral cooperation.[63] In return, the United States has benefited from Egypt's cessation of hostilities against Israel, strong support in the 1991 Gulf War (which was key to enlisting other Arab states in the coalition), routine approval of military overflights and naval transits, and secure sea lanes through the Suez. Egypt has long battled terrorism at home and has cooperated closely with the United States on a broad range of counterterrorism and law enforcement issues.[64] Egypt has also provided forces to a number of UN peacekeeping operations around the world, support to Operation *Enduring Freedom* in Afghanistan, training to Iraqi and Palestinian security forces, and security assistance to a number of African states. U.S. and Egyptian forces participate in combined military exercises, including deployments of U.S. troops to Egypt, and U.S. Navy ships regularly visit Egyptian ports. Egypt hosts Operation *Bright Star*, a biennial multinational military exercise.

Restoring this partnership to its potential will require renewed cooperation in areas of common interest and new efforts to overcome mutual mistrust and manage enduring policy differences. Both governments need to clarify their respective expectations and goals and give greater visibility to areas of cooperation as a way to bolster public support for the relationship. The annual bilateral Military Cooperation Committee meetings have focused on acquisitions and exercises. A new political dialogue, with a broader scope and participation than the earlier U.S.-Egypt Strategic Dialogue, should be undertaken to chart a new course for this partnership.[65] Renewed U.S.-

Egyptian cooperation to stabilize the Israeli-Palestinian conflict would be the best way to overcome some of the mistrust and enhance U.S. regional legitimacy. As a center of Arab culture, moderate political, intellectual, and religious figures in Egypt have broad influence and can be among the most effective voices for countering ideological support for terrorism in the Arab world. The Egyptian military remains a powerful institution, adamantly opposed to Islamist extremism, which also values the good working relationship it has developed with the U.S. Armed Forces over the past 20 years. This situation presents opportunities to enhance bilateral military cooperation, such as sharpening the operational objectives of the *Bright Star* exercises to meet pressing mutual security concerns. Over time, Egypt, together with other moderate governments in the region, could become a much fuller partner in stabilizing Iraq and in advancing common interests in the broader Middle East, North Africa, and the Mediterranean basin.

Jordan: A Partner in Peace

Jordan remains an important partner for the United States in the search for durable peace and political moderation in the Middle East, as it has been for much of the past four decades. While a small country with few natural resources, its tempered policies and location among hostile neighbors have often allowed it to help diffuse tensions. Relations with the United States were set back by the late King Hussein's tilt toward Iraq during and after the first Gulf War; however, Amman has since pursued a number of policies welcomed by Washington, including normalizing diplomatic and economic relations with Israel pursuant to a 1994 bilateral peace treaty, and supporting other Middle East peace efforts. Jordan has contributed to postconflict stabilization and relief efforts in Afghanistan and Iraq and provided training and equipment to the new Iraqi army and police forces. It has been a valued U.S. partner in combating terrorism and extremism, notably by taking steps to disrupt terrorist finances and operations, and arresting and prosecuting individuals linked to al Qaeda. Indeed, Jordan has also been a target of local terrorists and the al Qaeda affiliate Abu Mus'ab al-Zarqawi.[66]

Since 1952, the United States has provided Jordan with economic and military assistance totaling more than $9 billion. U.S. assistance has risen significantly since the mid-1990s to encourage Jordan's support for the Middle East peace process and the war on terrorism and to buffer it from the adverse effects of the Iraq war.[67] The U.S.-Jordanian Military Commission was established in 1974, and combined training exercises take place in Jordan on a regular basis. Jordan also received designation as a major non-NATO ally in 1996, giving it preferential access to U.S. defense articles and other military assistance. These U.S. assistance programs have helped Jordan advance its development and security, enabling it to remain a stable partner committed to advancing mutual interests in the Middle East.

Saudi Arabia and the Gulf States

Over the past decade, U.S. security partnerships in the Persian Gulf have included bilateral arrangements with, and military presence and prepositioning of equipment in, Saudi Arabia, Kuwait, and the other Gulf Cooperation Council (GGC) states; rudimentary engagement with the GCC as an organization; and support for the U.S.–U.K.–enforced no-fly and no-reinforcement zones in Iraq, all focused on safeguarding threats to key U.S. interests in the region. These partnerships were circumspect, for the most part. The United States did not guarantee the political survival of these regimes and even criticized their more egregious violations of international human rights standards, and the regimes often stood their distance from Washington on sensitive issues.[68]

Since 9/11 and the Iraq war, new attention has been given to threats emanating from the region, most prominently terrorism, but also proliferation of nuclear weapons and the acquisition of increasingly sophisticated missile systems. However, the lack of a broad and enduring political basis for cooperation with and among the Gulf States continues to limit what can be achieved. Each of the Gulf States has a different threat perception. While Saudi Arabia is uneasy about the growing ties of smaller Gulf States with the United States, the Gulf States are wary of Saudi ambitions and influence.[69] The areas in which their interests conflict may outnumber those in which they coincide. Even the imminent threat posed by Iraq just after the invasion of Kuwait could not fully overcome the rivalries and mistrust among GCC members or the reservations that many of them had regarding cooperation with outside forces. While continued turmoil in Iraq and Iran's quest for nuclear weapons and growing regional assertiveness are of considerable concern to all GCC states, it is unlikely to result in significant increases in their military capabilities, and it is far from clear that it will lead to common cause with each other or the United States. For example, the Saudis could respond to Iranian WMD acquisition by seeking countervailing capabilities of their own. All would prefer to see a U.S. dialogue with Iran. If this is not forthcoming, some Gulf leaders might find accommodation of Iran less costly than continued cooperation with the United States. Still, Gulf leaders have voiced growing concern about Iran's nuclear ambitions on military and environmental grounds and might, under some circumstances, tolerate U.S. military action to disrupt it. With regard to terrorism, while there is quiet tactical cooperation on specific cases and groups—and the Saudis in particular have fought a rather high-profile campaign against terrorists active within the kingdom—none of the Gulf monarchies is willing to embrace the Bush administration's prescription that democracy is the best way to address the root causes of terrorism. While resigned to the need for a continuing U.S. presence in the region as a stabilizing factor after the Iraq war, all the Gulf States in the long term want to see a much smaller U.S. footprint to deter potential threats from Iran or a resurgent Iraq.

Given Saudi Arabia's possession of the world's largest proven oil reserves and its leadership roles in the Islamic and Arab world, the U.S. relationship with the kingdom is pivotal.[70] The United States and Saudi Arabia have longstanding economic and defense ties, and a series of informal agreements, statements by successive U.S. administrations, and military deployments have demonstrated a strong U.S. commitment to its security.[71] Saudi Arabia was an important member of the coalition that evicted Iraqi forces from Kuwait and later hosted U.S. aircraft enforcing the no-fly zone over southern Iraq. While Saudi officials opposed the 2003 Iraq war, they reportedly allowed certain U.S. and British support activities to operate from their country. Following the war, Washington acceded to Riyadh's request that the roughly 5,000 U.S. military personnel stationed in Saudi Arabia be withdrawn from the kingdom, and the Combat Air Operations Center in the country was relocated to Qatar. The United States remains Saudi Arabia's leading arms supplier, having delivered over $22 billion in arms between 1997 and 2004.

While a strong supporter of Palestinian national aspirations with limited relations with Israel, the Saudi government has endorsed a number of proposals for Arab-Israeli peace, including the 2003 Quartet Roadmap, and in 2002 King Abdullah secured Arab League support for his "land for peace" approach to resolving the Palestinian-Israeli impasse. In 2005, Washington and Riyadh announced a new strategic dialogue to expand cooperation in several areas, including counterterrorism and military affairs. The Saudi leadership is well aware that 15 of the 19 September 11 terrorists were Saudi nationals, most from the same region, and that they are accused of fueling the *salafist* (Sunni Arab extremist) insurgency in Iraq. Saudi Arabia must be a part of any successful strategy to defeat Islamist extremism, but the ruling family will have to avoid appearing too closely aligned with the United States, as this is part of the reason they are also a target of al Qaeda. U.S. officials have commended improved Saudi cooperation in intelligence-sharing and disrupting terrorist networks and finances since 2003, although the 9/11 Commission found Saudi Arabia to be a "a problematic ally in combating Islamic extremism" because of certain domestic and foreign policies that help to foster extremism.[72] The Saudi government seems comfortable publicly condemning Islamist extremism and maintaining quiet intelligence and law enforcement cooperation. This may be the best that can be achieved given current political realities.

Cooperation with the Maghreb states—including Morocco, Tunisia, Libya, and Algeria—on counterterrorism, maritime security, and counterproliferation has advanced in recent years as a result of a growing convergence of interests on these issues and shifting strategic assessments by these governments.

The Way Ahead

The future of U.S. partnerships in this region will largely turn on how Washington completes its commitment to stabilize Iraq and succeeds in efforts to head off or preclude regional hegemony by a nuclear-capable Iran. Washington must also find the right balance between its commitment to Israel's security, efforts to promote a viable Palestinian state, and cooperation with other moderate governments in the region. The Palestinian issue is not the root cause of radical Islamist extremism, but it will be much easier for moderate Arab states to support U.S. policies on counterterrorism and regional security if they see the United States actively working for a just settlement and when they are seriously consulted on the direction of that process.

The Bush administration's vision for the Middle East and forceful promotion of democratic reforms have clearly met with resistance. Yet many leaders and elites in the region appreciate that adapting their traditional societies and social structures to the realities of globalization is essential to long-term prosperity and stability. The United States should continue to support gradual political and social transformation that will allow these countries to become better integrated into the global system without triggering an even greater Islamist rage, violent regime change, or anti-American backlash.

Another key challenge facing the United States will be shaping the size, visibility, and locations of the long-term U.S. military presence in the region to diminish the rage that it now engenders in the Muslim world. Many advocates of the 2003 Iraq war argued that the defeat of Saddam Hussein would allow for a smaller U.S. military presence in the region. The war and the ongoing insurgency in Iraq have brought even greater deployments and raised suspicions on the Arab street that the United States is actually planning for a sizable long-term military presence in Iraq. Maintenance of such a presence in Iraq, under almost any imaginable future, will remain a lightning rod for extremists throughout the region. In addition, there will be a continuing need to assess the demands of security in light of the erosion of Iraqi confidence in the legitimacy and effectiveness of their own government.

Over the long term, the United States needs to maintain the capability to respond to major conventional and WMD threats to its interests and to strike quickly and decisively against terrorist threats that partners in or near the Gulf region are unable to counter. It will also need to reassure regional partners that it will help them deter threats to their security, particularly if Iran does acquire nuclear weapons. These objectives could be achieved with a small permanent ground presence in the Gulf, together with ongoing naval operations and rotational deployments of air and ground forces to cooperative security locations for combined exercises and training with partners, and clear red lines about the U.S. responses terrorism and other acts of aggression.

Despite the challenges and limits discussed above, bilateral and multilateral partnerships, if properly structured, can advance vital U.S. interests in the broader Middle East. These partnerships can evolve based on habits of cooperation and patterns of trust. The Gulf governments and other friends in the region will likely remain wary of binding formal agreements that lock them into relationships that lack a foundation of trust. Given the absence of broad common interests, objectives, or threats, these habits of cooperation are more likely to develop in the context of multiple, overlapping mechanisms focused on narrower functional concerns. U.S. policy should continue to encourage friendly governments in the region to take somewhat greater responsibility for their own security, and it can advance this process through security cooperation activities that offer subtle advice rather than direction.

SOUTH AND CENTRAL ASIA

U.S. security cooperation with the states of South and Central Asia has gained new salience, given the war in Afghanistan, the requirements of U.S. global military strategy for unimpeded access to Eurasia, China's rise, and Central Asia's contribution to world energy supplies. A great deal of attention has been focused on the U.S. strategic partnership with India (treated in chapter 6 of this book). However, India and Pakistan (discussed in chapter 2) are essential partners in the struggle against terrorism. Cooperation with the states of Central Asia, earlier concerned with post-Soviet legacy issues, has lately focused on terrorism and transnational threats.

Pakistan

Washington and Islamabad have had an erratic partnership since 1947, with cycles of significant U.S. security and economic assistance to Pakistan alternating with breaks in cooperation, particularly after the 1965 Indo-Pakistan war and again after 1979 due to developments in Pakistan's nuclear program. Following the Soviet invasion of Afghanistan, the United States restored security and economic assistance as the two governments collaborated to bolster the Afghan resistance. However, relations remained strained and were marred by periodic violence against U.S. interests. Continued development of Pakistan's nuclear weapons program led to a suspension of all military and most economic assistance after 1990, and relations were further disrupted by Pakistan's 1998 nuclear test and the military overthrow of the democratically elected government in 1999.

Relations took a positive turn after September 11, when Pakistan agreed to support U.S. efforts to eliminate the Taliban regime in Afghanistan and enhance counterterrorism cooperation. In 2003, President Bush promised to develop a long-term relationship with Pakistan, pledging $3 billion in economic and military assistance over 5 years. The United States subsequently offered to provide $1.5 billion in foreign military financing between 2005 and 2009, making Pakistan one of the largest recipients of U.S. security assistance. This aid, coupled with Islamabad's designation as a major non-NATO ally in 2004, seeks to advance the modernization of the Pakistani armed forces. In March 2006, President Bush and Pakistani president Pervez Musharaff initiated a strategic partnership with regular high-level consultations on issues of mutual interest.[73]

While Pakistan has provided valuable assistance to the United States in combating terrorism, the partnership remains fragile. As discussed in chapter 2, Islamabad's tenuous hold over the Federally Administered Tribal Areas of Pakistan has allowed the region to remain a safe haven for Taliban forces conducting operations in Afghanistan. This problem, along with Pakistan's enormous development challenges and Musharaff's vulnerability to Islamist extremists and his crackdown in 2007 on civil dissent, all suggest that the U.S.-Pakistan partnership will remain vulnerable to intermittent disruptions for some time.

Central Asia

Following the collapse of the Soviet Union, the United States set out to develop security cooperation with the new states of Central Asia, particularly through NATO's Partnership for Peace, to strengthen their sovereignty and independence and to promote democratic reforms. The United States provided over $240 million and substantial technical assistance to help Kazakhstan eliminate Soviet nuclear warheads, weapons-grade materials, and supporting infrastructure. Authoritarian leaderships and resource constraints limited development of these partnerships. With the initiation of coalition military operations in Afghanistan, security cooperation with these states gained new urgency. Uzbekistan, Kyrgyzstan, and Tajikistan agreed to provide access to airfields and other support to U.S. and NATO forces participating in Operation *Enduring Freedom*.[74] However, relations with Uzbekistan soured following U.S.

criticism of the government's handling of the 2005 Andijan massacre, and access to the Karshi-Khanabad airfield was withdrawn in 2005. Political turmoil in Kyrgyzstan has also caused problems over operations at Manas. U.S. political support to democracy and human rights in Central Asia will continue to complicate cooperation with the region's autocratic governments on countering terrorism and other transnational threats. However, long-term U.S. interests in regional stability in Asia will be best served by continued promotion of gradual economic and political liberalization that will enable integration of Central Asia into the global economy. Given their much bigger stake and influence in the region, U.S. security strategy will need to engage Russia and China while remaining firmly supportive of Central Asian sovereignty.

EAST ASIA AND THE PACIFIC

Given the growing importance of East Asia to global stability and prosperity, sustaining the five U.S. treaty alliances in the region—Japan, the Republic of Korea, Australia, Thailand, and the Philippines—will remain one of Washington's central foreign policy priorities in the decade ahead. The Clinton and Bush administrations and their counterparts have made significant strides over the past decade to adapt U.S. alliances with Japan, Australia, and the ROK to new circumstances. However, sustaining these relationships as mature partnerships will require that the allies maintain candid, high-level political dialogues, further transform their armed forces, and redouble efforts to sustain domestic support. In light of the growing interest of East Asian governments in expanded regional cooperation, it will also be important to demonstrate how these alliances provide a stable context for and complement multilateral arrangements. Relations with Thailand and the Philippines have advanced in recent years on the strength of counterterrorism, humanitarian relief, and peacekeeping cooperation. Several partnerships in Southeast Asia are benefiting from practical cooperation on humanitarian activities and in combating terrorism and other transnational threats as well as the growth of democracy in the region.

All these efforts are intertwined with Washington's handling of several complex challenges, including the North Korean nuclear weapons program and potential instability on the Korean Peninsula; a rising China and cross-straits tension between China and Taiwan; the sustenance of regional cooperation in combating terrorism; the realignment and transformation of the U.S. military presence in the region; Japan's expanding role in international security affairs; and the promotion of peace and prosperity in Southeast Asia.

The U.S.-Japan Alliance

For close to half a century, the U.S.-Japan alliance and the U.S. military presence in Japan have served as the foundation for security, stability, and prosperity in East Asia. The 1960 Treaty of Mutual Cooperation and Security commits both countries to maintain and develop their capacities to resist armed attack and provide mutual assistance against certain attacks, as well as granting the U.S. Armed Forces access to facilities in Japan "for the purpose of contributing to the security of Japan and the maintenance of international peace and security in the Far East."[75] Forward-deployed forces in Japan have allowed the United States to maintain vital economic and strategic interests in the region, including security commitments to Japan, the Republic of Korea, and other Asian allies and friends. About 75 percent of the costs of the U.S. military presence in Japan are offset by the Japanese government through direct payments and indirect cost-sharing mechanisms.[76] For Japan, the alliance offers security consistent with its "peace constitution" at reduced costs (less than 1 percent of GDP), extended deterrence against potential WMD threats in the region, and safeguard against any future Chinese bid for regional hegemony. Without the alliance, Japan would face unattractive choices, including significant expansion of its defense capabilities, which could exacerbate regional tensions or trigger a destabilizing arms race that would force neighboring countries to choose sides.

At the same time, the alliance is a central pillar of U.S. global strategy and complements Tokyo's 2005 Integrated Security Strategy of fuller international engagement to prevent threats from reaching Japan. The U.S. ability to project power nearly halfway around the world from Japan was critical to the coalition's success in the 1991 Persian Gulf War. A decade later, the deployment of the USS *Kitty Hawk* to the Persian Gulf from Yokosuka, accompanied by Japan Maritime Self-Defense Force escort ships in Operation *Enduring Freedom* underscored the global significance of the U.S. presence in Japan and the mutual benefits of the U.S.-Japan alliance.

As the Cold War ended, doubts about the viability of and need for the alliance surfaced on both sides of the Pacific. In Japan, many questioned whether the costs of hosting U.S. forces were still warranted in the face of a diminished Soviet threat. In the United States, the legacy of bilateral trade and economic disputes in the 1980s, vocal Japanese opposition to the U.S. military presence, limited Japanese support during the 1991 Gulf War, and Tokyo's cautious response to the 1994 North Korean nuclear crisis caused many Americans to question Japan's value as an ally.[77] In response, the two governments worked to update the alliance to meet the challenges of the post–Cold War security environment and agreed in April 1996 to the Japan-U.S. Joint Declaration on Security. In September 1997, Japan issued the Guidelines for Japan-U.S. Defense Cooperation and subsequently enacted legislation that would allow Japan to provide the United States with rear-area support in "situations in areas surrounding Japan."[78]

Since 2001, Japan has assumed a greater role in support of international stability and security. At the time of the 1991 Persian Gulf War, Japan's security responsibilities extended only 1,000 nautical miles from the home islands. Developments since that time include the looming threat of North Korea's nuclear weapons and long-range missile programs and the growth of China's regional influence and military capabilities. Also, the 9/11 terrorist attacks challenged traditional assumptions regarding Japan's security environment, stimulated an evolution in thinking about Japan's security policies, and reaffirmed the strategic importance of the alliance with the United States. Much has been accomplished, but more needs to be done to transform the alliance into a global strategic partnership.

Convergent Strategic Assessments

The U.S.-Japan alliance has advanced on the basis of convergent assessments of the international security environment and a strong mutual conviction that the alliance enhances the security of both countries and the Asia-Pacific region and fosters global peace and stability. These assessments are reflected in the key national security documents of the alliance partners: the U.S. 2001 and 2006 Quadrennial Defense Review Reports and 2002 and 2006 National Security Strategies, and Japan's 2002 Defense White Paper, the October 2004 report of the Council on Security and Defense Capabilities, and the December 2004 New Defense Guidelines, as well as various bilateral statements.[79]

The 2001 and 2006 QDR Reports both focused on uncertainty as the defining feature of the contemporary global security environment—the United States could no longer know when, or from what direction, the country or its allies might come under attack. Security could be threatened by major war, asymmetric attacks by rogue states, the proliferation of weapons of mass destruction and ballistic missile delivery systems, or acts of international terrorism, possibly employing WMD.

Both reports envisioned Asia as "a region susceptible to large scale military competition," as the Bush administration wrestled with the best course for coping with China's rise. While it did not specifically mention China, the 2001 QDR focused heavily on the requirements of dissuading and deterring a possible "military competitor with a formidable resource base" in East Asia.[80] The 2002 National Security Strategy advocated cooperative ties with China, reflecting U.S. interest in ensuring Beijing's support in combating terrorism and on other global and regional security issues. The 2002 NSS opened the door to closer relations if China demonstrated a commitment to international norms and good neighborly relations, a theme that became a touchstone of U.S. policy in 2005 as the administration encouraged China to become a more transparent and responsible stakeholder in the international system, while hedging against less favorable outcomes.[81] Thus, the 2006 QDR Report called for steps to shape the choices of "countries at strategic crossroads" (most prominently China) to dissuade a major military competition and unveiled the concept of "tailored deterrence" to deal with "near peer competitors" and "regional challengers" such as North Korea.[82]

Twenty-four Japanese citizens were lost in the attacks on the World Trade Center, and Japan had prior experience with domestic terrorism—the 1995 sarin gas attack in the Tokyo subway system by members of Aum Shin Rikyo. The Japan Defense Agency's 2002 White Paper declared that the 9/11 terrorist attacks "defy not only the U.S., but also the freedom, peace and democracy of international society including Japan." The document noted that certain regional disputes, ethnic conflicts, and the proliferation of WMD, particularly possible terrorist acquisition of WMD, at a time of growing interdependence "have been recognized not merely as domestic issues, but as concerns of the international community as a whole." The White Paper highlighted Japan's obligations to UN Security Council Resolution 1363 to cooperate with the international community in the suppression of terrorist activity and recognized the leading role the United States played in this struggle.[83] Consensus on this assessment enabled Prime Minister Junichiro Koizumi to secure Diet passage in October 2001—and annual renewal through November 2007—of the "Anti-terrorism Special Measures Laws" that authorized Maritime Self-Defense Force ships to deploy to the Indian Ocean to provide logistical support to U.S. and coalition forces in Operation *Enduring Freedom*. When the U.S. Secretaries of State and Defense met with their Japanese counterparts for the first time after 9/11 at the December 2002 Security Consultative Committee session, they readily agreed to expand cooperation to combat terrorism and the proliferation of weapons of mass destruction, mentioning both North Korea and Iraq.[84]

Two major reports issued during 2004 reflected the emerging consensus in Japan that the contemporary international security environment required fundamental changes in the country's strategy and defense posture. In March, the ruling Liberal Democratic Party's Defense Policy Subcommittee issued a report that advocated amending Article 9 of the Constitution to reflect the legitimacy of a Japanese Self-Defense Force (SDF) role in collective self-defense, consolidation of crisis decisionmaking in the prime minister's office, enactment of a general law to support international peacekeeping, and enhancement of cooperation with the United States on new security threats.[85] The subcommittee report also advocated a major restructuring of the SDF to make it more flexible, and possible development of capabilities to strike enemy missile bases in the face of an imminent attack. In October, the Council on Security and Defense Capabilities, an advisory body to the prime minister chaired by Hiroshi Araki, issued its report. The "Araki Report" declared that the events of September 11 "marked the beginning of a new century for security affairs," noting the potential threats from both state and nonstate actors. The council recommended an "Integrated Security Strategy" for the defense of Japan and improving the global security environment, aiming "to prevent a direct threat from reaching Japan . . . and to reduce the chances of threats arising in various parts of the world with the aim of preventing such threats from reaching Japan or affecting the interests of Japanese expatriates and corporations overseas." [86] The strategy envisions use of both hard and soft power measures by Japan alone, in tandem with the United States, and in cooperation with the rest of the international community to improve the security environment and prevent the emergence of new threats. The commission report expressed concern with China's rise and the risks to Japanese and global security by a conflict over Taiwan.

Echoing the 2001 QDR Report, Japan's 2002 White Paper noted that "unpredictability and uncertainty have persisted" in East Asia as a result of the diverse national security perspectives of various governments; unsettled regional issues, particularly the continuing tension on the Korean Peninsula; and the presence of enormous military forces, including China's growing military strength. It concluded that the alliance with the United States and presence of U.S. forces remained essential to regional peace and stability. Thus, in the Asia-Pacific region, the two governments share a commitment to eliminating the threat posed by North Korea's nuclear program and peaceful reunification of the Korean Peninsula. While U.S. and Japanese leaders have endorsed a cooperative relationship with China, they have also jointly encouraged Beijing "to play a responsible and constructive role regionally as well as globally"; to seek "the peaceful resolution of issues concerning the Taiwan Strait through dialogue"; and "to improve transparency of its military affairs." They have also endorsed Russia's "constructive engagement" in the region and full normalization of Japan-Russia relations "through the resolution of the Northern Territories issue" and pledged mutual support for "a peaceful, stable and vibrant Southeast Asia."[87]

Japan's Expanding Security Role and the Alliance

A trend toward greater Japanese involvement in international security issues has been established over the past few years and will likely continue over the coming decade. However, given constitutional limitations, steps along this path have been fitful and sometimes required special legislation. In December 2001, the Diet amended the 1992 International Peace Cooperation Law, which set restrictive conditions for deployments and limited involvement to logistical support activities, to allow the SDF to undertake a range of core peacekeeping missions. The Diet later had to approve special measures so that 600 noncombat SDF engineers could support humanitarian and reconstruction operations in southern Iraq between February 2004 and July 2006.[88] Prime Minister Koizumi overcame domestic skepticism about the Iraq mission by arguing that the deployment was essential to bolster stability in the wider Middle East, the source of 90 percent of Japan's oil supplies, and to maintain alliance relations with the United States. In addition to support for the United States in Afghanistan and Iraq, the Koizumi government agreed to acquire and deploy missile defenses, participate in the Proliferation Security Initiative (Japan hosted an Initiative exercise in October 2004), enhance intelligence cooperation, and provide strong diplomatic backing for the U.S. position on North Korea's nuclear weapons program. Crisis management legislation passed by the Diet in 2003 and 2004 has further strengthened Tokyo's crisis response authorities and ability to work with the United States in areas surrounding Japan.[89]

Changing attitudes, particularly among Japanese in their 30s and 40s, toward Japan's international role, possible constitutional revision, and the exercise of the right of collective self-defense have underpinned these developments. Japanese public support for the alliance with the United States has remained strong over the past 40 years but has grown even stronger since 2002, with approval levels at 70 to 80 percent.[90] While favorable views of the United States in Japan fell in the year after the Iraq war from 74 percent to 68 percent and dropped further to 63 percent in 2006 polling, public trust in the U.S. defense commitment remains very high.[91] As for the U.S. military presence, a majority of Japanese surveyed in 2004 felt American bases should be reduced—49 percent "somewhat," but only 15 percent "greatly"—and 67 percent expressed the belief that the bases are important to Japan. Americans also have very positive views of Japan and the alliance. While 63 percent of the public had positive views of Japan in 2001, 69 percent of the public and 91 percent of opinion leaders characterized Japan as a reliable ally.[92]

SDF Transformation

Japan is also moving to transform the Self-Defense Forces to meet emerging security challenges. In December 2003, the Koizumi government called for a Defense Posture Review to ensure that the SDF is able to respond effectively to the threats of terrorism and the proliferation of weapons of mass destruction and ballistic missiles and to conduct proactive activities in support of international peace and stability. In December 2004, the government approved the resulting "National Defense Program Guideline for FY 2005 and After" (NDPG) and the related "Mid-Term Defense Plan [MTDP] FY 2005–2009."[93] These documents embraced the integrated strategy and force posture recommendations of the Liberal Democratic Party's Defense Policy Studies Subcommittee and the Araki Commission. The NDPG prescribes a major transformation of the SDF between 2005 and 2015 from its Cold War posture designed for defense of the homeland against full-scale invasion. It envisions a smaller (reduced from 162,000 to 155,000 personnel), more flexible, and mobile force with enhanced readiness. It notes the SDF must be able to cope with a diverse range of threats, including low intensity attacks in the vicinity of Japan, ballistic missiles strikes, terrorist actions, airspace intrusions, and attacks by guerrilla or special operations forces against offshore islands or critical infrastructure. To enhance the international security environment, the NDPG calls for active SDF participation in international peace operations and for intensified cooperation with the United States. To deal with the threat posed by ballistic missiles as well as more traditional state-based threats in areas surrounding Japan, it proposes to pursue ballistic missile defense systems and to strengthen the link to U.S. extended deterrence. It called for the creation of a Joint Staff Office (which was established in April 2006) to improve cross-service operational planning, enhanced intelligence collection and analytic capabilities, and qualitative improvements to the force through the acquisition of technology, particularly information processing and networking capabilities.

Transformation of the SDF's legacy force structure (which emphasized antitank, antisubmarine, and antiaircraft capabilities) and operational practices will take time. Budgetary constraints—including a 24.3 trillion yen (U.S. $234 billion at 2004 rates) ceiling set on the total MTDP, with annual budget growth decreasing—and the demands placed on social welfare spending by a rapidly aging population will limit resources available for transformation and extend its timeline. So, too, the 2004 NDPG did not fully address the sensitive issue of whether the SDF could be involved in collective self-defense actions, which limits their role in various regional and global operations. Nonetheless, the course charted by the NDPG and the programmatic recommendations of the MTDP will advance SDF transformation and enhance alliance relations.

At the October 29, 2005, Security Consultative Committee meeting, the United States and Japan reached a sweeping agreement to reshape the alliance in ways that reflect Japan's willingness to play a larger role in its own defense and in regional and global security.[94] This agreement established the framework for closer military ties by calling for more integrated contingency planning, collocating some U.S. and Japanese headquarters and units on the same bases in Japan, expanding combined military exercises in both countries, and enhancing intelligence-sharing, all steps designed to strengthen interoperability. To enhance combined missile defense activities, Japan agreed to find a site for deployment of a U.S. X-band radar, and the United States agreed to deploy additional capabilities (Patriot and Aegis) in and around Japan as appropriate.

Key Challenges Ahead

Much has been accomplished in recent years, but the gains are not set in concrete. The Shinzo Abe government was seen as likely to maintain the direction set by Koizumi. In a historic January 2007 speech to the North Atlantic Council, Prime Minister Abe noted that Japan and NATO share common values and responsibilities for dealing with global security challenges. Abe stated that Japan would "no longer shy away from carrying out overseas activities involving the SDF if it is for the sake of international peace and stability," and he pledged to expand cooperation with NATO in Afghanistan and elsewhere.[95] Yet this commitment to international engagement was a significant factor in Abe's surprise resignation 9 months later, following a difficult year in office marked by a series of political scandals and loss of control of the upper house of parliament in July by his Liberal Democratic Party (LDP). Abe cited his inability to break a parliamentary deadlock over extension of the antiterrorism legislation that authorized Japan's controversial naval mission in the Indian Ocean as the proximate reason for his resignation, and expressed the hope that his LDP successor could secure passage of the measure. However, the opposition Democratic Party of Japan remains firmly against the mission and sees it as a wedge issue to build political momentum and even force early general elections.[96]

Completion of the realignment of the U.S. military presence in Japan is essential to advancing future bilateral security relations. Enhanced alliance cooperation on regional and global security problems will also require further strengthening of Japan's institutional, legal, and military capabilities, as well as fostering domestic support for this role. The central strategic issues facing Asia and Japan—North Korea's nuclear weapons, Korean unification, and China's emergence as the region's dominant power—should keep the alliance as a core element of Japan's security strategy. That said, this does not mean that Japan's support for the alliance can be taken for granted. This is particularly the case if the United States fails to manage each of these issues—as well the local politics of realignment—to an outcome that protects Japan's security interests. Japan wants no part of an Asia dominated by China, but most Japanese also want to avoid a confrontation with Beijing.

Realigning the U.S. military presence in Japan. With regard to basing issues, Tokyo has focused on Okinawa, where public pressure for a significant reduction of U.S. forces has been intense for two decades. Discussions on the overall realignment of the U.S. presence in Japan began in 2003, in tandem with the internal U.S. Global Posture Review.

Implementation of the 1996 bilateral Special Action Committee on Okinawa (SACO) Final Report was an area of frustration for over a decade.[97] The report contained some 28 initiatives to reduce the impact of U.S. forces on the residents of Okinawa Prefecture, as well as procedural changes to the Status of Forces Agreement—all of which have been implemented. The heart of the SACO Report called for return of approximately 12,000 acres of land, contingent on relocation of various facilities within the Okinawa Prefecture. The centerpiece land return—the reversion of Marine Corps Air Station Futenma in a densely populated area of Ginowan city to Japan upon completion of a replacement facility elsewhere in Okinawa Prefecture— has been bogged down for years in Tokyo-Okinawa politics.[98] Meanwhile, discontent in Okinawa with operations at Futenma due to safety and noise concerns grew, and Tokyo's plans for construction of the replacement airfield through a land reclamation project across a coral reef met with intense local opposition.[99]

At the end of 2002, the United States and Japan launched the Defense Policy Review Initiative (DPRI) to advance alliance transformation, interoperability, and force realignment. After protracted and sometimes contentious negotiations, DPRI led to agreement on a detailed roadmap for the realignment of U.S. forces in Japan at the May 1, 2006, meeting of the Security Consultative Committee.[100] Among the issues addressed in the roadmap are realignment on Okinawa, including completion of a Futenma replacement facility in a less populated area off Cape Henoko and the relocation of approximately 8,000 Marine personnel to Guam; land returns and shared use of facilities; improvement in U.S. Army command and control capabilities; joint use of Yokota airbase; relocation of the U.S. Navy carrier airwing from Atsugi to the Marine Corps air station at Iwakuni; missile defense; and joint training. The roadmap commits Japan to contribute $6.09 billion in 2008 U.S. dollars toward the estimated $10.27 billion cost involved in the relocation of the Marines from Okinawa to Guam.

Timely completion of these realignment initiatives is essential to alliance transformation. This will be a challenge, as public opinion on Okinawa remains strongly opposed to the Futenma replacement.[101] The political leadership in Tokyo needs to make clear to the Japanese public, particularly on Okinawa, that realignment and transformation are not simply real estate transactions but also involve the enhancement of military capabilities and Japan's assumption of new responsibilities.

Alliance management. Further steps could be taken to strengthen high-level dialogue. During its first term, the Bush administration pursued a strategic dialogue between the Deputy Secretary of State and the Vice Minister of Foreign Affairs as a long-term planning mechanism to review regional and global developments, sustain strategic cooperation, and develop a common understanding and strategy toward China. In the second Bush term, this has been formally raised to the level of Secretary of State–Foreign Minister. However, in practice, the dialogue is now managed in the U.S. Government by the Under Secretary of State for Political Affairs. Meanwhile, in 2005, the U.S. Deputy Secretary of State initiated a strategic dialogue with China. While this has raised some concern in Japan that the United States is now paying greater attention to China and its economic dynamism, it is important to underscore in this context, and elsewhere, that the alliance with Japan—and the shared democratic values at its foundation—remains the pillar of U.S. regional and global strategy. Given Japan's increasing role in support of international security and the elevation in 2007 of the Japan Defense Agency to a cabinet ministry, defense officials should be included in the Strategic Dialogue to complement the alliance's existing "two plus two" structure.[102]

Missile defense cooperation. North Korea's continuing development of nuclear weapons and ballistic missile delivery systems stands as a direct threat to the security of Japan and the United States, making missile defense cooperation a critical element in advancing security and technology cooperation. In December 2003, the Koizumi government announced that Japan would acquire and deploy missile defense capabilities and continue participation with the United States in the development of missile defenses. The government earmarked 106.8 billion yen ($929 million) to initiate its missile defense acquisition in the FY 2004 budget. Spending on missile defense has been one area of steady growth in Japan's defense budget since that time. Driven by concerns of the growing threat from North Korea, it reached 182.6 billion yen ($1.5 billion) in FY 2007 to pay for early deployment of the Patriot Advanced Capability–3 (PAC–3) interceptor missiles and acquisition of Standard 3 missile interceptors for Aegis-equipped U.S. warships. Definition of the full program was a major focus of the NDPG and MTDP. The target date for the initial deployment of the missile defense system is 2008, and the system is scheduled to be fully operational in 2011. The missile defense decision marks a significant step forward in Japan-U.S. defense cooperation and integration, and it is complemented by the purchase of Aegis destroyers, licensed production of the PAC–3 missile, and joint research and development on advanced interceptors. Both governments have reaffirmed their commitment to missile defense cooperation, which allows both countries to hedge against the long-term challenge posed by China's continuing military buildup and modernization of its missile force. Greater cooperation in missile defense R&D and production would be facilitated by a decision to alter the Japanese government's arms export control policy. At the same time, the development and deployment of an operative missile defense system should not come at the cost of other elements of the U.S.-Japan security relationship, such as host nation support payments or SDF modernization.

Institutional development. To become a fuller partner in the alliance and the management of international peace and security, the Japanese government needs to continue to develop its national security institutions, military capabilities, and interoperability with U.S. forces. An important step in this process is the effort since April 2006 to enhance joint planning among the SDF branches. Combined planning with the United States concerning threats to Japan and contingencies in areas surrounding Japan should also be undertaken at the appropriate command levels, and the creation of a new U.S.-Japan Joint Task Force Headquarters at Camp Zama in 2008 should facilitate this.[103] Additional steps could be taken to improve intelligence-sharing and crisis coordination. Japan has created a National Security Council, but its capabilities for crisis management and policy development at the sub-cabinet level need to be further developed. Japan also needs a government-wide legal system to protect classified information from unauthorized release. All these measures would improve U.S.-Japan crisis management. Finally, the Japanese Diet should pass permanent, generic laws establishing generic principles to facilitate timely Japanese participation in international peace operations rather than relying on special legislation to authorize each engagement.

Sustaining Japanese political support for the alliance. While Japan's leaders seem open to increasing involvement in global security issues and have concerns about threats from North Korea and China, its citizens remain decidedly pacifist and uncertain about military engagement. Unlike South Korea, the U.S. global posture review and its call for greater flexibility in the use of stationed forces was not controversial in Japan because those forces have regularly undertaken off-island operations, and the Japanese are more wary of China. While Tokyo seems generally satisfied with the current consultation arrangements with respect to operations by U.S. forces in Japan, differences could still arise over controversial U.S. military actions supported by forces based in Japan. Political leaders in both countries could do more to emphasize to their constituents how the alliance and the U.S.-Japan strategic partnership support convergent interests in supporting democracy, prosperity, and stability in the Asia-Pacific region and across the globe.

The U.S.–ROK Alliance

The alliance between the United States and the Republic of Korea still enjoys strong support in both countries but is facing its most complex set of challenges since the Mutual Defense Treaty of 1953 was signed. Bilateral efforts to transform the alliance into a fuller, more equal partnership and articulate a common vision of its future course are taking place within the context of a complicated and paradoxical security environment marked by lingering North-South military confrontation, but with a diminished sense of threat in the ROK; fitful negotiations to eliminate North Korea's nuclear weapons program, as the South's economic engagement in the North deepened; ROK involvement in the global war on terrorism, but divided opinion over engagement of its forces in Iraq; and strong support for the alliance and the U.S. military presence, coupled with fears that these ties could draw South Korea into a confrontation with China. Seoul and Washington have differing perspectives on the main threats to security in Northeast Asia and on the role of the alliance in regional and global contingencies. On a divided peninsula, the Republic of Korea is itself marked by deep political and generational cleavages on a range of issues, including attitudes toward the United States and policy toward North Korea. For the first 50 years of the alliance, the North Korean threat loomed so large that U.S.–ROK differences were generally sublimated in the interest of unity. The strengthening of democracy in Korea, the development of a genuine opposition party, and emergence of a lively debate on foreign and national security issues in Korea have also made alliance politics more volatile.

Shifting Attitudes in South Korea

Anti-American sentiment in some segments of the South Korean population has strained alliance relations. As memories of American assistance in the Korean War and postwar reconstruction fade, frictions related to the ROK's continuing dependence on the United States for its security, and the sizable military presence associated with it, have become magnified. This dependence, coupled with their history of colonial rule during the first half of the 20th century, has left many Koreans with a deep sense of frustration over their inability to control their destiny.[104] Some segments of South Korean society feel that Washington has handled problems in the relationship, including certain incidents related to U.S. military operations in Korea and economic disputes, in an arrogant fashion.[105] The strident student protests and more nuanced anti-American sentiment voiced by some mainstream South Korean politicians in recent years do not pose a near-term threat to the alliance—more than 70 percent of the population favors maintaining or strengthening the relationship, and about 80 percent feel the U.S. military presence is important to South Korea's security. However, if the current polarization of South Korean attitudes toward the United States and North Korea along political and generational lines persists, it could erode the fabric of the alliance.[106]

A good part of the shift in attitudes toward the United States can be traced to the coming to political power of the "386 generation": people now in their 30s and 40s and who were born in the 1960s and educated during the period of protests for democratization in the 1980s. Two-thirds of South Koreans are now under age 40. The 386 generation is generally more nationalistic, outspoken, and questioning of U.S. intentions than their parents. The 386 generation is prominent in the administration of President Roh Moo-hyun, who supported the young democratic activists in the 1980s, and in the leadership of the progressive (center-left) Uri Party, which backs Roh and holds a large majority in the National Assembly. The 386 generation has no first-hand memory of the Korean War, but they did witness past U.S. support for authoritarian ROK governments and what they perceive as enduring U.S. unilateralism and lack of consultation in handling previous security crises on the peninsula. A number of intellectuals of this generation hold the view that U.S. policies facilitated Japanese hegemony over Korea between 1905 and 1945 and favored Japan over Korea after World War II. Some even believe that U.S. conduct of the Korean War led to the country's partition.[107] These perspectives have also been influenced by leftist teachers in secondary and higher education and inaccurate, polemical information on the Internet.

Developments since 2001, including the Bush administration's tough stance toward Pyongyang and skepticism of the ROK's Sunshine Policy of engagement with the North—coupled with the accidental killing in 2002 of two Korean schoolgirls by U.S. soldiers, who were subsequently acquitted of any wrongdoing—led to sharp drops in popular opinion about the United States. In U.S. State Department–sponsored surveys, South Koreans expressing favorable views of the United States declined from 66 percent in July 2001 to 47 percent in January 2003, and 59 percent felt bilateral relations were poor—the lowest reading in 15 years (see figure 7–2).[108] Over-

FIGURE 7–2. SHIFTING SOUTH KOREAN ATTITUDES

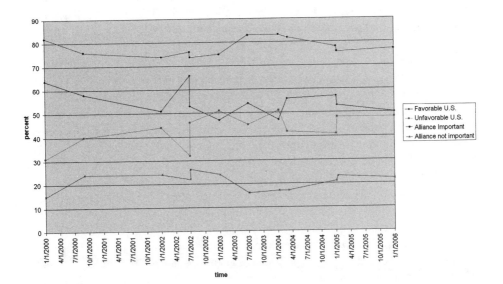

all attitudes toward the United States and bilateral relations have improved somewhat since 2005 but are more evenly divided than before 2001.[109] The generational differences are reflected in 2005 survey data showing that while 69 percent of those 50 and older held favorable views of the United States, opinion among those in their 30s (51 percent favorable, and 48 percent unfavorable) and 20s (52 percent favorable, 45 percent unfavorable) was more evenly split.[110] However, as concerns about the North Korean nuclear threat, reductions of U.S. forces in Korea, and the attendant potential of an economic downturn have grown, attitudes of younger Koreans, particularly those in their 20s, have become more positive toward the United States and the alliance.[111]

The military accident in 2002 led to near-unanimous support for revision of the Status of Forces Agreement, which was seen as institutionalizing the ROK's subordinate role in the alliance. Nonetheless, support for the U.S.–ROK alliance remains strong, particularly among older Koreans and members of the opposition Grand National Party. In 2005 and 2006 polling, large majorities continued to express support for the alliance, and about 80 percent believed the U.S. military presence was needed for Korea's security. More than 70 percent saw the United States as the most beneficial security partner for Korea over the next decade, and 69 percent believed the alliance should be maintained after unification. However, the intensity of support for the U.S. military presence had diminished significantly since 2000 (in 2005, 26 percent of those surveyed said it was very important, down from about 40 percent in the late 1990s).

South Korean views on North Korea were also divided—43 percent positive and 52 negative in early 2005—but this was a significant shift since 2001, when 73 percent viewed the North unfavorably.[112] Most South Koreans are not worried about a North Korean attack. They are concerned about the North Korean nuclear program and the possible collapse of the North, with the attendant potential for instability and economic dislocation throughout the peninsula. In 2005, 80 percent of South Koreans supported efforts to engage North Korea through the development of economic and cultural relations.[113] That same year, a majority of South Koreans (59 percent) believed that Pyongyang would surrender its nuclear program for a package of political and economic benefits. While there is broad support for U.S. and international efforts in the Six-Party Talks to eliminate North Korea's nuclear programs, most South Koreans favor an incremental approach featuring both carrots and sticks. In a 2004 survey, 27 percent of South Koreans blamed the United States for the lack of progress in the talks, and 70 percent lacked confidence that the United States would protect South Korea's interests in negotiations with the North. However, South Korean attitudes toward the North have hardened, and the Sunshine Policy has been tempered, in the aftermath of Pyongyang's October 9, 2006, nuclear test.[114]

A troubling trend is the surge in anti-Japanese sentiment in South Korea. In early 2005, 80 percent of South Koreans had unfavorable views of Japan, and 90 percent felt relations with Japan were poor. South Koreans see Japan (29 percent), as well as North Korea (13 percent) and China (12 percent), as potential threats to regional peace and stability over the next decade or more.[115] This sentiment is rooted in resentment over issues of history, the legacy of Japan's wartime occupation of Korea, as well as the reemergence of longstanding territorial controversies. However, particularly among elites, there is a fear that growing U.S.-backed Japanese involvement in management of regional and international security affairs could revive Japanese militarism and ambitions for regional hegemony. So, too, South Korean leaders and the wider population fear that what is perceived as Washington's strategic tilt toward Japan will make their country both less secure and less important to the United States.

Attitudes toward China, which has been the ROK's top export market since 2003, have fluctuated but reflect an abiding wariness. Beijing is now widely seen as a constructive partner in managing the North Korean nuclear problem and other aspects of regional security affairs. In a 2004 poll, South Koreans expressed equally positive feelings toward China and the United States (58 percent).[116] However, South Koreans also express lingering concerns about China's authoritarian political system and suspicions about its motives in Northeast Asia. The South Korean public and political leadership are well aware of China's history of domination of their country and know that China's rising economic and military power could at some point be used against Korean interests. In a May 2004 survey, 61 percent of respondents noted that China was the most important country from an economic standpoint, but 51 percent also saw China as a "competitive rival," and 78 percent said China's products would surpass Korean goods in 10 years.[117] The Korean public's perception of China as an economic and political rival has grown since 2005, particularly as China has stirred historical territorial disputes.

U.S. Goals and Strategy: North Korea

Dealing with the Democratic People's Republic of Korea's (DPRK's) nuclear program has also complicated alliance management issues with the ROK. The Bush administration has steadfastly defined North Korea's nuclear programs as a challenge to security in Northeast Asia and to international efforts to stem WMD proliferation, not as a bilateral issue between the United States and the DPRK. Since early 2003, the administration has emphasized that multilateral negotiations are the best way to resolve the problem, and, with Chinese assistance, the Six-Party Talks commenced in August 2003. The administration's diplomacy has succeeded in getting China, South Korea, Japan, and Russia to agree on the need for complete, verifiable, and irreversible dismantlement of the DPRK nuclear programs, which has helped to minimize, though not eliminate, North Korean efforts to create fissures within this coalition. Multilateral coordination has been hampered by differing interests and Pyongyang's efforts to play to South Korean sympathies and Chinese anxieties.

Given these challenges, progress in the Six-Party Talks has been limited and marked by several lengthy boycotts by the DPRK. At the end of the fourth round of talks on September 19, 2005, the Six Parties produced a joint statement of principles to guide negotiations. The statement was immediately subject to differing interpretations, particularly by the DPRK. However, the U.S. Government made clear its view of the main tenets, which were generally endorsed by all the other parties: all nuclear weapons and all elements of the DPRK's nuclear programs will be declared and completely, verifiably, and irreversibly dismantled; the DPRK will return, at an early date, to the Nuclear Non-Proliferation Treaty and come into full compliance with International Atomic Energy Agency safeguards; and various benefits, particularly the right to pursue nuclear energy for peaceful purposes at the "appropriate time," will only accrue to the DPRK when it has met these two obligations, demonstrated a sustained commitment to cooperation and transparency, and ceased proliferating nuclear technology.[118] The ROK government has been inclined to offer generous carrots to the North—including provision of energy and nuclear power early in the process—as a way to induce cooperation on the nuclear issue and to advance North-South reconciliation. Transforming the joint statement and the Initial Action Agreement of February 2007 on shutting down the Yongbyon reactor, discussed in chapter three, into an agreement acceptable to all six governments and the U.S. Congress will require a protracted and arduous diplomatic effort.

In addition to the nuclear issue, there remain differences between the United States and South Korea over policy toward Pyongyang including assistance, investment, and dealing with the regime's illicit activities. The ROK government rightly wants to play the leading role in managing relations with the North, including contingencies related to internal collapse. However, both governments recognize that the United States has unique experience and capabilities to find and secure the DPRK nuclear program in such a scenario. The two governments will need to continue to discuss integration of various crisis management plans and harmonization of these plans with combined operational military plans for the defense of South Korea. While the ROK has endorsed the principles of the Proliferation Security Initiative (PSI), it has yet to become a participant because of fears that engagement in certain PSI counterproliferation activities could have an adverse effect on relations with the North. U.S. and Japanese participation in any future PSI activities directed against North Korea would raise anxieties in the ROK government about various forms of North Korean retaliation against the South.

Rebalancing the Military Relationship

The two governments have agreed to the goal of a South Korean–led defense of the peninsula with the United States in a supporting role, but differences remain on the timing and ultimate structure of the new arrangements. Bilateral discussions on the future of the alliance (FOTA) between 2002 and 2004 focused on "legacy" issues including adjusting the U.S. footprint, transfer of certain conventional defense missions from U.S. to ROK forces, and enhancing combined defenses. In particular, the FOTA talks produced plans to shift U.S. forces deployed close to the demilitarized zone (DMZ) to consolidated bases south of Seoul and for transfer of the Yongsan Garrison in central Seoul and 59 other facilities to South Korean control. In tandem with the realignment, the ROK pledged to invest $10 billion to modernize its capabilities, and the United States committed to enhancements in firepower, air, and naval support valued at $11 billion and to maintain deterrence and support this evolving posture.[119]

In June 2004, before the either the Global Posture Review or the FOTA talks were completed, the U.S. Department of Defense notified the South Korean government of plans to withdraw 12,500 troops (about one-third of total deployments) from the peninsula by the end of 2005. This move followed a May 2004 decision to redeploy one of two U.S. combat brigades (3,600 troops) in the ROK to Iraq and sometimes contentious FOTA discussions. These developments surprised most Koreans and brought to the fore their conflicted feelings between the desire for and costs of a more self-reliant defense posture and the compromises attendant to continued reliance on the U.S. security guarantee. Korean officials worried about the ROK's ability to take on larger military missions and were concerned that the redeployments would mean that U.S. forces would no longer serve as the tripwire in mutual defense operations, leaving South Korea less rather than more secure. After several months of bilateral consultations, the governments agreed in October 2004 that the U.S. withdrawals and realignment would be stretched out through 2008 and plans to remove one artillery and one attack helicopter battalion would be cancelled.[120] The residual U.S. presence of 25,000 military personnel will be clustered around two hubs in the Osan-Pyongtaek and the Taegu-Pusan areas; however, the conditions for transfer of existing U.S. facilities and the acquisition of additional land for the consolidated bases by 2011 under the Land Partnership Plan, while agreed by both governments, remain contentious political issues in South Korea on environmental and legal grounds.

Greater self-reliance in defense has been a goal of South Korean governments since the 1970s. Investment of over $65 billion in several force improvement plans since that time has significantly enhanced the readiness and capabilities of the ROK army but did not fundamentally reduce the country's dependence on the United States. President Roh came to office in 2003 determined to reduce this dependency, consistent with South Korea's current prosperity and international stature, and to make the alliance a more balanced partnership. Roh advanced the concept of "cooperative, self-reliant defense" as a means for the South Korean government to realize greater control over its defense plans and decisionmaking and to reassure the public that, with improved capabilities, the ROK armed forces could provide for national defense even after the planned reduction and realignment of U.S. forces. President Roh and his advisors explained that the term *cooperative* underscored the intent both to maintain a transformed alliance with the United States and develop regional security cooperation in Northeast Asia.[121]

While ROK defense budgets have grown significantly in recent years, maintenance and personnel costs absorbed 66 percent of the 2004 and 2005 budgets, leaving only about 34 percent for required force improvements.[122] In an effort to achieve a self-reliant posture, the Korean Ministry of National Defense (MND) unveiled "Defense Reform 2020," a plan for qualitative transformation of the ROK defense establishment over 15 years. The 2020 plan calls for reducing standing forces by 26 percent but enhancing the capabilities of residual units through better joint planning and acquisition of state-of-the-art weapons and support systems. Force structure would be streamlined and include more professionals and fewer conscripts. Modernization would focus on improved mobility, situational awareness, and precision strike capabilities. The MND hopes to replace nearly every outdated major weapons platform; upgrade intelligence, surveillance, reconnaissance, and command and control systems; and purchase new air defense missiles and Aegis-equipped destroyers. To ensure effective oversight of expenditures, a new Defense Acquisition Program Administration will be established.

The 2020 plan calls for expenditure of U.S. $662 billion between 2006 and 2020, with 43 percent of those resources to be earmarked for force improvements. To sustain this program, MND estimates that defense spending would need to increase 9.9 percent annually from 2006 to 2010, 7.8 percent from 2011 to 2015, but only 1 percent from 2016 to 2020.[123] Under the ROK government's projections of 7 percent average annual GDP growth over the life of the reform program, MND estimates that the program would consume 2.6 to 3 percent of GDP until 2010, after which time the burden would decrease. Realization of Defense Reform 2020 will be a challenge for any South Korean government. Since the plan was issued, the Bank of Korea has projected lower out-year growth rates, and the potential for an economic downturn always exists. Pressures to control overall governmental expenditures and a general public skepticism about defense spending will likely remain impediments, absent a spike in concerns about North Korea. During the first half of the 2020 plan implementation, expenditures associated with the relocation of U.S. forces and the assumption of additional missions by ROK forces will likely raise MND operations and maintenance costs. Some analysts have questioned both the savings that can be achieved by cutting army personnel so steeply and the wisdom of taking such cuts before demographic trends require them, given the manpower-intensive demands of possible stabilization missions in the event of a North Korean collapse.[124] Several analysts assess that a truly independent ROK defense capability would require even greater defense spending.[125]

President Roh and his advisors have also made transfer of wartime operational command (OPCON) of ROK forces a touchstone of alliance transformation. In 2005, Roh began a public campaign for transfer of wartime OPCON of ROK forces, calling it a matter of regaining sovereignty and a valuable step in diminishing North-South tensions. Roh argued that projected improvements in ROK defense capabilities will allow the transfer.[126]

The United States supports the goal of Koreans playing a predominant role in their own conventional defense, including a change in command relationships. Washington's assessment is that ROK forces are capable of defending South Korea, with certain U.S. support. U.S. officials accepted the move from shared operational control under a combined headquarters to a system of independent, parallel national commands, as a natural next step in the evolution of the alliance and suggested that this could take place as early as 2009. This kicked off a firestorm of protests in Korea from opposition parties for former defense officials, who saw an OPCON shift by that date as premature and ill-advised, urging that further debate on timing be suspended until a new ROK government takes office in 2008. At the 38th U.S.–ROK Security Consultative Meeting, the ROK defense minister and then–U.S. Defense Secretary Donald Rumsfeld reviewed the results of a command relations study commissioned a year earlier and agreed to a roadmap that would transfer OPCON to the ROK after October 15, 2009, but not later than March 15, 2012.[127] In February 2007, Defense Secretary Robert Gates and Defense Minister Kim Jong-soo concluded an agreement that firmly established the transfer date as April 17, 2012. The two governments have agreed to develop a Strategic Transfer Plan. U.S. officials have underscored that the new command structure will maintain deterrence and combined U.S.–ROK defense of the Korean Peninsula, and that the United States will provide significant "bridging capabilities"—such as the command and control system of the Combined Forces Command—until the ROK achieves a fully independent defense capability. Sorting out a transitional command structure and long-term crisis management arrangements on the peninsula will require transparency, good faith, and flexibility by both governments, as well as candid discussions about handling sensitive issues relating to instability in North Korea.

Shaping a Broader Vision of the Alliance

U.S. and South Korean leaders have recognized that their mutual regional and global security interests, as well as a potential North-South rapprochement, require the development of a broader, long-term, vision for the alliance—one that expands its function from its present narrow peninsular focus.[128] Most ROK political leaders across the political spectrum believe their country's security and prosperity are still somewhat fragile and that the alliance with the United States remains an important safeguard against instability on the peninsula and a balancing factor in relations with China and Japan.

A majority of South Koreans also see shared democratic values and deep economic and personal ties as important underpinnings of the alliance. However, in contrast to Japan, the notion of the alliance serving purposes other than defense of the ROK is a relatively new concept in South Korean political discourse. For example, President Roh justified the unpopular deployment of 3,500 ROK military personnel in support of Operation *Iraqi Freedom* as a necessary manifestation of alliance solidarity and good faith, not a Korean contribution to protection of its own interests in Persian Gulf stability and energy supplies. Moreover, many on the left who object to the U.S. military presence are also skeptical of the benefits of the alliance for advancing South Korean interests. Without a shared vision of the future, both governments will have great difficulty making the case for the alliance to their publics.

Following the Future of the Alliance initiative, in late 2004 Washington and Seoul began the Security Policy Initiative (SPI), an interagency dialogue aimed at implementing agreements reached in the FOTA talks and developing a long-term vision of the alliance. The SPI reached a broad consensus on the main global and regional security challenges and produced agreement on a "Joint Study on the Vision of the ROK–U.S. Alliance" that describes how the alliance can contribute to peace and security on the Korean Peninsula, in the region, and globally.[129] Going forward, SPI will focus on articulating a vision for the future development of the alliance and a concept for operationalizing that vision, including the roles of each partner in fulfilling these objectives.

At the November 2005 Gyeongju Summit, Presidents Bush and Roh agreed to launch a ministerial-level Strategic Consultation for Allied Partnership (SCAP) to promote dialogue on bilateral, regional, and global issues of mutual interest. The two presidents noted that the alliance stands not only *against* threats but also *for* the promotion of the common values and interests in Asia and around the world.[130] At the first session of SCAP in January 2006, Secretary of State Condoleezza Rice and then-Foreign Minister Ban Ki-Moon set out an agenda for practical cooperation to promote democracy and human rights; counter terrorism and proliferation of WMD; prevent pandemic disease; enhance regional stability; and bolster multilateral peacekeeping, crisis response, and disaster management. The consultations will be followed by a subministerial dialogue.

A particularly contentious element of alliance transformation concerns *strategic flexibility*, a reference to off-peninsula operations by U.S. forces deploying from bases in Korea. Both the government and the broader public are concerned that U.S. operations from the ROK could draw the country into regional conflicts, particularly a confrontation with China over Taiwan, and that the global missions of U.S. forces might diminish their deterrent value on the peninsula. U.S. officials have sought to allay South Korean concerns on both accounts, noting that the concept is a two-way street that would also facilitate rapid movement of U.S. forces stationed elsewhere to the Korean Peninsula in a crisis. President Roh has acknowledged the logic behind strategic flexibility but has also affirmed that "USFK [U.S. Forces Korea] should not be involved in disputes in Northeast Asia without Korea's agreement. . . . We will never compromise on this."[131] At the January 2006 SCAP meeting, Secretary Rice and

Foreign Minister Ban issued a declaration formally acknowledging respect for the other's position.[132] Some South Korean analysts and politicians contend that this agreement requires amendment of the Mutual Defense Treaty, and hence approval by the National Assembly. In addition, the South Korean government would clearly like prior consultation on off-peninsula operations by units assigned to USFK, which could limit U.S. flexibility.

Another question on the horizon is clarifying how the alliance could complement any future Northeast Asian regional security cooperation or structure. Some in the ROK hope the Six-Party Talks could evolve into such a permanent forum for dealing with regional security issues, while others envision structures limited to countries in the region. President Roh has emphasized that his concept of "cooperative, self-reliant defense" would also allow for South Korea to act as a peaceful "balancing force" in a "cooperative security structure in the region based on the Korea-U.S. alliance."[133] This statement was quickly clarified by Blue House advisors as not suggesting any notion of South Korea balancing China and the United States. However, Roh continues to send mixed signals. Rather than endorse the notion that an adapted alliance with the United States can play a stabilizing role in Northeast Asia, Roh has chosen to advance more independent notions, warning of the need to "overcome old divisions" in the region. Roh and most South Koreans clearly fear aligning their country with the United States and Japan in any future effort to contain China.[134]

Sustaining the U.S.–ROK Alliance

In light of changing political and geostrategic landscapes, sustaining the U.S.–ROK alliance will require concerted bilateral efforts to continue transforming the relationship. Several efforts are essential to this goal.

Six-Party Talks and North Korea. Resolute but creative diplomacy in the Six-Party Talks remains essential to a durable resolution of the North Korean nuclear challenge, maintenance of peace and stability in Northeast Asia, and further adaptation of U.S. alliances with the ROK and Japan. It is essential for the United States and other governments to demonstrate that every effort has been made to resolve the nuclear issue peacefully. Unilateral or coercive actions may ultimately be necessary but could well come at the cost of public support for the alliance in the ROK. The key challenge for U.S. diplomacy will be to demonstrate a forthcoming public face and tactical flexibility while remaining firm on strategic outcomes. In the aftermath of Pyongyang's October 2006 nuclear test, Washington has reassured Seoul that its longstanding pledge of extended deterrence through the U.S. nuclear umbrella remains in effect. U.S. and South Korean leaders also need to initiate a more candid and transparent dialogue about North Korea leading to more coordinated policies. Otherwise, differences on this issue will continue to hamper adaptation of the alliance.

Shaping a fuller and broader partnership. The bilateral defense and foreign ministry dialogues are moving to adapt the alliance and develop a common vision to advance mutual interests. The U.S.–ROK Security Policy Initiative has produced agreement on a common vision of the alliance, but further effort on the part of both governments is required to broaden and deepen political support for a transformed alliance. If reshaped as an equal partnership between two democracies committed to defending shared values and common interests, the alliance could weather most developments in North-South relations or the region. Rather than being organized against a specific threat, it would serve a number of common Korean-American interests, including maintaining stability on the peninsula in the context of either a DPRK collapse or peaceful reunification; working with other Asian countries and institutions to enhance regional security cooperation; supporting international (UN) and other regional (Association of Southeast Asian Nations, NATO) efforts to stabilize failed states, combat terrorism, and slow WMD proliferation; and hedging against the emergence of an aggressive China. Such a vision of the U.S.–ROK alliance could engender the requisite political support on both sides of the Pacific. Indeed, it reflects the calls in South Korea for transforming the relationship into "a comprehensive, dynamic, and future-oriented alliance." This kind of a mature partnership with the United States would allow South Korea to extend its global influence.

Defense transformation and strategic flexibility. A transformed alliance should reflect the ROK's desire to achieve greater control over its own security and destiny while concurrently serving mutual regional and global interests. This will require further changes in command structures, procedures for contingency planning, and force posture. The Combined Forces Command will need to be replaced by a new mechanism to coordinate U.S. and ROK military operations.

A sustainable long-term U.S. posture in the ROK should be sufficient to assure Seoul of the mutual defense commitment, fill critical gaps in ROK capabilities, allow for rapid augmentation to repulse any aggressor, and provide the United States with a reliable foothold to support global defense operations. The U.S. contribution to defense of the ROK will shift from a heavy ground presence to reinforcements and firepower provided by air and naval forces. With regard to off-peninsula operations, given the ROK's desire to avoid any provocation of China, Seoul seems likely to want further clarification of the circumstances in which U.S. forces might act, as well as advance notification of unilateral operations by U.S. forces in Korea.

The alliance and regional security. Given China's growing influence on the Korean Peninsula and in the region and South Korea's commitment to good relations with Beijing, special efforts should be made to demonstrate how the alliance can support regional security cooperation. If Washington and Seoul fail to demonstrate how the alliance can serve this function, there is a danger that interest will grow in new, unproven structures for regional security cooperation to replace the alliance. Beijing continues to suggest that the U.S.–ROK alliance is an unnecessary anachronism in light of China's peaceful rise and efforts to bring peace to the peninsula. The Chinese have also advanced various ideas for a regional security architecture that would exclude the United States. Turning the Six-Party framework into a permanent regional security forum, which both governments agree could be pursued once the Six-Party Talks realize their primary mission, merits further examination by the analytic community.[135] In the interim, revival of the U.S.-Japan-ROK Trilateral Coordination and Oversight Group, which focused on North Korea policy, might be a useful mechanism to enhance trilateral cooperation on a broader range of issues.[136] Much as NATO's Partnership for Peace Program engaged Russia and other former Warsaw Pact countries in humanitarian and peacekeeping activities to build confidence in NATO's peaceful intent, perhaps trilateral participation in future humanitarian or peace support operation along with China and other Asian countries would be a way to demonstrate that both alliance relationships can contribute to regional security.

Diplomacy and public affairs. U.S. officials and the American media need to be sensitive to political and social change in South Korea and to the mounting frustration with Korean dependency on the United States. There is a tendency in Washington to exaggerate the extent of genuine anti-American sentiment in South Korea. U.S. public diplomacy needs to be more skillful in making the case for a transformed alliance, particularly with younger people in Korea. At the same time, the ROK government needs to be more outspoken in refuting irresponsible attacks against the United States in the South Korean media and public discourse and in explaining to its citizens how the alliance serves mutual interests. Enhancing the rather limited and formalized exchanges between South Korean legislators and their American counterparts could help deepen mutual understanding and strengthen support in both countries for the alliance.[137]

The U.S.-Australia Alliance: A Hardy Special Relationship

Australia is the oldest ally of the United States in the Asia-Pacific region, and the two countries have many common interests, shared democratic values, and a long history of working together. U.S.-Australia security cooperation is deep and multifaceted, akin to the U.S.–UK special relationship. The two countries have fought together in two World Wars, the Korean and Vietnam Wars, the 1991 Gulf War, and, more recently, in Afghanistan and Iraq. Both have experienced major terrorist attacks against their assets and citizens in the past years. The United States provides a robust security guarantee for Australia, including extended nuclear deterrence. Australia's small but effective armed forces contribute to mutual security in the Asia-Pacific region and around the world, and their capabilities are enhanced by access to U.S. weapons systems, defense technology, and military logistics support. There is extensive bilateral intelligence cooperation, including several joint facilities in Australia. The alliance enhances Australia's ability to work with and influence the United States and its status in world affairs.[138] The alliance helps anchor the U.S. role in Western Pacific security affairs and provides Washington a reliable partner for many common regional and global endeavors. That said, Australian support for U.S. policies, particularly vis-à-vis China, cannot be taken for granted.

The broad consultative and mutual security commitments in the Australia–New Zealand–United States (ANZUS) Treaty have allowed the alliance to adapt to changes in the international environment.[139] Founded as a safeguard against a militarily resurgent Japan, it became a bulwark against communist expansionism during the Cold War, and now serves to advance mutual global interests in an era of uncertainty and to balance potential rivalries in the Asia-Pacific region.[140] Since 1996, Washington and Canberra have retooled the alliance, undertaking joint operations in support of the UN peacekeeping in East Timor, tsunami relief, and counterterrorism and stabilization efforts in Afghanistan and Iraq. Australia and U.S. military forces also coordinate security cooperation and counterterrorism activities in the Philippines, Indonesia, and Malaysia. Australia still plays a leading role in security operations in East Timor, the Regional Assistance Mission to the Solomon Islands, and maritime security in the Pacific Islands. Annual meetings of defense and foreign ministers give the alliance strategic direction, with agreement to enhance intelligence cooperation, joint training and interoperability of military forces, and cooperative development of missile defenses. The Australian government has expressed support for rebalancing the U.S. military presence in the Asia-Pacific region, including the rotation of U.S. strategic bomber aircraft through Guam, and has agreed to regular visits to Australia by U.S. aircraft and combined training with the Australian Defence Force. The two governments are also exploring ways to assist coalition military operations and development of regional peace operations capacity.[141]

Important differences in population size, defense spending, and location influence alliance relations. Australia has only 20 million people, compared with nearly 300 million in the United States, in a country with about the same land mass. Australia's annual defense spending is about 3 percent of total U.S. spending. The Australian Defence Force numbers 52,000 regular forces plus some 20,000 reserves, including 5 army battalions and a special forces/commando regiment. Thus, Australia can best make niche contributions to alliance operations, including air tankers, special forces, certain types of electronic surveillance and intelligence, conventional submarines, and, in the future, highly capable early warning aircraft.[142]

Support for the alliance in both countries remains very strong. In a March 2005 public opinion poll, 72 percent of Australians said that the ANZUS alliance is either very or fairly important for Australia's security, while another survey of political leaders and voters after the 2004 federal elections put support at 84 percent.[143] There is strong bipartisan support for the presence of bilateral intelligence facilities, joint military exercises, and visits by U.S. military units—including nuclear-capable and -powered warships. There is also strong support for close cooperation with the United States in combating terrorism. However, Australians have not reached consensus on missile defense and their potential role in it—which is presently limited to research and testing. Neither political party would likely support establishment of a dedicated American military base in Australia.

For the first time since the Vietnam War, there is a debate in Australia about both the nature of U.S. power and U.S. expectations from the alliance. A contentious finding of a 2005 poll found that only 58 percent of Australians had positive feelings toward the United States, compared with 84 and 69 percent for Japan and China, respectively. Some of this decline can be attributed to divided opinion on U.S. policy toward, and Australian involvement in, Iraq. But there is also some concern about the nature of American power. Owen Harries, one of Australia's leading experts on the United States, noted that the enormous sympathy felt after September 11 evaporated quickly. While many Australians accept that the United States had to take forceful action against terrorism, Washington's unilateral application of military superiority has generated growing criticism and hostility.[144] In this context, there is also a sense among the Australian public that their government, as a junior partner in the relationship, has been a bit too compliant in dealing with Washington.

Japan is Australia's closest Asian partner, and the two governments have held strategic dialogues since 1990. While Australia maintains good relations with China and South Korea, bilateral relations with Japan are much deeper. This stance reflects an important convergence of U.S. and Australian strategic priorities in Northeast Asia. Australia has welcomed progress by the United States and Japan to transform their alliance as well as Japan's increasing contribution to regional security and promotion of greater trilateral cooperation. The three governments agreed in May 2005 that trilateral security discussions that were initiated in August 2002 at the vice ministerial level on a broad range of regional and global security issues will be elevated to the foreign ministerial level and sustained by more regular interaction of political directors.[145]

Outlook and Challenges

Australia will remain a staunch U.S. ally for the foreseeable future. The two nations share common approaches to terrorism, proliferation of WMD, and preventing the emergence of failed states. Although opposition leader Kevin Rudd ousted Prime Minister John Howard in late 2007, he is unlikely to pursue policies that would strain relations with the United States. However, Australia faces important challenges in its own neighborhood, which will have priority over supporting the United States in distant lands.[146] Given U.S. engagement in the Middle East and Central Asia, Washington will probably welcome a leading Australian role in addressing security challenges in Southeast Asia and the South Pacific.

Alliance relations could be strained if the United States were to place politically difficult demands on Australia in combating terrorism, seek military support that forced unacceptable risks, or try to draw it into a conflict with China over Taiwan. The Australian government and public are much less wary of China's rise than their American counterparts, and the absence of a common approach to Beijing may be the most explosive long-term threat to alliance solidarity. Australian officials have questioned whether the ANZUS Treaty would automatically apply in the event of a U.S. war with China over Taiwan, and only 21 percent of the public favor military support for the United States in that contingency. Washington would be on solid ground to invoke collective security provisions of Article IV in the face of an unprovoked

Chinese attack on the United States and would likely expect Australian assistance. If Canberra hesitated in either scenario, the alliance could be damaged, perhaps irreparably.

Washington cannot take Australian support for granted, particularly on forceful promotion of democracy. Given latent anxiety about U.S. power, Washington will need to take concerted efforts to convince the Australian public of both the necessity and legitimacy of U.S. policies. The close personal relationship of President Bush and Prime Minister John Howard smoothed management of U.S.-Australian cooperation on regional and global issues, but the advent of new leadership on both sides makes recent enhancements of bilateral, trilateral (with Japan), and other multilateral (with NATO) security consultations even more important in easing the political transition and fostering common security policies. These consultations should seek to enhance mutual understanding of the implications of China's rise and develop consensus on possible responses to regional crises.

U.S.-Thailand Alliance

The U.S.-Thailand alliance, which traces its origins to the 1954 Manila Pact (Southeast Asia Treaty Organization), enhances key regional and many global interests of both countries.[147] Thailand's stability and independence are important to the maintenance of peace in Southeast Asia. Thailand has been a staunch U.S. partner since the Vietnam War. Cooperation has strengthened in recent years and today includes joint efforts to counter terrorism, drug trafficking, and piracy. In 1999, Thailand joined forces from Australia and the United States to help stabilize East Timor, and in 2003 it sent engineers to Afghanistan, committing military forces outside Southeast Asia for the first time in over 50 years. To recognize the strength of the alliance, President Bush designated Thailand a major non-NATO ally in 2003.[148]

Thailand has been a consistent supporter of the U.S. military presence in Southeast Asia. The bilateral relationship grants the United States access to key facilities and prepositioning of supplies, which ease military operations and increase readiness in the region. Interoperability with Royal Thai Armed Forces has continued to grow, thanks to an extensive program of bilateral exercises, as well as Cobra Gold, one of the largest joint and combined training activities supported by U.S. Pacific Command in Southeast Asia. Cobra Gold is designed to ensure regional peace and strengthen the ability of the Royal Thai Armed Forces to defend their country or respond to regional contingencies. These exercises have recently included forces from Singapore and other Asian militaries.[149] The United States continues to assist the Thai armed forces with efforts to modernize and professionalize their armed forces and to improve defense installations.

U.S.-Philippines Alliance

U.S.-Philippine relations are based on shared history, commitment to democratic principles, and strong human and economic ties. After World War II, the Philippines became a lynchpin of U.S. security arrangements in the Western Pacific. The United States controlled 23 military installations, including Clark Air Base and the naval facilities at Subic Bay, for a lease period of 99 years. The U.S.-Philippine security relationship has evolved since the withdrawal of U.S. military bases in 1991–1992. The mutual security commitments of the 1951 U.S.-Philippines Mutual Defense Treaty were reaffirmed, and new terms for U.S. operations in the Philippines were established by the 1998 Visiting Forces Agreement.[150] This agreement helped overcome lingering suspicion by some in the Philippines that the United States was seeking to reestablish a military foothold and paved the way for revitalized bilateral military cooperation, including U.S. ship visits, large combined military exercises with Philippine forces, and counterterrorism operations. The annual Balikatan combined exercises seek to improve crisis action planning and counterterrorism capabilities of the Philippine armed forces, while enhancing interoperability with U.S. forces and demonstrating the U.S. security commitment.

Counterterrorism cooperation in recent years has led the bilateral security agenda. Sizable U.S. security assistance and military training missions have helped the Armed Forces of the Philippines disrupt the Abu Sayyaf terrorist group on Basilan Island off the coast of Mindanao. The United States and the Philippines have also intensified their law enforcement cooperation to combat terrorism. The Philippines was one of the first countries to send forces to Iraq, and in 2003, the United States named that country a major non-NATO ally. Despite the sudden withdrawal of Philippine forces from Iraq following the kidnapping of a Filipino citizen in 2004, alliance cooperation on counterterrorism and counterinsurgency will likely remain strong, as both governments share an assessment of the risks. However, Manila's increasingly close relations with China have raised doubts about its willingness to support the United States in a crisis over Taiwan. As with most U.S. allies in Asia, Manila wants to avoid having its military cooperation with Washington draw it into a confrontational relationship with China. The Philippines are unlikely to welcome a large permanent U.S. military presence or major operations from their territory any time soon.

U.S.–New Zealand Security Partnership

Though no longer treaty allies, New Zealand and the United States remain close partners and cooperate on a number of regional and global security issues. The two countries share many values and interests.[151] In the Asia-Pacific region, New Zealand has made valuable contributions to peacekeeping in East Timor and the Balkans and to reconciliation and reconstruction in the Solomon Islands. New Zealand has contributed to a number of UN peacekeeping missions, deployed special forces on three rotations in support of counterinsurgency operations in Afghanistan, provided support to stabilization and reconstruction efforts in Afghanistan and Iraq, and worked closely with the United States and other governments to track terrorist financing and slow the proliferation of nuclear weapons.[152]

As a small island nation remote from world trouble spots, New Zealand states it maintains a "credible minimum force" and places substantial reliance on its defense relationship with other countries, in particular Australia. Its defense capabilities have continued to erode, as the government has made only selected equipment upgrades, mostly for the army. However, in 2002, the government pledged to increase defense spending by 27 percent over 10 years to modernize defense equipment and infrastructure and increase its military personnel. Even if these enhancements in defense capabilities are realized, New Zealand will remain a fairly minor partner for the United States in managing regional and global security.

Emerging Partnerships in Asia

Several U.S. security partnerships in Southeast Asia are also growing. Singapore has consistently supported a strong U.S. military presence in the Asia-Pacific region and has emerged as a major security cooperation partner. In 1990, the two countries signed a memorandum of understanding (MOU) that allows U.S. access to Paya Lebar airbase and the Sembawang wharves. Under the MOU, a U.S. Navy logistics unit was established in Singapore in 1992; U.S. fighter aircraft deploy periodically to Singapore for exercises, and a number of U.S. military vessels visit Singapore. The MOU was amended in 1999 to permit U.S. naval vessels to berth at the Changi Naval Base, which was completed in early 2001. In July 2005, the two governments signed a Strategic Framework Agreement as a means to further deepen security cooperation.

Indonesia, the largest country in Southeast Asia and one that sits astride strategic trade routes, is an important security partner. Progress on democratization and human rights in Indonesia led to the lifting of congressional restrictions on security assistance in November 2005 and opened the way for U.S. support for military reforms and modernization, as well as for improvements to maritime security and disaster response capabilities. The United States and Indonesia are also building antiterrorism cooperation, and U.S. humanitarian and reconstruction assistance in the aftermath of the South Asian tsunami has improved bilateral relations. Recognizing their common interest in freedom of navigation and countering piracy and smuggling, Malaysia's government has supported the U.S. "Eyes in the Sky" initiative to increase combined aerial surveillance over the Strait of Malacca and has taken steps to enhance its own coastal policing activities. U.S.-Vietnam security cooperation and military-to-military contacts are progressing in a modest but positive direction, reflecting a number of common regional interests, including Vietnam's support for U.S. effective engagement in Southeast Asia.[153]

Mongolia has become a valued U.S. partner in promoting peace and combating terrorism. The United States has been helping Mongolia develop its peacekeeping capability since 1999. The Mongolian armed forces are contributing to peacekeeping in Sierra Leone and to stabilization of Afghanistan and Iraq. Washington is providing funding and other assistance to help Mongolia realize its desire to provide standby units for UN peacekeeping and to develop a regional peacekeeping training center outside Ulaanbaatar.[154]

WESTERN HEMISPHERE: A SHIFTING CONTEXT

The foundation of American strength stretches north and south beyond the territorial limits of the United States. The Western Hemisphere is the source of about half of U.S. oil imports as well as large percentages of imported electricity, natural gas, and other essential natural resources, agricultural products, manufactured goods, and human resources, on which the U.S. economy and society rely.[155] U.S. relations with its treaty ally, Canada, and partners in the Caribbean and Latin America are intertwined as never before as a consequence of economic integration, regional telecommunication and transportation revolutions, and a continuous process of demographic, cultural, and social integration that is also changing U.S. society. Here, the trade balance is highly favorable; the dollar is increasingly used as informal and formal currency, and U.S. democratic institutions and popular culture are still widely admired, despite mistrust and opposition to U.S. policies in much of Latin America. While the hemisphere is at peace, the United States and its neighbors need to deal cooperatively with many vexing and interrelated transnational problems: the illegal trade in people, money, drugs, arms, and intellectual property; environmental degradation; the spread contagious diseases; and, since September 2001, international terrorism. [156] These challenges affect various countries in the hemisphere differently, and habits of cooperation are not well established. Yet the future prosperity and security of the United States require good neighbors who also are effective partners. Both sides are uneasy about this growing interdependence, particularly the unavoidable perception of subordination to the United States, which will have to give way to greater mutual trust and assistance in order to improve and better integrate the region's surveillance and response systems and other essential mechanisms for addressing these complex threats.

U.S.-Canadian Security Relations

Cooperation between Washington and Ottawa is built on a firm foundation of good will between national political leaders and practical cooperation between government officials at all levels. This mutual confidence has long facilitated collaboration on trade and security as enshrined in the North American Free Trade Agreement (NAFTA), the new Trilateral Security and Prosperity Partnership, and the binational NORAD Agreement. In addition, there are mutual defense commitments under the North Atlantic Treaty.

U.S.-Canadian relations were somewhat strained after 2001 due to erratic official dialogue and public disagreements on a number of bilateral and international issues, including Iraq, the International Criminal Court, and the Kyoto Protocol. Canadian rejection of participation in the U.S. missile defense program in early 2005 and U.S. repudiation of a NAFTA ruling on Canadian softwood were two symptomatic jolts to the relationship. While security is at the top of U.S. concerns, Ottawa has often seemed more focused on trade and environmental issues.[157] More recently, there has been steady progress on cross-border law enforcement and counterterrorism programs, including implementation of the December 2001 Smart Border action plan, which enhances security while managing the flow of transit and trade; the March 2005 trilateral (with Mexico) Security and Prosperity Partnership of North America, which focuses on practical ways to help societies become healthier, safer, and more prosperous; and the renewal and expansion of the NORAD Agreement in 2006.

However, in the defense sector, stagnant defense budgets and limited modernization have further eroded the capabilities of the Canadian Forces (which diminished 50 percent since 1989) and raised concerns about their long-term interoperability with U.S. forces and the depth of the Canadian commitment to North American and transatlantic defense.[158] The government led by Prime Minister Paul Martin initiated efforts to address Canada's changing security landscape in 2004 with the country's first-ever National Security Policy (NSP). The NSP provided a blueprint for action in intelligence, threat assessment, emergency planning, public health, and border security. A key element in the revitalization of defense was the creation of a unified national command, Canada Command, reflecting the new priority given to domestic operations. The Conservative government led by Prime Minister Stephen Harper came to office in February 2006 and committed to strengthening ties with the United States and revitalizing the Canadian Forces.[159] The tone of Ottawa-Washington dialogue has improved, but it is unclear whether the minority Harper government can engender parliamentary support for strengthened security cooperation with the United States and the long-term plan to enhance Canadian defense capabilities.[160] In May 2006, Parliament approved by only four votes Harper's call for extension of the deployment of 2,300 Canadian troops to Afghanistan through 2009.[161]

For over 50 years, NORAD has been a unique locus of combined, binational aerospace defense planning and operations. However, after 9/11 and various natural disasters, both countries recognized the need to enhance coordination and integration of security measures in the land, maritime, and cyber domains. In advance of discussions on renewal of the agreement, a binational planning group at NORAD considered various options for establishing other mutual support compacts for joint and combined defense and assistance to civil authorities.[162] Expansion of NORAD responsibilities to these other domains is challenging because of sovereignty concerns and the multiplicity of civilian and law enforcement agencies, which have disparate capabilities and operational practices, on both sides of the border. However, the two governments agreed that better binational information and intelligence-sharing in all domains is essential and that U.S. Northern Command (USNORTHCOM) and its counterpart, Canada Command, should be the focal points for maritime operations and liaison with domestic agencies in each country. Following a vote by the Canadian Parliament in May 2006, the NORAD Agreement was expanded to integrated surveillance of the continent's maritime approaches and internal waterways to improve warning of terrorist and other threats in this domain.[163] The new agreement will allow intelligence on shipping and threats to the sea lanes to be sent directly to NORAD and Canada Command headquarters. The two commands can then develop procedures to integrate national efforts to enhance security in the maritime domain.

The other major issue on the bilateral defense agenda is Canada's future role in missile defense. Canadians occupy a geographic space that is critical to the defense of the continental United States from an array of missile threats. In early 2005, the Liberal government turned down the U.S. request for a broad endorsement of Washington's missile defense program, including deployment of antiballistic missile interceptors on Canadian territory. Treading carefully, given strong domestic opposition, the Harper government has said it is willing to negotiate with the United States on the missile defense program and then seek parliamentary approval of any agreement.[164] However, a majority of Canadians fear that missile defense will be costly, ineffective, and lead to the militarization of space. The opposition Liberal party is now firmly opposed. Harper took the position that he would await a U.S. proposal. It would be prudent for Washington to ask Canada for help with specific technical challenges and defensive weapons rather than a broad commitment to cooperation on missile defense. The United States and Canada worked out many thorny sovereignty-related issues over the first decade of NORAD's existence, and the debate over command and control and operations of a missile defense system will be equally challenging.

Washington and Ottawa need to sustain high-level dialogue to build consensus on common approaches to new security challenges and further adaptation of the alliance. Washington should take a flexible and comprehensive approach to security burden-sharing and be sensitive to Canadian sovereignty concerns in efforts to bolster defense of the North American homeland. U.S. officials should also recognize that Canadian security concerns encompass a wider array of realities, such as illegal fishing off Canada's shores, control of events along its Arctic frontier, and vulnerability to infectious disease. Canadians need to make a long-term commitment to defense modernization if they want to retain influence with the United States on security affairs.

Latin America and the Caribbean

Relations with countries in the southern part of the hemisphere are generally more circumspect, reflecting the pressures of diverse transnational problems that beset the region, as well as vacillations in Washington's attention and the increased sophistication of regional leaders in managing their international relations. The United States no longer dominates the region as it did for over a century. In the shadow of U.S. global primacy and persistent resentment of what is perceived as a self-serving exercise of power, growing subregional economic and security cooperation and an expanding array of economic and political partners outside the hemisphere are providing opportunities to reduce dependence on the United States. Some have started to look east, toward the countries of the European Union and Russia, and west, to China and other Asian states, for bilateral trade and military assistance.[165] The support of several U.S. administrations for economic policies that have failed to deliver equitable development has fed this resentment in some countries and fostered a new willingness to challenge Washington, as was seen at the contentious fourth Summit of the Americas in November 2005. Furthermore, the Bush administration's circumspect approach to multilateral institutions and the treatment of prisoners in Iraq and Guantanamo have further eroded U.S. moral authority among these less powerful governments that place great stock in international norms. The growing support for tougher immigration policies in the United States adds to the hemispheric divide. The decline of U.S. influence is epitomized by the unwillingness of 12 Latin American and Caribbean governments party to the International Criminal Court (ICC) to sign Article 98 Bilateral Immunity Agreements pledging not to seek prosecutions of U.S. citizens in the court. Absent this waiver, under the provisions of the American Service-members Protection

Act, these countries are ineligible for most non–drug-related U.S. assistance programs, including security assistance (Foreign Military Financing), professional military education (International Military Education and Training), and nonmilitary economic support funds.[166] The protection act is perceived in the region as another manifestation of U.S. bullying and sends a counterproductive signal to countries that have seen abuses by their own military and security establishments escape legal prosecution. Still, most Latin American leaders seek to maintain good relations with the United States and recognize the need for cooperation with Washington and their neighbors in tackling the region's new and traditional security problems.

The remarkable, albeit uneven, democratic transformation in much of the region over the past two decades is also facing new challenges. In many countries, there is growing frustration with ineffective governance, unaccountable leaders, corruption, worsening economic disparities, and inadequate social welfare programs. The crisis in democratic governance is reflected in a 2005 poll by the respected Chilean firm *Latinobarómetro*, which revealed that only about half of Latin Americans are firm supporters of democracy and only one in three is satisfied with the way their democracy works in practice. Those figures, which have been fairly constant in recent years, are significantly lower than those of a decade ago.[167] However, this does not appear to presage a disposition toward authoritarianism. With the exception of Peru, Ecuador, and Paraguay, majorities (62 percent) say that in no circumstances would they support a military coup, and 70 percent agree that whatever its problems, democracy is the least bad system of government. This erosion of confidence in democracy has been most pronounced in the Andean ridge, parts of Central America, and Paraguay. For example, a March 2006 UN poll in Peru revealed that 60 percent of those surveyed said they either did not know what democracy was or disliked it, and 13 percent said they would like a strong nondemocratic government. A similar poll in 2005 revealed that 87 percent said they were dissatisfied with democracy.[168] This frustration has fueled growing populism and support for vague concepts like the "Bolivarian Revolution" that promise an alternative to "brutal" integration into the global economy, greater economic equality, and a platform to resist U.S. domination.

The United States is the most important trading partner for Latin American and Caribbean nations, but movement toward equitable, durable partnerships will not be easy. If some of the mistrust can be overcome, the more prosperous and stable countries in the Southern Cone could become fuller partners with the United States in maintaining hemispheric and global security. However, the governments in the Andean ridge and the Caribbean basin continue to find it difficult to correct longstanding socioeconomic problems and counter those transnational forces that exploit weak governance. If the United States remains vague about its regional interests and fails to develop a modern concept for hemispheric partnership, it will find its southern neighbors continuing to diverge from Washington's agendas and beginning to exclude the U.S. Government from their policy deliberations.[169]

A Legacy of Mistrust

Public opinion of the United States in most of Latin America is quite negative, reflecting strong opposition to U.S. policies on the Iraq war, preemptive action, international institutions, and treatment of prisoners. A 2004 *Latinobarómetro* poll indicated that the United States had lost standing since 2000 in all but five Latin American countries. Only in El Salvador, Colombia, and Panama did polling show slightly favorable growth.[170] Since late 2005, opinions of the United States in the region have shown modest gains (except in Venezuela and Uruguay), perhaps as the anger over the Iraqi war fades. However, the figures are still far from the warmth of the late 1990s.[171] Central America remains a bright spot in this picture, perhaps buoyed by the 2005 free trade agreement and over U.S. $12 billion in remittances from nationals working in the United States. Sizable majorities (over 68 percent) of the populations in Central America surveyed in 2005 expressed positive attitudes toward the United States. In all the other Latin nations, positive views of the United States dropped anywhere from 6 to 31 percent between 2000 and 2005 (for example, from 73 to 53 in Mexico, from 68 to 53 in Brazil, and from 73 to 57 in Chile). Declines in positive perceptions of bilateral relations have fallen less steeply and have improved significantly in Colombia and more modestly in Central America. Overall, 61 percent of Latin Americans surveyed in 2005 expressed "little or no confidence" in the United States, while 31 percent expressed "some or a little."

Despite active north-south commerce, the United States is still seen as detached from and disinterested in the region. There is widespread belief that aside from Colombia, drug trafficking, and the war on terrorism, Latin America and the Caribbean do not figure in Washington's strategic thinking. Many Latin American officials understand the U.S. concern with terrorism, but it is not prominent in their daily agenda. The decline in U.S. development and disaster assistance to the region is often cited as another manifestation of Washington's narrow self-interest. U.S. officials argue that they have a coherent, common sense approach to the region, but the perception of indifference has broad support in Latin America nevertheless. Critics often cite the fact that a Chilean diplomat and Brazilian army general lead the UN peacekeeping mission in Haiti as proof that the United States has left its southern neighbors to fend for themselves.

While the characterization of the Bush administration's regional policy as disinterested and disengaged is wide of the mark, that perception needs to be deflected if the United States is to successfully adapt strategic relations with neighbors to meet common transnational threats. It is also worth noting that societies across the region distrust each other, as well as the United States. Historically, most governments have been so preoccupied with maintaining control and sovereignty that they have defined their interests defensively and followed zero-sum strategies in relations with neighbors. This lack of trust only reinforces a tendency toward suspicion of Washington's motives and ulterior agendas. While the modernizing influence of globalization and democratization has begun to change the Latin mindset, the past is still a factor in national foreign and security policies. The region's leaders face two conundrums. Should they compromise sovereignty by trusting neighbors to collaborate fully and honestly on politically sensitive issues that they cannot resolve alone? From the United States, they want greater attention to market access, investment, and shared expertise, all of which will enhance national credibility as a desirable partner in the global economy and will create jobs at home. Can this be achieved, however, without being overwhelmed in an asymmetrical relationship with the United States that negates their national interests and denies them freedom of action in bilateral and international affairs?

Toward a New Concept of Hemispheric Security

The job of building greater trust and mutual respect among leaders, security establishments, and publics is essential if there is to be effective regional security cooperation. In the past, U.S. policymakers have used separately or in combination diplomacy, trade initiatives, political development, economic and security assistance, counternarcotics programs, and, as a last resort, armed intervention and peace enforcement in their efforts to foster stability, peace, and prosperity in the Western Hemisphere. Even when Washington has sought UN or OAS support for its actions, U.S. initiatives have traditionally been pursued with an air of paternalism that has been a source of considerable friction and has tended to obscure important differences among various countries.

Nevertheless, the priorities of hemispheric accord have shifted over the years. During the Cold War, U.S. policymakers defined peace as the absence of an arms race between neighbors and dormant boundary disputes. In the post–Cold War era, the focus shifted to security and confidence-building between neighbors, creation of a nuclear-free zone in Latin America, and negotiated settlement of long-running internal wars. The emergence of a common economic and political vision, celebrated by the 1994 Summit of the Americas in Miami, introduced the concept that democratic institutions and modern, open economies can best maintain regional peace and prosperity. Washington's concept of stability has evolved in a similar direction. During the Cold War, the United States sought collective security with allies, some unsavory, that were capable and willing to shoulder responsibility for controlling events within their borders and minimizing access by the Soviet Union and Cuba. Today, U.S. policy seeks a region of democratic governments that are more likely to pursue free trade, uphold international law, resolve disputes peacefully, and collaborate against common threats posed by drug trafficking networks, gangs, and other transnational criminal groups. Bilateral and subregional cooperative mechanisms that can serve to deepen confidence and foster stronger partnerships, such as the Conference of Central American Armed Forces, are also welcomed. In a similar fashion, efforts to foster prosperity have shifted from helping countries individually with their economic development to a broader view of integrated subregions of open, free market democracies modeled on NAFTA.

As the region has become more integrated and seen the growth of democracy and free markets, interest has developed in formulating a hemispheric strategy for stability, peace, and prosperity. There have been regular presidential summits and greater activism by the OAS, epitomized by the completion of the 2001 Inter-American "Democratic Charter," which recognizes that democracy is essential for the social, political, and economic development of the peoples of the Americas.[172] So, too, the region has seen growing subregional cooperation and an emerging notion of a "South American Community of Nations," even if some countries remain somewhat tentative about political and economic cooperation.

The October 2003 OAS Special Summit on Security was a milestone in manifesting the commitment of governments in the region to work together under shared values, certain principles, and common approaches to build a safer and more secure region. This effort began in 1991 as a means to deal with transnational security challenges. The summit declaration endorsed a new "multidimensional" approach to security that recognizes both traditional and new threats, the priorities of each state and subregion, and the links between hemispheric security and global peace and security. It is built on a foundation of democratic values, respect for human rights, and national sovereignty. The declaration calls on countries to strengthen cooperation in existing OAS mechanisms, such as the Inter-American Committee Against Terrorism, to address security problems such as terrorism, transnational organized crime, trafficking, proliferation of WMD, natural and manmade disasters, and environmental degradation. Significantly, the declaration recognized the importance and utility of various inter-American instruments, including the Inter-American Treaty of Reciprocal Assistance (Rio Treaty). While Mexico withdrew from the treaty in 2001, calling it archaic, most countries agreed to assess it and other instruments related to collective security in the hemisphere, such as the relationship between the Inter-American Defense Board and the OAS. The declaration was a clear signal of the region's attempt to assert itself.[173]

Multilateral approaches to security in the hemisphere are still tentative, given enduring national differences and zero-sum thinking, but enhanced cooperation to advance stability, peace, and prosperity is possible, particularly on a subregional level. The composition of the UN stabilization mission in Haiti demonstrates that a few states, Brazil and Chile, see it in their interests to be more active in helping manage hemispheric and global security. The United States should actively encourage and support such regional initiatives that align with its security interests. Building on the foundation established by the Inter-American Democratic Charter, the United States should also bolster support for democratic freedoms and convince Latin leaders that they cannot be indifferent when their neighbors subvert them because subregional development and stability suffers. U.S. support for cooperation among Latin American and Caribbean states can help overcome the "us/them" tension that has neighbors defending themselves against a U.S. policy rather than cooperating to solve common problems.

Mexico, the Caribbean Basin, and Defense of the U.S. Southern Approaches

The 9/11 Commission recommended major improvements to the U.S. immigration system and to security of porous borders and ports of entry, working closely with Mexico and Canada to prevent terrorists from entering the country or launching attacks against the United States from the Western Hemisphere.[174] The U.S. Strategy for

Homeland Defense calls for an active, layered defense to deter, intercept, and defeat threats at a safe distance. The southern geographic approaches to the United States, comparable to the depth afforded by Canada to the north, encompass Mexico, the Caribbean archipelago, mainland Central America, and northern South America. There are two main maritime, air, and land corridors that originate in northern South America and run northwest to the United States. These are areas marked by relatively weak governance, porous borders, ungoverned spaces, and many transnational problems. The 25 countries of the Caribbean basin need to be factored into U.S. homeland defense plans; however, their governments have other priorities, resource shortages, and limited capabilities (see figure 7–3). Their security concerns include drug trafficking, organized crime, and immigration issues. Yet the potential for collusion among gangs, criminal networks, and terrorist organizations to advance their separate goals raises the stakes and calls for an integrated security strategy. Building on the OAS concept of multidimensional security, the United States should explore a strategy of integrated cooperation with and among countries in the Caribbean basin and Mexico to address these concerns in a holistic way. This effort could build on expanding subregional security cooperation among the countries of Central America and the Caribbean.[175]

Given its land and sea frontier of nearly 2,000 miles, U.S cooperation with Mexico to enhance mutual security is essential. However, the Mexican government is reluctant to engage in bilateral defense activities due to the weight of history with the United

FIGURE 7–3. AREA OF NOTIONAL MEXICO-CARIBBEAN BASIN SURVEILLANCE SYSTEM

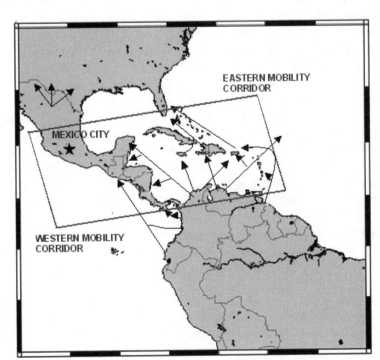

States, fear of subordination, and an inward-looking concept of national security. Mexico shuns strategic alliances and emphasizes the internal role of its armed forces for civic action in the countryside, security of critical infrastructure, disaster relief, and some law enforcement and antidrug operations. As a result, the current bilateral defense relationship is nonstandard and minimalist, characterized by few military-to-military contacts and low levels of military sales and assistance.[176]

Over the last decade, both governments have worked hard to overcome suspicions in order to become open, pragmatic partners in security relations. Mexican and U.S. law enforcement, immigration, and other agencies collaborate in border administration, intelligence, and information-sharing on transnational crime networks and terrorism. However, defense-to-defense contact has progressed slowly, complicated by organizational asymmetries. Unlike the U.S. Department of Defense, Mexico's military is organized into two departments under the leadership of two cabinet-level uniformed officers: the Secretary of National Defense, who has responsibility for the army and air force, and the Secretary of the Navy.[177] The senior position, the Secretary of National Defense, is the counterpart of not only the U.S. Secretary of Defense, but also the Chairman of the Joint Chiefs of Staff and the Secretary and Chief of Staff of the Army and the Air Force. The Secretariat of National Defense engages the Office of the Secretary of Defense and the Joint Staff. There is no natural entry point into Mexico's defense establishment for a U.S. combatant command. Decisionmaking on military policy and operations is closed and tightly controlled from Mexico City.

Mexican governments have not adapted traditional nationalistic tendencies that once served the country well to today's geopolitical and economic realities. Political leaders are struggling with conflicting goals and tendencies to develop a framework for national security. There are two competing schools of thought on defense. The passive, standard approach advocates remaining isolated, doing what is politically acceptable to appease the United States, and acting as a "doorstep defense" of its frontiers. The active approach argues that Mexico should think and act innovatively in expanding its security agenda, cooperating with neighbors, and improving the military's capacity to protect the approaches to the country.[178] Despite the unprecedented support the Mexican army and navy unexpectedly provided U.S. authorities to help victims of Hurricane Katrina in 2005, the weight of history, nationalism, and lingering concerns about subordination will continue to limit bilateral defense cooperation with Mexico.

Despite these impediments, there may be a way to build support for a multidimensional approach to enhancing mutual security in the Caribbean basin. This approach treats the region as a geostrategic whole rather than a collection of bilateral relationships and proceeds from the recognition that there is a direct correlation between disrupting entrenched trafficking and smuggling networks and countering terrorists. Proceeds from transnational crime are known to support terrorist organizations, and both exploit similar smuggling methods and transit routes. The focus would be on gaining control of ungoverned areas and stopping the illegal movement of drugs, arms, people, and money. The center of gravity would remain drugs from Colombia. If countries in the region improve public safety and the capacity to diminish the scourge of trafficking and smuggling networks of concern to them, U.S. vulnerability to terrorists eager to take advantage of ungoverned space and local instability decreases.

Rather than try to integrate Mexico and the Caribbean basin countries into a North American defense system, this concept seeks to encourage the development of a partnership with these countries to address interrelated transnational security concerns. Mexico could play a pivotal, even a leadership, role vis-à-vis its Caribbean neighbors. This Caribbean Basin Security Partnership could develop an air, maritime, and land surveillance and response system covering key corridors of concern. The heart of the partnership could be the "Mexico–Caribbean Basin Surveillance System," based in and led by Mexico and staffed by military, police, and intelligence officers from participating countries that would provide information to all participating governments. The system could exchange information with USNORTHCOM, Canada Command, NORAD, and other U.S. and Canadian authorities. It could build on existing subregional military and police cooperation, such as the Conference of Central American Armed Forces, the Eastern Caribbean Regional Security System, and the Association of Caribbean Commissioners of Police, as well as developments in regional consequence management cooperation. U.S. DOD, Coast Guard, and law enforcement assistance programs have helped some of these neighbors develop relevant operational capabilities. This partnership would give Caribbean basin states their own active, layered defense of their geographic approaches. As the zero-sum mentality to security in the region fades, it is possible to envision a series of interdependent homeland defenses in the region sharing information and know-how. The system would help member states exercise control over their maritime and air domains through enhanced early warning of transnational criminal or terrorist threats and by coordinating interdictions of illicit flows of goods, services, and people. National governments would remain responsible for military or police actions on their own territory.

A stable and secure hemisphere allows pursuit of U.S. global interests from a position of strength, enhances regional homeland security, and provides a context for enhancing regional prosperity and democracy. The United States needs to continue developing all facets of its cooperation with the governments of the Caribbean and Latin American states, particularly Colombia and Mexico, to combat an array of transnational threats in a more integrated fashion. The OAS Declaration on Security in the Americas provides a sound conceptual context for these efforts:

- Brazil, Chile, Colombia, and several countries in Central America have demonstrated a willingness and ability to become effective partners in managing security in the hemisphere and to contribute to global peacekeeping and stabilization operations.
- Given the weight of history and the asymmetries of interests and capabilities, progress, particularly with Mexico, will be fitful. One command realignment might help advance bilateral and regional security cooperation in the Caribbean basin. Mexico was placed in the USNORTHCOM area of responsibility for good reasons, particularly to facilitate planning for consequence manage-

ment along the U.S.-Mexico border, but defense of the remainder of the Caribbean basin rests with U.S. Southern Command, which is precluded from direct engagement with Mexico. A better arrangement might be to leave Mexico unassigned to a geographic command, making it the responsibility of the Joint Staff. This could ease dealings with the Secretaries of National Defense and the Navy, who consider the Joint Staff as their counterpart, and allow plans and missions to be implemented, with Mexico's understanding, through the most appropriate U.S. command.

A GLOBAL STRATEGY FOR ALLIANCE MANAGEMENT

As this chapter has argued, U.S. allies and partners share a stake in maintaining global stability and an open economic system. They often augment and complement U.S. power in significant ways in the advancement of these mutual interests. The efforts to adapt and sustain existing relationships and build new ones are paying concrete dividends by reducing the burdens on the United States in managing turmoil and promoting growth around the world. U.S. allies and partners are increasingly thinking and acting globally about security, as evidenced by the involvement of Japan, Australia, and South Korea in Afghanistan and the Persian Gulf and of NATO in Afghanistan and Africa. Still, better integration of the activities of U.S. alliances and partnerships across regional lines could create a global web of relationships for effective common action in dealing with key strategic challenges.

As more security problems, including terrorism, WMD proliferation, and dealing with weak states, have global consequences, U.S. partnerships need to adapt. U.S. allies and partners do not necessarily share Washington's threat assessments or strategies for dealing with these threats. There are also widening gaps between the military capabilities of the United States and all its partners, gaps that can be narrowed but will not be closed. Nonetheless, U.S. partners and allies bring invaluable capabilities that complement and augment U.S. efforts, from deterrence on the Korean Peninsula to irregular warfare in Afghanistan to peace operations in the Balkans. Orchestrating these efforts effectively will require innovative consultations—including with third parties and international organizations, new approaches to security cooperation, and greater political sensitivity in the conduct of U.S. global military operations.

- Allies and partners are playing a critical role in support of U.S. strategy in combating global terrorism. Real progress has been made in enhancing cooperation on homeland security and developing innovative forms of multilateral intelligence cooperation. The United States and its allies and partners have developed mechanisms for rapid consultations and operational coordination in the face of credible warning of such threats.[179]
- The most significant threat to U.S. and allied security is the specter of catastrophic terrorism using a weapon of mass destruction in a major urban area. Disrupting such threats in a timely fashion may require preemptive military

action against state or nonstate actors. Further U.S. diplomatic and legal efforts are needed to build consensus for this kind of action.[180] Mitigating the consequences of such attacks, which could easily overwhelm the capabilities of single government, calls for more concerted interagency planning and cooperation with all U.S. allies.

- Allied and partner engagement in stabilization, security transition, reconstruction, and humanitarian missions in the Balkans, Afghanistan, Haiti, and Africa makes important contributions to mutual security. U.S. allies and partners provided 71 percent of funding and 85 percent of the personnel for UN peacekeeping operations in 2003. As the 2006 Quadrennial Defense Review noted, the military has an important role to play in these missions, but successful efforts require development of new mechanisms for integrated civil-military cooperation, involving many agencies of governments as well as nongovernmental organizations.

- U.S. European and Asian allies, as well as Middle East partners, recognize that the stabilization of Iraq is critical to long-term security in the Middle East and mutual security. This assessment leaves open the prospect of a greater allied or partner involvement in the training of the Iraqi military and security forces and in building civil society and the rule of law there and elsewhere in the Middle East. These allies and partners have also provided important support in international efforts to halt Iran's nuclear program and moves to establish hegemony in the Middle East.

- Developing common approaches to China's rise and Russia's rebound as an "energy superpower" will remain a thorny problem in relation with Asian and European allies. Allies in both regions see opportunities for expanded economic and political engagement with China and do not want to be drawn into a conflict with Beijing over Taiwan. However, the political storm over the EU's deliberations in 2005 regarding lifting its post-Tiananmen arms embargo on China should not have been a surprise. The kinds of systems the Chinese might seek from Europe—advanced surveillance, command and control, and communications systems—are precisely what the Chinese need to develop networked capabilities to disrupt U.S. military operations. Given the multifaceted, global nature of China's rise, there is a need for high-level strategic dialogue on China between the United States and its European and East Asian allies to achieve some agreed principles or rules of the road.

- In an era of global security challenges and global force management, global patterns of interaction and cooperation among U.S. allies and partners and regional security institutions are also needed. NATO is expanding its partnerships into the Middle East and has developed effective operational cooperation with Australia, Japan, New Zealand, and South Korea in the conduct of counterinsurgency and stability operations in Afghanistan. NATO should take steps to formalize and add a consultative dimension to these new partnerships as a way to enhance their effectiveness and legitimacy.

- With growing interest in East Asia in new forms of regional security cooperation, it is incumbent upon the United States and its Asian allies to demonstrate how the alliances can serve broader regional interests. Trilateral U.S.–ROK–Japan participation in practical security cooperation with China and other countries in East Asia would be a way to demonstrate how both alliance relationships can contribute to regional security. Moreover, such cooperation could help temper rising tensions in relations between China and Japan and the ROK and Japan. Closer to home, the United States should encourage Mexico and the governments of the Caribbean and Central America to enhance their cooperation in dealing with transnational threats as a way to enhance homeland security throughout the Western Hemisphere.

- Finally, Washington's policies in Iraq and the war on terrorism have led to a precipitous drop in public opinion of the United States, even among some of its closest allies and partners. Expanding and better integrating these relationships will be a slow process until concrete steps are taken that restore confidence in Washington's leadership, strategic judgment, and moral authority.

Chapter Eight

Transforming Defense Strategy and Posture

CHRISTOPHER J. LAMB WITH CHARLES D. LUTES, M. ELAINE BUNN, AND CHRISTOPHER CAVOLI

G iven the complexity and dynamism of the international security environment described in previous chapters, transforming the defense establishment and U.S. Armed Forces remains a major strategic challenge for the rest of the decade and beyond. Years of sustained engagement in Iraq and Afghanistan are stretching U.S. ground forces particularly thin, wearing out equipment, interrupting training cycles, and depressing recruitment. Even if troop levels in these two countries can be reduced in the near future, it will take years to restore the force to peak readiness. This near-term requirement to recapitalize and "reset" the force is not the same thing as transformation, and the latter remains a high priority for the Nation's defense leadership over the longer term.

As a Presidential candidate in 2000, Governor George W. Bush campaigned on a promise to transform America's defense establishment and warfighting capabilities. In the Bush administration, Secretary of Defense Donald Rumsfeld made transformation his signature issue during his tenure at the Pentagon. More recently, resources and attention consumed by the global war on terror and decisions by the White House in 2006 to curtail the growth of defense spending have slowed the transformation agenda. Nevertheless, President Bush and Pentagon leaders remain committed to the transformation agenda. Indeed, they argue that transformation is necessary both to be successful in the war on terror and to deter and defeat future adversaries in an era of great uncertainty.[1]

Interest in military transformation predates the Bush administration. During the 1990s, consensus was growing that the Nation should put more emphasis on transforming its military, even as it was drawing down its force structure from Cold War–era levels. Many believed that the information revolution, stimulated by advances in modern computing power and associated effects, was fundamentally altering social, economic, and political affairs and would do the same for military capabilities. Defense leaders came to believe that transformation was necessary to exploit the information revolution for a dramatic increase in military capabilities. They thought transformation would be necessary to prepare for future adversaries who also would exploit the information revolution and use other asymmetric approaches (such as weapons of mass destruction [WMD], missiles, and advanced naval mines) to counter U.S. conventional military superiority.

By the mid-1990s, senior Department of Defense (DOD) officials were expressing interest in a revolution in military affairs that would transform military capabilities, and a supporting revolution in business affairs that would transform defense planning and resource allocation processes. The Clinton administration made transformation a major dimension of the *prepare* portion of a new defense strategy—shape, respond, prepare—that it articulated in the first *Quadrennial Defense Review* (QDR) *Report* in 1997. That report emphasized the importance of building a strong backbone of command, control, communications, computers, intelligence, surveillance, and reconnaissance systems, areas that were most obviously affected by the information revolution. However, at the time, Pentagon leadership did not otherwise make a sharp distinction between modernization programs already under way and transformed military capabilities. In other words, the tendency was to claim that all existing major acquisition programs help transform U.S. forces. During this period, most transformation progress was made in improving the rigor and scope of concept development and experimentation activities undertaken by the Services and U.S. Joint Forces Command (USJFCOM) to explore better means of warfighting.[2]

When the Bush administration took office, it articulated a more ambitious vision for the overall transformation effort. The breadth of the agenda was reflected in Secretary Rumsfeld's Transformation Planning Guidance, which defined *transformation* as:

> a process that shapes the changing nature of military competition and cooperation through new combinations of concepts, capabilities, people, and organizations that exploit our nation's advantages and protect against our asymmetric vulnerabilities to sustain our strategic position, which helps underpin peace and stability in the world.

This broad definition put transformation in a strategic context by noting that it includes the need to identify unique U.S. strategic strengths and potential vulnerabilities. Interestingly, the document also offered a more discriminating criterion that could be used to help adjudicate what is, and what is not, transformational and, hence, what programs would be favored in resource allocation decisions:

> Shaping the nature of military competition ultimately means redefining standards for military success by accomplishing military missions that were previously unimaginable or impossible except at prohibitive risk and cost.

The implication here is that modernizing military capabilities merely improves the ability to execute missions under existing standards of performance, while transforming military capabilities completely redefines the standards for success.[3] The Bush administration hoped to invest in the latter at the expense of the former and suggested that doing so eventually would produce capabilities that would render previous ways of warfighting obsolete, thus radically changing the measures of success in military operations overall.

Hence, transformation was defined both broadly, as a sweeping set of reforms designed to prepare the U.S. military establishment for a new era, and more narrowly, as a revolution in military operational art and science. The Transformation Planning Guidance provided a framework that covered both meanings when it describes the scope of transformation to include: "how we fight, how we do business inside the Department, and how we work with our interagency and multinational partners."[4] The narrower meaning of transformation boils down to "how we fight," while the broader transformation agenda also includes reforms in business processes and interagency and multinational relationships.

How much progress has been made on transformation, and what challenges lie ahead? Many would evaluate progress by reviewing transformational output to date—that is, revolutionary new military capabilities fielded or begun by the Bush administration. This approach would not be fruitful for two reasons. First, while the individual and collective value of various military capabilities is relevant, it is far more important to evaluate their trends and the choices they impose on defense leaders (issues considered in the closing section of this chapter). Second, as the Department of Defense leadership concluded in their 2006 *QDR Report* to Congress, the Pentagon is not producing sufficient transformational output to date and it must reform strategic decisionmaking in order to make more progress in this regard.[5]

Therefore, rather than evaluating a sample of new military capabilities, this chapter takes a broader, top-down view of transformation progress and challenges. It will consider three core transformation reforms initiated by the Pentagon that may well determine over time whether the United States can field and manage transformational military forces.[6] Joint operating concepts (JOCs) capture the most important changes in the way U.S. forces fight. A capabilities-based approach to defense planning and resource allocation is the most significant internal change in the DOD process that fields new capabilities to enable new warfighting concepts. *Global force planning* is a broad term coined here that involves new command and control relationships, global posture, and global force characteristics that exploit and enable transformed forces. The new command and control relationships include interagency and foreign partners and should allow the Pentagon leadership to better manage a new global force posture and forces with global capabilities.

An evaluation of the progress on these three important initiatives—joint operating concepts, capabilities-based approaches, and global force planning—demonstrates how challenging and far-reaching the transformation reforms initiated by the Bush administration are. This chapter also examines the strategic rationale behind transformation policy and how it has affected progress on the transformation agenda to date. To establish some context for discussing these subjects, a review of how the Bush administration's transformation agenda fits in with its broader defense strategy is in order.

The new strategy rolled out by the Bush administration in its 2001 *QDR Report* underscored the importance of transformation. The strategy called for dissuading future military competition, in part by experimentation with revolutionary operational concepts, capabilities, and organizational arrangements stimulated by a culture of innovation and risk-taking. Transformation was still understood to encompass both U.S. military forces and the defense establishment. What garnered the most attention and gave transformation more immediacy than previous efforts, however, was the willingness of the new administration to single out specific operational areas as keys to transforming U.S. forces. The *QDR Report* levied a requirement for transformation roadmaps that would specify timelines to develop capabilities to meet six key operational goals:

- protect the U.S. homeland and critical bases of operation
- deny enemies sanctuary
- protect and sustain power in access-denied areas
- leverage information technology to connect troops and their operations
- improve and protect information networks from attack
- enhance space operations.[7]

Early Bush administration defense planning and programming adjustments were designed to shift resources to these key operational areas. After the initial set of program and budget adjustments was executed in support of the transformation vision, increasingly difficult questions arose about the value of additional resource allocations in these areas. Concretely, how would additional investments in these priority areas produce a substantial return in the form of transformed capabilities?

FIGURE 8–1. BUDGET RISKS INHERENT IN CURRENT DEFENSE PROGRAM

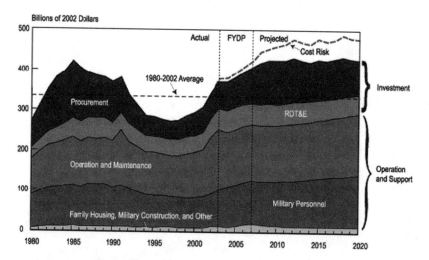

Source: Congressional Budget Office, "The Long-Term Implications of Current Defense Plans," January 2003, available at <http://www.cbo.gov/showdoc.cfm?index=4010&sequence=1&from=0>.

The challenge of identifying the type, timing, and amount of investments in transformational capabilities was exacerbated by the need to justify such resource allocations in the aftermath of the terrorist attacks on September 11, 2001. Responding to the terrorists generally, and the wars in Afghanistan and Iraq specifically, required significant increases in resources for current operations and led some to question whether DOD could both transform and fight the war on terrorism (see figure 8–1). Nevertheless, the Secretary of Defense steadfastly maintained that the Defense Department would do both at the same time and argued that it must do so since the possibility of terrorist WMD use was an example of the new security problems that demanded transformed military capabilities.

Congressional support for increases to the defense budget greatly reduced but did not eliminate the tension between a high operations tempo and transformation investments. Increasingly, DOD leaders were required to make tough judgments about where to cut back in order to maintain the pace of investments in the six priority transformation areas. The decisions to cut major Army programs, namely the Crusader self-propelled artillery system and the Comanche helicopter, are the most notable (but not the only) examples to date of where DOD accepted some increased risk in near-term operational capabilities in order to fund more transformational, longer-term capabilities. Indeed, other dramatic program cuts were made when the White House determined that the defense buildup had to be scaled back for fiscal reasons.[8] In order to manage, implement, defend, and assess the impact of such decisions, which invariably spark passionate debate within the Pentagon and Congress, it is important for DOD to have a well understood process that clarifies assumptions and generates analysis and evidence about where it is best to take and minimize risk while pursuing transformation.

Transformational capabilities are only obvious in retrospect. The conceptual struggle to comprehend and anticipate the changing character and conduct of war is always intense, as is the bureaucratic struggle to acquire resources in support of any given vision of the future. Transformation theorists argue that it is profitable, even indispensable, to have a rich competition among ideas, concepts, and prototype systems in order to stimulate innovation. Ultimately, however, some process for picking the most promising initiatives for major investment opportunities is necessary.

In recognition of this fact, DOD published the Transformation Planning Guidance in April 2003 to organize for managing transformation.[9] The document clarified senior leader and organizational roles and responsibilities for implementing transformation strategy. Among the most significant responsibilities, assigned by the Secretary of Defense, was the requirement for the Chairman of the Joint Chiefs of Staff, in coordination with the USJFCOM commander, to develop joint operating concepts that would depict how transformed forces will fight. These concepts would help senior decisionmakers choose between competing investment options by clarifying which capabilities are most useful. The objective was to ensure that strategy and joint warfighting concepts drove requirements and programs, rather than the other way around, as so often was the case in the past.

JOINT OPERATING CONCEPTS

The JOCs directed by the Secretary are intended to guide the transformation of the joint force so that it is prepared to operate successfully against the most important security threats the military will face in the next 10 to 20 years. Since new capabilities help make new concepts of operation possible, and new concepts in turn help guide the development of new capabilities, both concepts and capabilities need to be developed in light of one another. Thus, as the defense program rolls forward, year-to-year investments in capabilities can be made that both enable and are informed by concepts of how future forces will operate.

The Evolution of Joint Operating Concepts

Initially, the Secretary directed the Chairman of the Joint Chiefs of Staff to develop one overarching joint concept that would capture the broad outline of the new American way of war enabled by the emergence of information technologies. What emerged originally was called the *joint operations concept* and was constructed around the tenets of network-centric warfare and effects-based operations in a joint environment.[10] It emphasized high-quality shared awareness, dispersed forces, speed of command, and flexibility in planning and execution. The premise of the concept was that if U.S. forces fight first for information superiority (see figure 8–2), the future joint force commander would be able to bring all available assets together rapidly to achieve desired effects better. The concept assumed the availability of the requisite information and the existence of more agile and rapidly deployable forces that can:[11]

- achieve common understanding of all dimensions of the battlespace throughout the joint force
- make joint decisions and take action throughout the joint force faster than the opponent
- adapt in scope, scale, and method as the situation requires
- rapidly deploy selected portions of the joint force that can immediately transition to execution, even in the absence of developed infrastructure
- create and sustain continuous pressure throughout the battlespace for as little or as much time as it takes to accomplish strategic or operational aims
- disintegrate, disorient, dislocate, or destroy any opponent with a combination of lethal and nonlethal means
- conduct deployment and sustainment activities in support of multiple simultaneous, distributed, decentralized battles and campaigns
- accomplish all of the above in an interagency and multinational context.

This broad conceptualization of the new American approach to military operations made it clear that interoperability, information-sharing, and mobility will be accorded greater priority than in the past. However, the overarching concept was too broad to describe the approaches that U.S. forces will take to defeat different categories of threats, which require different capabilities. Accordingly, the Secretary also directed

FIGURE 8–2. CRITICAL NEED FOR INFORMATION SUPERIORITY

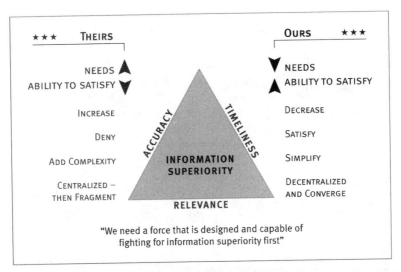

Source: Office of Force Transformation, "Elements of Defense Transformation," 16, accessed at <http://www.oft.osd.mil/library/library_files/document_383_ElementsOf Transformation_LR.pdf>.

the development of four subordinate joint operating concepts, which the Chairman assigned to combatant commanders for development as follows:[12]

- homeland security, developed by U.S. Northern Command
- strategic deterrence, developed by U.S. Strategic Command
- major combat operations, developed by U.S. Joint Forces Command
- stability operations, developed by U.S. Joint Forces Command.

These four concepts broadened the traditional focus of the defense establishment on deterring and winning wars. Major combat operations and strategic deterrence are traditional military competencies, but each required adjustment in light of new threats. The operating concept for major combat operations must account for adaptive adversary strategies designed to hamper U.S. power projection into its regions by holding bases and lines of communication at risk with new technologies and weapons of mass destruction. The strategic deterrence concept must account for the proliferation of WMD and their means of delivery. Stability operations, initially understood to encompass the range of problems engendered by irregular forces (terrorists, insurgents, saboteurs, and so forth) are not new, but they are increasingly important and constitute a problem set for which the American military lacks a uniform and well understood operating concept. Of course, the need for a new concept for homeland security has been manifest since the terrorist attacks on September 11.

FIGURE 8–3. JOINT CONCEPT RELATIONSHIPS

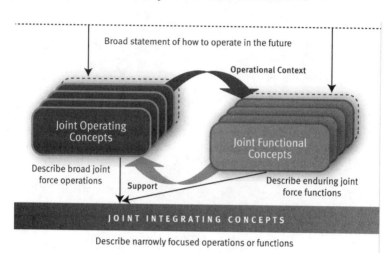

Derived from Department of Defense, Joint Operations Concept (DRAFT) (Washington: DC, TBD).

From the beginning, defense analysts debated whether these four concepts were sufficiently discriminating and relevant. Many thought that the concept for strategic deterrence should be better bounded, perhaps by focusing on WMD deterrence as opposed to deterrence of all threatening adversary behavior. Similarly, some argued that stability operations should be narrowed to focus exclusively on the problem of terrorism, and especially transnational terrorism. In addition, it was understood that the four concepts would still not be sufficiently detailed to allow individual capabilities to be assessed, so a third layer of supporting concepts that would elucidate more specific military missions (for example, air-to-air superiority, global strike, undersea superiority, forced entry, and logistics) would be required as well (see figure 8–3).[13]

The name of the overarching concept was subsequently changed from the *joint operations concept* to the *Capstone Concept for Joint Operations* to avoid confusion with the subordinate concepts in the JOC family.[14] The new capstone concept improves upon its predecessor by emphasizing the military contribution to an integrated effort with interagency and multinational partners to achieve national objectives. The other concepts are also being updated to reflect the new capstone concept and to address some of the previous criticisms.

The Four Major Joint Operating Concepts

The initial four concepts were the centerpiece of the Pentagon's efforts to develop joint operating concepts and a critical component of its transformation strategy. Despite the possibility that the concepts may be revised in the future to align them better with a more diverse or narrow categorization of security priorities, there is value in assessing progress to date on the four extant concepts.[15] Doing so illuminates some general problems and principles for concept development that are relevant regardless of the operating concept in question.

Homeland defense and civil support JOC. The obvious need for a concept for homeland security is complicated by the need for careful delineation between military and civilian responsibilities. The homeland defense and civil support JOC envisions a layered and comprehensive defense requiring geographical and functional integration.[16] The first layer of defense consists of efforts to neutralize threats in forward regions through major combat operations, preemptive attack, stability operations, and strategic deterrence. Next, joint forces counter threats that are transiting approaches to the United States, and do so as far from the homeland as possible, through surveillance and reconnaissance, missile defense, air defense, land defense, and maritime interception. Finally, the military must detect, deter, prevent, and defeat direct external threats to all U.S. states and territories, as well as support civilian agencies in mitigating the effects of catastrophic emergencies.

The Secretary directed that this JOC deal with the "seam of uncertainty" when roles and responsibilities of DOD and its civilian partners overlap. This emphasis is likely a byproduct of the Hurricane Katrina experience when military resources were available but withheld pending request from local agencies. The concept now emphasizes capabilities to develop shared situational awareness and an integrated U.S. Government effort, but it is a difficult challenge to delimit the military mission and devise appropriate means of coordination with the many other Federal and state agencies that will be involved in the event of attacks on the homeland. Consider, for example, air surveillance. Whereas the Federal Aviation Administration (FAA) is focused on civilian passenger craft that ostensibly want to cooperate with the FAA surveillance system, the military needs to consider stealthy airborne platforms that would attempt to avoid detection. Should the existing FAA system be upgraded to military detection standards, or augmented by existing or completely new military capabilities? These sorts of questions apply to many other aspects of homeland defense as well, including civil defense and consequence management operations. What is quite clear is that information will have to be exchanged rapidly between large numbers of government organizations. This in turn raises innumerable difficulties concerning the security, reliability, and declassification of information. Drafts of the concept have not been able to sort out such vexing issues, and despite improvements, the current concept is not sufficiently discriminating to be of much help in assessing the relative value of competing capabilities. Even if capability gaps are evident and clearly not the responsibility of the Department of Defense, a JOC cannot dictate which capabilities should be developed by other government agencies. Perhaps of greater concern are capability gaps that are not evident or well understood. The 2005 DOD *Strategy for Homeland Defense and Civil Support* has, as its second priority, the ability of the department to support civil authorities in multiple, catastrophic mass casualty chemical, biological, radiological, nuclear, and explosive incidents within the United

States.[17] Yet this JOC does not specifically address the difficult issues involved in dealing with multiple simultaneous events, including how events and resources would be prioritized.

Deterrence operations JOC. The deterrence operations JOC replaced an earlier strategic deterrence concept and is intended to address a broader range of potential adversaries and situations. Despite criticism that the original strategic deterrence JOC was overly broad and should be limited to deterring WMD use, the revised version retains the same broad focus on preventing any adversary actions that threaten vital interests of the United States.[18] In keeping with such a broad definition, the concept identifies similarly expansive objectives and means to accomplish them. The concept defines the objective of deterrence as decisive influence over adversary decisionmaking in order to convince the adversary to forego grievous courses of action against the United States. This objective can be achieved in three ways: by denying the adversary benefits, imposing unacceptable costs, or affecting his understanding of the consequences of his actions. Yet virtually every capability resident in the U.S. military is applicable to these endeavors.[19] In fact, defined so broadly, the concept must encompass not only the entirety of the U.S. military, but also all other instruments of national power (for example, diplomatic, informational, and economic).

The net effect of such breadth is the same high level of abstraction and lack of discrimination that marked the homeland defense concept. The consequences are the same, too: the concept does not come to grips with the most significant trends in deterrence, and it is not useful as a means of discrimination between alternative capabilities based on their utility for implementing the concept.

This concept acknowledges several significant deterrence challenges for U.S. military forces, including the increasingly diverse types of adversaries, weapons of mass destruction, and defenses that may be employed against them, all of which beg for a reassessment of strategic deterrence strategy. For example, despite some nonproliferation successes in 1990s, most notably in South America and South Africa, and more recent evidence that the danger of proliferation has been reversed in Libya and Iraq, the general trend remains that more countries, such as Iran and North Korea, are acquiring diverse sets of weapons of mass destruction and their delivery systems. Moreover, there has been a steady rise in the involvement of nonstate actors, some with the intent to proliferate and others with a desire to use WMD. The extensive supplier network of Pakistani scientist A.Q. Khan presents new challenges to traditional counterproliferation concepts, as does Osama bin Laden's professed desire to obtain and use a nuclear or biological weapon. Nonstate actors such as bin Laden are unlikely to be dissuaded or deterred by threats to hold traditional targets at risk. Even state actors may conclude they can use some chemical or biological weapons without precipitating a U.S. nuclear response. The concept does discuss the need to tailor deterrence options to this wide range of challenges but offers no prescriptions on how this should be done beyond the observation that enemy motives, intentions, and cultural predispositions must be well understood.

In addition, because of the growing accuracy of conventional weapons, it is possible to envision their use against nuclear weapons. In part because of these trends, the United States has opted to develop missile defenses and to change its approach to strategic deterrence, scrapping the historic reliance on the Anti-Ballistic Missile Defense Treaty and an offensive strategic triad of nuclear intercontinental ballistic missiles, submarine-/sea-launched ballistic missiles, and bombers. In its place is a new triad, consisting of offensive strike (conventional, nonkinetic, and nuclear), defenses (both active and passive), and a responsive infrastructure for maintaining and updating strategic capabilities. These changes, and the reality that an adversary can much more easily hold U.S. allies at risk than the United States (which was not the case in the Cold War, when the Soviet Union could hold both the United States and its allies at risk), demand a reconsideration of strategy for deterring weapons of mass destruction. Currently, the breadth of the concept means that this important issue goes unaddressed. As is the case with the homeland defense concept, a secondary effect of such a high level of abstraction is that the concept is not helpful for assessing the value of alternative strategic deterrence capabilities.

Finally, the concept's emphasis on tailored deterrence raises an important risk issue that the JOC should address. It is always important to understand and assess the adversary's intent and decisionmaking calculus. But to what extent should these assessments be relied upon to guide adjustments in relative capabilities? Before the first Gulf War, many analysts did not believe that Saddam Hussein would attack another Arab state, and they were proven wrong. Similarly, despite massive efforts to understand Soviet decisionmaking during the Cold War, the United States was caught by surprise when Soviet leadership permitted and eventually facilitated the collapse of the Soviet Union. To the extent that tailored deterrence requires much better knowledge of adversary decisionmaking, the concept must assess the capabilities required to build this knowledge, ways to assess the validity of foreign decisionmaking assessments, and means of mitigating risk should such assessments prove to be flawed.

Major combat operations JOC. The JOC for major combat operations envisions an effects-based approach to be used throughout the deployment, employment, and sustainment of the combined (joint and allied) force.[20] The concept is focused on a regional power with advanced military capabilities such as access denial, information operations, advanced conventional weapons, and weapons of mass destruction. It stresses that future large-scale military operations will be conducted in a distributed, collaborative environment, where precision and information dominance replace mass as the key enabler of success. U.S. forces will seek to defeat its adversaries through disintegration—integrated destruction and dislocation that break the enemy's will and ability to organize, adapt, and recover. In many ways, this continues the trajectory of warfare first established in Operation *Desert Storm* and most recently demonstrated by the speed and decisiveness of major combat operations in Iraq. Since it is an area increasingly well practiced by the United States, this concept is perhaps the best developed of the four. However, as with the others, it lacks much specificity and is mute on some of the more difficult issues that it should address.

For example, the reliance on information dominance raises difficult questions about how to preserve access and reliability of information and the extent to which information processing will occur at information hubs instead of on individual platforms.[21] The assumption that the adversary will use weapons of mass destruction and other antiaccess tactics raises questions about the advisability of fixed bases and the best way to ensure defense of critical transportation nodes. On a positive note, the current version of this concept fixes an earlier weakness by acknowledging an important lesson from the Iraq experience—the need to carry out combat operations in such a way as to facilitate a smooth transition to the stabilization phase of a major combat operation.

Military support to stabilization, security, transition, and reconstruction operations JOC. The 2006 revision of this JOC for military support to stabilization, security, transition, and reconstruction (SSTR) operations has some similarities to previous drafts but is startlingly and significantly different in one key respect. As with the previous draft of the stability operations JOC, the 2006 version addresses a wide range of cases in which a future joint force commander might use a joint force to conduct stability operations that precede, occur during, or follow conventional combat operations.[22] The JOC covers helping a severely stressed government avoid failure, recover from natural disaster, and build a "new domestic order" following internal collapse or defeat in war. It recognizes that stability operations can no longer be considered as preludes and aftermaths of major combat but instead will be addressed throughout all phases of a major combat operation—an emphasis that clearly arises from recent experience in Iraq. Perhaps reflecting institutional frustration over the disproportionate load the Department of Defense carries in Iraq, the concept clearly identifies the State Department as the lead U.S. Government agency in any SSTR operation and subordinates the military to a support role to either the State Department or the host country.

The 2006 version of the concept varies significantly from previous drafts in its treatment of irregular warfare. Previously, the concept emphasized the need to deal with irregular forces. It demonstrated sophistication in observing that there are a variety of potential stability spoilers, ranging from those motivated by greed to those with unwavering political or religious convictions, and notes that the former may be dealt with by a variety of means short of force. The concept included many of the historically validated attributes of success in stability operations: patience, perseverance, all-source intelligence, discriminating use of force, effective use of information, and, above all, the need to secure legitimacy and popular support for military operations.

The revised version changes the emphasis on irregular warfare dramatically. It acknowledges that the presence of armed insurgents constitutes a high-end SSTR operation but sidesteps the challenge of dealing with irregular forces by observing that a large supporting U.S. counterinsurgency/counterterrorist effort is counterproductive. It suggests only that a future joint force commander must "make substantial contributions to SSTR efforts as quickly as possible and then give way to other civilian agencies and host nation institutions." The concept avoids addressing the type of difficulties the United States is currently encountering in Iraq. Instead, more than 4 years after a difficult real-world experience in Iraq with serious national security implications, the Pentagon's leading conceptual effort on stability operations postponed dealing with irregular forces. Instead, a fifth JOC on irregular warfare is to be written at a later date.[23]

The focus on military support to other organizations for stabilization, security, transition, and reconstruction activities without specifically addressing irregular warfare is not helpful. Beyond the possibility of spontaneous mass civil unrest, as happened following the 1989 U.S. intervention in Panama, the threat or presence of irregular forces is the only factor that makes stability operations truly challenging and relevant to the Department of Defense. As a general rule, stability operations are routine activities without high stakes when there is no organized armed opposition bent on disruption. Stability operations complicated by resolute irregular forces, however, require a complex mix of relentless but precise lethal force and integrated application of nonlethal instruments of power. A concept is sorely needed that will address the central purpose of tactical combat operations in stability operations and be unequivocal about how force is to be applied.

Such a concept would benefit from unambiguous language such as that contained in an earlier classic on stability operations: the 1940 Marine Corps *Small Wars Manual*.[24] The manual notes that "in small wars, caution must be exercised, and instead of striving to generate the maximum power with forces available, the goal is to gain decisive results with the least application of force and the consequent minimum loss of life." The manual argues for an offensive spirit in tactical operations against irregular forces, but not so much because it is possible to destroy them completely as it is desirable to keep them on the run and dispersed so that the political process of reform may continue. In describing the strategy to be employed in small wars, the manual argues that "the solution of such problems being basically a political adjustment, the military measures to be applied must be of secondary importance and should be applied only to such extent as to permit the continuation of peaceful corrective measures." These and other passages in the *Small Wars Manual* explain unequivocally the strategic and tactical purpose of combat operations, which is a prerequisite for a more detailed description of the concept for defeating irregular forces.[25] Currently, the SSTR concept simply notes that maintaining a safe and secure environment for stability operations may require measured and discriminate offensive operations without specifically addressing how this should be accomplished.

Fundamental Attributes of a Good Joint Operating Concept[26]

The joint operating concept development process has undergone two major iterations. Yet the JOCs themselves remain insufficiently mature to guide DOD in making the fundamental choices required to develop transformational capabilities for the joint force. The JOCs suffer from some common problems that must be corrected if they are to fulfill their intended role as the "engines of transformation."

Discriminating definitions. All military problems, from weapons of mass destruction to guerrilla warfare, have similar and dissimilar characteristics. The overarching Capstone Concept for Joint Operations must focus on their similarities (for example, the need to provide security through threat or use of organized lethal force) and emphasize an approach that will be applicable to all employment of military force (for example, by emphasizing the importance of first securing critical information about the specific problem at hand in order to employ force effectively).

However, the underlying premise of the four specific joint concepts is that different approaches are required for military problems that are dissimilar in critically important ways. Each concept must come to grips with the defining characteristics of the military problem. Since invariably there is more than one way to solve a problem, deciding between alternative approaches to solve the core problem is the essence of a good operating concept.

Therefore, the first priority for an operating concept is delimiting the problem with a discriminating definition, something that the Transformation Planning Guidance failed to do. Instead, those charged with developing the concepts were allowed to produce their own definitions. They all opted for overly broad definitions that substantially overlap with one another and thus confuse the problem being addressed. Not surprisingly, the recommended approaches to the problem are so broad that they are not readily distinguishable and thus are not useful for discriminating between alternative capability sets. These joint operating concepts do not assist with strategic management of the defense program by making the choices among alternative capabilities more transparent. Instead, they confuse strategic management of the defense program by obscuring the differences between both the problem and potential solution sets.

Presumptive causal linkages. Joint operating concepts should describe how a future commander will plan, prepare, deploy, employ, and sustain a joint force against potential adversaries. In short, they will presume an understanding of what will produce a successful operation. Thus, a good operating concept will articulate a clear path of presumptively causal linkages for resolving a clearly defined problem. To do so, most military theorists begin by establishing a lexicon and associated framework of essential concept components[27] and then proceed to explain how the key conceptual elements are used to produce a solution to the military problem. In other words, the concept must provide a description of the objective (end) that includes the desired endstate and associated effects that are necessary to achieve the objective; an explanation of how the operation proceeds to produce the desired effects (ways); and identify the capabilities (means) necessary to execute the concept, preferably prioritized by their order of importance for success. Having failed to be sufficiently discriminating in the description of the objective, it is not surprising that all four major concepts developed to date tend to avoid presumptive causal linkages. Instead, they provide an inventory of possible means that vary in application, as circumstances seem to warrant. To some extent, joint operating concepts are situation-dependent, but the core idea requires explicit descriptions of how to execute the concepts rather than just a catalogue of possible means to employ.

Risk identification and mitigation. A good operating concept not only articulates ways and means, but also does so with a cognizance of alternatives and their presumed advantages and disadvantages. If it is a transformational concept, it must knowingly depart from current practices and be aware of how it incurs risk by doing so. For example, the German military innovators who advocated blitzkrieg tactics knew that their mobile forces penetrating deep behind enemy front lines were vulnerable to being cut off, starved for supplies, and defeated piecemeal. They estimated that their enemies would not be able to organize and move quickly enough to exploit this potential vulnerability, and they did everything possible to make sure this was the case.

A good concept, then, needs to identify ways to mitigate known risks and establish warning signs that it is failing to do so when the operations are actually undertaken. Going a step further, a set of metrics for assessing successful employment of a concept would assist with evaluating the contribution of any given capability to the concept's execution.

The second iteration of each of the four joint operating concepts attempts to identify an associated set of risks, and some of them discuss possible ways of mitigating those risks. Yet these risks tend to be described generally and are not specific to the concept of operations articulated. For instance, the major combat operations concept raises the possibility that a new generation of warfare might emerge or that the characterization of the future security environment might be inaccurate. To mitigate such problems, the JOC suggests broad investments as a hedge against alternative futures. These problems are endemic to defense planning and not particular to the JOCs chosen to guide U.S. military development.

If the Pentagon's joint operating concepts are to be effective tools for transformation, they must eventually become discriminating and detailed enough to allow identification and prioritization of transformation requirements in the defense program. They also must remain open to modification so they may incorporate new findings from experimentation and practical experience. Absent these characteristics, the joint operating concepts will not become engines of transformation, and a central element of the Pentagon's much-needed transformation to capabilities-based planning will remain missing as well.

A CAPABILITIES-BASED APPROACH[28]

The emphasis on new concepts of operation is fueled by the conviction that new military capabilities permit forces to be employed in dramatically different and more effective ways. Prior to his election in 2000, President Bush promised "a future force that is defined less by size and more by mobility and swiftness, one that is easier to deploy and sustain, one that relies more heavily on stealth, precision weaponry, and information technologies."[29] Since then, transformation theorists in the Pentagon have elaborated on this vision and promised an information-age military that will be less platform-centric and more network-centric, able to distribute forces more widely by increasing information-sharing via a secure network that provides actionable information at all levels of command.

Recent operations provide some evidence that this vision is already taking shape, as creative commanders in the field now exploit with good effect information systems developed and fielded by the Pentagon in the 1990s. The campaigns in Afghanistan and Iraq seemed to validate the new Pentagon catchphrase for transformation: "fight first for information superiority." A precise understanding of where friendly and enemy forces were, and the consequent ability to outmaneuver and attack the enemy rapidly and with great precision, were hallmarks in the combat phases of these operations. President Bush and the Pentagon leadership want to build on this progress and recognize that doing so would require a more systematic way to identify military capabilities that would best support transformation objectives.

The 2001 Quadrennial Defense Review emphasized that DOD needed to adopt a new approach to developing military forces, which it referred to as *capabilities-based planning*. Arguing that the United States could not know the origin of threats decades from now, QDR 2001 focused instead on the idea of anticipating the kinds of capabilities that an adversary might employ. A capabilities-based model would focus more on "how an adversary might fight than who the adversary might be and where a war might occur," and it would require identifying capabilities that U.S. military forces would need to deter and defeat adversaries who will rely on "surprise, deception, and asymmetric warfare to achieve their objectives."[30]

The 2001 QDR closely tied a capabilities-based approach to strategy but also made a reactive and proactive case for a capabilities-based approach that paralleled the case it made for transformation in general. It asserted that capabilities-based planning is necessary to prepare for a more diverse and uncertain set of security threats and to exploit information-age opportunities to produce transformational capabilities, such as advanced remote sensing and long-range precision strike.

Thesis: Abandon Atypical Threat Cases and Platform-centric Planning

The two-part strategic rationale used to justify capabilities-based planning has a lot of appeal, and it satisfied two longstanding complaints about defense planning. Critics of Pentagon planning during the 1990s protested that it focused exclusively on two archetypical threat cases that were actually anomalies: Korea and Iraq. If the United States had to fight on the Korean Peninsula, it would benefit from more than 20 immediately available, well-trained, and well-equipped South Korean divisions— not a circumstance likely to be true in most other plausible future contingencies. In the case of an Iraqi contingency, the United States would benefit from a massive amount of base infrastructure it developed in and around the Gulf region for precisely this purpose—again, not a circumstance likely to be repeated elsewhere. Critics argue that since the United States cannot predict precisely where it will have to fight, planning ought not to assume such a specific set of cases (see text box). Allowing the entire Pentagon planning system to be driven by these two atypical cases for almost 10

EXCERPTS FROM THE 1997 NATIONAL DEFENSE PANEL REPORT ON TWO-THEATER WAR PLANNING CONSTRUCT

- Current defense strategy states that U.S. forces should be capable of fighting two regional wars at almost the same time. . . . This two-theater war concept is predicated on the belief that the ability to fight more than one major war at a time deters an enemy from seeking to take advantage of the opportunity to strike while the United States is preoccupied in another theater.

- Our current forces, however, with the support of allies, should be capable of dealing with Iraq. . . . The risks in Korea remain high, but . . . as long as we retain the ability to introduce forces into the region, we have adequate combat power within the present force structure to deal with this threat. As a result, it is our judgment that our current force structure is sufficient for the regional threats that we see today.

- We are concerned that the [two-military-theater-of-war construct] may have become a force-protection mechanism—a means of justifying the current force structure—especially for those searching for the certainties of the Cold War era. . . . The two-theater construct has been a useful mechanism for determining what forces to retain as the Cold War came to a close. To some degree, it remains a useful mechanism today. But, it is fast becoming an inhibitor to reaching the capabilities we will need in the 2010–2020 time frame.

- The real issue is where we are willing to take risk. The current posture minimizes near-term risk at a time when danger is moderate to low. A significant share of the Defense Department's resources is focused on the unlikely contingency that two major wars will break out at once, putting greater risk on our long-term security. While we cannot identify future threats precisely, we can identify the challenges. Our priority emphasis (including resources) must go to the future.

Report of the National Defense Panel, "Transforming Defense: National Security in the 21st Century," December 1997, available at <http://www.fas.org/man/docs/ndp/part03.htm>.

years, they argued, resulted in force structure and program decisions optimized for an extremely narrow problem set.

The other common complaint about Pentagon planning that capabilities-based planning seemed to address was the tendency simply to react to the systems deployed by potential enemies. Over the course of the Cold War, critics argue, the Services increasingly defaulted to producing weapons that were qualitatively better than whatever the

Soviet Union deployed, irrespective of whether there might be a better way to accomplish the mission. Since the Soviet Union was the predominant threat, it was enough to show that any given system was better than whatever the Soviet Union had. After the demise of the Soviet Union, the United States celebrated with an extended military "procurement holiday" during the 1990s. When recapitalization of the force could no longer be avoided, critics worried that the Pentagon was about to spend the new decade modernizing its forces by pumping out advanced tanks, planes, and ships that best addressed the Cold War requirement to project power across the vast oceans and stop large, multiechelon mass armor attacks in the Soviet tradition. By emphasizing capabilities rather than threats, these critics hoped to shake off the old bottom-up, stovepiped acquisition processes that produced great individual platforms but ignored the larger issue of how joint forces communicate and operate together for greater effect. Critics wanted the Pentagon to invest more in information-age systems that would be inherently more capable, flexible, and, not incidentally, more applicable to a wider range of threats.

Antithesis: Bound Uncertainty

Although defensible, the two-part strategic rationale for capabilities-based planning is not without problems, some of which have retarded its implementation since the 2001 *QDR Report* was published. First, the assumption that it is easier to anticipate the tactics an adversary will use than it is to predict the identity of the adversary is open to challenge. Looking back at recent operations in Iraq and Afghanistan, one might argue that it would have been easier to predict the adversary location than the tactics. The United States contemplated attacking terrorist bases in Afghanistan during the 1990s, and Iraq was a well-recognized potential belligerent. As for enemy tactics, many would have predicted that the Taliban and al Qaeda would have quickly transitioned to a prolonged guerrilla struggle rather than attempt to hold on to major population centers. Also, many supposed that Saddam Hussein would not fight the United States again without employing weapons of mass destruction or using terrorism and information operations to disrupt the flow of U.S. forces through Persian Gulf ports. Only in retrospect did it become clear that he was either unable or unwilling to do so.

Another problem is that the enemy tactics identified in the *QDR Report*—surprise, deception, and asymmetric warfare—are notably vague. They seem tantamount to saying we need to be prepared for just about anything except what we currently think might be most likely. Indeed, the report claims that the "senior leaders of the Defense Department set out to establish a new strategy for America's defense that would embrace uncertainty and contend with surprise."[31] There is a problem with uncertainty as a strategic principle, however. Taken absolutely, it is the antithesis of planning. It is not possible to plan for that which cannot be anticipated, and it is not possible to distribute resources to priority solutions if there is no corresponding known problem set. The only way to avoid this dilemma is to identify solutions that apply equally well to any conceivable security problem. Future transformation capabilities are often described in vague ways that make them seem like easy and simple solutions to a wide variety of problems, but in reality they are not. Some capabilities obviously have broader applications than others, but difficult choices about which capabilities merit the most investment cannot be avoided.

Therefore, while it is understandable that the Pentagon leadership wanted to avoid the optimistic assumption that future adversaries would confront U.S. conventional force advantages head-on where U.S. forces have the greatest comparative advantage, just assuming the contrary does not get a defense planner very far. At worst, concentrating on uncertainty amounts to an abnegation of planning. The likely result is that less transparent and perhaps less rational influences will dictate allocation of limited resources.[32] The only real advantage of emphasizing the unpredictability of the security environment is that it should stimulate planners to consider a wider set of possible threat scenarios against which they can then measure the sufficiency of alternative future force and capability options.

Contrary to popular belief, however, the Pentagon already had a wide range of alternative scenarios before 2000. It did not typically analyze them for several reasons. Some of the scenarios did not involve large-scale force-on-force battles, and the Pentagon lacked a set of modeling and simulation approaches and tools to assess them effectively. In addition, although the strategy formally underscored the importance of atypical contingencies, in practice there were insufficient political will and analytic resources to investigate and act upon the requirements associated with anything other than the best-known warfighting scenarios.

Justifying capabilities-based planning by associating it with transformational output is also problematic. It is true that changing the focus of the discussion to capabilities rather than threats opens the door for redefining the most desired capabilities. Instead of military requirements being defined in terms of something similar to, but better than, whatever the most likely enemy has, the focus on capabilities tends to open the debate to include proposals for new ways to accomplish a mission and thus potentially support new transformational capabilities.

However, changing the terms of the debate does not guarantee that transformational capabilities will be identified and developed. If you believe that having the ability to kill enemy tanks is a good thing, and that the best antitank capability is another tank, you can ignore specific threat countries altogether, focus on desired antitank "capability," and still come up with a recommendation to build a bigger, heavier (and decidedly not transformational) tank. The same could be said about air-to-air superiority and fighter aircraft, and so on.

In short, contrary to *QDR Report* assertions, capabilities-based planning does not necessarily lead to the conclusion that the U.S. military needs "advanced remote sensing, long-range precision strike, transformed maneuver and expeditionary forces and systems, to overcome anti-access and area denial threats."[33] It only increases the possibility that these capabilities will be looked at seriously, particularly if the problem set (threat environment) is defined as robust antiaccess and area denial threats.

These flaws in the strategic justification for capabilities-based planning and the established thinking that it reflected had some unfortunate effects, which, ironically, may have delayed implementation of capabilities-based planning. The undue emphasis on uncertainty instead of variability in threat, and the erroneous implication that there was a dichotomy between capabilities and threats, retarded work on the Department's illustrative planning scenarios (now called defense planning cases). If threat was no longer important, why pay attention to illustrative threat cases?

Some proponents of capabilities-based planning understood the problem with un-bounded uncertainty and felt that some reference to threat cases was necessary. They still erred too much on the side of uncertainty by arguing that DOD should look at literally hundreds of cases and choose whatever capabilities most broadly applied to the greatest range of cases, irrespective of the importance of any given case. The problem with this approach is that it runs the distinct danger of suboptimizing for the most critical cases. Not all security problems have equal consequences if handled poorly. Failure in some cases would more seriously damage the country's security interests. Eventually, the Pentagon recognized this and settled down to building a prioritized set of threat cases with sufficient variability, but time was lost in the process.

Another problem arose from the tendency to confuse capabilities-based planning with a broad vision of transformational capabilities that would be equally valuable for a wide range of contingencies and missions. The tendency was to devalue the impor-tance of analysis and detailed studies about marginal utilities. What was probably needed, many felt, was a new vision to break the Pentagon out of its rut and lethargy. It soon became apparent, however, that the hard questions about where to invest mar-ginal defense dollars still benefit from good analysis. The key is to make sure that the analysis addresses the issues senior decisionmakers are concerned about and that it does so with transparent quantitative and qualitative input and methodologies that are appropriate to the subject matter. Transformation leaders eventually looked more fa-vorably on analysis, but the Pentagon has yet to improve significantly the quality and quantity of the analysis that it can produce in support of capabilities-based planning.

Synthesis: Agreement on Next Steps for Capabilities-based Planning?

The 2001 QDR emphasis on capabilities-based planning was advantageous in sev-eral respects. It served notice to institutional forces in the Pentagon that major changes in the planning, programming, and budgeting system used for decades would be forth-coming. It shifted the terms of the planning debate to allow serious evaluation of a wider range of possible contingencies as the basis for planning and alerted the Services that the usual justifications for their preferred major programs would be viewed skep-tically if not deemed sufficiently transformational. However, as noted, flaws in the strategic rationale for capabilities-based planning tended to retard its implementation.

Today, there appears to be a better appreciation for what capabilities-based plan-ning is and what it will require. Most now agree that capabilities-based planning is not an antidote to uncertainty and that completely divorcing threat and capabilities cre-ates a false and deleterious dichotomy. Planning in the 1990s focused too much on a couple of specific potential enemies, and in so doing perhaps ceded the initiative to other possible adversaries. However, it would be just as undesirable to go to the other extreme and conduct defense planning without reference to threats. Ignoring threat projections altogether means never being able to judge how much is enough, or how good is good enough. Specifically, it means no standards for the adequacy of the effects a capability can produce, and, more generally, it means no reference point for assessing the value of any given capability. In short, if the problem cannot be bounded, risk cannot be assessed or resources prioritized. The future threat environment may be less certain today than it was during the Cold War, but defense planners cannot escape the need to make judgments about the nature of the future security environment and the major problems that it will present for U.S. interests.

The great innovation in capabilities-based planning, therefore, was not the irrelevance of the threat in an uncertain world, but the importance of assessing and managing risk across a much more diverse problem set. Threat is not ignored; it is simply assessed with much greater variation, as are capabilities. It is important to look at variation in capabilities as well as threat. Defense officials need some means of evaluating the respective merits of alternative capability sets by objective standards, including the ability to test those capabilities across a broader problem set in order to assess their benefits and risks. The upshot is that capabilities-based planning will require the ability to assess and manage risk more self-consciously by looking at much greater variation in problem definition (threat) and in solutions (strategy, concepts of operation, and capabilities), all while paying attention to costs and resource constraints.

Next Steps for a Capabilities-based Approach

To accelerate implementation of a capabilities-based approach to defense planning and resource management, consensus is growing that the Pentagon will ultimately need to take several steps:

Establish an authoritative conceptual framework. First, a white paper or some other type of authoritative statement is needed to clear up much of the conceptual confusion surrounding capabilities-based planning. It should define the concept, its purpose, and its attributes.[34] Since the purpose of capabilities-based planning is to help senior decisionmakers adjudicate risks through their resource allocation decisions in an environment characterized by much greater variability in threats and capability options, the key to success is meaningful comparison of both risks and risk mitigation options.

Such comparison requires a conceptual framework, complete with taxonomy and lexicon to delimit and prioritize categories of threats and capabilities so that the debate about risk management can proceed on transparent and comprehensible terms. While the taxonomies and lexicon will change over time, it is virtually impossible to make comparisons across threats, mission areas, and platforms without a common set of reference points and terminology.

To be meaningful, the comparisons must use common qualitative and quantitative measurements of risk. Furthermore, the framework must distinguish between timeframes, since risk and capabilities evolve over time, and investments come to fruition in different time periods. For example, it is possible to forego near-term operational capability in order to prepare better for future threats. The framework must also distinguish between levels of analyses, since the variables relevant to threat, capabilities, and risk are different at the strategic, operational, and tactical levels of war.

Increase and organize joint analytic resources. Handling the variability in threat and capability options characteristic of a capabilities-based approach requires more robust joint analysis and a more integrated planning, programming, and budgeting system informed by that analysis than previously was the case. Today, the overwhelming majority of analytic capability in the Pentagon is owned by the Services, which conduct their own internal studies using their own data and models and without giving attention to broad trades across military capability areas. While useful to the Services, these studies do nothing for the senior decisionmakers who need to assess and evaluate options for alleviating risk. Thus, an immediate first step for implementing capabilities-based planning is to invest more resources in joint analysis at the strategic and operational levels. Reorganization also is required to ensure effective and efficient management of these resources. Currently, the scant joint analytic resources devoted to strategic and operational analysis are split between offices with different mandates and proclivities (the Joint Staff and multiple offices of the Office of the Secretary of Defense), either in the form of assigned personnel or dollars available for contractor support. It would be better to have these diverse organizations combine their resources under the same management with a common purpose and work more directly in support of senior decisionmakers.

Institutionalize an authoritative, transparent, and discriminating analytic system. Several building blocks are necessary for good analysis, each of which tends to suffer from lack of emphasis, transparency, discrimination, or some combination of these factors. The Pentagon needs authoritative planning cases instead of allowing Service and joint analysts to create their own preferred cases, and (as discussed above) it needs sufficiently discriminating and detailed joint operating concepts for how forces will be employed. It also needs risk metrics for evaluating the results of different concepts employed in different scenarios. The Pentagon needs more diverse modeling and simulation tools that can evaluate a wider range of military phenomena than just force-on-force combat results, including the impact of irregular warfare, information, and weapons of mass destruction. Finally, it needs authoritative and transparent data to populate its models and simulations so that decisionmakers are not presented with conflicting conclusions based solely on assumptions hidden in different data sets.

Implementing a capabilities-based approach to defense planning and resource allocation processes will not be easy. Those charged with doing so often note that it took a decade or longer to institute the current planning, programming, and budgeting system, and that working through the details of a capabilities-based approach will take at least as long. No doubt this is true, which is even more reason to move out quickly on the prerequisites for capabilities-based decisionmaking that are already apparent.

GLOBAL FORCE PLANNING

A well-developed capabilities-based approach to strategic risk assessment would certainly assist decisionmakers with one of the most complex and difficult areas of transformational import: global force planning. A striking characteristic of the 2001 QDR was its emphasis on global capabilities. The 1997 QDR noted the importance of remaining a global power with global presence and engagement, but said little about global capabilities other than mentioning the need for worldwide communications and a "globally vigilant intelligence system." The 2001 QDR adopted a strategy that exploits emerging global capabilities and demands more of them.

The new strategy assumed that U.S. forces postured and managed to contain defunct Soviet or late 20th-century regional threats could not efficiently respond to increasingly uncertain threats, some of which are most effectively dealt with on a global basis and with some global capabilities. The strategy's overall intent, therefore, was to provide the President with a wider range of military options to discourage aggression. To stimulate the development of such capabilities, the strategy adopted a much more demanding goal for deterring foreign adversaries in an increasingly uncertain world. Instead of relying on forward-deployed forces to absorb the shock of an enemy onslaught and hold on until more U.S. forces could be projected into theater, the new strategy required forward-deployed forces, augmented by global capabilities, to defeat the enemy attacks rapidly in a wider range of potential contingencies "with only modest reinforcement from outside the theater." And they needed to be able to do so in spite of enemy antiaccess and area-denial threats.

To achieve this ambitious goal effectively, changes are required in three core areas: command and control, posture, and capabilities. A new global dimension for each of these areas was emphasized in the 2001 *QDR Report*,[35] albeit not organized under the umbrella rubric of global force planning, a term used for convenience here. The report promised changes in how global forward-deployed and forward-stationed forces were postured to support forward deterrence better, and it promised supporting changes in global force capabilities that could immediately augment those forces. In addition to long-range strike aircraft and Special Operations Forces, which already are immediately available to supplement forward forces, the report noted that globally distributed capabilities and forces could also rapidly and precisely strike enemy targets at various distances.[36]

The report noted that the new strategy would require changes in how command and control over U.S. forces is exercised, including new command and control assets and integrated intelligence that would contribute to a "Global Command and Control System Common Operational Picture." It also called for a new joint presence policy that would "increase the capability and flexibility of U.S. forward-stationed forces and aid in managing force management risks," including setting up choices between different combinations of force packages (that is, cross-Service trades) based on which would best support presence and deterrence.

The emphasis on new global command and control arrangements and force presence policies, when combined, represents a new approach to global force management.

Along with global force posture and capabilities, global force management promises to have a sweeping impact on the way the United States will develop, deploy, and operate its military forces in concert with allies and partners.

GLOBAL FORCE MANAGEMENT

The new approach to global force management includes tools and policies for managing global deployment of forces and associated risk assessments, and new combatant commander responsibilities that involve a global span of control over some forces and missions. The two reforms, which are discussed separately below, are related. Combatant commanders with new global command responsibilities are expected to provide expert opinion and inputs for the global force management system overseen by the Pentagon and other national authorities.

New Tools and Policies[37]

The driving force behind global force management is the need to assess and manage risk better on a global basis. Doing so requires a more centralized approach to risk management. Geographic commanders do not have visibility over all the relevant factors affecting global risk. Someone with a broader field of vision must make judgments about where to accept and reduce risks. For example, if a combatant commander responsible for current operations in Iraq requests additional forces, granting the request would likely require accepting risk elsewhere. If the forces are taken from South Korea, the risk to the defense of South Korea from North Korea may increase. National authorities must consider whether moving an aircraft carrier or bomber wing forward to that part of the world, or repositioning other forces, is necessary to draw down that risk.

Making such risk assessments and decisions is difficult. To manage and assess such risks on a global basis, two general sets of reforms are required. First, the Pentagon needs tools and systems that would allow a near-real-time assessment of the location and readiness of all units around the globe, and second, it needs a rapid and joint means of assessing the risk associated with using those forces for different purposes. The Pentagon calls the set of tools and processes to support decisionmaking the *global force management process*,[38] and it continues to work on a prototype of the new system.[39]

When fully functional, the global force management process will be the essential analytic DOD tool for managing risk on a global scale. Previously, the practice was for the Secretary of Defense to apportion forces well in advance to geographic commanders who based their planning on the assumption that those forces would be available in the event of war. The real world is more complicated. Geographic commanders do not always get all the forces they desire, in which case they must adapt their plans quickly. Sometimes they get more than they expected or even needed to reduce risk to an acceptable level. The tendency is to push everything forward as fast as possible to the location of the immediate conflict, regardless of planning assumptions. When this happens, risk may increase elsewhere if adversaries believe the United States is overcommitted and unable to respond to their provocations.

Meanwhile, functional commands such as U.S. Strategic Command, U.S. Transportation Command, and U.S. Joint Forces Command, which have critical wartime missions as well, often complain that they do not get a large enough say in which forces receive priority for a higher state of readiness. The Chairman of the Joint Chiefs and Secretary of Defense need to be able to see and understand all these competing priorities and assess their import. Ultimately, they need to be able to advise the President with risk assessments that reflect current operational realities and not outdated assumptions. To improve their ability to manage all forces on a global basis and in near-real-time, the President and Secretary of Defense have also adjusted some of the combatant commander relationships, particularly where forces with global reach are concerned.

New Combatant Commander Relationships

The President, given his constitutional authority as Commander in Chief, ultimately has command and control of all U.S. forces. However, the President cannot oversee every military plan and operation on a day-to-day basis, nor can the Secretary of Defense. Combatant commanders, under the guidance of the Secretary of Defense and President, plan and prepare for potential military operations and, when necessary, command and control joint (and combined) military forces. In the past, the Pentagon organized U.S. combatant commands to deal with traditional contingencies occurring in one region or another, but those delineations are no longer satisfactory. Regional conflicts with significant escalation potential (especially to weapons of mass destruction) that could cut across regional boundaries—not to mention the war on terror—increase the need for global command and control. Consequently, U.S. defense leadership has begun to revise combatant commander responsibilities to deal with these cross-cutting issues better and to integrate military capabilities more effectively with other elements of national power—diplomatic, informational, and economic.

The Goldwater-Nichols Department of Defense Reorganization Act of 1986 shifted power and responsibilities from the military Services to geographic combatant commands. With its emphasis on jointness, Goldwater-Nichols gave geographic combatant commands more responsibility and authority, primarily so they could better address regional contingencies. Geographic combatant commands—U.S. European Command (USEUCOM), U.S. Pacific Command, U.S. Central Command, and U.S. Southern Command—were assigned the majority of general purpose forces with the expectation that most wars would be confined to one or another geographic area of responsibility. While functional commands existed, they had narrowly circumscribed roles and missions.[40] Prestige and power clearly resided with the geographic commands.

However, early in the Bush administration, Secretary Rumsfeld changed the nomenclature for the heads of the combatant commands from *commanders in chief* to *combatant commanders*. This was not merely a terminology change; it reemphasized civilian control of the military. The change reminded commanders that there is only one Commander in Chief in the United States—the President—and that the goal of the Unified Command Plan, which the President approves, is to ensure that the President and Secretary of Defense have a range of military options for dealing with whatever situations arise.

Beginning in 2002,[41] and continuing with changes over the next several years, the Bush administration made major changes to both geographic and functional/global commands, both creating new commands and altering the missions of others. These changes:

- created a new geographic command, U.S. Northern Command (USNORTHCOM), whose primary mission is homeland defense. The USNORTHCOM commander is responsible for land, aerospace, and sea defenses of the United States, and for providing military support to civil authorities if needed in the case of natural disasters, attacks on U.S. soil, or other civil difficulties.[42]
- expanded another geographic command, USEUCOM, with assignment of Russia[43]
- created a new functional/global command with the merger of U.S. Space Command into the U.S. Strategic Command (USSTRATCOM). In addition to the nuclear deterrence and space missions that the new USSTRATCOM inherited, it also was given four previously unassigned missions:[44] global strike, information operations, integrated missile defense, as well as command, control, communications, computers, intelligence, surveillance, and reconnaissance (ISR). Subsequently, USSTRATCOM was also assigned the mission of combating weapons of mass destruction.[45]
- moved the regional responsibilities of U.S. Joint Forces Command to USNORTHCOM and USEUCOM, freeing USJFCOM to focus on transformation and experimentation, interoperability, joint concepts, joint battle management/command and control, and global force management. This change underscored the point that geographic combatant commands do not "own" the forces assigned to them, but that they will be apportioned as the Secretary of Defense believes appropriate, given circumstances at the time.
- assigned U.S. Special Operations Command (USSOCOM), which has long both provided and managed the Special Operations Forces supplied to geographic combatant commands, the overall responsibility for the global war on terrorism, and not just when it involves Special Operations Forces.

With these changes, nonregional commands have been given expanded responsibilities for global missions that cross regional boundaries—altering the previous balance between geographic and global commands as well as expanding functional responsibilities as managers of joint capabilities—changing the previous balance between the Services as capability providers and combatant commands as force employers.

Key Questions Ahead

While the changes since 2002 have helped update the command structure to address 21st-century threats, the command structure may still require further changes in the face of current and future challenges. Several key issues are looming.

Geographic/global/functional balance. First, determining the proper balance in the future between geographic, functional, and global commands will be difficult. The increasingly global security environment raises important questions about how combatant commands should be organized. How should DOD organize for missions such as the war on terror or combating WMD—missions that inherently cut across geographic boundaries? What is the best way to command and control capabilities that may operate across multiple time zones and more than one geographic combatant command—such as global missile defense, space operations, global strike, or ISR? What sorts of command and control arrangements are needed for "speed of light" capabilities—such as information operations, or (potentially) lasers? As these questions illustrate, security challenges are increasingly global in nature but also require a deep understanding of local regional conditions.

Geographic commands and global/functional commands each have strengths and weaknesses. Geographic commands understand the conditions in the regions in which they operate—knowledge that may be essential to knowing how to assure allies, dissuade military competition, deter conflict, wage war, or secure the peace. However, some would argue that regional understanding is not an inherently military duty and is better handled by diplomats or intelligence officers. On the other hand, geographic commands may not have the in-depth knowledge about all capabilities they may be able to employ and may have to rely on either functional commands or Services to provide that expertise. They also lack the global perspective to look across multiple regions to assess implications of options and actions, since their responsibility and focus are a particular part of the world. Functional commands have in-depth knowledge of the capabilities for which they are responsible—such as special operations, global strike, or information operations—but lack the in-depth regional expertise about friends and adversaries in the regions. They also may not have a broad view of all the capabilities that can be brought to bear in a situation—since they primarily know the capabilities for which they are responsible. In their global role, however, they can look across regions and consider how actions and challenges in one geographic area may affect other areas.

USSOCOM and USSTRATCOM have a combination of functional as well as geographically global missions. Both are capability providers to geographic combatant commanders—USSOCOM providing Special Operations Forces, and USSTRATCOM providing global strike forces. Both are responsible for independent global missions that require a variety of capabilities, USSOCOM having the lead in the war on terror and USSTRATCOM for combating WMD. Some are concerned that giving a global mission to a functional force provider may lead it to apply the capability it owns without adequately considering other capabilities—along the lines of the adage, "When all you have is a hammer, every problem looks like a nail." If the war on terror is the Nation's highest priority, perhaps it merits its own global (but not functional) command.

Ultimately, retaining some mix of the three—geographic, functional, and global commands—with appropriate connectivity among them is desirable. Some operations, including engagement and stability operations, are best handled by geographic commanders. Others, including aspects of combating terrorism, missile defense, and countering WMD proliferation, require a global perspective (and a variety of capabilities) but also cognizance of differing regional conditions that must be taken into account. Some functional issues such as Special Operations Forces and information operations are best handled by joint capabilities providers (whether such joint capabilities providers are called *combatant commanders* or something else) but also need to be tempered by regional awareness.

Another possibility is to take the *combatant* out of all the combatant commands, so that they serve the enduring missions of peacetime planning, security cooperation, integration, coordination, and synchronization, and have fewer permanent joint task forces (JTFs) that, as needed, are responsible for executing wars. Recognizing that JTFs are actually the warfighters could reduce tension about who is supporting and who is supported among geographic/functional/global commands, since all would be in a support role to the actual warfighters for the duration of the conflict. Some find this idea impractical, arguing that it requires a four-star officer to build coalitions, fight wars, and demand the support needed for combat. However, recent precedent is that in the circumstances where the higher rank is deemed necessary, the JTF commander could be a four-star—for example, General George Casey, USA, took over as the Commander of Multinational Forces in Iraq in July 2004, replacing a three-star (Lieutenant General Ricardo Sanchez, USA). It has been the four-star officer in the region—General Casey and, now, General David Petraeus, USA—who is in charge of operations—not the four-star USCENTCOM commander headquartered in Tampa.

Interagency coordination. A second key issue will center on the need to move beyond combatant commander integration to true interagency integration. It has become commonplace to assert that addressing current and future strategic problems often requires integration among all instruments of national power—diplomatic, informational, military, economic, and legal. The question is how to make this integration real when the mechanisms for doing so are clearly inadequate. Interagency relationships are essential to the missions of all combatant commands, particularly in the pre- and postconflict stages. For instance, if the center of gravity for winning the war on terror is in influencing ideas and perceptions, that is not purely—or even primarily—a military function. The war in Iraq makes clear the downsides of not integrating military, diplomatic, informational, and reconstruction actions from the beginning. For commands such as USNORTHCOM, where support to civil agencies is a key mission, essential tasks cannot be performed without close coordination among Federal, state, and local government agencies. Interagency cooperation, in short, while always helpful, has now become indispensable for success.

Many combatant commands have joint interagency coordination groups (JIACGs) with interagency representation. While JIACGs are useful for bringing different agency perspectives together on a range of political-military matters, they are, as their name implies, coordination mechanisms. Civilian personnel assigned to the JIACGs operate mainly as liaisons for their home agencies and generally lack sufficient seniority and authority to speak definitively or give approval for their agencies.

A number of ideas have been advanced for how to improve interagency planning and operations, to include:

- creating a new independent government organization in Washington, DC, to integrate military and civilian planning[46]
- designating a Deputy National Security Advisor as the lead for integrating interagency planning for and implementation of complex operations and creating a new office and Crisis Action Teams in the National Security Council (NSC) to support this effort, as well as establishing planning offices in each agency[47]
- replacing geographic combatant command "proconsuls" with regional Embassy-like teams with all relevant agencies represented.[48]

Clarifying the roles and missions of various agencies in dealing with key security concerns, bolstering planning and operational capabilities of relevant civilian agencies, and enhancing the capacity of the NSC staff to integrate interagency planning and monitor policy implementation are promising and practicable approaches to achieving greater unity of effort. Ultimately, however, the U.S. Government must learn to collaborate across the various agencies that own requisite expertise for working complex foreign contingency operations in much the same manner that many American businesses have had to collaborate across organizational components (marketing, design, and engineering) to be successful in a dynamic and increasingly dangerous (or competitive) environment. Without such collaboration in Washington, DC, and in the field, it will not be possible to successfully execute missions in support of homeland security, the war on terror, combating weapons of mass destruction, or stability operations.

Working the seams. Efforts to resolve command and control issues within a combatant command at least benefit from clearly delineated responsibilities and chain of command. In contrast, command and control issues across combatant commands, where there may be overlapping or interrelated issues, and between combatant commands and non-DOD agencies, where there is no common chain of command (below the Presidential level) and little if any joint planning capability, are far more complex. There will always be boundary lines or seams between organizations, where one organization's responsibilities end and another's begin. Seams are not necessarily bad; they allow for a reasonable span of control and division of labor. Seams are where organizations are soldered together, and as long as they do not become stovepipes—impeding coordination and integration, or letting things fall through the cracks between them—then *seam* is not figuratively a four-letter word.

The issue is not eliminating seams, but preventing or mitigating their negative aspects: anything that prevents effective flow of information, intelligence, personnel, and units across boundaries, or competing mandates or lack of a common understanding of the objective, which leads to inefficient or contradictory activities. Making sure that the commander's intent is understood by all commands is more important than the division of responsibilities among them. There is probably any number of Unified Command Plan alignments, or interagency divisions of responsibility, that would be satisfactory.

It is more important that senior leaders—combatant commanders, the Secretary of Defense, agency heads, NSC staff—spend enough time working on issues that arise from organizations' intersection. That may mean that combatant commanders or organization heads focus on looking "across and up," and leave it to their deputies to "look down" and manage internal processes. To work the seams may truly require a cultural change, since the military tends to be most comfortable with clear lines of authority and a chain of command that is unambiguous and unequivocal. The problem is that a clear line of authority and command may not work well in the complexity of today's world, where everything is related to everything else, and the boxes are not so neat. There may be many situations where the operative words are *coordinate and collaborate* rather than *command and control*. Within DOD and commands, there needs to be increased emphasis on creating avenues for regular coordination and planning, both at the commander-to-commander level and at the working level.[49]

Toward a More Agile Global Posture

While new command relationships and management tools and systems are needed for global force management, a new global force posture is also needed to improve the ability to move forces quickly to problems areas that can only imperfectly be anticipated in advance. Many U.S. military units are still stationed in proximity to potential Cold War–era flashpoints—particularly in Europe, and more specifically Germany—that are now quite secure. Even Korea, which has remained a volatile area since the Korean armistice of 1953, has changed dramatically. As discussed in chapter seven, South Korea is now one of the world's largest economies (14th in terms of 2006 gross domestic product) and is capable of providing for much of its own defense. These changes in the security environment and allied capabilities led to a reexamination of Cold War assumptions about the location and structure of U.S. forces.

It is easy enough to conclude that U.S. Cold War–era overseas basing and force deployment are outdated; the much harder question is to determine precisely how force posture should be revised. Maintaining large numbers of ground forces in stable and powerful countries might be less important than making changes that would help consolidate relationships with new allies or better position U.S. forces for responses to new threats emanating from the arc of instability along the southern reaches of the Northern Hemisphere. Yet the specifics of precisely what moves to make, and how and when to make them, are exceedingly complicated and have required detailed review.

A year after the 2001 *QDR Report*, U.S. defense leadership initiated the Global Posture Review (GPR) to consider these issues and make recommendations on updating basing of U.S. military forces around the globe. Officials on and off the record predicted the largest basing changes since World War II, describing a network of far-flung staging bases to support highly mobile units that would deploy out of new training garrisons that would be strategically located and rotationally staffed. Inevitably, the result was a rising tide of expectations overseas. In Europe, speculation quickly followed that there might be brigade-sized bases with ports and airfields in Romania and Bulgaria, or major new training areas in Poland, or airfields in unnamed countries that could replace the American base at Ramstein. Over time, as speculation mounted, many countries inferred that political considerations would drive basing decisions, and they would be punished or rewarded for their actions regarding the war in Iraq or other U.S. policies. Many sources in Germany and Spain, for example, assumed that they would lose out on American bases due to their lack of support for operations in Iraq. In contrast, and especially among new U.S. allies in Central and Eastern Europe, expectations were clear that major (and lucrative) new arrangements with the American military were impending, in part because of their support for the U.S. operations in Iraq.[50]

As part of an effort to downplay exaggerated hopes or unwarranted concerns, U.S. defense and diplomatic officials sought to emphasize the strategic rationale for the repositioning. Moving forces from their traditional (especially Western European) bases to new foreign locations or back to the United States was touted as a way to avoid the onerous training restrictions U.S. forces faced with increasing frequency at their current bases. It would also be a method to avoid delays when host nations disputed the policies prompting the deployment of American forces. Most of all, however, the reposture was advertised as a way to increase U.S. strategic agility by moving troops closer to potential hot spots and thereby speeding their potential deployment.

Not surprisingly, given the strategic rationale proffered, countries with close proximity to the arc of instability speculated that they were well-positioned candidates for hosting U.S. forces, and many assumed bases would be built eventually. In particular, some countries in Central Asia and the Caucasus saw an opportunity to acquire American security guarantees or at least to strengthen defense relationships with the United States. Other, better established U.S. allies who seemed ill positioned to retain U.S. forces could not help but view proposed changes in light of their own domestic and international political concerns. Some countries, such as South Korea, expressed concern that decisions about repositioning U.S. forces would not sufficiently account for their strategic interests.[51] Others, such as Japan, saw an opportunity to revisit longstanding sources of irritation in current basing relationships.[52]

Modest initial changes and enduring challenges. Two years after the initial flurry of discussion, the Pentagon in August 2004 announced the results of the GPR. Some important and salutary changes were proposed. A logical construct for overseas deployment infrastructure was elaborated, foreseeing well-equipped, permanent main operating bases for the stationing of major forces, austere forward operating locations for the temporary staging and onward movement of forces, and cooperative security locations for use as intermediate staging bases. One additional aircraft carrier battlegroup and more submarines will be forward-stationed in the Pacific, dramatically cutting transit time for these platforms from their home bases to their anticipated areas of deployment. Also, for the first time since the Vietnam War, Guam will have the continuous presence of B–52 bombers on its shores.[53] Army forces in Korea have begun a long-overdue downsizing and relocation south of the Han River that better reflects the evolution of the North Korean threat and the advances made by the South Korean Defense Forces. Throughout the world, headquarters will be streamlined, redundant echelons of command eliminated, and forces reoriented toward global employment rather than regional focus.

Yet it must be said that the initial results of the Global Posture Review fell short of far-reaching expectations and concerns overseas. Contrary to early predictions of a posture review driven by politics or strategy, operational military logic has dominated the changes to date. Many of the early and more radical ideas for reposturing the military's global presence that had strong political or strategic rationale in the abstract proved less attractive when operational research demonstrated that they would contribute relatively little to the strategic agility needed to respond to the complex security environment in the next 25 years. Ultimately, most major reposturing decisions—that is, those involving relocation of brigade- or division-sized units—were made more on the basis of operational, not political or geostrategic, advantages.

This is particularly true with regard to ground forces, whose repositioning made up the bulk of the major proposals for unit relocation. Strategic agility of ground forces depends on the capability to deploy appropriately trained and ready forces to the problem area quickly. In this calculation, geography plays a role, but stationing forces closer to targets does not necessarily mean those forces can deploy to their targets more quickly. The effect of geography on the speed of deployment depends on three factors: proximity of deploying forces to the port of embarkation (sea or air); throughput at the ports of embarkation and debarkation; and distance to the target area.

These variables are not always controllable. Distance to the target area and the capacity of ports of debarkation will vary with the contingency. However, throughput at the port of embarkation can be considered a major factor when deciding whether or where to relocate forces. Throughput depends on infrastructure, such as ramp-space, crash-fire rescue equipment, materiel handling equipment, rail or road access, sustainment facilities for staging forces, communications ability, and traffic management systems. It is hard to see how reposturing U.S. ground forces currently based overseas would improve these variables.[54] Except for those in the United States, new locations probably would not offer the highly developed ports of embarkation U.S. forces currently enjoy. Black Sea ports in Bulgaria and Romania would be hard pressed to provide the sort of outload capacity found in Bremerhaven, Germany, or the Netherlands. Likewise, airbases near training areas in Bulgaria, Romania, or Poland would require major upgrade to equal even a medium-throughput facility in the West.

Proximity of deploying forces to the port of embarkation is also a controllable variable, one that depends on both raw distance and the capacity of the transportation infrastructure between the forces' garrisons and the port. Again, it is hard to see how significant improvements could be gained by moving major ground forces to locations in new countries. True, new locations might offer closer physical proximity of the deploying force to the port; however, given the state of transportation infrastructure outside of the United States and the modern countries where forces are currently located, it is not clear this proximity would compensate for a less developed outload capacity.

In any event, U.S. forces are already positioned close enough to major air and sea ports that "fort-to-port" transit is rarely the time-critical path in brigade-level deployment sequences. Throughput at the port itself and other nongeographic factors such as the pace of strategic decisionmaking, the time required to identify and outload cumbersome and diverse ground force equipment, aircraft flow plans, and even materiel handling equipment (for example, the size and number of forklifts available) usually drive the speed of deployment. Offsetting disadvantages of undeveloped port infrastructure and making the repositioning of ground forces advantageous require a significant decrease in distance to assumed targets. However, much of the early and most animated speculation surrounding the GPR involved moving ground forces fewer than 800 miles from their current locations. The costs in throughput and accessibility would be balanced against a mere 2-hour decrease in flight time—hardly worth the effort.

Indeed, while obviously dependent on the contingency in question, some studies suggest that moving forces to and through a port may take two to three times longer than the time required to actually transit to the conflict area. In the first Gulf War, for example, the Army's VII Corps, which left from 4 embarkation points in Europe, took 42 days to load up 40,000 pieces of equipment on the ships, and only 20 days of transit to the Middle East. In short, finding ways to expedite the outloading process for ground forces may have a higher payoff than repositioning them or even investing in new strategic transportation capabilities. At least this is the case with ground forces.

Repositioning naval and air forces can have greater advantages. These forces are platform-centric, and the fighting package deploys from a port, not through one. Especially for ships, with their slower transit speeds, this means that moving closer to an area of potential employment can significantly add to its strategic responsiveness. Not surprisingly, some of the major repositioning called for by the Global Posture Review concerns naval forces in the Pacific, where the distances from current bases to potential conflict areas are the greatest.

Training requirements also helped determine GPR results. To achieve strategic agility, the forces that deploy must be trained and ready. Training and maintaining a complex modern force require that three things be readily available: adequate space where the force can train, instrumented training areas, and high-level maintenance capabilities. Some countries seem willing to provide more space for more aggressive training than is possible in much of the United States or Western Europe. However, it is doubtful that this environmental permissiveness will be sustained over time, especially as countries of Central Europe integrate with the European Union. Furthermore, these countries lack the sophisticated training and maintenance systems needed to hone a modern force. As with deployment infrastructure, it is unlikely that the United

States could easily replicate the systems it already possesses or justify doing so. The (probably temporary) benefit to be gained by environmental permissiveness might not outweigh the disadvantage of lower-quality training infrastructure and maintenance. Although excellent training can be conducted in many nontraditional locations, their limitations in terms of instrumentation and professional personnel suggest they should be seen as supplements to the primary facilities the United States currently possesses at places such as Hohenfels and Grafenwoer in Germany.

Tradeoffs of global presence. Political considerations can and should affect strategic basing decisions. The presence of American forces affects relations with host countries and can be used as a valuable tool in reassuring friends and dissuading enemies. However, political considerations cut both ways. Political complications can also slow the speed of deployment when states limit U.S. options by foot-dragging or outright denial of transit, overflight, or deployment, notwithstanding agreements covering these issues that seem more permissive. State policies are politically determined and fluctuate over time, but large fixed infrastructure cannot fluctuate so easily. In the absence of the Soviet threat, which helped cement U.S. relationships with key allies, a more diverse range of opinions and responses to American requests for base usage is to be expected. Absent a strong and abiding strategic partnership with a country, it is increasingly precarious to forward deploy significant ground forces. Unless U.S. forces are mobile (amphibious or prepositioned materials afloat) or in locations that the United States reliably controls (for example, Guam or Diego Garcia), there is an increasing likelihood that local approval of deployments may not be granted. In this regard, the Global Posture Review actually concluded that political considerations reinforced military logic. Indeed, the largest movement of forces foreseen is the relocation of the better part of two ground divisions from Germany and a brigade from Korea to the United States—hardly the result anticipated abroad. The redeployment of heavy forces to the United States is a significant development, but one where political constraints on deployability were determined to be more important than the net effects of geographical location or the strategic-political effect of forward presence.

This is not to say that geostrategic positioning does not matter in a military sense; it matters greatly. Holding key ground and posturing for quick employment—and the consequent potential for improved deterrence—are important considerations influencing force locations. Ultimately, however, strategic agility is not simply a function of moving forces closer to the expected fight. Numerous other operational considerations must be taken into account. In the end, geostrategic reasoning ended up recommending a hierarchy of intermediate staging bases and ports of debarkation in forward locations with varying levels of operational capacity and fixed infrastructure. Unfortunately, the austere and almost temporary nature of these locations, some of which will consist of little more than a set of usage agreements, does not correspond well with the high expectations aroused by the announcement of the posture review.

Since the initial results of the GPR deflated many expectations, some of which were backed up with significant investments of political capital, the United States will need to mend some fences with potential partner states. In doing so, it should make an effort to demonstrate how cooperative security locations and forward operating locations can improve U.S. strategic agility and produce local benefits as well. Such improvements are not obvious. The United States needs to make a case for how rapid and locally contracted infrastructural improvements still have economic and political advantages, and how a smaller U.S. footprint in a host nation reduces political friction that hurts both the United States and the local government. Routine operational (or training) use of cooperative security locations and forward operating locations demonstrates the strategic reach they provide for U.S. forces and the deterrence value they hold for host nations. These activities can also enhance the transformation of host nation armed forces and improve their interoperability with U.S. counterparts. While not cost-free for U.S. forces, especially during times of high operational tempo, the political and strategic benefits justify the effort and would help smooth ruffled feathers in the wake of the initial results of the Global Posture Review.

Recalibrating the Capabilities Mix

The need for new global command and control relationships and a new global defense posture in part reflects the emergence of new capabilities with truly global reach. Capabilities that provide the potential for rapid and, in some cases, almost immediate response raise difficult command and control issues, but also make great contributions to the strategy goal of forward deterrence. National missile defense and global ISR capabilities were emphasized in the 2001 QDR, but the global reach of Special Operations Forces and some types of information operations also was noted. In addition, long-range bombers capable of precision bombing and the possibility of conventional intercontinental ballistic missiles and hypersonic vehicles that could deliver lethal payloads raise the promise of other global rapid response capabilities that support forward deterrence.

Risk management and force design. Some new global capabilities are extremely expensive and immediately raise complex investment and force design issues. Something must be given up in order to pay for building a future force that has more global intelligence, strike, and defense capabilities. What are the tradeoffs, and what force options make the most sense? This question must be answered on several levels.

At the strategic level, there may be tradeoffs between investments in a more elaborate and flexible set of overseas base options and in forces that are not dependent upon bases. Forces have differing levels of self-deployability and sustainment. Aircraft carriers are completely self-deployable, bringing all their combat power and, depending on the type of combat operations, weeks' or months' worth of supplies to sustain operations as well. They can also be replenished at sea when necessary. Fighter aircraft can deploy to theater with the aid of refueling tankers but then depend upon local bases to support their operations. Ground forces are the least self-deployable and sustainable unless configured in an expeditionary manner such as the Marines. The Marines deploy aboard their own ships and, once ashore, can sustain ground operations for about a month before major sustainment support is required.

Future options could make U.S. military forces more self-deployable and sustainable and less onerous for allies as well, but at quite some cost. For example, the Navy is experimenting with a sea-basing concept that would permit ground forces to attack their land objectives from a collection of naval platforms without the need for an operational pause to regroup after having captured an enemy port. One report noted that such a capability could be replenished from major bases within 2,000 miles of the operation (for example, Guam or Diego Garcia), or perhaps even directly from the United States. Such a capability would significantly reduce reliance on host nation support for bases.[55] Why invest a lot of resources in land bases that can only operate with the approval of the host nation government when the vast majority of the Earth's surface is within reach of internationally accessible sea lines?

Many observers believe a sea-basing capability makes sense in a period of shifting political relationships and loyalties. They believe it would be better to invest in more self-deployable and sustainable force capabilities than to incur the expense of trying to maintain a wide network of land bases that entail high political and material costs. Sea basing and mobile ballistic missile defense would be attractive to allies as well. They would be a less visible (and thus, in some cases, less politically onerous) form of American commitment, and their use would make the allied nation's key transportation nodes less attractive targets to the enemy.

Another potentially attractive operational-level trade is investing more in planning tools and transportation techniques that improve fort-to-port transit and port-to-foxhole movement, such as unit containerization and sense-and-respond logistics that reveal needs and allocate resources in real time. Such investments might make more sense than expensive efforts either to lighten Army forces considerably or to improve their strategic mobility by means of high-speed vessels or novel airship designs. As noted above, when the total time to move Army units from fort to foxhole is considered, it is not the actual transit to theater, but the movement to the port, on-loading, and subsequent off-loading and reorganization for combat that take the most time.

At the operational level, other tradeoffs in force design must be considered in light of growing global capabilities. Global force capabilities that have greater speed, range, and endurance generally have more flexibility to deal with surprise and enemy anti-access strategies. Some argue that the first priority for operational success is to safeguard rapid movement along global lines of communication (sea, air, space, and cyberspace). For example, Operation *Iraqi Freedom* used fewer than half the tactical airstrike sorties of *Desert Storm*, but the tanker-to-sortie ratio was double that of *Desert Storm*. In short, if U.S. forces control space, air, and sea lines of communication, and can defend and transit them freely, it will be far easier to get to the fight faster with the most powerful joint strike capability, including ground forces. The question is how to pay for such global reach capabilities. Some have argued that the United States can afford to downsize some of its extensive forcible entry force structure, which ranges from diverse Army airborne units to Marine Expeditionary Forces. Sacrificing some of this force structure in favor of flexible entry capabilities that expand the range of entry points an enemy must protect would vastly complicate the enemy's challenge of mounting an effective defense.

The argument that U.S. forces fight first for information superiority also raises questions about tradeoffs between global ISR capabilities and force structure that provides strike capability. If there is greater assurance of hitting a target because of more accurate and timely intelligence, fewer shooters are needed. A more specific tradeoff can be considered between global and theater ISR capabilities. Some prefer space-based ISR systems that can survey the entire globe in persistent fashion, while others argue that deployable, air-breathing theater ISR capabilities are better able to surge when demand is highest.

With respect to coalition operations, the greatest efficiencies may be possible from investments in command and control capabilities that permit U.S. forces to share such exquisite intelligence. Such investments might make allied forces much more capable and cost less than many other politically difficult and operationally less important interoperability initiatives such as common standards for logistics and transportation of military forces. Yet sharing command and control, and especially intelligence, is a security-sensitive and technically challenging enterprise. Usefully integrating the numerous sources of information available to the United States alone is a huge undertaking. Figuring out how to integrate allied intelligence and data sources and to share them through a multilevel security process that allows only partial access of information to different parties is a stupendously difficult challenge, but one with significant payoff.

Tactical capability trades must be considered as well. For example, some believe that mobility may be the best defense against area-denial weapons such as chemical agents that can be used to attack airbases and seaports. Rather than invest large amounts of resources in static chemical and biological defenses to protect key nodes like air and sea bases, more resources should be invested in long-range bombers, sea basing, and other global strike capabilities that are not so vulnerable to WMD. Similarly, since the easiest way to deliver weapons of mass destruction over significant distances is to use aircraft or missiles, many argue for greater investments in a combination of persistent theater ISR, hypersonic strike vehicles, and more robust theater air and missile defenses. These force capabilities, they argue, are more important perhaps than maintaining the size of the current tactical fighter forces, an area in which the United States currently holds a comfortable advantage.

Transformation's difficult trades. The range and complexity of the choices highlighted by the emergence of global force capabilities underscore the importance of institutionalizing a capabilities-based approach to defense decisionmaking. Just as defense planners must now take into account a far greater variability in threat, so must they also consider a more diverse range of capability options. Identifying areas to reduce and accept risk in a deliberate manner, supported by the best possible analysis, is a major challenge to senior decisionmakers.

Changes have already been made to facilitate the move to a capabilities-based approach. For example, in May 2003, DOD adopted a 2-year planning cycle so that it could use the off-year to focus on key defense planning issues, fiscal execution, and program performance. The Defense Department also has adopted an enhanced planning process that furthers the institutionalization of capabilities-based planning.[56]

The specific studies and trades considered by the department are classified,[57] but the process itself is described as being dependent upon the development of joint operating concepts, risk metrics, better models and simulations, and supporting databases. However, unless the process takes an integrated look at strategic as well as operational and tactical level choices, it is likely to produce an overly narrow set of options uninformed by their broader strategic implications.

CONCLUSION

Transformation of the U.S. defense establishment accelerated with the 2001 Quadrennial Defense Review and the strong backing of both the President and Secretary of Defense. Senior leaders remain committed to transformation, a commitment that is rooted in agreed-upon strategy considerations such as the need to prepare for a more diverse and uncertain set of security threats. However, the administration's emphasis on transformation changed somewhat in the 2006 Quadrennial Defense Review. The 2006 QDR put more emphasis on improving military capabilities through unity of effort—working more effectively with international and intragovernmental partners— than through exploitation of information-age technologies to meet the operational challenges identified in the 2001 QDR.

The change in emphasis no doubt reflects in part the demands of the ongoing war on terror and many global and regional security problems where the need to effectively collaborate with allies and to integrate all elements of national power is more critical to success than new technologies. The tension between successfully prosecuting the war on terror and preparing for future information-age threats will grow if the former absorbs increasing amounts of senior leader attention and near-term funding. There is always a tension between current operational costs and longer-term investments. Since the stakes are so high in the war on terror, if forced to choose between successful current operations and transformation investments, the former would be given the nod. For the time being, the Pentagon maintains it will not sacrifice success in current operations to safeguard the likelihood of successful transformation.

Certainly, the most difficult strategic tradeoffs can be avoided as long as the President and Congress are willing to support increased levels of Pentagon spending to fund current operations in the war on terror. Some believe this helps transformation, as expensive transformation capabilities can be initiated and developed to the point where they can compete with established and well-understood, albeit decidedly less revolutionary, capabilities. Other transformation theorists believe the infusion of resources from the war on terror perversely handicaps transformation. They argue that critical resource shortages are a necessary stimulus for transformation, and that as long as hard choices can be avoided, the Pentagon will default to lower-risk and less revolutionary options. Both views seem to capture some truth now. The Pentagon invested heavily in transformational starts without abandoning much near-term capability. The 2006 QDR did not substantially alter this pattern. Senior leaders managed to maintain current capabilities without sacrificing their transformation programs. They did so by cutting the size of air and naval forces while resisting pressure to increase ground forces in response to the demands of ongoing operations in Iraq and Afghanistan.

How the Pentagon will adjudicate risk when the tradeoffs between transformation, mere modernization, and current operations are more stark remains uncertain.

Other challenges to transformation are clearer. One challenge is conceptual clarity. Uncertainty is not a principle that can form the basis for defense planning. It is awkward to insist simultaneously, as the Pentagon has done, on the need to assume surprise as a condition of the future security environment and the need to invest heavily in global intelligence to reduce the chance of surprise. It is possible to argue for the flexibility to respond well to surprise while trying to reduce its likelihood, but there is a tension between the two. Why invest billions in global intelligence if the result is invariably surprise? Ultimately, limited resources must go to one area or another based on an assessment of where they do the most good. It is essential to make reasoned judgments about the future security environment and how to respond to the most critical anticipated problems.

The challenge for defense planners now is to cope with an increasingly diverse set of threats and the options for dealing with them. Sharply defining the essential elements of the security problems embodied by the JOCs would be helpful for illuminating choices and increasing the likelihood that joint operating concepts will fulfill their role as engines of transformation. Improving JOCs would also help accelerate the development of capabilities-based planning, which in turn is necessary to properly evaluate options for global force management, design, and posture. The need to assess and manage risk in light of far greater threat and capability variability is the raison d'être of capabilities-based planning. The significance of increased variability is that it heightens the complexity of defense planning and analysis. Complexity can be managed only by holding firm to several large, foundational ideas about what the future will demand (that is, relying on a vision of what circumstances require). Yet as already argued, even within the framework of a coherent vision, senior decisionmakers cannot make tough decisions about defense programs without supporting concepts, organizations, and new modes of analysis; at least, they cannot do so very well, neither substantively nor politically.

How one goes about transforming what is undisputedly already the world's greatest military power is bound to be highly contentious. It is critically important to have a transparent and well-understood process that generates analysis and evidence about where it is best to take and minimize risk while implementing transformation.[58] In this regard, there is a clear need to tighten up and accelerate joint operating concept development and to better institutionalize the other key elements of a capabilities-based approach into a new planning and resource allocation system. Such a system will be critically needed to support the difficult choices inherent in all transformation decisions, but especially for choosing between alternative force postures and designs under the aegis of global force planning, which puts established defense programs at risk and affects congressional constituencies across the United States, as well as numerous allied and friendly countries. As the 2006 QDR recognized, fully implementing a capabilities-based approach to planning and resource allocation will require more institutional reform than the Pentagon has been able to muster to date.[59]

Chapter Nine

Securing America's Future: Progress and Perils

STEPHEN J. FLANAGAN

B y any measure, the first years of the 21st century have been a tumultuous period for America—one dominated by the threat of terrorism, the wars in Afghanistan and Iraq, growing confrontations with known or suspected proliferators, and episodic explosions of mass violence in chronically unstable regions. The seven strategic challenges examined in this volume will test the skill, tenacity, and imagination of the Bush administration's successors and America's allies and partners in the coming decade and beyond. This chapter reviews the contributors' assessments and recommendations on policy and strategy. There are other global problems, including energy scarcity, pandemic disease, and climate change, that will also have an impact on American security. However, the seven challenges addressed here represent America's security and defense priorities. How effectively they are managed and resolved will influence whether future generations look back upon this era as a dangerous passage leading toward an eventually more peaceful global order or as a pathway spiraling downward into an ever more fragmented, violent world.

GLOBAL COUNTERINSURGENCY AGAINST TERRORISM

America's struggle against terrorism remains mired in controversy. Clearly, its most tangible achievement was the disruption of and damage to the al Qaeda leadership following the ouster of the Taliban regime in Afghanistan in late 2001. Equally important has been the creation of a de facto international counterterrorist coalition operating in the law enforcement, financial tracking, and military spheres. The U.S. Government has developed a national strategy for combating terrorism, along with plans and new intelligence and other organizations to implement it. National security components have improved their cooperation with law enforcement agencies. New civilian and military organizations for homeland security have been established, and they have developed a range of measures to prevent or respond to another attack.

Nevertheless, U.S. strategy for combating terrorism faces a number of major obstacles. The groundswell of global sympathy that the United States enjoyed in the immediate aftermath of the 9/11 attacks has largely dissipated, particularly since the invasion of Iraq and the ensuing insurgency. Many foreign governments have become disaffected with the U.S. approach to the struggle and are reticent to cooperate openly with Washington. Al Qaeda has proven resilient and transformed into a dispersed movement of affiliated *salafi* jihadist groups. A July 2007 National Intelligence Estimate on the terrorist threat to the United States acknowledged that the organization has managed to preserve or regenerate some of the key capabilities required to attack the U.S. homeland. Iraq has emerged as an epicenter for training and operations and a *cause célèbre* for radical extremists more generally. Combating this transnational insurgency will require close cooperation with foreign governments and an understanding of the nature of the appeal that the violent, radical Islamist movement seems to hold for disaffected segments of the Muslim community.

The struggle against terrorism will be prolonged and requires a delicate balance between efforts to disrupt and defeat terrorist networks and measures to counter their ideological appeal. An effective strategy must prevent terrorists from acting and at the same time break the connective tissues between the movement and the populations from which they draw strength. Considering the immense destructive power in the hands of modern terrorists, those combating them are compelled to seize the offensive by discovering, disrupting, and destroying terrorist cells before they can strike. However, the campaign must also discredit the jihadist theory that the current international order, dominated by the United States, explains the ills facing their target audience. Given that the conflict is about legitimacy, the established order can prevail only if it can convince uncommitted community members that it is prosecuting the struggle with legitimate means. Western strategic communications across cultural boundaries will have little effect in the battle of ideas unless authentic voices within Muslim communities offering compelling alternatives to jihadist ideology can be discreetly supported.

The strategic concept outlined in chapter two calls for synergy between actions designed to eradicate jihadist terrorists and their structures and those designed to isolate jihadists from the wider Muslim population. It calls for waging a number of tailored local counterinsurgencies in parallel as elements of a grand transnational counterinsurgency. Early action in a number of seemingly obscure places, long before violence erupts, will enhance the chances of success. The use of force should focus on eradicating specific terrorist assets or capabilities that pose a clear and present danger and should be led by host country forces if at all possible. To mitigate criticism of such operations, grassroots efforts to build global revulsion to terrorist methods should be bolstered.

With prudent defensive measures, regenerated international support, and effective management of shifting coalitions, it is possible to prevent terrorists from doing catastrophic harm to U.S. citizens and interests and from raising the temperature of intercultural confrontation to the boiling point. By strengthening control over undergoverned territories, helping other countries correct the legitimacy deficits under which their governments labor, lowering the ambient level of violence by working to resolve regional conflicts, and seizing the initiative to support better solutions to tangible grievances than those offered by the jihadists, U.S. strategy can make progress and ultimately eliminate the conditions that breed future jihadists.

COMBATING WMD THREATS

The proliferation of weapons of mass destruction (WMD)—particularly the specter of these weapons falling into the hands of terrorists—may well be America's gravest strategic challenge in the years ahead. In the post-9/11 context, the Bush administration, wary of "a perfect storm" of rogue regimes, terrorism, and WMD, has employed a muscular approach to eliminate the conditions before the storm fully matures. The record has been decidedly mixed.

Regime change and the shattering of state institutions in Iraq removed a WMD program that was actually moribund and whose reconstitution potential was vastly overestimated. The experience has made most U.S. and world leaders reluctant to contemplate preventive use of force against emerging WMD threats and has set a high standard for the intelligence required to gain support for preemptive use of force even against imminent threats. Iraq also demonstrated that the U.S. Armed Forces were ill equipped to deal with the complex missions of disabling and eliminating WMD, and progress has been slow in correcting these deficiencies. The U.S. Strategic Command now has responsibility for the mission, a standing joint task force will be created, and the Intelligence Community is implementing many of the reforms advocated by the 9/11 Commission. However, the U.S. capacity for detecting and removing a nation-state's WMD capability is little better than it was before 9/11, and countering the terrorist use of WMD requires further refinements in unconventional strategy and operations.

Libya's 2003 decision to foreswear nuclear weapons came as a consequence of years of economic sanctions, the impact of the Iraq example, and the discovery of the scope of their clandestine enrichment program. But the fact that Libya was much further along in fuel cycle development than previously suspected was also a wake-up call to the Intelligence Community. At the same time, the questionable safety and security of nuclear material in the former Soviet Union and the potential for instability in other countries that possess WMD remain grave concerns. The Nunn-Lugar Cooperative Threat Reduction (CTR) program has had some notable success, but up to two-thirds of Russia's weapons-grade material remains inadequately secured.

Iran and North Korea have pursued their nuclear development in order to gain a deterrent, and international negotiations to slow both programs have yielded few concrete results. The unwillingness or inability of the International Atomic Energy Agency, the United Nations (UN), and the world community to hold North Korea and Iran accountable for their Nuclear Non-Proliferation Treaty (NPT) obligations has diminished the treaty's utility. President Bush advanced proposals in 2004 to close loopholes in the NPT and other nonproliferation regimes, including tighter restrictions on export of sensitive technologies and expanding the G–8 Global Partnership to eliminate and secure sensitive materials. While progress on export controls has been limited, the Proliferation Security Initiative (PSI) has gained support as an effective multilateral instrument for preventing the transfer of critical WMD components between states.

Given the shortcomings of diplomacy and the nonproliferation regime, the Bush administration has not ruled out the use of force. However, given the demands of current counterinsurgency and stability operations in Iraq and Afghanistan, international opposition, and the retaliatory options that might be available to Tehran and Pyongyang, U.S. military action on any scale carries substantial risks. Limited missile or airstrikes against key WMD facilities are unlikely to have much impact, given that both countries have taken steps to disperse, hide, and harden these facilities, and attacks on leadership sites bring the risk of wider conflict and—in the Iranian case, at least—help the current regime to rally much-needed public support.

Meeting the WMD proliferation challenge requires a comprehensive strategy to address both the demand and supply problems to include strengthening of the nonproliferation regime, diplomatic engagement, and the threat of force. Given that these efforts could fail, it is essential to further refine the Bush administration's concept of tailored deterrence. In facing a nuclear North Korea or Iran, the United States will also have to pursue a tailored reassurance strategy to ensure that key allies and partners do not feel the need to develop their own deterrent. Efforts to strengthen and expand the CTR program beyond the former Soviet space, to include ensuring that participating countries fulfill their financial pledges, should be continued.

Given the potential for instability in a number of states with WMD programs, the international community needs to develop plans to quickly find and secure materials or weapons stockpiles to prevent them from falling into the hands of terrorists or nonstate proliferators. Further emphasis is needed on denying adversaries access to fissile materials and weapons in the first place. Extending the PSI model to corporate enterprises, financiers, and scientists could help prevent nonstate actors from obtaining critical technologies.

PROTECTING THE AMERICAN HOMELAND

There have been significant improvements since 2001 in U.S. preparedness to thwart catastrophic attacks on the homeland and address the consequences of natural or man-made megadisasters. The single most important advance has been the deepening understanding of terrorist threats. The National Counterterrorist Center is fusing information about international terrorist activities from many Federal agencies into integrated databases, which the Federal Bureau of Investigation combines with information on U.S. persons to create an integrated terrorist watch list. Officials have begun to evaluate more rigorously the actual vulnerabilities and preparations for mitigation and recovery. Many states have established command centers to integrate local, state, Federal, and private resources available in a crisis. Vulnerabilities in U.S. civil aviation systems have been reduced, making it more difficult for terrorists to hijack another aircraft. Federal stocks of smallpox vaccine stocks have grown to the point where nationwide coverage is now attainable. The lessons of Hurricane Katrina have led to important reforms in disaster preparedness. The Pentagon has given expanded authority to U.S. Northern Command to stage forces and equipment prior to the onset of a catastrophic disaster and launched a $1.5 billion initiative to improve medical countermeasures against genetically engineered biohazards, as well as new programs for improved interagency communications.

However, remedying a number of glaring shortfalls will require even better integration of the efforts of civilian authorities, the military, the private sector, and individual citizens. America's public health infrastructure remains woefully unprepared to deal with a major biomedical emergency. While preparedness activities have been spurred on by the administration's May 2006 *Implementation Plan for the National Strategy for Pandemic Influenza*, the pace of progress remains modest in relation to the threat. The U.S. public health system is not yet capable of executing a nationwide crash immunization program and still lacks a fully effective nationwide surveillance system to provide early warning that an attack has occurred. Given the increasing probability of genetically modified biological agents, the current system of developing and producing vaccines remains entirely inadequate.

The consolidation of 22 agencies into the Department of Homeland Security (DHS) was a major step toward integrating U.S. security. However, coordination among Federal, state, and local crisis response agencies remains problematic. Planning is still conducted by vertically stovepiped agencies that hamper integration and agility. State and local officials still wrestle with an inadequate appreciation of what Federal authorities can provide and with national security regulations that limit the number in their ranks who have access to intelligence and military information. On the military side, there is still strong reluctance to build a dedicated operational capability for catastrophic response, and no Department of Defense (DOD) field components have as their primary mission the task of aiding civil authorities. While DOD has created an Assistant Secretary of Defense for Homeland Defense, the U.S. Northern Command, a Joint Task Force Civil Support, two Response Task Forces (East and West), and the Guardian Brigade to command the defense of America, it has not actually created any new units specifically trained, equipped, and tasked to provide support to civil authorities in a crisis since the creation of the Chemical-Biological Incident Response Force in 1996.

The United States must address a number of challenges if it is to sustain momentum on homeland security. The most difficult long-term problems are structural. The legislation establishing the Department of Homeland Security did not include incentives to develop genuine interagency operations. Further steps should be taken to improve domestic response and coordination, starting with those agencies now located inside DHS and expanding to other all Federal agencies involved in preventing and responding to catastrophic events. There is also a need to improve crisis communication, planning, and coordination through regular training and exercises among all levels of government and with the American public to clarify the division of responsibility for security, response, and recovery. To deal with the biological threat, effective epidemiological monitoring should be developed nationwide by investing in state and local public health offices.

The international dimension of U.S. homeland security architecture could also be strengthened. A fresh look should be given to various ways of bolstering defensive barriers along the most likely geographic approaches to the American homeland. In May 2006, the United States and Canada agreed, in connection with indefinite renewal of their bilateral air defense cooperation under the North American Aerospace Defense Command (NORAD) agreement, to initiate integrated surveillance of the continent's maritime approaches and internal waterways to improve warning of terrorist and other threats. Across the Atlantic, effective security and transportation cooperation with European countries can be improved through closer U.S. cooperation with European governments and the European Union (EU) and by exploring the North Atlantic Treaty Organization's (NATO's) role to support civil authorities in areas where it has unique capabilities.

Looking south, the picture is more complex. The United States has many neighbors spread across a vast area that is prone to weak governance, rising crime, permeable borders, and the corrupting effects of chronic trafficking and associated transnational problems. Moreover, the quality of bilateral cooperation between these countries and the United States varies greatly. While the United States remains focused on terrorism, Central America and the Caribbean governments are most concerned with public order and criminal activities. However, these problems can be mitigated in complementary ways. Given its size and proximity to U.S. borders, Mexico's role will be pivotal. Instead of trying to integrate Mexico into a U.S-centric scheme— which will simply fuel Mexican neuralgia over subordination to the United States— Washington should find ways to encourage Mexico's leadership in the development of a Caribbean basin initiative on security and disaster response, based in and led by Mexico and staffed by military, police, and intelligence officers from participating countries. Once established and strengthened, this system could collaborate with NORAD as an equal command, providing a southern hub for international sharing and coordinated action.

Given the evolving threat environment, homeland security enhancements should rank at the very top of the priority lists of all levels of government in the United States over the next decade. Yet the national mood tends to vacillate between periods of casual distraction and bouts of heightened, sometimes panicky, vigilance. Absent any new political pressures for a major expansion of Federal authority, the only real public policy option available is to remedy shortfalls, with a view to making the current cumbersome system more robust. Such a strategy could well prove effective, provided the result is more genuine two-way communication between Washington and the states, based on a clearer mutual understanding of the kinds of circumstances that could trigger a massive Federal response.

DEFUSING CONFLICTS IN UNSTABLE REGIONS

The global nature of the contemporary security environment provides a compelling rationale for more concerted efforts at mastering another strategic challenge: building greater stability in the world's most chronically insecure regions. Along Latin America's Andean ridge, throughout much of sub-Saharan Africa, and across a vast arc from the Maghreb to Southeast Asia, the problems of weak governance, civil unrest, and episodic violence are all too common. These regions no longer fit the Cold War's stereotypes of being peripheral or backward. Amidst widespread poverty, one finds pockets of affluence and economic vibrancy. The bulk of the world's energy reserves are found in these regions; vital routes of global commerce run through them. Yet the volatility permeating parts of these areas feeds conditions in which insurgency and extremist ideologies can thrive. Regional conflicts often trigger massive human displacement; they are a boon to illegal trafficking; they can be a magnet for inflows of arms and, in some instances, mass destruction technologies. They are also incubators of disease pandemics, and in extreme cases, venues for genocidal violence, as witnessed in Rwanda more than a decade ago and, more recently, in Sudan's Darfur region.

As chapter five argues, the risks posed by regional volatility confound easy assessment. While the explosive potential of legacy conflicts (for example, the Taiwan Strait) cannot be discounted, the likelihood that a regional crisis would trigger a 1914-like confrontation among the great powers is much less than in previous eras. The aggregate number of conflicts and their direct human toll also appear to have declined. Still, there can be little room for complacency. Threatening scenarios are legion: aggression by dictatorial regimes against neighbors, preemptive strikes by would-be victims, escalation between nuclear-armed rivals, the collapse of a major energy supplier, and the spread of ethnosectarian conflict across permeable frontiers engulfing whole regions. Some of these scenarios are already etched into recent history; others remain hypothetical but very plausible. All of them amplify pressures upon the United States to take an activist posture in quelling regional instability.

"Exporting stability" is commendable as a policy goal but is extraordinarily difficult to achieve. The mix of essential tools—intelligence, diplomacy, military capacity, as well as humanitarian and developmental assistance—is not all that hard to identify. The real challenge lies in figuring out how to utilize these various instruments within the distinctive politics and culture of an individual region. Typically, strategies for stabilization will aim either to *contain* a conflict by denying outside support to combatant groups, to *engage* warring factions diplomatically with a mix of inducements or pressures, or to *compel* a desired outcome, most often through the direct or indirect uses of force. Compellent action via armed intervention is clearly the most risky; and in modern times, American attitudes toward the endeavor have been deeply ambivalent. U.S. experiences in Vietnam and Somalia have reinforced a strong preference for applying force decisively against clearly defined enemies rather than waging lengthy counterinsurgency or nation-building campaigns. But in warfare, as the saying goes, the enemy gets a vote too.

Afghanistan and Iraq: The Legacies

Each in its own way, the U.S.-led operations in Afghanistan (*Enduring Freedom*) and Iraq (*Iraqi Freedom*) have come to symbolize cautionary tales about the challenges of mounting effective stabilization in the wake of military intervention. As venues for external intervention, these two countries could not have been more different. Afghanistan was war-ravaged, desperately poor, illiterate, and largely rural. By contrast, Iraqi society, though despotically ruled, was more quiescent, highly urbanized, literate, and living amidst an extensive, albeit decaying, infrastructure. Geostrategically, Afghanistan is a remote hinterland while Iraq, endowed by oil wealth, occupies vital crossroads between the Arab and Persian worlds.

In light of these differences, it is ironic that Afghanistan turned out to be the more amenable venue for postconflict stabilization. Most Afghans had grown weary from years of fighting. Initial stabilization efforts were also aided by Pakistan's quick about-face, abandoning the Taliban; by the emergence of Hamid Karzai as a unifying leader from within the very Pashtun community that had produced the Taliban; and by the fortuitous fact that the capital city, Kabul, did not become a contested zone. In Iraq, by contrast, the optimism that surrounded preparations for the postinvasion phase of *Iraqi Freedom* quickly evaporated. The toppling of Saddam unleashed a number of unresolved ethnosectarian tensions. Any hope of building democratic order in Iraq has necessarily entailed shifting the reins of power from a long-privileged minority to a long-repressed majority, in effect convincing the winners to be generous in their victory and the losers to be gracious in accepting their minority status in a new dispensation. In Afghanistan, this kind of far-reaching adjustment was not required.

Plagued by crippling factionalism and extremist violence, Iraq's ability to hold together as a unified state looks problematic; it remains to be seen how the positive effects of the U.S. military "surge" into greater Baghdad during 2007 can be sustained. Afghanistan also faces an uphill struggle, albeit of lesser magnitude, with a resurgent Taliban operating in the southeast of the country and along mountainous Afghan-Pakistan border areas. In both cases, several lessons are clear:

- Postconflict stabilization activities must be accorded a priority commensurate with the task at hand, in much the same fashion that the United States considers the options and capacities of its foe when preparing to fight and win battles.
- Planning for the postwar phase must be based upon a rigorous assessment of alternative scenarios, on realistic assumptions regarding how "ripe" a country is for outside stabilization assistance, and, above all, a preparedness to commit the necessary resources to the mission. In hindsight, it is clear that Washington's ambitious "tear down and rebuild" strategy for creating post-Saddam governance in Iraq was incompatible with the security prong of the U.S. Iraq strategy, which foresaw a modest and quickly diminishing U.S. postwar military presence, aimed mainly at building the security capacity of local Iraqi forces.
- Persuading regional neighbors to see a stabilization campaign as being in their interests is a key to success. If neighbors have reason to be hostile, or if—as in Afghanistan's case—spoilers are able to gain cross-border sanctuaries, the process can founder until those backing the stabilization are able to drive wedges between spoilers and their external patrons.
- Multinational coalitions can be indispensable in terms of establishing an operation's legitimacy and sharing burdens, though at some cost to operational

flexibility. In nonpermissive environments, however, coalitions function best when their mission is to secure rear areas. Casting them as substitutes for U.S. military power in contested areas—as in southeastern Afghanistan—is bound to be a gamble.

Recalibrating the Paradigm

Managing America's conflicting impulses on regional stabilization poses a huge challenge for future U.S. policymakers. A "stay the course" approach clearly is under siege. Events unfolding in Iraq and Afghanistan are fueling a long-held view in American politics that nation building is a quagmire to be avoided at all costs. Moreover, U.S. allies and partners are stretched thin and losing their enthusiasm for the missions. Yet a shift away from active involvement in regional conflicts provokes a strong counterargument: the United States ignores these conflicts at its peril because chronic instability provides fertile ground for extremists and terrorists, endangers key partners, drives demand for WMD proliferation, and abdicates America's moral leadership wherever violence turns genocidal. Moreover, failing to help build local governance is simply imprudent since nothing will bar a recurrence of whatever problems provoked the intervention in the first place.

Ultimately, prevailing threat conditions or humanitarian concerns in the foreseeable future will generate pressures for the United States to be involved in large-scale stabilization activities. What is needed is a new strategic framework for such activities that offers better balance between direct intervention and indirect action, between U.S.-led operations and regionally led actions where the United States plays an enabling role, between a heavy military footprint and a lighter, more diverse, and sustained presence, and between the direct provision of essential stabilization assistance to affected populations and indigenous capacity building. U.S. regional stabilization activities should be guided by three overarching goals:

- Mitigating "fault-line" conflicts. By decoupling ethnosectarian conflicts from each other and from the global struggle that militant Islamists seek to advance, stabilization activity can help to shrink the recruiting pool for violent extremists and reduce their geographical room for maneuver. Done right, conflict stabilization contributes very directly to the larger counterterror campaign.
- Strengthening "anchors," plugging "gaps." By assisting large, modernizing states whose collapse would trigger massive human displacement, disruptions to global commerce, and/or the spread of militant nonstate actors, the United States can work collaboratively in a capacity-building mode on ways to help prevent the lateral spread of conflict.
- Building humanitarian protection. By helping to mobilize international capacity aimed at thwarting acts of genocide, the United States can act constructively on its humanitarian concerns in situations where national security interests are not directly implicated.

Achieving these goals will not be easy. America's military, diplomatic, intelligence, and foreign aid communities have viewed their primary missions in ways that give stabilization activities short shrift. Reformers at the Departments of State and Defense have begun to build a foundation for innovation, but well-intentioned policy provides no guarantee of the resources and high-level attention that effective implementation requires. Getting the U.S. house in order requires progress on the following priorities:

- Improving situational awareness. More rigorous conflict assessments, in line with those being piloted by the State Department, could serve as an important baseline for progress on generating balanced information collection requirements and analytic production.
- Building planning expertise. Improved planning across agencies requires a triumvirate of regional experts who know an affected area's sociopolitical environment, program managers who understand how key U.S. capabilities are resourced and utilized, and strategists who can bridge both worlds and offset the parochialism of the other two communities.
- Meeting doctrinal, equipment, and force sizing needs. The U.S. Army–Marine Corps collaboration on developing counterinsurgency doctrine provides a valuable assist to education and training on stabilization. However, equipment shortfalls—for example, for armored vehicles, nonlethal weapons, and air-defense countermeasures—need to be remedied; and how best to prepare, field, and protect civilian specialists in nonpermissive environments remains a difficult and unresolved question.
- Assisting governance-building activity. Both top-down aid, at the level of national ministries, and bottom-up assistance, where government is a provider of community services, are vital to ensuring that an enabled indigenous security sector does not overwhelm the government it is meant to support.
- Civil-military training. In any mission that requires personnel rotations, early familiarity with the mission's civil-military division of labor is essential if newly arriving personnel are to begin contributing more than they are absorbing. The highest priority for joint training would be for personnel to be embedded in ministries and deployed in civil-military field settings.
- Forging closer links to international and regional organizations. Washington has a compelling interest in working more closely with allies and partners to strengthen international capacity to meet an ongoing surge in expanding mission commitments, whether in Darfur, Lebanon, or other venues.
- Strengthening lessons learned. Greater priority should be accorded to innovating new methods for distilling experiences of previous as well as ongoing operations. U.S. Joint Forces Command is playing a useful role as a locus for integrated efforts, but the learning process overall is only as strong as its constituent parts, beginning with collection and ending up with acceptance, absorption, and dissemination by commanders and policymaking levels of government.

These priorities represent a starting point for overcoming the formidable institutional, political, and other barriers that stand in the way of major enhancements in U.S. stabilization capabilities. A posture of selective engagement built around the three strategic goals noted above may have the best chance of generating a broad consensus within an increasingly restive, ambivalent American body politic.

MANAGING GREAT POWER RELATIONS

Past ideological differences that constrained U.S. relations with China, Russia, and India have given way to a new pragmatism. How well the United States manages its relations with each country to build constructive relations and avoid the reemergence of rivalries and conflict will be a major test for American leadership in the decade ahead. Leaders of all three powers confront major domestic socioeconomic and governance challenges that can be best addressed in the context of a peaceful external environment. A major internal crisis in any one of them would be fraught with global consequences. While important strides have been made over the past decade in great power cooperation to combat terrorism, thwart WMD proliferation, and stabilize certain regional conflicts, differences with Washington over the proper handling of some of these issues, as well as divergent national interests on these and other matters (particularly promoting democratic governance as an instrument of foreign policy), will likely limit the scope for effective joint action.

This leads to some uncertainty about the role of these three powers in the international system over the next decade and how to best influence their evolution in positive directions. Working effectively with these powers will not be easy for U.S. leaders. These relationships lack a history of regular consultations, patterns of cooperation, and longstanding personal relationships. All three governments are wary of U.S. dominance in the international system, have criticized the U.S. exercise of its military power, and have concerns about the U.S. military presence in neighboring regions. China and Russia remain suspicious that adapted U.S. alliances and security partnerships will be used to the detriment of their security interests.

China: Engagement, Dissuasion, Deterrence

China presents the biggest challenges to and opportunities for U.S. policy. China has become increasingly important to a wide range of U.S. interests, while the United States is a key market for China and is uniquely positioned to facilitate or obstruct Chinese strategic interests. Given its economic power, geopolitical ambitions, and growing military capabilities, China is emerging as the only potential peer competitor to the United States in Eurasia and the world. U.S. strategy under the past three administrations has combined support for Chinese integration into global institutions as a way to influence Chinese internal and external behavior in positive directions with actions to maintain U.S. military capabilities and alliances as a hedge against the possibility of an aggressive China. Despite occasional crises, Sino-U.S. relations have seen remarkable continuity and stability during that period. Cooperation on shared regional and global interests has grown since 2001 in the wake of China's support for the war on terrorism and acquiescence to a number of other U.S. policies. However, several underlying tensions and potential conflicts are likely to strain relations in the coming decade:

- Chinese leaders are struggling to cope with vexing domestic social and governance problems. A political crackdown by Chinese leaders to maintain internal stability or eliminate challenges to Communist Party rule would raise the profile of human rights and civil liberties concerns in U.S. China policy. Chinese efforts to dampen a crisis through accelerated economic growth via increased exports would likely aggravate bilateral economic and political differences.
- Taiwan's growing sense of a separate identity, Beijing's robust military modernization efforts that are improving its ability to use force in a crisis, and heightened nationalism on both sides of the strait are eroding the stability of the cross-strait status quo. While China and Taiwan are likely to rely primarily on negotiations to pursue their long-term objectives, the possibility of a conflict and the growing U.S. role in cross-strait relations complicate the broader U.S.-China relationship.
- China's reluctance to discuss its nuclear force modernization plans and uncertainty about the ultimate size and effectiveness of U.S. missile defenses create a potential for misperception and the emergence of a strategic military competition. China's military modernization is moving faster than expected in the mid-1990s, which raises the stakes in a Taiwan confrontation and heightens concerns in Washington about Chinese ambitions. This negative dynamic might be tempered by greater transparency and an expanded dialogue on strategic forces issues.
- China's rapid economic growth, military restraint, and multifaceted engagement have increased its regional influence and allayed concerns in East Asia about its rise. This stance contrasts positively with perceived U.S. unilateralism and preoccupation with fighting terrorism. A broader U.S. foreign policy agenda with greater appeal to other countries and systematic employment of superior U.S. hard and soft power assets—for example, greater emphasis on economic development and on cooperation on nontraditional security issues of interest to Asian governments—would give the United States a stronger hand in this competition.
- China's sustained economic, technological, and military growth feeds concerns that it will eventually challenge the U.S. global position. These concerns are reinforced by the realpolitik worldview of Chinese leaders, the slow pace of political change in China, and growing nationalism, which could combine to trigger China's use of force with respect to Taiwan or a host of other unresolved maritime and territorial disputes.

Given these challenges and the range of U.S. interests at stake, the United States should pursue a nuanced hedging strategy of engagement, dissuasion, and deterrence to influence China's political evolution and long-term strategic choices in positive directions. This involves simultaneously cooperating with China to pursue common interests, engaging it to alter its internal and external behavior, and deterring it from unwanted military actions. Maintaining the balance between aggressively pursuing short-term U.S. economic and security interests and longer-term efforts to shape Chinese thinking about its global interests will be difficult. Leadership, vision, and patience will be necessary for the United States to take full advantage of the benefits that cooperation with China offers while successfully meeting the strategic challenges China poses to U.S. interests.

Russia: Balancing Cooperation and Competition

The U.S.-Russian relationship has fallen short of the partnership hoped for in the early 1990s as a consequence of a major shift in Russian domestic affairs, problematic external behavior, and efforts to counterbalance U.S. power. Limited cooperation in U.S.-Russia relations is now overshadowed by widespread U.S. disapproval of Russian domestic practices and mutual criticism of the other's behavior postures in the international arena. Russia, buoyed by high energy and commodity prices after a period of domestic turmoil and painful reforms in the 1990s, is seeking to capitalize on its newfound prosperity to attain a special place in the international system. A shadow of its Soviet strength with limited power projection capabilities, Moscow's military capabilities still dwarf those of its former Soviet neighbors, and its intelligence and security services remain active at home and abroad. Its newfound economic muscle, control of key transportation routes, and willingness to use energy trade for political coercion give it leverage in Eurasia. Russia's stature as a major nuclear power, permanent seat on the UN Security Council, and G–8 membership, coupled with its assertiveness, help it retain influence in the wider world. But the country's long-term economic and demographic picture remains quite bleak with a boom-bust cycle of development heavily dependent on external factors.

Russia's internal political trends will also complicate effective cooperation with the United States and Europe. Stability in Russian domestic politics during Vladimir Putin's administration has been accompanied by steady accumulation of authority in the hands of the federal government, a weakening of regional leaders and other political institutions, and the marginalization of civil society. However, this so-called vertical of power has failed to produce effective centralized governance and proven ineffective in dealing with various crises and social problems. Democracy is in retreat, but the country's openness to the outside world and widespread grassroots dissatisfaction with the government's performance suggest Russian society is changing. The Kremlin's concept of *sovereign democracy* signals that Russian leaders will resist external pressures for domestic political change and may resort to increasingly nationalist rhetoric for political mobilization. However, despite the Russian government's attempts at domestic consolidation, there remains considerable risk of domestic destabilization over the next decade that will render the country less governable.

Within this context, the United States faces three key challenges in dealing with Russia:

- U.S. interests will require Russian cooperation on various international issues—from Iran's nuclear ambitions to energy security. The United States will need to secure that cooperation while adhering to its fundamental principles and engaging Russian leaders and the general public in a candid dialogue about the importance of shared values for a true partnership. This dialogue may have to take place against the backdrop of further retreat from democracy in Russia or amid growing instability in parts of Russia. Reconciling U.S. interests with its principles in these circumstances will be a major challenge for U.S. foreign policy.
- Moscow's assertive behavior with respect to the former Soviet states could cause considerable damage to these countries and to U.S. interests in promoting their sovereignty and integration in the international arena. Russian fears of encirclement have spawned a broad political consensus favoring restoration of dominant influence over its periphery. However, Moscow's mixed record of involvement shows that it often lacks the capabilities or will to serve as a manager of regional security. Its assertiveness toward its former satellites has produced a backlash even among its closest allies. The challenge for the United States and Europe here is to achieve the right balance in relations with Moscow and its neighbors that would provide the latter much-needed support without unnecessarily antagonizing the former.
- While Russia continues to posture as a great power, its ability to implement ambitious international initiatives with respect to North Korea, Iran, and the Middle East has proven glaringly inadequate. The Putin era has had few diplomatic accomplishments, and Russia has no natural allies or friends. Its relations with the United States and Europe have grown strained; ties with China, while normalized on the surface, are increasingly wary; and partnerships with Japan and India remain elusive. The challenge here will be to secure Moscow's cooperation and give it a voice in major international fora, but without giving it the right of veto or forcing it into isolation and opposition to the international community.

U.S. policy toward Russia should take the long view and navigate carefully between two distinct postures: selective cooperation in areas deemed too important to be neglected, such as nuclear security, WMD proliferation, and terrorism; and neocontainment, which would place greater emphasis on the competition of ideas, geopolitical balancing, and even diplomatic isolation where U.S. and Russian interests diverge. U.S. efforts to vigorously contain or punish Russia would not only be of questionable effectiveness, but also could backfire and either harden the country's emerging anti-Western consensus or risk new destabilization.

India: Harmonizing Interests and Managing Expectations

The U.S.-Indian relationship is a work in progress. India's status as a relative newcomer to the club of major powers and the absence of geopolitical rivalries with the

United States make it the most likely of the three Eurasian great powers to become a full-fledged U.S. strategic partner. However, India's great power status cannot conceal the nation's poverty, uneven development, and growing pains. Whether and in what manner it will assume the global role that many futurists and policymakers see as inevitable based on a combination of demographic forces, developing military capabilities, economic expansion, and its political system remains unclear.

India is destined to be the world's most populous country by mid-century, but this demographic status also creates enormous political pressures to sustain economic development and domestic social cohesion. The Indian armed forces, the world's third largest, are professional, well trained, and provide both effective national defense and valuable contributions to international peacekeeping missions. However, the Indian military would require significant additional resources for modernization and power projection capabilities, improved interservice integration, and a shift from its territorial defense posture to support wider global interests that India and the United States have in common. The Indian economy has taken off in recent years, and India is expected to surpass the combined output of the European Union by 2035. However, the country's internal development has been uneven, and many economists believe India will have serious shortfalls unless it can overcome many structural problems and expand external trade and foreign investment. Within India's thriving multiparty, multiethnic, and multireligious democracy, there is a yearning for recognition as a major power, but no consensus on whether or how to apply the country's political, military, economic, or cultural power beyond the confines of South Asia. At the same time, Indians manifest a strong desire to preserve the country's unique identity and its independence from any international power bloc, and to balance rival powers rather than taking sides between them.

While there are substantial areas in which Indian and American interests converge— defeating terrorism, encouraging the spread of democracy and respect for human rights, and promoting prosperity—there are also areas of serious divergence, not the least of which involves relations with Pakistan. Even in cases where the two countries share common concerns, such as the growing presence and influence of China in Southeast Asia and the Indian Ocean, they do not have common assessments or strategies. There are also areas of direct competition, most notably as rival importers of hydrocarbon fuels.

- While the United States was willing to give symbolic recognition of India's great power status by accepting the reality of its possession of nuclear weapons and undertaking the U.S.-India Civil Nuclear Cooperation Initiative, it has thus far declined to go so far as to support India's top priority of attaining a permanent UN Security Council seat.
- On the military front, Indian leaders want access to U.S. military-related technology without restrictions or linkages of any kind. It remains to be seen how far Washington will be willing to go in advancing the nascent military and defense industrial cooperation.

- While India and the United States share many security interests in South Asia, countries in the region do not see Indian involvement as benign, which calls into question how effective India can be. The most pressing security problem confronting the United States in South Asia today—defeating the Pakistani and Afghan manifestations of the globalized jihadist insurgency—is one in which India can play only a marginal role, primarily due to enduring enmity in Indo-Pakistani relations. U.S. relations with India and Pakistan are inextricably intertwined and will continue to complicate the U.S.-Indian partnership.
- The Indian commitment to the United Nations as the primary if not the only source of international legitimacy is another potential cause of friction in the would-be strategic partnership. India has been and will remain reluctant to join coalitions of the willing to maintain global peace and stability.

All this counsels realistic expectations on both sides and avoidance of overtaxing the evolving U.S.-Indian strategic relationship. Whatever kind of power India becomes, the United States will benefit from positive relations. At the least, a strong India will preclude Chinese hegemony in Asia, but India is unlikely to be a deferential partner even on critical U.S. concerns outside South Asia. Forging a successful strategic partnership will require identifying where the two countries' interests converge, slowly building ties across a multitude of fronts, and developing mechanisms to manage differences in substance and style that that have previously strained relations.

Balancing U.S. Interests in Eurasia

Washington's efforts to forge more effective cooperation with China, Russia, and India will require careful balancing of diverse U.S. interests and principles. Given America's global reach and other asymmetries, each of these three countries has more at stake in promoting relations with the United States than in joining with each other to counterbalance American power. Russia and China are trying to limit U.S. engagement and democracy promotion activities in Eurasia, including through their wary cooperation with four Central Asian countries in the Shanghai Cooperation Organization (SCO). However, divergent interests among its members make it unlikely that the SCO will develop into an anti-U.S. alliance. The emergence, over time, of a stable Eurasia resting on three regional pillars and one global one would serve the interests of all four countries well.

ADAPTING ALLIANCES AND PARTNERSHIPS

A Global Web of Relations

To advance its interests in today's complex global security environment, the United States must continue to strengthen cooperation with allies and partners and expand and adapt these relationships to deal with new challenges. The 31 U.S. treaty allies, along with many close partners, form a capable core group of states that share a stake in maintaining global peace and stability. Despite differing policy approaches and a widening gap between U.S. and allied military capabilities, these countries can augment and complement U.S. actions in the advancement of mutual interests and help avoid military and political overextension. Moreover, allied and partner support and involvement grant greater legitimacy to U.S. actions, and sound alliance relations diminish the inclination of countries to counterbalance U.S. power. Effective consultations and security cooperation activities with allies and partners are essential to implementation of the U.S. global force realignment and long-term U.S. defense strategy. Better cross-regional integration of the activities of U.S. alliances and partnerships could create a global web of relationships for effective common action on key strategic challenges.

During its first term, the Bush administration's preference for shifting, ad hoc coalitions over alliances and regional security organizations strained relations with many longtime allies and partners who saw it as reflecting both a diminished U.S. commitment to existing security obligations and a propensity for unilateral action. During its second term, the Bush administration undertook essential steps to restore relations with European allies in the aftermath of disagreements over the Iraq war and to accelerate the process of adapting East Asian alliance relationships and building new partnerships around the world, with some noteworthy progress. However, much work remains to restore these relationships to their full potential.

Recalibrating the U.S.-European "Terms of Engagement"

NATO's transformation, begun in 1990, has continued since 2001. The Alliance has undertaken a range of new and challenging operations, streamlined its military command arrangements, developed a new Response Force for high-intensity expeditionary operations, absorbed seven new members, and broadened its dialogue and cooperation with partners in Eurasia and the greater Middle East. Still, NATO's future remains far from assured, as its members continue to differ on the nature of emerging threats, the role of force in international affairs, strategies for countering terrorism and WMD proliferation, burden-sharing with respect to operations in Afghanistan, NATO's global role, and relations with the European Union. These policy debates continue in the context of a widening gap between U.S. and European military capabilities, due to shrinking European defense budgets and operational constraints, political transitions in Europe, and doubts among European elites and publics about American leadership and values.

Transatlantic relations will continue to be concerned less with how Europe and America relate to one another, and more with how they cooperate in dealing with the rest of the world. To sustain the transatlantic relationship, the next administration faces three overarching challenges: to encourage a fragmented, often reluctant Europe to become as full a partner in managing global security affairs as it is in promoting development and demonstrate that the United States really welcomes such a partnership; to restore European confidence in American leadership post-Iraq; and to find the right institutional arrangements and division of labor, particularly bilaterally with the EU and between NATO and the EU, to advance many common interests.

Several specific steps seem warranted to adapt and recalibrate transatlantic security and defense cooperation:

- NATO's 1999 strategic concept needs to be updated to reflect the multifaceted, global nature of the security threats that Allies confront in the early 21st century, particularly terrorism, WMD proliferation, and stabilization of weak states, and a consensus needs to be reached on steps to address these new challenges. Allies should initiate efforts to prepare a new concept at the 2008 Bucharest Summit, while recognizing that the next U.S. administration will need some time to conduct a policy review and formulate its approach before completing work on a new concept.

- The Alliance should improve its planning and decisionmaking processes to include granting military authorities greater discretionary authority in preparing contingency plans, better integration of its military planning with the capabilities of various civilian actors (for example, the UN, EU, World Bank, and nongovernmental organizations) with whom NATO is working, and new political procedures to authorize military operations by a limited group of Allies with minimal operational oversight by countries not engaged.

- NATO and the EU need to improve their strategic dialogue and practical cooperation at all levels to help bring together their complementary talent, ideas, and resources to address major global security concerns. With growing EU involvement in security and defense matters, the United States also needs to maintain vigorous diplomatic engagement in Brussels and national capitals to ensure greater synergies and coherence regarding U.S. bilateral ties with EU member states and its ties with European institutions.

- Allied leaders have affirmed that NATO remains open to new members. An "open door" policy and active partnerships remain the best way for the alliance to promote positive reforms within and effective cooperation with neighboring nonmember governments. The Partnership for Peace should be transformed, adequately resourced, and better integrated with bilateral and subregional efforts to address new security challenges.

- NATO membership remains a divisive issue within Ukraine. However, continued allied support to Kyiv's defense, security sector, and other reforms, and active cooperation in the NATO-Ukraine Council can advance Ukraine's Euro-Atlantic integration and mutual security interests.

- Moscow continues to profess its openness to cooperation with NATO on common security concerns including counterterrorism, WMD proliferation, missile defense, and airspace management. Allies cannot ignore Russia's retreat from democracy but should remain willing to work with Moscow on such mutual security interests so long as it respects the sovereignty of its neighbors and other international commitments.

- NATO's decade-long dialogue with Mediterranean neighbors has borne few practical results, and it will take time to overcome unfamiliarity and suspicions among new partners in the broader Middle East. Nevertheless, NATO and the EU can build capacity in and limited cooperation with countries in the region through dialogue and training.

- Since 2001, NATO has undertaken operational military cooperation with Australia, New Zealand, Japan, and South Korea to counter terrorism and promote stability in Afghanistan and Iraq. NATO should develop mechanisms for routine political consultations with these and other capable democracies around the world; better integrate their armed forces into NATO-led operations where they elect to participate; and improve their interoperability with allied forces.

Balance in the Middle East

In the Middle East, U.S. security ties to Israel remain robust, but fragile partnerships with moderate Arab states have been strained by a number of policy differences, particularly about how to handle the ethnosectarian turmoil in Iraq. Cooperation with the Maghreb states on counterterrorism, maritime security, and counterproliferation has advanced in recent years as a result of a growing convergence of interests on these issues and shifting strategic assessments.

The future of U.S. partnerships in the Middle East will turn heavily on how successful Washington is in stabilizing Iraq and balancing its strong support of Israel's security with efforts to promote a durable resolution of the Israeli-Palestinian conflict. Washington should seek the help of moderate Arab governments in addressing both these challenges, while enhancing security assistance and cooperation with them in areas of common concern such as terrorism, security of energy flows, and offsetting the growth of Iranian power. Saudi Arabia and the other Gulf monarchies can be expected to provide quiet intelligence and law enforcement cooperation on countering violent extremist groups, but they will want to avoid appearing too closely aligned with the United States.

Any long-term U.S. military presence in the region must be reshaped to diminish the rage that it continues to engender in the Muslim world while still reassuring partners. The United States needs to maintain the capability to respond to major conventional and WMD threats to its interests, to support partners in disrupting certain terrorist threats, and to deter Iranian hegemony. These objectives could be achieved with a small permanent ground presence in the Gulf, together with ongoing naval operations and rotational deployments of air and ground forces to cooperative security locations for combined exercises and training with partners, and clear red lines about the U.S. responses to terrorism and other acts of aggression.

The Bush administration's efforts to promote democratic reforms in Iraq and the Middle East have met strong resistance. Yet many leaders and elites in the region appreciate that adapting their traditional societies and social structures to the realities of globalization is essential to long-term prosperity and stability. The United States should continue to support gradual political and social transformation that will allow these countries to become better integrated into the global system without triggering an even greater Islamist rage, violent regime change, or anti-American backlash.

South and Central Asia

U.S. security cooperation with the states of South and Central Asia has gained new importance, given the war in Afghanistan, the requirements of U.S. global military strategy, and Central Asia's contribution to world energy supplies. A new, multifaceted strategic partnership with India has been initiated, and Pakistan and Afghanistan have become partners in the struggle against terrorism.

While Pakistan has provided valuable assistance to the United States in combating terrorism, the partnership remains fragile. Islamabad's tenuous hold over its Federally Administered Tribal Areas has allowed the region to remain a safe haven for Taliban forces conducting operations in Afghanistan. This problem, along with Pakistan's enormous development challenges and Pervez Musharraf's vulnerability to domestic extremists and growing pressures to restore democracy, all suggest that the U.S.-Pakistan partnership will remain vulnerable to intermittent disruptions for some time.

U.S. political support to democracy and human rights in Central Asia will continue to complicate cooperation with the region's autocratic governments on countering terrorism and other transnational threats. However, long-term U.S. interests in regional stability will be best served by continued promotion of gradual economic and political liberalization that will enable integration of Central Asia into the global economy. Given their much bigger stake and influence in the region, U.S. security strategy will need to engage Russia and China while remaining firmly supportive of Central Asian sovereignty.

East Asia and the Pacific

Considerable progress has been achieved in adapting U.S. alliances in East Asia. Complex and difficult negotiations with Japan and the Republic of Korea (ROK) have resulted in agreement to transform the U.S. military posture in region, allowing Washington to meet the security challenges of the post-9/11 world while reinforcing defense commitments. Both Japan and the ROK have become more engaged in international security affairs; Japan, with deployments to the Indian Ocean, Iraq, and other parts of the Middle East, and the ROK with deployments to Iraq and Afghanistan. Similarly, Australia has supported the United States in Afghanistan and Iraq, while assuming greater responsibilities for stability in the South Pacific region.

Relations with other treaty allies (Thailand and the Philippines), as well as new partners in Southeast Asia (Singapore, Malaysia, Indonesia, and Vietnam), and Mongolia (relations) have advanced in recent years on the strength of growing cooperation in combating terrorism and other transnational threats, humanitarian relief, and peacekeeping cooperation.

The key strategic challenges for the United States and its allies in sustaining trans-Pacific security relationships will be to transform the alliances with Japan and South

Korea into fuller partnerships, rooted in shared interests and values and open to cooperation with other countries in addressing certain regional and global security concerns; to build consensus on dealing with China's rising influence and military capabilities; and to show how security ties with the United States provide a stable context for and complement multilateral regional arrangements. Sustaining these relationships as mature partnerships will require allies to maintain regular, high-level political dialogues, further transform their armed forces, and redouble efforts to sustain domestic support. Several specific challenges confronting U.S. alliances with Japan, South Korea, and Australia merit further discussion.

The U.S.-Japan Alliance

- The most immediate challenge in bilateral security relations involves implementation of the May 2006 agreement on realignment of the U.S. military presence in Japan, which will reduce some of the friction associated with that presence, enhance mutual security, and advance the transformation of Japan's Self-Defense Forces.
- Enhanced alliance cooperation on regional and global security problems will require further strengthening of Japan's national security institutions and legal authorities, military capabilities, and interoperability with U.S. forces.
- Cooperative development of ballistic missile defense technologies and concepts has become a critical element of bilateral security relations in light of North Korea's possession of nuclear weapons and ballistic missile delivery systems. This cooperation also provides a long-term hedge against modernization of China's missile forces. Integrating U.S. and Japanese capabilities to counter a range of possible attacks against either or both countries will require patient dialogue and careful planning.

The U.S.–ROK Alliance

- The U.S.–ROK Security Policy Initiative has produced agreement on a common vision of the alliance, but further effort on the part of both governments is required to broaden and deepen political support for a transformed alliance and move it forward. Reshaped as an equal partnership between two democracies committed to defending shared values and common interests, a mature alliance can advance many mutual Korean-American interests on the peninsula, stand against the emergence of an aggressive China, and effectively support international stability and security.
- South Korea's assumption of the leading role in the defense of the peninsula will require continuing improvements in ROK military capabilities as well as the development, by 2012, of new command structure to replace the present Combined Forces Command. The long-term U.S. posture in the ROK should

assure Seoul of an enduring defense commitment, fill critical gaps in ROK capabilities, allow for rapid augmentation to repulse any aggressor, and provide the United States with a reliable foothold to support global security operations.

- U.S. officials and the American media need to be sensitive to political and social change in South Korea, and U.S. public diplomacy needs to be more skillful in making the case for a transformed alliance, particularly with younger people in Korea. Contacts between the U.S. Congress and the ROK National Assembly are limited and should be expanded. The ROK government needs to be more outspoken in refuting irresponsible attacks against the United States in the South Korean media and public discourse and in explaining how the alliance serves mutual interests.

The U.S.-Australia Alliance

U.S.-Australia security cooperation rests on a solid political foundation and will remain deep and multifaceted for the foreseeable future. Australia's small but effective armed forces play a leading role in addressing security challenges in Southeast Asia and the South Pacific and provide valuable niche contributions to military operations around the world. Washington should avoid taking Australian support for U.S. policies, particularly vis-à-vis China in a Taiwan crisis, for granted. Enhancements of bilateral, trilateral (with Japan), and other multilateral (with NATO) consultations will help sustain the relationship during periods of political transition and foster common security policies.

Other Asian Alliances and Partnerships

Thailand remains a consistent supporter of the U.S. military presence in Southeast Asia, providing access to key facilities and prepositioning of supplies, and U.S. interoperability with Royal Thai Armed Forces has continued to grow. Counterterrorism cooperation has helped restore bilateral security ties with the Philippines, which will likely remain strong, given a shared assessment of the risks. However, Philippine nationalism will not support a large permanent U.S. military presence or major operations from its territory in the near future. At the same time, Manila's increasingly close relations with China have raised doubts about its willingness to support the United States in a crisis over Taiwan. New Zealand and the United States, though no longer treaty allies, remain close partners and cooperate on a number of regional and global security issues including peacekeeping and combating terrorism. Mongolia has become a valued partner in peacekeeping training and in combating terrorism.

Several U.S. security partnerships in Southeast Asia have the potential to grow. Singapore continues to value the U.S. military presence in the Asia-Pacific region and has extended expanded access arrangements to U.S. naval vessels and aircraft. Progress on democratization has led to restoration of U.S. support for Indonesia's military reforms and modernization and allowed for increased bilateral cooperation on maritime security and counterterrorism activities. Common interest in freedom of navigation and countering piracy and smuggling has advanced security cooperation with Malaysia. Similar regional interests are advancing U.S.-Vietnam security cooperation and military-to-military contacts.

Western Hemisphere

U.S.-Canadian Security Relations

Security relations between the United States and Canada remain on a firm foundation of good will and practical cooperation. Overall relations were somewhat strained after 2001 due to erratic official dialogue and public disagreements on a number of bilateral and international issues. More recently, there has been steady progress on cross-border law enforcement and counterterrorism programs, including implementation of the December 2001 Smart Border action plan, which enhances security while managing the flow of transit and trade; the March 2005 trilateral (with Mexico) Security and Prosperity Partnership of North America focused on practical ways to promote health, safety, and commerce; and the renewal and expansion of the NORAD aerospace defense agreement in 2006, to include integrated surveillance of the continent's maritime approaches and internal waterways. In the defense sector, stagnant defense budgets and limited modernization have further eroded the capabilities of the Canadian Forces and raised concerns about their long-term interoperability with the U.S. military and the depth of the Canadian commitment to North American and transatlantic defense.

Canada's first-ever National Security Policy (NSP), completed under the Paul Martin government in 2004, provided a blueprint for improving the country's capabilities in intelligence, threat assessment, emergency planning, public health, and border security to address 21st-century challenges. Another important step was the creation of a unified national command, Canada Command, with new priority given to domestic operations. The Conservative government led by Prime Minister Stephen Harper came to office in February 2006 committed to further strengthening ties with the United States and revitalizing the Canadian Forces. While the tone of Ottawa-Washington dialogue and day-to-day operational collaboration have improved, it remains unclear whether the minority Harper government can engender parliamentary support for strengthening military capabilities or for more contentious issues, including Canadian participation in the U.S. missile defense program.

Washington and Ottawa need to sustain high-level dialogue to build consensus on common approaches to new security challenges and further adaptation of the alliance. Washington should take a flexible and comprehensive approach to security burden-sharing and be sensitive to Canadian sovereignty concerns in efforts to bolster defense of the North American homeland. U.S. officials should also take into account the broad range of Canadian security concerns, including illegal fishing off its shores, control of events along its Arctic frontier, and vulnerability to infectious disease. Canadians need to make a long-term commitment to defense modernization if they want to retain influence with the United States on security affairs. Washington should seek

Canada's help with specific technical challenges and defensive weapons rather than a broad commitment to cooperation on missile defense. Many thorny sovereignty-related issues will have to be sorted out before missile defense cooperation can advance.

Latin America and the Caribbean

There has been uneven progress since 2001 in adapting security relations with other U.S. partners in the Western Hemisphere. While U.S. and Mexican law enforcement and immigration officials have developed pragmatic, albeit wary, cooperation on border security, military-to-military ties have remained minimal, due to institutional asymmetries and Mexican sovereignty concerns and fears of subordination. U.S. cooperation with Chile, Brazil, and several Central American and Caribbean governments on regional and transnational security concerns has produced concrete results and shows promise. U.S. support to Colombia's counterinsurgency efforts remains critical to strengthening that country and to containing and managing conflicts, narcoterrorism, and other transnational threats in the Andean ridge. Multilateral security cooperation in Latin America is progressing slowly, as habits of cooperation are not well established and many governments are uneasy about their growing interdependence. Traditional zero-sum thinking about national security concerns still restrains serious Latin collaboration.

U.S. security relations with most countries in Latin America have been constrained by partner concerns about Washington's exercise of its global primacy, its episodic engagement in the region, and differing approaches to transnational problems. The Bush administration's disinterest in multilateral institutions and the treatment of prisoners in Iraq and Guantanamo have eroded U.S. popularity and moral authority among these less powerful governments that place great stock in international norms. Frustration with ineffective national governance and U.S. support for economic policies that have failed to deliver equitable development have fostered populism, such as Hugo Chavez's "Bolivarian Revolution" in Venezuela, and a new willingness to challenge Washington. The growing support for tougher immigration policies in the United States adds to the hemispheric divide. Latin leaders have expanded subregional economic cooperation and economic and political engagement with partners outside the hemisphere to reduce dependence the United States. While U.S. influence in Latin America has declined markedly since 2001, most leaders in the region seek to maintain good relations with the United States, their most important trading partner, and recognize the need for at least intelligence-sharing with Washington in tackling new and traditional security problems.

The key challenges for the United States in advancing security cooperation in the hemisphere are to overcome lingering suspicions and doubts about its policies and commitment to the region and to build consensus on a comprehensive vision and strategy built on subregional security collaboration.

- The United States should continue developing all facets of its cooperation with the governments of the Caribbean and Latin America to combat an array of transnational threats in a more integrated fashion. The 1994 Summit of the Americas in Miami introduced the concept that democratic institutions and modern, open economies can best maintain regional peace and prosperity, a concept further affirmed by the 2001 Inter-American Democratic Charter. The 2003 Organization of American States Declaration on Security in the Americas, which built on these principles and regional support for a new, multidimensional approach to security, provides a sound conceptual context for these efforts.

- Brazil, Chile, Colombia, and several countries in Central America have demonstrated a willingness and ability to collaborate in managing security in the hemisphere and contribute to regional and global peacekeeping and stabilization operations. The United States should actively encourage and support such efforts by Latin American governments.
- The weight of history, nationalism, asymmetries of interests and capabilities, and lingering concerns about subordination will continue to limit bilateral defense cooperation with Mexico. However, the United States might seek to develop the partnership with Mexico and the Caribbean basin countries discussed above to address interrelated transnational security concerns and disaster response.

Security Partnerships in Africa

In the face of Africa's growing economic importance and continuing state weakness, the United States is nurturing partnerships with regional leaders in South Africa, Nigeria, Kenya, and Ethiopia, and supporting efforts by the African Union and subregional organizations to build African capabilities to maintain regional peace and stability and mitigate global terrorism. Creation of the new U.S. Africa Command will enhance American military engagement, contingency planning, and support to training activities.

A Global Strategy for Alliances and Partnerships

Efforts to adapt alliances and develop new security partnerships are paying concrete dividends. Allies and partners are playing a critical role in support of U.S. efforts to counter global terrorism and innovative mechanisms have been developed for intelligence-sharing and operational coordination to disrupt and mitigate attacks. Allied and partner engagement in stabilization, security transition, reconstruction, and humanitarian missions in the Balkans, Afghanistan, Haiti, and Africa makes important contributions to mutual security. U.S. allies and partners provide over 70 percent of the funding and personnel for UN peacekeeping operations.

In an era of global security challenges and global force management, new patterns of interaction and cooperation among U.S. allies and partners and regional security institutions are needed. NATO is expanding its partnerships into the Middle East and has developed effective operational cooperation with Australia, Japan, New Zealand, and South Korea in the conduct of counterinsurgency and stability operations in Afghanistan.

Cooperation among U.S. Allies and partners in East Asia also is continuing to evolve. Trilateral U.S.-Japan-Australia cooperation has developed on the strength of bilateral ties among the three governments and shared assessments of the security environment. Trilateral U.S.-Japan-India cooperation has sought to build on common regional concerns and shared democratic values. Renewal of trilateral U.S.–ROK–Japan cooperation, which existed with respect to North Korea contingency planning, could help advance the regional role of both alliance relationships and dampen animosities between Tokyo and Seoul.

Given growing interest in East Asia in new forms of regional security cooperation, it is incumbent upon the United States and its Asian allies and partners to demonstrate how these relationships can serve broader regional interests. Much as NATO's Partnership for Peace program engaged Russia and other former Warsaw Pact countries in humanitarian and peacekeeping activities to build confidence in NATO's peaceful intent, perhaps trilateral participation in future humanitarian or peace support operation along with China and other Asian countries would be a way to demonstrate that both alliance relationships can contribute to regional security.

The Bush administration's policies in Iraq and the war on terrorism have led to a precipitous drop in global public opinion of the United States, even among some of its closest allies and partners. Expanding and better integrating these relationships will be a slow process until concrete steps are taken to restore confidence in Washington's leadership, strategic judgment, and moral authority. It will require demonstrating a new willingness to listen to the views of other countries, and to work with them as partners in solving common problems.

TRANSFORMING DEFENSE STRATEGY AND POSTURE

Taking Stock

The Bush administration made transformation of the U.S. defense establishment a signature issue and put it in a new strategic context. Administration officials contended that in an era of great uncertainty, the United States needed to identify unique strategic strengths and potential vulnerabilities and systematically favor the latter in investment decisions. Their vision of transformation comprised sweeping reforms of DOD business practices, as well as accelerating a revolution in military operational art and science. In the 2006 *Quadrennial Defense Review* (QDR) *Report*, the Pentagon leadership concluded that DOD is not producing sufficient transformational output and must reform strategic decisionmaking. Rather than just look at output, chapter eight of this volume assesses three core transformation reforms initiated by the Pentagon that are likely to determine whether the United States can field and manage transformational military forces over the next decade: joint operating concepts (JOCs); a capabilities-based approach to defense planning and resource allocation; and global force planning.

The Bush administration's transformation agenda is informed by elements of its defense strategy, which calls for dissuading future military competition in part through experimentation with revolutionary operational concepts, capabilities, and organizational arrangements stimulated by a culture of innovation and risk-taking. In its 2001 *QDR Report*, the administration identified six specific operational areas as keys to transformation: defending the homeland, denying enemies a sanctuary, projecting power into denied areas, leveraging information technology for operations, protecting information networks, and enhancing space operations. It also mandated roadmaps to develop capabilities in these areas, along with the requisite shifts in resources.

Difficult questions about resource allocation to support transformation were compounded after 9/11 by the demands of operations in Afghanistan and Iraq and led some to question whether the Pentagon could simultaneously transform and fight the war on terrorism. However, former Secretary of Defense Donald Rumsfeld maintained throughout his tenure that DOD must do just that in order to prevail over terrorists and deter and defeat future adversaries. Congressional support for increases to the defense budget reduced but did not eliminate the tension between a high operations tempo and transformation investments. This led the Pentagon to accept some near-term risks in order to fund longer-term transformational capabilities. To improve management of the process, the Pentagon issued the 2003 *Transformation Planning Guidance*. That document called for, among other things, the Chairman of the Joint Chiefs of Staff, in coordination with the commander of the U.S. Joint Forces Command, to develop JOCs that would depict how transformed forces would fight in the future and help senior decisionmakers choose between competing investment options.

Joint Operating Concepts

The JOCs are intended to guide transformation, assuring that new concepts and capabilities evolve in an interactive way, so that the joint force is prepared to operate successfully against the most important threats of the next two decades. The objective is to ensure that strategy and joint warfighting concepts drive requirements and programs, rather than vice versa, as has often happened in the past.

An overarching Capstone Concept for Joint Operations and four subordinate joint operating concepts for homeland security, strategic deterrence, major combat operations, and stability operations have been drafted. A fifth JOC on irregular warfare is planned. Iterations of the Capstone Concept have sought to capture the broad outline of the new American way of war enabled by the emergence of information technologies and built on the tenets of network-centric warfare and effects-based operations. It emphasizes high-quality shared awareness, dispersed forces, speed of command, mobility, and flexibility in planning and execution. The premise of the concept is that if U.S. forces fight first for information superiority, commanders would be able to bring all available assets together rapidly to achieve desired effects better. It also emphasizes the military contribution to an integrated effort with interagency and multinational partners to achieve national objectives.

Chapter eight concludes that most of the JOCs lack sufficient specificity or fail to address several difficult issues. If the joint operating concepts are to be effective tools for transformation, they must eventually become discriminating and detailed enough to allow identification and prioritization of transformation requirements in the defense program. They also must remain open to modification so they may incorporate new findings from experimentation and practical experience.

A Capabilities-based Approach

The 2001 QDR also called for a new approach to developing military forces, *capabilities-based planning*, that would identify capabilities that U.S. military forces would need to deter or defeat a diverse range of future adversaries. This approach seeks to overcome two limitations of previous defense planning: that it focused exclusively on two archetypical threat cases that were actually anomalies—Korea and Iraq; and that it was too reactive to systems deployed by adversaries. The goal is to focus less on individual platforms and more on how joint forces could communicate and operate together for greater effect against a wider range of threats.

The assumption that it is easier to anticipate the tactics an adversary will employ than it is to predict their identity is open to challenge. In Afghanistan and Iraq, it would have been easier to predict the adversary than their tactics. In addition, the enemy tactics identified in the 2001 *QDR Report*—surprise, deception, and asymmetric warfare—are vague, implying the need to prepare for just about anything. Using uncertainty as a strategic principle is the antithesis of planning. Most planners now recognize that some reference to threat cases is necessary. The greater innovation in capabilities-based planning is recognizing the importance of assessing and managing risk across a much more diverse range of threats. Implementation of a capabilities-based approach to defense planning and resource allocation will take time, but chapter eight proposes several steps that could accelerate the process:

- A white paper could clear up much of the confusion surrounding capabilities-based planning. It should define the concept, its attributes, and purpose in comparison of both risks and risk mitigation options.
- Handling the variability in threat and capability options characteristic of a capabilities-based approach requires more robust joint analysis and a more integrated planning, programming, and budgeting system informed by that analysis than previously was the case.
- The Pentagon needs an authoritative, transparent, and discriminating analytic system and authoritative planning cases. It also needs sufficiently discriminating and detailed joint operating concepts for how forces will be employed and risk metrics for evaluating the results of different concepts employed in different scenarios.

Global Force Planning

The 2001 QDR concluded that uncertainty about the origins of future threats also requires development of global force planning and capabilities. The intent was to provide the President with a wider range of military options to discourage aggression. The concept adopted a much more demanding goal for deterring foreign adversaries by requiring forward-deployed forces, augmented by global capabilities, to defeat enemy attacks rapidly in a wider range of potential contingencies with only modest reinforcement from outside the theater. Achieving this goal requires changes in command and control, posture, and capabilities.

The new approach to global force management includes tools and policies for administering worldwide deployment of forces and associated risk assessments, and new combatant commander responsibilities that involve a global span of control over some forces and missions. Combatant commanders with new global command responsibilities are expected to provide expert opinion and inputs for the global force management system overseen by the Pentagon and other national authorities. The driving force behind global force management is the need to assess and manage risk better on a global basis, which requires a more centralized approach, including systems for near-real-time assessment of the location and readiness of all units around the globe, and for weighing the risks associated with using those forces for various purposes. The Pentagon calls the set of tools and processes to support decisionmaking the *global force management process*, and it continues to work on a prototype of the new system.

New Combatant Commander Relationships

In the past, the Pentagon organized U.S. combatant commands to deal with traditional contingencies occurring in one region or another, but those delineations are no longer satisfactory. Regional conflicts with significant escalation potential that could spill across regional boundaries—not to mention counterterrorism operations—increase the need for global command and control. Consequently, U.S. defense leadership has revised combatant commander responsibilities to deal with these cross-cutting issues better and to integrate military capabilities more effectively with other elements of national power. Beginning in 2002, the Bush administration made major changes to both geographic and functional/global commands, both creating two new geographic (Northern and Africa) and one functional/global (Strategic) commands and altering the missions of others. Nonregional commands have been given expanded responsibilities for global missions that cross regional boundaries—altering the previous balance between geographic and global commands as well as expanding functional responsibilities as managers of joint capabilities—changing the previous balance between the Services as capability providers and combatant commands as force employers. While the changes since 2002 have helped update the command structure to address 21st-century threats, the command structure may still require further adjustments.

- Determining the proper balance in the future between geographic, functional, and global commands will be difficult, particularly in handling global challenges. Retaining some mix of the three with appropriate connectivity among them is desirable. The commands will also find it difficult to balance noncombat responsibilities such as peacetime planning and security cooperation.

- The second challenge will be to move beyond integration of combatant commanders to interagency integration, as called for in the 2006 QDR and many other national strategy documents. Many combatant commands have established joint interagency coordination groups with personnel who can provide liaison to their home agencies, but achieving better "whole of government" efforts will require bolstering the planning and operational capabilities of relevant civilian agencies and enhancing interagency planning and policy implementation.
- Among various combatant commands and between the commands and non-DOD agencies, concerted effort is required to guard against inefficient or contradictory activities because of areas of overlapping or ill-defined responsibilities.

Building a More Agile Global Posture

The Bush administration concluded early in its tenure that changes in the security environment required a new global force posture to improve the agility of U.S. forces to move quickly to unanticipated hot spots and that improvements in allied capabilities allowed this to happen with reduced risk. Many U.S. military units are still stationed in proximity to potential Cold War–era flashpoints. In 2002, the Pentagon initiated the Global Posture Review (GPR) to review Cold War assumptions about the location and structure of U.S. forces and to make recommendations on realigning the basing of U.S. military forces around the globe.

In August 2004, the Pentagon announced the results of the GPR. It advanced a new construct for overseas deployment infrastructure including well-equipped, permanent main operating bases for the stationing of major forces, austere forward operating locations for the temporary staging and onward movement of forces, and cooperative security locations for use as intermediate staging bases. One additional aircraft carrier battlegroup and more submarines will be forward-stationed in the Pacific, dramatically cutting transit time for these platforms from their home bases to their anticipated areas of deployment. Also, for the first time since the Vietnam War, Guam now has a continuous presence of B–52 bombers on its shores. Army forces in Korea have begun a long-overdue downsizing and relocation south of the Han River that better reflect the evolution of the North Korean threat and the advances made by the South Korean Defense Forces. Throughout the world, headquarters will be streamlined, redundant echelons of command eliminated, and forces reoriented toward global employment rather than regional focus.

Yet the initial results of the Global Posture Review fell short of far-reaching expectations and fears overseas. Contrary to early predictions of a posture review driven by politics or strategy, operational military logic has dominated the changes to date. Many of the early and more radical ideas for reposturing the military's global presence that had strong political or strategic rationale in the abstract proved less attractive when operational research demonstrated that they would contribute relatively little to strategic agility. Since the initial results of the GPR deflated many expectations, the United

States needs to mend some fences with potential partner states. Washington should emphasize how these arrangements produce local economic and political benefits and point out that their smaller footprint reduces political friction with local communities. Moreover, routine operational (or training) use of these facilities demonstrates the U.S. commitment to the host country and can also enhance the transformation of host nation armed forces and improve their interoperability with U.S. counterparts.

Recalibrating the Capabilities Mix

New capabilities that provide the potential for rapid and, in some cases, almost immediate response raise difficult command and control issues, but also make valuable contributions to deterrence. National missile defense and global intelligence, surveillance, and reconnaissance (ISR) capabilities were emphasized in the 2001 QDR, but the global reach of Special Operations Forces and some types of information operations was also noted. In addition, long-range bombers capable of precision strikes and the possibility of conventional intercontinental ballistic missiles and hypersonic vehicles that could deliver lethal payloads raise the promise of other global rapid response capabilities that support forward deterrence. However, some of these global capabilities are extremely expensive and raise difficult investment and force design issues. Something must be given up in order to pay for a force with these capabilities. At the strategic level, there may be tradeoffs between investments in overseas bases for ground and air forces and in naval and long-range aircraft.

Future options, such as the Navy's concept for floating seabases, could make U.S. military forces more sustainable and less dependent on allies for overseas deployments, but at quite some cost. Many analysts believe such capabilities as seabases and shipborne mobile ballistic missile defenses make sense because they are impervious to shifting political developments in a host country and present that country with fewer risks and burdens. At the operational level, improvements in planning tools and transportation methods, such as high-speed vessels or novel airships, could improve strategic mobility.

Some have argued that the United States can also afford to downsize its extensive forcible entry force structure. Sacrificing some of this force structure in favor of flexible entry capabilities that expand the range of entry points an enemy must protect would vastly complicate the enemy's challenge of mounting an effective defense. The argument that U.S. forces fight first for information superiority also raises questions about tradeoffs between global ISR capabilities and force structure that provides strike capability. Another tradeoff exists between costly global and theater ISR capabilities. With respect to coalition operations, the greatest efficiencies may be possible from investments in command and control capabilities that permit U.S. forces to share detailed intelligence, rather than much more costly efforts to build interoperability.

Mustering Reforms for Transformation

Transformation of the U.S. defense establishment was accelerated by the 2001 Quadrennial Defense Review and the strong backing of both the President and

Secretary of Defense. The Pentagon's current leadership remains committed to transformation, although the 2006 QDR and subsequent guidance from Secretary Robert Gates placed new emphasis on improving military capabilities by enhancing management processes and working more effectively with international and intragovernmental partners and less on exploitation of information-age technologies. This change in emphasis reflects, in part, the demands of counterterrorism activities and other global and regional security problems where effective collaboration with allies and integration of all elements of national power are more critical to success than new technologies. The tension between successfully combating terrorism and preparing for future information-age threats will grow if the former absorbs increasing amounts of senior leader attention and new-term funding. The most difficult strategic tradeoffs could be avoided as long as the President and Congress are willing to support increased levels of defense spending to fund current operations in Iraq and Afghanistan. Thus far, the Pentagon has been able to invest heavily in transformational starts without abandoning much near-term capability. The 2006 QDR maintained this course by cutting the size of air and naval forces, while resisting pressure to increase ground forces in response to the demands of ongoing operations in Iraq and Afghanistan. How the Pentagon will adjudicate risk when the tradeoffs between transformation, mere modernization, and current operations are more stark remains uncertain.

Sharply defining the essential elements of the security problems embodied by the joint operating concepts would be helpful for illuminating choices and increasing their utility as engines of transformation. Improving JOCs would also help accelerate the development of capabilities-based planning, which in turn is necessary to properly evaluate options for global force management, design, and posture. The need to assess and manage risk in light of far greater threat and capability variability is the raison d'être of capabilities-based planning. The significance of increased variability is that it heightens the complexity of defense planning and analysis. Complexity can be managed only by holding firm to several large, foundational ideas about future demands on forces. However, senior decisionmakers cannot make tough decisions about defense programs without supporting concepts, organizations, and new modes of analysis.

MANAGING U.S. GLOBAL ENGAGEMENT

Policy and organizational initiatives since 2001 have led to important progress in addressing the seven strategic challenges explored in this book. However, much remains to be done to enhance global order and advance vital U.S. interests over the next decade.

A more successful counterterrorism strategy requires a synergy between actions designed to eradicate jihadist terrorists and their structures and those designed to isolate jihadists from the wider Muslim population. Enhancing security of the homeland calls for better integration of the efforts of civilian authorities, the military, the private sector, and individual citizens, as well as further steps to improve domestic response and coordination. Meeting the WMD proliferation challenge requires a comprehensive

Notes

CHAPTER ONE

[1] Arthur K. Cebrowski, "Transforming Transformation—Will It Change the Character of War?" Paper presented to the National Intelligence Council's *2020 Project*, Workshop on "Changing Nature of Warfare," May 25, 2004, Washington, DC, available at <http://www.cia.gov/nic/PDF_GIF_2020_Sup port/2004_05_25_papers/transformation.pdf>.

[2] Stephen J. Flanagan, Ellen L. Frost, and Richard L. Kugler, *Challenges of the Global Century* (Washington, DC: National Defense University Press, 2001), 8–10.

[3] The current age of globalization could be compared to that of the late 19th and early 20th centuries. World War I effectively ended the first era of globalization, and similar conditions exist for cataclysmic events to do the same to this one. See Niall Ferguson, "Sinking Globalization," *Foreign Affairs* 84, no. 2 (March/April 2005), 64–77.

[4] National Intelligence Council, *Mapping the Global Future: Report of the National Intelligence Council's 2020 Project* (Washington, DC: Government Printing Office, 2004), 10 (hereafter *Mapping the Global Future*).

[5] Thomas P.M. Barnett, *The Pentagon's New Map* (New York: G.P. Putnam's Sons, 2004).

[6] Thomas Friedman describes the "flattening" of the world as "connecting all the knowledge centers on the planet into a single global network, which—if politics and terrorism do not get in the way—could usher in an amazing era of prosperity and innovation." See Thomas L. Friedman, *The World is Flat: A Brief History of the Twenty-First Century* (New York: Farrar, Straus and Giroux, 2005), 2–47.

[7] U.S. Joint Forces Command, *The Joint Operational Environment: The World Through 2030 and Beyond* (September 4, 2006), 43, available at <http://www.dtic.mil/futurejointwarfare/strategic/joe_040906.doc> (hereafter *The Joint Operational Environment*).

[8] The *arc of instability* is the swath of territory running from the Andean Ridge and the Caribbean basin through most of Africa, the Middle East, and Central and Southeast Asia. The countries along this arc—often weak or failed states—have

been left far behind as the rest of the world is brought into the global economy. These countries have also been referred to as the "non-integrated gap." See Flanagan, Frost, and Kugler; and Barnett.

⁹ Flanagan, Frost, and Kugler, 9–10.

¹⁰ Robert P. Cincotta, Robert Engelman, and Danielle Anastasion, *The Security Demographic: Population and Civil Conflict After the Cold War* (Washington, DC: Population Action International, 2002), 12–13, available at <http://www.populationaction.org/resources/publications/securitydemographic/index.html#>. This study found that during the 1990s, countries in which young adults comprised more than 40 percent of the adult population were more than twice as likely as countries with lower proportions to experience an outbreak of civil conflict. States with urban population growth rates above 4 percent were about twice as likely to sustain the outbreak of a civil conflict as countries with lower rates.

¹¹ *Mapping the Global Future*, 13.

¹² Department of Defense, *The National Defense Strategy of the United States of America* (Washington, DC: Department of Defense, March 2005), 5.

¹³ Ibid.

¹⁴ United Kingdom, Ministry of Defence, The Development, Concepts, and Doctrine Centre (DCDC), *The DCDC Global Strategic Trends Programme, 2007–2036*, 3ᵈ edition, 56–59, available at <http://www.mod.uk/NR/rdonlyres/5CB29DC4-9B4A-4DFD-B363-3282BE255CE7/0/strat_trends_23jan07.pdf>.

¹⁵ See Charles D. Lutes, "New Players on the Scene: A.Q. Khan and the Nuclear Black Market," *eJournal USA: Foreign Policy Agenda* (Washington, DC: U.S. Department of State, March, 2005), available at <http://usinfo.state.gov/journals/itps/0305/ijpe/ijpe0305.pdf>.

¹⁶ See Department of Defense, *The National Military Strategy of the United States of America* (Washington, DC: Joint Chiefs of Staff, 2004), 4 (hereafter *National Military Strategy*).

¹⁷ Thomas X. Hammes, *Insurgency: Modern Warfare Evolves into a Fourth Generation*, Strategic Forum 214 (Washington, DC: National Defense University Press, January 2005).

¹⁸ Moises Naim, "The Five Wars of Globalization," *Foreign Policy* 134 (January/February 2003), 38–36.

¹⁹ *The Joint Operational Environment* (Draft), 14.

²⁰ *National Military Strategy*, 6.

²¹ *The Joint Operational Environment* (Draft), 60.

²² Ibid., 64.

²³ *Mapping the Global Future*, 95.

²⁴ Ibid., 17.

²⁵ Cebrowski.

²⁶ *National Defense Strategy*, 3.

²⁷ *Mapping the Global Future*, 16.

²⁸ *The Joint Operational Environment* (Draft), 62.

²⁹ *Mapping the Global Future*, 10.

30 Bruce Hoffman et al., "Headlines over the Horizon," *Atlantic Monthly* 292, no. 1 (July/August 2003), 84–90.

31 Dafna Linzer, "Iran Is Judged 10 Years From Nuclear Bomb," *The Washington Post*, August 2, 2005, A1, available at <http://www.washingtonpost.com/wp-dyn/content/article/2005/08/01/AR2005080101453_pf.html>; Office of the Director of National Intelligence, National Intelligence Estimate, "Iran: Nuclear Intentions and Capabilities" (Washington, DC: National Intelligence Council, November 2007), available at <http://www.odni.gov/press_releases/20071203_release.pdf>.

32 For a more expansive discussion, see Judith S. Yaphe and Charles D. Lutes, *Reassessing the Strategic Implications of a Nuclear-Armed Iran*, McNair Paper 69 (Washington, DC: National Defense University Press, August 2005).

33 Henry A. Kissinger, "China: Containment Won't Work," *The Washington Post,* June 13, 2005, 19.

34 Hoffman et al., 86.

35 Ibid., 87.

36 Johnnie Carson, *Shaping U.S. Policy on Africa: Pillars of a New Strategy*, Strategic Forum 210 (Washington, DC: National Defense University Press, September 2004).

37 Naim.

38 Sam J. Tangredi, *All Possible Wars? Toward a Consensus View of the Future Security Environment, 2001–2025*, McNair Paper 63 (Washington, DC: National Defense University Press, 2000). See also *The DCDC Global Strategic Trends Programme,* 76–85.

39 According to Colin S. Gray, "Surprise effect, not surprise, is the challenge." Colin S. Gray, "Transformation and Strategic Surprise" (Carlisle, PA: Strategic Studies Institute, April 2005), available at <http://www.carlisle.army.mil/ssi/pdffiles/PUB602.pdf>.

40 *Mapping the Global Future,* 93.

41 International Energy Agency, *World Energy Outlook 2006*, available at <http://www.worldenergyoutlook.org/summaries2006/English.pdf>, 1–3.

42 Jane Kay, "Report predicts climate calamity: All continents face drought, starvation, rising seas, panel says," *San Francisco Examiner,* April 7, 2007, available at <http://sfgate.com/cgi-bin/article.cgi?file=/c/a/2007/04/07/MNGTTP4OH11.DTL>.

CHAPTER TWO

1 *National Intelligence Estimate: The Terrorist Threat to the U.S. Homeland* (Washington, DC: National Intelligence Council, 2007), available at <http://www.dni.gov/press_releases/20070717_release.pdf>.

2 George J. Tenet, testimony before the Senate Select Committee on Intelligence, "The Worldwide Threat 2004: Challenges in a Changing Global Context," February 24, 2004, available at <cia.gov/cia/public_affairs/speeches/2004/dci_speech_02142004.html>.

3 *The National Security Strategy of the United States of America* (Washington, DC: The White House, 2006), 8. Donald H. Rumsfeld, "Foreword," *The National Mili-*

tary Strategic Plan for the War on Terrorism (Washington, DC: Chairman of the Joint Chiefs of Staff, 2006), 1 (hereafter cited as *NMSP–WOT*).

4   "Rumsfeld's War-on-Terror Memo," *USA Today*, October 22, 2003.

5   *Extremely small* does not mean negligible. In India in the 1980s, an estimated 4,000 Sikh militants out of a Sikh population of 20 million caused more than 15,000 deaths. If active terrorists make up that same percentage of the world's Muslim population, that would be 260,000 terrorists.

6   According to Bruce Hoffman, *Inside Terrorism* (New York: Columbia University Press, 1998), 17, the concept was first articulated by the Italian anarchist Carlo Pisacane. Mikhail Bakunin explained it in "Letters to a Frenchman on the Present Crisis" (1870): "We must spread our principles, not with words but with deeds, for this is the most popular, the most potent, and the most irresistible form of propaganda." Prince Pyotr Kropotkin seems to have been the first to use the exact expression *propaganda by deed* in his pamphlet *Revolutionary Government* (1880).

7   Letter, Ayman al-Zawahiri to Abu Mus'ab al-Zarqawi, July 9, 2005, released by Office of the Director of National Intelligence, October 11, 2005, available at <dni.gov/press_releases/letter_in_english.pdf>.

8   "Until [the whole world is under the sway of Islam], the world is divided into two: the House of Islam (*dar al-Islam*), where Muslims rule and the law of Islam prevails; and the House of War (*dar al-Harb*), comprising the rest of the world." Bernard Lewis, *The Political Language of Islam* (Chicago: University of Chicago Press, 1988), 73.

9   Shibley Telhami, "Understanding the Challenge," *Middle East Journal* 56, no. 1 (Winter 2002), 13.

10 Dennis Pluchinsky, "The Global Jihad," presentation at workshop on "Terrorism and Islamic Extremism in the Middle East: Perspectives and Possibilities," co-sponsored by the Center for Contemporary Conflict (Naval Postgraduate School) and Center for Naval Analyses, Alexandria, VA, February 22, 2005. Cited by permission of the author.

11 Francis Fukuyama, "The Neoconservative Moment," *The National Interest,* no. 76 (Summer 2004), 63.

12 George W. Bush, speech at Paul H. Nitze School of Advanced International Studies, Washington, DC, April 10, 2006, available at <whitehouse.gov/news/releases/2006/04/20060410-1.html>.

13 Theodore Karasik and Cheryl Bernard, "Muslim Diasporas and Networks," in Angel Rabasa et al., *The Muslim World after 9/11* (Santa Monica, CA: RAND Corporation, 2004), 441, observe that in some European countries only a fraction of nominal Muslims even bother to attend Friday prayers on a regular basis. Most want only to get on with achieving a better life in material terms and gaining a modicum of acceptance in the countries that have become their homes.

14 Robert Taber, *The War of the Fleas* (New York: Lyle Stuart, 1965), 20.

15 C. Christine Fair, "Islam and Politics in Pakistan," in Rabasa et al., 276.

16 Even in areas where governments normally function reasonably well, such groups have shown a greater nimbleness in responding to episodic lapses in regime

performance, as when they were able to get aid to victims of the December 2004 tsunami in Southeast Asia faster than the governments concerned.

[17] "Egyptian Islamist Leaders Fault Al-Qaida's Strategy," *Al-Sharq al-Awsat*, January 11–12, 2004 (translation by Foreign Broadcast Information Service accessed at <www.fas.org/irp/world/para/ig_bk.htm>).

[18] Max Weber, "The Fundamental Concepts of Sociology" (1913), in *The Theory of Social and Economic Organization,* ed. Talcott Parsons (New York: Free Press, 1964), 124–132.

[19] Alexander Bickel, *The Morality of Consent* (New Haven: Yale University Press, 1976), 16–17.

[20] Pew Global Attitudes Project, *A Year After Iraq War* (Washington, DC: Pew Research Center for the People and the Press, 2004), 19.

[21] Pew Global Attitudes Project, *Views of a Changing World* (Washington, DC: Pew Research Center for the People and the Press, 2003), 104.

[22] *A Year After Iraq War*, 10.

[23] Michael C. Hudson, *Arab Politics: The Search for Legitimacy* (New Haven: Yale University Press, 1977), 2.

[24] *Views of a Changing World*, 105.

[25] Pew Global Attitudes Project, *What the World Thinks in 2002* (Washington, DC: Pew Research Center for the People and the Press, 2002).

[26] *Views of a Changing World*, 34–40.

[27] David Fromkin, *A Peace to End All Peace: The Fall of the Ottoman Empire and the Creation of the Modern Middle East* (New York: Avon, 1990), 93.

[28] Thomas Carothers, "Democracy: Terrorism's Uncertain Antidote," *Current History* 101, no. 659 (2003), 406.

[29] Andrew Kohut, statement before the Senate Foreign Relations Committee, "American Public Diplomacy in the Islamic World," February 27, 2003, accessed at <people-press.org/commentary/print.php3?AnalysisID=63>; Shibley Telhami, "U.S. Policy and the Arab and Muslim World: The Need for Public Diplomacy," *Brookings Review* 20, no. 3 (Summer 2002), 47; Telhami, "Understanding the Challenge," 13–14.

[30] Lewis, 73, explains that an offensive jihad to spread the faith is an obligation on the Muslim community collectively (individual members may fulfill this obligation by paying taxes to support a professional army, for example), while a jihad to defend the Islamic community is a "personal obligation of every adult male Muslim." Modern jihadists assert that such a defensive jihad does not require a call to arms by a duly constituted political authority, but that does not seem to be the position of the classical jurists.

[31] Ted Robert Gurr, *Why Men Rebel* (Princeton: Princeton University Press, 1970), 13.

[32] Anne Speckhard, "Understanding Suicide Terrorism: Countering Human Bombs and Their Senders," in *Topics in Terrorism: Toward a Transatlantic Consensus on the Nature of the Threat,* vol. 1, ed. Jason S. Purcell and Joshua D. Weintraub (Washington, DC: Atlantic Council of the United States, 2005), 7.

[33] Telhami, "Understanding the Challenge," 9.

[34] David Thaler, "The Middle East: The Cradle of the Muslim World," in Rabasa et al., 92, 104.

[35] *Abrams v. United States*, 250 U.S. 616 (1919).

[36] *Arab Human Development Report 2003: Building a Knowledge Society* (New York: United Nations Development Programme, 2003), 54.

[37] Robert Satloff, *The Battle of Ideas in the War on Terror: Essays on U.S. Public Diplomacy in the Middle East* (Washington, DC: Washington Institute for Near East Policy, 2004), 30.

[38] *Salafism* is the movement within Sunni Islam that calls for stripping away practices and beliefs that *salafists* consider inconsistent with those of Muhammad's earliest followers. Not all rigorously conservative Sunnis are *salafists*, and not all *salafists* support the use of violence to achieve the movement's aims. Quintan Wiktorowicz and John Kaltner, "Killing in the Name of Islam: Al-Qaeda's Justification for September 11," *Middle East Policy* 10 (2003), 76–92, provides an incisive look at the ideological factions within the *salafi* movement. *Salafi* antiterrorist Web sites in English include Wahhabi Myth <wahhabimyth.com>, Salafi Publications <salafipublications.com>, Center for Victory of Islamic Da'wa <troid.org>, and Fatwa-Online <fatwa-online.com>.

[39] *NMSP–WOT*, 3.

[40] C. Christine Fair, "Militant Recruitment in Pakistan: Implications for Al Qaeda and Other Organizations," *Studies in Conflict and Terrorism* 27 (2004), 495.

[41] Fair, "Islam and Politics," 275–276.

[42] Christopher Matthews, *Hardball: How Politics Is Played—Told by One Who Knows the Game* (New York: Summit, 1988), 62.

[43] Letter, Abu Mus'ab al-Zarqawi, released by Coalition Provisional Authority, February 2004, available at <state.gov/p/nea/rls/31694.htm>

[44] *Quadrennial Defense Review Report* (Washington, DC: Department of Defense, 2006), 79.

CHAPTER THREE

[1] In the first Presidential debate on September 30, 2004, Senator John Kerry identified nuclear proliferation and weapons of mass destruction as the single most serious threat the Nation faces in the 21st century. President Bush agreed with that assessment but added the caveat "in the hands of a terrorist enemy." Commission on Presidential Debates, "The First Bush-Kerry Presidential Debate" (Miami, FL: September 30, 2004), available at <debates.org/pages/trans2004a.html>.

[2] *The National Security Strategy of the United States of America* (Washington, DC: The White House, September 2002), available at <whitehouse.gov/nsc/nss.pdf>.

[3] *The National Strategy to Combat Weapons of Mass Destruction* (Washington, DC: The White House, September 2003), available at <whitehouse.gov/news/releases/2002/12/WMDStrategy.pdf>.

[4] Federation of American Scientists, "Counterproliferation Initiative Presidential Decision Directive PDD/NSC 18, December 1993," available at <fas.org/irp/offdocs/pdd18.htm>.

5　Barry R. Schneider, *Radical Responses to Radical Regimes: Evaluating Preemptive Counter-Proliferation*, McNair Paper 41 (Washington, DC: National Defense University Press, 1995).

6　Department of Defense, "Joint Service Chemical and Biological Defense Program: FY 2002–2003 Overview," available at <acq.osd.mil/cp/cbd0vw02.pdf>.

7　*National Security Strategy*, 14.

8　Ibid., 15.

9　*Iraq's Weapons of Mass Destruction Programs* (Washington, DC: Director of Central Intelligence, October 2002), 1, available at <cia.gov/cia/reports/iraq_wmd/Iraq_Oct_2002.htm>.

10　Ibid.

11　Charles Duelfer, *Comprehensive Report of the Special Advisor to the DCI on Iraq's WMD: Key Findings* (Washington, DC: Central Intelligence Agency, September 30, 2004), available at <cia.gov/cia/reports/iraq_wmd_2004/index.html>.

12　The Commission on the Intelligence Capabilities of the United States Regarding Weapons of Mass Destruction, *Report to the President of the United States* (Washington, DC: U.S. Government Printing Office, March 31, 2005), available at <wmd.gov/report/transmittal_letter.html>.

13　Tommy Franks, *American Soldier* (New York: HarperCollins, 2004), 331.

14　Much of this discussion on WMD elimination is derived from the work of National Defense University's Center for the Study of Weapons of Mass Destruction. For a summary, see Rebecca K.C. Hersman, *Eliminating Adversary Weapons of Mass Destruction: What's at Stake?* (Washington, DC: National Defense University Press, 2004).

15　Franks, 399.

16　Hersman, 6.

17　*Quadrennial Defense Review Report* (Washington, DC: Department of Defense, 2006), available at <defenselink.mil/qdr/report/Report20060203.pdf>.

18　Barton Gellman and Dafna Lizner, "Unprecedented Peril Forces Tough Calls: President Faces a Multi-Front Battle Against Threats Known, Unknown," *The Washington Post,* October 26, 2004, A1.

19　"Unclassified Report to Congress on the Acquisition of Technology Relating to Weapons of Mass Destruction and Advanced Conventional Munitions, 1 July Through 31 December 2003" (Washington, DC: Director of Central Intelligence, 2003), available at <cia.gov/cia/reports/721_reports/july_dec2003.htm#1>.

20　George W. Bush, "Remarks by the President on the War on Terror," Oak Ridge National Laboratory, Oak Ridge, TN, July 12, 2004, available at <whitehouse.gov/news/releases/2004/07/20040712-5.html>.

21　The Commission on the Intelligence Capabilities of the United States Regarding Weapons of Mass Destruction, 252.

22　Ibid., 253.

23　The details on the BBC *China* seizure and the Khan network were derived from published sources. Specifically, see Bill Powell and Tim McGirk, "The Man Who Sold the Bomb," *Time,* February 14, 2005, 22–30. Also see Gellman and Lizner.

24 Pakistan Foreign Secretary Ahmad Khan announced the completion of a series of tests on May 30, 1998. See "Pakistan Conducts Additional Nuclear Test: Will There Be More?" CNN.com, May 30, 1998, available at <cnn.com/WORLD/asiapcf/9805/30/pakistan.nuclear/>.

25 See Sharon A. Squassoni, "Weapons of Mass Destruction: Trade Between North Korean and Pakistan," CRS Report for Congress, Number RL31900 (Washington, DC: Congressional Research Service, March 11, 2004).

26 Mark Landler, "Trafficking in nuclear arms called widespread: Chief UN inspector cites a 'Wal-Mart' in proliferation trading," *International Herald Tribune,* January 24, 2004, 1.

27 George W. Bush, State of the Union Address, Washington, DC, January 20, 2003, available at <whitehouse.gov/news/releases/2004/01/20040120-7.html>.

28 Mohamed ElBaradei, quoted by Roula Khalaf, "Concern over Iran's Nuclear Technology," *London Financial Times*, December 10, 2004, 1.

29 Paul Kerr, "IAEA: Seoul's Nuclear Sins of the Past," *Arms Control Today* 34, no. 10 (December 2004), available at <armscontrol.org/act/2004_12/Seoul.asp>.

30 Paul Kerr, "IAEA Investigating Taiwan and Egypt," *Arms Control Today* 35, no. 1 (January/February 2005), available at <armscontrol.org/act/2005_01-02/Egypt_Taiwan.asp>.

31 For an in-depth analysis, see Kurt M. Campbell, Robert J. Einhorn, and Mitchell B. Reiss, eds., *The Nuclear Tipping Point: Why States Reconsider Their Nuclear Choices* (Washington, DC: Brookings Institution Press, 2004).

32 George W. Bush, "Remarks by the President on Weapons of Mass Destruction Proliferation," Fort Lesley J. McNair, Washington, DC, February 11, 2004, available at <whitehouse.gov/news/releases/2004/02/20040211-4.html>.

33 Judith S. Yaphe and Charles D. Lutes, *Reassessing the Implications of a Nuclear-Armed Iran*, McNair Paper 69 (Washington, DC: National Defense University Press, 2005).

34 Secretary of State Condoleezza Rice, "Interview on the Charlie Rose Show," May 7, 2007, available at <http://www.state.gov/secretary/rm/2007/may/84460.htm>.

35 Edward Cody, "North Korea Nuclear Talks Adjourn Without Agreement," *The Washington Post*, August 7, 2005, A14; "Joint Statement of the Fourth Round of the Six-Party Talks," Beijing, September 19, 2005, available at <state.gov/r/pa/prs/ps/2005/53490.htm>; and Assistant Secretary of State Christopher R. Hill's statement at the Closing Plenary of the Fourth Round of the Six-Party Talks, September 19, 2005, available at <http://www.state.gov/r/pa/prs/ps/2005/53499.htm>.

36 U.S. Department of State, Bureau of Public Affairs, Fact Sheet, "North Korea: An Important First Step," February 20, 2007, available at < http://www.state.gov/documents/organization/80680.pdf>.

37 Paul D. Wolfowitz, "On Missile Defense," speech, Washington, DC, October 24, 2002, available at <defenselink.mil/speeches/2002/s20021024-depsecdef.html>.

38 *Quadrennial Defense Review Report*, 2006.

39 For a fuller examination of this concept, see M. Elaine Bunn, *Can Deterrence Be Tailored?* Strategic Forum 225 (Washington, DC: National Defense University

Press, January 2007), available at <http://www.ndu.edu/inss/Strforum/SF225/SF225.pdf>.

40   Quoted in David E. Sangar, "Behind the Urgent Diplomacy: A Sense Iran Will Get the Bomb," *The New York Times*, February 6, 2006.

41   James E. Goodby, Daniel L. Burghart, Cheryl A. Loeb, and Charles L. Thornton, *Cooperative Threat Reduction for a New Era*, Defense and Technology Paper 4 (Washington, DC: Center for Technology and National Security Policy, National Defense University, September 2004).

42   Ibid., 4.

43   "The Global Partnership's Third Anniversary," *Global Partnership Update* no. 7 (May/June 2005), 1, available at <sgpproject.org/publications/GPUpdates/GPUpdate%20June2005.pdf>.

44   Office of Management and Budget, "Budget of the United States Government, FY2006," available at <whitehouse.gov/omb/budget/fy2006/energy.html>.

45   Cooperative Threat Reduction Annual Report to Congress, Fiscal Year 2006, 1, available at <nti.org/e_research/official_docs/dod/2005/dod022805.pdf>.

46   See The White House, *National Strategy for Combating Terrorism,* February 2003; *National Strategy to Combat Weapons of Mass Destruction*, December 2002; and *National Strategy for Homeland Security,* July 2002.

47   Condoleezza Rice, "Dr. Condoleezza Rice Discusses the President's National Security Strategy," address given at the Waldorf-Astoria Hotel, New York, NY, October 1, 2002.

48   *Quadrennial Defense Review Report.*

49   Ibid., 51.

50   Ibid., 49.

51   "Implementing the 2006 Quadrennial Defense Review," proceedings of the 2006 Joint Operations Symposium, Institute for National Strategic Studies, National Defense University, Washington, DC, March 16–17, 2006, available at <ndu.edu/inss/symposia/joint2006/QDR%20Proceedings%20--%20FINAL.pdf >.

CHAPTER FOUR

1   Among the most notable of these efforts: The National Commission on the Terrorist Attacks Upon the United States, *The 9/11 Commission Report* (New York: Norton & Company, 2004); The White House, *National Strategy for Homeland Security* (Washington, DC: U.S. Government Printing Office, 2002); Department of Defense, *Strategy for Homeland Defense and Civil Support* (Washington, DC: U.S. Government Printing Office, June 2005); The White House, *The Federal Response to Hurricane Katrina Lessons Learned* (Washington, DC: U.S. Government Printing Office, 2006); U.S. House of Representatives, Final Report of the Select Bipartisan Committee to Investigate the Preparation for and Response to Hurricane Katrina, *A Failure of Initiative* (Washington, DC: U.S. Government Printing Office, 2006); The White House, *National Strategy for Pandemic Influenza* (Washington, DC: U.S. Government Printing Office, 2005), and its subsequent *Implementation Plan* (Washington, DC: U.S. Government Printing Office, 2006).

2   The White House, *National Strategy for Homeland Security*, ix.

3   See General Assembly of North Carolina, Session Law 2001–469, which went into effect on January 1, 2002, available at <http://www.ncga.state.nc.us/EnactedLegislation/SessionLaws/HTML/2001-2002/SL2001-469.html>.

4   Following the capture of Khalid Sheikh Mohammed, investigators uncovered detailed information about production plans for chemical and biological weapons. According to captured documents, certain members of al Qaeda had plans and the requisite materials to manufacture cyanide and two biological toxins, and were close to producing anthrax bacteria. Barton Gellman, "al-Qaida Near Biological, Chemical Arms Production," *The Washington Post*, March 23, 2003.

5   Jonathan Medalia, "Nuclear Terrorism: A Brief Review of Threats and Responses," Congressional Research Service, September 22, 2004, CRS–1.

6   Anonymous, *Through Our Enemies' Eyes* (Washington, DC: Brassey's, Inc., 2002; reprint, Michael Scheuer, *Through Our Enemies' Eyes* [Washington, DC: Potomac Books, 2006]), 187.

7   See Aaron Roper, "U.S. Ballistic Missile Defense Spending May Double," UPI, November 9, 2006, available at <http://www.spacewar.com/reports/US_Ballistic_Missile_Defense_Spending_May_ Double_999. html>.

8   Daniel Arnaudo, "Bush Cuts Threat Reduction Budget," *Arms Control Today*, April 20, 2007, available at <http://www.armscontrol.org/act/2007_3/ThreatReduction.asp>. See also Center for Defense Information, "Non-Proliferation and the FY 2005 Budget Request," available at <http://www.cdi.org/news/nuclear/ FY05-nonproliferation.pdf>.

9   U.S. Department of Homeland Security, press release, "President Signs FY 2007 Homeland Security Appropriations," October 4, 2006, available at <http://www.dhs.gov/xnews/releases/ pr_1159998463126.shtm>.

10 See U.S. Customs and Border Protection, CSI *Fact Sheet*, September 30, 2006. Available at <http://www.cbp.gov/linkhandler/cgov/border_security/international _activities/csi/csi_fact_sheet.ctt/csi_fact_sheet.doc.>.

11 *Through Our Enemies' Eyes*, 66.

12 Faisal Mohammad Ali, "Forgotten Hero of Bhopal's Tragedy," BBC News, December 2, 2004, available at <http://newswww.bbc.net.uk/2/hi/south_asia/4051755.stm>.

13 Philip Rucker, "Study Proposes Rerouting Hazmat Trains to Maryland," *The Washington Post*, April 5, 2007, B1.

14 "The 1993 Bombing: The First Attack on the World Trade Center," available at <http://911research.wtc7.net/wtc/bombing93/>.

15 Images of the devastation caused by this accident are available at <http://images.google.com/images?sourceid=navclient&ie=UTF-8&rls=GGLJ,GGLJ:2006-35,GGLJ:en&q=texas%20city%20ship%20explosion&oe=UTF-8&sa=N&tab=wi>.

16 For a fuller review of bioterrorism threats, see Henry S. Parker, *Agricultural Bioterrorism: A Federal Strategy to Meet the Threat*, McNair Paper 65 (Washington, DC: National Defense University Press, 2003), 15–17.

17 Laura Blumenfield, "Dissertation Could Be a Security Threat," *The Washington Post,* July 8, 2003, 1.

18 "Capitol Hill Anthrax Incident: EPA's Cleanup Was Successful; Opportunities Exist to Enhance Contract Oversight," Government Accounting Office Report, 03–686, June 2003, 10, available at <http://www.gao.gov/new.items/d03686.pdf>.

19 Col. John Boyd, USAF, developed this concept to describe the decision cycle in a fighter melee; he later showed how it applied to all levels of war.

20 A number of observers, including senior members of the House Intelligence Committee, have expressed concern that the Office of the Director of National Intelligence has added another layer of bureaucracy, but not fundamentally improved key capabilities or responsiveness of the Intelligence Community. See Scott Shane, "In New Job, Spymaster Draws Bipartisan Criticism," *The New York Times*, April 20, 2006, A1; and Walter Pincus, "Intelligence Redo Is Harshly Judged: A Judge Critiques 9/11 Overhaul, and Finds It Top-Heavy, *The Washington Post*, March 31, 2006, A17.

21 The Robert T. Stafford Disaster Relief and Emergency Assistance Act, P.L. 93–288, as amended, 42 U.S.C. §5121–5206 (2005).

22 *The Federal Response to Hurricane Katrina*, 54.

23 U.S. Department of Homeland Security, "The National Response Plan," December 2004, available at <http://www.dhs.gov/interweb/assetlibrary/NRPbaseplan.pdf>; updated May 2006, available at <http://www.dhs.gov/dhspublic/interapp/editorial/editorial_0566.xml>. The plan incorporates best practices and procedures from incident management disciplines—homeland security, emergency management, law enforcement, firefighting, public works, public health, responder and recovery worker health and safety, emergency medical services, and the private sector—and integrates them into a unified structure.

24 See The Center for Biosecurity, University of Pittsburgh Medical Center, available at <http://www.upmc-biosecurity.org/website/events/2001_darkwinter/index.html>.

25 Paul Ritvo et al., "A Canadian national survey regarding attitudes and knowledge regarding preventative vaccines," *Journal of Immune Based Therapies and Vaccines* 1, no. 3 (November 2003), available at <http://www.pubmedcentral.nih.gov/articlerender.fcgi?artid=280696#N0x82d11a 8.0x855f9d0>.

26 Post-9/11 deficiencies in public health infrastructure and workforce were detailed initially in Board of Health Promotion and Disease Prevention, Institute of Medicine, *The Future of the Public's Health in the 21ˢᵗ Century* (Washington, DC: National Academies Press, 2002); and more recently in Board of Health Sciences Policy, William Hooke and Paul G. Rogers, eds., *Public Health Risks of Disasters: Communication, Infrastructure, and Preparedness—Workshop Summary* (Washington, DC: National Academies Press, 2005). Lack of disaster preparedness training for Emergency Management System personnel was cited in a report of the Committee on the Future of Emergency Care in the United States Health System, *Emergency Medical Services: At the Crossroads* (Washington, DC: National Academies Press, 2006). And shortfalls in planning and funding for medical surge capacity in the face of a protracted biomedical crisis were chronicled in the American Hospital Association, testimony before the U.S. Senate Special Committee on

Aging, "Preparing for Pandemic Flu," May 25, 2006, available at <http://www.aha.org/aha/testimony/2006/060525-tes-pandemicflu.pdf>.

27   U.S. Department of Homeland Security, "The National Exercise Plan," available at <http://www.ojp.usdoj.gov/odp/exercises.htm>.

28   *The Federal Response to Hurricane Katrina*, 7–8.

29   Ibid.

30   Few images of Katrina's damage were more shocking than those showing dozens of New Orleans city buses under water in flooded parking lots, evidently because, according to Mayor Ray Nagin, their parking areas had been "high and dry throughout every storm that has ever hit the city of New Orleans. And we expected the same for this event. Unfortunately, those buses flooded also because 80 percent of the city went underwater." See *The Federal Response to Hurricane Katrina*, 185.

31   The Stafford Act, 42 U.S.C. §5170 (2005).

32   *The Federal Response to Hurricane Katrina*, 53–54.

33   See, for example, criticisms by VADM Thad Allen recounted in *The Federal Response to Hurricane Katrina*, 53.

34   U.S. House of Representatives, *A Failure of Initiative*, 15.

35   When queried about the President's question, 38 governors reportedly expressed objections. See Bill Nichols and Richard Benedetto, "Govs to Bush: Relief is Our Job," *USA Today*, October 2, 2005. As one governor opined: "I would never abdicate, nor would I expect any other governor to abdicate, the responsibility to protect the people of my state."

36   Department of Defense, *Quadrennial Defense Review Report*, February 2006, 23.

37   Trust for America's Health, "Ready or Not? Protecting the Public's Health from Disease, Disasters, and Bioterrorism, 2005," available at <http://healthy americans.org/reports/bioterror05/>. See also American Hospital Association, Testimony before the U.S. Senate Special Committee on Aging, note 23.

38   Centers for Disease Control, press release, "CDC Finds Flu Deaths Higher Than Previously Estimated," January 7, 2003, available at <http://www.cdc.gov/od/oc/media/pressrel/r030107.htm>.

39   Department of Defense, *Strategy for Homeland Defense and Civil Support*, iii.

40   For example, the National Guard has fielded 12 CBRNE Enhanced Response Force Packages (CERFPs), and Congress has authorized 5 more. Yet CERFP teams are not organized as units; they are task organizations that draw resources from various battalions that may or may not be located in the same state. Even these subunits do not have a primary mission of emergency response. Rather, their primary mission remains their traditional "wartime" mission in areas such as medical support, engineering, military police, and chemical defense. Thus, the emergency response mission to support first responders is only a secondary mission and cannot be regularly practiced as a unit. Some states are increasing the number of these units under state programs but none are making CBRNE response their primary mission.

41   See North American Aerospace Defense Command, Newsroom, "U.S., Canada Strengthen NORAD agreement," May 23, 2006, available at <http://www.norad.mil/newsroom/news_releases/2006/052306.htm>; and Parliament of Canada, *Hansard*,

39th Parliament, 1st Session, no. 15, May 3, 2006, 1820–2320, and no. 18, May 8, 2006, 1500.

42 For additional background on this idea, see John A. Cope, "Protecting the U.S. Southern Approach: A Prescription," *Joint Force Quarterly* 42 (3[d] Quarter 2006), 17.

43 U.S. Northern Command, "Role of NORTHCOM," available at <www.northcom.mil>.

CHAPTER FIVE

1 Daniel Yankelovich, Public Agenda Poll, "Confidence in U.S. Foreign Policy Index, Volume 3: Anxious Public Sees Growing Dangers, Few Solutions," Fall 2006, available at <http://www.publicagenda.org/foreignpolicy/pdfs/foreign_policy_index_fall06.pdf>.

2 Robert Cooper, *The Breaking of Nations: Order and Chaos in the Twenty-first Century* (New York: Atlantic Monthly Press, 2003), 77.

3 Director of Central Intelligence, Statement for the Record, Joint Inquiry Committee, Senate Select Committee on Intelligence, October 17, 2002.

4 Recent reports suggest, however, growing concern that al Qaeda is regaining operational capacity. In his annual threat assessment, former U.S. Director of National Intelligence John Negroponte stated that "al Qaeda's core elements are resilient." See John D. Negroponte, statement, Annual Threat Assessment of the Director of National Intelligence to the Senate Select Committee on Intelligence, January 11, 2007, 2. See also Mark Mazzetti and David Rohde, "Terror Officials See Qaeda Chiefs Regaining Power," *The New York Times,* February 19, 2007, A1.

5 The term *fault-line conflicts* was coined by Samuel P. Huntington in the mid-1990s to describe conflicts between states or groups with differing civilizational identities. See his *The Clash of Civilizations: Remaking of World Order* (New York: Touchstone, 1997), chapters 10–11. By certain measures, conflict trends since then somewhat belie Huntington's thesis regarding the increasing prevalence of such wars: large-scale fighting in the Balkans, the Caucasus, and southern Sudan subsided, while *intra*-civilizational violence surged in places like Congo, Darfur, and, more recently, Iraq, where Sunni Muslim insurgents and jihadists are pitted against Shi'a Muslim militias. Even so, the term is still apt as a label for conflicts driven by clashing identities—whether religious, ethnic, or broadly cultural—that can rally extremist support more widely.

6 *The National Security Strategy of the United States of America* (Washington, DC: The White House, September 17, 2002), 1.

7 The first Failed States Index provides rich narrative; see "Globalization at Work: The Failed States Index," *Foreign Policy* 149 (July/August 2005), 56–65; an updated and expanded index was compiled in 2006 by the Fund for Peace, available at <http://www.fundforpeace.org/ programs/fsi/fsindex.php>. As for the labels, "a premodern world" belongs to Robert Cooper, 65; "zone of turmoil and development" belongs to Max Singer and Aaron Wildavsky, *The Real World Order* (Chatham, NJ: Chatham House Publishers, 1993); "a non-integrating gap" belongs to Thomas P.M. Barnett, *The Pentagon's New Map: War and Peace in the 21st Century* (New York: G.P. Putnam's Sons, 2004); "southern belt of strategic instability" belongs to Stephen J. Flanagan, Ellen L. Frost, and Richard L. Kugler,

Challenges of the Global Century: Report of the Project on Globalization and National Security (Washington, DC: National Defense University Press, 2001); a "neo-Hobbesian world of turmoil" belongs to Hans Binnendijk and Richard L. Kugler, *Seeing the Elephant: The U.S. Role in Global Security* (Washington, DC: National Defense University Press and Potomac Books, 2006).

8 Failed States Index, 57.

9 For a vivid perspective on the phenomenon, albeit with dubious historical parallels, see John Rapley, "The New Middle Ages," *Foreign Affairs* 85, no. 3 (May/June 2006), 95–103.

10 For a good overview of the diverse actors on today's irregular battlefields, see Steven Metz, *Rethinking Insurgency* (Carlisle, PA: Strategic Studies Institute, U.S. Army War College, June 2007), 12–42.

11 Human Security Center, *Human Security Report 2005: War and Peace in the 21st Century* (Oxford: Oxford University Press, 2005), 14–41.

12 On June 28, 1914, Gavrilo Princip, a diminutive, sickly former student and a member of a secret Serb society, had gone into a café in Sarajevo after thinking he missed his chance to get a shot off at the Austrian Archduke, Franz Ferdinand, who was visiting the city that day (and who had already escaped a bomb earlier in the day). As fate would have it, the Archduke's car took a wrong turn by the café and had to back up the street in order to turn around. Princip was waiting. Had he not been successful, some other event almost surely would have produced the catalytic effect; but history never discloses its alternatives. As for parallels with our contemporary situation, clearly there are some. See Niall Ferguson, "Sinking Globalization," *Foreign Affairs* 84, no. 2 (March/April 2005). On the other hand, an ideologically driven power (for example, a Leninist Soviet Union) and a rigid alliance system are not part of the mix.

13 See Fareed Zakaria, "It's the Economy, Mr. President," *The Washington Post*, November 20, 2006, A17.

14 According to then–Director of National Intelligence John D. Negroponte: "Al Qaeda's core elements . . . continue to maintain active connections and relationships that radiate outward from their leaders' secure hideout in Pakistan to affiliates throughout the Middle East, northern Africa, and Europe." See Negroponte, Annual Threat Assessment, 2. Warnings regarding al Qaeda's ability to regenerate its ability to attack the U.S. homeland were reinforced in the National Intelligence Estimate, *The Terrorist Threat to the U.S. Homeland* (Washington, DC: Director of National Intelligence, July 2007), 1, available at <http://dni.gov/press_releases/20070717_release.pdf>.

15 The author is indebted to my colleague Joseph McMillan for drawing this distinction.

16 Chester A. Crocker, Fen Osler Hampson, and Pamela Aall, eds., *Leashing the Dogs of War: Conflict Management in a Divided World* (Washington, DC: U.S. Institute of Peace, 2007), 361.

17 Richard Haass applies this label to Iraq; see "The New Middle East: As the Iraq War helps bring the American era to a close, a new order will begin to emerge in the region," *Newsweek International*, January 8, 2007.

18 It is also true, however, that interventions in humanitarian crises have helped to advance national security objectives. The 1999 Australian-led operation in East Timor, awkward as it was for Jakarta, has had a generally salutary impact on Indonesia's long-term prospects for stability.

19 For a useful first step in this direction, see Stewart Patrick, "Weak States and Global Threats: Fact or Fiction?" *The Washington Quarterly* 29, no. 2 (Spring 2006), 27–53.

20 Thomas P.M. Barnett, "The Pentagon's New Map," *Esquire* 139, no. 3 (March 2003), 174.

21 Attributed to LTG Karl Eikenberry, USA, in Jim Hoagland, "The Key to Afghanistan: More Time," *The Washington Post*, September 24, 2006, B7.

22 Portions of this section are drawn from the author's "Regional Conflicts: Strategies for Quelling Violence and Prospects for Sino-U.S. Cooperation," presentation to a conference of the U.S.-China Project on Areas of Instability and Emerging Threats, Beijing, People's Republic of China, February 23, 2004, available at <http://www.acus.org/docs/0402-Regional_Conflicts_Strategies_Violence_Prospects_Sino-U.S._Cooperation.pdf>.

23 There is nonetheless a rich history of involvement in such adventures; see Max Boot, *The Savage Wars of Peace: Small Wars and the Rise of American Power* (New York: Basic Books, 2002).

24 Thus, realists and neoconservatives would debate whether interventions should be a venue for democracy promotion; liberal internationalists, realists, and neoconservatives would all differ over how much deference to pay to the United Nations in conducting interventions; and right-wing "America First" nationalists and left-wing pacifists might join together in fighting the others on whether interventions were necessary at all. And these are only just a few fault lines. For a rich exposition of how recent interventions have embroiled neoconservative thinkers with these other foreign policy approaches (albeit with somewhat different labels), see Francis Fukuyama, *America at the Crossroads: Democracy, Power, and the Neoconservative Legacy* (New Haven: Yale University Press, 2006).

25 Author's emphasis. *National Security Strategy*, 9.

26 *The National Security Strategy of the United States of America* (Washington, DC: The White House, March 2006), 14.

27 Ibid., 14–15.

28 This is not to say that American neglect is always resented. The author was once party to a conversation between two foreign diplomats from different countries. One bitterly complained to the other: "Why do the Americans always ignore us?" The other smiled and replied: "Ah, yes, but just wait until they start paying attention to you."

29 This is a broader application of a point aptly made by Ken Menkhaus following the Ethiopian invasion of Somalia in January 2007; see "Who Broke Mogadishu?" *Guardian Unlimited,* January 16, 2007, available at <http://commentisfree.guardian.co.uk/ken_menkhaus/2007/01/who_broke_mogadishu. html>.

30 Although it is worth pointing out that in some of these cases, the United States aided and abetted insurgency as much as countering it, especially so in Kosovo,

where the benefited local party was Muslim separatists under the banner of the Kosovo Liberation Front; in East Timor, which worked to the advantage of Christian separatists under Falantil banner; and Iraq, where the U.S. invasion inflated the sails of Shi'ite organizations long suppressed by Saddam.

[31] Australian terrorism expert David Kilcullen calls this *conflict disaggregation*. See George Packer, "Knowing the Enemy: Can Social Scientists Redefine the War on Terror," *The New Yorker*, December 18, 2006.

[32] For example, Mexico and Brazil would fall into this category of states of primary concern, along with Turkey, Egypt, Ethiopia, Nigeria, Pakistan, Bangladesh, the Philippines, and Indonesia.

[33] The most authoritative official exposition of this approach is found in the Long War concept. See U.S. Department of Defense, *Quadrennial Defense Review Report* (Washington, DC: Department of Defense, February 6, 2006), 11–12. For a sympathetic journalistic treatment, see also Robert Kaplan, "Intervention's Realistic Future," *The Washington Post*, November 22, 2006, A21.

[34] An authoritative statement on principles for military intervention aimed at this objective is spelled out in the Report of the International Commission on Intervention and State Sovereignty, *The Responsibility to Protect*, December 2001, xii–xiii.

[35] For background, see Stockholm International Peace Research Institute, *Armaments, Disarmament and International Security, 2002* (Oxford: Oxford University Press, 2002), 388–389. See also James A. Schear, "Global Institutions in a Cooperative Order," in *Global Engagement: Cooperation and Security in the 21st Century*, ed. Janne E. Nolan (Washington, DC: Brookings, 1994), 266–267.

[36] This concept was first established in the 1907 Hague Convention and developed in successive laws of war instruments; see Adam Roberts and Richard Guelff, eds., *Documents on the Laws of War*, 3d ed. (Oxford: Oxford University Press, 2000).

[37] Two examples are Operation *Fuerte Appoyo*, launched into Central America in October 1998 after a devastating hurricane killed 10,000 and threatened major population movements, and Operation *Atlas Response,* which was launched into Mozambique in March–April 2000, when three cyclones in the space of a few weeks inundated the country and threatened to undermine a weak state in the midst of an otherwise successful postconflict recovery.

[38] The best example is seen in the experience of the UN Protection Force in Bosnia-Herzegovina, whose vulnerabilities on the ground to Serb reprisal were so pronounced that they served as a disincentive to call for NATO airstrikes in response to violations of the safe-areas.

[39] Historically, the United States has also on occasion taken the view that central government is not the solution but the problem and has supported groups resisting central government authority; Nicaragua and Afghanistan (during the 1980s) and Kosovar Albanians are cases in point.

[40] Author's discussion with senior UN official, Sarajevo, October 1994.

[41] James A. Baker III and Lee H. Hamilton, *The Iraq Study Group Report* (New York: Vintage Books, 2006), 47.

42 Abu Musab Al-Zarqawi's strategy of sowing the seeds of sectarian war in Iraq—and in so doing triggering Shi'a violence against fellow Sunni insurgents—provides the most compelling example of sacrificing local interests as against the needs of the international jihad.

43 Robert Kagan, "Embraceable E.U.," *The Washington Post*, December 5, 2004, B7.

44 Within this last category is the problem of opium cultivation and methods of eradication or crop substitution in places like Afghanistan, Colombia, and Southeast Asia.

45 The author's favorite example draws from Cambodia. When at the end of the peace process in late 1993, the four Khmer factions could not agree on which side should have the honor of contributing a new chief of defense to lead the new royal Cambodian armed forces, they asked the Australian general officer who commanded the UN force to do the honors. He politely declined.

46 These roles can range from a neutral mediator, to an evenhanded (but not necessarily neutral) power broker, to "partisan" supporters who can deliver reluctant parties to a final deal, to funders and financial backers of a settlement.

47 Comments of General Joseph Hoar, USMC (Ret.); see Michael R. Gordon, "Millions for Defense, Barely a Penny for Djibouti," *The New York Times*, December 1, 2002, 10.

48 The author uses the term *compellence* as it was coined by Thomas C. Schelling in his classic work, *Arms and Influence* (New Haven: Yale University Press, 1966), 70–71.

49 James F. Dobbins et al., *The UN's Role in Nation-Building: From Congo to Iraq* (Santa Monica, CA: RAND Corporation, 2005), 117.

50 U.S. military resistance to the idea of shooting looters in Baghdad is well chronicled by Michael Gordon and Bernard Trainor in *Cobra II: The Inside Story of the Invasion and Occupation of Iraq* (New York: Pantheon Books, 2006), 478.

51 While there is merit to this argument, one must be careful about overdrawing it. The degree of local acceptance of, or hostility to, a nongovernmental organization's (NGO's) activities also depends on what the activity actually is, not just on who is supporting or protecting the activity. Thus, the international NGOs in Afghanistan that help educate young girls today are not engaging in politically or culturally neutral activities as far as Taliban remnants are concerned, and such programs would most likely have spurred violence from Islamic extremists whether or not the United States had intervened.

52 For a particularly good review, see Kenneth Katzman, *Afghanistan: Post-War Governance, Security and U.S. Policy,* CRS Report for Congress, updated January 11, 2007 (Report RL30588), 5–28.

53 Though less than achieving the demilitarization of Kabul, as called for by the Bonn Agreement, the International Security Assistance Force nevertheless played an essential role. See Barnett R. Rubin, Humayun Hamidzada, and Abby Stoddard, *Afghanistan 2005 and Beyond: Prospects for Improved Stability* (Clingendael: Netherlands Institute of International Relations, April 2005), 55.

54 David Rhode and James Risen, "CIA Review Highlights Afghan Leader's Woes," *The New York Times*, November 5, 2006, 12.

55 Barnett R. Rubin, "Saving Afghanistan," *Foreign Affairs* 86, no. 1 (January/February 2007), 74, 76. Rubin lays out some temporary supplemental measures that could be taken to bolster district level civil administration and the court system.

56 See Elizabeth Rubin's revealing travelogue, "In the Land of the Taliban," *The New York Times Magazine*, October 22, 2006, 86–175. Extremist attacks are increasing against Pakistani government targets as well. See Abdul Sattar, "Blast in Courtroom Kills 15 in Pakistan," *The Washington Post*, February 18, 2007, A22.

57 President George W. Bush, speech to the Nation, March 19, 2003, available at <http://www.whitehouse.gov/news/releases/2003/03/20030319-17.html>.

58 Donald H. Rumsfeld, "Beyond Nation-building," remarks at 11th Annual Salute to Freedom, New York City, February 14, 2003, available at <http://www.defenselink.mil/speeches/2003/sp20030214-secdef0024.html>.

59 Ibid. Regarding Iraq, Rumsfeld stated: "We have set up a post-war planning office to think through the problems and coordinate the efforts of coalition countries and U.S. government agencies." In fact, even at the time, it was clear that significant postwar planning had lagged badly behind planning for the forced entry phase.

60 Cancellation or "off-ramping" of force deployments into theater is well chronicled in Gordon and Trainor, *Cobra II*, 460–461.

61 See interview with then–National Security Advisor Condoleezza Rice, ibid., 142.

62 As former Secretaries of Defense Arthur Schlesinger and Harold Brown stated in a Pentagon review of detention operations in August 2004, the "war plan presupposed that relatively stability and security operations would precede a handover to Iraq's authorities." Quoted in Thomas E. Ricks, *Fiasco: The American Military Adventure in Iraq* (New York: The Penguin Press, 2006), 147.

63 Then–Army Chief of Staff General Eric Shinseki's estimate of "several hundred thousand" troops to exert "post-hostilities control" was substantially in excess of the 100,000 troops reportedly foreseen in the actual planning, triggering public disavowal by Deputy Defense Secretary Paul D. Wolfowitz. See Eric Schmitt, "Pentagon Contradicts General on Iraq Occupation Force's Size," *The New York Times*, February 28, 2003, A1. See also Gordon and Trainor, *Cobra II*, 102–103.

64 The firefight between a unit of the U.S. Army's 82[d] Airborne Division and Iraqi militants in Fallujah that reportedly left a number of dead and injured noncombatants falls into this category. For an account, see Gordon and Trainor, 462.

65 James Jay Carafano and Dana Dillon call this the "clean slate solution." See "Winning the Peace: Principles for Post-Conflict Operations," *Backgrounder*, no. 1859 (Washington, DC: The Heritage Foundation, June 13, 2005), 3.

66 As the Iraq Study Group assessed the problem of government capacity: "[M]ost of Iraq's technocrat class was pushed out of government by de-Baathification." Baker and Hamilton, 21.

67 Ibid., 8.

68 Complexities are well developed in Key Judgments, National Intelligence Estimate, *Prospects for Iraq's Stability: A Challenging Road Ahead* (Washington, DC: National Intelligence Council, January 2007), 2.

69 The vehicle for Karzai's initiative was a grand tribal assembly—the so-called Peace Jirga—bringing together populations along both sides of the troubled border. See

Taimoor Shah and Carlotta Gall, "Afghan Rebels Find Aid in Pakistan, Musharraf Admits," *The New York Times*, August 13, 2007, A1.

70 See General David H. Petraeus, USA, *Report to the Congress on the Situation in Iraq*, September 11, 2007, available at <http://www.mnf-iraq.com/index.php?option =com_content&task=view&id=13904& Itemid=1>.

71 Dave Kilcullen, "Anatomy of a Tribal Revolt," *Small Wars Journal* blog, August 29, 2007, available at <http://www.smallwarsjournal.com/ blog/2007/08/anatomy-of-a-tribal-revolt/>. Kilcullen provides rich insights into this phenomenon and offers recommendations for managing tensions between provincial-level actors and Iraqi government.

72 The strongest case for (qualified) optimism was made by Ambassador Ryan Crocker in September 2007, citing in part the frustration of Iraq's own political leaders as an incentive for change: "[T]here is a palpable frustration in Baghdad over the sectarian system that was used to divide the spoils of the state in the last few years. Leaders from all communities openly acknowledge that a focus on sectarian gains has led to poor governance and served Iraqis badly." See testimony of Ryan C. Crocker, Joint Hearing of the U.S. House of Representatives Committee on Foreign Affairs and the Committee on Armed Services, September 10, 2007, available at <http://www.state.gov/p/nea/rls/rm/2007/91941.htm>.

73 See Defense Science Board, *Transitions To and From Hostilities* (Washington, DC: Department of Defense, December 2004).

74 For a judicious, careful analysis of assumptions, see Nora Bensahel, "Mission Not Accomplished: What Went Wrong with Iraqi Reconstruction," *The Journal of Strategic Studies* 29, no. 3 (June 2006), 456–462.

75 See, for example, I. William Zartman and Saadia Touval, "International Mediation in the Post-Cold War Era," in Chester Crocker, Fen Osler Hampson, and Pamela R. Aall, *Managing Global Chaos: Sources of and Response to International Conflict* (Washington, DC: United States Institute of Peace Press, 1996), 452–453.

76 This is a definite congruence between success and failure in conflict stabilization and whether or not the capital city in a particular zone of conflict is itself on the front line. If it is—for example, Mogadishu, Sarajevo—then stabilization becomes much more problematic.

77 Remarks by General Anthony Zinni, USMC, "Beyond Jointness: The Civil-Military Dimensions of Peace Operations and Humanitarian Assistance," National Defense University, Washington, DC, 1999, 63.

78 The democratic process itself, as part of tear-down/rebuild strategy, posed its own set of challenges. Stephen Biddle makes the good point that rapid democratization is a recipe for polarizing already antagonistic communal groups. See Stephen Biddle, "Seeing Baghdad, Thinking Saigon," *Foreign Affairs* 85, no. 2 (March/April 2005), 8.

79 Examples where adroit diplomacy and pressure helped to divide rebel forces or spoilers from their regional patrons include the Khmer Rouge from the People's Republic of China and Thailand, in the early 1990s; the Croatian Serb militia from the Milosevic regime in 1995; and the Indonesian militia from Jakarta in East Timor in 1999. Recent developments suggest the possibility of a U.S. opening to

discussions with Iran and Syria regarding Iraqi stability; see Helene Cooper and Kirk Semple, "U.S. Set to Join Iran and Syria in Talks on Iraq," *The New York Times,* February 28, 2007, A1.

80 The White House, National Security Presidential Directive/NSPD–44, "Management of Interagency Efforts Concerning Reconstruction and Stabilization," December 7, 2005.

81 Office of the Spokesman, Transformational Diplomacy, Fact Sheet, January 18, 2006, available at <http://www.state.gov/r/pa/prs/ps/2006/59339.htm>. See also Condoleezza Rice, remarks at Georgetown University, Washington DC, January 18, 2006, available at <http://www.state.gov/misc/52620.htm>.

82 Department of Defense Directive 3000.05, "Military Support for Stability, Security, Transition, and Reconstruction (SSTR) Operations" (Washington, DC: Department of Defense, November 28, 2005), available at <http://www.dtic.mil/whs/directives/corres/pdf/d300005_112805/d300005p.pdf>.

83 For a useful assessment of the initial phase, see Gordon Adams, "Post-Combat Stabilization and Reconstruction: The Lessons for U.S. Government Organization and National Security Resource Planning," in *Iraq and America: Choices and Consequences,* ed. Ellen Laipson and Maureen S. Steinbruner (Washington, DC: Henry L. Stimson Center, July 2006), 145–151.

84 See Rajiv Chandrasekaran, "Iraq Rebuilding Short on Qualified Civilians," *The Washington Post,* February 24, 2007, A1. See remarks by General Peter Pace, USMC, Chairman, Joint Chiefs of Staff, to the Senate Armed Services Committee, February 6, 2007, available at <http://www.jcs.mil/chairman/speeches/070206SecDefSASC_Hearing.html>.

85 See Shawn Zeller, "On the Work Force Roller Coaster at USAID," *Foreign Service Journal*, April 2004, 33.

86 Ibid., 36. As of the end of fiscal year 2006, total full-time USAID employees numbered slightly over 2,400. Nearly two-thirds of these, however, were Washington-based staff. The author is grateful to Stewart Patrick, Research Fellow, Center for Global Development, for providing these figures.

87 See John Williamson, "The Washington Consensus as Policy Prescription for Development," lecture delivered at the World Bank, January 13, 2004, available at <http://www.iie.com/publications/papers/ williamson0204.pdf>.

88 For a full exposition on this theme, see Francis Fukuyama, *State Building: Governance and World Order in the Twenty-First Century* (London: Profile Books, 2005), 2–57.

89 For amplification, see the author's "Information Requirements in S&R Operations: What Do Inquiring Minds Want to Know?" presentation to a workshop on Communications, Information Systems and Networks in Support of Stabilization and Reconstruction Operations, National Defense University, October 28, 2004, available at <http://www.ndu.edu/ctnsp/S&Rworkshop1004/2_schear.pdf>.

90 NSPD–44, 2. Per the directive, the Secretary of State shall "coordinate (such) efforts with the Secretary of Defense to ensure harmonization with any planned or ongoing U.S. military operations across the spectrum of conflict."

91 Headquarters, U.S. Department of the Army and Marine Corps Combat Development Command, *Counterinsurgency*, U.S. Army Field Manual 3–24, Marine Corps Warfighting Publication 3–33.5, December 15, 2006.

92 For perspective on this problem, see Office of the Secretary of Defense, "Interim Progress Report on DoD Directive 3000.05—Military Support for Stability, Security, Transition and Reconstruction (SSTR) Operations," August 2006, 17.

CHAPTER SIX

1 *The National Security Strategy of the United States of America* (Washington, DC: The White House, March 2006), 35.

2 Condoleezza Rice, "Campaign 2000: Promoting the National Interest," *Foreign Affairs* 79, no. 1 (January/February 2000), 45–62.

3 Colin L. Powell, press conference following meetings with Chinese officials, Beijing, China, July 28, 2001, available at <state.gov/secretary/former/powell/remarks/2001/4327.htm>.

4 See the remarks on China in *The National Security Strategy of the United States of America*, September 17, 2002, available at <whitehouse.gov/nsc/nssall.html>; and in Richard N. Haass, "China and the Future of U.S.-China Relations," remarks to the National Committee on U.S.-China Relations, New York, December 5, 2002, available at <usinfo.state.gov/regional/ea/uschina/haaschina.htm>.

5 Jonathan Pollack was one of the first to articulate the logic of a hedge strategy in a 1995 working paper for the Council on Foreign Relations. A revised version was published as "Designing a New American Security Strategy for Asia," in *Weaving the Net: Conditional Engagement with China,* ed. James J. Shinn (New York: Council on Foreign Relations, 1996), 99–132.

6 Deputy Secretary of State Robert B. Zoellick, "Whither China: From Membership to Responsibility?" Remarks to National Committee on U.S.-China Relations, New York, September 21, 2005, available at <state.gov/s/d/rem/53682.htm>.

7 "Remarks by President Hu Jintao of The People's Republic of China at Welcoming Luncheon at the White House Hosted by President George W. Bush of the United States of America," April 20, 2006, available at <fmprc.gov.cn/eng/zxxx/t259220.htm>.

8 See Keith Crane et al., *Modernizing China's Military: Opportunities and Constraints* (Santa Monica, CA: RAND, 2005), 91–134; and Department of Defense, *Military Power of the People's Republic of China 2006* (May 2006), 18–21, available at <defenselink.mil/pubs/pdfs/China Report 2006.pdf>.

9 China's 2007 military budget announcement revealed that official defense spending for 2006 was actually 297.93 billion *renminbi* (RMB), or about U.S. $36.3 billion at the current exchange rate of 8.2 RMB per dollar. "China's defense budget to rise 17.8 percent in 2007," *People's Daily,* March 4, 2007.

10 Leonard S. Spector, Jing-dong Yuan, and Phillip C. Saunders, prepared statement for the U.S.-China Economic and Security Review Commission, Hearing on China's Proliferation Policies and Practices, July 24, 2003, available at <cns.miis.edu/research/congress/testim/testlsp.htm>.

11 This definition is adapted from Andrew Krepinevich and M. Elaine Bunn.

[12] "The cauldron boils," *The Economist*, September 29, 2005. Also see Murray Scot Tanner, "China Rethinks Unrest," *Washington Quarterly* 27, no. 3 (Summer 2004), 137–156.

[13] Yongding, "China's Color-Coded Crackdown," October 2005, available at <foreignpolicy.com/story/cms.php?story_id=3251>.

[14] "Quarterly Chronicle and Documentation," *China Quarterly*, no. 185 (March 2006), 215–217, 242–263.

[15] James A. Kelly, "Overview of U.S. Policy Toward Taiwan," testimony at a hearing on Taiwan, House International Relations Committee, Washington, DC, April 21, 2004, available at <state.gov/p/eap/rls/rm/2004/31649.htm>.

[16] This section draws upon Phillip C. Saunders, "Long-Term Trends in China-Taiwan Relations: Implications for U.S. Taiwan Policy," *Asian Survey* 45, no. 6 (November/December 2005), 970–991.

[17] William J. Clinton, "Remarks by the President to the Business Council," February 24, 2000, available at <hongkong.usconsulate.gov/uscn/wh/2000/022401.htm>; "Bush vows 'whatever it takes' to defend Taiwan," CNN.com, April 25, 2001, available at <archives.cnn.com/2001/ALLPOLITICS/04/25/bush.taiwan.03>.

[18] "Bush Reaffirms U.S. Commitment to One-China Policy," available at <usinfo.state.gov/xarchives/display.html?p=washfile-english&y=2003&m=December&x=20031209173641esuarKS0.2866632&t=xarchives/xarchitem.html>.

[19] Su-27 and Su-30 fighters, S–300 surface-to-air missiles, *Kilo*-class submarines, and Sovremenny destroyers equipped with advanced antiship missiles.

[20] See David Shambaugh, "A Matter of Time: Taiwan's Eroding Military Advantage," *The Washington Quarterly* 23, no. 2 (Spring 2000), 119–133; and Department of Defense, *The Military Power of the People's Republic of China 2006*, 50.

[21] Michael S. Chase, "U.S.-Taiwan Security Cooperation: Enhancing an Unofficial Relationship," in *Dangerous Strait: The U.S.-Taiwan-China Crisis*, ed. Nancy Bernkopf Tucker (New York: Columbia University Press, 2005), 162–185.

[22] See David M. Lampton and Kenneth Lieberthal, "Heading off the Next War," *The Washington Post*, April 13, 2004.

[23] This section draws upon arguments in Phillip C. Saunders and Jing-dong Yuan, "China's Strategic Force Modernization," in *China's Nuclear Future*, ed. Albert Willner and Paul Bolt (Boulder, CO: Lynn Rienner, 2006), 79–118.

[24] China's nuclear deterrent relies primarily on cave- and silo-based DF–4 and DF–5A intercontinental ballistic missiles (ICBMs). These missiles must be fueled and have warheads attached before launch, resulting in a force with low readiness and high vulnerability to attack. China's modernization program will deploy new solid-fueled, road-mobile ICBMs and submarine-launched ballistic missiles (SLBMs), resulting in significant improvements in launch preparation time, survivability, and accuracy. The DF–31, a road-mobile ICBM with a 7,250-kilometer (km) range that can reach parts of the western United States, began deployment in 2006. The DF–31 will probably be a single-warhead missile, although it may employ decoys or other countermeasures to penetrate U.S. missile defenses. China is also developing the DF–31A, a 12,000-km range missile expected to enter service in 2007.

Department of Defense, *Military Power of the People's Republic of China 2006*, 27; Howard Diamond, "Chinese Strategic Plans Move Forward with Missile Test," *Arms Control Today* 29, no. 5 (July/August 1999), 27, available at <armscontrol.org/act/1999_07-08/chija99.asp>. China has replaced older DF–5 ICBMs with new DF–5A variants that could potentially be fitted with multiple warheads or missile defense countermeasures. These land-based ICBMs will be supplemented by the Julang-2 (JL–2), an SLBM that will be deployed on the new JIN Class Type 094 ballistic missile submarine (SSBN), which should be operational by the end of the decade. John Wilson Lewis and Hua Di, "China's Ballistic Missile Programs: Technologies, Strategies, Goals," *International Security* 17, no. 2 (Fall 1992), 28; and Department of Defense, *Annual Report on the Military Power of the People's Republic of China* (Washington, DC: Department of Defense, 2003), 31, available at <defenselink.mil/pubs/20030730chinaex.pdf>. As a result, the number of Chinese missiles capable of reaching the United States is likely to increase from the current 18 to 26 to at least 50 to 60. This assessment assumes China would want significant numbers of both land- and sea-based missiles in order to diversify its delivery systems and guard against possible technological improvements that could reduce the survivability of its nuclear forces. Some of this expansion is dictated by the fact that the addition of just 2 Type 094 SSBNs would add 32 warheads to China's arsenal. A minimum of two submarines is necessary to keep one on operational patrol at all times; the U.S. Navy typically requires three submarines in order to have one operationally deployed at all times.

25 Alan D. Romberg and Michael McDevitt, eds., *China and Missile Defense: Managing U.S.-PRC Strategic Relations* (Washington, DC: The Henry L. Stimson Center, February 2003); Paul H.B. Godwin and Evan S. Medeiros, "China, America, and Missile Defense: Conflicting National Interests," *Current History* 99, no. 638 (September 2000), 285–289; Charles Ferguson, "Sparking a Buildup: U.S. Missile Defense and China's Nuclear Arsenal," *Arms Control Today* 30, no. 2 (March 2000), 13–18.

26 Missile Defense Agency, "A Day in the Life of the BMDS," 3[d] ed., 2005, 23, available at <mda.mil/mdalink/pdf/bmdsbook.pdf>.

27 Because the size of the planned U.S. ballistic missile defense system is still unclear, Chinese analysts have focused more on the political intentions behind U.S. system deployments rather than the technical capabilities of the initial systems.

28 Department of Defense, "Findings of the Nuclear Posture Review," January 9, 2002, available at <defenselink.mil/news/Jan2002/020109-D-6570C-001.pdf>.

29 See Brad Roberts, "China-U.S. Nuclear Relations: What Relationship Best Serves U.S. Interests?" (Arlington, VA: Institute for Defense Analyses, 2002), available at <dtra.mil/about/organization/china-usrelations.pdf>.

30 See Peter Brookes, "The Case for Missile Defence," *Far Eastern Economic Review*, September 7, 2000, 33.

31 Department of Defense, *Annual Report on the Military Power of the People's Republic of China* (Washington, DC: Department of Defense, 2005), 36, available at <defenselink.mil/news/Jul2005/d20050719china.pdf>; and Phillip C. Saunders,

"China's Future in Space: Implications for U.S. Security," Space.com (May 2005), available at <space.com/adastra/china_implications_0505.html>.

[32] Banning Garrett, "The Need for Strategic Reassurance in the 21st Century," *Arms Control Today* 31, no. 2 (March 2001), 9–14, available at <armscontrol.org/act/2001_03/garrett.asp>.

[33] Alexandra Harney, Demetri Sevastopulo, and Edward Alden, "Top Chinese general warns US over attack," *Financial Times*, July 14, 2005.

[34] Evan S. Medeiros and M. Taylor Fravel, "China's New Diplomacy," *Foreign Affairs* 82, no. 3 (November/December 2003), 22–35.

[35] See, for example, "Premier: China's development to benefit Asia," Xinhua, November 11, 2003, available at <http://www2.chinadaily.com.cn/en/doc/2003-11/02/content_277694.htm>.

[36] David Zweig and Bi Jianhai, "China's Global Hunt for Energy," *Foreign Affairs* 84, no. 5 (September/October 2005), 25–38; Phillip C. Saunders, *China's Global Activism: Strategy, Drivers, and Tools*, Occasional Paper No. 4. (Washington, DC: National Defense University Press, 2006).

[37] Donald H. Rumsfeld, remarks to the International Institute for Strategic Studies, Singapore, June 4, 2005, available at <defenselink.mil/transcripts/2005/tr20050604-secdef3002.html>.

[38] Joshua Cooper Ramos, *The Beijing Consensus* (London: Foreign Policy Centre, 2004), available at <fpc.org.uk/fsblob/244.pdf>; and Joshua Kurlantzick, "Cultural Revolution: How China Is Changing Global Diplomacy," *New Republic*, June 27, 2005, 16–21.

[39] Including claims to the Spratly Islands, disputes with Japan over the Senkaku/Diaoyu Islands and the East China Sea, and disputes with Vietnam over the Paracel Islands.

[40] See James J. Przystup and Phillip C. Saunders, *Visions of Order: Japan and China in U.S. Strategy*, Strategic Forum No. 220 (Washington, DC: National Defense University Press, 2006), available at <www.ndu.edu/inss/Strforum/SF220/SF_220.pdf>.

[41] Russian Central bank Web site, <cbr.ru/eng/main.asp>.

[42] See commentary by Fiona Hill, "Putin, Yukos, and Russia," *The Globalist,* December 1, 2004, available at <brookings.edu/views/articles/hillf/20041201.htm>.

[43] On Russian investment needs, see Nadejda Makarova Victor, "Global Natural Gas Market and Russian Gas Supply," available at <iis-db.stanford.edu/evnts/4454/Russian_Gas_March_14.pdf>.

[44] Yevgeniy Yasin, "*Vklyuchilsya Mekhanizm Tormozheniya Modernizatsii*" ("The Mechanism of Slowing Modernization Has Kicked In"), available at <liberal.ru/article.asp?Num=392>; Vladimir Milov, "*Gazovyy Prezident*" ("The Gas President"), *Novaya Gazeta*, December 26, 2005, available at <2005.novayagazeta.ru/nomer/2005/97n/n97n-s17.shtml>; Nadejda M. Victor, "Russia's Gas Crunch," Washingtonpost.com, April 6, 2006, available at <washingtonpost.com/wp-dyn/content/article/2006/04/05/AR2006040501954.html>.

[45] See Nicholas Eberstadt, "The Demographic Factor as a Constraint on Russian Development," Seminar Series Paper, available at <ndu.edu/inss/Repository/

INSS_Proceedings/Russian_Power_Apr03/RussianPower_Eberstadt_AY02-03.pdf>.

46 Central Intelligence Agency, "Russia: Economy," *The World Factbook*, available at <cia.gov/cia/publications/factbook/geos/rs.html#Econ>.

47 Central Intelligence Agency, "Russia: People," *The World Factbook*, available at <https://www.cia.gov/library/publications/the-world-factbook/geos/rs.html#People>.

48 Ibid.

49 See Robert Parsons, "2005 in Review: Russia's Centralization Gathers Pace," December 23, 2005, Radio Free Europe/Radio Liberty, available at <rferl.org/featuresarticle/2005/12/ace0524f-7ade-4a60-be05-ccf14183ae07.html>.

50 "Rival Rallies over Russian Reform," BBC News, February 12, 2005, available at <news.bbc.co.uk/2/hi/europe/4260117.stm>; Steven Miller and Dmitri Trenin, eds., *The Russian Military: Power and Policy* (Cambridge: The MIT Press, 2004).

51 Richard Ericson, "The Post-Soviet Russian Economic System: An Industrial Feudalism?" Bank of Finland Institute for Economies in Transition, available at <bof.fi/bofit/eng/7online/abs/pdf/bon0800.pdf>; on lawlessness in the Russian heartland, see Peter Finn, "For Russians, Police Rampage Fuels Fears," March 27, 2005, available at <washingtonpost.com/wp-dyn/articles/A4009-2005Mar26.html>.

52 Vladislav Surkov, "*Suverenitet—Eto Sinionim Politicheskoy Konkurentnosposobnosti*" ("Sovereignty Is a Synonym of Political Competitiveness"), February 22, 2006, available (in Russian) at <http://www.edinros.ru/news.html?id=111148>.

53 Yuliya Latynina, "*Trotskistsko-Berezovskiy Protsess*" ("A Trotskiite-Berezovskiy Trial"), *Yezhednevnyy Zhurnal*, August 28, 2007, available (in Russian) at <http://www.ej.ru/?a=note&id=7357>.

54 "Russia Revises Military Doctrine to Reflect Global Changes," March 6, 2007, available at <http://www.spacewar.com/reports/Russia_Revises _Military _Doctrine_To_Reflect_Global_Changes_999.html>.

55 Anatoliy Tsyganok, "*Razgovory o Perevooruzhenii Rossiyskoy Armii—mif*" ("Talk about rearmament of Russian Army is a myth"), June 30, 2006, available (in Russian) at <tsiganok.ru/publications/esmi/doc/176/>.

56 For the latest statement on this subject, see Ministry of Defense of Russia, *Current Tasks of Development of the Armed Forces of the Russian Federation* (Moscow: Russian Ministry of Defense, October 2003).

57 Ibid.

58 In March 2006, Russia and Georgia signed an agreement on withdrawing Russian troops from Georgia by 2008 ("Russia, Georgia Sign Agreements on Military Base Withdrawal," Moscow News, March 31, 2006, available at <mosnews.com/news/2006/03/31/georgiabases.shtml>); the implementation of such agreements in the past has proven controversial.

59 The Kremlin's favorite candidate in the 2004 presidential election, Victor Yanukhovich, staged a political comeback in July 2006, following the March 2003

parliamentary election, but his return to politics appears to be due as much to Ukrainian domestic factors as to Russian intervention.

60 See "*Kitayskiy Faktor v Novoy Strukture mezhdunarodnykh otnosheniy i Strategiya Rossii*" ("The China Factor in the New Structure of International Relations and Russia's Strategy"), Nikitsky Club, available at <nikitskyclub.ru/article.php?idpublication=4&idissue=32>.

61 Council for Foreign and Defense Policy, "*Novoye Osvoyeniye Sibiri I Dal'nego Vostoka*" ("New Conquest of Siberia and Far East"), available at <svop.ru/live/materials.asp?m_id=6752&r_id=6878>.

62 Aleksei Arbatov, *Bezopasnost': Rossiyskiy Vybor* (Security: Russian Choice) (Moscow: EPICenter, 1999), 305–307.

63 Jackson Diehl, "Crumbling Before Putin," Washingtonpost.com, June 19, 2006, available at <washingtonpost.com/wp-dyn/content/article/2006/06/18/AR2006061800901.html>; Anatol Lieven, "Putin versus Cheney," *International Herald Tribune*, May 11, 2006, available at <iht.com/articles/2006/05/11/opinion/edlieven.php>.

64 National Intelligence Council, *Mapping the Global Future: Report of the National Intelligence Council's 2020 Project* (Washington, DC: U.S. Government Printing Office, 2004), 8–10.

65 "Background Briefing by Administration Officials on U.S.-South Asia Relations," Office of the Spokesman, Department of State, March 25, 2005, available at <state.gov/r/pa/prs/ps/2005/43853.htm>.

66 R. Nicholas Burns, "The U.S. and India: An Emerging Entente?" remarks prepared for the House International Relations Committee, September 8, 2005, available at <state.gov/p/us/rm/2005/52753.htm>.

67 See, inter alia, Strobe Talbott (the chief advocate of closer U.S.-Indian relations in the Clinton administration), "Good Day for India, Bad for Nonproliferation," Yale Global Online, July 21, 2005, available at <yaleglobal.yale.edu/display.article?id=6042>; Robert Einhorn, statement before the House International Relations Committee, October 26, 2005; Michael Krepon, statement before the Senate Foreign Relations Committee, November 3, 2005; George Perkovich, "Faulty Promises: The U.S.-India Nuclear Deal," *Policy Outlook,* September 2005.

68 *Mapping the Global Future,* 32.

69 As of mid-2005, more than 6,000 Indian soldiers were deployed with such missions.

70 Janes' Sentinel Security Assessment—South Asia, June 21, 2007. Calculations are based on the budget as stated in rupees, not taking into account an inflation rate of some 5 percent.

71 Central Intelligence Agency, "India: Military," *The World Factbook*, available at <cia.gov/cia/publications/factbook/geos/in.html#Military>; International Institute of Strategic Studies, *The Military Balance 2007* (London: International Institute for Strategic Studies, 2007).

72 Lok Sabha Standing Committee on Defence, *Ministry of Defence Demands for Grants (2004–2005): First Report* (New Delhi: Lok Sabha Secretariat, 2004), 20–21.

73 Lok Sabha Standing Committee on Defence, *Ministry of Defence Demands for Grants (2007–2008)* (New Delhi: Lok Sabha Secretariat, 2004), 68, 95, 118–121.

74 The army and the Defence Committee appear to believe that the problem is caused by too-short terms of service for new officers and a lack of job training to prepare them for post-service life. This analysis seems open to question.

75 Jane's Sentinel Security Assessment—South Asia, November 17, 2005. Ability to sustain the force in combat is complicated by the diverse sources of equipment, which not only suffer from technical interoperability but also are designed to operate on the basis of radically different logistic doctrines. C. Christine Fair, "U.S.-Indian Army-to-Army Relations: Prospects for Future Coalition Operations," *Asian Security* 1 (April 2005), 162.

76 Ibid., 159–160.

77 Lok Sabha Defence Committee (2007), 62.

78 Some modest steps toward jointness have been taken, such as the creation of an embryonic Integrated Defence Staff and a unified Defence Intelligence Agency.

79 The Indian approach to civilian control of the armed forces grows out of a constitutional philosophy that the state must be safeguarded not only from an unruly military but also from partisan politics run amuck. This safeguard, embodied in the 1950 constitution of India, is provided by the Civil Service of India, of which the Indian Administrative Service is the elite component. The service is considered independent of the government of the day and is bound to execute the laws and policies of the republic even in the face of ministerial direction to the contrary.

80 International Monetary Fund, *World Economic Outlook Database*, April 2007, available at <http://www.imf.org/external/pubs/ft/weo/2007/01/data/index.aspx>.

81 Ibid.

82 Central Intelligence Agency, "India: Economy," *The World Factbook*, available at <cia.gov/cia/publications/factbook/geos/in.html#Econ>; Stephen Philip Cohen, *India: Emerging Power* (Washington, DC: Brookings Institution Press, 2001), 28.

83 Angus Maddison, *The World Economy: A Millennial Perspective* (Paris: Organization for Economic Co-operation and Development, 2001), 203.

84 John Adams, "India's Economy," in *Understanding Contemporary India*, ed. Sumit Ganguly and Neil DeVotta (Boulder, CO: Lynne Rienner, 2003), 112; Cohen, 28.

85 *Mapping the Global Future,* 47.

86 "President, Prime Minister of India Discuss Freedom and Democracy," White House press release, July 18, 2005, available at <whitehouse.gov/news/releases/2005/07/20050718-1.html>.

87 Rahul Bedi, "India-U.S. Conduct Air Exercise Amid Protests," *Jane's Defence Weekly,* November 23, 2005.

88 Sumit Ganguly, "International Relations," in *Understanding Contemporary India*, 103–105.

89 Ibid., 104.

90 *The Statesman's Year-Book, 1865* (London: Macmillan, 1865); Maddison, 183–184.

91 Cohen, 9–10.

92 Ibid., 14, 18–19.

93 Stephen J. Blank, *Natural Allies? Regional Security in Asia and Prospects for Indo-American Strategic Cooperation* (Carlisle, PA: Strategic Studies Institute, 2005), 9.

[94] And which cannot realistically be offset even if the United States succeeds in helping India develop the kind of civilian nuclear power industry that Americans evidently consider too dangerous for the United States itself—a formulation that opponents of the U.S.-Indian relationship will be quick to seize on if an Indian nuclear power plant suffers a Bhopal-like mishap.

[95] Cohen, 22.

[96] Siddarth Srivastava, "India Reaches Out to Afghanistan," Asia Times Online, August 30, 2005, available at <atimes.com/atimes/South_Asia/GH30Df01.html>.

[97] Ashley J. Tellis, "South Asia: U.S. Policy Choices," in *Taking Charge: A Bipartisan Report to the President Elect on Foreign Policy and National Security—Papers*, ed. Frank Carlucci, Robert Hunter, and Zalmay Khalilzad (Santa Monica, CA: RAND, 2000), 88, cited in Tellis, *India as a New Global Power: An Action Agenda for the United States* (Washington, DC: Carnegie Endowment for International Peace, 2005), 9.

[98] Ashley J. Tellis, "Smoke, Fire, and What to Do in Asia," *Policy Review* 100 (April/May 2000), 27.

[99] Foreign Secretary Shyam Saran, presentation at Carnegie Endowment for International Peace, December 21, 2005.

[100] Ganguly, 100.

[101] National Security Strategy 2006, 36.

[102] Shanghai Cooperation Organization, "Declaration on Fifth Anniversary of Shanghai Cooperation Organisation," Article IV, Shanghai, June 15, 2006, available at <sectsco.org/502.html>.

CHAPTER SEVEN

[1] See Stephen J. Flanagan, Ellen L. Frost, and Richard L. Kugler, *Challenges of the Global Century: Report of the Project on Globalization and National Security* (Washington, DC: National Defense University Press, 2001), 14–15.

[2] As former Secretary of Defense Donald H. Rumsfeld framed the issue in September 2001 concerning steps to keep the coalition together on Afghanistan, "The mission determines the coalition. And the coalition must not be permitted to determine the mission." See "Defense Secretary Rumsfeld Speaks in Washington," CNN transcript, September 23, 2001, available at <http://transcripts.cnn.com/TRANSCRIPTS/0109/23/se.02.html>.

[3] The 2002 National Security Strategy noted that America would implement its strategy by "organizing coalitions—as broad as practicable," and that NATO could create coalitions under its own mandate or "contribute to mission-based coalitions." *The National Security Strategy of the United States of America* (Washington, DC: The White House, September 17, 2002), 10, 25–26, available at <http://www.whitehouse.gov/nsc/nss.html>.

[4] Department of Defense, *Quadrennial Defense Review Report*, February 6, 2006, 6, 83–89, available at <http://www.defenselink.mil/pubs/pdfs/QDR20060203.pdf>.

[5] Department of Defense, Office of the Assistant Secretary of Defense (Public Affairs), "Global Posture," testimony as prepared for delivery by Secretary of Defense Donald H. Rumsfeld, Senate Armed Service Committee, September 23,

2004, available at <http://www.defenselink.mil/speeches/2004/sp20040923-secdef0783.html>.

6 See National Intelligence Council, *Mapping the Global Future* (Washington, DC: U.S. Government Printing Office, 2004), 56–61; and Robert Samuelson, "The End of Europe," *The Washington Post*, June 15, 2005, A25.

7 This assessment focuses on U.S.-European relations, although Canada is among the founding members of NATO.

8 See Pew Research Center, Global Attitudes Project reports. Since 2002, of the West European countries surveyed, only in the United Kingdom did more than half of the respondents have a positive view of the United States. Latest survey issued June 13, 2006, accessed at <http://pewglobal.org/reports/display.php?PageID=825>.

9 See U.S. Department of State, "European Cooperation with the United States in the Global War on Terrorism," testimony of Cofer Black, Coordinator for Counterterrorism before the Senate Foreign Relations Committee, Subcommittee on European Affairs, March 31, 2004, available at <http://www.state.gov/s/ct/rls/rm/2004/30983.htm>; and Dana Priest, "Help from France in Key Covert Operations," *The Washington Post*, July 3, 2005, A1.

10 NATO, "The Alliance's Strategic Concept agreed by the Heads of State and Government participating in the meeting of the North Atlantic Council," November 8, 1991, paragraphs 10–12, available at <http://www.nato.int/docu/basictxt/b911108a.htm>.

11 During the 1990s, several factors tempered the effects of the demise of the Soviet threat and highlighted the continued utility of strong transatlantic military links, including the 1991 Gulf War, which demonstrated how NATO's patterns of military cooperation improved allies' ability to fight together in a "coalition of the willing" outside Europe; hedging against revanchism in Russia, given its vast arsenal and uncertain political direction; and the escalating Balkan conflicts, which showed that interstate and intrastate wars within Europe were still possible.

12 Jean-Marie Colombani, editorial in *Le Monde* (Paris), September 13, 2001.

13 As a rule, terrorist groups operating in these countries or against their interests did not seek to inflict hundreds or thousands of casualties.

14 Despite consensus on the threat during the Cold War, many European allies emphasized the forward defense part of NATO strategy in contrast to the U.S. embrace of flexible response, including the possibility of early use of nuclear weapons. Conversely, European officials who disagreed adamantly with the United States on how to proceed on Iraq in 2003 were quick to emphasize that they did not dismiss the dangers posed by a WMD-armed Iraq. During the 1999 Kosovo crisis, there were heated debates within the Alliance on whether it could act collectively and militarily to end the ethnic cleansing without preexisting UN authorization. Arguments by the United States and several other allies in favor of moving ahead without such authorization eventually carried the day, but allies wrangled over the conduct of military operations. See Wesley K. Clark, *Waging Modern War: Bosnia, Kosovo, and the Future of Combat* (New York: Public Affairs, 2001), 215–216.

[15] Robert Kagan, "Power and Weakness," *Policy Review*, no. 113 (June/July 2002). In fairness, Kagan and others (both Americans and Europeans) acknowledge the risks of overgeneralizing these differences.

[16] This is not always the case in practice—or even in theory. For example, in a July 2002 defense policy statement to the French National Assembly, Prime Minister Jean-Pierre Raffarin noted that France "wants to conserve the capability to act alone if its own interests and its bilateral commitments so dictate." British Prime Minister Blair has repeatedly made a similar point. For example, he told a Polish audience in May 2003, that "[t]he argument that Britain . . . could not in the future support military action in Iraq without Europe's permission is completely untrue."

[17] In fact, the United States did ask for and receive both collective NATO assistance *and* support from individual allies for operations in Afghanistan. For an explanation of U.S. views on the role of NATO in the war on terrorism, see statement by Deputy Secretary of Defense Paul D. Wolfowitz at NATO Defense Ministers meeting, September 26, 2001, available at <http://www.defenselink.mil/transcripts/2001/t09272001_t0926na.html>. No Allied minister suggested that NATO lead the coalition against al Qaeda and the Taliban.

[18] *National Security Strategy of the United States of America*, 15–16.

[19] Figures from NATO International Staff, Force Planning Directorate, "NATO-Russia Compendium of Financial and Economic Data Relating to Defence," December 18, 2006, available at <http://www.nato.int/docu/pr/2006/p06-159e.pdf>. Averages exclude Luxembourg and Iceland, and from 1999 include the Czech Republic, Hungary, and Poland, which joined the alliance that year.

[20] European Defence Agency, "An Initial Long-term Vision of European Defence Capabilities and Needs," October 3, 2006, available at <http://www.eda.europa.eu/ltv/061003%20-%20EDA%20-%20Long%20Term%20Vision%20Report.pdf>, 23.

[21] See R. Nicholas Burns, "NATO and the Future of Trans-Atlantic Relations," remarks in Oslo, Norway, January 26, 2004, available at <http://nato.usmission.gov/ambassador/20040126_Oslo.htm>.

[22] Figures in current dollars.

[23] Specific improvements included the areas of chemical, biological, radiological, and nuclear defense; intelligence, surveillance, and target acquisition; air-to-ground surveillance; command, control, and communications; combat effectiveness, including precision-guided munitions and suppression of enemy air defenses; strategic air and sea lift; air-to-air refueling; and deployable combat support and combat service support units.

[24] NATO, "Prague Summit Declaration," November 24, 2002, paragraph 4g, available at <http://www.nato.int/docu/pr/2002/p02-127e.htm>.

[25] The NATO Response Force (NRF) can number up to 25,000 troops in a brigade-sized land component. It also has a naval task force comprised of a carrier battlegroup, an amphibious task group, and a surface action group, as well as an air component capable of 200 sorties per day. Allies agreed at the November 2006 Riga Summit to share the costs of airlift for short-notice deployments of the NRF. It is a rotational force to which allies must commit replenishments to meet evolving requirements. See NATO Office of Public Affairs, NATO Update, "NATO

Response Force Declared Fully Operational," November 29, 2006, available at <http://www.nato.int/docu/update/2006/11-november/e1129c.htm>.

26 See Steve Sturm, "Matching capabilities to commitments," *NATO Review* (Spring 2005), available at <http://www.nato.int/docu/review/2005/issue1/english/military_pr.html>.

27 EU regulations, such as the "stability clause" limiting public deficits to 3 percent of GDP, are an additional constraint. Several EU governments—including Germany, France, Italy, and Belgium—are considering the idea of exempting defense expenditures from the 3 percent deficit ceiling.

28 See Michèle A. Flournoy and Julienne Smith, *European Defense Integration: Bridging the Gap Between Strategy and Capabilities* (Washington, DC: Center for Strategic and International Studies, October 2005), 72–79, available at <http://www.csis.org/media/csis/pubs/0510_eurodefensereport.pdf>.

29 The A400M is a case in point. At the April 2003 French-German-Belgian-Luxembourg summit on European defense, the four leaders specified that participation by EU states in their proposed European Security and Defense Union "will involve participation in major European equipment programs such as the A400M." A few days later, the Airbus consortium, apparently ceding to political pressure, awarded the contract for building the A400M engines to a European group, although its bid reportedly was significantly higher than its North American competitor.

30 This so-called Berlin Plus formula assures the EU access to NATO operational planning and includes cooperation in the areas of defense planning, the loan of certain NATO capabilities and common assets to the EU, and the possible use of NATO commands for EU-led operations.

31 A May 23, 2005, article in the French daily *Le Figaro* seemed to capture this sentiment when it stated: "Having been on the scene [in Darfur] for six months, but not very visibly, the European Union does not want to see NATO, a newcomer in the region, steal the show."

32 While the United Kingdom and France in theory could jointly lead a complex peacekeeping mission, there is as yet little evidence that they share sufficiently close strategic visions of when, where, and how the EU's military capability should be used. In June 2003, the EU undertook its first autonomous operation, codenamed *Artemis*, whereby 1,400 troops operating under French command headquarters (Framework Nation) were sent to quell ethnic unrest in the town of Bunia in the eastern part of Democratic Republic of Congo. This mission was taken over by a UN force in September. See report to the Council of the European Union, available at <http://ue.eu.int/cms3_fo/showPage.asp?id=605&lang=EN&mode=g>.

33 Speaking at a conference in early 2006, French Defense Minister Michèle Alliot-Marie said that NATO was best suited to handle "heavy, long-duration operations, where the U.S. is involved, while ESDP is better adapted to lighter, more flexible 'quick strike' operations and civil-military actions." See "Intervention de Madame Michèle Alliot-Marie, ministre de la défense français, devant la Conférence pour la Politique de Sécurité de Munich," February 4, 2006, available at <http://www.defense.gouv.fr/sites/defense/decouverte/le_ministere/ministre_de_la_defense/declarations/2006/fevrier/conference_pour_la_politique_de_securite_le_040206>.

This reflects a more circumspect vision of the proper scope of ESDP missions than Paris has sometimes advanced. However, at the same event, British Defense Minister John Reid cited a less rigid division of labor, noting: "We must have a more grown up [NATO–EU] relationship that recognises the reality that NATO will be working alongside the EU and others in future operations, as in Darfur." John Reid, "Speech at the 42[d] Munich Conference on Security Policy," February 4, 2006, available at <http://www.securityconference.de/konferenzen/rede.php?menu_2006=& menu_konferenzen=&sprache=en&id=167&>.

[34] On April 29, 2003, the leaders of Belgium, France, Germany, and Luxembourg agreed to establish an EU operational planning staff in the Brussels suburb of Tervuren. While proponents argued that such a staff was essential if the EU were to undertake autonomous operations, opponents, particularly the United Kingdom, argued that the EU could use a national headquarters and augment it with planners from contributing countries, as happened in the EU mission to Bunia. This was seen in Washington as a duplicative structure that added little to capabilities. Later that year, EU leaders worked out a compromise whereby the EU set up a small cell of operational planners at NATO's Strategic Headquarters Allied Powers Europe to ensure smooth coordination between EU and NATO when the former borrows NATO assets; a new planning unit with civil/military elements was established in the EU's Military Staff; and the EU agreed to normally rely on national headquarters to plan autonomous missions, unless the EU Council unanimously decided to use the EUMS, particularly for integrated civil/military missions. See Charles Grant, "Reviving European Defence Cooperation," *NATO Review* (Winter 2003), 7–10, available at <http://www.nato.int/docu/review/pdf/i4_en_review2003.pdf>.

[35] Leo G. Michel, "NATO and the EU: Improving Practical Cooperation," report of the workshop organized by the Institute for National Strategic Studies, National Defense University, in partnership with the Finnish Ministry of Defense, March 21–22, 2005, available at <http://www.ndu.edu/inss/Repository/Outside_Pub lications/Michel/NATO-EU_Workshop_Final_Summary.pdf>.

[36] Council Joint Action 2004/55/CFSP, "On the Establishment of the European Defence Agency," *Official Journal of the European Union*, July 12, 2004, L245/17–28 (English), available at <http://ue.eu.int/uedocs/cmsUpload/l_24520040717 en00170028.pdf>.

[37] See Pew Global Attitudes Project, "America's Image Slips, But Allies Share U.S. Concerns Over Iran, Hamas," June 13, 2006, available at < http://pewglobal.org/ reports/display.php?PageID=825>.

[38] In Bosnia, 14 (of 26) PFP partners participated in IFOR, and 3 later joined SFOR. Sixteen partners have participated in KFOR in Kosovo. The PFP Planning and Review (PARP) process introduced interoperability objectives in 1996 to permit partners' forces to operate with allies. Later known as Partnership Goals (PGs), these guidelines sought to foster development of specific armed forces and capabilities that partners could offer in support of NATO operations and permit partners greater participation in planning. See Jeffrey Simon, *Partnership for Peace: Charting a Course for a New Era*, Strategic Forum 206 (Washington, DC: National Defense University Press, March 2004), available at <http://www.ndu.edu/ inss/strforum/SF206/SF206.pdf>.

39 Albania, Armenia, Azerbaijan, Bulgaria, Estonia, Georgia, Kazakhstan, Latvia, Lithuania, Macedonia, Romania, Slovakia, and Ukraine have generally contributed small contingents (11 to 300 troops) to *Iraqi Freedom*. Romania, which became a NATO member in 2004, deployed up to 860 troops in Iraq.

40 John Tefft, Deputy Assistant Secretary for European and Eurasian Affairs, "Ukraine's Election: Next Steps," testimony before the House International Relations Committee, December 7, 2004, available at <http://www.state.gov/p/eur/rls/rm/39542.htm>.

41 Public opinion polls conducted by the Razumkov Centre for Economic and Political Studies in Ukraine between 2002 and 2005 reported nationwide support between 21 and 33 percent, with opposition ranging from 32 to 49 percent. However, these polls also showed how polarizing this issue is with support in the western "orange" part of the country ranging from 65 (2002) to 49 (2005) percent, while support in the pro-Russian eastern and southern regions was only at 33 (2002) to 8 (2005) percent. Some polls in 2006 have shown national support as low as 12 percent. See also Steven Woehrel, "Ukraine's Orange Revolution and U.S. Policy," Congressional Research Service, April 1, 2005 available at <http://www.usembassy.it/pdf/other/RL32845.pdf>.

42 Mediterranean Dialogue countries are Algeria, Egypt, Israel, Jordan, Mauritania, Morocco, and Tunisia. Members of the Gulf Cooperation Council are Bahrain, Kuwait, Oman, Qatar, Saudi Arabia, and the United Arab Emirates. Four of the six GCC countries—Bahrain, Qatar, Kuwait, and the United Arab Emirates—have joined the Initiative. For background on both initiatives, see NATO, Public Diplomacy Division, "Security Cooperation with the Mediterranean Region and the Broader Middle East," available at <http://www.nato.int/docu/secCoMed/secopmed-e.pdf>.

43 Department of Defense, "2004 Statistical Compendium on Allied Contributions to the Common Defense," tables D–4 and D–9, available at <http://www.defenselink.mil/pubs/allied_contrib2004/allied2004.pdf>.

44 European Defence Agency, "An Initial Long-term Vision of European Defence Capabilities and Needs," 6.

45 See Center for Technology and National Security Policy and Institute for National Strategic Studies, *Transatlantic Homeland Defense*, Special Report (Washington, DC: National Defense University Press, May 2006).

46 See Leo G. Michel, *NATO Decisionmaking: Au Revoir to Consensus?* Strategic Forum 202 (Washington, DC: National Defense University Press, August 2003), available at <http://www.ndu.edu/inss/strforum/SF202/SF202.pdf>.

47 See Clark, *Waging Modern War*, 215–216, 422–425.

48 See Jeffrey Simon and Eugene Rumer, *Toward a Euro-Atlantic Strategy for the Black Sea Region,* Institute for National Strategic Studies Occasional Paper 3 (Washington, DC: National Defense University Press, April 2006).

49 NATO Press Release (2006) 150, "Riga Summit Declaration," November 29, 2006, paragraph 17, available at <http://www.nato.int/docu/pr/2006/p06-150e.htm>.

50 Ibid., paragraphs 11–13.

51 See Ivo Daalder and James Goldgeier, "A Global NATO," *Foreign Affairs* 85, no. 5 (September/October 2006), 105–113.

52 During the 59th session of the UN General Assembly in 2004, Israeli votes coincided with those of the United States 98 percent of the time. Comparable figures for Australia, the United Kingdom, and Japan were 90, 89, and 87 percent, respectively. See U.S. Department of State, "Voting Practices in the United Nations—2004," available at <www.state.gov/documents/organization/44415.pdf>.

53 Clyde R. Mark, *Israel: U.S. Foreign Assistance*, Congressional Research Service, Report IB85066, April 26, 2005, 1–12, available at <http://fpc.state.gov/documents/organization/47088.pdf>. In 2004, Israel received a total of $2.68 billion from U.S. foreign assistance accounts: about $2.14 billion in Foreign Military Financing, $477 million in Economic Support Funds, $49 million in immigration grants, and $13.1 million in other assistance.

54 Jeremy M. Sharp, "U.S. Foreign Assistance to the Middle East: Historical Background, Recent Trends, and the FY 2007 Request," Congressional Research Service Report RL32260, updated December 21, 2006, available at <http://opencrs.cdt.org/document/RL32260/2006-12-21%2000:00:00>.

55 Barbara Opall Rome, "Israel, U.S. Test Compatibility of Arrow-Patriot Interceptors," *Space News*, March 14, 2005, available at <http://www.space.com/spacenews/archive05/IsraelMD_031405.html>.

56 Clyde R. Mark, "Israeli–United States Relations," Issue Brief IB82008, Congressional Research Service, updated November 9, 2004, 10–11.

57 The British government proposed the idea of British-Israeli strategic cooperation in 1950, but Israel rejected the suggestion. In 1954, Israel initiated contacts aimed at the possibility of joining NATO or establishing a formal bilateral defense treaty with the United States, two ideas that have resurfaced from time to time. See Yair Evron, "An Israel-United States Defense Pact?" *Strategic Assessment* 1, no. 3, Jaffe Center for Strategic Studies, Tel Aviv University, October 1998, available at <http://www.tau.ac.il/jcss/sa/v1n3p2_n.html>. The idea of NATO membership has resurfaced in recent years in the context of containing Iran. See Ronald Asmus, "Contain Iran: Admit Israel to NATO," *The Washington Post*, February 21, 2006, A15.

58 In the May 2003 Pew Global Attitudes survey, which covered 21 countries, pluralities or majorities in every country except the United States expressed the view that American policies in the Middle East favor Israel over the Palestinians too much. Jodie T. Allen and Alec Tyson, Poll Analysis, "The U.S. Public's Pro-Israel History In Mid-East Conflicts, Americans Consistently Side with Israel," Pew Research Center, July 19, 2006, available at <http://pewresearch.org/obdeck/?ObDeckID=39>.

59 Mark, "Israeli-United States Relations," 13–14. The State Department also notified Congress of possible Israeli misuse of U.S.-supplied cluster munitions against civilian areas of Lebanon in the summer of 2006. See Glenn Kessler, "Israel May Have Misused Cluster Bombs, U.S. Says," *The Washington Post*, January 30, 2007, A13.

60 See Charles Krauthammer, "Israel's Lost Moment," *The Washington Post*, August 4, 2006, A17.

61 The ABC News/Washington Post Poll, August 3–6, 2006, and CNN Poll conducted by Opinion Research Corporation, August 2–3, 2006, cited in the Polling Report, available at <http://www.pollingreport.com/israel.htm>.

[62] Abdel Monem Said Aly, "An Ambivalent Alliance: The Future of U.S.-Egyptian Relations," Saban Center Analysis, Number 6, January 31, 2006, 15–17; Abdel Monem Said Aly, "The Future of U.S.-Egyptian Relations," presentation at the Saban Center for Middle East Policy, The Brookings Institution, June 9, 2004, available at <http://www.brookings.edu/fp/saban/events/saidaly20040609.htm>.

[63] Jeremy M. Sharp, "Egypt: Background and U.S. Relations," Report RL33003, Congressional Research Service, June 14, 2006, 27–29.

[64] U.S. House of Representatives, Committee on International Relations, Subcommittee on the Middle East and Central Asia, 108th Cong., 2[d] Sess., Hearing, "The Future of U.S.-Egyptian Relations," statements of David Satterfield, Deputy Assistant Secretary of State for Near Eastern Affairs, and Rose Likens, Principal Deputy Assistant Secretary of State, Bureau of Political-Military Affairs, U.S. Department of State, 18–23, 46–52. In 2003, the two governments established a Counterterrorism Joint Working Group.

[65] Abdel Monem Said Aly, "An Ambivalent Alliance," 23, and "Strengthening the U.S.-Egyptian Relationship," Council on Foreign Relations Press, May 2002, available at <http://www.cfr.org/publication/8666/strengthening_the_usegyptian_relationship_a_cfr_paper.html?breadcrumb=default>.

[66] U.S. Department of State, *Country Reports on Terrorism 2006*, April 2005, 136–138, available at <www.state.gov/documents/organization/65472.pdf>.

[67] Alfred B. Prados, "Jordan: U.S. Relations and Bilateral Issues," Issue Brief IB93085, Congressional Research Service, April 26, 2006, 11–12.

[68] This section draws heavily on analysis by Joseph McMillan. See Joseph McMillan, "The United States and Gulf Security Architecture: Policy Considerations," *Strategic Insights* 3, no. 3 (March 2004), available at <http://www.ccc.nps.navy.mil/si/2004/mar/mcmillanMar04.asp>.

[69] See Judith S. Yaphe, "Gulf Security Perceptions and Strategies," in *The United States and the Persian Gulf*, ed. Richard D. Sokolsky (Washington, DC: National Defense University Press, 2003), 37–59.

[70] For a review of the complexities involved in managing the U.S.-Saudi relationship, see Joseph McMillan, *U.S.-Saudi Relations: Rebuilding the Strategic Consensus,* Strategic Forum 186 (Washington, DC: National Defense University Press, November 2001), available at <http://www.ndu.edu/inss/strforum/SF186/sf186.pdf>.

[71] Alfred B. Prados, "Saudi Arabia: Current Issues and U.S. Relations," Issue Brief IB93113, Congressional Research Service, February 26, 2006, 1–2.

[72] 9/11 Commission, *The 9/11 Commission Report: Final Report of the National Commission on Terrorist Attacks Upon the United States* (Washington, DC: W.W. Norton, 2004), 371, available at <http://www.9-11commission.gov/report/index.htm>.

[73] The White House, Office of the Press Secretary, Fact Sheet, "United States and Pakistan: Long-term Strategic Partners," Mach 4, 2006, available at <www.state.gov/p/sca/rls/fs/2006/62592.htm>.

[74] Uzbekistan provided access to Karshi-Khanabad airfield for special operations, combat search and rescue, and theater lift units. Kyrgyzstan provides access to Manas International Airport as a hub for a variety of air activity supporting operations

in Afghanistan. Tajikistan gives the United States overflight rights, as well as emergency landing and refueling privileges and a base for a small French unit. See Jim Nichol, "Uzbekistan's Closure of the Airbase at Karshi-Khanabad: Context and Implications," CRS Report for Congress, October 7, 2005, available at <http://digital.library.unt.edu/govdocs/data/2005/upl-meta-crs-7519/RS22295_2005Oct07.pdf>.

[75] The 1951 Security Treaty Between Japan and the United States provided the initial basis for the alliance and allowed for the presence of U.S. Armed Forces "in and about" Japan "to contribute to the maintenance of international peace and security in the Far East and to the security of Japan against armed attack from without." It was replaced by the 1960 Treaty of Mutual Cooperation and Security, which commits both countries to maintain and develop their capacities to resist armed attack in common. It declares that an armed attack on either country in territories administered by Japan will be considered dangerous to the safety of the other. However, Japan was relieved of any obligation to defend the United States if it were attacked outside of Japanese territories because of limitations on its armed forces under Article 9 of the Japanese constitution. It also grants the U.S. Armed Forces access to facilities in Japan "for the purpose of contributing to the security of Japan and the maintenance of international peace and security in the Far East. See "Treaty of Mutual Cooperation and Security between Japan and the United States of America," signed January 19, 1960, available at <http://www.mofa.go.jp/region/n-america/us/q&a/ref/1.html>.

[76] This figure recognizes both direct, on-budget payment of U.S. stationing costs and off-budget forgone revenue from taxes, rents, or other charges. Japan provided $3.2 billion in direct cost sharing during 2002. See U.S. Department of Defense, "2004 Statistical Compendium on Allied Contributions to the Common Defense," table E–5, available at <http://www.defenselink.mil/pubs/allied_contrib2004/allied2004.pdf>.

[77] See Balbina Y. Hwang, "Japan's New Security Outlook: Implications for the United States," Heritage Foundation Backgrounder, no. 1865, July 7, 2005, 2, available at <http://www.heritage.org/Research/AsiaandthePacific/bg1865.cfm>.

[78] Government of Japan, Ministry of Foreign Affairs, "The Guidelines for U.S.-Japan Defense Cooperation," September 23, 1997, available at <http://www.mofa.go.jp/region/n-america/us/security/guideline2.html>.

[79] *Quadrennial Defense Review Report*; *The National Security Strategy of the United States of America,* chapter 6; Japan Defense Agency, *The Defense of Japan 2002 (Summary)*, August 2002, available at <http://www.jda.go.jp/e/pab/wp2002/0101.htm>; and Council on Security and Defense Capabilities Report, *Japan's Vision for Future Security and Defense Capabilities* (hereafter cited as the Araki Report), October 4, 2004, available at <http://www.jiaponline.org/resources/japan/security/Japan%20CSDC%20Report.pdf>.

[80] *Quadrennial Defense Review Report.*

[81] Robert B. Zoellick, Deputy Secretary of State, "Whither China: From Membership to Responsibility?" remarks to the National Committee on U.S.-China Relations, September 21, 2005, available at <http://www.state.gov/s/d/rem/53682.htm>.

The 2006 National Security Strategy articulated the hedging strategy, see *The National Security Strategy of the United States of America*, 40–42, available at <http://www.whitehouse.gov/nsc/nss/2006/nss2006.pdf>.

82 *Quadrennial Defense Review Report*, 27–31.

83 *The Defense of Japan 2002*, 1–2.

84 U.S. Department of State, "Joint Statement, U.S.-Japan Security Consultative Committee," December 16, 2002, available at <http://www.state.gov/r/pa/prs/ps/2002/16007.htm>.

85 Liberal Democratic Party of Japan, Defense Policy Subcommittee, National Defense Division, Policy Research Council, "Recommendations on Japan's New Defense Policy," March 30, 2004, English translation available at <http://www.jimin.jp/jimin/saishin04/pdf/seisaku-006E.pdf>.

86 Araki Report, 4–11.

87 U.S. Department of State, "Joint Statement, U.S.-Japan Security Consultative Committee," February 19, 2005, available at <http://www.state.gov/r/pa/prs/ps/2005/42490.htm>.

88 Prime Minister of Japan, "The Outline of the Basic Plan Regarding Response Measures Based on the Law Concerning the Special Measures on Humanitarian and Reconstruction Assistance in Iraq," December 9, 2003, accessed at <http://www.kantei.go.jp/foreign/policy/2003/031209housin_e.html>.

89 See James J. Przystup, *U.S.-Japan Relations: Progress Toward a Mature Partnership*, Institute for National Strategic Studies Occasional Paper 2 (Washington, DC: National Defense University Press, 2005), 7.

90 Juliana Gittler, "Polls: Japanese Still Welcoming American Stay," *Pacific Stars and Stripes*, October 19, 2006. According to a survey conducted in May and June of 2006 sponsored by the U.S. Embassy in Tokyo, 80 percent of respondents said they favored or strongly favored the alliance. A similar poll in 2004 found 68 percent of those Japanese surveyed had the same views. The polling sponsored by the Embassy is supported by a variety of other survey data.

91 Pew Survey, June 13, 2006.

92 Ibid.; and Ministry of Foreign Affairs, "2006 Image of Japan Study in the U.S. (Summary)," August 2006, available at <http://www.mofa.go.jp/region/n-america/us/survey/summary2006.html>.

93 Embassy of Japan press releases, December 21, 2004, "National Defense Program Guideline for FY 2005 and After," available at <http://www.us.emb-japan.go.jp/english/html/pressreleases/2004/NDGP.pdf>; and "Mid-Term Defense Build-Up Plan FY 2005–2009 (outline)," available at <http://www.us.emb-japan.go.jp/english/html/pressreleases/2004/MTDBP.pdf>.

94 U.S. Department of Defense, U.S.-Japan Security Consultative Committee Document, "U.S.-Japan Alliance: Transformation and Realignment for the Future," October 29, 2005, available at <http://www.defenselink.mil/news/Oct2005/d20051029document.pdf>.

95 Shinzo Abe, speech at the North Atlantic Council, "Japan and NATO: Toward Further Collaboration," January 12, 2007, available at <http://www.mofa.jp/region/europe/pmv0701/nato.html>.

[96] Radio Free Europe/Radio Liberty News, "Afghanistan: Abe Resignation Throws Japan's Mission Into Uncertainty," September 12, 2007, available at <http://www.rferl.org/featuresarticle/2007/09/0d0ec920-d00d-42d9-886f-321aaf79eff8.html>.

[97] The SACO Report can be accessed on the Ministry of Defense Web site under the Defense Policy tab at <http://www.mod.go.jp/e/index_.htm>.

[98] The SACO Report originally envisioned relocation of Futenma to a sea-based facility within 8 years, but local communities rejected the plan, and the entire project stalled. In 2002, the Government of Japan and the Okinawa Prefecture reached agreement on a basic plan calling for relocation to a dual use military-civilian landfill facility; construction, however, has yet to begin, and the Government of Japan does not envision completion before 2015.

[99] Julia Yonetani, "Does the U.S. Need a New Marine Air Station on Okinawa? Voices of Resistance," *Japan Focus* no. 124 (June 2004), available at <http://www.japanfocus.org/article.asp?id=123>.

[100] Joint Statement by Secretary of State Condoleezza Rice, Secretary of Defense Donald H. Rumsfeld, Japanese Minister of Foreign Affairs Taro Aso, and Japanese Minister of State for Defense Fukushiro Nukaga, following a meeting of the United States–Japan Security Consultative Meeting, Washington, DC, May 1, 2006, available at <www.state.gov/secretary/rm/2006/65523.htm>. The United States–Japan Roadmap for Realignment Implementation is available at <http://www.state.gov/r/pa/prs/ps/2006/65517.htm>.

[101] Hisane Masaki, "Okinawa plan for U.S. forces inches ahead," *Asia Times*, January 24, 2006, available at <http://www.atimes.com/atimes/Japan/HA24Dh01.html>.

[102] The Araki Report also wisely recommended that U.S.-Japan cooperation in dealing with new transnational security threats and in the areas around Japan utilizes the Comprehensive Mechanism under the Security Guidelines to integrate the efforts of a wide array of military, civil, and police agencies. See Araki Report, 14. The Japan Defense Agency became the Japan Defense Ministry on January 9, 2007.

[103] Richard Halloran, "A Monumental Change in Japan," *Real Clear Politics*, September 4, 2006, accessed at <http://www.realclearpolitics.com/articles/2006/09/a_monumental_change_in_japan.html>.

[104] Seok Hyun Hong, Ambassador of the Republic of Korea to the United States, "The Korea-U.S. Alliance: A Vision of Common Interests and Ideals for the Next Half Century," address at the Center for Strategic and International Studies, Washington, DC, May 11, 2005.

[105] For a discussion of the underlying sources of Korean attitudes toward the United States, see Georgetown University, School of Foreign Service, Asian Studies Program, and the Korea Society, "Korean Attitudes Toward the United States: The Enduring and Endured Relationship," Summary Conference Report by David I. Steinberg, January 30–February 1, 2003, available at <http://www.koreasociety.org/FYI/Korean_Anti-Americanism_Conference_Summary.pdf>.

[106] See Nae-Yong Lee and Han Wool Jeong, "Fluctuating Anti-Americanism and the Korea-U.S. Alliance," *International Studies Review* 5, no. 2 (October 2004), 30.

[107] For an incisive discussion of anti-Americanism in Korea and concerns of the 386

Generation, see Kun Young Park, *A New U.S.-ROK Alliance: A Nine-Point Policy Recommendation for a Reflective and Mature Partnership*, CNAPS Working Paper Series (Washington, DC: Brookings Institution, September 2005), 22–24, available at <http://www.brookings.edu/fp/cnaps/papers/park20050907.pdf>.

[108] U.S. Department of State, Office of Research, Opinion Analysis, "Trends in South Korean Opinion of the U.S.," M-42-03, April 9, 2003, 1–2.

[109] "South Koreans' Continued support for U.S. Security Ties," M-15-06, February 22, 2006. Lee and Han (29) note that several independent South Korean surveys showed a rise in support for a stronger alliance in 2003 and 2004.

[110] See U.S. Department of State, Office of Research, Opinion Analysis, "South Korean Views of U.S. Show Partial Recovery," M-62-05, June 6, 2005, 1–2.

[111] Lee and Han, "Fluctuating Anti-Americanism," 34–35.

[112] Ibid., 3.

[113] In a May 2005 poll, only 13 percent of South Koreans surveyed saw North Korea as a threat to regional peace and stability. Ranking their security concerns about North Korea, 41 percent cited the North's nuclear weapons program, 30 percent the collapse of the North and a massive refugee flow, and only 5 percent worried about the prospect of North Korea supplying terrorists with weapons of mass destruction. Only 29 percent feel the North's nuclear program poses an immediate threat to South Korea's security, and 25 percent believe it poses no direct security threat but worry it could limit foreign investment. U.S. Department of State, Office of Research, Opinion Analysis, "South Korean Public Shows Continued Support for 'Engaging' the DPRK," M-61-05, June 3, 2005, 1.

[114] Kyung Bok Cho and William Sim, "South Koreans Go Cold on Sunshine Policy Toward Nuclear North," Bloomberg News, October 27, 2006, accessed at <http://www.bloomberg.com/apps/news?pid=20601080&sid=aK1WY6cLY_.Y&refer=asia>.

[115] In 2005, the numbers were Japan 29, North Korea 13, and China 12. In 2006, the figures were Japan 17, North Korea 14, and China 14.

[116] See Chicago Council on Foreign Relations, *Global Views 2004: Comparing South Korean and American Views on Foreign Policy*, 2004, 16, available at <http://www.ccfr.org/globalviews2004/sub/pdf/Global_Views_2004_US_Korea.pdf>.

[117] "Public Opinion Polls About China," *Dong-a Ilbo*, May 4, 2004, available at <http://english.donga.com/srv/service.php3?biid=2004050493898&path_dir=20040504>.

[118] Assistant Secretary of State Christopher R. Hill's Statement at the Closing Plenary of the Fourth Round of the Six-Party Talks, September 19, 2005, available at <http://www.state.gov/r/pa/prs/ps/2005/53499.htm>.

[119] U.S. House of Representatives, Committee on International Relations, "The U.S.–ROK Relationship," prepared statement of Deputy Under Secretary of Defense for Asian and Pacific Affairs Richard Lawless, September 27, 2006. Under this plan, the 2^d Infantry Division, the main U.S. ground combat force in the ROK, and the 8th Army Headquarters would relocate to consolidated bases in the Osan-Pyongtaek region. Some of these adjustments had been under consideration since the early 1990s under the East Asian Strategy Initiative (EASI), an effort of the Bush administration to develop a comprehensive vision of the Alliance for the long term

following the collapse of the Soviet Union and the changes in East Asian security at that time. EASI included a 10-year plan to reduce U.S. troops from 135,000 to about 98,000 by the end of 1995. The EASI also called for redefinition of U.S. alliances in the region.

[120] During the first phase in 2004, 5,000 troops, including the 2[d] Brigade Combat Team of the 2[d] Infantry Division and associated units, were withdrawn (after a year in Iraq, the 2[d] Brigade redeployed to Fort Carson, Colorado, in 2005). During the second phase, 2005–2006, the United States redeployed another 5,000 troops (3,000 in 2005, 2,000 in 2006), comprising combat units, combat support and combat service support units, units associated with mission transfer areas, and other support personnel. In the third and final phase, 2007–2008, the United States will redeploy 2,500 troops consisting primarily of support units and personnel. See Department of Defense News Release, 995–04, October 6, 2004, available at <http://www.defenselink.mil/releases/2004/nr20041006-1356.htm>.

[121] Office of the President, Republic of Korea, "Address by President Roh Moo-hyun on the 58th Anniversary of National Liberation," August 15, 2003, and "Address by President Roh Moo-hyun on the 55th ROK Armed Forces Day, October 1, 2003," available at <http://english.president.go.kr/cwd/en/archive/archive_list.php?meta_id=en_speeches&m_def=3&ss_def=1>. See also Hoon Noh, *South Korea's Cooperative Self-reliant Defense: Goals and Directions*, KIDA Papers no. 10 (Seoul, Korea: Korean Institute for Defense Analyses, April 2005).

[122] The ROK defense budget increased by 9.9 percent in 2005 ($20.08 billion) and 10 percent in 2006 ($22.9 billion). Juhyun Park, *Medium-Term Expenditure Framework and Year 2005 Defense Budget*, KIDA Papers no. 9 (Seoul, Korea: Korean Institute for Defense Analyses, March 2005).

[123] The 2020 Plan calls for 9.9 percent annual growth in defense spending 2006–2010, 7.8 percent 2011–2015, and 1.0 percent 2016–2020. See Republic of Korea, Ministry of National Defense, *Defense Reform 2020*, E-book, December 2005, available at <http://www.mnd.go.kr/mndEng/DefensePolicy/DefenseReform 2020/ebook/index.jsp>; and Han Youg-sup, "Analyzing South Korea's Defense Reform 2020," *The Korean Journal of Defense Analysis* 18, no. 1 (Spring 2006), 116–117.

[124] Bruce W. Bennett, *A Brief Analysis of the Republic of Korea's Defense Reform Plan*, RAND National Defense Research Institute Occasional Paper, 2006, 21–23, 37–39, available at <http://www.rand.org/pubs/occasional_papers/2006/RAND_OP165.pdf>.

[125] Bennett, 23–26; and Han, 127. The MND's original 2020 plan was $725.55 billion and called for 11 percent growth in defense spending in 2006–2010.

[126] "Roh Renews Call for Return of Wartime Command," *The Chosun Ilbo*, October 2, 2005, available at <http://english.chosun.com/w21data/html/news/200510/200510020005.html>.

[127] Department of Defense, "The 38 Security Consultative Meeting Joint Communiqué," Washington, DC, October 20, 2006, available at <http://www.defenselink.mil/news/Oct2006/d20061020uskorea.pdf>.

[128] Joint Statement Between the United States of America and the Republic of Korea,

"Common Values, Principles, and Strategy," May 14, 2003, available at <http://www.whitehouse.gov/news/releases/2003/05/20030514-17.html>.

129 "The 38 Security Consultative Meeting Joint Communiqué," paragraph 8.

130 "Joint Declaration on the ROK-U.S. Alliance and Peace on the Korean Peninsula," November 17, 2005, available at <http://www.whitehouse.gov/news/releases/2005/11/20051117-6.html>.

131 Min Seong-jae, "Roh limits role of USFK in Asia," *JoongAng Ilbo*, March 9, 2005, available at <http://joongangdaily.joins.com/200503/08/2005030822183218799 00090309031.html>.

132 At the January 2006 SCAP meeting, Secretary of State Condoleezza Rice and Foreign Minister Ban Ki-moon issued a declaration that the ROK "respects the necessity for strategic flexibility," while the United States pledged that in implementing strategic flexibility, it "respects the ROK position that it shall not be involved in a regional conflict in Northeast Asia against the will of the Korean people." U.S. Department of State, Office of the Spokesman, Media Note 2006/70, "United States and the Republic of Korea Launch Strategic Consultation for Allied Partnership," January 19, 2006, available at <http://seoul.usembassy.gov/rok20060119.html>; Min Seong-jae, "Roh limits role of USFK in Asia." Chinese officials have played into this debate in the ROK, noting that they accept the presence of U.S. forces in the ROK for bilateral security, but those forces should never be directed at a "third party." See "Chinese Ambassador Cautious on US Military Flexibility," *The Korea Times*, March 22, 2006, available at <http://times.hankooki.com/lpage/nation/200603/kt2006032216222011990.htm>.

133 Hong Speech, May 11, 2005; and Shim Jae-yun, "President Opposes Role for USFK in regional Conflicts," *The Korea Times*, March, 8, 2005, available at <http://times.hankooki.com/lpage/nation/200503/kt2005030819023111950.htm>.

134 Ser Myo-ja, "The Alliance: Is it in Trouble?" *JoongAng Ilbo*, April 25, 2005, available at <http://joongangdaily.joins.com/200504/24/200504242300387939 900090309031.html>; and "Roh Warns U.S. Against Dividing Northeast Asia," *The Chosun Ilbo*, September 16, 2005.

135 Ibid. From the same conference, see particularly the paper by Chung Kyung-yun, "Strategies for Institutionalization of Multilateral Military Cooperation in Northeast Asia," 81–111.

136 James L. Schoff, *Tools for Trilateralism: Improving U.S.-Japan-Korea Cooperation to Manage Complex Contingencies* (Herndon, VA: Potomac Books, 2005).

137 Jason W. Forrester, *Congressional Attitudes and the Future of the U.S.-ROK Alliance* (Washington, DC: Center for Strategic and International Studies, May 2007), available at <http://www.csis.org/media/csis/pubs/070504_congressionalattitudes_final.pdf>.

138 Government of Australia, Department of External Affairs, Canberra, *Advancing the National Interest, Australia's Foreign and Trade Policy White Paper*, chapter 6, "Strengthening our Alliance with the United States," updated January 17, 2006, available at <http://www.dfat.gov.au/ani/chapter_6.html>.

139 The Alliance is codified in the trilateral 1951 treaty between Australia, New Zealand, and the United States. Government of Australia, Department of External Affairs, Canberra, Security Treaty between Australia, New Zealand and the United States

of America [ANZUS], signed San Francisco, September 1, 1951, entry into force generally, April 29, 1952. Australian Treaty Series, 1952, no. 2 (Canberra: Australian Government Publishing Service, 1997), available at <http://canberra. usembassy.gov/anzus/anzus.pdf>. Article III calls for consultations in the face of various security threats. Article V commits the parties, in the face of an armed attack on any one of them, to take actions to meet common dangers in accordance with each governments' constitutional processes.

[140] Alexander Downer, Minister for Foreign Affairs, Government of Australia, Department of External Affairs, "The Australia-United States Alliance and East Asian Security," speech given at the University of Sydney Conference, Sydney, June 29, 2001, available at <http://www.dfat.gov.au/media/speeches/foreign/2001/010629_fa_us_alliance.html>.

[141] U.S. Department of State, Embassy Canberra, "U.S., Australia to Cooperate on Missile Defense, Troop Training," transcript of press conference following the AUSMIN Meeting, July 7, 2004, Washington File, EPF405 07/08/2004, available at <http://usembassy-australia.state.gov/hyper/2004/0708/epf405.htm>; and "U.S., Australia Security Alliance Retools To Meet Modern Threats," text of communique from the 20th AUSMIN Meeting, November 17–18, 2005, Washington File, EPF502 11/18/2005 (2280), available at <http://usembassy-australia.state.gov/hyper/2005/1118/epf502.htm>.

[142] See Paul Dibb, *U.S.-Australia Alliance Relations: An Australian View*, Strategic Forum 216 (Washington, DC: National Defense University Press, August 2005).

[143] Ivan Cook, *Australians Speak 2005: Public Opinion and Foreign Policy* (Sydney: The Lowy Institute for International Policy, March 2005), 2, 14–15, available at <http://www.lowyinstitute.org/Publication.asp?pid=236>. Ian McAllister, *Representative Views: Australian Opinions on Security* (Barton, Australia: Australian Strategic Policy Institute, June 2005). In a 2001 poll, 90 percent of Australians surveyed saw the alliance as important.

[144] Owen Harries, *Understanding America* (Sydney: Centre for Independent Studies, 2002), 30.

[145] U.S. Department of State, Embassy Canberra, "U.S. Security Talks with Australia, Japan To Intensify, Rice Says," transcript of remarks by Secretary of State Condoleezza Rice and Australian Foreign Minister Alexander Downer after their meeting, May 4, 2005, Washington File, EPF304 05/04/2005, available at <http://usembassy-australia.state.gov/hyper/2005/0504/epf304.htm>.

[146] See Dibb, *U.S.-Australia Alliance Relations*.

[147] The United States and Thailand are among the signatories of the 1954 Manila pact of the former Southeast Asia Treaty Organization (SEATO). Article IV(1) of this treaty provides that, in the event of armed attack in the treaty area (which includes Thailand), each member would "act to meet the common danger in accordance with its constitutional processes." Despite the dissolution of SEATO in 1977, the Manila pact remains in force and, together with the Thanat-Rusk communique of 1962, constitutes the basis of U.S. security commitments to Thailand. See U.S. Department of State, Bureau of East Asian and Pacific Affairs, Background Note, Thailand, October 2005, available at <http://www.state.gov/r/pa/ei/bgn/2814.htm>.

[148] The major non-NATO ally designation recognizes, formalizes, and encourages the continuation of a cooperative relationship with a U.S. military partner. It does not generally embody a qualitatively new relationship, nor is it an indication that the United States will automatically provide significantly more advanced military technology.

[149] U.S. Embassy Thailand, press release, "Cobra Gold 2005 Joint Exercise," May 2–13, 2005, available at <http://bangkok.usembassy.gov/news/press/2005/nrot018.htm>.

[150] The Treaty is available at <http://www.dfa.gov.ph/vfa/frame/frmmdt.htm>. Article IV stipulates that "Each Party recognizes that an armed attack in the Pacific Area on either of the Parties would be dangerous to its own peace and safety and declares that it would act to meet the common dangers in accordance with its constitutional processes." The Visiting Forces Agreement is available at <http://www.dfa.gov.ph/vfa/content/Vfa.htm>.

[151] U.S. Department of State, Embassy Wellington, "Background Notes, New Zealand, September 22, 2005, available at <http://www.state.gov/r/pa/ei/bgn/35852.htm>. In the face of growing concern about nuclear testing in the South Pacific, the Labour government elected in 1984 banned visits by nuclear-armed and nuclear-powered warships to New Zealand ports. This stance prevented practical alliance cooperation, and after extensive efforts to resolve the issue proved unsuccessful, the United States suspended its ANZUS security obligations to New Zealand in 1986. Even after President Bush's 1991 announcement that U.S. surface ships do not normally carry nuclear weapons, New Zealand's legislation prohibiting visits of nuclear-powered ships continues to preclude a bilateral security alliance with the United States. The U.S. Government would welcome New Zealand's reassessment of its legislation to permit a return to full ANZUS cooperation.

[152] Phil Goff, New Zealand Ministry of Defense, "Transformation of a Small Defence Force to Meet Today's Security Environment," speech at the National Defense University, Washington, DC, April 20, 2006, available at <http://www.beehive.govt.nz/ViewDocument.aspx?DocumentID=25536>.

[153] U.S. Department of State, Bureau of East Asian and Pacific Affairs, "Testimony of Deputy Assistant Secretary Eric G. John on Human Rights in Vietnam," Subcommittee on Asia and the Pacific and Subcommittee on Africa, Global Human Rights and International Operations of the Committee on International Relations, March 29, 2006, available at <http://usinfo.state.gov/eap/Archive/2006/Mar/30-801916.html?chanlid=eap>.

[154] Ambassador Pamela J. Slutz, "United States-Mongolia Relations: A New Era of Comprehensive Partnership," address to the Academy of Management, Ulaanbaatar, January 12, 2006, available at <http://mongolia.usembassy.gov/01/12/06.html>.

[155] U.S. Department of Energy, *Petroleum Supply Annual, 2004,* volume 1, table 21, June 2005, available at <http://www.eia.doe.gov/oil_gas/petroleum/data_publi cations/petroleum_supply_annual/psa_volume1/psa_volume1.html>.

[156] Moises Naim, "Five Wars of Globalization," *Foreign Policy* 82, no. 1 (January/February 2003), 28–37.

[157] Derek H. Burney, "Canada-U.S. Relations: Are We Getting it Right?" address to

the Ranchman's Club, Calgary, November 17, 2005, available at <http://www.cdfai.org/PDF/Canada-US%20Relations%20Are%20We%20Getting%20it%20Right.pdf>.

[158] See comments of Dwight Mason, former co-chairman of the U.S.-Canadian Permanent Joint Board on Defense, in Canadian Defence and Foreign Affairs Institute, Conference Publication, "Canadian Defence and the Canada-U.S. Strategic Partnership," September 2002, 65–66, available at <http://www.cdfai.org/PDF/can-us_strat-partners.pdf>.

[159] Speaking notes for the Honourable Gordon J. O'Connor, Minister of National Defence, at the Conference of Defence Associations Institute Annual General Meeting, February 23, 2006, available at <http://www.forces.gc.ca/site/Newsroom/view_news_e.asp?id=1860>.

[160] Elinor Sloan, "The Strategic Capability Investment Plan: Origins, Evolution and Future Prospects," Canadian Defence and Foreign Affairs Institute, March 2006, 26, available at <http://www.cdfai.org/PDF/The%20Strategic%20Capability%20Investment%20Plan.pdf>.

[161] Doug Struck, "Canada Votes to Extend Mission in Afghanistan," *The Washington Post*, May 18, 2006, A18.

[162] Jason Proulx, "Group Studies U.S.-Canada Defense Relationship," *Armed Forces Press Service*, November 3, 2005, available at <http://www.defenselink.mil/news/Nov2005/20051103_3230.html>.

[163] See North American Aerospace Defense Command, Newsroom, "U.S., Canada strengthen NORAD agreement," May 23, 2006, available at <http://www.norad.mil/newsroom/news_releases/2006/052306.htm>; and Parliament of Canada, *Hansard*, 39th Parliament, 1st session, no. 15, May 3, 2006, 1820–2320, and no. 18, May 8, 2006, 1500.

[164] CTV News, "Harper open to missile-defence talks with U.S.," January 11, 2006, available at <http://www.ctv.ca/servlet/ArticleNews/story/CTVNews/20060112/elxn_harper_missile_060111/20060113?s_name=election2006&no_ads=>.

[165] See Bernd Mützelburg, "Europe and Latin America—Toward a Strategic Partnership?" Herbert-Quandt-Stiftung, 24th Sinclair House Debate, *Europe and Latin America—Toward a Strategic Partnership?* (Frankfurt: Societäts-Verlag, 2005), 71–75.

[166] The countries sanctioned under APSA are Barbados, Bolivia, Brazil, Costa Rica, Ecuador, Mexico, Paraguay, Peru, St. Vincent and the Grenadines, Trinidad and Tobago, Uruguay, and Venezuela. See Juan Forero, "Bush's Aid Cuts on Court Issue Roil Neighbors," *The New York Times*, August 19, 2005. As of August 2006, Chile had not ratified the treaty establishing the International Criminal Court.

[167] "Democracy's ten-year rut: The *Latinobarómetro* poll," *The Economist*, October 27, 2005, available at <http://www.economist.com/printedition/displayStory.cfm?story_id=5093522&fsrc=RSS>.

[168] Monte Reel, "A Tough Talker Woos Peru's Poor," *The Washington Post*, April 2, 2006, A18.

[169] The English-speaking Caribbean countries have approached cooperation warmly since gaining independence after World War II. Their common heritage and politi-

cal culture, membership in the British Commonwealth, and similar challenges to governing small states have encouraged formal subregional economic and security collaboration, such as the Caribbean Community and Common Market, although in practice, national capacities and priorities often vary, as does the attractiveness of cooperation with the United States.

[170] See Marta Lagos, "The Image of the United States in Latin America: *Latinobarometro* 1995–2004," presented at the Miami Herald's Americas Conference, September 30–October 1, 2004, accessed at <http://www.latinobarometro.org/fileadmin/documentos/articulos_y_documentos/Presentaci%F3n%20Miami%20The%20Image%20of%20USA.pdf>.

[171] "Democracy's ten-year rut: The *Latinobarómetro* poll," and Corporation *Latinobarómetro*, "*Latinobarómetro* Report 2005," available at <http://www.latinobarometro.org/uploads/media/2005_02.pdf>.

[172] Organization of American States, "Inter-American Democratic Charter," September 11, 2001, available at <http://www.oas.org/charter/docs/resolution1_en_p4.htm>.

[173] Organization of American States, Special Conference on Security, "Declaration on Security in the Americas," Mexico City, Mexico, October 28, 2003, available at <http://www.oas.org/main/main.asp?sLang=E&sLink=../../documents/eng/officesinmemberstates.asp>. For a discussion of the negotiation of the declaration, see Ambassador Miguel Ruiz-Cabañas, Permanent Representative of Mexico to the OAS and Chairman of the OAS Committee on Hemispheric Security, "Review of the OAS Special Conference on Security," Colleagues for the Americas Series, Institute for National Strategic Studies, National Defense University, November 21, 2003, available at <http://www.ndu.edu/inss/Repository/INSS_Proceedings/Colleagues_for_the_Americas/Colleagues_2003_11.pdf>.

[174] 9/11 Commission, 390.

[175] John A. Cope, "A Prescription for Protecting the U.S. Southern Approach," *Joint Force Quarterly* 42 (3d Quarter 2006), 17–21.

[176] Of the military services, the Mexican navy, *Marina*, is the most active and works primarily with the U.S. Coast Guard to block narcotics and other smuggling activities. The Mexican navy also has purchased numerous U.S. excess defense articles. *Marina* has direct contact with the Joint Interagency Task Force–South in Key West, Florida, on narcotics issues and informal contact with U.S. Northern Command.

[177] The secretariats are military organizations. The army is by far the largest and is politically the most influential service. A small marine corps is part of the navy. Special operations forces are in the Secretariat of National Defense.

[178] Raúl Benítez-Manuat, *Mexico and the New Challenges of Hemispheric Security* (Washington, DC: Woodrow Wilson International Center for Scholars, 2004); and unpublished comments of Oscar Rocha, the Joaquin Amaro Foundation for Strategic Studies, "Mexico-U.S. Defense Relations," Institute for National Strategic Studies Workshop, "The Caribbean Sea and Its Border Areas in U.S. Homeland Defense," National Defense University, Washington, DC, August 16, 2005.

[179] Dana Priest, "Help From France Key in Covert Operations," *The Washington Post*, July 3, 2005, 1.

[180] For a discussion of the international legal and other considerations that make the case for antiterrorist military intervention and other preventive actions, see Joseph McMillan, *Apocalyptic Terrorism: The Case for Preventive Action*, Strategic Forum 212 (Washington, DC: National Defense University Press, November 2004), available at <http://www.ndu.edu/inss/strforum/SF212/SF212_Final.pdf>.

CHAPTER EIGHT

[1] The White House, "Revitalizing National Defense," August 28, 2007, available at <http://www.whitehouse.gov/infocus/defense/>.

[2] For the Department of Defense's own assessment of its transformation performance for this period, see William S. Cohen, "Emerging Operational Concepts Quadrennial Report, 1996–1999," Report to Congress, September 2000. The report was required by Section 486 of Title 10, United States Code, which directed the Secretary to submit a quadrennial report on emerging operational concepts, new organizational arrangements, and acquisition strategies used to harness emerging technologies, capabilities, and changes in the international order. The report was a gentle prod from Congress to get DOD to move faster on transformation.

[3] One example was the U.S. Army's campaign to revolutionize its ability to fight at night with the aid of night-vision devices and precise geolocation devices. All other land forces had to adapt to this innovation or risk being rendered obsolete.

[4] *Transformation Planning Guidance* (Washington, DC: Department of Defense, April 2003). The *Transformation Planning Guidance* was drafted in the Office of the Under Secretary of Defense (Policy) and signed by the Secretary of Defense.

[5] Department of Defense, *Quadrennial Defense Review Report* (Washington, DC: Department of Defense, 2006), 1.

[6] This chapter analyzes salient aspects of defense transformation and assumes a rudimentary knowledge of defense affairs. For a more general overview of the current administration's transformation agenda and its critics, see Ronald O'Rourke, "Defense Transformation: Background and Oversight Issues for Congress," Congressional Research Service Report for Congress, updated June 1, 2006.

[7] The March 2005 National Defense Strategy changed this list from six operational goals to eight operational capabilities, most notably adding "operating from the global commons," "improving proficiency against irregular challenges," and "increasing capabilities of partners, international and domestic." Other modifications are consistent with the original list.

[8] Greg Jaffe and Jonathan Karp, "Military Cuts Target Old Ways of War: Pentagon Budget Proposal Would Hit Navy, Air Force; Shipbuilders Face Squeeze," *The Wall Street Journal*, January 25, 2005, 3.

[9] *Transformation Planning Guidance,* 3, advertised senior leadership commitment to transformation, articulated a strategic rationale for transformation, and described a strategy for pursuing transformation, all in order to "mobilize the rest of the

Department and stimulate the bottom-up innovation required for successful transformation." It was intended to establish a process that would "define transformation investments that address future risk with enough specificity that they can be balanced against the other three primary risk areas identified in the Quadrennial Defense Review: force management, operational, and institutional risk."

10 *Network-centric warfare* has been defined as "the combination of emerging tactics, techniques, and technologies that a networked force employs to create a decisive warfighting advantage." Department of Defense, Office of Force Transformation, *Military Transformation: A Strategic Approach* (Washington, DC: Office of Force Transformation, 2003). U.S. Joint Forces Command has defined *effects-based operations* as "a process for obtaining a desired strategic outcome or 'effect' on the enemy, through the synergistic, multiplicative, and cumulative application of the full range of military and nonmilitary capabilities at the tactical, operational, and strategic levels."

11 Department of Defense, *Joint Operations Concepts* (Washington, DC: Department of Defense, November 2003).

12 *Transformation Planning Guidance*, 15.

13 Currently, the Pentagon has two categories of supporting concepts: joint functional concepts (JFCs) and enabling concepts called joint integrating concepts (JICs). A JFC describes how the future joint force will perform a particular military function. The current set of JFCs includes force application, protection, battlespace awareness, command and control, focused logistics, network-centric operations, force management, and training. JICs provide more specificity and a narrower focus. JICs describe fundamental tasks, conditions, and standards required to conduct narrow missions that support the broader JOCs and JFCs. Their level of detail permits more rigorous assessment of alternative capabilities. JICs have been developed for forcible entry operations and undersea superiority, and future JICs will include global strike operations, sea-basing operations, air and missile defense, joint command and control, joint logistics, and joint urban operations.

14 Department of Defense, *Capstone Concept for Joint Operations: Version 2.0* (Washington, DC: Department of Defense, August 2005).

15 The Pentagon's 2006 Quadrennial Defense Review (QDR) categorizes future security problems in four areas: traditional large conventional force attacks, irregular attacks by terrorists and insurgents, catastrophic attacks involving weapons of mass destruction by terrorists or rogue states, and disruptive challenges, such as breakthrough technologies or other novel nontechnical asymmetric tactics. The joint operating concepts could be aligned with these categories, although it is difficult to envision a concept for disruptive challenges, which operationally would seem to be highly situation dependent and best dealt with as an intelligence and research and development challenge. The QDR depicts four strategic problems: "defeating terror networks," "preventing hostile states and non-state actors from acquiring or using weapons of mass destruction," "defending the homeland in depth," and "shaping the choices of countries at strategic crossroads."

16 Department of Defense, *Homeland Defense and Civil Support Joint Operating Concept,* Draft Version 1.7 (Washington, DC: Department of Defense, July 2006).

See also Department of Defense, *Homeland Security Joint Operating Concept* (Washington, DC: Department of Defense, February 2004).

[17] Department of Defense, *Strategy for Homeland Defense and Civil Support* (Washington, DC: Department of Defense, 2005), available at <http://www.defenselink.mil/news/Jun2005/d20050630homeland.pdf#search+%22Homeland%20Defense%20Strategy%22>.

[18] Department of Defense, *Deterrence Operations Joint Operating Concept,* Draft Version 1.9 (Washington, DC: Department of Defense, July 2006). See also Department of Defense, *Strategic Deterrence Joint Operating Concept* (Washington, DC: Department of Defense, February 2004). For a critique of the latter, see Christopher J. Lamb, *Transforming Defense*, Institute for National Strategic Studies Occasional Paper (Washington, DC: National Defense University Press, September 2005), 8.

[19] The concept identifies both direct and enabling means. *Direct means* include force projection, nuclear strike, active and passive defenses, global strike, strategic information operations, inducement operations, and space control. *Enabling means* include global situational awareness, command and control, overseas presence, and allied/coalition military cooperation and integration.

[20] Department of Defense, *Major Combat Operations Joint Operations Concept,* Draft Version 1.9 (Washington, DC: Department of Defense, June 2006).

[21] The question of information redundancy and whether platforms ought to retain sufficient information-processing capability to enable them to fight independent of the network is a critical issue. Some might argue that it is too detailed for an operating concept or that it need not be addressed in such an early version of the concept.

[22] Department of Defense, *Stability Operations Joint Operations Concept* (Washington, DC: Department of Defense, September 2004).

[23] As this book went to press, the new and revised JOC on irregular warfare reportedly had been written and was awaiting approval. Department of Defense, *Military Support to Stabilization, Security, Transition, and Reconstruction Operations Joint Operating Concept (JOC)*, Draft version 1.9 (Washington, DC: Department of Defense, June 2006).

[24] The rise of modern insurgencies in the past 50 years has been characterized as a new form of warfare called *fourth-generation warfare*. This form of warfare has been particularly vexing for U.S. forces in Vietnam, Lebanon, Somalia, and most recently in Iraq. Critics of defense transformation argue that high-technology, information-age warfare is inappropriate for this type of adversary. See Thomas X. Hammes, *Insurgency: Modern Warfare Evolves into a Fourth Generation*, Strategic Forum 214 (Washington, DC: National Defense University Press, January 2005).

[25] U.S. Marine Corps, *Small Wars Manual* (Washington, DC: U.S. Government Printing Office, 1940), chapter I, 1–9(f), 1–16(c); chapter II, 2–5.

[26] For a good discussion of military concepts and how they should be written, see John F. Schmitt, "A Practical Guide for Developing and Writing Military Concepts," Working Paper #02–4, Defense Adaptive Red Team (McLean, VA: Hicks and Associates, December 2002).

27 Some would consider the classic principles of war (for example, mass, objective, security, simplicity) to be a good starting point. Others prefer the core military elements championed by some Army sources (sense, move, shoot, communicate, protect, sustain). A more recent example of an organizing framework is the three domains of warfare identified by the Pentagon's Office of Force Transformation: cognitive, informational, and physical. The Office of Force Transformation asserts that the nexus of these three domains is the capabilities necessary to conduct network-centric warfare.

28 The Quadrennial Defense Review referred to a capabilities-based strategy, approach, model, and force. Our concern here is primarily with planning, so the term *capabilities-based planning* is used. Ultimately, a broader term, such as *approach*, is probably more appropriate since certainly the scope of reform exceeds planning.

29 George W. Bush, quoted in the *Transformation Planning Guidance*, 3.

30 *QDR Report*, September 30, 2001; section on "A Capabilities-Based Approach," 13–14. The link drawn between capabilities-based planning and transformation is made even more explicit in the foreword to the report:

> Adopting this capabilities-based approach to planning . . . entails adapting existing military capabilities to new circumstances, while experimenting with the development of new military capabilities. In short, it requires the transformation of U.S. forces, capabilities, and institutions to extend America's asymmetric advantages well into the future.

31 Ibid., 3.

32 Examples of such influences are service parochialism, special pleading by select offices within the Office of the Secretary of Defense, and imprecise studies based on faulty methodologies or data.

33 *QDR Report*, 14.

34 Such a document was called for at a recent Pentagon-sponsored symposium on capabilities-based planning. See Military Operations Research Society, Capabilities-based Planning Workshop, Outbrief (Long Version), November 16, 2004.

35 Global posture and capabilities received somewhat more attention than global force management in 2001, but subsequently it has become a major area of interest and activity in the Pentagon.

36 *QDR Report*, 26.

37 The description of new tools and processes to support global force management is drawn primarily from the Operational Risk section of the 2004 Secretary of Defense *Annual Report to the President and the Congress*, available at <http://www.dod.mil/execsec/adr2004/index.html>. The Secretary's 2005 report simply mentions that work continues on the Global Force Management process and tools.

38 Ibid., 33–34:

> The Global Force Management process, now being developed, will provide insights into the global availability of forces, allowing military planners to do quick-turn, accu-

rate assessments of how force changes will affect our ability to execute plans and evaluate associated risk. These assessments, in turn, will help us match the right force capabilities to emerging missions while providing visibility to stress on the force caused by frequent deployments away from home station.

See also the 2005 Secretary of Defense *Annual Report to the President and the Congress,* 11.

39 According to the 2004 Secretary of Defense *Annual Report to the President and the Congress*, the Pentagon formally assigned roles and responsibilities for the new global force management process in 2004, and work is under way on improving force structure data and providing new risk assessment methodologies. A prototype of the new system using the Army is to be completed in fiscal year 2005, at which time the new global force management process will be represented in the "Forces for Unified Commands" document, which formally assigns forces to combatant commanders.

40 They were as follows: U.S. Transportation Command to support geographic combatant commands with transportation; U.S. Special Operations Command to support other commands with Special Operations Forces; and U.S. Strategic Command to provide nuclear weapons and deterrence. U.S. Joint Forces Command (formerly U.S. Atlantic Command) had both functional (joint experimentation) and geographic (U.S. and Atlantic Ocean) responsibilities.

41 See briefing on the Unified Command Plan of 2002 at <www.defenselink.mil/transcripts/2002/t04172002_t0417sd.html>.

42 Some would say USNORTHCOM is a functional command with a geographic command's name.

43 Russia had previously not been assigned to a combatant commander's area of responsibility but had been in the portfolio of the Chairman of the Joint Chiefs of Staff.

44 These "missions" could be seen more as capabilities.

45 This change was made by a Secretary of Defense executive order and has not yet been written into the Unified Command Plan.

46 Anthony C. Zinni, "Civil-Military Cooperation in a Time of Turmoil," speech at the Center for Strategic and International Studies, Washington, DC, December 7, 2004.

47 Clark A. Murdock et al., *Beyond Goldwater-Nichols: Defense Reform for a New Strategic Era*, Phase I Report (Washington, DC: Center for Strategic and International Studies, March 2004), 63.

48 This option might be either in addition to or instead of having geographic combatant commands, with regional political-military issues and security cooperation handled by the new interagency organizations—in which case operations could be under the command and control of joint task forces or functional and/or global combatant commands.

49 One measure of merit for evaluations might be, "How many times did you talk to your counterpart in another command or agency each week?"

50 By way of just one example, Madrid's *La Razon* reported on September 13, 2004,

that Spain would lose U.S. bases to Portugal and Italy because of Spain's decision to withdraw its forces from Iraq. See FBIS, EUP20040913000281. The article claimed that Naples would be the new headquarters of the U.S. Naval Forces Europe and that Gaeta (Sicily) would keep the U.S. Sixth Fleet originally offered to Rota (Cadiz), Spain. Furthermore, it reported that Oeiras (Lisbon) would host the standing structure of the planned North Atlantic Treaty Organization Response Force, and therefore Lisbon would also become the Joint Headquarters under the command of the vice admiral of the Sixth Fleet.

51 See Jong-Heon Lee, "U.S. Intent Questioned: Seoul Seen as Base for Role in China-Taiwan Fight," *The Washington Times*, December 3, 2004, 17. Lee relates how a South Korean legislator raised concerns that the U.S. intention was to use South Korea as a base for potential military operations in the event of a conflict between China and Taiwan. However, the same article demonstrated that American diplomacy was having some effect. It noted that Foreign Minister Ban Ki-moon said South Korea was not opposed to U.S. forces playing a greater role in Northeast Asia unless it meant a weakening of the combined defense posture for ensuring peace and stability on the Korean Peninsula. Mr. Ban stated, "I admit the necessity of what the Americans call strategic flexibility," and noted that the global security situation had changed in the past 50 years.

52 See Anthony Faiola, "Japan Plans to Press U.S. on Troops: Foreign Minister Seeking Reduction of 'Burden' on Okinawa," *The Washington Post*, October 6, 2004, 24. Faiola reported that the Japanese Foreign Minister, Nobutaka Machimura, said he would press his country's case for reducing what he called "the excessive burden" placed on Okinawa by the presence of U.S. troops while leaving adequate forces in Japan to promote security in the region.

53 Katie Worth, "B–52 Bombers Arrive: Andersen to Host Continuous Rotation of Aircraft," *Pacific Daily News* (Guam), February 23, 2004.

54 See Frances M. Lussier, "Options for Changing the Army's Overseas Basing," Congressional Budget Office Report, May 2004, especially 47. Lussier concludes that options for restationing of Army forces overseas would only make small improvements in the Army's strategic responsiveness, at least with respect to Germany. In part because of an excellent German transportation network (that the United States has invested in), the time required to deploy Army heavy units by sea to many potential trouble spots is not significantly shorter from Eastern Europe than it is from Germany. It also takes much longer to deploy a heavy brigade combat team from Eastern Europe than to deliver the prepositioned set of equipment that is maintained on board ships at Diego Garcia in the Indian Ocean.

55 Defense Science Board, Report on Sea Basing, August 2003, accessed at <www.acq.osd.mil/ dsb/reports/seabasing.pdf>.

56 *Annual Defense Report to the President and the Congress*, 39.

57 Unfortunately, one important trade area associated with global intelligence became public recently. See "Disclosures about Program to Develop Spy Satellites Could Prompt Investigation," *The Wall Street Journal*, December 13, 2004, 5.

58 For example, Members of Congress and their staffs wanted to see the operational analysis that drove the Pentagon's decision to cancel the Crusader self-propelled

artillery system. More recently, in an open forum discussion with defense writers, Undersecretary of Defense for Policy, Douglas J. Feith, promised that the Defense Department would provide lawmakers with analysis that would put proposed defense program cuts into context. Apparently, the promise emerged in response to speculation about the fate of Lockheed-Martin's C–130 program, which has numerous and powerful proponents on Capitol Hill. See Shailagh Murray, "Bush Faces Pentagon Gunfight: Proposed Weapons-System Cuts Stir Republican Opposition," *The Wall Street Journal*, February 1, 2005, 4.

[59] For one discussion of a necessary prerequisite for capabilities-based planning, see Christopher J. Lamb and Irving Lachow, *Reforming Pentagon Strategic Decision-making*, Strategic Forum 221 (Washington, DC: National Defense University Press, July 2006), available at <http://www.ndu.edu/inss/Strforum/SF221/SF221.pdf>.

About the Contributors

EDITORS

Stephen J. Flanagan is Senior Vice President and Director of the International Security Program at the Center for Strategic and International Studies (CSIS). Prior to joining CSIS in June 2007, he served for 7 years as Director of the Institute for National Strategic Studies and Vice President for Research at the National Defense University (NDU). Dr. Flanagan has held several senior positions in government, including Senior Director for Central and Eastern Europe at the National Security Council, National Intelligence Officer for Europe, and Associate Director of the State Department's Policy Planning Staff. He also has held academic and research appointments at Harvard University's John F. Kennedy School of Government, the International Institute for Strategic Studies, and the Council on Foreign Relations. He is widely published and is co-editor, most recently, of *The People's Liberation Army and China in Transition* (NDU Press, 2003).

James A. Schear is Director of Research at the Institute for National Strategic Studies at NDU. From 1997 to 2001, he served as Deputy Assistant Secretary of Defense for Peacekeeping and Humanitarian Affairs. His previous public service includes assignments as an advisor to the United Nations (UN) Secretariat and to UN missions in Cambodia and the former Yugoslavia (1990–1995). Dr. Schear has held research appointments at Harvard University, the Brookings Institution, the Carnegie Endowment for International Peace, the International Institute for Strategic Studies, the Aspen Institute, and the Henry L. Stimson Center. During 2006, he served as an expert to the Iraq Study Group, co-chaired by former Secretary of State James Baker and Representative Lee Hamilton.

CONTRIBUTING AUTHORS

M. Elaine Bunn, a Senior Research Fellow at INSS, specializes in strategic policy and directs the Institute's Future Strategic Concept Program. Prior to joining NDU, Ms. Bunn held a number of positions in the Office of the Secretary of Defense, including as a member of the Senior Executive Service, and Principal Director for Nuclear Forces and Missile Defense Policy. She was with the RAND Corporation from 1998 to 2000 on a Department of Defense exchange assignment. During 2001, she co-chaired a nuclear panel for the Secretary of Defense, framing issues for the 2001 Nuclear Posture Review. She has published a number of policy papers and journal articles on strategic concepts and defense policy and strategy.

Christopher Cavoli, LTC, USA, is the Associate Director of the Program for Security, Stability, Transition, and Reconstruction Operations at the George C. Marshall European Center for Security Studies, in Garmisch, Germany, where he specializes in security and counterinsurgency studies. Prior to his current assignment, he commanded 1st Battalion, 32d Infantry of the 10th Mountain Division, with responsibility for Nangarhar, Laghman, Nuristan, and Kunar Provinces in Eastern Afghanistan. He also served as Senior Military Fellow at INSS and as Deputy Executive Assistant to the Chairman of the Joint Chiefs of Staff. LTC Cavoli's career background includes Foreign Area Officer, airborne, and light infantry experience. Prior to Operation *Enduring Freedom*, his operational assignments included Operations *Provide Comfort* (Iraq) in 1991 and *Joint Forge* (Bosnia) in 1999–2000.

John A. Cope, COL (Ret.), USA, is a Senior Research Fellow in INSS, specializing in Western Hemisphere security affairs, U.S. policy for Latin America and the Caribbean, civil-military relations, and defense education. Before retiring from the Army, Colonel Cope served in the State Department's Bureau of Inter-American Affairs, U.S. Southern Command, U.S. Army South, U.S. Army War College, and the 101st Airborne Division. His recent work has focused on examining security cooperation in the Caribbean Basin as an integral part of U.S. homeland defense, studying U.S. defense relations with Canada and Mexico, assessing U.S. Colombia policy, and measuring progress and risks of Colombia's Democratic Security.

Thomas X. Hammes, Col (Ret.), USMC, completed 30 years in the Corps in 2005. He served at all levels in the operating forces to include command of a rifle company, weapons company, intelligence company, infantry battalion, and the Chemical Biological Incident Response Force. He was also Assistant Chief of Staff for Plans, I Marine Expeditionary Force. He participated in stabilization operations in Somalia and Iraq. His final tour in the Marine Corps was as Senior Military Fellow at INSS. He is the author of *The Sling and the Stone: On War in the Twenty-First Century* (Minneapolis: Zenith Press, 2004) and numerous articles and opinion pieces. He is currently reading for a DPhil in Modern History at Oxford University.

Christopher J. Lamb, a Senior Research Fellow at INSS, specializes in U.S. defense strategy, requirements, plans, and programs, with particular emphasis on force transformation and capabilities-based planning. Prior to joining INSS, Dr. Lamb served as the Deputy Assistant Secretary of Defense for Resources and Plans from 2001 to 2004. At INSS, Dr. Lamb also serves as Director, Research and Analysis, for the Project on National Security Reform, a collaborative effort with the Center for the Study of the Presidency and several other public policy research institutions. A well-known authority on special operations, he is co-author (with David Tucker) of *United States Special Operations Forces* (New York: Columbia University Press, 2007).

Charles D. Lutes, Col, USAF, a Senior Military Fellow at INSS, specializes in combating the proliferation of weapons of mass destruction (WMD) as well as strategic concept development, counterterrorism, and interagency coordination. He is the lead investigator for the Institute's Spacepower Theory Project. Colonel Lutes' prior assignment was as chief of the WMD division under the Joint Staff Plans and Policy Directorate. On the operations side, he has logged more than 3,000 hours piloting C–5s and KC–135s and has commanded an operational support squadron. He is co-author (with Judith Yaphe) of *Reassessing the Implications of a Nuclear-Armed Iran,* McNair Paper 69 (NDU Press, 2005).

Joseph McMillan is a Senior Research Fellow at INSS specializing in counterterrorism, security assistance, the greater Middle East, and South Asia. Before joining NDU in 2001, he served in the Department of Defense in a variety of assignments, including Principal Director for Russia, Ukraine, and Eurasia and Principal Director for Near Eastern and South Asian Affairs in the Office of the Secretary of Defense. Mr. McMillan is a career member of the Senior Executive Service. He is editor of *In the Same Light as Slavery: Building a Global Antiterrorist Consensus* (NDU Press, 2006).

Leo G. Michel, a Senior Research Fellow at INSS, specializes in the North Atlantic Treaty Organization (NATO), the European Union, and transatlantic security issues. Prior to joining the Institute, Mr. Michel served in the Office of the Secretary of Defense as a member of the Senior Executive Service and Director for NATO Policy. He also held a faculty appointment at the Geneva Centre for Security Policy in Geneva, Switzerland. Before joining the Department of Defense in 1986, Mr. Michel served as an intelligence analyst, a staff member of the U.S. House of Representatives, and a reporter for French news media. Mr. Michel served as a U.S. Navy officer during 1969–1972.

James J. Przystup, a Senior Research Fellow at INSS, specializes in Asian security issues in general and the U.S.-Japan and the U.S.–Republic of Korea security relationships in particular. Prior to his service at NDU, Dr. Przystup served as the Director of the Asian Studies Center at The Heritage Foundation. His public service includes assignments on the Policy Planning Staff at the Department of State and in the Office of the Secretary of Defense as Director for Regional Security Strategies on the Policy Planning Staff. In 1983–1984, he served as the Deputy Director of the Presidential Advisory Commission on U.S.-Japan relations. From 2005 to 2007, he co-directed the Policy Research Group, an advisory group supporting a joint initiative to update the U.S.–Republic of Korea alliance.

Eugene B. Rumer, a Senior Research Fellow at INSS, is a specialist on Russia and other states of the former Soviet Union. Previously, Dr. Rumer served as a member of the Secretary's Policy Planning Staff at the Department of State, and as Director for Russian, Ukrainian, and Eurasian affairs at the National Security Council. Prior to entering government service, he worked for the RAND Corporation for 8 years, first as an analyst based in Santa Monica, California, and later as a Senior Staff Member and resident representative in Moscow, Russia. He is co-author (with Dmitri Trenin and Huasheng Zhao) of *Central Asia: Views from Washington, Moscow, and Beijing* (Armonk, NY: M.E. Sharpe, 2007) and author of *Russian Foreign Policy Beyond Putin,* Adelphi Paper 391 (London: Institute for International Strategic Studies, forthcoming).

Phillip C. Saunders, a Senior Research Fellow, specializes in China and East Asian security issues and coordinates the work of NDU's Center for the Study of Chinese Military Affairs. Prior to joining INSS, he served as Director of the East Asia Nonproliferation

Program, Center for Nonproliferation Studies, at the Monterey Institute of International Studies, where he taught courses on Chinese politics, Chinese foreign policy, and East Asian security. Dr. Saunders has conducted research and consulted on East Asian security issues for the Woodrow Wilson School at Princeton University, the Council on Foreign Relations, RAND, and the National Committee on U.S.-China Relations. Among his recent published works is *China's Global Activism* (INSS Occasional Paper 4, 2006).

Index